THE SELECTED WORKS OF ANDREW LANG

VOLUME 2

THE SELECTED WORKS OF ANDREW LANG

VOLUME 2

Literary Criticism, History, Biography

EDITED BY
Andrew Teverson, Alexandra Warwick
and Leigh Wilson

EDINBURGH
University Press

Edinburgh University Press Ltd
The Tun – Holyrood Road, 12(2F) Jackson's Entry,
Edinburgh EH8 8PJ

www.euppublishing.com

Typeset in 10.5 pt Monotype Bembo
by Isambard Thomas, and
printed and bound in Great Britain by
CPI Group (UK) Ltd, Croydon CR0 4YY

A CIP record for this book is available from the British Library

ISBN 978 1 4744 0023 7 (hardback)
ISBN 978 1 4744 0024 4 (webready PDF)
ISBN 978 1 4744 0450 1 (epub)

General Introduction

When Andrew Lang died in 1912, and for some time after, even the most sympathetic commentators remarked on the disappointment inherent in his now completed *oeuvre*. The most scathing was Henry James, writing to Edmund Gosse in November 1912:

> Where I can't but feel he should be brought to justice is in the matter of his whole 'give-away' of the wonderful chance he so continually enjoyed (enjoyed thanks to certain of his very gifts, I admit!) give-away, I mean by his cultivation, absolutely, of the puerile imagination and fourth-rate opinion, the coming round to that of the old apple-woman on the corner as after all the good and the right as to any of the mysteries of mind or of art.[1]

Both were publically more generous to Lang, as were the many obituaries and commemorative writings, but in introducing the published versions of the first ten years of the Andrew Lang Lectures,[2] Adam Blyth Webster, Professor of English Literature at St Andrews, admits that:

> Through much, through most, of what had been written about him there ran the admission that he had done many things gracefully and some exceedingly well, but also the wonder, regretful or complaining, not that he should have done so much but that, it seemed, he had failed to do more.[3]

For many, though, it was not so much that they wished Lang had done more, rather that he had done less, and concerned himself with just one area; usually, for each commentator, the area that most concerned themselves. His friend George Saintsbury wrote of Lang's ability:

> It may be that in one way it did not concentrate itself enough—did not leave two or three big books instead of thirty or forty little ones; and in another concentrated itself too much by writing not very small books on subjects which might have been adequately treated in not very long essays.[4]

Saintsbury concluded his assessment:

> 'Selections', of course, suggest themselves and have been suggested. It would be possible to conceive not merely one but more than one which would supply reading of the most refreshing kind. But it would be an extraordinarily difficult job; and while selections often fail to satisfy their readers, this selection would be so unlikely to satisfy the selector that he would probably never get it finished.[5]

Saintsbury's words indicate the sense that is present over and over again in those who discuss Lang, that he is, simply, unmanageable, both in the volume of his production and in its variety. The volume is undeniable: he started his career as a reviewer for *The Academy* in 1874 and he wrote for the *Daily News*, the *Morning Post* and the *Saturday Review* producing hundreds of reviews over more than two decades.[6] For *Longman's Magazine* (with which he was so closely associated that he repeatedly had to tell readers that he was not the editor), he wrote 240 columns, occasional articles, poetry and fiction; he produced more than 500 columns for the *Illustrated London News*, as well as essays for the *Cornhill Magazine*, *Fraser's Magazine*, the *Fortnightly Review*, the *Contemporary Review*, *Blackwood's Edinburgh Magazine*, *Harper's*, *Macmillan's*, the *St. James's Gazette*, *The Pilot*, *The Critic* and numerous others. His work was also published in American journals and newspapers and was widely syndicated in the English-language press around the world.

Aside from the periodical and newspaper work, Roger Lancelyn Green, Lang's only biographer, lists more than 200 publications under Lang's name: poetry and fiction, translations, histories, biographies, collections, works on anthropology, mythology, folklore, literature and many introductions to works by others, including every volume of the complete works of Scott and Dickens.[7] The range and variety seems to have defeated possible critics as well as potential editors. After the commemorative pieces that appeared in 1912 and 1913 and the personal notes in the autobiographies of those that knew him, only the Lang Lectures kept his work in view and even they became intermittent after 1934. The centenary of his birth in 1944 drew some brief articles and a radio programme was broadcast on the fiftieth anniversary of his death.[8] John Gross, one of the few later twentieth-century critics that mentions Lang, called him 'a don lost to journalism'[9] and in 1984 Harold Orel, in his book on Victorian literary critics, concludes in almost the same words as writers sixty years earlier: 'For all his wisdom and gracefulness of style, Lang's legacy to our age is … a disappointment, and less than it might have been.'[10] In the 1980s Marysa Demoor carried out invaluable work on his letters[11] and while there was a smattering of works on Lang,[12] on the whole most twentieth-century scholars tacitly agreed with his obituaries, and no collections or editions of his work have ever appeared.[13]

There is, however, an indication of what might be the real reason for the neglect in the first Lang Lecture, delivered by George Gordon in 1927. He says that:

> It is worthwhile to observe how instinctively Lang settled, in the studies of his time, on the adventurous, the mysterious, the problematic; on the frontier of subjects, where new work was being done, and on sciences in the making ... the conditions of his performance have not always been understood.[14]

In the late nineteenth century the sciences and other disciplines were struggling for definition, working for greater clarity of boundaries and objects of study rather than less. Lang's refusal of such segregation placed him awkwardly in the intellectual milieu of his own time and further stranded his work as those boundaries between academic disciplines hardened in the twentieth century. It is only recently that it has become possible, in George Gordon's words, to understand the conditions of Lang's performance. Firstly, the digitisation of catalogues and material (particularly periodicals) has made the location of his sprawling mass of work far easier, but more importantly over the last forty years or so, the *fin de siècle*, the period of his prime, has become one of particular interest for scholars from a number of disciplines. The developing interest in the gothic, in the construction and rise of consumer capitalism, in the histories of science and technology, in the genealogies of modernism, in the constructions of modern identities around, in particular, gender, sexuality and ethnicity, in the development of the idea of professionalisation, all have given a preeminence to the period as the origin of a particular kind of modernity and have found significance in exactly the adventurous, the mysterious and the problematic topics that fascinated him. Thus we can see Lang anew as the complicated and sometimes contradictory scholar that he was, both a Victorian man of letters and one who worked in and on the boundaries between subjects in a way that anticipated the interdisciplinary studies of the later twentieth century.

Fittingly for a man at the intersection of so many fields, he was born at the edges of two nations, in the Border country of Scotland. Lang's nationality has been rather scornfully treated by some; Henry James, in his correspondence with Gosse, accuses Lang of affecting an 'extraordinary voulu Scotch provincialism'[15] and more recently Margaret Beetham has suggested that he 'performed' Scottishness in a way that was typical of the English upper class.[16] Neither of these views is true; Lang felt himself to be a Scot, a member, as he puts it, of a 'small nationality'[17] and never entirely at home in England. He spent as much time as he could in Scotland and gathered a good deal of folkloric material as well as accounts of contemporary and historical psychic phenomena. Though his longer works on Scottish history were published later in his career, beginning in the 1890s, there is Scottish material throughout his work, indeed, among his first published pieces was a collection of Scottish nursery tales.[18]

The same longevity is apparent in his other interests too. In 1863, the same year as the nursery tale collection, he also published a piece on 'Spiritualism Mediaeval and Modern', and it was decades later, in 1911, when he became President of the Society for Psychical Research. He studied classics at Balliol and became a Fellow of Merton in 1868 and while there he published poetry and worked on translations of Aristotle and Homer, but the Merton library records show that he also read the newest work in other subjects, such as anthropology. He read E. B. Tylor's important work *Primitive Culture* (1871) in 1872 and he met Tylor in the same year.[19] At the end of his life he was still researching and writing on the same topics. *The World of Homer* came out in 1910, in which he offered further evidence in support of his assertion that the *Odyssey* and the *Iliad* were the work of a single author, against the dominant view that they were patchwork texts by several hands, and *Method in the Study of Totemism* was published in 1911. He was also translating folk and fairy tales long before the first of his highly popular Fairy Books came out in 1889, and the last of the series of twelve appeared only two years before his death.

It was after his unexplained departure from Oxford,[20] however, that he began the career that brought him to public attention and to a central place in late nineteenth-century literary life. His contemporaries admired his wit and learning, even those like George Bernard Shaw whose political positions were far from Lang's own,[21] and the *Daily News* had a list of subscribers who wanted only issues with Lang's articles sent to them.[22] He soon became a powerful figure, dominating journals and newspaper columns, instrumental in the careers of other writers (such as Henry Rider Haggard) and popular with the reading public. It was also in this arena that the debates occurred that perhaps did the most damage to Lang's reputation as a literary critic. His review of Thomas Hardy's *Tess of the D'Urbervilles* in 1892, his criticism of the work of Émile Zola and his long-running skirmish with W. D. Howells and others over the value of Romance led to the caricature of him that James articulates to Gosse: of dismissing important new novelists and willfully cultivating 'puerile imagination and fourth-rate opinion' in his many readers.[23]

There may have been resentment of Lang's success in the turn against him that occurs in the 1890s; James and Gosse were not the only writers jealous of their status in the competitive literary world. Publically Lang continued to engage confidently in sharp debates in all the areas of his interests, but privately he expressed increasing lack of certainty about his own worth. In this, as in so much else, Lang is a contradictory figure. He was a very public man and by no means isolated from the social world. Among many connections that he made, he originally introduced James to Gosse, and both to Robert Louis Stevenson. He was also one of the first to notice

Rudyard Kipling, introducing him to Haggard, and he brought together George Saintsbury and Austin Dobson. His reserve, however, is a striking feature of all accounts of him,[24] and he demonstrates an almost pathological privacy. He consistently advised his correspondents to destroy his letters – 'Burn this or some beast will publish it, some day, for ten bob'[25] – and was insistent that no biography of him should be written, instructing his wife to destroy all his papers after his death.[26] He seems to have found socialising painful and upsetting; a remark in a letter to Haggard is typical of many such comments that he makes: 'I came back a week ago [to London] – I hate the place as much as ever, and have no craving for Society; a lot of people I don't want, and who don't want me. I envy Robinson Crusoe.'[27]

His personal and social diffidence translated into an insistence on his outsider status in relation to the subjects on which he wrote. In his letters it is often difficult to tell whether he considers himself a great writer and thinker or a talentless and shallow mind, and in his 1890 essay *How to Fail in Literature* (see Volume 2, pp. 275–90), the failure that he details is actually the description of a highly successful career not unlike his own. The tacking back and forth between these positions is found not just in his journalism but in his writings on other subjects too. In his historical and anthropological work he often stresses his amateur status and suggests that he has no real right to be intervening in the debate, while simultaneously asserting his position in confident terms and questioning the place of those apparently better qualified. In his correspondence this is also evident; a letter to his friend Anna Hills in 1891 is typical:

> I'm doing a book on Homer, and nobody will ever read it, even if I finish it. I have to do over again, and more systematically most that I did last year. This is dull work, and impels me to vivacities of expression about the German commentators. Of all the bustards, the blind owls, the German Homeric critic is the most bewilderingly imbecile. We were at a dance last night: I don't dance and I knew nobody (and do not wish to do either).[28]

He expresses lack of confidence in the eventual success of his work, switches to assertion of the stupidity of existing authorities and then drops immediately into a social scene that exactly mirrors the exclusion yet superiority of his scholarly position.

In the light of this, Lang's attitude to the institutions of culture is unsurprising. When, in the 1890s, there was agitation for the formation of an authoritative cultural body similar to the Académie française, Lang mocked the idea, yet in 1906 he accepted election to a Fellowship of the British Academy, which had finally been established in 1902. When the Academic Committee of the Royal Society of Literature was formed in 1910[29] Lang was among the original group selected (and he accepted), but he wrote to Clement Shorter; 'Thanks for electing me an Academician, but my place, if anywhere, is in the Anthropology lot',[30] while elsewhere he despairs that he will be remembered only for 'totems'.[31] Similarly, writing to Oliver Lodge after the Society for Psychical Research asked Lang to be their President for 1911, he makes light of his credentials for the job, suggesting that they amount only to his need for 'something' about which to 'jaw', and saying that he is 'a mere littérateur (as the hap'ny papers say)'.[32] It would seem that he used the range of his disciplinary interests to disclaim full membership of any of them, but it is exactly in this borderline position that the value of Lang's work appears. It also perhaps explains the lack of attention to his legacy; his refusal of allegiance meant that no school saw him as 'one of their own' and continued to tend to his memory.

Although public recognition continued to be offered and his writing continued at an enormous rate, in his last years Lang, who had always been physically rather frail, became much more so and seemingly beset with depression and anxiety. According to Marie Belloc Lowndes, Mrs Lang had found her husband's behaviour strange:

> He declared that awful calamities were about to befall Europe, and that almost everything for which he cared would be destroyed, especially university buildings and libraries. He further said the little money they possessed would probably be taken from them … even when he was dying, he had tried to make her promise she would leave the old world and settle in America.[33]

At the same time Charles Longman wrote to Haggard concerned for Lang's health and his 'strange depression about public affairs', particularly the strikes that were taking place.[34] The melancholic tendency noted by his friends and his often-stated aversion to 'politics' converged, with his wife claiming only two days after his death 'it was really the strikes that killed him.'[35] Whatever the personal reasons and political conservatism that this might show, it also shows that Lang recognised the change that was happening and saw the shape of the twentieth century: European wars, a greater social democracy and America as the future. Born on a geographical borderland, he died in a temporal one and his work illuminates much of the intellectual conditions of the emergence of the new world from the old.

On the death of his brother Lang wrote 'I know it is for the best, not to survive ourselves',[36] and that wish was almost fulfilled. His house in St Andrews has no plaques, there is no memorial to him, even his gravestone in the old cathedral precincts of St Andrews does not have his name on it. His vast body of work is little known and he is consistently relegated to the footnotes of all the disciplines in which he wrote. These two volumes of selections of his writings are an attempt to address that neglect and to enable his work to be read in a new light; one that shows him in a crucial place in turn-of-the-century intellectual life. Mindful of Saintsbury's prediction that a selection from Lang 'would be so unlikely to satisfy the selector that he would probably never get it finished', and given that a Complete Works would probably occupy about fifty volumes, much has necessarily been omitted from the current volumes. The principle of the selection has been to pick out the pieces most representative of Lang's originality and complexity, and to illustrate his position on contemporary topics of debate. We have not included any of Lang's own poetry or fictional writing, his newspaper leaders or reviews. He also wrote many essays on individual writers and, with the exception of the piece on Zola and the more general surveys in Volume 2, these too have been excluded. Enthusiasts of golf, cricket and fishing will be disappointed at the omission of his many pieces on those subjects. His journalism has been selected where it bears more directly on particular topics, such as Scotland or the business of writing, and where longer essays are also presented, but there remains a great deal of more general interest that does not appear here. A number of the longer pieces included have, in addition, been edited to eliminate repetition and to show the range of his ideas more clearly in relation to each other. It is our hope that the reader *will* be unsatisfied and so look further into the wealth of material that remains.

Andrew Teverson
Alexandra Warwick
Leigh Wilson

Introduction to Volume 2

> There was a time when it was impossible to make a remark on a subject of literature without thinking or being reminded of Mr Andrew Lang. That time is past, and I cannot say I regret it. It is not well to have a dictator of letters, and this one did not (I think) use his power advisedly. A graceful and at times a somewhat invertebrate writer, I think he took less pains than it was possible to take in the ordering of his prejudices by the rules of justice. This would not have mattered in an irresponsible critic, but if such things matter at all, and perhaps they don't, in a critic of wide influence, direct and indirect, it mattered a good deal. The prejudices were not unamiable in themselves, being mainly those of 'the gentlemanly interest,' but they were hardly presented in a manner conforming.[1]

George Street's assessment of Lang was published in *Blackwood's Edinburgh Magazine* in 1898 and, despite the obitural tone of the writer, Lang lived for another fourteen years and continued writing on the subject of literature. In fact, the work that appeared just a few days before his death was his *History of English Literature: From 'Beowulf' to Swinburne* (1912). The description of Lang's influence is not exaggerated and nor is Street's frustration unique; many contemporary and later writers commented on what they saw as Lang's lack of a serious engagement with literary criticism or a critical engagement with serious literature. Part of this irritation is directed perhaps less at Lang than at the state of literature, criticism, education and reviewing at the end of the nineteenth century. In both nineteenth- and twentieth-century commentators there is frequently a sense that someone should have taken up the mantle of Matthew Arnold and forged a manifesto for such work and, for some, the frustrated hope that this might have been Lang. At worst, Lang is accused of encouraging the rise of degraded taste. John Gross, for example, writes in 1969 that,

> for the majority of the members of the library-lending public [Lang] brought words of comfort. At a time when the serious novel and the best-seller seemed to be drifting irretrievably apart, here was a critic who simply conjured away the whole problem of relative values—he refused again and again to recognize that distinctions have to be drawn between art and entertainment, between adult readers and children, between good books and bad books.'[2]

Gross is effectively only repeating Henry James's damning assessment of nearly fifty years earlier, that Lang cultivated 'fourth-rate opinion' such as might have been held 'by the old apple woman on the corner.'[3]

Lang's position in relation to the reading public is much more complex than this, as was the period with which his career coincided, and his writing illustrates clearly the tensions and confusions of the questions about the difference between writing and literature, the function of criticism against the practice of reviewing, the uses of literature and the place of culture that circulated in the *fin-de-siècle* literary world. In his writings on Scotland, history and biography too, he shows not only the complexity and interdisciplinary nature of his own thought but illuminates the contemporary debates on the subjects in ways that neither James, Gross nor many others allow.

Critics and Criticism

Complaints about the sorry condition of literary criticism were already present in the 1880s. Grant Allen, writing in the *Fortnightly Review* in 1882 says:

> criticism is now reduced to such a dead level of mediocrity and impotence as it has never before known. Not, of course, scholarly criticism, art criticism, theatrical criticism; not, above all religious criticism, which plays so large a part in the great underlying struggle of our age. Our present question narrows its bounds to the consideration of criticism applied to books.[4]

Allen's article was only one of a number by a range of prominent people who worried at the question of fiction and the state of criticism across two decades. Robert Louis Stevenson's 'A Gossip on Romance' appeared in *Longman's* in November 1882; Walter Besant's 1884 lecture on 'The Art of Fiction' produced responses from Lang, Stevenson, James and others.[5] In 1891 the topic was still current and the *New Review* conducted two symposia in its pages: 'The Science of Fiction', with contributions from Besant, Paul Bourget and Thomas Hardy, and 'The Science of Criticism', with James, Lang and Edmund Gosse.[6] What was at stake in this 'era of discussion' as James called it[7] was not just the nature and place of fiction, but the competence, or otherwise, of criticism and individual critics.

Lang's clearest sustained statement appears in 'The Science of Criticism', although the principles are re-stated very frequently elsewhere, sometimes just as a few lines in an article on another topic, but always consistently: 'The only kind of Criticism worth reading or writing is that which narrates the adventures of an ingenious and educated mind in contact with masterpieces'.[8] At worst it passes the time, at best it 'does for art and works of art what art does for nature and the works of nature. It clears our eyes, it heightens and intensifies and makes more select our pleasures.'[9] The problem as far as Lang is concerned is that much contemporary criticism is not of the best sort, partly because the work with which it deals is itself of an inferior kind. He ends with a direct jibe at 'Mr Henry James and Mr Saintsbury', suggesting his own loftiness above the material with which critics are confronted, but also indicating the intensely competitive and personalised nature of the debate. His tone throughout is typical: managing to suggest that none of the matter under discussion is of any real value, that his own contribution is paltry and even amateur, yet at the same time that both his opinion and the topic are of great importance.

Lang's critical principles were, fundamentally, those of Matthew Arnold. He was not afraid to criticise Arnold's practice or his poetry,[10] and it seems that he did not make much of Arnold's lectures while a student at Oxford,[11] but he believed, as Arnold did, that the classical works were the best foundation for understanding literature. He refers frequently to Aristotle's *Poetics*, Horace's *Ars Poetica* and Longinus's *On the Sublime*, cornerstones of the education of the literary elite. These were works that Lang knew very well, having written translations or prefaces to all three texts. For him the classics were Arnoldian 'Culture'. As he writes about Homer: 'to forget Homer, to cease to be concerned and even curious about Homer, is to make a step towards a new barbarism' and 'To keep up, to diffuse, as far as we may, interest in the best literature, is the duty of all who have been educated and called to this task.'[12] In the same essay he refers to the copyist monks of the Middle Ages and remarks that 'they, too, were out of harmony with their age, but they were working for the age which was to come.'[13] He voices exactly in this way Arnold's conception of the function of poetry and of the function of criticism, where criticism, the diffusion of the best existing literature, is necessary because, in times of inferior literary production, criticism must hold the place of the poetry-to-come. Lang's essays on the literature of the nineteenth century all suggest that he believes that his is not a great age, but that decline is neither permanent nor inevitable. He suggests that the duty of the critic is to the future; in Arnold's words, to the 'promised land, towards which criticism can only beckon.'[14]

It is partly for this reason that Arnold also disavows practical action and, by implication, politics:

> Everything was long seen, by the young and ardent amongst us, in inseparable connection with politics and practical life … Let us try a more disinterested mode of seeing them; let us take ourselves to the serener life of the mind and spirit … and not, as soon as we get an idea, be running out with it into the street and trying to make it rule there.[15]

This cultivation of disinterestedness is evident in Lang. There is a clear statement of his position in 'Poetry and Politics', published in 1885 in *Macmillan's Magazine,* in which he suggests that an Arnoldian position of serenity has been reached but is now endangered:

> In the happy Truce of the Muses, which now enables us to judge a poet on his literary merits, Mr Courthope has raised a war-cry which will not, I hope, be widely echoed ... [he] has brought back the howls of partisans into a region where they had long been silent. One cannot but regret this intrusion of the factions which have 'no language but a Cry' into the tranquil regions of verse.[16]

This argues very precisely against both party politics applied to literature and the distraction from the purely poetic that such discussion produces. Personal political belief is not a good position from which a critic can start, nor are the beliefs of poets of any use as a measure of their achievements. He is equally opposed to 'novels with a purpose':

> Let us suppose that an author ... has a just and natural desire to reform the world ... a novel is not the place for them. A novel is not a treatise. Many things that need be said should be said simply, directly, with all authorities and evidence. They ought not to mixed up with flirtations, love affairs, and fanciful episodes. They may be true, but, presented in a romance, they may be most mischeviously misunderstood and perverted ... 'Nana', for example, may contain what we should know, and circumstances which we should endeavor to rectify. But a reform of morals would not be aided by letting 'Nana' circulate in English among the readers of Miss Yonge.[17]

As well as Arnold, this aversion to politics is owed equally to the French writer Charles Sainte-Beuve, on whose journalistic practice Lang consciously modelled his own. Sainte-Beuve published his series of topical columns, *Causeries du lundi,* in the newspaper *Le Constitutionnel* for two decades between 1849 and 1869. Writing in France in the immediate aftermath of 1848, the year of revolutions in Europe, and in the long shadow of the French Revolution, Sainte-Beuve's columns constantly inveighed against agitation in both the form and content of literature:

> A dreadful rivalry, a sort of furious contest, has begun in recent years among the strongest men in this potent all-consuming and inflammatory literature. The serial mode of publication, which demands that each new chapter should stun the reader, has forced the tone and feeling of the novel to a desperate and eventually unsustainable extremity of pitch. Let us calm down a little.[18]

For Sainte-Beuve, the critic is the agent of restraint in the immediate moment and thus has a responsibility to preserve the currents of what is best during turbulent times while waiting for the restoration of order. Arnold was no less conscious of the possibility of social unrest and of the necessity of some cohering agency that, like Sainte-Beuve's, both restrains and defers and Lang follows both. Indeed, in 'Politics and Men of Letters' he warns explicitly of the dangers of 'men of letters' on the basis of their involvement in the Reformation and the French Revolution.[19]

In his article for *The Pilot,* 'Politics and Men of Letters' (1900), Lang recognises the mixed nature of the political ideas of many writers, and his own political views were similarly inconsistent. Like many, he remained conscious of what he calls the 'Social Question', displaying a generalised fear of the mass at the same time as a paternalistic sympathy for some individuals and causes. In his 'At the Sign of the Ship' column in *Longman's Magazine* in April 1886 he writes in a Carlylean vein, lamenting the loss of the dignity of work that is suffered by the unemployed and supporting the policy of emigration as the solution. Anti-emigrationists are accused of 'class-hatred'.[20] The same issue of *Longman's* announces that the magazine's initiative to raise money to provide wagons for the supply of inexpensive food to the unemployed has been receiving 'handsome' subscriptions.[21] The subscription list for the 'Donna', as the campaign was called, always appeared directly after the 'Ship' column and such was Lang's influence on the magazine that it could not have done so without his approval. We also find Lang encouraging his readers to send work to a needlewomen's co-operative and linking this project to Walter Besant's novel *The Children of Gibeon*, which depicted the sufferings of workers in the East End of London and was then being serialised in the magazine.[22] Earlier in the same year he writes passionately in support of Besant's proposition of a 'People's Palace' for the benefit of that same deprived district.[23] He showed concern for individuals too, assisting 'X', the working man with whom he published the essay 'The Reading Public' in the *Cornhill Magazine* in 1901, out of unemployment into work as a proof corrector. Yet despite these instances, Lang was certainly no radical, affecting a non-political stance and tending rather to apply an anthropological analysis to 'the problem of poverty' and concluding that history shows us that 'human nature' militates against equality:

> To be sure the starving Fuegians are all equally badly off, and if one man gets a blanket the tribe divides it into equal rags on the spot, and according to First Principles. But then that communistic tradition is not ideally delightful, and implies equality of starvation. To such a state, however, a system of equal and common property would necessarily reduce the boasted Aryan race, and thus our descendants would struggle out of it into civilization again, and so on, *da capo*.[24]

As this suggests, Lang was, in many ways, fundamentally conservative and perhaps became more so in his last years. He may or may not have been killed by the fear of social unrest,[25] but in her edition of his letters to American correspondents, Marysa Demoor suggests that at the end of his life Lang wanted to move to America, and was only stopped by his wife's refusal.[26] His letters to the American academic Brander Matthews give an interesting slant to his pessimism, but also to his perception of the United States as the place of newness and political modernity. In 1888, long before the reported disillusionment of his later years, he writes to Matthews, 'It will be jolly to meet you in summer, but I'm sick of England, and would rather be in America',[27] and again in November 1889, 'This country has gone to the devil: I expect to end my days, if I am permitted so to do, under the Stars and Stripes, which I think will be the British flag of the future.'[28] At a time when American writers like Henry James, and a little later T. S. Eliot, were crossing the Atlantic in the other direction seeking more traditional values, Lang seems to have had at least some desire to embrace the new.

Lang's politics were also complicated by his Scottish identity. He was a monarchist but refused, only half-jokingly, to recognise Victoria as Queen because, in his Jacobite view, she had no proper claim to the throne. Of course, an anti-political stance is an ideological position in itself, but Lang's method is perfectly illustrated in 'Poetry and Politics'. In response to William Courthope's claim that the work of Homer, Milton and Virgil 'can readily be analysed into their elements', he asserts absolutely that it cannot and that this is, in fact, the very test of poetry. If it can be analysed (like Pope's work) it is not poetry. Reason, or argument, has no place, the 'matter is not for argument but for perception.'[29] After this assertion of the innate sensibility that enables perception, he says that we 'follow our tastes, incapable of conversion' but then veers away from examining the origin of those tastes, warning, 'All this, however, is an attempt to plumb "the abysmal depths of personality."'[30] Instead, he equates understanding with feeling and then places it beyond the realm of enquiry: in the inmost self, the abysmal depths. While this has its basis in Arnoldian disinterestedness it comes to be, in Lang, an almost pathological aversion to examination of the personal both in himself and others.

Lang's impersonalness is a consistent feature of accounts of him: Kipling wrote that he was 'as detached to all appearances as a cloud'.[31] It is more than the 'Oxford manner' of languid detachment that his friend Sidney Colvin described,[32] and Haggard, one of his closest friends, suggested that his aloofness covered a deep melancholy.[33] Despite his admonitions to correspondents to destroy his letters, many of them do survive, though it is hard to see what he thought so 'hasty, indiscreet, inaccurate' [34] about them as they withdraw from expression even, or especially, at moments of extreme emotion. On the death of Haggard's young son he writes a short note: 'Dear Haggard, I am more sorry than I can say. I don't like to say anything. Nothing can be more cruelly sad. God bless you. Yours ever A Lang.'[35] On the death of his brother Thomas, Lang writes to Haggard a brief account of Thomas's cricketing and college career, and concludes: 'I tell you because you are a good fellow, if ever there was one, and so was he, but please do not reply on this matter.'[36] Elsewhere, in his essay on Tennyson he remarks, 'Concerning the affection between him and Arthur Hallam one does not care to speak; the topic is not for comment, and certainly not for mine',[37] and he uses the same example again in a letter to Brander Matthews, where he mentions personal writing with distaste but also some unconscious self-revelation. Writing to Matthews about J. M. Barrie's book on Barrie's mother, he says:

> Nobody but a very reserved shy Scot could have written the Mother book, but I really believe it is no worse than *In Memoriam*, or any other personal expressions of affection. I certainly could not take money for it, and I daresay he won't.[38]

This intense aversion to emotional expression, self-revelation and revelation of the self in others shapes his criticism and reviewing. While it follows Arnold's rejection of 'depth-hunting' that he saw as a manifestation of the Romantic sickness of self-absorption, it also echoes Sainte-Beuve's 'personal method' where biography is relevant, but only in what might be thought of as the public details of a writer's life. The facts of Walter Scott's Scottishness, for example, are of relevance to his work, but his romantic life is not.[39] Although in his work on ghosts and psychic phenomena he is interested in the psychology of credence, he concentrates that in a socio-historical or anthropological account of the evolution of certain types of belief, rather than speculating on personal and individual motivation. His remark 'more claymores, less psychology'[40] is often used as the damning summary of his failure to appreciate the modern novel, but Lang's apparent rejection of psychology is only of what he thought to be groundless and ultimately prurient speculation on the private lives of individuals, real or fictional. It is, for him, not properly scientific and no better than the harmful gossip and sensational revelations that he saw as features of the worst kind of New Journalism.

In this anti-individualism he stands apart from the Paterian Aestheticism expressed in the artistic movements of the *fin de siècle* that included writers like Oscar Wilde. Lang's relation to Aestheticism and the Decadents (and indeed Wilde himself) is interesting in his near silence on the subjects. At Oxford he knew Pater, and Pater himself referred to Lang as 'my friend' and sent him *Studies in the History of the Renaissance* when it was published in 1873, the year before Lang left Oxford. Twenty years later he wrote in a letter, 'Time was when I admired Mr Pater inordinately, and Rossetti beyond measure, but one can introduce some limit to one's worship. A good deal in fact.'[41] His aversion to Aestheticism seems to have set in rather quickly; he met Stevenson in the winter of 1873–4 and his initial dislike was due to the latter's appearance: 'Long cape. Long hair. Queer hat. Damned queer. Hands: white, bony, beautiful. Didn't like the cape. Didn't like the hair … seemed another aesthete [Sidney] Colvin had discovered. Didn't like him.'[42] Lang does not mention Wilde[43] even though some of their interests might seem to coincide: Wilde published a book of fairy tales, *The Happy Prince* (1888), and a long piece on criticism, 'The Critic as Artist' (1891) which had first appeared in two parts under the title 'The True Value and Function of Criticism' in the *Nineteenth Century* in July and September 1890. Wilde certainly knew Lang's work from their shared illustrator Jacomb Hood.[44] Yet although he distances himself quite firmly from the positions of Aestheticism or Decadence, Lang was not critical of them, in fact he defended the Young Man, and specifically Henry James, against Robert Buchanan's ranting attack on the movements in the figure of 'The Modern Young Man'.[45] That defence shows that his coolness towards Aestheticsm and his partiality for adventure stories were not rooted in degenerationist ideas, and he did not see the romance as a crucial defence against the declining virility of contemporary manhood, as others did.

Realism, Romance and the Reading Public

If Lang rejected the Oxford influence of Pater, many of his ideas, including those on romance, are derived from his university years. Matthew Arnold, according to his biographer Lionel Trilling, passed for a Hegelian 'probably without ever having read him', [46] and the same can be suggested of Lang, though, unlike Arnold, we do know that he did actually read Hegel.[47] Lang was in the centre of Oxford Hegelianism at its most intense point. Benjamin Jowett, who had studied Hegel in Germany as a young man, was the dominating presence in Oxford and Lang met him first aged 14. He writes of Jowett:

> He was the tutor of two of my uncles, and my own. I have frequently walked and talked with that best and most loyal of friends: in town, in the country, at Oxford, as a boy, an undergraduate, a fellow of my College, and after leaving Merton for good, I saw much of the Master.[48]

Lang was also tutored by Thomas Hill Green (who had been Jowett's student) and was contemporary with A. C. Bradley at Balliol, his brother F. H. Bradley at Merton and William Wallace at Merton. All, particularly Green and Wallace, were important scholars of Hegel, and their translations, readings and applications of his philosophy were fundamental to the development of versions of Idealism in late-Victorian intellectual and social life. Jowett was Regius Professor of Greek; his introduction of Hegelian philosophy into the study of the classics and his synthesis of it with Darwinian ideas of evolution had a profound influence on its teaching at Oxford and, it seems, on Lang.[49]

Lang produced three books on Homer: *Homer and the Epic* (1893), *Homer and his Age* (1906) and *The World of Homer* (1910). These are published late in his career, but he had produced many earlier articles[50] and in them all he begins from the same position: that Homer was one person and that he wrote the *Odyssey* and the *Iliad* in the sixth century BCE. In this, he was at odds with contemporary scholarship, where the prevailing view was that the works were a composite by many different hands, produced over a much longer period. His argument is that the works are a 'complete and harmonious picture of an age', a historical unity, and that the epic can only present 'a unity of historical ideas if it be the work of one age.'[51] Such unity is also dependent on the poet. The Preface to *Homer and the Epic* begins, 'The Homeric question, the question of the unity of authorship, is a literary problem.'[52] Such harmonious perfection can only be the work of one mind expressing its age.

Though he takes issue with 'the Germans' frequently throughout his work on Homer, Hegel is never mentioned, yet Lang's view is a precise echo of his in this respect. In his long genealogy of the epic Hegel writes:

> an epic poem as an actual work of art can spring from one individual only … the spirit of an age or a nation is indeed the underlying efficient cause, but the effect, and actual work of art, is only produced when this cause is concentrated into the individual genius of a single poet.[53]

Hegel's translator also notes he was 'in advance of his time when he repudiated the Homeric scholarship of his contemporaries.'[54]

It is also in Hegel's ideas on the epic that there may be an answer to those writers frustrated by Lang's apparent failure to engage with the novel on a serious level. Hegel writes: 'In the other spheres of our present national and social life there is opened up in the domain of epic an unlimited field for romances, tales and novels.'[55] For him, such modern works are in the 'domain of epic' but with a crucial difference:

> it is quite different with romance, the modern popular epic. Here we have completely before us again the wealth and many-sidedness of interests, situations, character, relations involved in life, the wide background of a whole world, as well as the epic portrayal of events. But what is missing is the *primitive* poetic general situation out of which the epic proper proceeds. A romance in the modern sense of the word presupposes a world already prosaically ordered.[56]

For Lang the novel is interesting, but he did not really believe that it mattered; like Arnold he thought poetry was the place where true culture could be found and through which the civilised harmonious serenity of Homer could again be achieved. The novel, then, matters only as entertainment, an 'anodyne' as he called it.[57] His attraction to romance, rather than manifesting an incorrigible taste for rubbishy adventure tales, can be explained as a drawing towards the place where the spirit of the classical epic can still be found in a 'prosaically ordered' world. If, as Lang says, 'the epic, in the Odyssey, becomes a romance, the best of all romances'[58] then the best of modern romances approach most closely to the ideal form. Lang's frequent statements about 'boys' books' or his suggestion that the boy is a kind of ideal reader have often been quoted in proof of the anti-intellectualism of his literary pleasures.[59] This too can be seen differently in relation to Hegelian ideas. Hegel writes: 'in epic proper the childlike consciousness of a people is expressed for the first time in poetic form.'[60] During the nineteenth century ideas of the child and of childhood changed and in their most complex form become deeply enmeshed in post-Darwinian sociology and anthropology, where a strong equation is made between the developmental stages of the individual through childhood, adolescence and adulthood and the development of humanity in general through analogous states. This has far-reaching consequences, most obviously in emerging ideas of race and class and the formation of new hierarchies of social and global dominance, but Lang is not among those who ascribe moral weight to different stages. For him, childhood, or its analogue the primitive, is neither an inferior condition nor a sign of degeneration, but contains the possibility of the persistence of the poetic in the prosaically ordered world. He contests the notion that romance is just swashbuckling adventure 'only met with in Central Africa or on the Spanish Main'. Rather, it is 'that element which gives a sudden sense of the strangeness and the beauty of life; that power which has the gift of dreams.'[61]

In some sense, then, romance for Lang is 'sublimated anthropology' as George Stocking claims,[62] but there is a stronger reason embedded here for his antipathy towards Realism. Hegel, continuing his comments on the modern popular epic, observes that:

> all the more scope may be given to the poet the less he can avoid bringing into his descriptions the prose of real life, though without for that reason remaining himself on the ground of the prosaic and commonplace.[63]

Again it is possible to see a relationship to Lang's position. Lang's critique is actually of what would now be called Naturalism, rather than Realism as defined in contemporary terms. He had a high estimation of much of what is today more usually called Realism, such as the work of Dickens; it was the Naturalism of writers like Zola for which he had such a profound dislike. He was also unsympathetic to British writers in a similar style, like George Moore and George Gissing. He wrote of the latter's 'perverted idealism' and complained that 'he selects unhappy things and pushes to unhappy conclusions'.[64] In all his essays and remarks on Realism and Naturalism, Lang never denies that the people, events and situations represented exist, nor contends that the works in which they appear are wrong or even bad. In 'Literary Anodynes' (1888), for example, he writes: 'I do not say that these philosophies of all things in three volumes have no right to exist.'[65] His objection was not, in Hegel's terms, to the prose of real life but to the writer choosing to remain on the ground of the prosaic and not seeking within it the 'poetry' of epic or romance.

The frequency of Lang's return to comment on Zola is revealing. This is not simply because Zola was a convenient representative of Naturalism, nor because his novels were a current subject of review and discussions in newspapers and magazines. Zola clearly troubles him; in his first long essay on him in 1882 he begins with a familiar Langian gesture of quarantine, placing his subject outside his concern. Here it is the foreigners, the Russians, Dutch, Italians, Spanish, Danish, Norwegians, Germans and even Americans who appreciate Zola, while 'England alone holds aloof … our unfortunate Puritanism, alas! prevents us from understanding M. Zola and the joys of *naturalisme*'. He says that:

> a minute critical study is impossible in English … but it is not impossible to indicate and criticize M. Zola's literary ideas, which now make so much stir; to describe his method; to trace the history of his success; and even to point out certain qualities of real value, certain passages of distinction and of beauty in his romances.[66]

Lang admires Zola's technique and his writing and manifestly thinks him better than many contemporary English novelists. He admires, too, Zola's conviction and tries to separate him from responsibility for his uncritical worshippers and imitators. He recognises Zola as not prurient, but as highly moral, and that his morality is right. In the *Illustrated London News* in 1894 he defends him against a very personal attack by George Moore, making Moore seem petty and vain in comparison with Zola, who he calls 'a great incongruous brute force'.[67] His note on Zola's death in 1902 opens with an admission that he owes Zola an apology, though precisely for what it is not quite clear. His conclusion seems to be that Zola was a great writer and a great moralist, but that his artistic project was fundamentally misconceived precisely because it was a 'moral mission', thus 'his whole method was a blunder in art but behind it was that genius which takes endless trouble'.[68] Even in this short note Lang returns to the metaphors he often uses in discussion of Naturalism: the microscope, the laboratory and the dissecting room. Zola 'saw everything too big',[69] as if his own eye were the microscope. Elsewhere he says directly of Zola: 'This word "science" is always in his mouth, and it does not seem to occur to him that art and literature are one thing, and science quite other.'[70] Zola's real offence is not to know these things, but to reveal them, to 'sow broadcast, the knowledge of secret and nameless iniquities.'[71]

Lang's position, then, on Realism and romance is more complex than has been allowed; made up of a number of different elements. His loyalty to his friends, often noted in memoirs, plays a part as Stevenson and Haggard had both pitched in to the debate in print rather earlier than Lang[72] and were roundly attacked. Haggard was personally criticised, notably by W. T. Stead, who accused him of plagiarism. Lang's article of 1887, 'Literary Plagarism', is a defence of his friend as much as it is a statement of his own position. Lang also enjoyed a tussle in print and, having found an adversary in the American critic and novelist William Dean Howells who wrote for *Harper's* magazine, he took every opportunity to disagree with him on romance and other topics. Howells later conceded that his had been 'a losing fight' and that 'the monstrous rag-baby of romanticism was as firmly in the saddle as it was before the joust began'.[73]

Lang's position with regard to science is not as straightforward as his critique of Zola may suggest. While he rhetorically disdained the scientific when he came across it in the literary, in other areas of his writing he explicitly strove to be considered 'scientific'; to be methodical, logical, faithful to the dictates of the evidence, to be properly inductive. Lang's anthropological work, and his writing on anthropology as a method, asserts again and again that anthropology is a science to the extent that it works according to these principles. In 'Science and Superstition' in *Magic and Religion* (1901), Lang sets out his vision of scientific method, and goes on to argue that anthropology has to follow this if it is to be taken seriously:

> We all know what we mean by science; science is 'organised common sense.' Her aim is the acquisition of reasoned and orderly knowledge. Presented with a collection of verified facts, it is the part of science to reduce them to order, and to account for their existence in accordance with her recognised theory of things. If the facts cannot be fitted into the theory, it must be expanded or altered; for we must admit that, if the facts are verified, there is need for change and expansion in the theory. The 'colligation' of facts demands hypotheses, and these may not, at the moment of their construction, be verifiable ... Our hypotheses then must be consistent with our actual knowledge of nature and of human nature, and our conjectured causes must be adequate to the production of the effects.[74]

However, while this does suggest a straightforward sense of scientific empiricism, Lang often used the case of anthropology in his defence of psychical research, whose scientific status was strongly contested. Lang links the two disciplines in a way that urges, against this contestation, its claims to be a science. As anthropology, now a respectable science, was once on the margins of science, so is psychical research: 'Anthropology has herself but recently emerged from that limbo of the unrecognised in which Psychical Research is pining.'[75] Lang is clearly suggesting that psychical research, too, will one day emerge from such limbo and be considered a science. Lang defended psychical researchers against the scorn of some scientists, as in his repudiation of the criticisms of the anatomist Charles Sedgwick Minot.[76] At the same time, elsewhere, Lang seems frustrated with psychical research for its very scientific language and attempts at rigour. This knot of positions can be seen clearly in Lang's essay 'Ghosts Up To Date', published in *Blackwood's Edinburgh Magazine* in 1894, where he prefaces his account (and implicit defence) of psychical research as a science with a lament for the scientising of ghosts:

> The most frivolous pastimes have now a habit of degenerating into scientific exercises ... even ghost stories, the delight of Christmas Eve, have been ravaged and annexed by psychology. True, there are some who aver that the science of the Psychical Society does not hold water; but, in any case, it is as

> dull and difficult as if it were some orthodox research dear to Mr Herbert Spencer. To prove this fact, I had marked for quotation some remarks, by eminent ghost-hunters, on the provinces and parts of the brain, on the subjective and the objective, the conscious, the reflex, the automatic ... which would frighten off the most intrepid amateurs...If we must understand all that kind of thing before we can enjoy a ghost story, we who are middle-aged may despair.[77]

His review of Émile Zola's book on Lourdes is another case that illuminates Lang's complex veering between the scientific and the supernatural with the effect of blurring the distinctions between them, even as he calls for those distinctions. He describes Zola's detailing of all the conflicting interests (commercial, spiritual, psychological, fraudulent) at play on the pilgrimage site and agrees with him that all are present, but suggests that Zola finds himself in the same position as the Church: 'the difficulty of the Church (without irony) is to restrict the miraculous'; in order to maintain some premium on them 'there really ought to be an economy in miracles'.[78] If scarcity value is necessary to maintain miracles like those at Lourdes through restriction both of the occurrence and the explanation of the miraculous, then this is also true of literature. About Stevenson's revelation of how he wrote 'The Wrecker' Lang says:

> many readers may actually enjoy seeing the toy taken to pieces, may be pleased to watch the disintegration of the puppets. It is an odd taste, but it may be a taste which is prevalent. We are too curious; we have too much of the scientific spirit even in our pleasures.[79]

Similarly, in an essay on style Lang says 'we set up an unknown God called style, which we ignorantly worship' but that the ignorance is somehow necessary and inevitable: 'how the thing was done by Shakespeare and by the Greeks you cannot by searching find them out.'[80] Criticism, then, is bound to fail if conceived of as an analytic project. An 'economy of miracles' has to be practised: if it is possible to see how it is done, then that writing is not the greatest, and if the mechanisms are revealed the power of the marvellous is weakened. 'Science' can tell us about the conditions of the emergence of literature, its changing form and function, but in the matters of style and effect the marvellous has to remain in tension with explanation.

There also appears to be a question of gender at work in Lang's attitude to both criticism and the writing of Realism, in so far as they are presented as neither manly nor gentlemanly pursuits. Lang's conception of gentlemanliness is not prudish. In 'The Evolution of Literary Decency' (1900) his question is: 'Why did decency, or prudery if anyone pleases, come *suddenly* into vogue between 1770 and 1800?'[81] Crucially, he rejects any notion that this is a reflection of 'a sweeping purification of "Society"' and locates it entirely within the social function of literature, which then acquires its own momentum, re-evaluating literature of the past as well as producing new forms in the present. Thus Lang suggests that Fielding becomes 'indecent' as the morality of his work is embedded in his comedy and Victorian morality can only recognise the serious. Morality and prudery are firmly separated and the latter condemned as a false, fashionable emotional attitude. In 'Literary Decency' he places the blame on the rise of middle-class women readers who enjoyed 'sentiment, didacticism, and romance, and terror' but also on 'the Wesleyan Reformation acting on the middle classes far beyond the bounds of the Wesleyan communion.'[82] Lang's description of the Wesleyan movement is perceptive, identifying it as essentially romantic in that it is rooted in public manifestation of feeling and emotion. Thus we come to a rather familiar position: the distrust of women, emotion and femininity and the tangling of the three in a manner that is typical of many at the *fin de siècle*.

Lang's aversion to the teaching of literature appears to be partly based in his recognition of it as a subject for women. In the last decades of the nineteenth century the active assertion by women of rights to education, rewarding work, self-determination in matters of property and personhood caused very noticeable reaction. Lang demonstrates very clearly the elements of this reaction – an aversion to knowing women in both senses: he does not wish to know about them, and he does not wish them to manifest their knowledge, on certain subjects at least. In 'Realism and Romance' (1887), for example, he writes of the Realists:

> If I were to draw up an indictment, I might add that some of them have an almost unholy knowledge of the nature of women. One would as lief explore a girl's room, and tumble about her little household treasures, as examine so curiously the poor secrets of her heart and tremors of her frame.[83]

A 'Sign of the Ship' column from 1896 is further revealing. It is a complicated piece in which he repeats the literary decency argument around Lady Eastlake's 1847 review of *Jane Eyre* in which she says that 'no virtuous woman could have written *Jane Eyre*'. Lang's piece begins as an account of changing practice (1847 is represented as the distant past), continues as a kind of gallant defence of Brontë's honour and concludes with heavy sarcasm:

> We ought to be thankful for our modern advantages and the surprising additions to our knowledge of the bad side of human nature and the obscurer maladies which beset the human frame that we owe to lady novelists. Before we knew them, like Falstaff, we 'knew nothing.'
> They unflinchingly expose vice, adding none of the allurements of humour, or style, or taste, or even grammar. Nothing but good, properly considered, can come of such maids and matrons, and their rampages in romance.[84]

It appears that, in a confused fashion, Romance is identified with masculinity and Realism/Naturalism with femininity (or at least ungentlemanliness), rather than with men and women. Lang makes no distinction between earlier male and female writers, indeed, in 'Victorian Literature' he names four 'great masters of the novel': Dickens, Thackeray, George Eliot and Charlotte Brontë. He also admires Jane Austen, against contemporary popular taste, but perhaps precisely because she refuses 'Analysis or Passion, or Realism, or Naturalism, or Irreverence, or Religious Open-mindedness'.[85] His scorn for some women writers is part of his dislike of Realism; women Realists and their 'real' women are in some way worse than their male counterparts. His attitude is manifest in the female characters he most admired. He is attracted to iconic women of history: Helen of Troy, Mary, Queen of Scots and Joan of Arc, about all of whom he wrote fiction and non-fiction. Robert Rait, in his eulogy to Lang, describes him more than once as 'chivalrous' in his historical writings,[86] but this is less true of his history, where he is careful to respect the facts, than it is of his responses to fiction. He reserved special reverence for Haggard's Ayesha ('She' of the 1886 novel), writing to Haggard: 'You can't expect me to be in love with all your women; a heart devoted to Ayesha has no room for more.'[87] For Lang, the ideal woman was neither worldly nor of this world. He writes tellingly in an article on Shakespeare's comedies:

> Everyone, it may be supposed, has his favourite lady in Shakespeare, among his women every man meets that soul kindred to his own, and immortally longed for, whom we do not generally find in this little life, though perhaps she may welcome us in another.[88]

It is a confrontation with the anti-Helen, or anti-Ayesha, that produced one of Lang's most notorious clashes: his review of Thomas Hardy's *Tess of the D'Urbervilles*. Generally, Lang refused to review newly-published books he did not like; 'there is little pleasure in criticising where one is not in full sympathy with the subject',[89] he wrote, and he often expressed similar sentiments. His review of *Tess* concludes by saying quite clearly that the book may well be good, but it is not to his taste.[90]

Although initially Hardy appears to have been more upset by another notice in the January number of the *Saturday Review*, it was Lang's review to which Hardy responded (naming Lang) in the preface to the fifth edition of *Tess*, and privately he wrote:

> Lang's article on 'Tess' in the New Review is, of course, Langy. If Andrew, with his knowledge and opportunities, had a heart instead of a hollow place where his heart ought to be, he would by this time have been among the immortals of letters instead of in the sorry position of gnawing his quill over my poor production. Or, if accident forced him to this business, he would have felt the smallness of stopping to pick out the trivial incidents of a first edn of a book of 140,000 words, and would have put his finger on the real faults of the story.[91]

Robert Louis Stevenson hated the novel and he and Lang corresponded on the topic,[92] rather more frankly than in Lang's review; later in the year of the review of *Tess* he wrote to Stevenson: 'Hardy can't even look at a flint quarry but he falls to talking about phalluses.'[93] The reason for their shared dislike seems to have been the representation of women and of sexuality, rather than failure to recognise the novel's literary merit, as the majority of Lang's published response to Hardy's preface is concerned with the figure of Tess herself.[94]

A short essay of Lang's from 1891 is equally illuminating in this respect. It is almost a coda to the earlier 'Realism and Romance' and although entitled 'Notes on Fiction' it is actually about the place of love in the novel. He opens with Samuel Johnson's definition of the novel as a tale 'usually of love' and then, using a statistical survey of publishing in 1889, calculates that as 1,040 novels were published in that year, the public was 'provided [with] about 8000 studies of the passion of love' in one year alone. He then begins to separate the 'masters of English fiction', about whom he says 'character and incident are their materials, not character as dominated by the passion of love'.[95] Women writers, he suggests, are more convincing of the reader (he excludes Mary Braddon, but includes Rhoda Broughton and Charlotte Brontë). Conviction, he decides, is produced by the 'unnamed gift' that can make us 'believe as we read' as opposed to 'mere descriptions'. Immediately, this gift is shown as the gift of (some) children and 'the novelist must never, in this sense, put away childish things'. His conclusion is that 'the greatest English novelists live by anything rather than their love stories.'[96] In 'Realism and Romance' we see what he means by his discussion of 'boys' books'. After his praise of Stevenson and Haggard he writes:

> Mr Stevenson and Mr Rider Haggard have both written novels, have both written boys' books. Personally, I prefer their boys' books to their novels. They seem happier in their dealings with men than with women, with war rather than love.[97]

What Lang is perhaps confessing to in 'Realism and Romance', 'Notes on Fiction', 'Literary Anodynes' and elsewhere is the preference for the company of men, which in itself is a description of the dwindling male sphere in which life and fiction are invaded by real women and women realists; the last retreat is to the world of the boys' book. Lang is certainly not alone. Fiction of the 1880s and 1890s is marked by stories and novels 'without a petticoat in the whole history'.[98] In the complex negotiations of gender in the late nineteenth century, the apparent withdrawal from femininity is frequently a withdrawal from adult sexuality or adulthood altogether. In Lang's case, with his emotional privacy and seeming aversion to people in general, the dimension of gender becomes more complicated to discern. As well as his respect for some dead women writers, he also encouraged the career of at least one living: Alice Shield, with whom he collaborated on *The King Over the Water* (1907). His many letters to Anna Hills show her to be not just a close friend but an intellectual equal as they exchange books and ideas and he consults with her on his work.

It is not women that he dislikes, but the emotionality and more specifically the adult sexuality with which they are associated. The vehemence of Lang's stand against Realism and against the representation of love can perhaps be explained in part by this very personal position, and in turn we can begin to see again the confusion of elements that shapes his literary criticism. His inheritance of Hegelian and Arnoldian philosophies from his Oxford education combines with his own deep aversion to the exploration of the 'abysmal depths of personality' to make his literary work obstinate and self-denyingly limited in a way that his work in other fields is not. There are indications that he was perhaps conscious of this, most noticeably in his frequent return to Zola. In the piece written on Zola's death, it seems that the apology that he feels is owed is not so much to Zola as to a more general audience. He acknowledges that it is possible for a moral man to intervene in public affairs, as Zola did in the Dreyfus case, and comes close to suggesting that he may himself have misconceived his own moral duty in his pathological privacy, as he does again in 'Politics and Men of Letters'.

Lang also had a complex relationship to 'the people', strongly espousing a kind of democracy of literature while excluding explicitly political discussion about it. He is also faced with a problem familiar to many late Victorians – the people. Even in versions of socialist thought this is visible; despite a political commitment to 'the people' as an idea, as actual persons they are less tolerable. Lang is by no means a socialist, but he is deeply interested in 'peoples', and their societies, histories and beliefs. Grant Allen originally suggested the phrase 'the romance of anthropology' to describe the works of Haggard and Stevenson, and in doing so may well having been picking up Lang's association and influence on those writers.[99] Despite his deep knowledge, Lang cannot, however, overcome the disparity between what might be called the 'folk' and people as individuals. This is apparent in his attitude to the 'reading public'. In his anthropology his description of early societies as 'communistic' is rarely pejorative and seems rather to be illustrating the extent to which 'early peoples' might be early but they are not primitive (in its pejorative sense). In both *Myth, Ritual and Religion* (1887) and *The Making of Religion* (1898) he is keen to show that the practice of Aboriginal peoples of sharing what they have so that no-one is without pre-dates missionary intervention, and that it is evidence that they have ethics. In fact he quotes the belief of the elders that young men, after contact with whites, lose this selflessness and generosity. He concludes: 'So much for the anthropological dogma that early theology has no ethics.'[100]

Longman's Magazine, from its first appearance in 1882, addressed itself to the new reading public (in part produced by the 1870 Elementary Education Act), as Charles Longman put it, to the 'immense class [that] exists amongst us'.[101] In Longman's words there is a clear sense of that class being separate from his, and Lang's, own, yet existing in very close promixity to it.

Although the cheaper price of his magazine (at sixpence it was half the price of other monthly journals) did not attract the literate working classes as hoped, it continued to expound a broadly democratic literary mission. Julia Reid has suggested that Lang's advocacy of romance was partly motivated by this democratising impulse, but that under pressure from contemporary social problems of class and gender, *Longman's*', and Lang's, 'enthusiasm for "mass culture" breaks down and is displaced onto a nostalgic, pastoralised populism.'[102]

It seems to be true that other work published in *Longman's* during the 1890s does tend towards the pastoralised populism that Reid identifies, but Lang's case is perhaps more complex. His view was never that the romance was the form appropriate for the non-intellectual's less refined sensibility, but rather that the reader deserved better than what he saw as the trash of much contemporary fiction. Despite the caricatured view that critics like Margaret Beetham propagate,[103] Lang was not an undiscriminating champion of genre fiction; he did, for example, estimate the early work of Henry James rather highly.[104] It is also true that after 1900 a certain exasperation with the reading public is apparent in his work. In a short piece in *The Pilot* in 1901 he writes about footnotes, suggesting that the 'bookish man revels in them', but that 'the "general" reader cannot endure them. They distract the attention of the general reader (which is about as concentrated as that of a kitten)'.[105] In the same year he writes in the 'Ship' that 'the increase in the number of readers has begotten a class of printed trash',[106] but in both articles he suggests the responsibility of *all* readers and writers and persistently asserts that the reading public deserves better material than it is receiving. For him, romance is that better material, because it is the form in which 'the people' or the folk can be expressed at their best, as they were in the ancient form of the epic.

There is a continuity of thought here with his anthropological work. Whereas some critics like Beetham have asserted that 'Lang subscribed to a hierarchy which was not only racial but specifically national',[107] this is demonstrably not the case. He departed rather quickly from Edward Tylor's progressivist narrative as proposed in *Primitive Culture* (1871) and consistently suggests both a continuity of so-called 'primitive thought' and the equal validity of primitive beliefs and practices as ways of representing and interacting with the world.[108] In all his work there is implicitly as well as often explicitly an assertion that 'reality' is plural and that more than one thing can be true at any time. In writings on psychic phenomena he clearly describes the complex forces that are present: deliberate fraud, commercial interest, contestation by different social groups, materiality, the 'other' – all can be in operation without any one being 'true' and rendering the others false. In literature, for Lang, there is good writing and bad writing in purely stylistic terms, but there is no hierarchy of forms or genres, just as there is no hierarchy in social or racial existence. Thus it is not so much a question of democracy as pluralism. Lang's pluralism leads him to what appears to be, and sometimes is, a democratic position, but equally it does not necessarily entail any action in the world.

The Business and Institutions of Literature

Late nineteenth-century journalism is an intensely self-conscious business, often appearing almost as interested in itself as it is in other subjects. Lang is similarly self-conscious of his 'trade' and illuminating of the crowded and changing world of publishing and its current concerns, taking a decided stand, for example, against the 'New Journalism'.[109] He knew well the 'Grub Street' image and the associated figure of the 'hack', not least in their inheritance from eighteenth-century models of periodical culture. He is conscious of writing as a business located in material conditions, as we see in the opening statement of 'The Science of Criticism', where he describes it as 'the form of skilled labour which is occupied in writing about other men's books, old or new.'[110] He clearly identifies it as *work*, and in a number of articles, and particularly in his *Longman's Magazine* column 'At the Sign of the Ship', he writes frequently of what he calls 'Literature as a Trade'.[111] In this he participates in all the contemporary debates. Although he frequently mentions the poor remuneration that writers receive, refers to the 'sweated labour' of writing and inveighs against the lack of international copyright law (which enables American publishers to reprint work without payment), he is against any attempts, such as those of Walter Besant with the Society of Authors, to redress these wrongs through collective action. In his 'Sign of the Ship' column of July 1893, he is responding directly to the Congress of Authors assembled in Chicago and which Besant was attending. His language is all of the market, but he concludes in something of a muddle between asserting the writer as an independent trader and a person driven by the Muse to create. He is of the opinion that any protectionism or unionisation would distort the natural competition of the market and that writers should continue to sell their work as and when they can, and for the best price they can command. He is confused, however, by a notion of genius that is sometimes coupled with commercial acumen. As he puts it in *How to Fail in Literature* (1890):

> Some have the gift, the natural incommunicable power, without the ambition, others have the ambition but no other gift from any Muse. This class is the more numerous, but the smallest class of all has both the power and the will to excel in letters.[112]

How to Fail in Literature strongly expresses a sense of writing as a craft and it is an odd mixture of stylistic and professional advice, where failure simultaneously seems to be 'the goal of ignorance, incompetence, lack of common sense, conceited dullness, and certain practical blunders' [113] and thus the deserved fate of the talentless, but also a mark of honour for the genuinely inspired.

Lang was ambivalent, too, about 'professional' recognition in the form of honours and appointments. In his speculations on the idea of an Academy, he gives his own list of those he imagines might be selected 'on the French principle'. Although he lists Thomas Hardy, George Meredith, Mr Swinburne, Leslie Stephen and Robert Bridges, Lang notes that 'there is not one literary gent in the Forty' and says that 'an Academy does not exist in the interests of what the public calls Literature, but in the interests of learning, research, science, style, and such trifles.'[114] He clearly places himself as a 'literary gent', that is, a professional writer, on the side of the public against the academics and respected authors. Yet when the Academic Committee of the Royal Society of Literature was formed in 1910 [115] Lang accepted the election to the founding group. He also seems to have been close on a number of occasions to professional positions in the field of literature. In a letter of 1889 he writes that he had considered applying for the Chair at Glasgow but that it would be too much work, though in a second letter he is at pains to says that 'the Crown' had offered the post and he had turned it down.[116] Roger Lancelyn Green suggests that Lang was a candidate for the Merton Professorship in 1885; he certainly wrote sharply in *The Academy* at the suggestion that 'popular writers should not occupy the position' saying that:

> a man of real capacity and knowledge … is sometimes driven into periodical literature just because he is *not* endowed. He must write what people at large can read, or he must starve; and this necessity sadly limits the time and energy he can bestow on unremunerative labours of a more 'solid' and 'serious' description.[117]

He was proposed as Warden of Merton in 1903[118] and Philip Waller suggests that Lang was possibly a candidate for Poet Laureate in 1892.[119] He received honorary doctorates (from St Andrews in 1885 and Oxford in1904), but his formal teaching, such as in the post of Gifford Lecturer at St Andrews, was on anthropology. At Oxford he lectured on English history and on anthropology, not on literary subjects. He stood against the establishment of English as university subject, posing the question directly: 'Can English literature be made, and should it be made, the subject of teaching and examination in the Universities?' Lang's answer on both counts is, emphatically, 'no'.[120]

Through the later nineteenth century 'English' as literary study began to appear gradually in the universities' extension schools, attended largely by women and lower-middle-class men, while in the universities themselves it existed mainly as philology or history, or a combination of both. The introduction of literary English in universities was a troubled process, opposed by many within them. Plans for a new School of English Language and

Literature were approved at Oxford in 1893, 'with no clear agreement having been reached on its nature or purpose'.[121] The Merton Professorship of English Language and Literature established in 1885 had gone to a philologist, despite a general belief that it should go to a literary scholar. At Cambridge English emerged more gradually (and less controversially) than at Oxford, but had no literary Chair until 1911 (and its first holder was a classicist, A. W. Verrall), only becoming an independent School of English in 1917. All departments were still beset by what Chris Baldick calls 'the problem of teaching a subject with no appropriate factual (and above all examinable) staple'[122] and no recognisable 'method'. In his inaugural lecture as King Edward VII Professor at Cambridge in 1912, Sir Arthur Quiller Couch was still voicing a resistance to 'method' which to him smacked of science, as well as a distaste for private opinions being expressed in public, and yet still asserting the existence of the intensely personal recognition of the intangible '*thing*' of literature.[123]

Lang would probably have concurred with all of Quiller Couch's remarks.[124] He believed that literature cannot be taught because the ability to produce or appreciate it is innate and only some improvement can be gained in perfecting the craft: 'the majority cannot be taught literature, and the minority need no teaching.'[125] Further, he rejects the possibility that other subjects have any relevance to literature. His long essay 'Examinations in Fiction' [126] imagines what English exam papers might look like should such intersections with history, politics, religion or economics be allowed to occur. The result is amusing, not least because most of the questions would not look out of place on a contemporary university English course. In literary study, then, Lang seems stubbornly to refuse the incursion of other disciplines in a manner that is at odds with his agile movement across disciplinary boundaries in his other work. Perhaps in the end it was only in literature that he felt himself to be professional; in all his other work he assumes the persona of the amateur outsider and this was hardly a position he could pretend to claim in the arena of literature.

Scotland, History and Biography

Lang's writings on history and biography are also clearly ways of attempting to understand Scotland and the Scottish people, almost all of them being concerned with figures and events in Scottish history. There had been a resurgence of interest in Scotland and its culture after Walter Scott, most famously manifested in Queen Victoria's enthusiasm for tartan and the Highlands. The Bannantyne Club, to which Scott belonged, was dedicated to the publication of Scottish historical documents, and Scott's contemporary and Club member Patrick Fraser Tytler produced his pioneering history between 1828 and 1843, doing much to increase knowledge and interest in the country, though definitely not voicing any desire for devolution.

Tytler concluded his history in the year 1603, with the union of the crowns in the accession of James VI of Scotland and I of England after the death of Elizabeth I. Other nineteenth-century historians, such as John Hill Burton and Peter Hume Brown, followed a similar line, writing in high patriotism but nevertheless concluding their histories in 1748 with the act of political union and a sense of Scotland becoming, as Hill Burton put it, 'completely fused into the great British Empire'.[127] Although Lang's own histories also stop short of what he referred to as 'a dangerously close approach to many "burning questions" of our day',[128] he refuses to regard Scotland as assimilated. Rather than assert this in political or economic terms in his history, he expresses this belief in his other areas of interest, continuing to investigate the distinct identity of the Scottish people. He wrote biographies of Prince Charles Edward Stuart (Bonnie Prince Charlie) and Mary Queen of Scots, and his more contemporary biography is of the Scotsman John Gibson Lockhart, who had written the monumental life of Walter Scott.

Lang loved the work of Scott and of Robert Louis Stevenson as much for its Scottish language and settings as for its romance. Lang firmly identified himself as Scottish and it is interesting that much of his work is concerned with the investigation of the possible existence of universal human patterns of experience and belief and the manifestations of those in particular and specific contexts; this could easily be seen as part of an attempt to understand the complexity of his own identity. He certainly dismisses race as an explanation of specificity. Unlike many of his contemporaries, he did not subscribe to the belief in hierarchies of race; in fact he rejects 'race' as a form of social existence too distant in the past to be of relevance:

> Let us repeat that the relations of race to poetic or other mental qualities is a mystery– that *verae causae*, as of environment and historical circumstances, must be exhausted before we can claim this or that gift as a gift of race. Races have too long been mixed, and the history of race is too profoundly obscure.[129]

He argues strongly, however, for the influence of the rooted experience of environment and historical circumstances; in his *History of Scotland* (published in four volumes, 1900–7) he asserts that 'the Celtic note' is 'not of race, but of an isolated life in lonely forests or hills, a life led by a dispossessed or unsuccessful people.'[130] Far from being an affectation or performance, Lang's interest in and identification with Scotland is completely consistent with his intellectual work and his effort in so many fields to explore the complex intersections of human experience and its manifestation in culture.

Lang came to the writing of history late and through literature, in fact through Stevenson. Stevenson, by then living in Samoa, had asked Lang to send him Scottish historical material to use in a novel. While researching, Lang came across documents in the British Museum that seemed to suggest that the spy for the British government in the company of Bonnie Prince Charlie was, shockingly, the chieftain of a clan of Jacobite supporters: Alexander McDonnell of Glengarry. He sent copies of the letters and manuscripts to Stevenson, who began to write a story based on them. It was unfinished when Stevenson died in December 1894 and the papers were returned to Lang, who published his work on them as *Pickle the Spy, or, the Incognito of Prince Charles* in 1897. The book sold well, going into three editions within three months, and part of the reason for the sales was the controversial nature of Lang's claim that a Jacobite hero was in fact a traitor to the cause. It was unexpected, too, from the staunchly Scottish Lang who expressed his Jacobite sympathies frequently, both publicly and privately. He wrote, for example, in a letter to Henry Newbolt: 'A cove at Windsor asked me to revere the Queen. How could I? I rise and follow Charlie.'[131] He was hurt by the accusations of disloyalty, but remained doggedly attached to the evidence. As John Buchan said of him 'He did not, in Dr Johnson's phrase, love Scotland better than the truth',[132] and as he wrote himself 'Whatever you do, don't write the history of people who want not to know the facts and regard history as the process of conserving their illusions.'[133]

After *Pickle* he continued to write historical essays and books, all of them on a similar pattern which involved the production of evidence to question previously held views, or illusions, about significant figures in Scottish history. He nevertheless understood the illusions and rather yearned to be able to share them. He writes in his biography of Charles Stuart:

> Charles is loved for his forlorn hope: for his desperate resolve: for his reckless daring, the winning charm that once was his: for bright hair, and brown eyes: above all as the centre and inspirer of old chivalrous loyalty, as one who would have brought back a lost age, an impossible realm of dreams. Romance was in Charles' blood ... of this world his kingdom never was, and could not be; but he was and is lord of the region of dreams and desires.[134]

The biography goes on to show all of Charles's failures and weaknesses, but Lang's own wish for history to conform more closely to the model of romance is obvious and self-conscious, even as he denies that wish to himself and his readers alike. As can be seen in his analysis of Zola at Lourdes, it is his work in literature and mythology that allows him to understand the impulse of people to create such illusions, and he boasts that 'I am the first historian to introduce anthropology and psychical research as to miracles, also facts derived from angling and bearing on a miracle of St Columba'.[135]

His iconoclasm continued in his other historical work, driven by the same simultaneous desire to share the illusion and present the truth that would destroy it. He wrote privately of Mary, Queen of Scots: 'My sentiment is in favour of her, and my reason is against her.'[136] Having initially believed that parts of the Casket Letters were forged to incriminate Mary in the death of her husband Lord Darnley, he then changed his mind, convinced by evidence in Thomas Henderson's 1905 biography of the Queen. In 1911, re-reading his own book, he then concluded that the case against Mary was, at best, not proven. Demoor suggests that from his correspondence we can see that privately he always believed Mary guilty, but that he bowed to the evidence.[137]

In historical and biographical works his personal and political sympathies are evident; he is drawn to individuals rather than groups, he is clearly a monarchist and he favours Catholics over Presbyterians but, as with Charles and Mary, he is scrupulous with evidence that contradicts his sympathies. John Knox is a figure who tests the tensions of Lang's personal and intellectual positions and he found it difficult to reconcile the character of Knox with the religious and social change that the movement brought. While he realised that Scotland owed its freedom of belief and thought to the Reformation, he also stressed the many shortcomings of the new church and of Knox himself. In the 1952 Lang Lecture William Croft Dickinson suggests that he did not like the narrow bigotry and fanaticism of Presbyterianism and also that 'he feared its democratic nature and distrusted its virility. His sympathies were always with an aristocracy, and Knox, for good or ill, raised a people.'[138] During his research for his *History of Scotland* he was repulsed by his discoveries about Knox. He wrote to Herbert Maxwell 'I never heard of a more fraudulent medium than Knox'[139] and 'that man had the soul of a penny society journalist, and he knew he was a funk.'[140] He later wrote tellingly to the historian Robert Rait:

> It is mournful to reflect that the man who tried to dupe us with such transparent fables was such a vigorous cloud-compelling heart, in fact I never knew anything more saddening than the whole story, as if Zeus Aristophanised with human fortunes. He had the right end of the stick, he gave a shove in the right direction, so blindly, so clumsily, so hypocritically and so antichristianly, so to speak – and probably a Christian could not have done the job.[141]

Bringing his knowledge of mythology and psychical research to bear on history, he identifies Knox in the same way as Charles and Mary, as the product of a willing collusion between the people and an image. Knox, as a 'fraudulent medium', is culpable of deliberate fostering of the illusion, but Lang seems to suggest that this was ultimately beneficial to Scotland and its people, as though fantasies or alternative realities can bring about actual change. As with his thinking on romance, 'illusion' is hardly escapist, it is a version of the real that becomes, or can become, the truth.

The power exerted by dreams and visions on material political realities is also important in Lang's work on Joan of Arc. Jeanne d'Arc, as Lang nearly always called her, was something of an obsession for Lang. He published a privately printed pamphlet, *The Voices of Joan of Arc* (1895), and in the same year wrote on her in 'The Voices of Jeanne d'Arc'.[142] The pamphlet, which was reprinted as an essay in *The Valet's Tragedy, and Other Studies* (1903), is a reading of the representation of Jeanne in Shakespeare's *Henry VI, Part I*, and at the end of the essay Lang compares Jeanne to contemporary mediums, as he does in the later essay 'The Three Seeresses (1880–1900, 1424–1431)' (1900).[143] Lang's interest in and devotion to her were offended and provoked by the publication at the beginning of 1908 of *Vie de Jeanne d'Arc* by Anatole France, the French poet, journalist and novelist. France, a strong critic of the power of the Church in France, argued that Jeanne's visions and voices were not authentic, but suggested to her by malign and manipulative priests. Lang challenged France's assertions, his principal argument being that France's work was bad history, and asserts very clearly what he believes the discipline should be. He stresses the importance of rigorous method and scrupulous use of evidence and castigates France for his sloppiness. As well as this, France's ostensible siding with a disenchanted modernity is challenged by Lang in his defence of Jeanne. In his article in the *Scottish Historical Review* in 1908, Lang accuses France of being 'perpetually mythopoeic; he keeps on inventing legends not to be found in his authorities'.[144] France, in other words, may be materialist, but he is not scientific. It is Lang, rather, who brings rigour and method to the evidence, yet his conclusion is that Jeanne's marvels were genuine. This paradoxical union in Lang's work generally of the rigorously scientific in the aid of the marvellous can be seen in a note to his poem 'A Scot to Jeanne d'Arc', written in January 1894 (and one of three poems[145] he wrote on the subject):

> It is not easy for any one to understand the whole miracle of the life and death of Jeanne d'Arc, and the absolutely unparelleled grandeur and charm of her character, without studying the full records of both her trials, as collected and published by M. Quicherat, for the Société de l'Histoire de France.[146]

Historical method is here vital in obtaining not a disenchanted view of the world, but a knowledge of the marvellous.

It is clearly the case, then, that Jeanne represented for Lang something more than a chance to assert a rigorous historical method. As here, she seems to be for him one of a handful of cases which offered tangible evidence that human faculties are more than those assumed by materialist science. His book for children, *The Story of Joan of Arc* (1906) begins with the assertion that she 'was perhaps the most wonderful person who ever lived in the world'.[147] In *The Maid of France* (1908), he acknowledges that sometimes even science cannot explain Jeanne's marvels: 'If there are incidents in her later career which science, so far, cannot explain, I shall not therefore regard them as false. Science may be able to explain them on some future day; at present she is not omniscient'.[148] His passionate defence of Jeanne is also part of Lang's sense of his Scottishness, and his feeling for the meaning of Scottish history. In 'A Scot to Jeanne d'Arc' (1894) he exonerates Scotland for any part in the injustice done to her:

Not upon the shame,
Whose sires were to the Auld Alliance true;
They, by the Maiden's side,
Victorious fought and died;
One stood by thee that fiery torment through … [149]

Fittingly perhaps, the work that Lang left unfinished at his death was a collaboration with his brother John on the stories, folklore and landscapes of his childhood in Scotland, *Highways and Byways in The Border.* In that, he circles round to his beginning and to the interests that sustained him throughout his life and career.

Chronology of the life and major works of Andrew Lang

1844
Born (31 March) in Selkirk on the Scottish Borders to John Lang and Jane Plenderleath Sellar Lang.

***c.*1852–4**
Attends Selkirk Grammar School.

1854–61
Attends the Edinburgh Academy.

1861–3
Attends St Andrews University.

1863
Co-founds and edits the *St Leonards Magazine* at St Andrews University.

1863–4
Transfers to the University of Glasgow to compete for the Snell Exhibition Scholarship to Oxford University. Awarded scholarship.

1865–8
Attends Balliol College, Oxford University, reading Classics under Benjamin Jowett. Graduates first class in 'Classical Moderations' (1866) and 'Greats' (1868).

1869–75
Fellow at Merton College, Oxford University.

1872
Ballads and Lyrics of Old France (poetry collection).

1872
Reads E. B. Tylor's *Primitive Culture.*

1872–4
Spends winters on the French Riviera to recover from a lung infection. Meets Robert Louis Stevenson (31 Jan 1874).

1873
(May) Publishes his first scholarly essay on folklore, 'Mythology and Fairy Tales' in the *Fortnightly Review.*

1874
Begins writing regularly for *The Academy.*

1875–c.1895
Writes regular leaders in the *Daily News* and the *Saturday Review.*

1875–1911
Contributes entries for the *Encyclopaedia Britannica*, eventually writing for the ninth, tenth and eleventh editions.

1875
(17 April) Marries Leonora Blanche Alleyne.

1875
Leaves Merton College and settles in London at 1 Marloes Road, Kensington.

1877
Publishes letters in *The Academy* (1 and 15 December) concerning the foundation of a Folk-Lore Society.

1878
Foundation of the Folk-Lore Society, and publication of the first volume of the *Folk-Lore Record* (subsequently the *Folk-Lore Journal*) with Lang's long essay 'The Folk-Lore of France'.

1879
Publishes with S. H. Butcher the translation *The Odyssey of Homer Rendered into English Prose.*

1882
Helen of Troy (epic poem).
The Black Thief (play).

1883
Publishes with Ernest Myers and Walter Leaf *The Iliad of Homer, a prose translation.*

1884
Publishes his first book on folklore, *Custom and Myth.*
The Princess Nobody: A Tale of Fairyland (children's book, using drawings by Richard Doyle).
Ballads and Verses Vain (poetry collection).
Introduces Margaret Hunt's translation *Grimms' Household Tales* with the Essay 'Household Tales'.

1885
Rhymes à la Mode (poetry collection).

1886–1905
Writes the monthly column 'At the Sign of the Ship' in *Longman's Magazine.*

1886
Books and Bookmen (literary essays).
Letters to Dead Authors (epistolary literary criticism and pastiche).
In the Wrong Paradise (stories).
The Mark of Cain (novel).

1887
First edition of the anthropological work *Myth, Ritual and Religion.*
Publishes *He* anonymously with Walter Herries Pollock, a parody of Henry Rider Haggard's novel *She.*
Publishes an edition of William Adlington's translation of Apuleius, *The Most Pleasant and Delectable Tale of the Marriage of Cupid and Psyche*, with a substantial introduction.

1888
Grass of Parnassus (poem collection).
The Gold of Fairnilee (children's book).
Editor of *Perrault's Popular Tales* (1888), which includes a substantial introductory essay.

1888–9
President of the Folk-Lore Society.

1889–1910
Publishes twelve anthologies of fairy tales known as the 'coloured fairy books' beginning with *The Blue Fairy Book* (1889) and *The Red Fairy Book* (1890).

1891–7 & 1905–12
Regular contributor to the *Illustrated London News.*

1889
Prince Prigio (children's fantasy novel, first of the 'Chronicles of Pantouflia').
Letters on Literature (epistolary literary criticism).
Lost Leaders (selected journalism).

1890
The World's Desire (novel, with Henry Rider Haggard).
Publishes his first biography, *The Life, Letters, and Diaries of Sir Stafford Northcote.*
How to Fail in Literature (satirical advice for writers).

1891
The International Folk-Lore Congress is held in London with Lang as President.
Essays in Little.

1892–1912
Regular contributor to *Blackwood's (Edinburgh) Magazine.*

1892–4
Editor of the *Waverley Novels* by Walter Scott (48 vols).

1893
Homer and the Epic (classical literary criticism).
Prince Ricardo of Pantouflia (children's fantasy novel, second of the 'Chronicles of Pantouflia').
Collaborates with Rider Haggard on the novel *Montezuma's Daughter*.
Publishes an edition of *Kirk's Secret Commonwealth* with a substantial introduction.

1894
Ban and Arrière Ban (poetry collection).
Publishes his first book-length investigation of spiritualism *Cock Lane and Common Sense*.

1895
My Own Fairy Book (collected children's stories).

1896
A Monk of Fife (novel; historical romance).
The Life and Letters of John Gibson Lockhart (biography).

1897
The Book of Dreams and Ghosts (history of psychical phenomena).
Publishes his investigation of the identity of the spy for the English codenamed 'Pickle', *Pickle the Spy; or the Incognito of Prince Charles*.
Modern Mythology (study of mythological interpretation).
Editor of *The Works of Charles Dickens* (34 vols).

1898
The Making of Religion (anthropological study on the origins of religion).
Parson Kelly (novel, with A. E. W. Mason).

1899
The Homeric Hymns (translation).
Second edition of *Myth, Ritual and Religion*, revised and enlarged.

1900–7
Publishes four volumes of *A History of Scotland from the Roman Occupation to the Suppressing of the Last Jacobite Rising*.

1900
Prince Charles Edward Stuart (biography).

1901
The Mystery of Mary Stuart (historical study).
Magic and Religion (anthropological study).
Alfred Tennyson (biography).

1902
James VI and the Gowrie Mystery (historical study).
The Disentanglers, last single authored novel.

1903
The Valet's Tragedy, and Other Studies in Secret History (accounts of historical mysteries).
Social Origins (anthropological study).
Collaborates with Rider Haggard on the novel *Stella Fregelius*.

1904
(22 June) Made honorary Doctor of Letters by Oxford University and appointed Ford Lecturer in English History.

1905
John Knox and the Reformation (historical study).
The Secret of the Totem (anthropological study).
Adventures Among Books (literary criticism and autobiography).

1906
The Story of Joan of Arc (historical study for children).
New and Old Letters to Dead Authors (epistolary literary criticism).
Life of Sir Walter Scott (biography).
Portraits and Jewels of Mary Stuart (study in art history).
Homer and his Age (classical literary criticism and history).
Elected Fellow of the British Academy.

1907
Tales of a Fairy Court (children's book).

1908
The Maid of France: Being the Story of the Life and Death of Jeanne d'Arc (biographical and historical study).

1910
The World of Homer (classical literary criticism and history).
Sir Walter Scott and the Border Minstrelsy (literary history and criticism).
Elected founding member of the Academic Committee of the Royal Society of Literature.

1911
Method in the Study of Totemism (anthropological study).
Elected president of the Society for Psychical Research.
A Short History of Scotland.

1912
A History of English Literature (literary history/criticism).
Shakespeare, Bacon and the Great Unknown (literary history/criticism).
Sees his family's death omen, a ghostly cat.
(20 July) Dies at Banchory in Aberdeenshire aged 68 of a heart attack.

1923
Posthumous publication of *The Poetical Works* (4 vols) edited by Leonora Lang.

A Note on the Text

The first published version of the text has been used for all pieces reproduced here, with two exceptions. Lang rarely revised his work, even when it was published multiple times and in multiple locations. The exceptions are *Myth, Ritual and Religion* (first published 1887, second edition 1899) and *The Making of Religion* (first published 1898, second edition 1900), where Lang did revise the second editions. As his changes are useful indications of the development of his thought, the second edition of each has been used here, with the changes made indicated in endnotes.

Lang's spelling and punctuation have been kept, as have the original styles of presentation, which vary according to the practice of the publisher, journal or newspaper in which the work appeared. The only exception to this is the consistent editorial use of single inverted commas throughout. Obvious typesetting errors have been silently corrected, but other editorial interventions are indicated in square brackets.

Where Lang has used languages other than English, we give translations in the endnotes, except in those instances where words or phrases are very familiar to English speakers, or where Lang has given his own translation.

Original footnotes have been retained except where ommissions are indicated in endnotes. Where they are correct, no additional information has been added. Where they are incorrect, or if Lang's use of different editions is confusing, the correct or additional information is given in endnotes. In particular, Lang seems to have used different editions of E. B. Tylor's *Primitive Culture* without indicating which. For ease of reference, citations of the first edition (1871) have been provided on those occasions where Lang paraphrases or directly quotes from it.

Of the letters included included here, only the letters to William James have been previously published (in Marysa Demoor, *Friends Over the Ocean: Andrew Lang's American correspondents, 1881–1912*, Ghent: Rijksuniversiteit Gent, 1989). Others are reproduced from the manuscript copy. Dating of the letters reproduced and those referred to in the introductions is speculative. Lang never put a year on his letters, and frequently no month or date either. Some letters remain with original envelopes bearing legible postmarks, but otherwise internal evidence has been used to date previously unpublished letters.

Lang's poor handwriting obstructs certainty about all words in the letters, and where words are truly illegible, this is indicated in square brackets. Where there is some uncertainty about a word, the most likely reading of it has been given and a question mark in square brackets follows it.

Where it will assist in the identification of the stories Lang refers to, 'tale type' references have been given in the section headings and endnotes. These refer to entries in the tale type indexing system developed by Antti Aarne and Stith Thompson in the early twentieth century, and reworked by Hans-Jörg Uther in 2004. As is conventional, the tale type reference numbers are given with the prefix ATU (Aarne/Thompson/Uther), and in every case the citation may be found in Uther, *The Types of International Folk Tales*, FF Communications 284 (Helsinki: Suomalainen Tiedeakatemia Scientiarum Fennica, 2004). Frequently mentioned proper names of people or groups do not have a footnote, but can be found in detail in the appendices.

Acknowledgements

Thanks to the following for their generous help: Susan Halpert and Heather Cole, Houghton Library, Harvard University; Elaine Miller, Catriona Foote and Dr Norman Reid, Special Collections, University of St Andrews; Dr Chris Morton and Philip Grover, Pitt Rivers Museum, University of Oxford; Jonathan Smith, Trinity College Library, Cambridge; Peter Meadows, Department of Manuscripts, Cambridge University Library; Moira Marsh at the Wells Library, Indiana University; staff of London Library; staff of the British Library; staff of Senate House Library, University of London.

Thanks to the Department of English, Linguistics and Cultural Studies, University of Westminster and to the Research Capability Fund of the Faculty of Arts and Social Sciences, Kingston University for their generous financial contributions.

Thanks also to: Simon Avery, Monica Germanà, Louise Sylvester and Martin Willis for well-timed encouragement; Jackie Jones for her support during a difficult beginning; Bill Gray for his thorough reading and good advice; Debra Kelly and Valerie Chambon for help with the French; Catriona Macdonald; Jonathan Metzer for help with the Greek; Kate Simpson for shared frustration with Lang's handwriting; Diane Stafford for care with the copy-editing; Izzie Thomas for care with the typesetting; Em Warwick for biographical notes; Simone Coxall, David Cunningham and Toby Litt.

For permission to reproduce Lang's letters to Oliver Lodge, William James and E.B. Tylor, thanks to: SPR archive, Cambridge University Library; Houghton Library, Harvard University; Manuscript Collection, Pitt Rivers Museum, University of Oxford.

I

CRITICS AND CRITICISM

This section shows Lang's position in the world of reviewing and criticism of the late nineteenth century and illustrates his own views of some of the topics of the time. 'Poetry and Politics' was first published in *Macmillan's Magazine* 53:314 (December 1885), pp. 81–8 in response to William John Courthope's book *The Liberal Movement in English Literature* (London: John Murray, 1885). Courthope and Lang were contemporaries with similar careers: both studied Classics at Oxford, published poetry and were part of the journal culture of the 1880s and 1890s. Courthope also wrote on literature and history, contributing to many of the same journals as Lang, including *Blackwood's Edinburgh Magazine*. Courthope became editor (with Alfred Austin) of the explicitly politically conservative *National Review* in 1883, and upon his appointment to the Professorship of Poetry at Oxford in 1895 Lang harshly criticised the first volume of Courthope's book *History of English Poetry*, see 'At the Sign of the Ship', *Longman's Magazine* 26:155 (September 1895), pp. 541–50. Lang states again his views on writers, critics and politics in 'Politics and Men of Letters', first published in *The Pilot* (21 April 1900), pp. 220–1.

Plagiarism was another contentious topic and Lang's article 'Literary Plagiarism' was published in *Contemporary Review* 51 (June 1887), pp. 835–40. The context of the article is Lang's defence of Henry Rider Haggard. Haggard had published an attack on Realism, 'About Fiction' in the *Critical Review* in February 1887, upon which the influential journalist W. T. Stead, writing in the *Pall Mall Gazette* (11 March 1887), accused Haggard of plagiarising his novels, and Lang and Haggard of the offence of 'log-rolling', meaning the mutual public promotion of each other's work. Lang's 'At the Sign of the Ship' column at this time also contains discussion of both plagiarism and 'log-rolling', for example in *Longman's Magazine* 9:50 (December 1886), pp. 216–20. The popular novelist Marie Corelli, supported by Stead, was also vociferous on the issue and the character of the powerful reviewer David McWhing in her novel *The Sorrows of Satan* (London: Methuen, 1895) is at least partly modelled on Lang.

The 'At the Sign of the Ship' column on critics was first published in *Longman's Magazine* 10:57 (July 1887), pp. 329–31. This column is part of Lang's long-running skirmish with the American writer William Dean Howells. Howells began writing for *Harper's* in October of 1885 and Lang, who had been the paper's English editor, was sacked a month later. Howells started a causerie, the 'Editor's Study', in *Harper's* at exactly the same time as Lang began his own in *Longman's* in January 1886. The two men clashed over many topics, but principally over the role of the critic and in the Realism versus romance debate (see section 2 of this volume, 'Realism, Romance and the Reading Public', p. 92). The second 'Sign of the Ship' column in this section was also first published in *Longman's Magazine* 16:95 (September 1890), pp. 569–72, and is part of the skirmish with Howells. Howells was only to write for another two years in *Harper's*; his contract expired in 1892. Lang wrote a barbed farewell and a short poem about Howells in his 'Sign of the Ship' column, *Longman's Magazine* 19:114 (April 1892), pp. 682–4.

'The Science of Criticism' was first published in the *New Review* 4:24 (May 1891), pp. 403–8. This formed part of two 'symposia' conducted by the *New Review* in 1891. The first was on 'The Science of Fiction' with contributions from Walter Besant, Paul Bourget and Thomas Hardy, and the second was 'The Science of Criticism' with Lang, Henry James and Edmund Gosse. The symposia themselves were part of what James called 'the era of discussion' about the nature of fiction and the function of criticism during the 1880s and 1890s. Grant Allen had published 'The Decay of Criticism', in the *Fortnightly Review* 31:183 (March 1882), p. 39 and Robert Louis Stevenson's 'A Gossip on Romance' appeared in *Longman's* in November of the same year. There was a steady rumbling of the debate during the following year, and in April of 1884 Walter Besant gave a lecture on 'The Art of Fiction' which attracted several responses, including one from Lang ('The Art of Fiction', *Pall Mall Gazette* 30 (April 1884), pp. 1–2). The lecture itself appeared in print in May and both Henry James and Stevenson responded in *Longman's* in the autumn and winter (Henry James 'The Art of Fiction', *Longman's Magazine* 4:23 (September 1884), pp. 502–21 and Robert Louis Stevenson, 'A Humble Remonstrance', *Longman's Magazine* 5:26 (December 1884), pp. 139–47). The same personalities, with the addition of others like Henry Rider Haggard, William Dean Howells, Vernon Lee and George Saintsbury, continued the discussion with its overlapping concerns about the theory, practice and ethics of the novel and criticism throughout the next decade.

'Poetry and Politics', *Macmillan's Magazine* 53:314

(December 1885), pp. 81–8

The separation of literary criticism from politics appears to have been a gain both to politics and to literature. If Mr. Swinburne, for example, speaks unkindly about kings and priests in one volume, that offence is not remembered against him, even by the most Conservative critic, when he gives us a book like 'Atalanta' or 'Erechtheus.' If Victor Hugo applauds the Commune, the Conservative M. Paul de Saint Victor[1] freely forgives him. In the earlier part of the century, on the other hand, poems which had no tinge of politics were furiously assailed, for party reasons, by Tory critics if the author was a Whig, or had friends in the ranks of Whiggery.* Perhaps the Whiggish critics were not less one-sided, but their exploits (except a few of Jeffrey's)[2] are forgotten. Either there were no Conservative poets to be attacked, or the Whig attack was so weak, and so unlike the fine fury of the Tory reviewers, that it has lapsed into oblivion. Assuredly no Tory Keats died of an article, no Tory Shelley revenged him in a Conservative 'Adonais,' and, if Lord Byron struck back at his Scotch reviewers, Lord Byron was no Tory.

In the happy Truce of the Muses, which now enables us to judge a poet on his literary merits, Mr. Courthope has raised a war-cry which will not, I hope, be widely echoed. He has called his reprinted essays 'The Liberal Movement in English Literature,'[3] and has thus brought back the howls of partisans into a region where they had been long silent. One cannot but regret this intrusion of the factions which have 'no language but a Cry'[4] into the tranquil regions of verse. Mr. Courthope knows that the title of his essays will be objected to, and he tries to defend it. Cardinal Newman,[5] he says, employs the term 'Liberalism' to denote a movement in the region of

* Compare Maginn's brutal and silly attack on Shelley's 'Adonais,' recently reprinted in Maginn's 'Miscellanies', Sampson Low and Company.

thought. Would it not be as true to say that Cardinal Newman uses 'Liberalism' as 'short' for most things that he dislikes? In any case the word 'Liberal' is one of those question-begging, popular, political terms which had been expelled from the criticism of poetry. It seems an error to bring back the word with its passionate associations. Mr. Courthope will, perhaps, think that the reviewer who thus objects is himself a Liberal. It is not so; and though I would fain escape from even the thought of party bickerings, I probably agree with Mr. Courthope in not wishing to disestablish anything or anybody, not even the House of Lords. None the less it is distracting, when we are occupied for once with thoughts about poetry, to meet sentences like this: 'Life, in the Radical view, is simply change; and a Radical is ready to promote every caprice or whim of the numerical majority of the moment in the belief that the change which it effects in the constitution of society will bring him nearer to some ideal state existing in his own imagination.'[6] Or again: 'How many leagues away do they' (certain remarks of Mr. Burke's[7]) 'carry us from the Liberal Radicalism now crying out for the abolition of the hereditary branch of the Legislature?'[8] and so on. One expects, in every page, to encounter the deceased wife's sister, or 'a cow and three acres.'[9] It is not in the mood provoked by our enthusiasm for the hereditary branch of the Legislature, it is not when the heart stands up in defence of the game laws, that we are fit to reason about poetry. Consequently, as it appears to me, Mr. Courthope, in his excitement against Radicalism, does not always reason correctly, nor, perhaps, feel correctly, about poetry.

As far as I understand the main thesis of Mr. Courthope's book, it is something like this. From a very early date, from the date certainly of Chaucer, there have been flowing two main streams in English literature. One stream is the Poetry of Romance, the other is the Poetry of Manners. The former had its source (I am inclined to go a great way further back for its source) 'in the institutions of chivalry, and in mediaeval theology.' The other poetical river, again, the poetry of manners, 'has been fed by the life, actions, and manners of the nation.' One might add to this that the 'life and actions' of our people have often, between the days of the Black Prince and of General Gordon,[10] been in the highest degree 'romantic.' This mixture, however, would confuse Mr. Courthope's system. Drayton's 'Agincourt,' Lord Tennyson's 'Revenge' may be regarded at will, perhaps, as belonging to the poetry of romance, or the poetry of national action. Mr. Courthope does not touch on this fact, but the reader will do well to keep it in mind, for reasons which will appear later.

The fortunes of the two streams of poetry have been different. The romantic stream was lost in the sands of Donne, Crashaw, Cowley, and the rest,[11] but welled up again in the beginning of our own century, in Scott, Coleridge, and others. The poetry of manners, on the other hand, had its great time when men, revolting from the conceits of degenerate romanticism, took, with Pope, Dryden, Thomson, and Johnson, to 'correctness,' to working under the 'ethical impulse.' Now the 'correctness' and the choice of moral topics which prevailed in the eighteenth century were 'Conservative,' and the new burst of romantic poetry was 'Liberal,' and was connected with the general revolutionary and Liberal movement in politics, speculation, and religion. Finally, Mr. Courthope thinks that 'the Liberal movement in our literature, as well as in our politics, is beginning to languish.' Perhaps Mr. Chamberlain[12] and his friends are not aware that they are languishing. In the interests of our languishing poetry, at all events, Mr. Courthope briefly prescribes more 'healthy objectivity' (the words are mine, and are slang, but they put the idea briefly), and a 'revival of the simple iambic movements of English in metres historically established in our literature.'[13]

In this sketch of Mr. Courthope's thesis, his main ideas show forth as, if not new, yet, perfectly true. There is, there has been, a poetry of romance of which the corruption is found in the wanton conceits of Donne and Crashaw. There is, there has been, a poetry of manners and morals, of which the corruption is didactic prosiness. In the secular action and reaction, each of these tendencies has, at various times, been weak or strong. At the beginning of this century, too, a party tinge was certainly given, chiefly by Conservative critics, to the reborn romantic poetry. Keats cared as little as any man for what Marcus Aurelius[14] calls 'the drivelling of politicians,' but even Keats, as a friend of 'kind Hunt's,'[15] was a sort of Liberal. But admitting this party colouring, one must add that it was of very slight moment indeed, and very casually distributed. Therefore, one must still regret, for reasons which will instantly appear, Mr. Courthope's introduction of party names and party prejudices into his interesting essays.

It is probably the author's preoccupation with politics which causes frequent contradictions, as they seem, and a general sense of confusion which often make it very hard to follow his argument, and to see what he is really driving at. For example, Scott, the Conservative Scott, whom Mr. Courthope so justly admires, has to appear as a Liberal, almost a revolutionary, in verse. Mr. Courthope quotes Coleridge's account of the origin of Lyrical Ballads as the first note of the 'new departure,' which I have called the 'Liberal Movement in English Literature.' Well, but the Tory Scott was an eager follower of Coleridge's; he played (if we are to be political) Mr. Jesse Collings[16] to Coleridge's Mr. Chamberlain. This, by itself, proves how very little the Liberal movement in literature was a party movement, how little it had to do with Liberalism in politics.

Again, when Mr. Courthope is censuring, and most justly censuring, Mr. Carlyle's grudging and Pharisaical[17] article on Scott, he speaks of Carlyle as a 'Radical,' and finds that 'our Radical Diogenes' blamed Scott 'because he was a Conservative, and amused the people.'[18] Now Carlyle, of all men, was no Radical; and Scott, as a Conservative, is a queer figure in a Liberal movement. Another odd fact is that the leaders of the Liberal movement 'steeped themselves' in the atmosphere of feudal romance. Whatever else feudal romance may have been, it was eminently anti-Radical, and, to poetic Radicals, should have been eminently uncongenial. Odder still (if the Liberal movement in literature was a party movement to any important extent) is Mr. Courthope's discovery that Macaulay was a Conservative critic. Yet a Conservative critic Macaulay must have been, because he was in the camp opposed to that of Coleridge and Keats. Macaulay was a very strong party man, and, had he been aware that his critical tastes were Tory, he would perhaps have changed his tastes. Yet again, Mr. Courthope finds that optimism is the note of Liberalism, while 'the Conservative takes a far less sanguine view of the prospects of the art of poetry,' and of things in general. But Byron and Shelley, in Mr. Courthope's argument, were liberal poets. Yet Mr. Courthope says, speaking of Shelley, 'like Byron, he shows himself a complete pessimist.' For my own part (and Mr. Courthope elsewhere expresses the same opinion), Shelley seems to me an optimist, in his queer political dreams of a future where Prometheus and Asia shall twine beams and buds in a cave,[19] unvexed by priests and kings – a future in which all men shall be peaceful, brotherly, affectionate sentimentalists. But Mr. Courthope must decide whether Byron and Shelley are to be Conservatives and pessimists, or Liberals and optimists. At present their position as Liberal pessimists seems, on his own showing, difficult and precarious. Macaulay, too, the Liberal Macaulay, is a pessimist, according to Mr. Courthope. All this confusion, as I venture to think it, appears to arise, then, from Mr. Courthope's political preoccupations. He shows us a Radical Carlyle, a Conservative Macaulay; a Scott who is, perhaps, a kind of Whig; a Byron, who, being pessimistic, should be Conservative, but is Liberal; a Shelley, who is Liberal, though, being pessimistic, he ought to be Conservative. It is all very perplexing, and, like most mischief, all comes out of party politics. It is less easy to demonstrate, what I cannot help suspecting, that Mr. Courthope's great admiration of the typical poetry of the eighteenth century comes from his persuasion that that poetry, like Providence, 'is Tory.' This may seem an audacious guess. I am led to make it partly by observing that Mr. Courthope's own poems, especially the charming lyrics in 'The Paradise of Birds,' have a freedom and a varied music, extremely Liberal, extremely unlike Johnson and Thomson, and not all dissimilar to what we admire in the Red Republican verse of Mr. Swinburne. Now, if Mr. Courthope writes verse like that (and I wish he would write more), surely his inmost self must, on the whole, tend rather to the poetry he calls Liberal, than to that which (being a politician) he admires as Conservative, but does not imitate. All this, however, is an attempt to plumb 'the abysmal depths of personality.'[20] We are on firmer ground when we try to show that Mr. Courthope expresses too high an opinion of the typical poetry of the eighteenth century. Now this really brings us face to face with the great question, Was Pope a poet? and that, again, leads us to the brink of a discussion as to What is poetry? On these matters no one will ever persuade his neighbours by argument. We all follow our tastes, incapable of conversion. I must admit that I am, on this point, a Romanticist of the most 'dishevelled' character; that Pope's verse does not affect me as what I call poetry affects me; that I only style Pope, in Mr. Swinburne's words, 'a poet with a difference.' This is one of the remarks which inspire Mr. Courthope to do battle for Pope, and for Thomson, and Johnson, and the rest. Mr. Matthew Arnold, too, vexes Mr. Courthope by calling Pope and Dryden 'classics of our prose.' Why are they not poets? he asks; and 'Who is a poet if not Pope?' Who? Why from Homer onwards there are many poets: there are 'many mansions,'[21] but if Pope dwells in one of them I think it is by courtesy, and because there are a few diamonds of poetry in the fine gold of his verse. But it is time to say why one would (in spite of the very highest of all living authorities) incline to qualify the title of 'poet' as given to Pope. It is for a reason which Mr. Courthope finds it hard to understand. He says that Mr. Matthew Arnold and Mr. Swinburne deny Pope the laurel without assigning reasons. They merely cry, in a despotic fashion, *stet pro ratione voluntas*.[22] They do not offer argument, or, if they argue, their arguments will not 'hold water.' But Mr. Courthope himself justifies the lack of argument by his own reply to certain reasonings of Wordsworth's. 'Your reasoning, no doubt,' says Mr. Courthope to the Bard of Rydal, 'is very fine and ingenious, but the matter is one not for argument, but for perception.'

Precisely; and so Mr. Arnold and Mr. Swinburne might answer Mr. Courthope's complaints of their lack of argument, –'The matter is one not for argument, but for perception.'[23] One feels, or perceives, in reading Pope, the lack of what one cannot well argue about, the lack of the indefinable glory of poetry, the bloom on it, as happiness is, according to Aristotle, the bloom on a life of goodness. Mr. Swinburne, avoiding 'argument,' writes, 'the test of the highest poetry is that it eludes all tests. Poetry in which there is no element at once perceptible and indefinable by any reader or hearer of any poetic instinct may have every other good quality ... but if all its properties can easily or can ever be gauged and named by its admirers, it is not poetry, above all it is not lyric poetry, of the first water.'[24] In fact, to employ the terms of Mr. Courthope's own reply to Wordsworth, 'the matter is one not for argument, but for perception.' Now this 'perceptible and indefinable' element in poetry is rarely present in Pope's verse, if it is ever present at all. We can 'gauge and name' the properties of Pope's verse, and little or nothing is left unnamed and ungauged. For this reason Pope always appears to me, if a poet at all, a poet 'with a difference.' The test, of course, is subjective, even mystical, if you will. Mr. Courthope might answer that Pope is full of passages in which he detects an indefinable quality that can never be gauged or named. In that case I should be silenced, but Mr. Courthope does not say anything of the sort. Far from that, he says (and here he does astonish me) that 'the most sublime passages of Homer, Milton, and Virgil, can readily be analysed into their elements.'[25] Why, if it were so, they would indeed be on the level of Pope. But surely it is not so. We can parse Homer, Milton, and Virgil; we can make a *précis* of what they state; but who can analyse their incommunicable charm? If any man thinks he can analyse it, to that man, I am inclined to cry, the charm must be definable indeed, but also imperceptible.

[...]

In the long run, perhaps, as Mr. Courthope says, Mr. Swinburne 'only proves by his argument that the poetry of Byron is of a different kind from the poetry of Wordsworth and Shelley, and that he himself infinitely prefers the poetry of the two latter.'[26] Unluckily argument can prove no more than that the poetry which we 'infinitely prefer' is of a different kind from the poetry of Pope and Johnson, and even from most of Thomson's. One cannot *demonstrate* that it is not only of a different kind but of an infinitely higher kind. That is matter for perception. But this one may say, and it may even appear of the nature of an argument, that the poetry of 'a different kind,' which I agree with so much more competent a judge as Mr. Swinburne in preferring, is not peculiar to any one people, or time, or movement. It is *quod semper, quod ubique, quod ab omnibus*.[27] I find this flower on the long wild, frozen plains and steppes, the tundras, of the Finnish epic, the 'Kalevala': [28] – 'The cold has spoken to me, and the rain has told me her runes; the winds of heaven, the waves of the sea, have spoken and sung to me, the wild birds have taught me, the music of many waters has been my master.' So says the Runoia,[29] and he speaks truly, but wind and rain, and fen and forest, cloud and sky and sea, never taught their lesson to the typical versifiers of the Conservative eighteenth century. I find their voices, and their enchantment, and their passion in Homer and Virgil, in Theocritus, and Sophocles, and Aristophanes, in the *volkslieder*[30] of modern Greece, as in the ballads of the Scottish border, in Shakespeare and Marlowe, in Ronsard and Joachim du Bellay,[31] in Cowper and Gray,[32] as in Shelley and Scott and Coleridge, in Edgar Poe, in Heine,[33] and in the Edda.[34] Where I do not find this natural magic, an 'element at once perceptible and indefinable,' is in the 'Rape of the Lock,' 'The Essay on Man,' 'Eloisa to Abelard,' 'The Campaign' – is in the typical verse of the classical and Conservative eighteenth century. Now, if I am right in what, after all, is a matter of perception, if all great poetry of all time has this one mark, this one element, and is of this one kind, while only the typical poetry of a certain three generations lacks the element, and is of another kind, can I be wrong in preferring *quod semper, quod ubique, quod ab omnibus*?[35]

The late Rector of Lincoln College[36] (a Liberal, to be sure, alas!) has defined that which we consciously miss in Pope and Johnson as 'the element of inspired feeling.' Perhaps we cannot define it, and perhaps it is going too far to say, with the Rector, that 'it is by courtesy that the versifiers of the century from Dryden to Churchill are styled poets.'[37] Let us call them 'poets with a difference,' for even Mr. Courthope will probably admit (what he says Mr. Swinburne has 'proved' about Byron) that they are poets 'of a different kind.' Then let us prefer which kind we please, and be at rest. We, who prefer the kind that Homer began, and that Lord Tennyson continues, might add, as a reason for our choice, that our side is strong in the knowledge and rendering of Nature. Wordsworth, in a letter to Scott,* remarked that Dryden's was 'not a poetical genius,' although he possessed (what Chapelain, according to Théophile Gautier,[38] *especially* lacked), 'a certain ardour and impetuosity of mind, with an excellent ear.' 'But,' said Wordsworth, 'there is not a single image from nature in the whole body of his works,' and, 'in his translation from Virgil, wherever Virgil can be fairly said to have had his eye upon his object, Dryden always spoils the passage.' So, it is generally confessed, does Pope spoil Homer, Homer who always has his eye on the object. I doubt if Chapman,[39] when he says –

> 'And with the tops he bottoms all the deeps,
> And all the bottoms in the tops he steeps,'

gives the spirit of a storm of Homer's worse than Pope does, when he remarks –

> 'The waves behind roll on the waves before.'

Or where does Homer say that the stars –

> 'O'er the dark trees a yellower verdure shed,
> And tip with silver every mountain head?

> 'And all the stars show plain'

says Homer, and it is enough. The 'yellower verdure,' and the silver, and the rest of this precious stuff comes from Pope, that minute observer of external nature. Mr. Courthope numbers Dryden, with Shakespeare, Chaucer, and Scott, among poets with 'the power of reproducing the idea of external nature.'[40] It may be my unconscious Liberalism, but I prefer the view of that eminent Radical, William Wordsworth. Mr. Courthope elsewhere asserts that the writers of the best poetry of the eighteenth century (meaning Pope, I presume, and the rest), 'faced nature boldly, and wrote about it in metre directly as they felt it.'[41] Probably, by 'nature,' Mr. Courthope means 'human nature,' for I cannot believe that Pope, boldly facing Nature on a starlit night, really saw a 'yellower verdure' produced by 'that obscure light which droppeth from the stars.'

Before leaving the question of the value of typical eighteenth century poetry, one would recall Mr. Courthope's distinctions between the poetry of manners and national action, and the poetry of romance. I said that there

* Lockhart's 'Memoirs of the Life of Sir Walter Scott,' ii. 89.

was much romance in our national actions. Now, outside the sacred grove of Conservative and classical poetry, that romance of national action has been felt, has been fittingly sung. From the Fight of Brunanburh, to Drayton's 'Agincourt,' from Agincourt to Lord Tennyson's 'Revenge,' and Sir Francis Doyle's 'Red Thread of Honour,'[42] we have certain worthy and romantic lyrics of national action. The Cavalier poets[43] gave us many songs of England under arms, even Macaulay's 'Armada' stirs us like 'Chevy Chase,' or 'Kinmont Willie.'[44] The Conservative and classical age of our poetry was an age of great actions. What, then, did the Conservative poets add to the lyrics of the romance of national action? Where is *their* 'Battle of the Baltic,'[45] or their 'Mariners of England'? Why, till we come to Cowper (an early member of 'the Liberal movement,') to Cowper and the 'Loss of the Royal George,'[46] I declare I know not where to find a poet who has discovered in national action any romance or any inspiration at all! What do we get, in place of the romance of national adventure, in place of 'Lucknow' and 'The Charge of the Light Brigade,'[47] from the classical period? Why, we get, at most, and at best,

'Though fens and floods possessed the middle space
That unprovoked they would have feared to pass,
Nor fens nor floods can stop Britannia's bands,
When her proud foe ranged on their border stands.'* [48]

I recommend the historical and topographical accuracy of the second line, and the musical correctness of the fourth. Not thus did Scott sing how –

'The stubborn spearsmen still made good
Their dark impenetrable wood,'[49]

and I doubt if Achilles found any such numbers, when Patroclus entered his tent,

'And he was singing of the glorious deeds of men.'[50]

The Conservative age, somehow, was less patriotic than the poets of 'the Liberal movement.' Space fails me, and I cannot join battle with Mr. Courthope as to the effect of science on poetry, and as to the poetry of savage times and peoples, though I am longing to criticise the verses of Dieyries and Narrinyeries,[51] and the *karakias* of the Maoris, and the great Maori epic,[52] so wonderfully Homeric, and the songs of the Ojibbeways and Malagasies.[53] When Macaulay said, 'as civilisation advances, poetry almost necessarily declines,'[54] I doubt if much Dieyri or Narrinyeri verse was present to his consciousness. But this belongs to a separate discussion.

I have tried to show that, by introducing political terms into poetical criticism, and by having his eye on politics when discoursing of poetry, Mr.

---

* Of course there are better things than this in the 'Campaign' of the inspired Mr. Addison.

Courthope has not made obscure matters clearer, and has, perhaps, been betrayed into a strained affection for the Conservative and classical school. His definition of what gives a poet his rank, 'his capacity for producing lasting pleasure by the metrical expression of thought, of whatever kind it may be,'[55] certainly admits Pope and some of his followers. But, as a mere matter of perception, I must continue to think them 'poets with a difference,' different from Homer, Sappho, Theocritus, Virgil, Shelley, Keats, Coleridge, and Heine. This is the conclusion of a romanticist, who maintains that the best things in Racine, the best things in Aristophanes, the best things in the Book of Job, are romantic. But I willingly acknowledge that the classical movement, the Conservative movement, the movement which Waller[56] began and Pope completed, was inevitable, necessary, salutary. I am not ungrateful to Pope and Waller; but they hold of Apollo in his quality of leech, rather than of minstrel, and they 'rather seem his healing son,' Asclepius, than they resemble the God of the Silver Bow.[57] As to the future of our poetry, whether poets should return to 'the simple iambic movements' or not, who can predict? It all depends on the poets, probably unborn, who are to succeed Mr. Matthew Arnold and Lord Tennyson. But I hope that, if our innumerable lyric measures are to be deserted, it may be after my time. I see nothing opposed to a moderate Conservatism in anapaests,[58] but I fear Mr. Courthope suspects the lyric Muse herself of a dangerous Radicalism.

'Literary Plagiarism', *Contemporary Review* 51

(June 1887), pp. 835–40

According to a recent biographer of Byron, originality can be expected from nobody except a lunatic, a hermit, or a sensational novelist. This hasty remark is calculated to prejudice novelists, lunatics, and hermits. People will inevitably turn to these members of society (if we can speak thus of hermits and lunatics), and ask them for originality, and fail to get it, and express disappointment. For all lunatics are like other lunatics, and, no more than sane men, can they do anything original. As for hermits, one hermit is the very image of his brother solitary. There remain sensational novelists to bear the brunt of the world's demand for the absolutely unheard-of, and, naturally, they cannot supply the article. So mankind falls on them, and calls them plagiarists. It is enough to make some novelists turn lunatics, and others turn hermits.

'Of all forms of theft,' says Voltaire indulgently, 'plagiarism is the least dangerous to society!'[1] It may be added that, of all forms of consolation, to shout 'plagiarism' is the most comforting to authors who have failed, or amateurs who have never had the pluck to try. For this reason, probably, a new play seldom succeeds but some unlucky amateur produces his battered old MS., and declares that the fortunate author has stolen from *him*, who hath Fortune for his foe. Indeed, without this resource it is not known how unaccepted theatrical writers would endure their lot in life. But if stealing is so ready a way to triumph, then humanity may congratulate itself on the wide prevalence of moral sentiments. So very few people greatly succeed (and scarce any one who does not is called a thief) that even if all successful persons are proved robbers, there must be a lofty standard of honesty in literature. On the other hand it is a melancholy fact that the very greatest men of all – Shakspeare, Molière, Virgil (that furtive Mantuan), Pausanias,[2]

Theocritus, and Lord Tennyson – are all liable to the charge of theft, as that charge is understood by the *advocatus Diaboli*.[3] It is a little odd, not only that our greatest are so small, but that our smallest – the persons who bark at the chariot of every passing triumph – are so great. *They* have never stolen, or nothing worth stealing, or nothing that any one would buy. But Dante: why, the whole idea of a visit to Hell, and a record of it, was a stock topic in early mediaeval literature. But Bunyan: every library possesses, or may possess, half a dozen earlier Progresses by earlier Pilgrims. But Virgil: when he is not pilfering from Homer or Theocritus (who notoriously robbed Sophron) he has his hand in the pocket of Apollonius Rhodius. No doubt Bavius and Maevius[4] mentioned these truths in their own literary circle. No doubt they did not gloss over the matter, but frankly remarked that the 'Æneid' was a *pastiche*, a string of plagiarisms, a success due to Court influence, and the mutual admiration of Horace, Varro,[5] and some other notorious characters. Yet the 'Æneid' remains a rather unusual piece of work.

Some one, probably Gibbon, has remarked about some crime or other, that it is 'difficult to commit, and almost impossible to prove.'[6] The reverse is the truth about plagiarism. That crim e is easy to prove, and almost impossible to commit. The facility of proof is caused by the readiness of men to take any accusation of this sort for granted, and by the very natural lack of popular reflection about the laws that govern literary composition. Any two passages or situations, or ideas, that resemble each other, or are declared to resemble each other when they do not, are, to the mind of the unliterary person, a sufficient basis for a charge of plagiarism. These circumstances account for the ease with which plagiarism is proved. Yet it is difficult, if not impossible, to commit. For he who is charged with plagiarism is almost invariably guilty of a literary success. Now, even the poorest and most temporary literary success (say that of a shilling novel) rests on the production of *a new thing*. The book that really wins the world, even for a week, from its taxes, and politics, and wars and rumours of war, must be in some way striking and novel. The newness may lie in force of fancy, or in charm of style, or in both; or in mere craftsman's skill, or in high spirits, or in some unusual moral sympathy and insight, or in various combinations of these things. In all such cases, and always, it is what is new, it is the whole impact of the book as one thing, that enables it to make its way to the coveted front. Now, what is stolen cannot be new; it can be nothing but the common-places of situation, and incident, and idea – each of them as old as fiction in one shape or other. Not the matter, but the casting of the matter; not the stuff, but the form given to the stuff, makes the novel, the novelty, and the success. Now, nobody can steal the form; nobody, as in the old story (or nobody except a piratical publisher), can 'steal the brooms ready-made.'[7] The success or failure lies not in the materials, but in the making of the brooms, and no dullard can make anything, even if he steals all his materials. On the other hand, genius, or even considerable talent, can make a great deal, if it chooses, even out of stolen material – if any of the material of literature can be properly said to be stolen, and is not rather the possession of whoever likes to pick it up.

On this view of the matter, the only real plagiarism is that defined in the Latin dictionary. *Plagiarus*, 'a man-stealer, kidnapper' so used by Cicero and Seneca.[8] Secondly, 'a literary thief (one who gives himself out to be the author of another's book).' Martial uses the word (i. 52): –

'My books, my Quintian, to thee
I send – if I may call them mine–
For still your Poet, who but he,
Recites them, – well, if they repine,
In that their slavery do thou
Come to their rescue and befriend them,
And raise the hue and cry, and vow
The hand that wrote them now doth send them,
You'll aid them much by this relief.
And bring confusion on the thief!'[9]

Here 'thief' is *plagiarius*, and a thief the rival poet is, for he gives himself out to be the author of another's book, and steals it ready-made.

This is the only perfect plagiarism, according to the definition – namely, the claiming of a work of art which belongs to another man. Now, plainly this kind of plagiarism is rare, nor would it be easy to mention a case in which it has been successful. In a number of novels we meet the story of a man who comes into possession of a book in manuscript, perhaps the deposit of a friend, and who publishes the work as a performance of his own. Such a man is a *plagiarius*: he casts his net (*plaga*) over the property of another. In real life it might be impossible to find an example of success in this kind of robbery. There are, unluckily, plenty of men and women who take credit, among their relations and friends, for the authorship of anonymous books which have been successful. They are 'claimants' like the Tichborne pretender,[10] rather than successful plagiarists. The case of George Eliot and 'Adam Bede' is well known. There was a person named Liggins who gave himself out for the author, and even reaped some social if not pecuniary benefit. In the same way, but on a smaller scale, there were various pretenders to the honour of having written a certain essay in the *Saturday Review*, 'The Girl of the Period.'[11] According to the actual writer, one of the pretenders was a clergyman. About twelve years ago an admired poet had great trouble with a married lady who asserted that the poet's real name was her assumed *nom de guerre*.[12] Her husband, naturally, was well deceived by this fair *retaria*[13] and caster of the *plaga* over other people's poems. Though it has nothing to do with the question of plagiarism, let us commiserate unlucky persons of letters whose real names, somehow, sound like assumed names. It is a misfortune they can scarcely recover from, and probably many people in the country still believe that Lord Lytton wrote 'Evan Harrington' and 'Richard Feverel.'[14]

Mr. Liggins did not succeed in the long run, nor does literary history, perhaps, contain a single example of the triumph of a literary Perkin Warbeck.[15] Only in very unusual and fantastic circumstances could he hope to keep the goods he stole ready-made. In the last novel on this situation, the pretender had every reason to believe that the true author of the MS. was drowned at sea. Unlucky and ill-advised pretender! The sea invariably gives up her dead – in novels. Short of such an unexpected accident as the sea's not giving up her dead, how is the true plagiarist to feel comfortable with his stolen goods? Almost his only chance, and that a bad one, would be by way of translation from some little-known language. Not long ago a story or novel by a modern author was published in a periodical. Presently the editor got a letter from a correspondent, offering to furnish 'the sequel of your little tale from the Basque' or whatever the original language may have been. Yes, it is very difficult to find a language safe to steal from. Let me confess that, in a volume of tales written by way of holiday tasks, I once conveyed a passage from the Zulu. There could not have been a more barefaced theft, and no doubt, in the present inflamed condition of the moral sense, somebody would have denounced me, had the tale been successful. But as long as you do not excite the pretty passion of envy, you may drive the Zulu cows unnoticed. There were only about three lines in the passage after all. The coolness of plagiarism has occasionally been displayed on a larger scale, as when a novelist boldly took a whole battle scene out of Kinglake's 'History of the Crimean War.'[16] *He* was found out, but he did not seem to care much. Probably this particularly daring theft was a mere piece of mischief – a kind of practical joke. What other explanation can be given of Mr. Disraeli's raid on M. Thiers, and the speech about General Saint-Cyr?[17] Of course, Mr. Disraeli could have made a better speech for himself. Thefts of this kind, like certain literary forgeries, are prompted by the tricksy spirit of Puck. But the joke is not in good taste, and is dangerous to play, because the majority of mankind will fail to see the fun of it, and will think the thief a thief in sober earnest. Only a humorous race would have made a God of Hermes, who stole cattle from the day his mother cradled him.

From these and similar cases, the difficulty, the all but impossibility, of successful plagiarism becomes manifest. If you merely use old ideas (and there are no new ideas), and so produce a fresh combination, a fresh whole, you are not a plagiarist at all. If you boldly annex the novel ready-made, either by way of translation, or publication of a manuscript not your own, you are instantly found out, and probably never get back your reputation. It appears that Mr. Charles Reade, in the 'Wandering Heir' 'bodily appropriated' twenty or thirty lines of a little-known poem of Dean Swift's, descriptive of fashionable life in Dublin. Mr. Reade appears to have used this poem in such a way as to make the public think it was his own composition. If he did, he acted, to say the least, with very great rashness. He reckoned without the unsuccessful novelist, and the unsuccessful novelist's family. Of course he was 'denounced as a plagiarist by two anonymous writers, who afterwards turned out to be a not very successful rival novelist and his wife.' These 'lynx-eyed detectives' do, pretty often, 'turn out to be' unsuccessful novelists and their kinsmen. Mr. Reade then uttered loud cries of wrath, and spoke of 'masked batteries manned by anonymuncula, pseudo-nymuncula, and skunkula.'*

He contended that to transplant a few lines out of Swift, and to weld them with other topics in a heterogeneous work, was not plagiarism, but one of every true inventor's processes, and that only an inventor could do it well. The whole affair was not worth much consideration, but Mr. Reade's theory of what a true inventor might lawfully do was certainly a little advanced. A lump of such a brilliant manufactured article as a poem by Swift would be apt to look incongruous even in a true inventor's prose, and certainly was appropriated ready-made. If Swift's notions about Dublin society had been adopted, and had informed the prose of Mr. Reade, a legitimate use would have been made of the material. Or, if Mr. Reade had said, 'the Dean of St. Patrick's wrote thus on the subject,' then once more the propriety of the quotation would have been unimpeachable. But perhaps the former of these suggestions will be demurred to by our moralists. There appears to be an idea that a novelist must acknowledge, in a preface or in footnotes, every suggestion of fact which comes to him from any quarter. For example, I write a novel in which a man is poisoned by *curari*.[18] Am I to add a note saying, 'These details as to the Macusi tribe are extracted from Wallace, from Bates, and from Brett's "Indians of Guiana" (London: Bell and Daldy. 1878). I have also to acknowledge the kind assistance of Professor Von Selber of Leiden. For another and earlier example of a somewhat similar use of this drug, the curious may consult "Le Crime de l'Omnibus", by M. Fortuné du Boisgobey, to whose practice, however, science may urge certain pathological objections.'

This kind of thing is customary and appropriate in books of learning, but it seems incredible pedantry to demand such explanations from authors of works of fancy. When the scene of a story and the manners of the peoples described are not known to a novelist by personal experience, he must get his information out of books. For example, any reader of the first volume of Mr. Payn's 'By Proxy'[19] might fancy that Mr. Payn had passed his life in the Flowery Land. But this is believed to be a false impression, caused by the novelist's ingenious use of works of travel. Is he bound to acknowledge every scrap of information in a preface or footnote? The idea is absurd. A novel would become a treatise, like Bekker's 'Charicles.'[20] The effect of this conscientiousness may be studied in the 'Epicurean' of the late Mr. Thomas

* 'How Charles Reade Worked' St. James's Gazette, May 3, 1887.

Moore,[21] where there are plentiful citations, on every page, of Egyptologists – for the most part exploded. The story would be better without the notes, which are useless in the age of Maspero and Mariette.[22] Of course, if any novelist can make his notes as delightful as Sir Walter Scott's, the more he gives us the better we shall be pleased – provided they come at the end of the volume.

All ideas are old; all situations have been invented and tried, or almost all. Probably a man of genius might make a good story even out of a selected assortment of the very oldest devices in romance. Miss Thackeray made capital stories out of the fairy tales,[23] that are older than Rameses II, and were even published by a scribe of that monarch's. Give Mr. Besant or Mr. Stevenson two lovers, and insist that, in telling these lovers' tale, the following incidents shall occur:

A sprained Ankle.
An Attack by a Bull.
A Proposal in a Conservatory watched by a Jealous Rival.
A Lost Will.
An Intercepted Correspondence.

Even out of these incidents it is probable that either of the authors mentioned could produce a novel that would soothe pain and charm exile. Nor would they be accused of plagiarism, because the ideas are, even by the most ignorant or envious, recognised as part of the common stock-in-trade.

Now, it is a fact that almost every notion and situation is as much part of the common stock-in-trade as those old friends. The 'Odyssey' for example, might be shown to contain almost all the material of the romance that is accepted as outside of ordinary experience. For instance, in 'She' we find a wondrous woman, who holds a man in her hollow caves (note the *caves*, there are caves in Homer), and offers him the gift of immortality. Obviously this is the position of Odysseus and Calypso. Rousseau remarked that the whole plot of the 'Odyssey' would have been ruined by a letter from Odysseus to Penelope. Rousseau had not studied Wolf; but had letters been commonly written in Homer's time, the poet would have bribed one of Penelope's women to intercept them. Homer did not use that incident, because he did not need it; but all his incidents were of primeval antiquity, even in his own time; he plagiarized them from popular stories; he stole the Cyclops almost ready-made.*

There are, doubtless, exceptions to this rule of the universality and public character of the stock of fiction. These exceptions are rather of an empirical sort, and should be avoided chiefly for the sake of weak brethren, who go about writing long letters in the newspapers. A few instances may be given from personal experience. A novelist once visited the writer in high spirits. Certain events of a most extraordinary nature had just occurred

* Gerland: 'Alt-Griechische Märchen in der Odyssee'.

to him, events which would appear incredible if I ventured to narrate them. My visitor meant to make them the subject of a story, which he sketched. 'But you *can't*' I said; 'that's the plot of 'Ferdinand's Folly'[24] and I named a book which had just arrived *sub luminis oras*.[25] He had not heard of 'Ferdinand's Folly,' but he went away sad, for he was a young man that had been robbed of a great opportunity. But he was presently consoled by receiving a letter from another author, a gentleman of repute in more than one branch of literature. 'I have just read your "Daisy's Dream",' said this author, 'and I find that there is a scene in it which is also in my unpublished work, "Psamathöe"'.[26] He then described the scene, which certainly did appear of glaring originality – if anything could be original. 'Nobody will believe two people could have invented this; and what am I to do?' said the second unfortunate author; and indeed I do not know what he did, or whether 'Psamathöe' was punished by an early doom for her unconscious plagiarism. The study of the diffusion of popular tales seems to show that there is no incident which may not be invented over and over again – in Siberia, or Samoa. These coincidences will also occur in civilized literature; but some examples are so astonishing that the small fry of moralists are certain to shout 'Stop thief.' On the whole, an author thus anticipated had better stop before they shout, but it was the merest accident that gave pause to the two novelists of these anecdotes. Alas! unconscious of their doom, the little victims might have published.

Another very hard case lately came under my notice. A novelist invented and described to me a situation which was emphatically new, because it rested on the existence of a certain scientific instrument, which was new also. The author was maturing the plot, when he chanced to read a review of some new work (I never saw it, and have forgotten its name), in which the incident and the instrument appeared. Now, may this author write his own tale, or may he not? If he does (and if it succeeds), he will be hailed as abandoned rogue; and yet it is his own invention. Probably it is wiser to 'endure and abstain;' otherwise the 'lynx-eyed detectives' will bring out their old learning, and we shall be told once more how Ben Jonson stole 'Drink to me only with thine eyes' from – Pisitratus![27] This I lately learned from a newspaper.

Thus it appears that, although plagiarism is hardly a possible offence, it is more discreet not to use situations which have either made one very definite impression on the world of readers, or which have been very recently brought out. For example: it is distinctly daring to make a priest confess his unsuspected sin in a sermon. The notion is public property; but everyone is reminded of Hawthorne's 'Scarlet Letter'.[28] Thus the situation is a thing to avoid; as certain measures – that of 'In Memoriam' for example – are to be avoided in poetry. The metre is everybody's property, but it at once recalls the poem wherein the noblest use was made of it. Again, double personality is a theme open to all the world: Gautier and Poe and Eugène

Sue[29] all used it; but it is wiser to leave it alone while people have a vivid memory of Dr. Jekyll and Mr. Hyde. It is not inconceivable that an author might use the old notion as brilliantly and with as much freshness as Mr. Stevenson has done; it is certain that if he tries, he will be howled at by the moral mob. A novelist may keep these precautions in his mind, but if, though he writes good books, he is not a bookish man, he will be constantly and unwittingly offending people who do not write good books, although they are bookish. Thus it lately happened to me to see an illustration of an unpublished work, in which a wounded and dying warrior was using his last force to break, with singular consequence, the weapon that had been his lifelong companion. I knew (being bookish) the incident was perfectly familiar to me, but I could not remember where I had met it before. It haunted me like the names which you try to recover from faithless memory, and one day it flashed on me that this incident was at least eight hundred years old. But I leave (not its source, for the novelist who is no bookman had probably never tasted of that literary fountain) but the place of its early appearance, to be remembered or discovered by any one who is curious enough to consult his memory or his library. But here another question arises: let it be granted that the novelist first found the situation where I found it, and is there any reason in the world why he should not make what is a thoroughly original use of it? The imagination or invention needed for this particular adaptation was at least as vivid and romantic as the original conception, which, again, might occur, and may have occurred, separately to minds in Japan and in Peru.

I have chiefly spoken of plagiarism in fiction, for there is little need to speak of plagiarism in poetry. Probably no man or woman (apart from claiming a ready-made article not their own) ever consciously plagiarized in verse. The smallest poetaster has too much vanity to borrow on purpose. Unconsciously even great men (Scott confesses in one case) have remembered and repeated the ideas or the rhythm of others. In a recent Jubilee Ode one reads (indeed it is quoted in a newspaper article on plagiarism):

> 'Deep-based on ancient right as on thy people's will
> Thy rule endures unshattered still.' [30]

The debt to the Laureate's verse[31] is not to be mistaken; but no less unmistakable is the absence of consciousness of this in the author. When I was a freshman, and when Mr. Swinburne was the new poet, I wrote a (most justly unsuccessful) Newdigate,[32] in which I thought there was a good line. Somebody's hands were said to be

> 'Made of a red rose swooning into white.'

This seemed 'all wery capital,' like matrimony to Mr. Weller,[33] till I found, in 'Chastelard,'[34] somebody's hand

> 'Made of a red rose that has turned to white,'

The mind of the unconscious plagiarist had not been wholly inactive, as the word 'swooning' shows, but it was a direct though unintentional robbery. No robberies, in verse, are made, I think, with more *malice prepense*[35] than this early larceny.

On the whole, then, the plagiarist appears to be a decidedly rare criminal, whereas charges of plagiarism have always been as common as blackberries. An instructive example is that of Molière and 'Les Précieuses.' Everything in it, cried Somaise and De Villiers, is from the Abbé de Pure, the Italians, and Chapuzeau.[36] But somehow none of these gallant gentlemen did, in fact, write 'Les Précieuses Ridicules,' nor anything that anybody except the Molièriste ever heard of.

The laudable anxiety of the Somaises of all time for literary honesty would be more laudable still if they did not possess a little vice of their own. It is not a vice of which any man is the *fanfaron*:[37] the delicate veiled passion of Envy. Indeed, these lynx-eyed ones have a bad example in their predecessor, Mr. Alexander Pope. Mr. Pope had a friend who became an enemy – Mr. Moore, who took the name of Smythe. This Mr. Moore-Smythe wrote a comedy, 'The Rival Modes,' played in 1727, wherein the persons occasionally dropped into poetry, printed in italics. On March 18, 1728, an anonymous correspondent in the *Daily Journal* accused Mr. Pope of having plagiarized certain verses from this comedy, and published them in the third volume of his 'Miscellanies':

'Tis thus that vanity coquettes rewards,
A youth of frolics, an old age of cards ' –

and so forth. There was no doubt that these verses, after appearing in the 'Rival Modes,' came out in Pope's 'Miscellanies.' But in 1729, in the enlarged edition of the 'Dunciad' Pope quoted the anonymous letters (there were two), and maintained that the verses were his own, and that Moore-Smythe was the plagiarist. He had given Smythe leave to use them (the men had once been on good terms), and had suggested their withdrawal later. Pope then, on a quarrel with Smythe, published them, and antedated them (1723), 'in order to found or support the charge of plagiarism against Smythe.' And Mr. Alexander Pope himself (like Conkey in 'Oliver Twist') was his own anonymous accuser, bringing the charge against himself, that he might retort it on the luckless Moore-Smythe. But Mr. Moore-Smythe was in one respect well advised: he made no reply.

Though it appears from this anecdote, as told in Mr. Carruthers' Life of Pope,[38] that people who bring charges of plagiarism are not invariably of a delicate morality, yet a review of the whole topic cannot but console the moralist. Mr. Matthew Arnold assigns to morality but a poor seven-eighths in the composition of human life. But we see that morality has far more interest and importance than this estimate allows. A masterpiece of mere art in poetry or fiction might be published (I wish it were probable) without exciting one hundredth part of the interest provoked by the charge of stealing half a page. Thus we learn that Art is of no importance at all in comparison with Conduct. A good new book is murmured about at a few dinner parties. A wicked new action – say the purloining, real or alleged, of twenty lines – is thundered about from the house-tops and flashed along all the network of electric wires from London to San Francisco. While men have this overpowering interest in morals, who can despair of humanity?

'At the Sign of the Ship', *Longman's Magazine* 10:57

(July 1887), pp. 329–31

'Then, are we Critics of no use in the world?' Mr Howells has been asking in *Harper's Magazine*. He does not appear to be very certain that we are. 'Perhaps criticism does some good we do not know of' he says, in a spirit of agnosticism. 'They say it does one good,' murmured Nicholas of ancient days, when he was crossing the Channel in a gale. 'But,' he added, 'I'd rather be done good to some other way.'[1] This is probably the feeling of many authors. Perhaps criticism does them good. But they would rather be done good to 'some other way.' Let me try to point out to the proud race of authors how criticism does them good. In the first place, it stops some of them in their first rush (which is always wild, like a salmon's) and turns them from a business in which they are of no avail. The present babbler humbly believes that his very earliest criticism of a novel had this valuable effect. The review set forth that there was only one excuse for publishing such a bad novel: the thing might be palliated if the novelist wished to commit a crime on his own account, and then to bring in the novel as proof of insanity. The idea, of course, would not be original, it would be borrowed from *Married Beneath Him*.[2] The author then wrote to me, thanking me for the kind frankness of my remarks and the consideration I had obviously bestowed on his work. He asked what intellectual pursuit I would recommend to him. This was how an author should take criticism! I replied that I thought he might have a turn for writing sonnets, and perhaps he had; in any case he did not again invade the shores of old Romance. Here, then, was one good action to the credit of the humble but not absolutely heartbroken Critic.

Critics do plenty of other good deeds; of course I don't want to boast, but merely to encourage Mr. Howells. Nobody could go on being a Critic if he thought the profession useless. For example, the Critic, like Sister Anne, is on a watch-tower, and the public, like Madame de la Barbe-Bleue, is below, anxiously awaiting some new genius.

'Anne, ma sœur Anne, ne vois-tu rien venir?'

Too often the Critic has to reply, *'Je ne vois rien que le soleil qui poudroye, et l'herbe qui verdoye.'*[3]

But, once and again, the Critic *does* see somebody coming, somebody not yet visible to the public below. Perhaps it is a company of Woodlanders, marching beneath the Greenwood Tree.[4] Perhaps, through the dust, it is Inkosi-kaas,[5] that glitters yonder, far away. Perhaps it is a boy travelling with a Donkey, or Prince Florestan voyaging from Bohemia, or Master Bultitude running away from Rodwell Regis.[6] Now and again the Critic hears a wandering Minstrel beneath the Tower; the voice is new, the voice is faint, but it is clear and musical. Then do you think that the Critic is not as glad as Sister Anne when she marked the coming of the Dragoon and the Mousquetaire? Sure that Mousquetaire was of M. d'Artagnan's company.[7] This good thing, then, the Critic does or may do; he spies the new genius trudging on, alone and unknown; he welcomes him, he announces him; sometimes it is long before the Public gives a hearing, but the Critic, at least, offers the stranger a chance. Doubtless he is apt to cry the reverse of 'Wolf,'– to cry 'Lamb' (let us say) when there is not really a fresh essayist of that force, or to herald a poet who turns out a poetaster. These blunders will happen, yet does the Critic (to vary the metaphor) fulfil the functions of that watchman who, from afar, beheld the beacon flashing to Mycenae, across the isles.[8] Without Critics, many a young author might never win a hearing, and many a painter might exhibit in vain.

A third good that the Critic does (now and then) is not always acknowledged by the author. The Critic induces him to improve his work. Mr. Howells, indeed, says that 'with the youngest and weakest author criticism is quite powerless against his will to do his own work in his own way.' Well, in 1833 Lord Tennyson was a very young, though anything but a 'weak' author. His poems were criticised in a variety of tones, often bumptious and brutal. But criticism was not powerless. Let any one compare, for example, the 'Palace of Art' in the edition of 1833, with the 'Palace of Art' in the last edition, and both with the contemporary reviews. Undeniably the poet has taken his Critics' advice. Where are

'Isaiah with fierce Ezekiel,
Swarth Moses by the Coptic sea,
Plato, Petrarca, Livy, and Raphaël,
And eastern Confutzee!'

Does the Soul any longer, regardless of expense, 'light white streams of dazzling gas'? And where is the famous water-rat? And where is the Man in the balloon who 'takes his flags and waves them to the mob,' and thus opens the 'Dream of Fair Women'? Or 'the little room so exquisite'? These and many another thing the Critics disliked have passed quietly away; the Critics were right and the poet knew it. But how the Critics, with that immortal volume of 1833 before them, could see the spots on the dawning sun, or listen for the frogs among the nightingales, does yet amaze a Critic of to-day. They were not many who applauded the new voice, for even Critics are mortal, and often slumberous and stupid. However, some apology has been made for them, poor fellows.

'At the Sign of the Ship', *Longman's Magazine* 16:95

(September 1890), pp. 569–72

It is time that the line should be firmly drawn between criticism and reviewing. In the August number of *Harper's Magazine* (which, by the way, contains a thrilling account of Custer's last fight[1]) Mr. Howells does not seem to draw this line. He once more endeavours to abate the insolence of 'critics', assures them that criticism has usually tried to depress originality, tells them that, being anonymous, they are tempted to be savage, and, generally, labours to make them 'know their place.' To myself he seems to overrate their influence – and their savagery. The ordinary anonymous reviewer is (as the Scotch lassie said of a modest lover) 'senselessly ceevil.'[2] He is good-natured to a degree. Occasionally he hits hard, and sometimes below the belt. Occasionally he may have a bad motive – a motive of envy, spite, or personal dislike. But on the other hand, as Mr. Thackeray said, authors should make up their minds to a great deal of 'honest enmity,' and 'to be abused for good as well as bad reasons.'[3] This is a hard lesson for authors, yet they should learn it. The anonymous is not necessarily, nor often, the dishonest reviewer. Mr. Howells tells a parable of a journal, the *Clarion* which 'is opposed to So-and-So's book.' Now if a reviewer lets his editor impose a task on him, if he attacks the books merely because the *Clarion* is opposed to them, he is selling his soul extremely cheap. But I believe such a bargain is rare. If the reviewer finds that he differs from the literary policy of his paper, he says, 'Send the book to some other man.' It is a mistake, to be sure, for a journal to have a 'policy' about an author's books at all; each should be judged on its merits. But there is no need, in any case, for the reviewer to dissemble. After reviewing for many years, I myself can only recall two cases in which an editor made any suggestions. One of the books was Mr. Rossetti's first poems, the other was a volume of Mr. Matthew Arnold's. The editor in each case said, 'If you don't like the work send it back, for I *do*'. I did like it in each instance; but had I disliked it, no harm would have been done. Nobody's conscience would have been wronged. So much for honesty, and, as for savagery, many signed French criticisms appear more amusingly cruel than the excesses of our anonymous press. For various reasons one might agree with Mr. Howells, and wish that all reviews were signed. But the public is of another opinion, and a reviewer can always act on Mr. Howells' excellent advice, and say nothing, anonymously, that he would hesitate to put his name to. Most of the names would be quite unknown, would tell the reader and author very little.

In short, the brief contemporary 'notice' is not criticism. It may be merely an item of literary news, or a brief summary – a useful thing in itself – or it may be a puff, or it may be a spiteful insult. It has not room to be a studied criticism, nor is the knowledge of any man so encyclopaedic that he can do a dozen books briefly, yet each with the touch of a specialist. The consciousness of this, and human kindness therewith, makes most reviewers good-natured. An author gets little good or bad from them. About familiar and prolific writers they keep little *clichés* on stereotyped forms. For my own part I know exactly what the reviewer will say about any new venture of my own. 'The versatile and industrious Mr. L. New field. Accustomed lightness of touch. Desultory. Inaccurate. May be read without fatigue. Opinions may still be divided as to Mr. L.'s conclusions.' That is the humour of it; not exhilarating, but quite kindly and harmless. And what more has a man a right to expect? If I have developed a theory about the religion of the Patagonians, what can Jones, who does the notices in the *Clarion* know about the matter? What can he care about the matter? He has to turn out a score of lines of copy, and it were irrational vanity in me to expect him to study half a library, and wring his brow with thought over me and my Patagonians. Or if I write a novel – which may fate forbid – it is a thousand to one that I neither excite Jones's enthusiasm, nor drive him to a fury of indignation. That is reserved for more powerful and passionate authors, who should be proud of ecstatic praise or violent condemnation – from Jones. They have, in either event, made Jones 'sit up,' as the saying is, and that is something. I only once remember having made him assume this attitude, with a translation of a Greek poet, and he hit out at me rarely. The subject of punishment merely giggled, and it were well for all authors to laugh instead of sitting down gravely to call Jones a treacherous savage, or going about to discover his name and habitation. Who cares where he is, or who he is? He has a right to his opinion, and one likes to hear him express it as if he meant it. But Mr. Howells appears to be wounded when people differ from his views of what fiction ought to be, and prove by the energy of their exclamations that he has hit them.

He is always hitting me, for one, because to me criticism seems more valuable and other than he thinks. I mean reasoned and considered writing on the tried masterpieces of the world, or even ingenious and entertaining writing about new books. To have a clever and accomplished man telling you, in his best manner, what thoughts come into his mind after reading even a new novel, is no trifling pleasure among the pale and shadowy pleasures of the mind. The topic may be Dante, or may be only Marie Bashkirtseff,[4] yet the ideas which it helps to suggest to a competent and well-read critic are agreeable, and not mere value-less verbiage. This is apart from his verdict of praise or condemnation: what one enjoys is not the verdict, but the insight into another nature. Not that even the verdict is wholly worthless; it attracts your attention to the book discussed ; you can read it and make up your own mind. One does not condemn a book unseen, because the *Scots Thistle* or the *Bungay Beacon*[5] has disparaged it. The public which reads is not so easily led, and the larger reading public elects its own favourites in contempt, or in ignorance, of reviews. A very much smaller public reads real criticism, ancient or modern, of Sainte-Beuve, of Villemain, of Aristotle, of Dionysius of Halicarnassus, for that matter,[6] and thence derives matter for thought. It is among the most innocent occupations of leisure, and, to men who themselves are authors, is among the most useful. Mr. Howells says that Canon Farrar[7] says he has learned nothing from his critics. Possibly not, but there are authors and authors, critics and critics. Would Mr. Howells say he could learn nothing from Longinus, from Horace, from Boileau, from Goethe? Does he, in turn, expect to teach nothing? Clearly he expects, or wishes, to teach a good deal, and, if he can do this as a critic, he should not despair of criticism.

For lack of signed names, Mr. Howells says, a journal is made to seem inconsistent. Once, for example, as he reminds us, there was a tiff between Mr. Thackeray and the *Saturday Review*. As far as my memory goes, the Saturday had objected to Mr. Thackeray's habit of talking about himself, and taking you into his confidence. No doubt he carried this to excess in his decline, as in *Philip* and the *Roundabout Papers*. He was always sensitive, as even modern authors occasionally are, and he replied by inventing the mild nickname of the *Superfine Review*. Now, on the other hand, says Mr. Howells, the *Saturday* is a champion of Mr. Thackeray's genius, and this looks inconsistent. Circumstances have altered, that is all; the genius remains, the old opponent is converted, and probably does not mind being inconsistent. Mr. Gladstone lately blamed Wellhausen's[8] inconsistency because in twenty years he has altered his opinion about the date of the Psalms. In twenty years even Mr. Gladstone may have altered his mind on some matters, and probably the *Review* which once had a dispute with a great living writer is not discredited because it admires his excellencies, and does not lay the former stress on the faults of his early old age.

'The Science of Criticism', *New Review* 4:24

(May 1891), pp. 403–8

Let us define criticism as the form of skilled labour which is occupied in writing about other men's books, old or new. If Sainte-Beuve wrote on Dante, that is Criticism; and if a paragraphist in a newspaper compose a column of printed matter out of the prefaces of new books which he has not read, that is Criticism also. It is Criticism which discovers that Homer's works were compiled, in about five hundred years, by about fifty different authors.[1] And it is Criticism which finds out that Mr. Smith or Mr. Brown steals his successful novels from Bishop Berkeley or Thomas Moore.[2] The former is an example of the Higher Criticism,[3] the latter of the lower species, and, really, both seem about equally valuable. It is not easy to find a common factor in Criticism, in the studies of which Aristotle and Longinus, Matthew Arnold and Sainte-Beuve, are masters, while unsuccessful lady novelists and uneducated pressmen form, perhaps, the majority of the school. All of them write about the work of other people, all distribute praise and blame; these are points common to all critics, though in reading, knowledge, taste, and temper there is every sort of diversity. All critics are contemplating works of literary art through the medium of their own temperaments, looking at them with their own eyes, estimating them by their own standard. Yet the writings of some critics are eternal possessions; always good to know and to live with, like the *Poetics* of Aristotle, or the *Ars Poetica* of Horace, or the Treatise of Longinus on the Sublime. The writing of other critics, daily or weekly, are often so ignorant, so prejudiced, so spiteful, so careless, that perhaps no printed matter is more entirely valueless and contemptible. It may be said that the topics with which the ordinary reviewer deal, the books on which he pronounces judgment, are not much better than the judgments he pronounces. This is very true, but it seems a pity that bad books should not be barren, but should beget bad reviews. That great George Dandin,[4] the public, has willed it so.

Perhaps the only kind of Criticism worth reading or writing is that which narrates the adventures of an ingenious and educated mind in contact with masterpieces. The literary masterpieces of the world are so rich, so full of beauties, so charged with ideas, that some or many of these must escape most readers. We wander as in a world full of flowers: we cannot gather all, nor observe all. It is pleasant and profitable to hear the experiences of another in the same paradise, of another whose temper, whose knowledge of the world and of books, are very different from our own. We may agree with what he tells us, or may differ, but even in our difference we feel that we learn much, that our mind is moved to new activities. Thus, for example, if a critic's chief duty is to be correct, to be sound in his judgments, it is plain that neither Mr. Matthew Arnold nor, to take a modern instance, M. Jules Lemaître[5] is always an impeccable critic. Mr. Arnold's 'Lectures on Translating Homer', a most lively and enlivening book, was vitiated (to my taste) by his extraordinary zeal for the English hexameter. It also contained many examples of his pet form of injustice. He chose an admirable passage from Homer, and as bad a passage as he could find from a ballad or from Scott: he placed them beside each other and drew conclusions. How a critic could ever persuade himself that this childish process was an argument we are not able to guess. But, on the other hand, the Lectures were full of deeply thought and keenly felt ideas on and impressions from Homeric poetry. Homer's admirers were delighted with new, and sound, and well expressed reasons for their admiration. In the same way M. Jules Lemaître confesses to more ignorance and more prejudice than, perhaps, he would like his enemies to charge him with. But he possesses, in his happier days, a sympathy, an urbanity, a wit, and even a literary enthusiasm (for Lamartine and Racine), which cover a number of sins in the eyes of an Englishman. Thus, it is not sober soundness and correctness and sagacity alone that make the critic. It is rather originality, individuality, the possession of wide knowledge and of an interesting temperament, that enables a writer on books to write what shall be valuable. For writing *about* writing is not in itself a very noble profession, nor one very well worth devoting time and labour to, though the greatest writers, Goethe, Wordsworth, Hugo, Scott, have not disdained it. The laws and processes of all arts are interesting to artists, and to others who, without possessing genius, have knowledge, and taste, and discrimination. Criticism does very little, if anything, for any art, but man is so made that he takes pleasure in having his say. This 'say' is Criticism, and, at worst, Criticism adds some agreeable hours to life, offers some pleasant matters of thought, brings us nearer to some great minds than we can come when we study their creative work alone; and so far, I suppose, Criticism has a *raison d'être* and needs no defence of its existence. Few persons, I presume, can look back on their first reading of Lessing's *Laocoon*[6] without pleasure, without remembering how their outlook was widened, how their ideas were clarified, how they had gained more in a few hours from a book than they could have extracted from experience in years. It is a commonplace thing to say, but it is true: that good Criticism does for art and works of art what art does for nature and the work

But we are writing about excellent critics, men of taste, learning, temper, urbanity, and wit. The works of such authors, from Aristotle to Hazlitt,[7] are, I suppose, very little read; are only read, as a rule, by people who have to occupy themselves professionally with literature, or who live much of their lives in literature's pale and shadowy, but enduring pleasures. The kind of Criticism which the world really reads is to be found in reviews of all sorts and sizes. 'It is an ill bird which fouls its own nest,'[8] and heaven forbid that I should speak ill of the mystery of reviewing, whereby many of us make our inglorious, but not dishonourable, bread and butter. There are good reviews among the multitude which the Press, daily and weekly, brings to the birth. There are even reviews by men who are masters of their subjects, and who can give an author new facts, or new matter for thought. There are amiable reviews, which do their best to procure a hearing for a book admired by the reviewer. There are severe reviews, which honestly dance upon a book which the critic does not admire. There are candid, and temperate, and funny reviewers, for all of whom authors and readers may be thankful. They help (a little) to sell a book, or (a little) they help to prevent its sale. Theirs are the verdicts of public tasters, that is all, or nearly all. Occasionally modern reviews are essays worth reading. If the reviewer be a student and competent, he can hang a charming article on the revival of an old play or the success or failure of a new play. Even the review of a novel may show good manners, wit, knowledge, a happy knack of bringing ideas together, and of elucidating the grounds of liking and disliking. I cannot agree with Mr. Besant's theory that critics never instruct and never encourage an author. That they often encourage and often discourage authors, experience shows us. That they instruct is more difficult to prove, because an author must, at all costs, be himself; and the best advice may be bad, if it makes him self-conscious, makes him try to be other than himself. On the whole, reviewing by instructed and competent men and women is not worthless, I hope, to the public, to publishers, or to authors. On the other hand, a great proportion of our innumerable reviews are written by the ignorant, the hasty, the spiteful, the careless, the incompetent. Some reviewers are merely flippant on all occasions; always with the same weary old second-hand flippancy, a bad imitation of a manner that never was good. Such are they who tell in a dozen lines of forced fun the plot of a novel. It may be a bad novel, but the best will not stand this process. Other reviewers there are, who appear to conceive gratuitous and causeless hates and loves for authors whom they never met, nor are likely to meet. They distribute blame or praise with a queer kind of personal *animus*, for which they probably could not account themselves.

The book reviewed is the last thing in their minds. They are denouncing or applauding their own personal ideal of the author. A good deal of envy, hatred, malice, and all uncharitableness goes into the manufacture of reviews, all combined in an aspic of ignorance. For the ignorance of the ordinary reviewer is only equalled by his confidence, and by the audacity with which he delivers his brawling judgments on a book, after a glance at the preface. In brief, reviewing may be, and often is, done by gentlemen and scholars, but it is, perhaps, as frequently the mere expression of ignorant and careless and envious dulness. And how could it be otherwise? Here is a hungry and eager nobody, who has never done, and never will do, anything. He has a pen in his hand, he has the work of someone who has made money and a name before him, and what is to prevent him from writing a review which amounts to a yell of 'Yah!'

At the best, I suppose Criticism does authors very little good. Archdeacon Farrar, I think, though I have not the reference at hand, once told the world that Criticism had done *him* no good.[9] This, perhaps, is an extreme case. But reviewing may do one's books good, if it be favourable. It may, if it be sincere and competent, give the public a hint as to what to read and what to avoid, though the public usually prefer its own selections. On a lower level, if it be witty (which is not common), Criticism may amuse, and to amuse a few readers is not wholly to waste time, ink, and paper. Such seem to me to be the humble duties of everyday reviewing work. You may benefit a new author a little, though, to be sure, in doing so you make all Grub Street[10] detest him. You may cause a pretender to dance at the Torture Stake,[11] though this again is an entertainment in which only the young braves and the squaws should take part. You should, at least, be 'indifferent honest,'[12] and speak your mind. Here is an opportunity for a story about that eminent female critic, Mrs. Carter, the learned lady and the translator of Epictetus.[13] On September 5th, 1746, Mrs. Carter wrote to Miss Talbot. She had been reading the *Odyssey*, and thought it a very mean performance. 'It really does not seem of any great importance to the reader whether Telemachus hung his clothes upon a peg, or was sloven enough to throw them on the floor; or whether Mr. Trulliber (I have forgot his Greek name) took exact care of the hogs. If it was not an incontestable fact that Milton wrote *Paradise Regained*, one could never believe Homer wrote the *Odyssey*.'[14]

Here we find Mrs. Carter an honest, if not, perhaps, an acute or sympathetic critic. But her Editor, a clergyman, tells us that 'Mrs. Carter's criticism was not designed for the public;'[15] she would have spoken very differently if she had written for the public. In that case Mrs. Carter would have been dishonest, a knave: we prefer her honest, and not very wise. Let all critics imitate the out-spoken private manner of Mrs. Carter, remembering, also, to avoid the literary arts unknown to Mr. Clough. 'He had not yet traduced his friends, nor flattered his enemies, nor blamed what he approved, nor praised what he despised.'[16] Criticism would be more amusing if all critics were like Mrs. Carter; it is vain to hope that they will all be like Mr. Clough. But, when all is said, I own that I can scarcely conceive of a topic less momentous than Criticism. We are all but *Goniobombukes*;* though some buzz a little longer or louder than others, and in a more spacious corner. Who reads Boileau now, and is Quintilian much in men's minds?[17] Does Mr. Pinero consult the

> 'Prefaces of Dryden,
> For these our critics much confide in?'[18]

Where is Burke on the Sublime,[19] and where is Mr. Morritt's *Vindication of Homer*, and Blackwell's treatise on the same author?[20] Quite a mild little poem or a third-rate play outlives and outlasts most of our Criticism, and the critic's lot, on the whole, is not a happy one. Perhaps Mr. Henry James and Mr. Saintsbury[21] find it more satisfactory business than I do.

* For the benefit of Grub Street, let us translate this hard word. It means 'persons who buzz in a corner.'

'Politics and Men of Letters', *The Pilot*

(21 April 1900), pp.220–1

As a rule men of letters of all degrees abstain from intruding conspicuously on the field of politics. But every now and then a band of them, or an individual, feels impelled to expression, and the expression is more noticed by virtue of its rarity. *Mon âne parle*! exclaims the public, like the prophet, but it seldom adds, *et même il parle bien.*[1] The literary recluse is not often on the popular side: when he shouts, it is generally 'with the smaller mob.' So he is, of course, in the wrong. In fact, the student is in a dilemma. If he abstains wholly from political expression, he is regarded as a contemptuous dilettante. If he speaks out, he is marked as an unpractical person, labelled a 'faddist,' and advised to return to his crucibles, his dictionaries, his metaphysics, or other wares. The only exception is made when he shouts, or, like Mr. Kipling and other poets, sings on the popular side.

Though I labour under these disabilities myself, I do not think them unnatural or entirely unjust. Other men – say, solicitors, barristers, doctors and the clergy – are in daily and close touch with active human beings. *Our* 'days among the dead are past'; from them, and from historical precedents, we partly draw our opinions of current affairs. We come to conclusions based on analogies, and no analogy can ever be a perfect fit, or, at least, the perfection of the fit will not be admitted by opponents, Thus, for example, one may feel (to put it in the least annoying way) that if we sympathise with Scottish, Swiss, Italian, Dutch and Polish thirst for national Independence, there may, perhaps, be something to be said for the motives of the Boers.[2] Am I dreaming, or did not Mr. Gladstone himself once express sympathy with the Soudanese and their struggles to be free?[3]

The student, who has heard his fellow-countrymen applaud the Greeks, the Hungarians, William Tell, Kosciusko,[4] and the rest, finds that

Independence is very well, but *not* if it is Independence of England. We are to wish well to Finns and Armenians, but not to any race which opposes itself to *us*. There does appear to be a lack of humour in our national attitude, but to think so may be the mere absurd result of dreamy recluse and bookish pursuits. These enervating habits blind us, perhaps, to the practical interests of our country, or make us conceive of them the wrong way. Or again, even if we are in the right, our words carry no weight, and it may be wiser to abstain from words. I cannot but sympathise with the old Hebrew Kings, when members of their literary class, the prophets, insisted on directing the foreign policy of the nation. Such people are apt to be idealists, and I confess that an empire guided by idealists would have singular fortunes. You could hardly conduct any ordinary business on the principles of idealism, which the student is certain to want to apply to the greatest affairs. Our rivals in business, private or public, do not apply them; there is no reciprocity. Suppose that a man of letters suddenly inherits a landed estate that pays, or a coal-mine. His natural impulse is to collect his farmers, or miners, and say, 'Now just put down, each you, what you reckon will remunerate you for your toil, and after that, we shall think of what remains over for the owner of the ground.' These things are not often done, but such are the principles which a life of study is apt to implant. Politics, home and foreign, we would conduct on the same sportsmanlike lines, but the great public does not think the matter practicable. I must frankly confess that, as there would be no chance of international reciprocity in a policy of this magnanimous description it is probable that the thing cannot be managed. Again, a sense of humour is usually fatal. Only the fugitive and cloistered man of letters, as a rule, can see his country as other nations see it, and of course, other nations cannot see themselves as we see them. Were this vision suddenly to be made manifest to France, Germany, England, America, and so on, diplomacy would become hysterical. There would be no end to the disturbance. Apologies from everybody to the rest of the world would pour into and out of every Foreign Office. Such would be the chaotic results of government by unpractical persons who do endeavour (with much discomfort) to see things as they are; who do try to emancipate themselves from the patriotic bias. It is exceedingly unpleasant to be thus emancipated. Hazlitt was free from the patriotic bias, and his life was wretched. Scott was entirely controlled by the bias of patriotism, and he could rejoice in successes which, to Hazlitt, were gall and bitterness. Which man of letters was in the right? Probably now one and now the other, as circumstances altered. To a thoughtful mind it does seem impossible that our country (whichever country it may be), should be *always* in the right, whatever it does or has done. But the fortunate conviction that it *is* in the right usually possesses the public mind. Then it is pretty vain for the possessor of the thoughtful mind to write to the papers and say that the country is in the wrong; and that, as a patriot, he wishes to enter on some other course. The pensive protestor is only informed that he is a 'crank.' I dare say that Amos and Jeremiah[5] were called 'cranks' in some Hebrew equivalent for that term of reproach.

The world has an advantage, in another way, over literary politicians. They may have written – on subjects non-political – matter which does not inspire confidence in their logic and reassuring powers. Thus, if the voting public had read and weighed diligently the contributions of Mr. Gladstone to the Homeric Controversy,[6] I seriously doubt if confidence in his political arguments would not have been shaken. The celebrated statesman's essays in Biblicial [sic] Criticism might have produced a similar effect. But the voting public of either party did not approach, in its myriads, the literary and critical works of Mr. Gladstone. He was practically regarded as purely a politician, and perhaps this was fortunate, perhaps not. But when a man of letters plunges into politics, then his books generally yield smooth pebbles which any one can sling at him, and which hurt. For these and other reasons I conceive that the student should, like Brer Wolf, 'keep on a saying nuffin,'[7] where politics are concerned; for wisdom, if it speaks in the streets, is not marked, except by 'brick-bats, drowned puppies and dead rats.'[8] Of course there are contrary examples, as of Swift and Burke – not to mention the living – but Swift and Burke, dwelling in the main current of affairs, occupied a position different from that of the ordinary (or extraordinary) poet, essayist, novelist, or historian.

Here I shall be reminded that those great and beneficent movements, those fertile sources of human happiness and welfare, the Reformation and the French Revolution were, to a considerable extent, the work of men of letters. Without Erasmus[9] and his criticism, certainly the Reformation would have lacked a foundation in scholarship, and would have missed the stimulus of an admirable irony. But, unhappily, the example does but prove how little we bookmen consult our happiness by interfering in practical affairs. Poor Erasmus was unaffectedly pained when he saw his countrymen cutting each other's throats, and inflicting on each other the most ferocious tortures, all in the cause of his own ideas. He felt much like a barndoor hen that had hatched cockatrices. Let us lay this lesson to heart. For my own part, if I had discovered a way of proving to absolute demonstration that all our ideas of religion and morals, and society are absurd, and that the Decalogue[10] is monstrously immoral, should think twice, or even thrice, before publishing my results. This attitude may not be scientific; certainly it is not scientific; but why, pray, if there is no such thing as morality, should I be loyal to science? Erasmus did not think of this in time; the gaiety of his disposition carried him away. He had not allowed for the practicalness of the public, which carries ideas, once perceived, to the point of arson and massacre. Afterwards he was sorry, and said as much. But he is not without excuse. The public so seldom perceives an idea! Nevertheless we ought to beware of letting ideas loose on the world. The French Revolution not only devoured its children (like Kronos)[11] but also a few of its literary parents. Literary men for forty years had rushed into the discussion of the foundations of all things, as usual, in the spirit of the pure idea. The idea, put into practice, raged like a fire, or the measles in the virgin field of a savage population. It swallowed up kings and creeds, and *philosophes*, who had bargained for no such matter. These are melancholy warnings that we ought to leave politics to the practical man and the professed politician; confining our activity to the silent exercise of the franchise. Our politics are like Colonel Newcome's, who so puzzled a deputation; or like those of Burns, Jacobite and also Jacobin, Divine Right coupled with the Rights of Man, the Bonny Lass o' Albany wedded to Tom Paine. Or we leap from Pantisocracy at one bound to Toryism, like Southey.[12] In short, where politics are concerned, most men of letters are like children, and though 'of such is the Kingdom of Heaven,' such are not the state of this world. In our present posture of affairs, literary men are making themselves heard. I do not precisely wish to enlist under Mr. Kipling's banner. On the other hand, the amenities of Mr. Robert Buchanan[13] are unpersuasive. Great is silence.

2

REALISM, ROMANCE AND THE READING PUBLIC

The growth of a 'reading public' in the latter decades of the nineteenth century produced much debate about the proper form and content of novels and the value of popular fiction. The growth in the reading public was partly prompted by the 1870 Elementary Education Act, which raised levels of literacy in the working classes. The moral effect of novels on middle-class women had long been a concern and this now extended to the working class. Lang was often accused by his contemporaries (and since) of encouraging an appetite for low-quality genre fiction and dismissing important and more challenging work, such as that of Henry James, Thomas Hardy and particularly Émile Zola. 'Realism and Romance' was first published in the *Contemporary Review* 52 (November 1887), pp. 683–93 and is the best-known of Lang's articles on fiction and his strongest statement in the debate. 'Literary Anodynes', first published in the *New Princeton Review*, 6:2 (September 1888), pp. 145–53, and 'Romance and the Reverse', first published in *St. James's Gazette* (7 November 1888), pp. 3–4, both continue the discussion of romance and participate in the more general debate on the nature of fiction being conducted on both sides of the Atlantic during the 1880s and 1890s (see also section 1 this volume, Critics and Criticism'. pp. 54–89). 'The Evolution of Literary Decency' was first published in *Blackwood's Edinburgh Magazine* 167:1013 (March 1900), pp. 363–70 and shows Lang's position on the question of morality in literature.

The voice of one member of the reading public is heard in the article co-published by Lang and 'X' entitled 'The Reading Public' *(Cornhill Magazine* 11:66 (December 1902), pp.783–95). The name of X is not known and the article is not co-written, as Lang only introduces and concludes X's piece, but the collaboration came out of correspondence that had arisen after X wrote to Lang in 1901 in appreciation of his work. X was a factory worker in Birmingham and when, after some years of correspondence, X lost his job, Lang assisted him financially by paying for small writing jobs and eventually helped him find a place as a proof corrector. Extracts of their correspondence are to be found in an article published by X after Lang's death in the *Cornhill Magazine* 33 (November 1912), pp. 684–94. Another working-class correspondent was C. M. Falconer who, up to his death in 1907, amassed what seems to have been a complete collection of Lang's work and to whom Lang dedicated his collection of articles *Adventures Among Books* (London: Longmans, Green and Co., 1905).

'Realism and Romance', *Contemporary Review* 52

(November 1887), pp. 683–93

The question attributed to St. Bernard, 'Whither hast thou come?'[1] is agitating critical and literary minds. There has seldom been so much writing about the value and condition of contemporary literature – that is, of contemporary fiction. In English and American journals and magazines a new Battle of the Books[2] is being fought, and the books are the books of the circulating library. Literary persons have always revelled in a brawl, and now they are in the thick of the fray. Across the Atlantic the question of Novel or Romance – of Romance or Realism – appears to be taking the place of the old dispute about State Rights,[3] and is argued by some with polished sarcasm, by others with libellous vigour. One critic and novelist makes charges, as desperate as that of Harry Blount at Flodden,[4] into the serried ranks of the amateurs of adventurous legend. Another novelist and critic compares his comrade to Mrs. Partington with her broom[5] sweeping back the tide of Romance: the comparison is of the mustiest. Surely – a superior person may be excused for hinting – contemporary literature is rather over-valued, when all this pother is made about a few novels. There have been considerable writers before Mr. Marion Crawford,[6] and, if we are to love books, the masterpieces of the past might seem to have most claim on our attention. But the world will not take Mr. Matthew Arnold's advice about neglecting the works of our fleeting age. I would make a faint and hypocritical protest against regarding the novels of the moment as the whole of literature, before I plunge into the eddying fray. 'Children of an hour,' I would say to my brethren, 'it is not of literature ye are writing so busily, but of the bookish diversions of the moment.' Literature is what endures, and what will endure: of all the novels we fight over in Reviews and at dinner-tables, will even the impulses and methods and sentiments endure? In changed and modified form doubtless they will go on living 'like the rest of us', but a little toss of the dust that settles on neglected shelves will silence all our hubbub. Therefore do not let us exaggerate the merit of our modern works; only three or four of them will be raised into that changeless world where 'Tom Jones' is and the 'Bride of Lammermoor,' where 'Esmond' is and 'Pickwick.'[7] This warning is merely a matter of conscience and caution, lest one should be confused with the person of wide reading – whose reading is confined to the monthly magazines. All of us, in fact, are like the men of Homer's age – the latest songs, the last romances are dearest to us, as to the Ithacan wooers of old time.

> 'For novel lays attract the ravished ears
> But old the mind with inattention hears'

as the ingenious Mr. Pope translates it.[8] However much we may intellectually prefer the old books, the good books, the classics, we find ourselves reading the books of the railway stall. Here have we for travelling companions 'The History and Adventures of Joseph Andrews and his Friend, Mr. Abraham Adams' (1743) on one side, and 'Lady Branksmere'(1887), by the author of 'Phyllis,'[9] on the other. The diverting author of 'Phyllis' will pardon me for thinking Henry Fielding a greater author than she, but it is about the charming Margaret Daryl, in her novel, that I am reading just now, and *not* about the brother of Pamela. We are all like that, we all praise the old and peruse the new; he who turns over this magazine is in no better case.

> 'Hypocrite lecteur, mon sembable, mon frère!'[10]

After this confession and apology, one may enter the lists where critical lances are broken and knights unsaddled; where authors and reviewers, like Malory's men 'lash at each other marvellously.'[11] The dispute is the old dispute about the two sides of the shield. Fiction is a shield with two sides, the silver and the golden: the study of manners and of character, on one hand; on the other, the description of adventure, the delight of romantic narrative. Now, these two aspects blend with each other so subtly and so constantly, that it really seems the extreme of perversity to shout for nothing but romance on one side, or for nothing but analysis of character and motive on the other. Yet for such abstractions and divisions people are clamouring and quarrelling. On our side, we are told that accurate minute descriptions of life as it is lived, with all its most sordid forms carefully elaborated, is the essence of literature; on the other, we find people maintaining that analysis is *ausgespielt* (as Mr. Bret Harte's critical shoeblack says),[12] and that the great heart of the people demands tales of swashing blows, of distressed maidens rescued, of 'murders grim and great', of magicians and princesses, and wanderings in fairy lands forlorn.[13] Why should we not have all sorts, and why should the friends of one kind of diversion quarrel with the lovers of another kind? A day or two ago, at a cricket match, I was discussing literary matters with an amateur of fourteen, the inheritor of a very noble name in English literature. We were speaking of Mr. Stevenson's 'Kidnapped.' 'I don't care for anything in it but the battle in the Round House' said this critic. I ventured to remark that I thought the wandering on the hills with Alan Breck was very good. 'Then it is good – for you,' answered the other, and that is the conclusion of the whole matter. That is good which is good for each of us, and why should I quarrel with another gentleman because he likes to sadden himself o'er with the pale cast[14] of Dostoieffsky, or to linger long hours with M. Tolstoi in the shade, while I prefer to be merry with Miss Margaret Daryl, or to cleave heads with Umslopogaas or Sir Lancelot in the sunshine? What can be more ludicrous than to excommunicate Thackeray, because we rejoice in Dickens; to boycott Daisy Miller because we admire Ayesha?[15] Upon my word, I hardly know which of these maidens I would liefer meet in the paradise of fiction, where all good novel-readers hope to go: whether the little pathetic butterfly who died in Rome or she who shrivelled away in the flame of Kôr. Let us be thankful for good things and plenty of them; thankful for this vast and goodly assembly of people who never were; 'daughters of dreams and of stories,' among whom we may all make friends that will never be estranged. Dear Dugold Dalgetty, and dear Sylvestre Bonnard, and thou, younger daughter of Silas Lapham, and Leather-stocking, and Emma Bovary, and Alan Breck and Emmy Sedley, and Umslopogaas, and Sophia Western[16]– may we meet you all! In the paradise of fiction there shall he 'neither bond nor free,' neither talk of analysis nor of romance, but all the characters of story that *live* shall dwell together deathless.

'Our heroes may sleep not, nor slumber,
And Porthos may welcome us there.'[17]

What is good, what is permanent, may be found in fiction of every *genre*, and shall we 'crab' and underrate any *genre* because it chances not to be that which we are best fitted to admire? I, for one, admire M. Dostoieffsky so much, and so sincerely, that I pay him the supreme tribute of never reading him at all. Of 'Le Crime et le Châtiment,'[18] someone has said that 'it is good – but powerful.' That is exactly the truth; it is too powerful for me. I read in that book till I was crushed and miserable; so bitterly true it is, so dreadfully exact, such a quintessence of all the imaginable misery of man. Then, after reaching the lowest deep of sympathetic abandonment (which I plumbed in about four chapters), I emerged, feeling that I had enough of M. Dostoieffsky for one lifetime. The novel, to my thinking, is simply perfect in its kind; only the kind happens to be too powerful for my constitution. I prefer a cigarette to that massive weed, with a Spanish name, on the enjoyment of which Mr. Verdant Green, greatly daring, ventured at a freshman's wine.[19] To what purpose, then, should I run down Russian novels as tedious and lugubrious? As far as I have wandered across the steppes and *tundras* of Russian fiction, it is vast, wind-swept; chilly, with dark forests and frozen expanses, and, here and there, a set of human beings at unequal war with destiny, with the Czar, with the laws of the universe, and the nature of things. Nothing can be more true, more masterly, more natural. But it is not exhilarating, and is not salutary for a nature prone to gloom, and capable of manufacturing its own pessimism on the premises without extra charge. The same remarks (purely personal) apply to certain English and American novels. There is a little tale 'A Village Tragedy,' by Mrs. Woods,[20] – which I view with dread. I know I shall drift into reading it, and adding another stone to the cairn which we all pile so assiduously on the dead body of our youth, on our festivity, on our enjoyment of existence. The worst, not the best of it, is that these legends are all 'ower-true tales',[21] and are often written with admirable care and attention. Again, there are stories in which the less desirable and delightful traits of human character are dwelt on, as it were by preference, till a man feels almost as merry as if he had been reading Swift's account of the Yahoos. For example, there is Mr. Howells's 'Modern Instance.' Here is a masterly novel, and a true picture of life, but of what a life! All the time one is reading it, one is in the company of a Gentleman of the Press, who is not, and is not meant to be, a gentleman in any other sense of the word. He is mean, and impudent, and genial, and unabashed; he has not the rudiments of taste or of breeding; he distresses and diverts one beyond endurance. But even he is an angel of good company compared with his passionate, jealous, and third-rate wife, who may match, as a picture of the wrong sort of woman, with Thackeray's Mrs. Mackenzie. The whole book is a page torn out of life, as people say, and it has wit as well as veracity and observation. Yet it makes one miserable, as Thackeray does not make one miserable, because the book contains no Clive, no Fred Bayham, no Colonel Newcome, no J. J., and no portly father of J. J. No admiration, however enthusiastic or personal, of modern stories of adventure can blind one to the merits of works of Realism like 'A Modern Instance,' or 'Le Crime et le Châtiment,'or 'The Bostonians.'[22] These are real, they are excellent; and if one's own taste is better pleased by another kind of writing, none the less they are good for the people whom they suit; nay, they should be recognised as good by any one with an eye in his literary head. One only begins to object if it is asserted that this *genre* of fiction is the only permissible *genre*, that nothing else is of the nature of art. For it is evident that this kind of realism has a tendency to blink many things in life which are as real as jealous third-rate shrews and boozy pressmen. Of course the distinguished chiefs of Modern Realism do not *always* blink what is pleasant, gay, sunny, and kindly in human nature. The Misses Lapham, or the Miss Laphams[23] (grammarians may choose), seem to me delightful girls, despite their education. The Lady of the Aroostook[24] was (as the young critic might say) a brick. So was Verena, the fair lecturer in

'The Bostonians.' But (to my mind) the tendency of Realism in fiction is often to find the Unpleasant Real in character much more abundant than the Pleasant Real. I am a pessimist myself, as the other Scot was 'a leear,'[25] but I have found little but good in man and woman. Politics apart, men and women seem almost always to be kind, patient, courteous, good-humoured, and well-bred in all ranks of society – when once you know them well. I think that the Realists, while they certainly show us the truth, are fondest of showing that aspect of it which is really the less common as well as the less desirable. Perhaps mean people are more easily drawn than generous people; at all events from the school of Realists we get too many mean people – even from a Realist who is as little a Realist as the king was a royalist – from M. Zola. These writers appear not to offer up Henry Fielding's prayer to the Muse, 'Fill my pages with humour, till mankind learn the good nature to laugh only at the follies of others, and the humility to grieve at their own.'[26] There is not much humour in their works, and little good humour is bred of them. That is the difference between work like Thackeray's, where there are abundant studies of the infinitely little in human nature, and work like that of many modern amateurs of Realism. 'It takes all sorts to make a world,' and all sorts, by virtue of his humour, Thackeray gives us. He gives us Captain Costigan and Harry Foker, as well as the crawling things in 'Lovel the Widower.' He gives us gentlemen and ladies, as well as tuft-hunters[27] and the George Brandons of this world. Fielding and Scott have this humour, this breadth, this greatness. Were I in a mood to disparage the modem Realists (whereas I have tried to show that their books are, in substance, about as good as possible, granting the *genre*), I might say that they not only use the microscope, and ply experiments, but ply them, too often, in *corpore vili*.[28] One does not dream of denying that they do exhibit noble and sympathetic characters – now and then. But happy, and jolly, and humorous people they hardly ever show us; yet these have their place among realities. And, on the whole, they do prefer to be busy with the rarer sort of realities, with the Cousines Bettes.[29] And they show a sort of cruelty and coldness in their dealings with their own creations. If I were to draw up an indictment, I might add that some of them have an almost unholy knowledge of the nature of women. One would as lief explore a girl's room, and tumble about her little household treasures, as examine so curiously the poor secrets of her heart and tremors of her frame. Mr. Christie Murray,[30] an admirable novelist, has said this, and said it well. Such analysis makes one feel uncomfortable in the reading, makes one feel intrusive and unmanly. It is like overhearing a confession by accident. A well-known book of M. E. de Goncourt's[31] is full of the kind of prying that I have in my mind. It is perhaps, science – it may be art: and to say that it is extremely disagreeable may be to exhibit old-fashioned prejudice. Good it may be, clever it is; but it is not good for me.

So much one who is not of their school may say for the Realists of our time. Of their style one would rather say little, because naturally each has his own style. The common merits, on the whole, are carefulness, determined originality, labored workmanship in language, and energetic nicety of speech. The natural defects that attend these merits are inverted adjectives, 'preciousness', affection, 'a nice derangement of epitaphs.'[32] For one I do not much object to these errors, or I might be obliged to dislike Charles Lamb and Sir Thomas Browne.[33] But I do object to the occasional apparition, among all the chiseled niceties, of a burly piece of newspaper slang, of a gross palpable provincial idiom, or a *cliché* of the American reporter. Style, by all means, let us have, but don't let it be so mixed. The realistic style is now and then mixed – that is the pity of it.

In trying to estimate modern, especially English and American, realistic fiction as a whole, one has first to admit that it is never fair to do anything of the sort. It is a rough, clumsy way of dealing, to give a name or a nickname to crowd of writers, and then to decide offhand upon their common qualities. Many of them may object to the name of Realists altogether. They all vary as much as other people in their natural talent, education and character. But, as far as any modern English and American novels have been written with an avowed artistic purpose, and that purpose the unrelenting minute portraiture of modern life and analysis of modern character, the unrelenting exclusion of exciting events and engaging narrative, we may say that these novels, though often full of talent, are limited in scope, and are frequently cramped in style. The pretension that all modern novels should be composed in this *genre*, and that all others are of the nature of original sin, seems to be an impossible pretension.

At this moment the strife is between Realism thus understood and the partisans of stories told for the story's sake. Now, there is no reason at all why stories told for the story's sake should not be rich in studies of character – peopled by men and women as real as Mr. and Mrs. Bartley Hubbard,[34] both of whom you may (if you are unlucky) meet any day, The 'Odyssey' is the typical example of a romance as probable as 'The Arabian Nights,' yet unblemished in the conduct of the plot, and peopled by men and women of flesh and blood. Are we to be told that we love the 'Odyssey' because the barbaric element has not died out of our blood, and because we have a childish love of marvels, miracles, man-eating giants, women who never die, 'murders grim and great,' and Homer's other materials? Very well. 'Public opinion' in Boston may condemn us, but we will get all the fun we can out of the ancestral barbarism of our natures. I only wish we had more of it. The Coming Man[35] may be bald, toothless, highly 'cultured,' and addicted to tales of introspective analysis. I don't envy him when he has got rid of that relic of the ape, his hair; those relics of the age of combat, his teeth and nails; that survival of barbarism, his delight in the last battles of Odysseus, Laertes' son. I don't envy him the novels he will admire, nor the pap on which he will feed bearsomely, as Mr. John Payne says of the vampire.[36] Not for nothing did Nature leave us all savages under our white skins; she has wrought thus that we might have many delights, among others 'the joy of adventurous living', and of reading about adventurous living. There is a novel of Mrs. Burnett's, 'Through One Administration'[37] which the civilized person within me, the Man of the Future within me, heartily delights to peruse. It is all about a pretty, analytic, self-conscious American married lady, and the problem is to discover whom she is in love with, and why. Is it her husband, or the soldier, or the Government clerk? Does she know which it is herself? As they are all 'moral men' like Werther, and 'would do nothing for to hurt her'[38] the excitement, to a civilized mind, is extremely keen. They all talk about their emotions for ever, and the pleasure which this affords to the Man of the Future in each of us is almost too poignant. I nearly cried when a property Red Indian (not *coram populo*,[39] of course) scalped the true lover, and coded the tale. But the natural man within me, the survival of some blue-painted Briton or of some gipsy, was equally pleased with a true Zulu love story, sketched in two pages, a story so terrible, so moving, in the long, gallant fight against odds, and the awful unheard-of death-agony of two Zulu lovers, that I presume no civilized fancy could have invented the incidents that actually occurred. If one were wholly civilized and 'cultured' to the back-bone (if one may mention that feature), the savage tale would have failed to excite. If one were all savage, all Zulu, 'Through One Administration' would leave one a little uninterested. The savage within us calls out for more news about the fight with the Apache, or Piute, who killed the soldier-man.

The advantage of our mixed condition, civilized at top with the old barbarian under our clothes, is just this, that we can enjoy all sorts of things. We can enjoy 'John Inglesant'[40] (some of us), and others can revel in Buffalo Bill's Exhibition.[41] Do not let us cry that, because we are 'cultured' there shall be no Buffalo Bill. Do not let us exclaim that, because we can read Paulus Silentiarius and admire Rufinus[42] there shall be no broadside ballads nor magazine poetry. If we will only be tolerant, we shall permit the great public also to delight in our few modern romances of adventure. They may be 'savage survivals' but so is the whole of the poetic way of regarding Nature. The flutter in the dovecots of culture caused by three or four boys' books is amazing. Culture is saddened at discovering that not only boys and illiterate people, but even critics not wholly illiterate, can be moved by a tale of adventure. 'Treasure Island' and 'Kidnapped' are boys' books written by an author of whose genius, for narrative, for delineation of character, for style, I hardly care to speak, lest enthusiasm should seem to border on fanaticism. But, with all his gifts, Mr. Stevenson intended only a boys' book when he wrote 'Treasure Island' and restored Romance. He had shown his hand, as a novelist of character and analysis, in 'Prince Otto.' But he did not then use just the old immortal materials of adventure. As soon as he touched those, he made a boys' book which became a classic, and deserved to be a classic. 'Kidnapped' is still better, to my taste, and indeed Scott himself might have been the narrator of Alan Breck's battle, of his wanderings, of his quarrel with the other Piper. But these things are a little over the heads of boys who have not the literary taste. They prefer the adventure of Sir Harry and the other Allan[43] in Kukuana-land or in Zu-Vendis. We may not agree with their taste, but that is their taste. Probably no critic would venture to maintain that the discoverer of Kôr has the same literary qualities as the historian of John Silver. It seems a pity, when we chance to have two good things, to be always setting one off against the other, and fighting about their relative merits. Mr. Stevenson and Mr. Rider Haggard have both written novels, have both written boys' books. Personally, I prefer their boys' books to their novels. They seem happier in their dealings with men than with women, and with war than with love. Of the two, Jess appears to me real, and the wife of Mr. Stevenson's Prince Otto shadowy. But Mr. Haggard's savage ladies are better than his civilized fair ones, while there is not a petticoat in the whole history of 'Kidnapped' or Treasure Island'. As for 'she' herself, nobody can argue with a personal affection, which I entertain for that long-lived lady.

> 'The holy priests
> Bless her when she is riggish,'

Shakespeare says of Cleopatra,[44] and like the holy priests, I can pardon certain inconsequences in Ayesha. But other moralists must find her trying; poor Ayesha, who 'was a true lover,' though she did not therefore, like Guinevere, 'make a good end.' Apparently female characters are not the strong point either of Mr. Haggard or of Mr. Stevenson, as far as they have gone. Consequently it is difficult to compare those agreeable writers with, let us say, M. E. de Goncourt or Mr. Howells. Nor is there much reason in comparing them with each other. Mr. Stevenson is a born man of letters, a born student of style. Since Thackeray no English author has been gifted with or has acquired a manner so perfect, so subtle, so original. And yet he has plenty to say, though he can say it so well, 'which is strange.' Unlike Sir Walter Scott, he can write English as well as he can write Scotch, and, since Scott, no one has written Scotch like him. If any short story comes second to the tale of 'Wandering Willie,' it is 'Thrawn Janet.' In addition to all these accomplishments, Mr. Stevenson possesses an imagination which touches that of Edgar Poe, on one side, and of M. Anatole France on the other. He can be as witty as Mr. George Meredith,[45] or humorous as Burns, as sad as Night, and as jolly as the Jolly Beggars. Perhaps his 'Night with Villon' is the most perfect of modern short studies in romance. One cannot be too thankful for a writer with such various endowments. There is no sense in comparing them with Mr. Haggard's gifts: he only resembles Mr. Stevenson in natural daring and inventiveness, and in having written admirable tales of adventure. He is as far as possible from being a born student, or a born master of style. He does not see the world through books, and he writes like a sportsman of genius. Thus one cannot pretend to criticize the style of the Romantic school, as (to a certain extent and with limitations) we may criticize the style of the Realistic school. There is, there can be, no Romantic school. Any clever man or woman may elaborate a realistic novel according to the rules, and may adopt the laborious use of inverted adjectives. But Romance bloweth where she listeth,[46] and now she utters her message to a student and a master of words, like Mr. Stevenson, through whom the tale reaches us, 'breathed softly as through the flutes of the Grecians.'[47] Now, again, Romance tells Mr, Haggard her dreams beside the camp-fire in the Transvaal, among the hunters on the lulls of prey, and he repeats them in a straightforward hunter's manner, and you believe in the impossible and credit adventures that never could be achieved. As works of art, the books of these two writers do not invite comparison, but both are inspired by that same venturous maid of Helicon, who somewhere learned the history of Odysseus' wanderings, and revealed them to the man of Chios.[48] Let us be grateful for all good things in literature, and not reject one because it lacks the grace or the glory of another. We are not to sneer at a good story, because the narrative might be better graced. How much Scott cared for style, or even for grammar, is but too manifest, even to persons who have not examined his manuscripts, wherein there is scarce an erasure or an alteration. Sir Walter reeled it off at a white heat. Thackeray's manuscripts are of a different aspect; what Balzac's were like all readers of literary anecdote know very well. To every man his own method, his own qualities, his own faults. Let us be grateful for the former, and a little blind to the latter.

Whatever the merits and demerits of modern English romance, one thing is certain. It is now undeniable that the love of adventure, and of mystery, and of a good fight lingers in the minds of men and women. They are stirred by the diamonds and the rich ingots, the 'Last Stand of the Greys' (a chapter from actual history), the bland John Silver, and the malevolent Gagool. The moral is manifest enough. The moral is not that even the best boys' book are the highest class of fiction, but that there is still room for romance, and love of romance, in civilized human nature. Once more it is apparent that no single *genre* of novel is in the future, or at least in the near future, to be a lonely literary sultan, lording it without rival over the circulating libraries. But to argue, therefore, that there is no more room for the novel of analysis and of minute study of character would be merely to make a new mistake. There will always, while civilised life endures, and while man is not yet universally bald and toothless – there will always be room for all kinds of fiction, *so long as they are good.* A new Jane Austen would be as successful as a new Charles Kingsley. Moreover, it will always be possible to combine the interest of narrative and of adventure with the interest of character. This combination has been possible in the earliest literature. If we take the saga of the Volsungs and Niflungs,[49] we find the union already perfect. What can be more barbaric than the opening of the Saga? Perhaps even Mr. Rider Haggard would not introduce a hero whose brother was a serpent, or a hero who turned into a wolf and bit off an old lady's tongue, and became the father of a family of little wolves. Yet this very saga has the characters of Sigurd and Gudrun; the immortal scene of the discovery of wronged and thwarted love; the man's endurance of it; the woman's revolt, and all the ruin that she drew on herself, her lord, her lover, and her kin. There is no more natural, true, and simple picture of human nature, human affections and passions, in Balzac or in Shakespeare, than that scene from a savage tale which begins with the loves and hates of serpents and she-wolves. What could be combined in an entrancing whole by a minstrel of Chios, by a saga-man of Lithend, need not be kept apart in modern fiction. We may still have excellent studies of life and character, with little of the interest of story in them. We may still have admirable romances, in which the delight of adventure far exceeds the interest of character, or, very often, the elegance of style. And we may still have novels, like many of Scott's, in which character, and life, and adventure are so mingled in a whole, that we can scarce tell which of them charms us most. There is even room for the novel of disquisition and discussion of life, as no admirer of Fielding, and Thackeray, and George Eliot will deny. Some of us will be better pleased by one kind, some by another. All will be good for some of us, if they are good in their kind. Why should persons of this taste or that give themselves airs, as if they only were the elect? A man need not hate 'M. Lecoq' because he delights in 'Manon Lescaut.' A man may have his hours for 'Madame Bovary,' and his hours for 'Le Cardinal,' and his hours for 'Le Crime de l'Opéra.'[50] 'There is one glory of the sun, and another glory of the moon;' let us contemn none of the heavenly bodies. I have heard Mark Twain[51] called a 'Barbarian'. This will not make me say that 'Huckleberry Finn' is better than a wilderness of 'Prophets of the Great Smoky Mountain.'[52] But I will admit that I greatly prefer old Huck, that hero of an Odyssey of the Mississippi. I can even imagine that a person of genius might write a novel 'all about religion,' or all about agnosticism, which might be well worth reading. I don't expect to live to see that romance, but it may come, for the novel is a perfect Proteus,[53] and can assume all shapes, and please in all. The lesson, then, is that it 'takes every sort to make a world,' that all sorts have their chance, and that none should assert an exclusive right to existence. Do not let us try to write as if we were writing for *Homo Calvus*,[54] the bald-headed student of the future. Do not let us despise the day of small things, and of small people; the microscopic examination of the hearts of young girls and beery provincial journalists. These, too, are human, and not alien from us, nor unworthy of our interest. The dubitations of a Bostonian minister may be made as interesting, by one genius, as a fight between a crocodile and a catawampus, by another genius. One may be as much excited in trying to discover whom a married American lady is really in love with, as by the search for the Fire of Immortality in the heart of Africa. But if there is to be no *modus vivendi*,[55] if the battle between the crocodile of Realism and the catawampus[56] of Romance is to be fought out to the bitter end – why, in that Ragnarôk,[57] I am on the side of the catawampus.

'Literary Anodynes', *New Princeton Review* 6:2

(September 1888), pp. 145–53

The whole world seems lately to have resolved itself into a commission on fiction. With an extreme and owl-like gravity mortals write essays in which fiction is treated as if it were, or should be, the last word of humanity. The first recorded word of man was not absolutely accurate, and his last may also be fictitious, but in the mean time one may protest that novels are not a kind of *Novum Organon*.[1] They cannot contain, and they need not pretend to contain, the whole sum of mortal thought, knowledge, and experience, with a good deal of prophecy thrown in. Yet this attempt is what many earnest novelists are coming to. You take up one book from the library, or you even buy it, and lo! it contains a new religion, or what the author (who may not have deeply studied the history of creeds) thinks is new. The next three volumes are a parable of how 'life may be lived well,' when the old morality has been superseded in favour of the new morality – socialism and free love. Now, one may live to see socialism tried, but, to a mature person, it is a great comfort that free love will not affect him. The newer and higher moralists may take the property of the elderly citizen, but they (the young ones at least) will not fall on his neck and embrace him as he takes his walks abroad. This reflection is comforting, but it prevents one from reading novels about how we are to live when we all do as the more emotional of our authors think we ought to do. A third romance neither tells us what we ought to believe, nor the truth as it is in Mr. Mudie's,[2] nor how we ought to behave when that state of things arrives which Carew foresaw and prophesied in *The Rapture*.[3] The third novel describes, with dismal minuteness, the loves of a piano-tuner and a lady teacher in a high-school. The loves come to nothing, and so does the interest, but the record is so conscientiously dismal that perhaps it is a masterpiece. In any case, it makes the reader wish that he had never been born, or, at all events, that the author had never been born. The fourth venture with the box from the circulating library[4] may try to enliven us with the more seamy side of the life of a married couple, whose attempts to divorce each other are paralyzed by the interventions of that malignant being, the Queen's Proctor. To explain his functions in English society is not for a critical, but still chaste and untarnished, pen: I must refer the studious to the learned pages of modern romance.

Here, then, are four kinds of novels – four popular kinds. Here is the novel of the new religion, the novel of the new society that declines to have any religion, the novel of dismal commonplace, and the novel of the divorce court. Can any poor man or woman who reads romance for amusement, and because it serves as an anodyne, get diversion, or comfort, or oblivion (except in slumber), from any of these? I do not say that these philosophies of all things in three volumes have no right to exist. 'We have all a right to exist, we and our works,' as even Mr. Matthew Arnold admitted.[5] But people have also a right to exist who read novels for the purpose of being amused, and of forgetting. Now, what does an able-bodied voter, or a sensible lady, want to forget, in this age of ours? Why, he (or she) wants to forget everything to be read about in the newspapers (except in Sporting Intelligence), and everything to be heard about from the pulpit, and everything in real life that saddens and perplexes. A man wants his novel to be an anodyne. From the romancer he demands what the wife of Thon of Egypt gave Helen, – nepenthe,[6] – the draught magical which puts pain and sorrow out of mind. Is this a selfish, unfeeling demand? It seems to me that one might as rationally call the timely tendency to sleep at night unfeeling and selfish. Are not some fourteen hours of the day enough wherein to fight with problems, and worry about faiths, and rend one's heart with futile pities and powerless indignations? Leave me an hour in the day, not to work in, or ponder in, or sorrow in; but to dream in, or to wander in the dreams of others. Into these dreams, printed and bound, let as little of truth come as may be; let me forget the sweating system, and the European situations, and party government, and a phantom fleet, and a stunted army.[7] Let me forget that 'miracles do not happen'; carry me where they *do* happen. Let me forget that nobody marries his true love; bear me to that enchanted realm where, as the ballad says,

'Oh, ye may keep your lands and towers,
Ye have that lady in your bowers;
And ye may keep your very life,
Ye have that lady for your wife!'[8]

Weary me no more, for this hour, with your shades of theological opinion; let me be happy with that god of the old French tale, that 'god who loveth lovers.'[9] Close the veil on the brutes who kick women to death, and raise the curtain on gallant deeds, and maidens rescued, and dragons and duennas discomfited. Pour out the nepenthe, in short, and I shall not ask if the cup be gold chased by Mr. Stevenson, or a buffalo-horn beaker brought by Mr. Haggard from Kukuana-land, or the Baron of Bradwardine's Bear,[10] or the 'cup of Hercules' of Théophile Gautier, [11] or merely a common café wine-glass of M. Fortuné du Boisgobey's or M. Xavier de Montépin's.[12] If only the nepenthe be foaming there, – the delightful draught of dear forgetfulness, – the outside of the cup may take care of itself; or, to drop the metaphor, I shall not look too closely at an author's manner and style, while he entertains me in the dominion of dreams. Opium-smokers do not care for marble halls; they can have visions in a hovel. Novel-reading, as here understood, is confessed to be a kind of opium-smoking. But it has none of the ill effects of that other narcotic; it may be taken with temperance; it cheers, and it does not inebriate, except the very young. As a very small boy, I once made and consumed, with distasteful results, certain cigarettes. This I did, not that I liked smoking, but because Captain Mayne Reid's[13] heroes made and smoked cigarettes. They also took scalps, and fought grizzly bears, and associated with earless trappers. Circumstances made it impossible for me to imitate those feats, but I could and did roll cigarettes, and make arrows with stone heads. This was an example of the inebriation of romance, but only very small boys are affected in this way. The mature can take a grown person's dose of fiction with impunity. Judges are notorious novel-readers; yet I never heard that they fled from their wedded wives to woo strange maidens because such things are done in romance. Prince Bismarck, probably, never assassinated any one in all his days (whatever M. Henri Rochefort may think), [14] yet Gaboriau is held to be the Prince's favourite author. 'The world is too much with us,'[15] and the world must be still more with Prince Bismarck. That is why, no doubt, he enjoys novels which are not of any world, still less of his own distinguished *monde*.[16] These dukes of Gaboriau's, who shoot people in low cabarets from the best of motives, and all because of the consequences of some affair that occurred in the First Crusade, or at the time of the Revocation of the Edict of Nantes,[17] are dwellers in no world but fairy-land.

To get into fairy-land – that is the aspiration of all of us whom the world oppresses. Mr. Howells may assure us that the part of modern fiction is to make to-day more actual, more real, to show us the kind, ugly, manly face of life – I do not quote his words, but the general sense of them. Well, Fiction may do that if she can, may do it for people who do not find to-day a great deal too actual for their taste already, who do not see the face of life at too close quarters. But many – the majority, one fancies – want to forget to-day now and then, to live a while unconditioned by time and space and evolutions. The old roads to fairy-land are lost: you may walk nine times 'widdershins'[18] round any fairy gnome, and the door will not open into that enchanted climate. The Fairy Queen will not 'borrow' us, as she borrowed

Tamlane,[19] but how we wish she would! We cannot reach that land of glad appearances, where none but the foolish cared to see that all the beautiful dames were mere shells and semblances, and the Queen herself but the ghost of dread Persephone.[20] Cut off from the fairy world, tied down to a world in which there are but few exceptions, at best, to the workings of the laws of Nature, we are driven into the domain of make-believe and of romance. In fiction we have the interest of realistic photographs of the life we know too well, realistic studies of the development of characters like our own petty characters, thwarted passions, unfulfilled ambitions, tarnished victories over self, over temptations, melancholy compromises, misery more or less disguised, dull dinner-parties, degraded politics. This is the stuff of the fiction that calls itself natural and real – this, and the study of blind forces of society, blind uneasy movements of the unhappy collective mass of mankind. To write about all this in novels may be considered a kind of moral and artistic duty; to read about it may be regarded as a discipline. I deny the duty: let the press and the pulpit and the platform see to it. I don't want the discipline; enough of it one gets every day, and too much. The discipline is a *discipline* in the old sense, – a constant self-flagellation; the wearing, voluntarily, of an iron chain studded with spikes. So true is this that, as the world unavoidably gets more terribly real and earnest, romance and literary anodynes will be more and more in demand. When the Civil War began in England, when things were at their sharpest and hardest for that season, we find Lovelace recommending Sidney's *Arcadia* to his Lucasta.[21] An escape into a peaceful world of shepherds and singers was what this gallant soldier asked, and what all of us who continue to read will soon be asking from the Muse of Fiction. Very great skill and art may be expended in drawing people exactly like our tormented and bewildered selves, with experience like our own; but this art will give us neither joy nor any rest. A person who is yet young enough to feel the distresses of the heart, and who is actually feeling them, will hardly be able to read a novel in which these regrets and disasters are too minutely studied, in which he sees his own tortured face as in a glass. He will want something very different, as Carlyle felt the need of Marryat's novels[22] in the literary misfortune of his life. The course of things at present makes for disorder and unhappiness. Nobody but the stormy petrels[23] of our race can enjoy this. We are driven, perforce, to the shores of old or new romance, and are compelled to care less for the feelings and emotions and thoughts of fictitious characters, than merely for a sequence of exciting events. We are concerned, in fiction, with what happens, if it be forcibly described, rather than with what is suffered or thought by the fictitious persons of the tale. Happily, the world is well supplied with books in which plenty of unusual events are made to happen with sufficient frequency and lack of verisimilitude. From the *Odyssey* to the *Arabian Nights*, from those to *Don Quixote*, to Sir Walter Scott, to Dumas, to Mr. Stevenson, to the *Mystery of the Hansom Cab*,[24] if you please, or to *Mr. Barnes of New York*,[25] there be records enough of the deeds that never were done. An eminent English novelist, a student of character, has just remarked to me that, in ten years, the romance of impossible adventure 'in fairy lands forlorn'[26] will be extinct and out of fashion. On the other hand, if this genre be well done after its kind, it can never cease to hold its readers. Sindbad has outlived a thousand tales of analysis, or of realism, or of religious maundering, and will outlive them all. The eternal child in the human breast will never cease to demand this sort of entertainment, and there will always be somebody to take the child on his knee and tell him a story.

Look at *Mr. Barnes of New York* and its myriads of readers. What attracted them? A picture of actual life, knowledge of the world, knowledge of the human heart, a well-graced style, sagacious reflections? Nothing of the kind: merely a rattling narrative; merely another shake of the old kaleidoscope of romance, in which the familiar glittering bits of coloured glass have fallen into a more or less novel arrangement. Not every one can shake the kaleidoscope so that the bits of glass shall dispose themselves cleverly, but he who can will ever find men, women, and boys eager to pay for a look into his peep-show. This is the reason of the success of M. Fortuné du Boisgobey and of M. Xavier de Montépin. The former scarcely takes the trouble, as a rule, to give the kaleidoscope a new shake. Give him a murder, a mutilated body, a fast young man with a good heart, a selection from the *demi-monde*,[27] an *ingénue*,[28] a duel, a diving-bell, and a game of baccarat[29] – with these and a villain (who generally cheats at cards), M. Fortuné du Boisgobey and his public are content. He gives his little tube a toss, the baccarat and the duel assume new relations to the murder and the *ingénue*, and lo! the novel is written. It is not very high art, – far from that, – but you go on reading because things do really occur in the tale, because you are curious, and because your curiosity makes you forget your work, forget your sorrow, forget 'problems,' metaphysical, social, religious, financial, or political. You are wrapped in a cloud of the author's *nugae*, and *totus in illis*.[30] It is the same with the admirable M. Xavier de Montépin. How many young ladies have I seen him throw out of the window of railway carriages, and over bridges! How often have I assisted at a kidnapping of the heroine, who, being spirited away to some lonely criminal bower, cannot be boring one with love scenes for some considerable time at least! How many wills have I witnessed, – forged wills; how many blameless *ouvriers*[31] have I seen arrested on false charges; of how many murders, in sepulchres and in four-wheeled cabs, have I not been the delighted spectator! Heaven forbid that one should compare these rapid and facile ingenuities to the works of artists in romance – of Scott, or (in his strange field, the churchyard,) of Edgar Poe, or of Alexandre the Great.[32] But as long as the *feuilleton*[33] helps one through a rainy evening or a long railway journey, and banishes thought and kills time, these great enemies, let us never be ungrateful to the *feuille-*

ton. Whereas, if one assails the dreary evening or the railway journey with a much more pretentious naturalistic or analytic novel, one might as well spend the time with one's own saddest thoughts and most bitter memories.

The world is aware of this, though it may hide its knowledge, and judges and maid-servants alike prefer a pleasant dip into the well of oblivion, the well of romance that keeps these rare shadows floating on its waves. A pitcher of water from this well it was, no doubt, that Venus sent Psyche to bring for her.[34] Shall we not be thankful to the bold adventurers who carry it home for us, for the tired and unimaginative? They may bring it, like Scott, in a golden pitcher, or, like the author of *Mr. Barnes of New York* in a travelling-flask, but it is the right water for our present thirst. To take a strong example: one feels incapable, without a resolute struggle, of sitting down to the tremendous Tolstoi, or the dismal Dostoiefsky, or the latest Scythian or Servian novelist. But one takes up Sir Walter's last, and not his best, *Count Robert of Paris*, and one is a boy again, back among the mysteries of the Byzantine Court, and nearly as happy with the Varangian as with Quentin Durward[35].What is this magic of the story-teller, that makes D'Artagnan and Athos our life-long friends, that keeps us as curious on a fifth reading as when we knew not what was about to happen to Porthos or Aramis?[36] These gentry deal with no social problems, but with the accidents of adventurous life as they arise: they never preach; they never hunt for epigrams till the reader is as tired of the chase as the author must have been. They offer us no new religion in three volumes; they do not even attack the old; in fact, our ancient friends in Scott and Dumas compete neither with the newspaper nor with the thoughtful monthly magazine. A constant competition with these dismal educational forces makes the serious novel of to-day so tedious and so uninviting. Even with the *Society Journal* do even the most serious novels compete, and you feel that they are full of personalities understanded of a few, and that the rest of the world is howling for a 'key.' Let him use the key who will, and thread the labyrinth, and listen to the wisdom, and canvass the problems. The great world will in the long run prefer even a wild legend from the *Family Herald* or will go wandering with Sindbad again in the Diamond Valley, or with Aladdin in the rich vaults underground, will haunt the House of the Seven Gables,[37] or dwell in the lichened Old Manse of many Mosses.[38] The more part of us, above all, the silent and uncritical multitude, are lovers of the Fairy Queen, and wilfully dwell in the land of illusion and romance. Glamour is better than truth sometimes, and moonlight than daylight; and the dear folk who never were, Porthos and Leather-stocking, Dugald Dalgetty and Locksley,[39] are more substantial than the shadows of ourselves who fill the earnest modern novel with the shadows of our sorrows and the thin echo of our complaints. These are the sad ghosts, and unholy, whom it is wiser to shun, for the company of happier and gayer unsubstantialities.

Consider, for example, M. Daudet's novel *L'Immortel* which appears at this moment, as I write. What an industrious dulness, what a leaden weight above the gay fantastic talent of the author of *Tartarin de Tarascon*. I have read articles in which M. Daudet was talked of as the impeccable and faultless novelist, and 'they were friends of ours,' as Aristotle says, [40] when he differs from Plato, 'who brought forward this opinion.' M. Daudet is a charming writer when he treats of his own South and his happy southern countrymen. But when he writes as a Parisian of Paris, truly from the literary cup he offers us it is pleasure to abstain. It is a comfort to speak one's mind about M. Daudet's later novels. They appear to me to combine the temper of the society journalist with the over-anxious research of words, which is the joy of the 'art-critic.' M. Daudet has observation, but it is too sedulously minute; he has wit, but it has become too bitter and unkind; he has knowledge of the world, but how much of that knowledge even a foreigner may glean from the *Figaro* or *Gil Blas*.[41] The old Latin saw says that 'indignation makes verses';[42] not poetry, of course, but verses. Indignation, even when it is not envy in disguise, does not make good novels. The humour and the good-humour which Fielding implored the muse to lend him, are absent wholly from M. Daudet's *L'Immortel*. It is an angry study, through a microscope, of the tempers and intrigues of Parisian literary society, or, at least, of the official class of literary people. There is not one noble, or generous, or unselfish character in the book, scarce even one honourable motive. The plot, what there is of it, is borrowed from a thread-bare stupid old scandal, – the anecdote of the mathematician who bought the forged autographs. A mathematician might do that, but M. Daudet's hero, or victim, is not a mathematician. As a professed historian and man of letters, he could hardly have made this colossal blunder in his own province; if he had strayed into mathematics, then, doubtless, he might equally have blundered. All the other characters, except, perhaps, the jolly painter who cares not for things academic, are a joyless, loveless, faithless company of mean intriguers. They are, as a rule, corrupted by the Academy;[43] they are mean, lustful, avaricious, larcenous, and you lay down this piece of *naturalisme* with the certainty that it is eminently unnatural, as unnatural as the leaden and deluged July whose rain beats the windows as I write.

You cannot make a good novel out of bitterness, ill-temper, sarcasm, the hunt for adjectives, the study of unredeemed mental and moral depravity, and a collection of venerable and virulent anecdotage. It is not a very good world that we live in, or we would be less eager to leave it for the world of Leather-stocking or of Allan Quatermain. But a world in which old literary cretins would accept the dishonour of their daughters for the chance of a vote in an election to the Academy, seems distinctly a worse world than that in which we live and move. Of the two kinds of pictures, the frankly imaginative and impossible is more true and real than the other, – the naturalistic, the realistic, the world of the reporter of the 'society' press. It may be urged that to come back to common life after a long-drawn interview with M. Daudet's characters is like escaping from the Inferno into Purgatory. Perhaps; but why should we voluntarily visit the Inferno at all? Like most literary questions, this is, ultimately, a question of taste, and cannot be argued further. But, for my own part, when I hear M. Daudet and his followers praised as if they were worthy to sit in the chair of Cervantes[44] or of Fielding, I am glad to remember that it is always easy to fall back on the Waverley Novels, or to look forward to the next batch of boys' books, or even to beg, or buy, or borrow a volume of the *Family Herald* or a narrative by the author of *The Leavenworth Case*.[45] These, or any other literary anodynes, are needed to make one forget the vivisection of academic monstrosities performed by M. Daudet. Certainly the maddest of impossible plots is better than the stale story of M. Chasles and his collection of forged autographs, with which M. Daudet attempts to enliven our leisure.[46] 'Not here,' O Tartarin, 'are haunts meet for thee.'[47] Not by these verities will mankind be made merrier, or better, or wiser, though grateful they may be that things are not so bad, nor men and women so vile, as in M. Daudet's novel.

'Romance and the Reverse', *St. James's Gazette*

(7 November 1888), pp. 3–4

In his essay entitled 'M. Zola on the Side of the Angels,'[1] Mr. George Moore is kind enough to ask me to awake and let M. Zola in. Myself and others, it seems, are asleep and unconscious that the distinguished Frenchman is 'knocking at the door with the lamp of Romance.' A reminiscence of a picture by Mr. Holman Hunt[2] seems to be trotting in the critic's mind – rather an incongruous reminiscence. Speaking for oneself, one may observe that one has been awake all the time – awake enough to know what sort of lamps, new or old, M. Zola has to sell. If it is not a commonplace of criticism that M. Zola is occasionally a *fantaisiste*, if not essentially a *Romanticiste*, one does not know a common-place when one sees it. The passages in his earlier work in which he is nearly at his best are the early chapters of 'La Fortune des Rougon' and of 'La Faute de l'Abbé Mouret.' The former is as idyllic as M. Zola knew how to make it; the latter is as fantastically romantic as nature permits M. Zola to be. The conservatory in 'La Curée' is another example of M. Zola's romantic experiments. It is probable that he took greater pleasure in composing these pages than in the studies which remind Mr. Moore of Rabelais – Rabelais of all authors – and of Swift. There is a great deal of dirt in Rabelais, and more in Swift; but in both cases it is not separated from humour; and M. Zola has as much humour as Mr. Gladstone, with none of his sensitive delicacy. The question, however, is not so much about M. Zola, who has often been discovered 'lone sitting by the shores of old Romance,'[3] lamp and all; but about what Romance is, and where it may be found. Mr. Moore seems to think that there exist people who have 'finally decided that romance consists solely of digging holes in Africa and blowing up pirates on the Spanish Main.' Nobody can tell what strange persons may exist on this globe; and some there may be who are capable of this kind of opinion. Mr. Moore, himself, gives a much better definition of Romance. It is 'rather the eternal aspiration after such overflowing measure of strength, fortune, and love, as life has got for giving.' Perhaps a later scholiast will read *n* in place of *g* in Mr. Moore's essay – 'as life has *not* for giving'. Either reading will do well enough. If we accept such a definition of Romance, it will cover Porthos and Monte Cristo:[4] Porthos, who satisfies the aspiration for strength, Monte Cristo who satisfies the aspiration for wealth; but who satisfies the aspiration for an overflowing measure of love? Perhaps Romuald, the chosen of Clarimonde in 'La Morte Amoureuse.'[5] But here we come to the difficulty about the *n* and the *g*, the 'not' and the 'got.' Life has *not* for giving the love of 'La Morte Amoureuse.' He who aspires to it is *impossibilium cupitor*,[6] and his romance will land him frankly in the impossible. It does not follow that all romance is concerned with impossibilities – very far from it; but it is only the impossible that can satisfy human aspirations: we all cry for the moon; and we can only meet the moon, like Endymion, in a dream. 'Blessed I call him who sleeps and wakes not, even Endymion,' says the lover in Theocritus. The Latmian[7] is lapped for ever in a vision of these impossible felicities, and these adventures never to be achieved, which are in the land of Faery. Sometimes it is the function of Romance to transport us thither, and to lull us for an hour with dreams of the impossible. Not that all impossibilities are romantic. In M. Zola's last novel it appears (according to Mr. Moore) that 'the Archbishop took orders on the death of his wife.' This has an air of the Impossible, however you like to take it; for surely the gentleman must have been in orders before he was the Archbishop; – and if he was in orders he could hardly have a wife. I presume that M. de Hautcoeur was a married layman, who, after the death of his wife, took orders and became an Archbishop.

What romance is, perhaps nobody will ever be able to define. We think we know it when we meet it, and it is not only met with in Central Africa or on the Spanish Main. Romance appears to be, in literature, that element which gives a sudden sense of the strangeness and the beauty of life; that power which has the gift of dreams, and admits us into the region where men are more brave and women more beautiful and passions more intense than in ordinary existence. A million of novels about the Spanish Main may not be so romantic as a dozen lines spoken on the moonlit terrace of Belmont.[8] A single movement or speech of a girl in 'Silas Lapham' may be as romantic as the singing of Gunnar in his grave[9] – while it lasts. In his new novel M. Zola seems to have introduced a very old romantic situation:

> She was but a vestment maker,
> And a stained-glass painter he.[10]

At least, Mr. Moore says he was disguised as a painter of stained glass. The situation is as old as King Cophetua;[11] the young person in the moonlit garden is older than 'Aucassin et Nicolette.'[12] Whether the literary results are romantic or not, depends on the genius of M. Zola, he has used the fine old materials, and Mr. Moore says he has used them well. From Mr. Moore's 'cursive analysis' the novel seems a good kind of sentimental romance. M. Zola has written sentimental romance before now – he may do it again; but it will not be so popular as 'Nana.'

Romance, then, to return to the general question, may be found everywhere. Virgil is full of it; so is Racine. But there is an obvious difference between the sense of the word 'romance' as an element in literature, in poetry, and the sense in which we use the word when we say that this book or that is 'a romance.' The distinction between 'a romance' and an ordinary novel is a distinction of convenience. There may be plenty of romance in a book which we call a novel, and a book which we call a romance may signally fail to be romantic. Perhaps it would be more scientific to use the word 'novel of Adventure' for what is commonly called a romance. If the former term is employed, we expect hair-breadth escapes, fights, perhaps the supernatural. Romances of adventures descend as it were, from fairy-tales, from Apuleius,[13] from the knightly stories of the Middle Ages. Beauty, Magic, Hidden Treasure, Giants, if you can manage them, Fairies, if they will come to your call, are the stuff of a romance of adventure. But it is plain to every person of common literary sense that 'romance' may inform any work of imaginative literature from 'Athalie'[14] to 'Le Rêve.' And it is equally obvious that profusion of adventure no more makes a work 'romantic' – if the writer lacks vision – than the profusion of squalid incident and detail make a book 'realistic' if the writer lacks the sense and grasp of realities. It is odd enough that in 'Consuelo,'[15] a romance, the most romantic passage contains nothing more adventurous than the arrival of two strolling musicians in a moonlit garden. In no prose can the sense of the beauty and mystery of the world be more suddenly heightened. It may be remarked we think of the Odyssey as a romance, the first and greatest of all; while we never think of the Iliad by such a name. Yet both are full of warlike adventure, and the Iliad contains as much of the supernatural as the Odyssey. The difference lies, perhaps, in the fairy style of the Odyssey, and in the wanderings among untrodden lands peopled by goddesses and ogres. Half of the action passes out of the known world, where all of the action of the Iliad is placed. The undiscovered or rarely visited lands have always given Romance verge and space enough; and thus it is not improbable that even Central Africa and the Spanish Main possess advantages which may be underrated. Adventures are to the adventurous; and impossibilities may seem less impossible in regions of which we know little, though of them we have heard much that is marvellous.

'The Evolution of Literary Decency', *Blackwood's Edinburgh Magazine* 167:1013

(March 1900), pp. 363–70

'Take away your bonny Afra Behn,'[1] said the old lady who, about 1810, borrowed, and vainly tried to read, the novels that had been the delight of her youth. Very few persons now peruse 'Astraea,'[2] who trod the stage so loosely; very few know whether she was more indiscreet than the novelists of the eighteenth century or not. Mrs Behn died in 1689: she had been the wife of a Dutchman, and, in one of her tales, she assures us that it is quite a mistake to suppose that a Hollander cannot love. This remark, and the circumstance that she anticipated Mrs Beecher Stowe in taking a negro for her hero in one novel,[3] are all that my memory retains of the romances of Astraea. They certainly did not leave a distinct and separate stain on my imagination.

The familiar anecdote of the old lady whose age rejected as impossible the romances which had delighted Society in her youth, supplies a text for a curious speculation. Wherefore had taste altered so radically in the space of one life-time? It is a natural but inadequate reply that taste always does alter in sixty years. Thus Lady Louisa Stuart, who was born about 1760, found, about 1820, that Richardson's novels, when read aloud, provoked inextinguishable laughter. In her youth people had wept or sighed over 'Pamela': now people mocked, and she mocked with them. Such changes of taste make the pathetic seem absurd, or make what Molière meant to be comic seem pathetic, at least to refined critics. But we are concerned with a change at once deeper and far more sudden – a change in morality rather than in style or sentiment. English literature had been at least as free-spoken as any other, from the time of Chaucer to the death of Smollett. Then, in twenty years at most, English literature became the most 'pudibund,'[4] the most respectful of the young person's blush, that the world has ever known.

Now, this revolution was something much deeper than the accustomed process which makes the style and the ideas of one generation seem antiquated and uncongenial to the readers of the next. We quite understand why Mr Guy Boothby[5] is preferred, say, to Thackeray, and Mr Henty to Marryat,[6] by the young. Youth detests what it thinks 'old-fashioned,' and is puzzled by traits of manners with which it is unfamiliar. But custom will presently stale the authors of to-day, and that change of taste will not correspond at all to a change which, in some twenty years, altered the whole tone and character of a national literature. Why, and owing to what combination of causes, did the very plain speech of our first famous novelists in the eighteenth century become a stumbling-stone to readers of some thirty years later? Why did decency, or prudery if any one pleases, come *suddenly* into vogue between 1770 and 1800? Why were such poems as Suckling's ballad of a marriage[7] published, about 1810, with lines and half-stanzas omitted? How are we to account for Bowdler?[8] The change of moral taste was really as great as the change of opinion about witchcraft, which arose between 1680 and 1736. Mr Lecky has written at length about that revolution,[9] but nobody, as far as I remember, has discussed the other alteration – Bowdler's alteration – in the matter of moral taste. In the first place, it did not correspond with a regular sweeping purification of 'Society.' Nobody will say that the Regency, the age of Bowdler, was much more moral than the early part of the reign of George I., the age of Wilkes.[10] Yet, between 1760 and 1770 we had Smollett and Sterne for living novelists, while in 1780–1815 we had Miss Edgeworth, Godwin, Miss Austen, Mrs Shelley, Galt,[11] and Scott. Writers more delicate in language and in description cannot be, nor could writers be much looser and coarser than those of the previous generation. The change of 1770–1814 lasted till quite recently. Novels were intended to lie 'on the drawing-room table,' and were meant to be fit for the young person. So stern were parents about 1840–1870 that they managed to find Thackeray 'improper,' and we all remember Thackeray's own remark that, since Fielding, nobody had dared to draw a man.[12] Colonel Newcome must have been born about 1800, and the Colonel revolted naturally against Joseph Andrews and Tom Jones. By our time, of course, taste has altered, and lady novelists introduce situations which, I verily believe, would have made Astraea herself blush vermilion. But even now the *language* of the most advanced writers is far indeed from attaining the simple breadth of Smollett or Fielding, though many modern ideas expressed in fiction would have made Roderick Random exclaim in virtuous indignation. We have had novels fit to accompany Petronius in the library of Lord Strutwell.[13]

A curious point in this evolution is the difference which it exhibits in France and in England. In England, Fielding and others felt it necessary, or desirable, to add coarsenesses to Molière. In France, the translation of 'Tom Jones' (1749) was at first prohibited in the interests of virtue. The French dramatists of the great age of Louis XIV are as decent, as 'mealy-mouthed,' as the dramatists of Greece. The dramatists of the contemporary Restoration in England, and of Queen Anne's reign, were notoriously coarse and lewd. The remonstrances of Addison and the 'Spectator'[14] had no effect on Fielding and Smollett. But, just when the old coarseness of these masters was dying out in England, the literature of France, in Diderot, Crébillon *fils*,[15] and many others, began greatly to outdo what our novelists had dared. The *régime* of conscious Virtue and of the *philosophes*[16] in France rather encouraged than checked such books as Voltaire's unspeakable 'Pucelle'.[17] People thought 'La Pucelle' amusing!

A classical example of the change in England is Charles Lamb's anecdote about the young lady who looked over his shoulder as he was reading 'Pamela.' She soon went away, and Lamb says that there was a blush between them. This may have occurred about 1815, and 'Pamela' had been the very manual of Virtue from 1740 to 1780, or thereabouts. It was put into the hands of ingenuous youth, and even of children. Richardson himself was the mere model of the proprieties, and thought Fielding 'low.' Diderot put Richardson on the same shelf as Moses. 'Pamela' was written, as Scott says, 'more for edification than for effect.'[18] Anticipating the modern clergy who preach on Miss Corelli and Mr Hall Caine,[19] Dr Sherlock praised 'Pamela' 'from the pulpit.' The novel was said to 'do more good than twenty sermons,'[20] though Lady Mary Wortley Montagu thought it more mischievous than the works of Rochester.[21] Scott also reckoned it apt rather to 'encourage a spirit of rash enterprise' among hand-maidens than of 'virtuous resistance.'[22] As a matter of fact, a generation or two later, 'Pamela' made Lamb's young friend uncomfortable. She got up and went away. She belonged to the new age of Miss Austen, Miss Edgeworth, and Sir Walter. Nor need we, even in this emancipated time, wonder at Lamb's young lady. I doubt if many even of our daring writers would have the courage (the lack of humour they have) to write several of the scenes which Richardson wrote, and which the clergy applauded from the pulpit.

Lately I saw a contemporary picture of a very scantily draped Pamela, aroused by fancying she heard Mr B. under the bed. It was not to be called a moral work of art, and I fear that 'Pamela' owed much of its success to qualities which doubtless made no conscious part of Richardson's design. Indeed, as we read it we 'laugh in a strange and improper manner,' like the wife of Mr Arthur Pendennis on one occasion.[23] Quite rapidly, in some sixty years, 'Pamela' lost her reputation, became little better than one of the wicked, frightened away the virgins whom she was meant to edify, and sank into 'a deplorably tedious lamentation,' as Horace Walpole declares,[24] read only by conscientious students of eighteenth-century literature. The reason is not merely that the lowly characters are slavish, as Scott observes. The reason is that, to our changed taste, 'Pamela' is both prurient and coarse. Even 'Clarissa' is obsessed, through all its intolerable length, by one dominant idea, and leads up to a catastrophe which we cannot contemplate with patience. Once more I doubt if our youngest and ablest writers would dare to subject a noble lady to the martyrdom of Clarissa, or would be admired by the general public if they did.

It is well known that Dr Johnson, though he read straight through 'Amelia,' told Hannah More that she ought to be ashamed of saying that she had read 'Tom Jones.' One cannot guess what fly had bitten the Doctor. 'Tom Jones' is a really moral work, if we set aside Fielding's leniency towards one inexcusable adventure of Mr Jones's. I presume that Fielding was reprobated because he was humorous. Even now we find the advanced, and virtuous, and earnest applauding the most squalid horrors of M. Zola and others, while they would fly in horror from Gyp.[25] And why? Obviously because M. Zola is absolutely devoid of wit and humour (which Gyp possesses), and therefore may be as abominable as he pleases. Has he not a lofty moral purpose! So, in fact, had Fielding, but, alas! he was humorous, all unlike Richardson, Zola, Ibsen, and Tolstoi. 'Joseph Andrews' not only makes us laugh, but encourages every generous virtue. Still, Joseph was 'low,' and 'Pamela,' in some incomprehensible way, was elevating. Even now, nobody dares to approach the broad and physically coarse methods of Fielding. We do not think it at all comic that Sophia should fall in an unbecoming manner from her horse, nor can we even imagine why Fielding thought it comic. So far the change is all for the better, indeed I am apt to think that it was generally for the better, except in such extreme instances as when the prudery of James Ballantyne spoiled the whole sense of 'St Ronan's Well'; or when Jeffrey induced Dickens to make clotted nonsense of 'Dombey and Son'[26] *vile damnum*[27] in the latter case. It does not appear to me that our ebullient novelists ought really to be hampered by limitations which do not seem to have been resented by Homer, Sophocles, Virgil, Moliére, and Racine. But our problem is, not the good or evil results of certain restraints on freedom of language and incident, but the wonderfully sudden rise of these restraints between 1770 and 1790. In 1771 Smollett published 'Humphry Clinker,' distinctly his best book. The brutality of 'Roderick Random,' the infamous ferocity of 'Peregrine Pickle,' are here mollified and mellowed. But, except in the works of M. Zola or of Swift, there are few passages in literature, if any there are, so physically and so needlessly nauseous as certain of the early letters of Matthew Bramble.[28] Everything disgustful that medical practice could suggest to a brutal fancy is here set forth with elaborate care. There is something of the ape, of the Yahoo, in these passages attributed to the pen of an honourable and benevolent country gentleman. On the chapter of Smells, 'Smelfungus,' as Sterne called Smollett, is as copious as M. Zola or M. Guy de Maupassant.[29] Nobody seems to have objected, as some purists did object to the freakish contemporary lubricities of Sterne. All these great eighteenth-century writers revelled joyously in the necessarily grotesque physical side of human nature. It was primely witty to half-poison somebody with a surreptitious dose of medicine. Homely articles of everyday life were constantly dragged in to get a laugh, articles that the most emancipated novelist of to-day keeps out of his daring pages. And, in thirty years, all these amusing objects, and scores of sets of comic or sensual situations, had become even more impossible in fiction than they are to-day. Even the author of 'Tom and Jerry'[30] would have given them a wide berth in England, and few authors, except M. Armande Silvestre,[31] venture on them in France. In 1740 Dickens would have had cheap and nasty resources, and would have used them, while the Dickens of 1840 shunned them even more scrupulously than most men.

One cannot imagine a change more rapid and more radical. We had not been a prudish people. Chaucer, Shakespeare, Dryden, Congreve, Smollett, Burns, Sterne, are at the opposite extreme from the prudish. Why did we become so dainty between Smollett's death (1771) and the rise of Mrs Radcliffe (1789)? We cannot attribute the revolution to the influence of feminine authors (such as Mrs Radcliffe, Miss Edgeworth, and Miss Austen), for feminine influence, in Mrs Manley, Mrs Heywood, and Afra Behn,[32] had tended in quite an opposite direction. Moreover, it is ladies to-day who throw their caps highest over the windmills, both in licentiousness of idea and physical squalor of theme, always, of course, for lofty moral purposes. Again, one cannot see that Society was more delicate when Rowlandson drew than when Hogarth [33] boldly designed spades *as* spades. The Court of the Regency was not purer than the early years of the Regent's worthy father. People were as naughty as when Lady Vane published the 'Memoirs of a Lady of Quality.'[34] Yet everything Smollettian and Rabelaisian was banished clean out of literature, and has never returned. Those persons are very young and ill-informed who think that the change is 'Early Victorian.' That theory, if correct, would be intelligible; but the revolution was really late Georgian: it arose in an age of heavy courtly licence, an age when popular life was nearly as rough as it had been in 1740. Yet quite a large class of topics was now banished, not only from books, but from conversation between the sexes. Burns, as a peasant, was probably the last poet who was allowed to take, or who took, his full swing. Byron was reprobated; and Leigh Hunt was gibbeted (hypocritically, I fear) for the 'Story of Rimini.' None of the three would have been much censured forty years earlier.

I have stated the problem, but I do not pretend to solve it. I remember no Jeremy Collier, and no Addison,[35] who set about reforming the coarseness of taste, just after Smollett's day; and it does not seem that Jeremy or Addison, when they tried, really produced much effect. The 'Spectator,' in Lamb's situation on Primrose Hill,[36] might, indeed, have proved as embarrassing as did 'Pamela' herself. Nor did foreign influences produce the revolution, for France was then hurrying into what had been the English extreme.

If I must make a guess, I would hazard the theory that the change was caused by the rise of a larger reading middle class, especially by the increase in the numbers of women of the middle classes, and in the country, who read books. They had not hitherto been literary: they had simply been housewives and stitchers; good mothers, not bookish. At no time had their class been so free, in conduct or conversation, as the women in 'Society' and in London. What they avoided in life, they disliked in literature. They now began to get into contact with literature through book clubs. There were regular societies of provincial Blues, not spotted by town or court. Moreover, we must probably allow a good deal for the many and far-reaching influences of the Wesleyan movement,[37] and of the Anglican Church as affected thereby. The red-faced parsons, absorbent of port and of ale, the Parson Trullibers,[38] died out. What can Mrs Trulliber have read? Nothing, probably; but the wives of the Henry Tilneys[39] did read, and doted on Cowper as well as on Clara Reeve[40] and Mrs Radcliffe. Moreover, even Sterne, with his 'sentiment,' made people desire fiction which could touch the heart as well as amuse, and they got it, in Mackenzie's 'Man of Feeling' and 'Julia de Roubigné.' Shelley, in boyhood, tried to set the example of didactic novels, meant, he says, to inculcate his metaphysics and morals. When once sentiment, and didacticism, and romance, and terror (as in Mrs Radcliffe and other favourites of Miss Catherine Morland[41]) came in, and were found delightful, humour and libertinism went out. Broad farce was not in harmony (despite Dickens) with sentiment and the wilfully didactic, nor with 'the horrid,' with spectral castles, and inquisitorial dungeons. Smollett had thought such attractions dead for ever, but he was wrong. They revived, they were hugely popular, they held the field, and horseplay went out. Miss Burney, again, could not be expected to sin in the direction of Astraea, yet she could interest and amuse without such gambols. There were no humorous novelists, or none who are now remembered as authors of stories, between the days of Smollett and Miss Edgeworth. There arose a forgotten school of historical novelists. So nobody was tempted to use the old, simple, animal expedients for getting a laugh. Thus the new and great generation of Scott and Miss Austen had no temptations to coarseness or licentiousness, even a moderate freedom would have been fatal, and modern critics may think Scott and Miss Austen 'senselessly decent.'[42]

On the whole, the most obvious and probable cause of the sharp and sudden revolution of taste was probably what we may call the Wesleyan Reformation acting on the middle classes far beyond the bounds of the Wesleyan communion. Wesley's movement was really (though he did not know it) part of the Romantic movement: it began in an asceticism, and in an emotion, and in 'supernormal experiences' after the model of the ideals of the medieval Church. Romanticism itself (in spite of some old French romances) is, in essence, 'a delicate thing'; knights amorous and errant are all unlike the festive wanderers of Fielding and Smollett. The squires of romantic lovers are no Straps nor Partridges, and the knights understand 'the maiden passion for a maid,'[43] in a sense unknown to the lovers of Sophia, Emilia, and Narcissa. The new middle-class lady novel-reader could not put up with the infidelities of Tom Jones, Roderick Random, and Peregrine Pickle. She felt personally insulted (and no wonder) by their behaviour. From all these influences, one ventures to conjecture, the singular and rapid change in taste, and the decent limitations on literary art (limitations hitherto conspicuously absent from English fiction), drew their origin. That the once Puritan middle classes deserve most of the praise is a theory strengthened by the example of America, where prudery as to the use even of simple harmless phrases (for example, you 'retire,' in America: you never go to bed) irritated Dr Oliver Wendell Holmes.[44] American literature is assuredly neither licentious nor coarse. But these hypotheses may be inadequate or erroneous, in which case the problem becomes vastly more curious and interesting. A problem it is: the generation of Scott's father saw nothing out of the way or reprehensible in literary forms which the authors of Scott's generation might, and, of course, did enjoy, but dared not, and cared not to follow. Sir Walter himself was an ardent admirer of Smollett, whom at one time he was constantly quoting. But Scott's own heroes never once wander from the strict path of a solitary virtuous attachment. His one heroine who, in fact, had transgressed from the path of Dian,[45] was, if I may say so, violently shunted back into it, owing to the prudery of Ballantyne, some of whose MS. notes on Scott's proof-sheets prove him to have possessed 'a nice morality.' Henceforward every hero was a Galahad, till Mr Rochester broke away from the rule and Richard Feverel fell into the ancient errors of Captain Booth.[46] Even now a hero's confessions are less startlingly explicit than those of Roderick Random; and nobody would pretend to interest us in a Peregrine Pickle, or even in a Pamela. The change, which was born full grown, has lasted for a century in England, which had previously set the very opposite example. It was a change due not merely to the moral revolution that sprang from the Wesleys, but to a general revolt, all along the line, in favour of the ideal and the spiritual, and against the godless commonplace and brutality of the early Hanoverian time. The new materialism of science has probably fostered the new 'emancipated' literature of the *strugforlifeur*[47] of M. Daudet. Thus reactions succeed each other; but on the whole, in fiction, and not looking at the worse than Smollettian vulgarity of such plays as 'Lord Quex,'[48] the tendency to a new licence seems to have expended itself.

Andrew Lang and 'X', A Working Man, 'The Reading Public', *Cornhill Magazine* 11:66

(December 1901), pp. 783–95

The Reading Public was an entity for which Coleridge entertained the greatest aversion and contempt. Perhaps his motive was that, whatever the public read, it certainly did not read the works of S. T. Coleridge, neither did it rapidly exhaust the editions of his friend Wordsworth.

[...]

However, the public would not read Coleridge, so Coleridge despised his 'reading public.' The truth is that poetry was not really what the public of 1804–1820 wanted, though by purchasing largely of Scott and Byron it gave a false impression that poetry was its delight. The public, unconsciously, thirsted for novels and no novels were given unto it. Therefore it fell back on the tales in verse of Scott and Byron, just because they were tales, though rhymed. Wordsworth, Keats, Reynolds and Coleridge gave no *story*; none knows who married Christabel, if anybody, or what the other mysterious lady had to make in the matter;[1] and there is no love interest in 'The White Doe of Rylstone.'[2] So all these were neglected, while the rhymed novels of Scott and Byron 'sold like hot cakes,' to use an impressive phrase of Mr. Kipling's applied (see advertisements)[3] to the romances of Mr. Guy Boothby.

When once the Waverley novels began, in 1814, the public showed its real taste by at once ceasing to buy poetry. Even in 1842 Tennyson 'made a sensation' in the trade by selling–500 copies of his poems!

One of the firm of Longmans, testifying before a Parliamentary Committee about 1834[4] declared that from 1814 onward people left off forming libraries and buying erudite books. All was now novels and popular manuals of cheap science and twopenny history, as at present. The reading public in short, had only purchased poetry and history because between Mrs. Radcliffe and Scott there was an entire dearth of readable prose fiction. Thus the reading public was virtuous for want of temptation, and, even when virtuous, would not read Keats, Wordsworth and Coleridge. Now S.T.C. knew that he was 'a wonderful man' as Wordsworth said, and that the reading public was entirely indifferent to his merit. He was obliged to write for the newspapers! Contrasting his conscious merits with the public neglect, he conceived that lifelong and often-expressed contempt of his for 'the reading public.' He had the secret of the painful earth mapped out in his mind, so he thought, yet there was no encouragement to publish. The world cared no more for his solution of the secret than, according to Mark Twain, housemaids care for the 'Immortality of the Soul.'[5] Nor do I think that the world was wrong in this want of interest.

Many, perhaps most, artists, and all authors (except the authors, who enjoy 'booms'[6]) share the sentiments of Coleridge. I am conscious that my own opinion of the reading public would be much more cordial if the public adored my work. As they adore those of – several quite inferior writers. On analysing this mood, like the hero of 'Happy Thoughts,'[7] I detect traces of egotism. Possibly others are not much more to be trusted; but we are all vexed when what we sincerely admire, the work perhaps of total strangers, is neglected, while what we contemn has the market assigned to hot cakes. Our intellectual interests and those of the reading public are distinct. I cannot understand why the historical essays of Mr. Horace Round [8]are less eagerly purchased than the novels of Mr.—. These I really cannot read at all; I fume, I throw the book often into the fire, or often into the water; while an essay on Knight's Fees, or Glamorgan's Treaty[9] (nice character for a novel, Glamorgan!) holds me as with the glittering eye of the Ancient Mariner.

Another grievance I have against that otherwise exemplary institution, the London Library. Entering its stately hall, I find old, fourth-rate, three-volumed novels to right, to left, and in front of me. But I cannot get the 'Journal of the Anthropological Institute.' The library ceased to subscribe after 1890. How like the reading public that is! Here we are with at least as much Empire as we know what to do with, an Empire teeming with millions of subjects, from the myriads of an ancient civilization in India to the dark crowds of Central Africa, the chivalrous Maoris, the waning hordes of Australia (the earliest-known representatives of humanity) the tribes of British Columbia, with their extraordinary institutions, and so forth. And here, on the other side, a periodical (the 'J.A.I.') which contains the results of scientific study of the inhabitants of our Empire. Even in a practical way, not to speak of scientific interest, it is worth while for us, and it is our duty, to know about them and their condition. But the reading public, the London Library public, does not want to know, will not collectively give a guinea (or a couple of guineas) annually, to procure the means of knowledge. Meanwhile the shelves are full of forgotten novels in three volumes. In the same way, in the library of an ancient seat of learning, an old haunt of professors and the learned, I have often found my paper-knife the first that ever burst into books, from works of 1760 to those of Mr. Max Müller,[10] which surely are not arid and 'rebarbative' like those Central Australian deserts which only the regretted Mr. David Carnegie[11] ever explored.

Such facts as these do not redound to the credit of the reading public. Authors who approach that public with almost anything but novels appear to think but lowly of its knowledge and powers of attention. The popular books on history and biography, especially in 'series', deliberately avoid references to authorities, without which I do not see how history, at least, can be written or read to any purpose. The writers make distinct and trenchant statements on points most complex and disputed, without indicating their sources, and their reading public loves to have it so. They are like the chiefs of – I forget what nasty island tribe – who intoxicate themselves by swigging the juice of a root, which the women extract by the simple process of chewing. Their 'intellectual pabulum' is presented to the public ready chewed, to save public time and thought. The results are hastily swallowed; and are readily forgotten. I lately read a book on a difficult theme, in which the author conciliated his customers by repeated assurance that he was nearly as ignorant as they could be – only a book or two ahead of them. Nor was he too modest.

The question arises, Who do read what? Certainly, the majority of persons engaged in education read very little beyond what they have to 'get up' for their classes and lectures. At the Universities, the teaching bodies, apart from the time spent in teaching, pass laborious hours in attending ceaseless meetings of committees. The late master of Balliol[12] (who made time for his own work – who knows how?) once attended two simultaneous meetings. It was a kind of 'bilocation' as in the case of saints. The practical man reads all the newspapers, nothing else. Millions of readers peruse only cheap illustrated magazines, which are often wonderfully good, but do not pretend to be literature. Intelligent ladies in the country read quantities of miscellaneous things without an order or an aim, just what the librarian chooses to put into their boxes.[13] The circulating libraries often do not send a book of any special sort; when asked for, 'It is out,' and it never gets an innings. In place of it are sent six-shilling novels which nobody asked for. The wearied applicant at last forgets about the book she wanted, and asks for another and does not get it. As to *buying* a book, he or she would usually as soon think of buying a boa-constrictor, unless he is specially a book-collector. I have had the amusement of seeing a volume of my own sold for 7*l.* 10*s.*, a volume which, for twenty years the public would not have at three-and-six. The bookseller helps. Lately a Swedish lady sent for one or two books of mine to 'the trade' of a large town in this country; she then wrote to me complaining of being told that *all* my books were out of print. Now an author cannot reach the public, and the public cannot get at an author, while booksellers adopt this vigorous policy.

The public, I hasten to say, is no more really indifferent than it ever was. Our learned ancestors would not have formed the libraries which still occupy the shelves of some country houses if any alternative had been open to them. They purchased classics, and folios and quartos and learned stumpy duodecimos,[14] because except for a few 'roguish French books' such as Mr. Pepys[15] loved, they could get nothing else. There were no circulating libraries till about the middle of the eighteenth century, and these are described in 'The Rivals.'[16] There were a few illustrated cheap magazines, no flood of novels at six shillings. And there was a prejudice to the effect that a gentleman ought to possess books. One glances at the volumes in old country-house libraries, and asks 'Did people read them?' Very little is said about them, certainly, in old collections of letters, except by people like Horace Walpole. But it was correct to own books; they have not, assuredly, been thumbed.

Reading, after all, is not a human duty. Very dull are the deserving people who read for conscience' sake, and actually form themselves into societies to encourage each other and keep up their spirits. The only reading worthy of the name is done 'for human pleasure', and pleasure is not a duty. To that pleasure only a small minority are sensitive, and I do not think they ought to give themselves airs. They have a taste which some are born with and others without. Judges usually read a great deal. Mr. Darwin and Prince Bismarck [17]were devoted to novels; Napoleon was an omnivorous and rapid reader, conquering whole libraries. Most novelists do not read – oh, the funny 'authorities' whom a certain historical novelist cites with honest pride! – nor, naturally, do reviewers read. Many *grandes dames de par le monde*[18] read abundantly; many statesmen do, and some boys, girls, under-graduates and spinsters. I doubt whether the clergy are studious, as many men of the sword decidedly are. In most towns there are studious tradesmen, and lawyers who are dungeons of rare learning. Miners form clubs to read Mr. George Meredith and other superior authors – so one hears.

Concerning artisans and what they read, I have received a statement from a labourer in one of our large towns. He happens to be a bookworm. I was brought into communication with him through an article of mine in the *Cornhill Magazine* on 'Examinations in Fiction.'[19] He answered some very difficult questions set in the old Oxford tract on the School of *Literae Fictitiae*.[20] I asked him about the amount and kind of study done by his laborious comrades: men who have very little leisure, and not, probably, more intellectual energy left for reading than most men engaged in commerce. He replied, and it ought perhaps to be said that he wrote amongst constant interruptions, and in loquacious company rather hostile to literary composition. What he says about his order is much akin to what most of us might truly say about our own, as far as the pursuit of literature is concerned.

'What Working-Men Read – And Don't Read.'

If one wished to obtain information as to what working-men read – and by that term I refer to men who work with their muscles for a daily or weekly wage – a visit to a free library and a chat with the librarian would seem to be the surest means of attaining that end. I doubt, however, whether the statistics obtained thus could be fairly considered sound, as a large proportion of the borrowers from free libraries are shopkeepers, clerks, assistants, &c., people who cannot strictly speaking, be described as members of the working-class. The working-man certainly does patronise the free libraries, but not to such an extent as would warrant us in attempting to gauge his literary consumption by the returns in the books of those institutions. The lending department does not gain his appreciation so much as the reading room, where you will find him engaged with the newspaper or the monthly magazines; of the latter I have noticed that he prefers those with the most profuse illustrations. Personally, I look upon free libraries as a boon to working-men who have a taste for good literature without the necessary means to purchase expensive books, and I regret that working-men generally are not better acquainted with the vast funds of instruction, recreation, and amusement here ready to their hands.

Personal association with working-men, both at the workshop and in their homes, is better qualified to give one a pretty correct idea of what they do and do not read and it may not be out of place to mention what my own tastes in reading are, as a labourer. For a working-man I have been rather a voracious reader since leaving school at the age of eleven, and I have dipped, more or less deeply, into every class of literature. Many books I have borrowed from free libraries, and I owe those institutions a debt of gratitude; but my favourites are contained in my own humble bookcase, and a motley-looking lot they are: all sizes of volumes, in all shades and styles of binding; most of them picked up from second-hand book stalls and in many cases showing signs of wear and tear. There are Aeschylus, Shakespeare and Lamb's 'English Dramatic Poets', Milton, Byron, Cowper, Shelley, Tennyson, and Longfellow among the poets; as philosophers Carlyle and Bacon; in political economy, Adam Smith; and as novelists, Scott, Dickens, Thackeray, and Fielding together with a couple of volumes of English history, and a score or so of the lesser lights of literature. My prime favourite among these 'literary friends' are Shakespeare, Longfellow, Carlyle, and Dickens, but none of them is kept for ornamental purposes; they are all read.

A working-man's – and especially a labourer's – income does not allow him to purchase many copyright works, so my acquaintance with present-day writers is derived through the agency of the lending library, and is mainly confined to novelists, of whom I may mention Sir Walter Besant, George Meredith, Thomas Hardy, Rider Haggard, and Hall Caine among others I have read, but must beg to be excused from expressing a preference for any one of them.

It is not to be assumed that working-men generally take an interest in the authors I have named; on the contrary I should find a difficulty in naming a dozen workmen of my acquaintance with whom I could discuss for half an hour all or any of the books in my small library. Were I to take an average working-man and leave him alone for an hour or two in a room containing my books and a year-old newspaper, I dare wager that on my return I should find him reading – if he were reading at all – the ancient newspaper. I recently heard a fellow workman remark that he had been to hear a debate between a Spiritualist and a Freethinker, [21] and, deeming that was rather an unusual form of amusement, I entered into conversation with him, during which he told me he had read a few of Dickens's and Marryat's books. He had never read any of Scott's works, so I lent him 'Ivanhoe'. A week or two later he returned it, and on my asking him his opinion of it, he confessed he had not read it through because 'there were so many characters in it that he found it impossible to remember them all.' He offered to lend me a book, which he said I was sure to like, and it turned out to be a volume entitled 'Wit and Humour', consisting of a collection of the paragraphs usually to be found in the (alleged) humorous column of the weekly newspaper. When I declined the offer, the expression on his face showed that he pitied my lack of appreciation of the humorous, and after I had read aloud to him what I considered to be a very choice extract from one of Mark Twain's books, without raising more than a perfunctory smile, the emotion was mutual.

Still, I have known a few working-men who did take some interest in good literature. There was one – he was a labourer too – whose most treasured literary possession was a paper-covered second-hand volume of Shakespeare's plays. I believe he knew almost all the plays by heart, and he would argue by the hour on the subjects of Hamlet's 'nor-nor-west' madness , or whether Falstaff really deserved such a bad character as many good people credit him with. He believed Shakespeare's to be the greatest mind of all time; and living not a great way from the bard's birthplace and being well acquainted with many of the legends concerning him, he considered that the poet's alleged appreciation of good ale rather enhanced than detracted from his merits. My friend was a little perturbed a few years ago when the American, Donelly, was attempting to prove Bacon's authorship of Shakespeare's work,[22] and he requested from me the loan of Bacon's 'Essays'. When he returned the book his mind was at rest. Bacon, he said, was a wise and clever man but he could not have written 'Hamlet', in spite of all the Donellys and cryptograms in the world. Shakespeare was not his only author though; he had a great admiration for Dryden's 'Virgil,' Pope's 'Odyssey' and the poetry of Byron and Longfellow. He also read much of Dumas (translated) and Dickens, though he did not care a great deal for Scott as a novelist.

Another workman friend reads nothing absolutely but fiction and poetry, and possesses an extensive stock of both. His library is contained in a good-sized wooden box, where the books are dumped one on top of another in a manner which must prove inconvenient when he wishes to obtain a particular volume which happens to be at the bottom of the box. He believes he has acquired a considerable knowledge of English history by means of the historical novel and his favourite writers are Harrison-Ainsworth, Charles Kingsley, and Scott, while among the English poets he prefers Macaulay and Tom Hood.

A gunmaker friend of mine holds a high opinion of Gray's 'Elegy'– an opinion which I share – and the verses of a minor poet, Kirke White; but I never discovered that he occupied his leisure moments with any other literature except the daily paper. I accompanied him to his lodgings one evening, and there got into conversation with his landlady (she was a dress-maker and her husband was employed in a small-arms factory), who surprised me greatly by talking learnedly about geology; in fact she treated me to quite a lecture, which she illustrated with pieces of rock that lay on the chimney-piece. Drifting from geology to literature, amazed me by remarking that her favourite writers were Carlyle and Dante (the latter, of course, translated). She was a great exception to the ordinary run of working-women, of whom my experience is that they read little, that little being fiction not of the best kind.* Therefore it came somewhat in the nature of a shock to me to find a working-woman taking an interest in Carlyle's 'Sartor Resartus' and Dante's 'Inferno', and I felt inclined to hide my diminished head, for I could boast no acquaintance with Dante beyond what I had read of him in Carlyle's 'Miscellaneous Essays.'

If, however we take a more extensive field for observation than is furnished by a mere personal acquaintance with workingmen, I think the lending-libraries attached to all adult Sunday schools will render a fair estimate of what the more intelligent of the working-class read. The schools are largely attended by the better class of working-men who have the privilege of borrowing books for a mere nominal charge – about a halfpenny a week in most cases – and a vote of the scholars is usually taken as to what new books shall be purchased. Still, an examination of the records kept of the books lent by these libraries is calculated to give one a very high opinion of the literary taste of the scholars. At one of the schools that I

* Alas, how like the sex! – A.L.

attended for about two years, I took some little interest in the library, and frequently assisted the librarian in his duties. The principal feature of the library at this school was a rather numerous collection of volumes of poetry by English and American poets, but with the exception of one – Bret Harte's poems – there was little demand for them. Our library contained but a few historical and scientific works, but even so, the number might have been reduced to a cipher without depriving any borrower of his favourite class of literature. The fiction department was pretty well patronized, Dickens, Scott, Lytton, Wilkie Collins, Jerome K. Jerome and Rider Haggard being most appreciated. There was quite a run on Lytton's novels, while 'Artemus Ward his Book'[23] and Jerome's 'Three Men in a Boat' seldom returned to the library except to be taken out by a fresh borrower. But the books which were most eagerly sought after in this department were the novels of a lady author whom I shall have occasion to refer to again.

This school, whose average attendance was upwards of 400, was situated near to a large railway goods-yard, and a good proportion of the scholars were railwaymen.

Another adult Sunday school that I know is connected with an important engineering concern, and was intended originally, I believe, solely for the employés of the firm, who still number quite five-sixths of the scholars; but at the present time outsiders also are invited to attend. It recently became my duty to overhaul the library of this school, in order to ascertain what books were damaged or incomplete so that they might be replaced by new ones, and I thus had a splendid opportunity of learning the literary preferences of these engineering scholars by the marks of usage – or non-usage – which the volumes bore, as well as by the librarian's record.

There were about 1,000 volumes in this library, most of them presented by the heads of the firm, and quite one-fourth – rather a disproportionate amount, I thought – were bound volumes of magazines of a semi-religious character. The magazines, some of which had been a considerable number of years in the library, were in excellent condition, and – possibly because their bulky size rendered them cumbrous to carry – did not appear to be much read, the most popular, or rather the least neglected, being those containing illustrations. This library, unlike the last mentioned, could boast of but a meagre collection of poetry, there being no more than five poets represented, viz. Shakespeare, Goldsmith, Scott, Longfellow, and Eliza Cook,[24] and the first-named seemed to have received the lion's share of what scanty appreciation had been bestowed here; the others were dusty, but showed no traces of service. So far as my knowledge of working-men extends, I can say that they care little or nothing for poetry, and I venture to suggest that if any twenty working-men, taken haphazard, were requested to give an opinion as to which were the greater poem, Gray's 'Elegy' or Kipling's 'Absent-minded Beggar', the verdict of at least fifteen would be given in favour of the latter. Longfellow's 'Village Blacksmith' might run Kipling's creation somewhat closer in the poetical regard of the British workman; still I am inclined to think it would have to take second place.

In the history and biography section, comprising some 150 volumes, a 'History of the Jews,' by Milman, had received some attention, together with Molesworth's 'History of England,' but J. R. Green's 'Short History of the English People'[25]– a work which should not have lacked appreciative readers – had not been outside the bookcase more than twice. The 'Works of Josephus,' 'History of Rome,' and the works of other historians, ancient and modern, on the shelves of that library may suffer from the ravages of time, but it does not appear probable, from present indications, that they will ever become dilapidated through the ardour of too-appreciative history-students – in this generation at least. In biography, a 'Life of Wellington'[26] seemed to share premier position in the affection of readers with Smiles's 'Lives of the Engineers.'[27] One can readily understand the preference for the last-named, considering the occupation of the scholars; but why the biographies of Robert Stephenson[28] and Thomas Carlyle were comparatively neglected, and such books as 'Lives of British Reformers'[29] and 'Industrial Biography'[30] totally ignored is hard to conjecture. The 'Diary' of quaint old Samuel Pepys seemed never to have been moved since the date of its introduction to the library, so thick was its covering of dust.

Among the scientific works, 'Elements of Geology,' by Sir Charles Lyell, 'Nature Study,' 'Planetary and Stellar World,' 'Hydraulic Engineering,' and 'Experiments in Steel'[31] had a few, a very few, students.

Of the volumes devoted to travel, which were not over numerous, 'Cook's Voyages' enjoyed the greatest measure of popularity.

Hitherto I had found no volumes so damaged by active service as to need replacement; but now I came to the fiction department and gathered from the battered condition of many of the books that here, at any rate were authors who suited the tastes of the scholars. The works of Lytton, Lever and Charles Kingsley had received a considerable amount of attention and of the latter's books 'Hypatia' had more readers than 'Hereward the Wake' or 'Westward Ho!' – a fact which I thought rather curious. Charles Reade's 'It's Never too Late to Mend' – the only example of that author – was less favoured than the novels of the foregoing three writers; but George Eliot's 'Romola' and 'The Mill on the Floss,' with Jane Austen's 'Sense and Sensibility,' appeared to be the least popular book in this department. Scott's novels – some ten or twelve volumes – showed signs of hard usage, but two editions – not quite complete – of Dickens's books were in worse condition, and these two authors were evidently well read. Henry Cockton's 'Valentine Fox'[32] had no lack of readers – among the younger scholars, I should suppose – as was evidenced by its worn cover and thumb-marked pages; and on the last shelf of the library were some twelve or fourteen volumes in the very last stages of dilapidation awaiting removal by the waste -paper dealer. These books were all by one writer, the lady author who was such a favourite at the other adult school library, Mrs. Henry Wood.[33] A reference to the returns showed that these novels were by far the most popular books in the library, and duplicates were on order to replace the tattered old ones, which had been kept till they almost fell to pieces. I confess the taste of these engineering scholars puzzled me: Mrs. Henry Wood's books literally worn to rags, and George Eliot and Jane Austen unappreciated! I endeavoured to explain the matter by a mental suggestion that doubtless the men took these books home for their wives to read.

On the whole, then, the result of my experience and observations among working-men is that their acquaintance with English literature is slight and mainly confined to fiction – not always of the best. I know for a fact that the daily paper and a few periodicals of the 'bits' variety constitute practically the whole literature of many of the working-class. Working-men read rather to beguile an idle moment than to increase their stock of knowledge, and so like something that will excite their interest or stir the emotions without requiring any special effort of the understanding.

[Lang:] I think my friend's description applies to every class of society, as regards literature and the love of it. To know Shakespeare by heart is as rare in Universities as it is railway-works and factories. To be wearied at the day's end and read nothing that demands more concentrated attention than an illustrated magazine, is only human nature. We, whose business it is to read and write have all the day, the fresh morning hours, for what is our delight as well as our study; and really we have no more grounds for despising people otherwise engaged because they do not read than Sir William Richmond[34] has for despising me because I do not occupy my spare hours in drawing in water-colours. The artisans appear, in their choice of novels, to be much on the general level; as regards Fielding, Scott, Thackeray, Marryat, and Dickens, infinitely above the level of many cultured persons. Mrs. Henry Wood is more popular, in all ranks, than Miss Austen. We may remember what Dean Stanley said about that masterpiece, 'East Lynne.'[35] Thackeray himself preferred novels strong, sweet and hot, rather like the port of which Tennyson said, 'It's strong, and it's black and it's sweet – sterling qualities, if not those of the most refined vintages.'[36]

One cannot seriously expect the large majority of mankind to be enthusiastically interested about the manners and customs of the Dieri[37] (though I remain shocked by the London Library), nor to excite themselves over the Philosophy of the Unconscious[38] or the mediaeval Cnichtengild.[39] *Our* 'days among the dead' are past, but the public, like Huckleberry Finn 'has no use for dead persons.' *We* live in a world of paper, under a firmament of ink, but it would not be fortunate if all mankind dwelt on such a planet. One book seems to be little known: the authorised translation of the Hebrew Scriptures. A young student in the Oxford History School recently asked me what the Puritan meant by saying, at the Restoration, that England 'hankered after the fleshpots of Egypt'! This student was deep in Hobbes and Stubbs and Clarendon, but had never read Exodus. Religion apart, people should know about Israel in Egypt, for there is an opera on the subject,[40] and it might happen to be matter of reference in conversation.

In other ages, literature and even science were relatively fashionable. French and English society twittered about 'vortices' and des Cartes, about sonnets and 'portraits', about Locke and Condillac and Montesquieu.[41] But novels and cheap picture magazines did not then compete so powerfully with more refined or more serious things. That old world possessed no 'Tit-Bits',[42] and is no more to be admired for not reading such literature almost exclusively than my friends, the Dieri, are to be applauded for the temperance of a tribe that possesses no native alcoholic stimulants.

3

ON WRITERS AND WRITING

In this section are examples of Lang's work on contemporary fiction and poetry and the question of writing itself. He wrote a great deal on individual authors, sometimes in introductions to editions, such as Scott, Dickens and Dumas, for whom he wrote prefaces to every volume of their complete works. Frequently, too, he published articles on individual writers, such as those later collected from the *St. James's Gazette* in *Letters to Dead Authors* (London: Longmans, Green and Co., 1886), or on writers generally, as in those from the American newspaper *The Independent* collected in *Letters on Literature* (London: Longmans, Green and Co., 1889). The two essays selected here, 'Of Modern English Poetry' (*Letters on Literature*, pp. 1–24) and 'Victorian Literature', give Lang's assessment of contemporary authors. The first was originally for an American readership and the addressees of the letters are not real persons but imaginary correspondents representing types of Americans. 'Victorian Literature' appeared in *Good Words* (38 (January 1897), pp. 91–5), a publication established in 1860 intended to provide appropriate reading for Sundays and directed at evangelicals and nonconformists, particularly of the lower middle class. Although it contained religious material it also published fiction and non-fiction articles suitable in tone.

The essay 'Émile Zola' was first published in the *Fortnightly Review* 31:184 (April 1882), pp. 439–52. It is Lang's longest and most substantial engagement with the work of Zola, though he writes frequently on him, see for example: 'Romance and the Reverse', this volume, pp. 112–114; 'An Apology for M. Zola', *Illustrated London News* 104:2864 (10 March 1894), p. 94; 'M. Zola on Lourdes', *Illustrated London News* 105:2893 (29 September 1894), p. 407 and on Zola's death, *Longman's Magazine* 41:241 (November 1902), p. 93. The essay shows the seriousness with which Lang considered Zola's work as well as further illustrating Lang's own position on the proper treatment of reality in novels.

'The Supernatural in Fiction', 'Notes on Fiction', and the two pieces from the *Illustrated London News* show Lang's ideas on the technique of writing and the difficulties of producing convincing effects in fiction. 'The Supernatural in Fiction' was published in *Adventures Among Books* (London: Longmans, Green and Co, 1905), pp. 271–80. In the acknowledgements, Lang suggests that this article may originally have appeared in *The Idler*. This is not the case, and it may not previously have been published as it has not been possible to locate any earlier publication. 'Notes on Fiction' is from *Longman's Magazine* 17:100 (February 1891), pp. 453–8, 'Behind the Novelist's Scenes' from the *Illustrated London News* 101:2778 (16 July 192), p. 83 and 'The Mystery of Style' from the *Illustrated London News* 102:2809 (18 February 1893), p. 216.

'Émile Zola',
The Fortnightly Review 31:184

(April 1882), pp. 439–52

In the autumn of 1879 Paris was covered with yellow posters, bearing, in huge black letters, the word NANA. Everywhere *Nana* met one – on the walls, in the newspapers, on the boards which cover the backs and breasts of the unfortunate race of 'sandwich men.'[1] Even in the shops of dealers in cigars the ends of the flexible pipes of india-rubber which supply smokers with the sacred gift of fire were covered with inscriptions to this effect – *Lisez*[2] *Nana! Nana!! Nana!!!* M. Zola has said about the friends of M. Victor Hugo, that they are well skilled in the art of the puff preliminary.[3] It was evident that the publishers of M. Zola himself were not unlearned in this art. Stimulated by the orgies of advertisements which heralded *Nana*, I cherished the ambition to write a critical essay on the author of *L'Assommoir* and his works. No such study, I believe, existed then in English. Our country is left behind in what M. Zola calls the march of the great literary movement. The Russians have composed volumes on M. Zola. The Italians have produced, so M. Paul Alexis informs us in his recent biography of M. Zola,[4] no less than fifteen works consecrated to his genius. He is relished in Denmark and Norway. M. de Sanctis has lectured on his novels at Naples.[5] In Holland, Dutch professors have written volumes on M. Zola; and learned Germany has contributed freely to the new science of Zolaology. Spain is not altogether inert; America has purchased 100,000 volumes of a crude translation of *Nana*. England alone holds aloof from this vast movement. The cause of our isolation is only too obvious. Our unfortunate Puritanism, alas! prevents us from understanding M. Zola and the joys of *naturalisme*.[6] I feared that it would be so as soon as I began the serious study of M. Zola's productions. One had not read many of M. Zola's novels before it became quite manifest that the English public would never take with pleasure to their author. 'Moi, je suis malade! Ce Zola me rend positivement malade!'[7] – M. Sarcey[8] is reported to have exclaimed at the first night of M. Zola's play, *Thérèse Raquin*. The English reader was certain to share the sensations of M. Sarcey, whose 'sturdy good sense' has been praised by M. Zola himself. A minute critical study of *Nana* and *La Curée* is impossible in English. But it is not impossible to indicate and criticize M. Zola's literary ideas, which now make so much stir; to describe his method; to trace the history of his success; and even to point out certain qualities of real value, certain passages of distinction and of beauty in his romances. M. Paul Alexis has made this task comparatively easy by publishing his *Émile Zola: Notes d'un Ami*. M. Alexis is one of several comparatively young writers who surround and worship M. Zola in his country house at Médan. M. Zola himself once said very hard things about *les illustres inconnnus*[9] who, according to him, surround M. Victor Hugo. The poet lives, it seems, in 'a little court' of adorers. M. Zola has now his own 'little court' of men who imitate and admire him, and M. Paul Alexis is the spokesman of these worshippers. His biography of M. Zola is not, perhaps, a diverting book, but it has an interest of its own. Most people who write (that is, almost every one nowadays) have a certain curiosity about the method of authors of distinction. This curiosity M. Alexis satisfies. He does more, he enables us to estimate the precise value of what M. Zola calls his *naturalisme*, and to appreciate the real worth of all his boasted *documents*.[10]

[. . .]

In 1865 M. Zola began to contribute to the press, and wrote in a Lyons paper the somewhat strident and ungracious criticisms which he afterwards published as *'Mes Haines'*. M. Zola is a warrior from his youth up, and in all his criticisms he attacks the theory that Art has a right to select pleasant subjects, to reject what is antipathetic, and to produce what is agreeable. As early as 1865 he was crying out for *documents* for science, for analysis, for minute observation in literature. We shall presently see, and the spectacle will be amusing enough, what Zola understands by analysis and by scientific observation. In the meantime it must suffice to note that, even in 1865, M. Zola was lifting up his testimony, and was dealing faithfully with all right-hand backsliders and left-hand fallers-off from the truth as it is in experimental, analytic, naturalistic, and scientific literature. In 1865, too, M. Zola showed that he had the courage of his convictions. He published a work which we have not succeeded in obtaining, *La Confession de Claude*. So scientific, experimental, and naturalistic was this volume, that M. Zola was 'wanted' by the police. He therefore left M. Hachette's establishment,[11] and, as he had now made a little reputation for himself, he chose literature as a profession. He wrote for M. Villemessant in *L'Événtment* and made a great noise by some criticisms of the Salon.[12] This may be described as scandal

No. 2, the first of M. Zola's profitable scandals having been caused by *La Confession de Claude*. His enemies accuse him of aiming deliberately at this sort of notoriety, but M. Zola himself regards the hostile tumult which his books excite merely as part of the martyrdom of genius. Balzac, he says, was 'stoned and crucified *comme le messie de la grande école du naturalisme*.'[13] M. Zola does not shrink from sharing the martyrdom of Balzac, saint and confessor.

We need not linger over M. Zola's fortunes as a journalist, nor attempt to exhume novels like *Les Mysterés de Marseille*. We now arrive at the date of M. Zola's first serious and laborious work, *Thérèse Raquin*, finished in 1867. The story was suggested by a review which M. Zola wrote of *La Vénus de Gordes*. In that edifying work a wife and her lover kill the husband, and are tried for their crime. In his review M. Zola suggested that it would have been a happier thought to make the crime escape the justice of men, and find its punishment in the remorse of the guilty pair, for ever united, and never to be 'delivered from the body of this death.'[14] The idea has been cleverly used by Gaboriau in *Le Crime d'Orcival*,[15] but M. Zola naturally treats it in his own very different manner. He has deliberately chosen the meanest characters, the most repulsive environment which his memory or his imagination could suggest.

[. . .]

There was a good deal of scandal (scandal No. 3) about *Thérèse Raquin*, 'Advertised by this controversy, the book sold pretty well,' says M. Alexis, with his usual eye to business. M. Zola wrote twice or thrice to M. Sainte Beuve to ask what he thought of *Thérèse Raquin*. M. Sainte Beuve's answer will be found in his *Correspondance* (vol. ii. p. 314). He said that the novel was remarkable and conscientious, but that the description of the horrors of the Passage du Pont Neuf was overdone and fantastic. He objected to the remorse of Thérèse and Laurent as improbable. And he asked whether it was necessary always to describe what is hideous and vulgar. This is a question to which the naturalists have really found no answer. In his new volume, *Une Campagne*, M. Zola replies to M. Renan, that he and his school are like surgeons, and prefer unhealthy subjects. They have no interest in what is normal and natural. This admission shows the true value of *naturalisme*. In some of his later works, however, M. Zola has introduced passages in which there is a certain relief; he has revived his old love of the country, and has almost outdone Paul and Virginia[16] in one episode. But, as a rule, he and 'those about Zola' prefer to describe passions so base, characters so detestable, scenes so unnatural in their wickedness that they make *Thérèse Raquin* seem almost idyllic. And, indeed, it has never vied in popularity with M. Zola's more mature stories of the same edifying sort.

Before approaching the long series of *Les Rougon-Macquart*, in which M.

Zola is working out in practice his aesthetic theories, it may be well to gain a clear notion of what these theories really are. They are explained in four or five volumes of collected criticisms, and in the preface to *Thérèse Raquin*.

M. Zola, defending himself against the charge of being an immoral writer, says that, in *Thérèse Raquin*, his object was entirely scientific. This word 'science' is always in his mouth, and it does not seem to occur to him that art and literature are one thing, and science quite other. Ben Allen and Bob Sawyer had a purely scientific aim in the medical conversation which alarmed Mr. Pickwick.[17] But, as that gentleman reminded them, the details of the dissecting-room, innocent in themselves, need not be discussed in the drawing-room. M. Zola is the impenitent Bob Sawyer of fiction, with none of Mr. Sawyer's amusing qualities. His aim, he says, was scientific. He goes on to observe that it would be fair to describe him as 'a writer who has forgotten himself in human corruptions, as a surgeon might do in a dissecting-room.' That is just what we complain of: M. Zola is always losing himself in the scientific contemplation of human corruption, and he publishes the result of his meditations in novels. His theory of what the modern scientific novel should be is set forth at great and tedious length in an essay called *Le Roman Expérimental*. Literature, at least the literature of our age, should be science, M. Zola thinks, and he illustrates what science should be by quoting long passages from Claude Bernard.[18] First, the man of science (and therefore the novelist) must be an observer. There is nothing new in that; all novelists, in their degree, have observed the world which they describe. But M. Zola's ideal novelist must make 'personal discoveries,' and must keep huge note-books full of the record of his investigations. This was Flaubert's method. M. Zola himself gradually fits great bundles of notes into his novel, according to M. Alexis. M. Zola points with pity to George Sand's[19] practice of writing her novels without any notes at all. As a matter of fact, we imagine that most writers of fiction keep some record of their reading and their observations. In a novel by no means naturalistic, Mr. Payn's *By Proxy*,[20] it is plain that the very minute and humorous description of Chinese life must have been distilled by the author from wide reading. Mr. Pinero,[21] too, has recently informed the world that dramatists keep collections of notes; and M. Daudi[22] a *naturaliste* by the way, is a great note-taker. Yet one may doubt whether Miss Austen, an innocent *naturaliste* if ever there was one, a close and minute observer, kept any written 'documents.' But the virtue of a French *naturaliste* is to amass notes as copious as those which Mr. Casaubon collected for *The Key of all Mythologies*.[23] It must be admitted that M. Zola is not always true to his own doctrine of 'personal discoveries.' He has written one novel, *La Curée*, on the rich financiers of the empire; one, *Son Excellence Eugène Rougon* on the politicians of the empire; and one, *Nana*, on the loose society of the empire. Into none of these three worlds –finance, politics and the world of *Nana* – had M. Zola ever entered. For his politic book, M.

Alexis says he crammed 'un livre très documenté, *Souvenirs d'un valet de chambre.*'[24] What a characteristic trait of the *naturaliste* this is! He cannot listen at certain key-holes himself, but he relies on the babbling of a lacquey out of place. Before he wrote Nana he 'appealed to the *souvenirs*' the chaste recollections of his friends. He was 'coached' by 'a very experienced man of the world,' who told him the dirty stories now gravely recorded in Nana for the edification of a hundred thousand citizens of the United States, now reading *Nana* in a crib. One is informed that the theatrical details in Nana are absurd. M. Zola's perfect novelist must not only make 'observations' like these, but experiments. When this statement is examined, it appears that the novelist, having determined on a character and an environment, must introduce, in his fancy, some new circumstances, and ask, 'In these circumstances how would the character act?' Surely every novelist who ever stained paper has necessarily made 'experiments' of this sort. So far, we see nothing novel in M. Zola's *aesthetic*, except his demand for copious notebooks. He goes on to define art as the reproduction of nature, and of life as conditioned by the temperament of the artist. Again, there is nothing new in this definition; only we must deplore the temperament of a writer who is almost always compelled to choose his subjects in 'human corruption.' The world is rich in beautiful lives, noble characters, 'Fair passions and bountiful pities, And loves without stain.'[25] We must presume that M. Zola and most other French *naturalistes* are unable, through an unhappy temperament, to see much of things and people 'lovely and of good report,'[26] and are compelled 'to lose themselves in human corruption.' Or, we must take it that M. Zola and his peers like to write on scandalous topics, because scandal brings notoriety and money. It is a disagreeable dilemma. But, even if we grant to M. Zola that the object of the art of fiction is 'the scientific knowledge of man,' we fail to see why that knowledge should dwell so much on man's corruption, and so little on the nobler aspects of humanity. M. Zola confesses, in so many words, that the novel, as conceived of by him, is a work of 'practical sociology.'[27] It is a pity that, like some other sociologists who do not write novels, M. Zola takes so much of his knowledge of society at second hand, and puts himself in danger of being 'crammed' by humorous persons whom he interrogates. But humour is a quality of which M. Zola does not even suspect the existence. To be brief, the 'experimental' or 'naturalistic' romance 'continues and completes physiology, and substitutes for the study of man in the abstract, the study of natural man as conditioned by his environment, and by physico-chemical laws.'[28]

Strong in this aesthetic theory, such as it is, this theory that art is science, and that anecdotes are 'documents,' M. Zola began to construct the series of novels called, in general, *Les Rougon-Macquart*. The scientific datum was the transmission of hereditary characteristics and their modification. There are few subjects more obscure. M. Zola, in 186–9, 'crammed' the topic of 'heredity,' reading especially Lucas's *Traité de l'Hérédité Naturelle.*[29] Different motives, according to M. Alexis, impelled M. Zola to begin his great series of novels, 'The History of a Family under the Second Empire.' He wished, very naturally, to have a secure source of income. This was to be provided by an arrangement with a publisher. The bookseller was to pay the author £240 a year for two yearly novels. The arrangement was complex in its details, and proved impossible in practice. When three or four of the stories had appeared, M. Charpentier became the publisher of the series. His dealings with M. Zola are a bright chapter in the sombre records of publishing. But M. Zola's ambition, even more than his interest, urged him to attempt the history of the Rougon-Macquart. He wished to leave a great work behind him, and to this task he bent himself with rare energy; and singleness of purpose. The least sympathetic critic must admit that, granting the genre, the History of the Rougon-Macquarts is a great, though gloomy, work. M. Zola has laboured, as a rule with a ruthless conscientiousness. After making himself master, as he believed, of the lore of hereditary transmission of character, he thought out his vast scheme, and drew up that family tree of the Rougon-Macquart, which was published eight years later in *Un Page d'Amour.* The family of Rougon-Macquart is like a seedy modern House of Atreus.[30] In place of the awful Atê, the Fate which dwells in Tiryns and Mycenae,[31] it is the curse of inherited character that broods over and dominates the line of Rougon-Macquart. The tree springs from a rotten root, and bears apples of Sodom and fruits of corruption.

[…]

The series of novels follow the fortunes of these people and their descendants, born to an inheritance of ignorance, madness, and debauch. Here one is naturally tempted to ask why a family of this sort should have been selected by a *naturaliste*? Surely there are houses in which honour, truth, temperance, courtesy, and love of knowledge are inherited qualities? But there would have been no market, perhaps, for the annals of such families. M. Zola, had he devoted himself to the study of an honourable house, would have become a French follower of Miss Yonge,[32] who has anticipated his scheme of drawing up the family tree of her characters. Again, one cannot but suppose (granting the theory of heredity), that the characteristics of long-forgotten and perhaps reputable ancestors might have reappeared in the Rougon-Macquart. Evolutionists will admit that their pedigree went back for hundreds of thousands of years, through thousands of ancestors, and any Rougon-Macquart might 'throw back' to decent progenitors lost in the mists of antiquity.

[…]

The book had no success; none of the series had really been successful on a grand scale. Another man might have been discouraged: M. Zola took counsel with himself, produced *L'Assommoir.* The story made his fortune. It was talked of everywhere. Even before it appeared as a complete volume, it provoked a protest, in the name of art and of decency, from Mr. Swinburne. To me, I confess, the *L'Assommoir* appears a dreadful, but not an immoral book. It is the most powerful Temperance tract that ever was written. As M. Zola saw much of the life of the poor in his early years, as he once lived, when a boy, in one of the huge lodging-houses he describes, one may fear that *L'Assommoir* is a not untruthful picture of the lives of many men and women in Paris.

[. . .]

In this narrative M. Zola spares us nothing. He writes in the slang of the people. He gloats over the amours of hatters, and the jests of undertakers. He tosses out the contents of the washerwoman's bucket; he makes his laundresses fight a hideous and indecent battle, one is beaten, as Villon anticipates him by saying:

> 'As linen is that lies
> In washer's tubs for bats to smite.'[33]

He takes you into the festering garrets of unclean workpeople, and describes the details of trades which he has obviously 'read up' for the purpose. Even when his wedding party of workpeople in their strange holiday best lose themselves in the Louvre, there is not a redeeming stroke of humour in M. Zola's story. In place of a character or two, such as Dickens would have drawn or invented, in place of Mr. Swiveller or Sam Weller, M. Zola copies and repeats the blasphemies of the slums. He steadily and gradually degrades his characters to unspeakable and undreamed-of depths of corruption. This is history, perhaps, or science; M. Zola thinks, not only that it is literature, but that all modern literature should be more or less like this. It is difficult to see why people read *L'Assommoir* if they avoid it: if they have not some professional reason for studying it, as they might study criminal statistics, or books of medical jurisprudence. But the book has had an enormous success, a success only excelled by *Nana*, a story of which little need be said. M. Zola has maintained that books like his exercise a moral function. *'Être maître du bien et du mal, régler la vie...n ...'est-ce pas lá être les ouvriers les plus utiles et les plus moraux du travail humain?'*[34] In Nana this moralist simply repeats at second hand, and strings together in a narrative incredibly dull, a number of abominable anecdotes. The book appeals to the basest curiosities. It cannot be called an alluring description of vice, but it does gloat on, and sows broadcast, the knowledge of secret and nameless iniquities. Literature and science alike refuse to acknowledge this last unclean fruit of the tree of Rougon-Macquart.

[. . .]

In M. Zola we find, to conclude, a writer with a method and an aim, a workman conscientious according to his lights; not without poetry, not without a sense of beauty, but more and more disinclined to make use of these qualities. In all his work you see the 'joins', and know where the 'notes' come in. It is part of his method to abstain from comment; never to show the author's personality, never to turn to the reader for sympathy. He is as cold as a vivisectionist at a lecture. His conception of modern literature, as science in disguise, did much to spoil the later work of George Eliot. His own knowledge of the literature of the world appears to be scanty; his judgments – as when he calls Scott 'a clever arranger – whose work is dead' – do not deserve to be discussed. His lack of humour is absolute, a darkness that can be felt. Finally, temperament, or system, or desire of success, or all combined, make several of his stories little better than a Special Reporter's[35] description of things and people that should not be described.

'Of Modern English Poetry',
Letters on Literature
(London: Longmans, Green and Co., 1889)

To Mr. Arthur Wincott, Topeka, Kansas.

Dear Wincott, –You write to me, from your 'bright home in the setting sun,'[1] with the flattering information that you have read my poor 'Letters to Dead Authors.' You are kind enough to say that you wish I would write some 'Letters to Living Authors;' but that, I fear, is out of the question.

A thoughtful critic in the *Spectator* has already remarked that the great men of the past would not care for my shadowy epistles – if they could read them. Possibly not; but, like Prior, 'I may write till they can spell'– an exercise of which ghosts are probably as incapable as was Matt's little Mistress of Quality.[2] But Living Authors are very different people, and it would be perilous, as well as impertinent, to direct one's comments on them literally, in the French phrase, 'to their address.'[3] Yet there is no reason why a critic should not adopt the epistolary form.

Our old English essays, the papers in the *Tatler* and *Spectator*, were originally nothing but letters. The vehicle permits a touch of personal taste, perhaps of personal prejudice. So I shall write my 'Letters on Literature,' of the present and of the past, English, American, ancient, or modern, to *you*, in your distant Kansas, or to such other correspondents as are kind enough to read these notes.

Poetry has always the precedence in these discussions. Poor Poetry! She is an ancient maiden of good family, and is led out first at banquets, though many would prefer to sit next some livelier and younger Muse, the lady of fiction, or even the chattering *soubrette*[4] of journalism. *Seniores priores:*[5] Poetry, if no longer very popular, is a dame of the worthiest lineage, and can boast a long train of gallant admirers, dead and gone. She has been much in courts. The old Greek tyrants loved her; great Rhamses[6] seated her at his right hand; every prince had his singers. Now we dwell in an age of democracy, and Poetry wins but a feigned respect, more out of courtesy, and for old friendship's sake, than for liking. Though so many write verse, as in Juvenal's time, I doubt if many read it. 'None but minstrels list of sonneting.'[7] The purchasing public, for poetry, must now consist chiefly of poets, and *they* are usually poor.

Can anything speak more clearly of the decadence of the art than the birth of so many poetical 'societies'? We have the Browning Society, the Shelley Society, the Shakespeare Society, the Wordsworth Society – lately dead. They all demonstrate that people have not the courage to study verse in solitude, and for their proper pleasure; men and women need confederates in this adventure. There is safety in numbers, and, by dint of tea-parties, recitations, discussions, quarrels and the like, Dr. Furnivall and his friends keep blowing the faint embers on the altar of Apollo.[8] They cannot raise a flame!

In England we are in the odd position of having several undeniable poets, and very little new poetry worthy of the name. The chief singers have outlived, if not their genius, at all events its flowering time. Hard it is to estimate poetry, so apt we are, by our very nature, to prefer 'the newest songs,' as Odysseus says men did even during the war of Troy.[9] Or, following another ancient example, we say, like the rich niggards who neglected Theocritus, 'Homer is enough for all.'[10]

Let us attempt to get rid of every bias, and, thinking as dispassionately as we can, we still seem to read the name of Tennyson in the golden book of English poetry. I cannot think that he will ever fall to a lower place, or be among those whom only curious students pore over, like Gower, Drayton, Donne, and the rest. Lovers of poetry will always read him as they will read Wordsworth, Keats, Milton, Coleridge, and Chaucer. Look his defects in the face, throw them into the balance, and how they disappear before his merits! He is the last and youngest of the mighty race, born, as it were, out of due time, late, and into a feebler generation.

Let it be admitted that the gold is not without alloy, that he has a touch of voluntary affectation, of obscurity, even an occasional perversity, a mannerism, a set of favourite epithets ('windy' and 'happy'). There is a momentary echo of Donne, of Crashaw, nay, in his earliest pieces, even a touch of Leigh Hunt. You detect it in pieces like 'Lilian' and 'Eleanore,' and the others of that kind and of that date.

Let it be admitted that 'In Memoriam' has certain lapses in all that meed of melodious tears; that there are trivialities which might deserve (here is an example) 'to line a box,' or to curl some maiden's locks, that there are weaknesses of thought, that the poet now speaks of himself as a linnet, singing 'because it must,' now dares to approach questions insoluble, and again declines their solution. What is all this but the changeful mood of grief? The singing linnet, like the bird in the old English heathen apologue, dashes its light wings painfully against the walls of the chamber into which it has flown out of the blind night that shall again receive it.[11]

I do not care to dwell on the imperfections in that immortal strain of sympathy and consolation, that enchanted book of consecrated regrets. It is an easier if not more grateful task to note a certain peevish egotism of tone in the heroes of 'Locksley Hall,' of 'Maud,' of 'Lady Clara Vere de Vere.' 'You can't think how poor a figure you make when you tell that story, sir,' said Dr. Johnson to some unlucky gentleman[12] whose 'figure' must certainly have been more respectable than that which is cut by these whining and peevish lovers of Maud and Cousin Amy.

Let it be admitted, too, that King Arthur, of the 'Idylls,' is like an Albert[13] in blank verse, an Albert cursed with a Guinevere for a wife, and a Lancelot for friend. The 'Idylls,' with all their beauties, are full of a Victorian respectability, and love of talking with Vivien about what is not so respectable. One wishes, at times, that the 'Morte d'Arthur' had remained a lonely and flawless fragment, as noble as Homer, as polished as Sophocles. But then we must have missed, with many other admirable things, the 'Last Battle in the West.'

People who come after us will be more impressed than we are by the Laureate's versatility. He has touched so many strings, from 'Will Waterproof's Monologue,' so far above Praed, to the agony of 'Rizpah,' the invincible energy of 'Ulysses,' the languor and the fairy music of the 'Lotus Eaters,' the grace as of a Greek epigram which inspires the lines to Catullus and to Virgil. He is with Milton for learning, with Keats for magic and vision, with Virgil for graceful recasting of ancient golden lines, and, even in the latest volume of his long life, 'we may tell from the straw,' as Homer says, 'what the grain has been.'[14]

There are many who make it a kind of religion to regard Mr. Browning as the greatest of living English poets. For him, too, one is thankful as for a veritable great poet; but can we believe that impartial posterity will rate him with the Laureate, or that so large a proportion of his work will endure? The charm of an enigma now attracts students who feel proud of being able to understand what others find obscure. But this attraction must inevitably become a stumbling-block.

Why Mr. Browning is obscure is a long question; probably the answer is that he often could not help himself. His darkest poems may be made out by a person of average intelligence who will read them as hard as, for example, he would find it necessary to read the 'Logic' of Hegel.[15] There is a story of two clever girls[16] who set out to peruse 'Sordello,' and corresponded with each other about their progress. 'Somebody is dead in "Sordello,"' one of them wrote to her friend. 'I don't quite know who it is, but it must make things a little clearer in the long run.' Alas! a copious use of the guillotine would scarcely clear the stage of 'Sordello.' It is hardly to be hoped that 'Sordello,' or 'Red Cotton Night Cap Country,' or 'Fifine,' will continue to be struggled with by posterity. But the mass of 'Men and Women,' that unexampled gallery of portraits of the inmost hearts and secret minds of priests, prigs, princes, girls, lovers, poets, painters, must survive immortally, while civilization and literature last, while men care to know what is in men.

No perversity of humour, no voluntary or involuntary harshness of style, can destroy the merit of these poems, which have nothing like them in the letters of the past, and must remain without successful imitators in the future. They will last all the better for a certain manliness of religious faith – something sturdy and assured – not moved by winds of doctrine, not paltering with doubts, which is certainly one of Mr. Browning's attractions in this fickle and shifting generation. He cannot be forgotten while, as he says,

'A sunset touch,
A chorus ending of Euripides,'

remind men that they are creatures of immortality, and move 'a thousand hopes and fears.'[17]

If one were to write out of mere personal preference, and praise most that which best fits one's private moods, I suppose I should place Mr. Matthew Arnold at the head of contemporary English poets. Reason and reflection, discussion and critical judgment, tell one that he is not quite there. Mr. Arnold had not the many melodies of the Laureate, nor his versatile mastery, nor his magic, nor his copiousness. He had not the microscopic glance of Mr. Browning, nor his rude grasp of facts, which tears the life out of them as the Aztec priest plucked the very heart from the victim. We know that, but yet Mr. Arnold's poetry has our love; his lines murmur in our memory through all the stress and accidents of life. 'The Scholar Gipsy,' 'Obermann,' 'Switzerland,' the melancholy majesty of the close of 'Sohrab and Rustum,' the tenderness of those elegiacs on two kindred graves beneath the Himalayas and by the Midland Sea; the surge and thunder of 'Dover Beach,' with its 'melancholy, long-withdrawing roar;' these can only cease to whisper to us and console us in that latest hour when life herself ceases to 'moan round with many voices.'

My friends tell me that Mr. Arnold is too doubting, and too didactic, that he protests too much, and considers too curiously, that his best poems are, at most, 'a chain of highly valuable thoughts.'[18] It may be so; but he carries us back to 'wet, bird-haunted English lawns;'[19] like him 'we know what white and purple fritillaries the grassy harvest of the river yields,'[20] with him we try to practise resignation, and to give ourselves over to that spirit

'Whose purpose is not missed,
While life endures, while things subsist.'[21]

Mr. Arnold's poetry is to me, in brief, what Wordsworth's was to his generation. He has not that inspired greatness of Wordsworth, when nature does for him what his 'lutin'[22] did for Corneille, 'takes the pen from his hand and writes for him.'[23] But he has none of the creeping prose which, to my poor mind, invades even 'Tintern Abbey.' He is, as Mr. Swinburne says, 'the surest-footed'[24] of our poets. He can give a natural and lovely life even to the wildest of ancient imaginings, as to 'these bright and ancient snakes, that once were Cadmus and Harmonia.'[25]

Bacon speaks of the legends of the earlier and ruder world coming to us 'breathed softly through the flutes of the Grecians.'[26] But even the Grecian flute, as in the lay of the strife of Apollo and Marsyas,[27] comes more tunably in the echo of Mr. Arnold's song, that beautiful song in 'Empedocles on Etna,' which has the perfection of sculpture and the charm of the purest colour. It is full of the silver light of dawn among the hills, of the music of the loch's dark, slow waves among the reeds, of the scent of the heather, and the wet tresses of the birch. Surely, then, we have had great poets living among us, but the fountains of their song are silent, or flow but rarely over a clogged and stony channel. And who is there to succeed the two who are gone, or who shall be our poet, if the Master be silent? That is a melancholy question, which I shall try to answer (with doubt and dread enough) in my next letter.

My dear Wincott, – I hear that a book has lately been published by an American lady, in which all the modern poets are represented. The singers have been induced to make their own selections, and put forward, as Mr. Browning says, their best foot, anapaest or trochee,[28] or whatever it may be. My information goes further, and declares that there are but eighteen poets of England to sixty inspired Americans.

This Western collection of modern minstrelsy shows how very dangerous it is to write even on the English poetry of the day. Eighteen is long odds against a single critic, and Major Bellenden, in 'Old Mortality,' tells us that three to one are odds as long as ever any warrior met victoriously, and that warrior was old Corporal Raddlebanes.[29]

I decline the task; I am not going to try to estimate either the eighteen of England or the sixty of the States. It is enough to speak about three living poets, in addition to those masters treated of in my last letter. Two of the three you will have guessed at – Mr. Swinburne and Mr. William Morris. The third, I dare say, you do not know even by name. I think he is not one of the English eighteen – Mr. Robert Bridges. His muse has followed the epicurean maxim, and chosen the shadowy path, *fallentis semita vitae*,[30] where the dew lies longest on the grass, and the red rowan berries droop in autumn above the yellow St. John's wort. But you will find her all the fresher for her country ways.

My knowledge of Mr. William Morris's poetry begins in years so far-away that they seem like reminiscences of another existence. I remember sitting beneath Cardinal Beaton's ruined castle at St. Andrews, looking across the bay to the sunset, while some one repeated 'Two Red Roses across the Moon.' And I remember thinking that the poem was nonsense. With Mr. Morris's other early verses, 'The Defence of Guinevere,' this song of the moon and the roses was published in 1858. Probably the little book won no attention; it is not popular even now. Yet the lyrics remain in memories which forget all but a general impression of the vast 'Earthly Paradise,' that huge decorative poem, in which slim maidens and green-clad men, and waters wan, and flowering apple trees, and rich palaces are all mingled as on some long ancient tapestry, shaken a little by the wind of death. They are not living and breathing people, these persons of the fables; they are but shadows, beautiful and faint, and their poem is fit reading for sleepy summer afternoons. But the characters in the lyrics in 'The Defence of Guinevere' are people of flesh and blood, under their chain armour and their velvet, and the trappings of their tabards.

There is no book in the world quite like this of Mr. Morris's old Oxford days when the spirit of the Middle Ages entered into him, with all its contradictions of faith and doubt, and its earnest desire to enjoy this life to the full in war and love, or to make certain of a future in which war is not, and all love is pure heavenly. If one were to choose favourites from 'The Defence of Guinevere,' they would be the ballads of 'Shameful Death,' and of 'The Sailing of the Sword,' and 'The Wind,' which has the wind's wail in its voice, and all the mad regret of 'Porphyria's Lover'[31] in its burden. The use of 'colour-words,' in all these pieces, is very curious and happy. The red ruby, the brown falcon, the white maids, 'the scarlet roofs of the good town,' in 'The Sailing of the Sword,' make the poem a vivid picture. […]

'The Blue Closet,' which is said to have been written for some drawings of Mr. Rossetti, is also a masterpiece in this romantic manner. Our brief English age of romanticism, our 1830, was 1856–60, when Mr. Morris, Mr. Burne Jones,[32] and Mr. Swinburne were undergraduates. Perhaps it wants a peculiar turn of taste to admire these strange things, though 'The Haystack in the Floods,' with its tragedy, must surely appeal to all who read poetry.

For the rest, as time goes on, I more and more feel as if Mr. Morris's long later poems, 'The Earthly Paradise' especially, were less art than 'art manufacture.'[33] This may be an ungrateful and erroneous sentiment. 'The Earthly Paradise,' and still more certainly 'Jason,' are full of such pleasure as only poetry can give. As some one said of a contemporary politician, they are 'good, but copious.'[34] Even from narrative poetry Mr. Morris has long abstained. He, too, illustrates Mr. Matthew Arnold's parable of 'The Progress of Poetry.'

> 'The Mount is mute, the channel dry.'[35]

Euripides has been called 'the meteoric poet,'[36] and the same title seems very appropriate to Mr. Swinburne. Probably few readers had heard his name – I only knew it as that of the author of a strange mediaeval tale in prose – when he published 'Atalanta in Calydon' in 1865. I remember taking up the quarto in white cloth, at the Oxford Union, and being instantly led captive by the beauty and originality of the verse.

There was this novel 'meteoric' character in the poem: the writer seemed to rejoice in snow and fire, and stars, and storm, 'the blue cold fields and folds of air,'[37] in all the primitive forces which were alive before this earth was; the naked vast powers that circle the planets and farthest constellations. This quality, and his varied and sonorous verse, and his pessimism, put into the mouth of a Greek chorus, were the things that struck one most in Mr. Swinburne. He was, above all, 'a mighty-mouthed inventer of harmonies,'[38] and one looked eagerly for his next poems. They came with disappointment and trouble.

The famous 'Poems and Ballads' have become so well known that people can hardly understand the noise they made. I don't wonder at the scandal, even now. I don't see the fun of several of the pieces, except the mischievous fun of shocking your audience. However, 'The Leper' and his company are chiefly boyish, in the least favourable sense of the word. They do not destroy the imperishable merit of the 'Hymn to Proserpine' and the 'Garden of Proserpine' and the 'Triumph of Time' and 'Itylus.'

Many years have passed since 1866, and yet one's old opinion, that English poetry contains no verbal music more original, sonorous, and sweet than Mr. Swinburne wrote in these pieces when still very young, remains an opinion unshaken. Twenty years ago, then, he had enabled the world to take his measure; he had given proofs of a true poet; he was learned too in literature as few poets have been since Milton, and, like Milton, skilled to make verse in the languages of the ancient world and in modern tongues. His French songs and Greek elegiacs are of great excellence; probably no scholar who was not also a poet could match his Greek lines on Landor.[39]

What, then, is lacking to make Mr. Swinburne a poet of a rank even higher than that which he occupies? Who can tell? There is no science that can master this chemistry of the brain. He is too copious. 'Bothwell' is long enough for six plays, and 'Tristram of Lyonesse' is prolix beyond even mediaeval narrative. He is too pertinacious; children are the joy of the world and Victor Hugo is a great poet; but Mr. Swinburne almost makes us excuse Herod and Napoleon III by his endless odes to Hugo, and rondels to small boys and girls.[40] *Ne quid nimis*,[41] that is the golden rule which he constantly spurns, being too luxuriant, too emphatic, and as fond of repeating himself as Professor Freeman.[42] Such are the defects of so noble a genius; thus perverse Nature has decided that it shall be, Nature which makes no ruby without a flaw.

The name of Mr. Robert Bridges is probably strange to many lovers of poetry who would like nothing better than to make acquaintance with his verse. But his verse is not so easily found. This poet never writes in magazines; his books have not appealed to the public by any sort of advertisement, only two or three of them have come forth in the regular way. The first was 'Poems, by Robert Bridges, Batchelor of Arts in the University of Oxford. *Parva seges satisest.* (A small crop suffices) London: Pickering, 1873.'

This volume was presently, I fancy, withdrawn, and the author has distributed some portions of it in succeeding pamphlets, or in books printed at Mr. Daniel's private press in Oxford. In these, as in all Mr. Bridges's poems, there is a certain austere and indifferent beauty of diction and a memory of the old English poets, Milton and the earlier lyrists. I remember being greatly pleased with the 'Elegy on a Lady whom Grief for the Death of Her Betrothed Killed.' […]

In his first volume Mr. Bridges offered a few rondeaux and triolets, turning his back on all these things as soon as they became popular. In spite of their popularity I have the audacity to like them still, in their humble twittering way. Much more in his true vein were the lines, 'Clear and Gentle Stream,' and all the other verses in which, like a true Etonian, he celebrates the beautiful Thames […]

I cannot say how often I have read that poem, and how delightfully it carries the breath of our River through the London smoke. Nor less welcome are the two poems on spring, the 'Invitation to the Country,' and the 'Reply.' In these, besides their verbal beauty and their charming pictures, is a manly philosophy of Life, which animates Mr. Bridges's more important pieces – his 'Prometheus the Firebringer,' and his 'Nero,' a tragedy remarkable for the representation of Nero himself, the luxurious human tiger. From 'Prometheus' I make a short extract, to show the quality of Mr. Bridges's blank verse:

> 'Nor is there any spirit on earth astir,
> Nor 'neath the airy vault, nor yet beyond
> In any dweller in far-reaching space
> Nobler or dearer than the spirit of man:
> That spirit which lives in each and will not die,
> That wooeth beauty, and for all good things
> Urgeth a voice, or still in passion sigheth,
> And where he loveth, draweth the heart with him.'

Mr. Bridges's latest book is his 'Eros and Psyche' (Bell & Sons, who publish the 'Prometheus'). It is the old story very closely followed, and beautifully retold, with a hundred memories of ancient poets: Homer, Dante, Theocritus, as well as of Apuleius.

I have named Mr. Bridges here because his poems are probably all but unknown to readers well acquainted with many other English writers of late days. On them, especially on actual contemporaries or juniors in age, it would be almost impertinent for me to speak to you; but, even at that risk, I take the chance of directing you to the poetry of Mr. Bridges. I owe so much pleasure to its delicate air, that, if speech be impertinence, silence were ingratitude.

'Victorian Literature', *Good Words* 38

(January 1897), pp. 91–5

Her Majesty's reign, already longer than that of any *anointed* monarch[1] of England,* has necessarily coincided with the production of an enormous mass of literature. We speak of the Victorian as we speak of the Elizabethan, or of the Augustan, or of the Georgian Age. To a seeker for hasty generalisation, the late Victorian Age will be remarkable for the wide diffusion of instruction, and the parallel decline and decay of most of the arts. We may not be able to discover any connection of cause and effect between the teaching of art and literature in hundreds of schools, colleges, institutions, and the accompanying frivolity, feebleness, and fantastic waywardness of painting; the frivolity, fantastic waywardness and ignorance of much popular literature. Compare the art of Reynolds, Gainsborough, Hoppner, Romney, Cotman,[2] with our Royal Academy, or our cheap impressionism. Compare Fielding with the various Amuraths[3] who succeed each other as the most popular novelists. The more we chatter about art, the worse is our performance. The more we prate of method and style in letters, the more does a large part of the public rejoice in certain romances which, in various proportions, combine all the blatancies, all the vulgarities, all the faults of taste and of morals. The more we educate, the lower is the standard of critical conscientiousness and critical learning, till a reviewer, in a highly respectable journal, actually does not know how many volumes there are in the work submitted to his judgment – the number being one!

There are, of course, exceptions, and all literary work of to-day is not frivolity or fustian, or earnest journalism 'standing,' like the Abomination of Desolation, 'where it should not.'[4] The Victorian Age, in fact, can give a

* The longest reign (may it soon yield its pride of place) is that of an uncrowned king, James III.

good account of itself, though certain existing tendencies deserve what has been said of them in the mass. The age has many glories, though education, in being diffused, has, perhaps unavoidably, been spread uncommonly thin.

When her Majesty ascended the throne, there had fallen a lull in poetry. The great time was over: Scott, Shelley, Byron, and Keats were dead. Wordsworth was long past his prime; Southey was nearing his pathetic end; Landor[5] was not listened to; Coleridge had ceased to sing; even Milman[6] had relapsed on prose; nothing was heard but the unregarded twitterings of minor minstrels – mostly women. Yet, even before the Queen's reign began, three thin, unread or ridiculed volumes of 1830 and 1833 had given assurance of poets – Tennyson and Browning. To hold in our hands the slim Tennysonian volumes of 1830 and 1833, and 'Pauline,' affects us as we are affected when we stand by the wells and springs of mighty rivers. In Lord Tennyson's earliest verses, even the defects indicate an attempt to revive the rich fantastic Elizabethan style, though that style had reached the author not uncontaminated by the affectations of Leigh Hunt and of Keats' earliest efforts. Beyond and above these things was perceptible the poet's original strain, an accent hitherto unheard; perceptible, too, was his intense natural genius for romance. 'Mariana,' had it stood alone, gave earnest of a great poet, a master of emotions, of words, of verbal music. In the same way, 'Pauline' heralded the arrival of a poet who should probe 'the abyssmal depths of personality.'[7] In both Tennyson and Browning there showed that which was temporary, and of their age – Victorian, accompanied by that which was personal to their genius, and that which was permanent, eternal, of the same essence as the noblest things in human literature. Through the whole careers of these great writers the two streams may be traced, the Victorian and the universal. Tennyson is Victorian in his 'Miller's Daughter,' his 'Locksley Hall,' his 'Queen of the May,' in much of his 'Princess' and 'In Memoriam,' and in many passages of the 'Idylls.' Browning, again, is Victorian in his perpetual arguing all round about him, in most of his religious reflections, in his preoccupation with 'problems.' Precisely in the same way, Shakspeare is Elizabethan in his euphuism, his quibbles, serious or comic, in his designed and fantastic obscurities (George III was well inspired in what he said about Shakspeare[8]); while he is universal and eternal in his poetry and his humour, in Macbeth, Hamlet, Falstaff, Rosalind, Jacques. Lucretius,[9] once more, is temporary and of his age in his epicurean system; he is personal and eternal in his glance at the wonder and beauty and mystery of the world; in that beating of his wings against the *flammantia moenia mundi*.[10]

For Tennyson and for Browning, as for Shakspeare and Lucretius, probably, the temporary element in their work was the chief interest of contemporaries to whom the essential and universal elements of poetry were of slight concern. No doubt, after 1842, it was his Victorian verses, his 'Queen of the May,' and his attempts at philosophising on popular doctrines and questions that won the greater part of his popularity for

Tennyson. No doubt Browning's faults, his obscure essays at profundity, pleased the professional Browningists. Both, however, will live for their permanent qualities of magic, of music, of romance; for 'all the charm of all the muses, flowering often in some lonely word'[11] of Tennyson as of Virgil. In the same way the rude, audacious vigour of romance, passion, and adventure in Browning's 'Men and Women' has already outlived the ponderous blank verse treatises of his later volumes.

These two great men are, of course, the chief literary glories of the Victorian Age; while it is the poetry of the 'Scholar Gipsy,' of 'Sohrab and Rustum,' of a hundred magical passages and pictures, not the cold and resigned philosophy of Matthew Arnold that promise him a measure of immortality. We are still too near Mr. William Morris, Mr. Swinburne, and Mr. Rossetti to attain anything like a dispassionate view of their qualities and defects, though in each we may undoubtingly observe traces and touches of what is essential and enduring. In each, too, we mark the temporary, the sign-manual of their epoch, in voluntary archaism or wilful fantasy. At present, 'the Muse has gone away',[12] or is making rather unpromising experiments under various evanescent foreign influences. For we live in an age of 'booms,'[13] and it is easy for people with little reading, and a strong love of posing, to flutter themselves over cheap French, or Russian, or Norse, or Lithuanian notorieties. The exiguity of contemporary education must produce such effects in persons who have never read Shakspeare, Milton, Homer, and Sophocles, but who have seen a great deal about Verlaine, Ibsen, Maeterlinck, and the Decadents[14] in the newspapers and the reviews which are 'up to date.' It is not hard to be 'up to date' by neglecting all that has gone before us, and it is as easy to be 'cultured' by reading certain critics, as to learn slang from the *Sporting Times*. Such are the natural consequences of a divorce between solid education and literature.

The world is too much with us – the brawling, snatching, excited world of to-day – and this is incompatible with greatness and permanence in literature. We pay this penalty for democracy, telegrams, newspapers, popular education, 'and why waste words,' remarked Alcibiades sweetly, 'on admitted absurdity?'[15] But the very democracy which Alcibiades thus described was producing, in a whirl of excitement, the greatest of literatures. We are not doing that, and the confusions of our age seem to make that impossible. However man does not live by literature alone – far from it; and some time, somehow, there may be compensations. Moreover, it is not popular and general conditions of any sort which produce literature, a thing born of the inscrutable genius – the wind blowing as it listeth[16] – which breathes on certain rare persons, born now and again into the world. Thus, if our current criticism be, as on the whole it is, ignorant, indolent, and partial, what are we to say of the criticism which ridiculed, abused, and insulted Wordsworth, Coleridge, Keats, Shelley, and even, on occasions, Scott? The conditions which result in great literary productions are so obscure that lovers of literature should never despair. In the darkest hour there may arise some 'new Avatar,'[17] just as times of leisure and cultivation may be hopelessly barren of genius. For 'encouragement' has little to do with the matter. State patronage may only endow poetasters, so the State very wisely leaves literature out in the cold. The public did not purchase the poems of Wordsworth, Keats, Shelley, or Coleridge any more than it would now reward their modern peers, if there were any such minstrels. The public prefers lay sermons in novels, if earnest, or tattle about the Royal Family, or 'Sporting Scraps.' As Mr. Birrell asks, 'What, in the name of the Bodleian, has the general public to do with literature?'[18] Like virtue, literature is its own reward.

After poetry, the literary imagination finds its best field in history. The Victorian age has its Macaulay, Carlyle, and Froude, all men of imagination who exercised that faculty freely on the real events of the past. For those who have a peevish desire to know what the real events were, the age can produce Mr. Gardiner.[19] The other great writers give us drama of the most moving and delightful sort, based on actual records, and highly coloured according to the taste and fancy of the author. In this kind of imaginative history the Victorian age is probably superior to any other. The scientific spirit reached the writers mentioned just enough, and not too much. All of them worked industriously at manuscript sources. It may be that Macaulay and Mr. Froude, especially, are not on 'our side,' our heroes may not be theirs, and we may adore what they burned. In both we recognise prejudices amounting to judicial blindness sometimes, and in Mr. Froude we regret a congenital incapacity for accuracy, while Mr. Carlyle, to be sure, was the vigorous special pleader for his Heroes. Mr. Carlyle may even be called immoral, and perhaps he is, in his adoration of Force: But even though we be Jacobites,[20] Mariolaters,[21] or moralists, to these authors we owe pictures incomparably vivid and brilliant of events incomparably dramatic. As Ancient Pistol[22] ate and swore, we read and remonstrate, but we go on reading. A Tory Macaulay would be delightful, and here is, indeed, a niche for any ambitious young writer to fill. But a Whig Macaulay, a Puritan Froude, a Calvinist Carlyle are all benefactors of bookish mankind. It was in vain that Mr. Freeman[23] scolded; even if one agrees with his ideas, with his tone nobody ought to agree. At present the study of history is overspecialised, or, at least, specialists are many. Writers who can reach, and hold, and instruct the person of ordinary intelligence are conspicuously absent. But laudable industry is collecting, criticising, and making accessible the materials for the imaginative historian, when he arrives. In these labours the later Victorian age is laudably employed, and the State does its duty with the Historical Manuscripts Commission.[24]

By literature, at this moment, the public and the reviewers chiefly mean novels. In this branch of *belles lettres*[25] we may proudly aver that the Victorian age has been what the Elizabethan age is in drama. How the

Elizabethan public was able to appreciate the noblest poetry in the noblest style, how that style came to be 'in the air,' so that every playwright had, in less or greater measure, the gift of expression, of lofty and coloured and passionate language, was a mystery to Scott, and a mystery it remains. We can only endure Shakspeare, on the stage, by aid of *spectacle* and *engouement*[26] for one or two popular actors, while Marlowe, Ford, Chapman, and Webster[27] would 'spell ruin.' We have, confessedly, no contemporary drama of literary excellence. We are translators, and adapters, or buffoons, or we appeal to an undramatic and non-literary kind of perverted ethical speculation with 'problem plays,' and esoteric dilemmas about the relations of the sexes. The language of these performances has nothing to do with literature, while dramas of literary merit, like 'Atalanta in Calydon,' or 'Chastelard,'[28] never, of course, see the footlights. Why these things should be thus is a topic on which men might write ingeniously for ever. People go to the theatre to be diverted, to see scenery and dresses; to be in the fashion; to get improper 'problems' placed before their eyes. Poetic drama does not amuse people, and 'Charley's Aunt' is still running![29] We must take things as we find them, or write poetic dramas which people will care to see, an ambitious task of which the present critic feels himself incapable. Mr. Louis Stevenson, like the sturdy moralist he was, did not content himself with grumbling. In alliance with Mr. Henley,[30] he wrote (among other things) 'Beau Austin,' and where is 'Beau Austin?'[31] Why did the literary public, whereof the male portion accepted Mr. Stevenson as a novelist, fail to encourage him as a dramatist? Who can say? It is the age of novels, not of dramas. If Shakspeare or Marlowe had written a novel, probably the Elizabethan public would not have been purchasers.

On the other hand, for good or evil, ours is the age of novels. Scott just lived to welcome and applaud Bulwer Lytton's 'Pelham;' he died just four years too early to applaud and welcome 'Pickwick.' With 'Pickwick' began her Majesty's reign, and how nobly that reign has prospered in the art of fiction everybody knows. The art has had a curious history, a curious intermittent existence. There were English novels, of course, before Richardson's and Fielding's, but not one of them holds its ground, unless we reckon as a novel the masterpieces of Bunyan and De Foe. With Fielding and Richardson the art is full-grown. Time nor custom can stale nor wither the immortal and rejoicing vitality of 'Tom Jones.' I chance to have been reading, simultaneously, 'Tom Jones' and 'Jane Eyre.' The elder work, earlier by a century exactly, seems to me far the more modern, if by more modern we mean the more full of actual character and breathing life and dialogue, which might be spoken today. As much may, perhaps, be said for Smollett, Richardson, Goldsmith, and Sterne. There is something universal, personal, and friendly in their characters, in the life which they depict. The salt has not lost its savour, as the salt of most novels is apt to do. But these great masters, oddly enough, left no schools, or the scholars are forgotten.

The play was still a rival of the novel and poetry after Burns and Cowper, Scott (by his poems) and Wordsworth, kept the novel in a subordinate place. People spoke of it with contempt, as the study of milliners and ladies' maids, in spite of Godwin and Mrs. Radcliffe. Then came 'Waverley,' and since 1814 the novel has been infinitely the most popular, almost the only popular form of English literature. It is not only that Scott raised up imitators. Galt and Lockhart had been 'ettling at'[32] Scotch novels before or contemporary with 'Waverley' (1814). Miss Austen, quite uninfluenced by Sir Walter, was his young contemporary. A form, a *genre* of literature, was discovered, which the British public, still not wholly demoralised by newspapers, could enjoy. Sir Walter (as has been said) lived to welcome Bulwer Lytton, and 'Pickwick' appeared but four years after his death. Since then the flood of novels has never ceased. We have always had either great masters, Dickens, Thackeray, George Eliot, Charlotte Brontë, or writers of a high though secondary rank, Charles Reade, Anthony Trollope; or a great body of entertaining and ingenious novelists, whom it is too early to call great masters, as at this moment. The elders of the Victorian age are, perhaps, more or less obscured today, partly by the inevitable reaction, partly by the temporary qualities of 'up-to-dateness,' which helped to obtain their contemporary vogue.

The defects of Dickens, like the defects of Scott, were perfectly visible to the critics of their own generation. An old *Blackwood* article, 'A Remonstrance with Boz,'[33] says just what we think now. The *Saturday Review* seems to have kept a critic to represent, forty years ago, the modern set of objections to Dickens.[34] His caricature, his mannerisms, his inexpensive pathos (in which, at all events, he firmly believed), his *clichés*, or stereotyped effects, his blank verse – it is not today for the first time that these have been discovered and blamed. Like other men, Dickens was worked too hard. Fiction is not a profession like another. Dickens and many of his successors have treated it like a profession, to the diminution of their own glory. The temporary, the 'topical,' the didactic, make up too much of his work. Taste has changed, and people are fastidious as to the books of the past who can eagerly swallow the most vulgar fustian in some of the mysteriously popular novelists of the present.

Under these disadvantages, the great name of Dickens labours, and Thackeray is blamed for preaching too much, as he undeniably does. He wrote only of the society in which he lived; he did not make amateur dives into the social strata of which he was not a born denizen. Limited he was, but within his limitations, and granting his aims, which is only justice, he reached a perfection only rivalled by that of Fielding. 'Vanity Fair,' 'Esmond,' 'Barry Lyndon,' will, to all appearance, hold their own with the masterpieces of the eighteenth century. Perhaps we can hardly say so much of any other Victorian novelist. The versatility of Bulwer Lytton, the veracity of Trollope, the abundant vigour of Charles Reade and Charles

Kingsley, do not seem to have that touch of immortality which makes eternal the great novelists of the eighteenth century, with Scott, Miss Austen, and Thackeray. About George Eliot and Charlotte Brontë one hesitates, excellent, and original, and strong as they are. Perhaps they have seen their best times of appreciation, whereas one feels a subjective, and of course fallible certainty, that 'Esmond' must live as long as literature lasts. In any case, put it at the lowest, the roll call of the dead Victorian novelists is illustrious and inspiring, and matter for gratitude.

Of the living, it is all but impossible to speak, and of the latest dead, Mr. Stevenson, we can only say here that he was worthy to come after Thackeray and Sir Walter; a finished writer like the former, a born story-teller and romanticist like the latter. But for the living also we may be grateful. So abundant is their variety, so healthy, on the whole, is their energy, and so obviously evanescent is the bombast of contemporary A, the verbiage of contemporary B, the absurdity of ideas in a noisy few, the dilettante squalor of another regiment. We have still, thank heaven, novelists of humour, sympathy, delicacy, observation, and novelists who can tell a plain tale of adventure and event, and novelists who can make history live again. A reviewer might like to praise his favourites among contemporaries (their name, happily, is Legion[35]), or to make game of his *bêtes noires*[36] (like Sir Richard Strachan, one is 'longing to be at them'[37]), but individual taste and predilection, and antipathy, come far too much into the matter for the occasion.

It should have been said, it were unjust not to say it, that though perhaps nobody is writing great verses (great by the standard of Tennyson), many living poets will probably live in a few pieces, their best: and surely the fortunes of Lovelace, Suckling, Hamilton of Bangour, and Graham of Gartmore[38] – the immortality of a song or a sonnet – are not things to be despised. It would be invidious to mention the contemporaries, more numerous than in many other ages – who may look forward to this measure of renown. For the rest, the Victorian age has, in Mr. Ruskin, a literary figure for which we in vain seek a parallel, and the same may be said of the late Mr. Pater. One so popular, the other so esoteric, they are both unique and unprecedented, at whatever rate they may be estimated by posterity.

As to scientific writings in all their varieties, as to philosophy, from Mr. Herbert Spencer to the late Mr. Green,[39] these lofty intellectual exercises are not precisely literature, and it is not as a master of style that the great Darwin[40] claims our admiration. When science, popular science, boils over into fiction, we have only to regret the circumstance, and turn to something more genuine. But the decent limitations which forbid us to discuss the living and working, in a brief survey of the literature of sixty years, make it impossible to say much about science out of place, preaching out of season, and the very English tendency to pervert fiction into tracts and disquisitions. Our race has had the love of sermons in its blood ever since the

Reformation. The sermons of new novelists, as a rule, would have led their authors, of old, to the block or the stake, but they are sermons for all that, and their number is not the most creditable feature in the later Victorian literature. They are proof at once of deficient humour, and of the want of historical perspective, which makes the moment hide the great Shakspeare of time. Thus blinded some critics clamour for the photographic representation of the ordinary and commonplace, a kind of 'realism' which is inevitably doomed to the briefest conceivable existence.

'Notes on Fiction'
Longman's Magazine 17:100
(February 1891), pp. 453–8

Dr. Johnson defines the novel as a tale 'usually of love' and there is no doubt that most novels since the Greek romances, have been very full of this passion. In his *English Novel during the Time of Shakespeare*, M. Jusserand[1] gives some statistics as to the preponderance of fiction in modern English literature. In 1885 there were more books of theology than novels, but novels took the first place in 1887, 1888, 1889. In the last year, 1,040 novels were published. This gives us, at the very least, the stories of 2,080 human hearts; but it would be more fair to multiply the number of novels by nine, allowing for four 'first lovers' in each, the villain (generally attached to the heroine), and four unsuccessful adorers, male or female. Thus the year 1889 may have provided about 8,000 studies of the passion of love, as it is fair to make allowance for novels in which treasure, or murder, or theology was the main interest. Thus it would seem as if what is called the 'love-interest' were the main attraction of romance, and yet there seems reason to doubt whether this is not a mere statistical illusion. It is frequently said, by novelists themselves, that what the great majority of their readers like is a love story; that their success is assured if they can only make their love scenes attractive. Of course this is a strain on the energies of the most vigorous novelist. A man can only write really well out of his own experience. Now novelists, as Mr. James Payn has assured an anxious world, 'live like other men, only more purely.'[2] It is, therefore, clear that their experience must be limited, and that when they have made copy out of their own emotions they must draw on their imagination. We see how Sir Walter Scott, the most reticent of men where his own heart was concerned, inspired himself, as to his heroines, by recollections of that one lady who broke his heart, after which, as he says, it was 'handsomely mended.' She is the heroine of *The Lay of the Last Minstrel*, of *Old Mortality* and of *Redgauntlet* at least, while I fancy that Scott's own unhappy love inspires Rebecca of York in *Ivanhoe*. Most of his other love affairs are children of fancy, and are unessential, and more or less conventional. They are part of the mere 'business' of the novelist, and, except in *The Bride of Lammermoor*, where tradition gave the situation, the story would really be almost as well without them. Flora MacIvor is a strong character, but not by reason of her loves, and the same is true about Di Vernon. It is the adventures of Harry Gow, or of Quentin Durward, that hold us, not the affairs of the heart which led these gentlemen into their adventures. Not only does this seem to be true about Scott, but it is true about most of the men who are the masters of English fiction. Character and incident are their materials, not character as dominated by the passion of love. Richardson may be called an exception, but Richardson was almost entirely a woman's author. *Clarissa*, even, can scarcely be called a love story; love were the wrong name for the passion of Lovelace. In Fielding's *Amelia* there is plenty of love, but Fielding, like King Candaules of Lydia, was 'in love with his wife,'[3] and Booth and Amelia are married before the tale begins. Tom Jones is, indeed, in love, like all who read about him, with Sophia; but the heart of Thomas was hospitable, and his adventures have many another interest besides that of pure affection.

Turning to the late masters, the slight part which love has in the success of Dickens need scarcely be insisted on. There is always a love affair, or more than one, but, except perhaps in the case of Dora,[4] the love affair is not what we remember best, is never what we read Dickens for. Humour and pathos, caricature, mystery, incident – all these, and not love, are his strong points. In the case of Thackeray, the 'love-interest' is infinitely stronger, the passion being usually thwarted and often unhappy, as in Emmy Osborne, Dobbin, Pen, Clive, Henry Esmond, Philip, and so on. Though we may remember best, and enjoy Colonel Newcome and Captain Costigan, the swain Foker (himself deserted and unfortunate), Major Pendennis, and a score of others, still the unhappy passions of Thackeray's heroes are so admirably and sympathetically touched that, in this respect, he excels both Dickens, Scott, and Fielding, and his novels really are tales of love. But if we turn to modern times and Mr. Stevenson, it is, of course, no such matter. People say that Mr. Stevenson has written 'no regular novel;' and he has not; that is to say, none in which love is the chief consideration. The Master of Ballantrae would have been nearly, if not quite, as complete, even without his gallantries with his brother's wife. On the other side, love must still be lord of all with Mr. Trollope. Mr. Black[5] is divided between love, salmon, scenery, and yachting, but we remember the scenery, the yachting, and the salmon best. Mr. George Meredith has excelled in love scenes, as in the charming passages of *Richard Feverel*, or the unhappy love of Dahlia;[6] but, even with him, human character in general and at large much preponderates. It is needless to say that, among all the merits of both the Kingsleys,[7] their love passages are among the least memorable. In short, 'Love is a great Master,' as Malory[8] says and illustrates nobly in his Lancelot and Guinevere; but the great masters in fiction have not been among his chief adepts. Our race cannot be for ever dallying with Amaryllis in the shade, or with the tresses of Neæra's hair.[9] The great Northern genius produced one perfect scene of passion in the 'Volsunga Saga,' the loves of Brynhild and Sigurd,[10] but the sagas in general prefer litigation to love; first fighting, then lawsuits are their interest, then ghosts and magic. Love bends the story to his will; he has his fatal stroke in the battle; but the scalds do not linger over scenes of love, nor over the exhibition of human character as influenced by love.

This case can be made out well enough, as far as the men novelists of England are concerned; the women, on the other hand, have usually excelled just where men have been less conspicuously successful. Thus, Miss Broughton,[11] more than any living novelist in England, probably, can make the reader distinctly and decidedly feel that her characters are many fathoms deep in love, and can even make us understand why they should be so. Anybody might, nay, everybody must fall in love with her Elizabeth in *Alas*, or sympathise with the people who do. The passion of her Joan is as true in its way as that of Miss Austen's Ann Elliot. Perhaps love is not the *forte* of Miss Braddon,[12] who powerfully interests her male readers in Murder, and her lady students in Millinery. Charlotte Brontë, again, can make her people very thoroughly in love: there is no mistake about Jane Eyre and Lucy Snow. But who remembers the amours in the novels of Mr. Wilkie Collins? Charles Reade and Mr. Besant have here more of the feminine talent: their people are in love, no mistake about it; and Beatrice, in Mr. Haggard's novel of that name, leaves no room for doubt about her sentiments. Yet there is a great mass of English fiction, and of the best fiction, in which the passion is little more moving to the readers than an algebraical formula. A is in love (X) with B, who is – £ s. d.[13] Hence certain actions and adventures on the part of A and B and others. But it is the adventures and actions consequent on the alleged, but not felt or obvious, presence of X that agitate the reader's mind, not X itself. He may be told by the author that X is carried to the *nth*. We accept his statement as part of the formula, but he never makes us feel it. Who, for example, cares for X in the works of Captain Hawley Smart?[14] It is not love, but the feats of horsemanship prompted by X, the bets, and intrigues, and nobbling of horses, that carry us on with them. This is, perhaps, rather an extreme example of the presence of love in novels as a mere formula. But, if the reader will abandon his mind to the consideration of this topic, he will probably discover that love, as a passion, is nearly as rare in fiction as, shall we say, in fact? He may discover that the greatest artists have in this region either comparatively failed or have been comparatively indifferent. We are speaking about English fiction, of course; the French have been more successful in touching this passion. We have no Manon

Lescaut in English, and M. Bourget and M. Maupassant[15] are here the masters of most English novelists. They are infinitely more sentimental, and so is M. Zola, in *Un Page d'Amour*, but M. Daudet is less of an amorist, and the 'love-interest' is rarely, or never, the essential interest of his novels, with the exception of *Sappho* and its squalid sentiment.

The great difficulty in writing of the passion in a novel is, of course, to make it seem *real*. This is a difficulty which probably must be the more felt by an author as he approaches the age when, according to Rochefoucauld, he should never talk as if love were an affair with which he could have any concern.[16] Thus Thackeray, in *Philip*, talks as if he took merely a posthumous interest in the affection. A man's real interest, much more than a woman's, is apt to betake itself in other directions, and an elderly novelist must write about the heart of youth with little more enthusiasm than about the tarts and toffee of boyhood. But this difficulty of making the matter in hand seem *real* of course attends the novelist in all his adventures. How is it done? What is the unnamed gift by which a person of no style or culture can tell a story, can make us believe as we read, while another author, full of all accomplishments, puts us off with mere descriptions in place of substantial men, women, and things? The novelist, of course, must have *conviction*; must convince himself first, as children do when they play at being pirates, hunters, knights of old, explorers, and so forth. The novelist must never, in this sense, put away childish things. As a very small boy, the present essayist could never 'play at horses,' for example, from a reasoned certainty that he was *not* a horse, and that his team, if he drove, were only other small boys and girls. Any one who remembers similar lack of illusions may as well give up the idea of writing novels. He may have observation; he will scarcely have sympathy with the puppets of his fancy; he may write like an angel, he will never persuade anybody to believe his narrative. It seems that a novelist sometimes may possess the power of carrying conviction, and sometimes may lack it. For example, M. Daudet has it to some extent in *Le Nabab*. In *Jack* he lacks it, to my mind, altogether. One sees much too plainly how Jack was made. One sees memories, or seems to see them, of *David Copperfield*.The story reads as if the author had said: 'I will try those situations in French, with a different and more sentimental bias.' The school where Jack is sent is not at all like Dotheboys Hall[17] (well, after all, it is a good deal like a French Dotheboys Hall), and the master, the sham poet, is not Mr. Murdstone,[18] but he reminds one of Mr. Murdstone. One has, throughout, an impression that everything has been carefully preconceived, studied, described, crammed for – that it is not spontaneous. I know, of course, that there was a real Jack, with whom M. Daudet was acquainted, and it is not impossible that he may never have read *David Copperfield*. But the impression remains; we know that we are to be melted and wrung with pity; we see the mechanism too clearly, we know how it is all done, we catch glimpses of the author with his note-book and in his study. The consequence is that much less artistic work is often much more true work of art. An artist who did not like a picture was asked what it wanted. 'It wants *that*' said he, snapping his finger on his thumb. We can hardly get nearer to what we wish to express. 'Jack' wants *that*! or we feel as if it wanted it. But, again, this may be partly because M. Daudet has told the world how he wrote his novels; he has taken them behind the scenes. This is really a dangerous frankness. The public likes such confessions, and, perhaps, when once it has read them, forgets them. A famous and very successful recent novel failed with a certain class of readers because, by the accident of circumstances, they felt as if they had been behind the scenes, as if they knew it all beforehand, and were reading a thrice-told tale. It is certainly rash in authors to take readers into their confidence, to show them the materials out of which their work was made, and the processes of the making. The result will seem to them a mosaic, not a picture, or perhaps it will beguile them no more than a study in Berlin wools.[19] But such examples are unusual. Generally the want of conviction in the reader comes of want of conviction in the author. He must believe before he can make us believe; and this is a special gift, possessed by many people who are nothing less than literary – by the boatman or shepherd who tells you a legend – and which is wanting wholly in the deliberate and accomplished author. It is, perhaps, most frequently absent in the love affairs of novels, and that is why the greatest English novelists live by anything rather than their love stories. Here, as usual, Shakespeare is supreme, and his lovers love with all their hearts and souls.

'Behind the Novelist's Scenes', *Illustrated London News* 101:2778

(16 July 1892), p. 83

In his new novel, 'The Wrecker,' Mr. Stevenson[1] speaks of the pleasure which children take in breaking their toys. They want 'to see how it is done,' they explore the sawdust with which the doll is stuffed, and the sand which makes the toy cobbler work, and they unscrew the wheels of their watches. This is the scientific instinct in an early form. Later, the same kind of curiosity inspires men to pry into the circulation of the blood and the mechanism of the brain. These organs and fluids work on, whether we know how it is done or not. In another guise, this painfully inquiring spirit urges people to ask how novels are 'done,' and Mr. Stevenson very good-naturedly, rather than very wisely, tells them in his 'epilude,' as a Scotch poet amusingly called it.[2] 'If 'prelude,' why not 'epilude'?' he asked himself. The reason was not obvious to him. Nor is the reason for Mr. Stevenson's explanation very obvious. He and Mr. Lloyd Osbourne[3] thought of a wreck peopled by the wrong crew – that was the primitive cell or germ of the narrative. Then they worked in descriptions of life and manners drawn from experiences in the Forest of Fontainebleau, in Edinburgh, in the isles of the Pacific, in San Francisco, in Australia. Well, to be told all this may please the curious, but I confess to feeling uncomfortable and 'disilluded' when I am thus taken behind the scenes. The author breaks up his own toy, and shows us the strings and the sand. It is an excellent toy, though I keep wishing that so much of the sand had not been shed on board of the Flying Scud, or rather that it had not been shed in that particular way. 'Mine is a beastly story,' says Mr. Carthew,[4] and 'beastly' it is. The murder of unresisting men, merely because their evidence would be inconvenient, is a crime for which one has no sympathy and can even make no excuse. A novelist might have arranged for a fair fight, as he was inevitably compelled to kill people. If he had not killed them, some may urge, there would have been no story and no mystery. But they might have died, as far as one can see, with arms in their hands. They might have made an attack on the specie of the castaways, who might have defended it with success. They would still be homicides and the justifiable nature of their deeds would have been difficult or impossible to prove, so we would have had our mystery, as at present. Probably the difficulty here was that the scene would have looked like a repetition of a scene in 'Treasure Island.'[5] Doubtless, there were other difficulties. We may also say that, after the fighting in the cabin, which was unforeseen, Carthew and his men, being armed, could have seized the ship, worked her out of the lagoon, and adroitly marooned the other crew in various islets, finally 'piling up' their vessel on a convenient isle, where they could wait to be taken off under false names. There would thus be the same mystery, which is essential to a 'police novel,' without a set of cold-blooded murders. The Carthewsians would, as far as one can see, have been at least as safe from detection as in the present case, and nobody, except the sanguinary Irishman, Mac, would have been guilty of murder. A man like Carthew simply could not have lived with that sin on his soul: he must have died of drink, or committed suicide, or given himself up to justice. He could not have taken it lightly, at Barbizon, or in Persia. This is the way in which it strikes one: one does not believe that Dodd and Urquart could have got over the horror and condoned it, as they did. Possibly what looks like an error in structure is part of a philosophy of life. Mr. Stevenson and Mr. Osbourne may have wished to show the soul of good in things evil, as in the scoundrelly lawyer, and the soul of evil in things good, as in Carthew.

However, this is a digression. The main question is: Should a novelist break up his own toy, and take us behind his own scenes? The sense of reality, the illusion, is difficult enough to preserve without deliberately destroying it. M. Daudet has done his best to destroy the reality of his own novels by telling us in his memoirs how it was done, what real persons and events suggested Numa Roumestan and Jack[6] and the other characters of his tales. On the face of them, they were bits of reporter's work, carried to the highest power; but M. Daudet, who did not manage to hide the strings, openly displays his *ficelles*.[7] The difficulty of *not* seeing the strings must always be felt by contemporary readers, who are more or less acquainted with the novelist's life and environment. To Oxford readers the strings in 'Robert Elsmere'[8] were inevitably very manifest. Mr. Stevenson's essays show some of his strings, even to those who are not fortunate enough to be more familiar with his adventures. Long ago, Hogg and many others could recognise fragments of Scott's conversation in the Waverley Novels. Laidlaw and others had hunted with him, on the hills above Loch Skene, the goat of 'The Black Dwarf.' Mr. Skene of Rubislaw had suggested the Jews in 'Ivanhoe.' The original death of Brian the Templar had occurred, not in the lists at Templestowe, but in the Parliament House of Edinburgh. The talk about 'long' and 'short' sheep was drawn from a well-remembered conversation, and so with many other incidents. All novels are necessarily patchwork, composed by imagination working on the treasures of memory. That novel is, so far, the best in which this work is least obvious. Dickens did not tell us, in his lifetime, how much of 'David Copperfield' was autobiographical. Had he done so, in a preface or an epilogue, he would, so far, have been showing us the seamy side of the novel, the loose, formless threads; he would have been taking us behind the scenes, and displaying Micawber without that jewel, his eyeglass, and his other graces. One's pleasure in fiction is always hurt when one recognises blocks of raw fact in the material. Of course, an author who is constantly being accused of plagiarism is, in a way, compelled to give his 'sources,' as the learned have it – to quote his authorities. These remarks are, after all, perhaps too individual; many readers may actually enjoy seeing the toy taken to pieces, may be pleased to watch the disintegration of the puppets. It is an odd taste, but it may be a taste which is prevalent. We are too curious; we have too much of the scientific spirit even in our pleasures. Yet, even to the unscientifically minded, how much pleasure and breathless curiosity there is in 'The Wrecker'!

‘The Mystery of Style’, *Illustrated London News* 102:2809

(18 February 1893), p. 216

In *Atalanta*, which one naturally buys for the sake of ‘David Balfour,’[1] there is an article by Mr. Watson on ‘The Mystery of Style.’ A mystery indeed it is, and a mystery Mr. Watson leaves it. What in the world do we mean by ‘style’? What is the Greek for style? What is the Latin for it? Had the ancients any word, or set of words, to express this idea, about which so much is written? We set up an unknown god called style, which we ignorantly worship. If one had to define style, one would probably define it as the best manner in which a thing can be done. There is style in fencing, style in golf, style in cricket: we know it when we see it. Grace combined with economy of effort goes far to make up style in these pastimes. There is a best way of attaining the ends aimed at, and that best way is natural to some people, not to others. Their movements are free, fluent, swift, classical, without eccentricity or stiffness, or over-exertion or flourish. Anyone who has seen Mr. Edward Lyttelton bat or Mr. Egerton Castle fence, or Ayton[2] drive a ball at golf, has seen style. But nobody, perhaps, will maintain that the best style is always productive of the most valuable results. No man chooses Dr. Grace[3] as a model of style at cricket, but it is he who gets the runs; and at other sports we find that style is by no means everything – that it does not make up for the want of a good eye and strong muscles; that these can do better without style than style can do without them. Thus, a person singularly gifted may do a thing not in the best way, yet better than it is done by others whose way is that of perfection.

Let us try the analogy in literature. Mr. Watson says, and many people say, that style is ‘the great antiseptic in literature, the most powerful preservative against decay.’ By ‘style’ he means ‘a peculiarly distinguished air and carriage,' wherein is recognised 'serenity based on strength.' This is all very interesting, but one doubts whether many authors have not escaped decay without possessing 'style,' thus understood. One might select Thucydides, Aristotle, and Tacitus as writers who, in Mr. Watson's formula, have 'a style,' but not style with a large S. The style of Thucydides is often akin to that of Mrs. Gamp.[4] The style of Tacitus not 'serene': he is always jerking in an epigram. As for the style of Aristotle, to use one of Tacitus's epigrams, it is conspicuous by its absence. Yet all these authors are full of vitality, by dint of their strength, spirit, and wisdom. These are not the predominant qualities of Virgil, who does live by virtue of that undefinable style, by his lines and half-lines, which breathe in music unrivalled and unapproached all the desire and all the melancholy of human kind. He lives by his style, the others live in spite of theirs. Of course, Mr. Watson's proposition cannot be converted: he does not say that, because all which has style lives, all which lives has style, in his sense of the word. What that sense may be it is hard to understand. The Romans had more, he thinks, of the grand style than the Greeks. He cannot intend this to apply to their art: Roman art is only Graeco-Roman – an imitation, a scholar's work; and the same is true of their poetry and prose, and drama and religion. They did things on a bigger scale; they were better lawyers, fighting men, engineers, but to say that they were a people in a better style than the Greeks is to confess a taste for the ponderous. The Germans fall under Mr. Watson's censure as having no style, or 'if they have, it is a demmed style,' as Mr. Mantalini[5] would have said. But, surely, art apart, our Teutonic kin are in rather a grand style as human beings. The Reformation was a large piece of work: so is, and so was, their Empire. When it comes to books, one must know German better than I do before offering an opinion. But as to Burns not having style, being indifferently well acquainted with *his* language, I cannot agree with Mr. Watson. It is an admirable Scotch style – the right word always in the right place. On the other hand, the style of the Waverley Novels, except in Scotch and in dramatic dialogue, is, frankly, an unconsidered thing. Yet the novels do not seem to need this 'antiseptic.' They have vitality enough to do without it. Mr. Watson praises Mr. Ruskin's style. Is it serene? Is it 'aristocratic'? Is it restrained? *Ma foi*! I doubt if that Corinthian eloquence will last long: if that rhetoric is an antiseptic; if that matter is stated in the best and simplest manner. So, too, of Milton, 'admittedly and indisputably our highest summit in style.' Milton's style is 'an army with banners,'[6] always marching in a stately progress, adorned, as I think Mr. Lowell says, with the spoils of all antiquity, with trophies from ancient song and old civilisations. It is rich, musical, studied, ornate, always advancing to a triumph, but who can put it above Shakspere's style, which is so flexible, so sweet, so full of change, so naturally adapted to each vicissitude, so prompt to rise, to fall, to glide, to murmur, to thunder, to ring like the clarion, to sigh like the lute, and yet is always so unstudied, so natural an expression of each moment's moods? Milton is not only an artist, but he knows it, and insists that you shall know it, with an eagerness most un-Virgilian, with a conscious insistence. You know whence he mined his gold, where he conquered his trophies, from what subject poets he levied his array; but you think of none of these things in reading Homer or in reading Shakspere. To prefer Milton is like preferring the Romans – an admirable poet, an extraordinary people, but neither in style nor in anything else the 'roof and crown of things.'[7] They made great efforts, and you are conscious of their exertions; you even see, to some extent, as in Gibbon, how the thing is done. But how the thing was done by Shakspere and by the Greeks you cannot by searching find out: with them, not with Milton, is the real mystery of style.

‘The Supernatural in Fiction’, *Adventures Among Books*

(London: Longmans, Green and Co., 1905)

It is a truism that the supernatural in fiction should, as a general rule, be left in the vague. In the creepiest tale I ever read, the horror lay in this – *there was no ghost!* You may describe a ghost with all the most hideous features that fancy can suggest – saucer eyes, red staring hair, a forked tail, and what you please – but the reader only laughs. It is wiser to make as if you were going to describe the spectre, and then break off, exclaiming, ‘But no! No pen can describe, no memory, thank Heaven, can recall, the horror of that hour!’ So writers, as a rule, prefer to leave their terror (usually styled ‘The Thing’) entirely in the dark, and to the frightened fancy of the student. Thus, on the whole, the treatment of the supernaturally terrible in fiction is achieved in two ways, either by actual description, or by adroit suggestion, the author saying, like cabmen, ‘I leave it to yourself, sir.’[1] There are dangers in both methods; the description, if attempted, is usually over-done and incredible: the suggestion is apt to prepare us too anxiously for something that never becomes real, and to leave us disappointed.

Examples of both methods may be selected from poetry and prose. The examples in verse are rare enough; the first and best that occurs in the way of suggestion is, of course, the mysterious lady in ‘Christabel.’

> ‘she was most beautiful to see,
> Like a lady of a far *countrée*.’[2]

Who was she? What did she want? Whence did she come? What was the horror she revealed to the night in the bower of Christabel?

[…]

What was it – the 'sight to dream of, not to tell'? Coleridge never did tell, and, though he and Mr. Gilman[3] said he knew, Wordsworth thought he did not know. He raised a spirit that he had not the spell to lay. In the Paradise of Poets has he discovered the secret? We only know that the mischief, whatever it may have been, was wrought. […]

If Coleridge knew, why did he never tell? And yet he maintains that 'in the very first conception of the tale, I had the whole present to my mind, with the wholeness no less than with the liveliness of a vision,'[4] and he expected to finish the three remaining parts within the year. The year was 1816, the poem was begun in 1797, and finished, as far as it goes, in 1800. If Coleridge ever knew what he meant, he had time to forget. The chances are that his indolence, or his forgetfulness, was the making of 'Christabel,' which remains a masterpiece of supernatural suggestion.

For description it suffices to read the 'Ancient Mariner.' These marvels, truly, are *speciosa miracula*[5] and, unlike Southey, we believe as we read. 'You have selected a passage fertile in unmeaning miracles,' Lamb wrote to Southey (1798), 'but have passed by fifty passages as miraculous as the miracles they celebrate.'[6] Lamb appears to have been almost alone in appreciating this masterpiece of supernatural description. Coleridge himself shrank from his own wonders, and wanted to call the piece 'A Poet's Reverie.' 'It is as bad as Bottom the weaver's declaration that he is not a lion, but only the scenical representation of a lion. What new idea is gained by this title but one subversive of all credit – which the tale should force upon us – of its truth?'[7] Lamb himself was forced, by the temper of the time, to declare that he 'disliked all the miraculous part of it,'[8] as if it were not *all* miraculous! Wordsworth wanted the Mariner 'to have a character and a profession,'[9] perhaps would have liked him to be a gardener, or a butler, with 'an excellent character!'[10] In fact, the love of the supernatural was then at so low an ebb that a certain Mr. Marshall 'went to sleep while the "Ancient Mariner" was reading,'[11] and the book was mainly bought by seafaring men, deceived by the title, and supposing that the 'Ancient Mariner' was a nautical treatise.

In verse, then, Coleridge succeeds with the supernatural, both by way of description in detail, and of suggestion. If you wish to see a failure, try the ghost, the moral but not affable ghost, in Wordsworth's 'Laodamia.' It is blasphemy to ask the question, but is the ghost in 'Hamlet' quite a success? Do we not see and hear a little too much of him? Macbeth's airy and viewless dagger is really much more successful by way of suggestion. The stage makes a ghost visible and familiar, and this is one great danger of the supernatural in art. It is apt to insist on being too conspicuous. Did the ghost of Darius, in 'Æschylus', frighten the Athenians? Probably they smiled at the imperial spectre. There is more discretion in Caesar's ghost –

> 'I think it is the weakness of mine eyes
> That shapes this monstrous apparition,'[12]

says Brutus, and he lays no very great stress on the brief visit of the appearance. For want of this discretion, Alexandre Dumas's ghosts, as in 'The Corsican Brothers,' are failures. They make themselves too common and too cheap, like the spectre in Mrs. Oliphant's novel, 'The Wizard's Son.' This, indeed, is the crux of the whole adventure. If you paint your ghost with too heavy a hand, you raise laughter, not fear. If you touch him too lightly, you raise unsatisfied curiosity, not fear. It may be easy to shudder, but it is difficult to teach shuddering.

In prose, a good example of the over vague is Miriam's mysterious visitor – the shadow of the catacombs – in 'Transformation; or The Marble Faun.' Hawthorne should have told us more or less; to be sure his contemporaries knew what he meant, knew who Miriam and the Spectre were. The dweller in the catacombs now powerfully excites curiosity, and when that curiosity is unsatisfied, we feel aggrieved, vexed, and suspect that Hawthorne himself was puzzled, and knew no more than his readers. He has not – as in other tales he has – managed to throw the right atmosphere about this being. He is vague in the wrong way, whereas George Sand, in *Les Dames Vertes*,[13] is vague in the right way. We are left in *Les Dames Vertes* with that kind of curiosity which persons really engaged in the adventure might have felt, not with the irritation of having a secret kept from us, as in 'Transformation.'

In 'Wandering Willie's Tale' (in 'Redgauntlet'), the right atmosphere is found, the right note is struck. All is vividly real, and yet, if you close the book, all melts into a dream again. Scott was almost equally successful with a described horror in 'The Tapestried Chamber.' The idea is the commonplace of haunted houses, the apparition is described as minutely as a burglar might have been; and yet we do not mock, but shudder as we read. Then, on the other side – the side of anticipation – take the scene outside the closed door of the vanished Dr. Jekyll, in Mr. Stevenson's well-known apologue. They are waiting on the threshold of the chamber whence the doctor has disappeared – the chamber tenanted by what? A voice comes from the room. 'Sir,' said Poole, looking Mr. Utterson in the eyes, 'was that my master's voice?'[14]

A friend, a man of affairs, and a person never accused of being fanciful, told me that he read through the book to that point in a lonely Highland chateau, at night, and that he did not think it well to finish the story till next morning, but rushed to bed. So the passage seems 'well-found' and successful by dint of suggestion. On the other side, perhaps, only Scotsmen brought up in country places, familiar from childhood with the terrors of Cameronian myth, and from childhood apt to haunt the lonely churchyards, never stirred since the year of the great Plague choked the soil with the dead, perhaps they only know how much shudder may be found in Mr. Stevenson's 'Thrawn Janet.' The black smouldering heat in the hills and glens that are commonly so fresh, the aspect of the Man, the Tempter of the Brethren, we know them, and we have enough of the old blood in us to be thrilled by that masterpiece of the described supernatural. It may be only a local success, it may not much affect the English reader, but it is of sure appeal to the Lowland Scot. The ancestral Covenanter [15] within us awakens, and is terrified by his ancient fears.

Perhaps it may die out in a positive age – this power of learning to shudder. To us it descends from very long ago, from the far-off forefathers who dreaded the dark, and who, half starved and all untaught, saw spirits everywhere, and scarce discerned waking experience from dreams. When we are all perfect positivist philosophers, when a thousand generations of nurses that never heard of ghosts have educated the thousand and first generation of children, then the supernatural may fade out of fiction. But has it not grown and increased since Wordsworth wanted the 'Ancient Mariner' to have 'a profession and a character,' since Southey called that poem a Dutch piece of work,[16] since Lamb had to pretend to dislike its 'miracles'? Why, as science becomes more cock-sure, have men and women become more and more fond of old follies, and more pleased with the stirring of ancient dread within their veins? As the visible world is measured, mapped, tested, weighed, we seem to hope more and more that a world of invisible romance may not be far from us, or, at least, we care more and more to follow fancy into these airy regions, *et inania regna*.[17] The supernatural has not ceased to tempt romancers, like Alexandre Dumas, usually to their destruction; more rarely, as in Mrs. Oliphant's 'Beleaguered City,' to such success as they do not find in the world of daily occupation. The ordinary shilling tales of 'hypnotism' and mesmerism are vulgar trash enough, and yet I can believe that an impossible romance, if the right man wrote it in the right mood, might still win us from the newspapers, and the stories of shabby love, and cheap remorses, and commonplace failures.

'But it needs Heaven-sent moments for this skill.'[18]

4

SCOTLAND, HISTORY AND BIOGRAPHY

In Lang's work history, biography and Scottishness are deeply connected, and there are strong relationships, too, with his work on folklore, mythology and psychical research. The Celtic Revival of the late nineteenth and early twentieth centuries drew his interest and he considered it both in relation to literature and to his anthropological theories of the origins of peoples and their beliefs. His introduction to Walter Scott's novel *Waverley, Or 'Tis Sixty Years Since* strongly places Scott's work in the language, landscape and traditions of Scotland. It was first published as the introduction to volume 1 of the Border Edition of the *Complete Works of Sir Walter Scott* (London: Macmillan, 1893), pp. lxxxi–cxi. Lang wrote separate introductions for each of the twenty-four volumes of the edition, the last in the year of his death, 1912. There are numerous other published pieces on Scott, including one of the *Letters to Dead Authors* (London: Longmans, Green and Co., 1886), pp. 152–61, and the short *Life of Sir Walter Scott* (New York: Charles Scribner, 1906). *Sir Walter Scott and the Border Minstrelsy* (London: Longmans, Green and Co., 1910) is a long and detailed consideration of the content and authenticity of the ballads in Scott's collection.

The short pieces from Lang's column 'At the Sign of the Ship' selected here show some of the range of Lang's writings on Scotland and the connections that he makes with psychic phenomena as well as his fierce defence of the Scots language and identity. These were first published in *Longman's Magazine* 9:49 (November 1887), pp. 107–9, *Longman's Magazine* 28:165 (July 1896), pp. 320–2 and *Longman's Magazine* 28:166 (August 1896), pp. 416–22. His detailed consideration of the question of the Celt, 'The Celtic Renascence', first appeared in *Blackwood's Edinburgh Magazine* 161:976 (February 1897) pp. 181–91 and he returns to it in the introduction to *A Study in Nationality* (London: Chapman and Hall, 1911), pp. iii–xx. The author of the book, John Vyrnwy Morgan (1860–1925), was a Welsh Congregationalist minister. He had published a number of books on Welsh history and theology before *A Study in Nationality* and went on to produce several more, including *The Philosophy of Welsh History* (London: John Lane, 1914), *The Church in Wales in the Light of History* (London: Chapman & Hall, 1918) and *The Welsh Mind in Evolution* (London: H. R. Allenson, 1925). Morgan was not in favour of Home Rule (in Ireland or in Wales) but believed Wales had prospered in the union in a way that would not have been possible if it had remained independent. He also thought that equality and a distinct identity within the union were important, and he argued for a Welsh Office and a Minister for Welsh affairs. Although these views are very like those of Lang on Scotland, it is not known how Lang came to write the introduction or whether the two men knew one another. Lang wrote many prefaces and introductions simply because he was asked by the author or publisher. The introduction is very precisely dated '29th October 1911' and, given the speed at which Lang wrote, it is possible that he produced it on that day. No correspondence between Lang and the author has been located.

Lang's biographies are of figures in Scottish history: John Knox, Mary Queen of Scots, Prince Charles Edward Stuart, or those closely connected, such as John Gibson Lockhart who was Scott's biographer (*The Life and Letters of John Gibson Lockhart*, 2 vols, London: John C. Nimmo, 1897). He sets out some of his principles in the writing of biography in 'At the Sign of the Ship' (first published in *Longman's Magazine* 28:163, May 1896, pp. 101–5).

In all his historical and biographical work, as well as on psychical research and anthropology, Lang is insistent on the matters of evidence and accuracy, frequently taking issue with other scholars on these points. 'History As She Ought To Be Wrote' was first published in *Blackwood's Edinburgh Magazine* 1006:166 (August 1899), pp. 266–74. One of Lang's principal adversaries in his historical work was J. A. Froude. Froude's books were popular but Lang regarded him as inaccurate in matters of fact and argued with him on a number of topics, including Mary, Queen of Scots. Lang published a good deal of work on her. He begins with the historical mystery of the 'Casket Letters', in *Longman's Magazine* 21:123 (January 1893), pp. 320–8 and returns to it again in *The Pilot* (28 July 1900), and writes at length on the same topic in *The Mystery of Mary Stuart* (London: Longmans, Green and Co.,1901), where he admits to having changed his position since his first article. His piece 'New Light on Mary Queen of Scots' was first published in *Blackwood's Magazine* 182:1001 (July 1907), pp. 7–27 and Lang was also responsible for the entry on the Casket Letters in the eleventh edition of the *Encyclopaedia Britannica* (1910). Mary is the main subject of volume 2 of Lang's *A History of Scotland* (Edinburgh: William Blackwood and Sons, 1902) and his *A Short History of Scotland* (Edinburgh: William Blackwood and Sons, 1911). He also wrote an article, 'Portraits and Jewels of Mary Stuart' in the *Scottish Historical Review* 3:10 (January 1906), pp. 129–56.

The other principal subject of his historical and biographical work is Joan of Arc, on whom he wrote frequently, including an illustrated book for children, *The Story of Joan of Arc* (London: T. C and E. C. Jack, 1906). The article selected here, 'M. Anatole France on Jeanne d'Arc' (*Scottish Historical Review* 5:2 (1908), pp. 41–9) again shows his combative style in argument and his attention to matters of evidence. The extracts from his book *The Maid of France: Being the Story of the Life and Death of Jeanne d'Arc* (London: Longmans, 1908) (Preface, pp. v–xiii and Introduction, pp. 10–15), like the biographies of Mary, Queen of Scots and Charles Edward Stuart, further examine the place of myth in history as well as illustrating his interest in psychical phenomena and the question of their real existence and effects.

'The Celtic Renascence', *Blackwood's Edinburgh Magazine* 161: 976

(February 1897), pp. 181–91

What is called 'the Celtic Movement,' in recent literature, is, no doubt, part of the general agitation in Celtdom.[1] But the form, and aims, and ideas of the 'Celtic Renascence' come from the influence of two men – M. Renan, who may be called the Moses of the proceedings, and Mr Matthew Arnold, who was the eloquent Aaron. We shall briefly examine their part, mainly prophetic, before criticising the conquering legions who now march under Mr William Sharp, Miss Fiona Macleod[2] (who may be aptly likened to the inspired Miriam), Professor Geddes,[3] and other leaders, through the Promised Land of New Celtic Literature.[4]

Monsieur Renan was the original conductor of the march. After Macpherson's 'Ossian' took its present lowly place in critical opinion,[5] after Scott's Highlanders made their final charge –

> 'And cast the useless targe aside,
> And with both hands the claymore plied'[6]

Celtic studies were mainly left to Celtic scholars in Ireland, England, France, Germany, and Wales. But Monsieur Renan, a Breton and a scholar, was also a *vulgarisateur*, a populariser of many things. In his 'Essais de Morale et de Critique' (1859) he republished (the piece has recently been translated by Mr Hutchison)[7] his 'La Poésie des Races Celtiques,' also a study of 'The Poetry of the Exhibition.' In the latter work he blamed those who 'limit their sympathies to forms of the past'; in the former he dwelt on the Poetic Past of the Celts. They had a great, or at all events a copious, literature. M. Renan praised Owen Jones's collection, the 'Myvyrian Archaeology,' and the delightful 'Mabinogion' translated by Lady Charlotte Guest.[8] He expatiated on the secular distressfulness of the Gael and Cymry[9]: *de la vient sa tristesse*.[10] Infinite delicacy, a thirst for the ideal not to be quenched by whisky, – these are other Celtic qualities. 'Call not their taste for intoxication a gross indulgence; never was a more sober people!' The Celt, being ideal, must get drunk: it is part of the pleasant unconscious poetry of his nature, as Harold Skimpole says;[11] whereas your beery Teuton – German, Scotch, or English – is a mere sensual lout. The Bretons sought in hydromel[12] what St Brandan and Peredur[13] pursued in their own manner, the vision of the world invisible. *We* 'drink for drinkee,' *they* 'drink for drunkee,' as the negro said.[14]

In this comparative psychology of liquor we may, perhaps, detect a slight national bias. The Celtic genius, on the whole, is neither glad nor sad –'*ni triste, ni gaie*.' There is in the Celt no Teutonic *enivrement de carnage*,[15] as in the Norse or German sagas, or the works of Mr Haggard, – which opinion of M. Renan's we conceive to be incorrect. The Celtic blood is responsible for Jeanne d'Arc (of whose Celtic origin nothing can even be conjectured). 'Without knowing it, she was more Celtic than Christian.'[16] This is a very fair specimen of Neo-Celtic assumption. It is based on the Fairies of Domremy:[17] now fairies are not specially Celtic, and Jeanne professed her entire disbelief in them at her trial. 'She was prophesied of by Merlin'; but, contrary to the orthodox opinion of the contemporary clergy, before the Council of Constance, Jeanne boldly declared that of Merlin she had the poorest opinion. 'She did not recognise Pope or Church,'– though she appealed to the Pope and the Council of Basel! In a note M. Renan moderates these Celtic opinions, later exaggerated by Henri Martin.[18] Still, we already perceive the Celtic tendency to claim whatever is excellent in a certain way as 'Celtic,' even if the facts are wrong, and the so-called Celt, La Pucelle,[19] is a native of the more or less originally Teutonic Marches. For the rest, M. Renan justly asserts for his Celts delicacy of fancy, love of the pre-Christian supernatural, and high antiquity of tradition, all these blending into the great Arthurian cycle of romance.

Mr Arnold followed, and expanded, M. Renan's ideas in his 'Lectures on the Study of Celtic Literature' (1867). With much that Mr Arnold said every lover of literature, and of a life not wholly 'practical,' will agree. His information, though he had not the Celtic tongues, was wider than the rather scanty lore which M. Renan displayed. But he argued in the usual way. He quoted Taliesin's[20] lines on his own metamorphoses, as essentially Celtic, and did not observe the very similar and equally poetical passage in the 'Kalewala,' the 'epic poem' (so called) of the Finns. Now Finns are not Celts, yet the features of delicacy, love of nature, love of the supernatural and of magic, and the tone of defeated melancholy, which charm us in Finnish old popular poetry, are precisely the things which charm us in the poetry of the Celt. These beauties come of the loneliness, the contact with nature, the fond dwelling on the past, the living in fantasy, which circumstances have forced on both Celts and Finns. They are rather the result of environment and of history than of race, they being 'Aryans' like the rest us, and the Finns being Ugrians.[21] Into the problematic lore about the distinctive shapes of the Celtic and Teutonic skulls we must decline to go; it is quite enough talk of 'Celtic, Teutonic, Greek *genius*,' as of a thing determined by *race*. The Celtic genius is emotional, Mr Arnold said, and unscientific, though, if necessary, Neo-Celts could doubtless prove Celtic blood in Newton and Darwin as easily as Dean Swift and Mr Louis Stevenson. 'The Celt has not produced great poetical works,' but his poetry has 'an air of greatness' and 'snatches of singular beauty and power.'[22]

From the Celtic element in our population (according to Arnold) English poetry got style, melancholy, natural magic, if not from the Celtic element, Mr Arnold asks, then where did it get them? We shall not, with some ethnologists, say 'from a Finnish substratum.' The ethnological question as what proportion of Celtic blood survived 'the English conquest,' outside of Wales, Cornwall, and the Highlands, nobody can answer. There would be intermarriages twelve hundred years ago. But, when the Celtic language and Celtic personal names vanished the surviving Celts would sink into the lowest grades of population. What have these grades done for poetry south of the Tweed?[23] Almost nothing! Their ballads and tales are notoriously flat and prosaic, doubtless the result of circumstances and of surroundings. But it is plain that such Celts as survived the English conquest would chiefly, if not exclusively, survive in what is the least imaginative and poetical of social strata. This they have not leavened, as far as our knowledge goes, and it is therefore unlikely that they leavened most the classes which have produced English poetry, the very classes into which they must have survived least.

Finding style in Icelandic literature, and not in the 'Nibelungen Lied',[24] Mr Arnold actually deduced it from Celtic settlers in Iceland, before the Norse occupation! Lord Strangford denied the facts,[25] but Neo-Celts may make what they can out of Icelandic and Scandinavian contact with the Islands and Ireland.* Mr Arnold then places Milton, Taliesin, and Pindar[26] among poets 'intoxicated with the passion for style.' But Pindar was not a Celt; and what proof have we, except his 'passion for style,' that Milton owed anything to Celtic blood? If we have, in Celtic poetry, Llywarch Hen's passionate aversion to old age,[27] we have also that of Alcaeus, of Mimnermus, of the author of Ecclesiastes,[28] – none of them Celtic precisely. If we have 'the Titanic' in Manfred and Lara, we have it in Prometheus.[29] Aeschylus was not a Celt, nor was Alfieri or Leopardi,[30] perhaps. To be sure, Miss Fiona Macleod talks of a 'Hellenic Celt,' but these are idle words.

Mr Arnold now discriminates 'the faithful way of handling nature, the Greek way, and the magical way,' which is Celtic. Keats had 'the Greek way,'

* Islay appears to be on Mr Arnold's side as to a Celtic settlement in Iceland. Mr Craigie, in 'Arkiv för Nordisk Filologi,' x. 149, shows that Celts learned much from Scandinavians, and taught very little.

but Keats was not a Greek, and could not read Greek. If he had also the Celtic way, is that because he was a Celt – because of 'the Celtic element'? If he could get the Greek way, untaught of and undescended from Greeks, why in the world should he not be born with the Celtic way, with no aid from a drop of Celtic blood? Shakespeare had 'the Greek note' as well as 'the Celtic note,' and, as a Greek element in Elizabethan England is out of the question, we must suppose that it is not *race* which gives Greek potentialities to Englishmen. Then why should *race* give them Celtic potentialities? Macaulay was Celtic enough – a reverend Highland ancestor of his tried to sell Prince Charles – yet Mr Arnold selects Macaulay as a contemner of Celtic MSS., and as a prize Philistine. Where does Celticism come in here? But if Macaulay had written like Keats, the Neo-Celts would have explained his gift as a Celtic inheritance.

The sum of Mr Arnold's argument is this: he finds certain qualities in Celtic poetry, he does not find them in German, though he does discover a few in Icelandic poetry. He recognises them all in the poetry of England (where there must be some Celtic blood), and he attributes these qualities to the Celtic element in the English, and even in the Icelanders. That these qualities exist in poetry where Celtic elements of race do not occur (as among Finns and Slavs), that Greek qualities abound where Greek elements of race are absent, that the historical circumstances and local conditions of the English – a maritime people – have not been those of the Germans, and may have helped to differentiate English from German poetry, are facts which do not weigh with Mr Arnold. Our style, our melancholy, our natural magic, must all be due to an imperceptible strain of the blood and the inherited qualities of the Celt, though our Greek qualities are *not* derived from the blood of the Greeks. Such arguments as these need only to be stated. They are not scientific, they would not satisfy science yet they have a pseudo-scientific ethnological air. In fact, they are Popular Science. It is impossible to disprove them: we *may* have a Celtic drop in our veins, and that Celtic drop *may* carry with it Celtic qualities in poetry. But it is certain that these qualities are not exclusively Celtic, and if there be 'Greek notes,' it is certain that these may be developed by poets with no Greek blood or training. Thus Mr Arnold's Celtic theory, if not demonstrably untrue, is, at least unproved and superfluous.

We now turn to Mr Arnold's successors, and first to Mr William Sharp, as a critic and editor of Macpherson's 'Ossian'.* Mr Arnold asserts that Macpherson's 'Ossian', after all deductions, has 'the very soul of the Celtic genius in it.' Wordsworth, despite his own 'natural magic,' denounced the book as worthless bombast, without any single truth to nature in it. We need not decide where poets disagree, but we may examine Mr Sharp's Introductory Essay. However low our opinion of Macpherson's 'Ossian'

* Centenary Edition. Patrick Geddes, Edinburgh

may be, it was a book with remarkable fortunes. A reprint edited by a Celtic scholar would have filled a place in the controversy on epic national poems. Macpherson really takes rank between Verkovitch[31] for Bulgaria and Lönnrot[32] for Finland, though nearer Verkovitch. A comparatively brief historical introduction might have explained the evolution of Macpherson's 'Ossian 'both in the English and the Gaelic. Mr Sharp offers no such guide: his introduction is mainly an attempt to summarise the ideas of Mr Alfred Nutt, of Campbell of Islay, and of Mr Hector Maclean.[33] We do not wish to press hard on an editor engaged in a work desirable, itself, and we shall not make sport out of the differences between Mr Sharp's account of Mr Nutt's views and the very necessary correction of his account in the *corrigenda*. Mr Nutt is alive to care of himself, but Islay is dead and we may be allowed to emend Mr Sharp's hurried, or confused, and certainly most bewildering version of Islay's ideas.

For instance (p. xvii), Mr Sharp writes thus: 'Professor O'Curry[34] says' something not unimportant. Since O'Curry, as quoted by Mr Sharp, yields no meaning, we turn to Islay, whose Ossianic theory Sharp is trying to summarise. Islay avers that O'Curry 'nowhere' says what Mr Sharp makes him say. Again, Mr Sharp writes that the first book in the Irish characters was printed in 1571 and 'so far it appears that Gaelic Scotland was ahead of Ireland in the literary race, for the first known Gaelic book was printed in Edinburgh.'

We confess to having been totally puzzled by this argument. The first Irish book printed appeared in 1571; but Scotland must have been earlier in the field, *because* 'the first Gaelic book was printed in Edinburgh.' Where is 'the therefore'? as Squire Western[35] says. Mr Sharp is guiding the unlearned Sassenach[36] into the Celtic Paradise, but the Sassenach flounders into this logical Slough of Despond.[37] 'Where is the therefore?' he asks. Well, Islay gives the date of the first Gaelic book, printed in Edinburgh, as 1567, whereas the first Irish book is of 1571. That is the reason why Islay thinks Gaelic was in print before Irish, but the date is exactly the fact which Mr Sharp omits.

Indeed, readers of Mr Sharp must be warned that, without Islay's essay in the hand, Mr Sharp's is absolutely unintelligible. Either he has failed to understand Islay (a writer who demands close attention), or he has summarised him with unfortunate haste and carelessness. Here is a singular example. Mr Sharp observes: 'At this day men still point out Dun Finn in Arran, and explain "Ar-ainn" to mean "Ar-fhinn", Fin's land ... Inseabh-Gall, the Hebrides, were so called from their Norse masters.' *This, then, proves that Scotland was considered to be the land of Fionn eighty years before Macpherson published anything*. Where is the proof?

The explanation, given by Islay, but omitted by Mr Sharp, is simply that the Fairy Minister, Mr Kirk of Aberfoyle, quotes or composes, in his Gaelic translation of the Psalms (1684), four lines in which the Highlands are called 'the generous land of Fionn.' Kirk 'flourished' at the time of the Revolution of 1688. His quatrain proves the point. Mr Sharp omits the proof.[38]

Islay's final opinion, or one of his final opinions, is given thus: 'I do not assert that the poet's name [the poet of the Gaelic 'Ossian' printed in 1807] was Ossian. I deny on good grounds that it was James Macpherson. I maintain that a poet, and a Scotch Highlander, composed all these Gaelic lines separately, if not together; and ... it is possible that there may be fragments of sentimental poetry, different from the popular ballads, more modern, but certainly older than 1730,' – this in spite of 'modern language, and English idioms.'

Mr Sharp does not add Islay's statement (he really wavered in a candid, if confusing way), that 'this is my own opinion,' but that, as no man 'is a fair judge of a written language in which he does not think,' he 'prefers the opinion' of a Highland shoe-maker. *He* says, '*This is not the old stuff*'.

We agree with the shoemaker. Macpherson's 'Ossian' 'is not the old stuff,' nor anything like it. The truth is that Islay, in 1872, withdrew from the half-hearted hankering after authenticity in Macpherson's 'Ossian' which he allowed to appear in his essay of 1862. No one could guess this from Mr Sharp's text, and in his *corrigenda* he tells the reader that the essay of 1862 is 'adequate and more easily procurable.' But he does not say that Islay, in 1872, declared that his later studies had 'turned the authenticity upside down.'*

We offer another instance of Mr Sharp's odd summary of Islay's ideas: 'If the statement of Mr MacGilvray, given at page 50 of the dissertation prefixed to the large edition of "Ossian" (1807), is not a deliberate falsehood, there is an end of the argument which makes Macpherson the author.' Now, what is Mr MacGilvray's statement? Mr Sharp does not tell us. Mr MacGilvray had said (according to Islay) that 'the very poems which were translated and published, "Fingal", "Temora", and many others, were collected in Gaelic in Scotland, from the people, long before 1760, and these were subsequently compared with Macpherson's published translations at Douay, by Mr Farquharson, the collector of the Gaelic, who did not know Macpherson, and the translations were found ... to be, in the main, translations as far as they went.'

Then where is Mr Farquharson's manuscript? 'It was torn, and leaves were used by the Douay students to light their fires.' It is like the poll-book of the disputed Irish election. 'It fell into the broth, and the dog ate it.'[39] So much for the statement of Mr MacGilvray, which Mr Sharp might have given, it is so deliciously Celtic.

In fact, there are old *ballads* about Ossianic heroes, but no *epic* has ever been found. Morven, the kingdom thereof, is unknown outside Macpherson's book, unknown in traditional songs or stories. As to style, Islay gives a correct rendering of a Gaelic 'run' or conventional passage, and then

* 'Leabhar na Feinne', p. xxxiv

does it into Macpherson's peculiar species of fustian.* 'The difficulty,' he says, 'would be to find an audience nowadays' for such trash. Into fragments of a genuine old ballad, Macpherson (or, if you please, an unknown predecessor about 1680–1730) foisted 'a vague but masterly word-picture of a landscape'– *à la* Mr Whistler[40] – 'through which stalk the *half-described indistinct* features of gloomy warriors ... The ballad is simple and natural; the epic [Macpherson's 'Ossian'] is laboured and artificial, and it is no translation, according to my definition of the word, but it is like something elaborated and built up out of the materials of one or more ballads.' As the shoemaker says of this very piece, 'Temora,' 'Cha'n'e so an seann stugh' ('It is not the old stuff'). The stuff is, in place of the genuine mythical opening of the ballad, 'The blue waves of Erin roll in light. The mountains are covered with day. Trees shake their dusky heads in the breeze. Grey torrents pour their noisy streams,' &c., *κ.τ.λ*, *u.s.w.*[41] Macpherson, some other impostor, gave us this, while cribbing his outline and some materials, from the old ballad. Macpherson's character for probity, in the affair of the Stuart Papers in the Scots College,[42] does not enable us to place much confidence in his assertions.

Mr Sharp admits that 'Ossian' of Macpherson is not a genuine rendering of ancient originals, that he 'works incoherently' upon a 'genuine but unsystematised, unsifted, and fragmentary basis,' and adds that 'if he were the sole author he would be one of the few poetic creators of the first rank,'– a class of men who never wrote fustian, we may add, never produced what Mr Sharp justly censures as 'clumsily constructed, self-contradictory, and sometimes grotesquely impossible.' Yet this 'Ossian' is informed by 'the antique spirit,' which 'gives it enduring life, charm, and all the spell of cosmic imagination.' Mr Sharp also commits himself to the sentiment that 'no single work in our literature has had so wide-reaching, so potent, and so enduring an influence.' But, among his curious *errata*, he hedges his statement thus, 'no single work *of its kind*.' There is no other work 'of its kind' in English (except Ireland's Shakespearian forgeries, or Chatterton's sham Old English);[43] in Bulgarian we believe that M. Verkovitch supplied an example.

Leaving Mr Sharp and Mr Arnold on one side, Wordsworth and Islay on the other, to settle the question of the literary value of 'Ossian' 'as she is wrote' by James Macpherson, we may surely say that Mr Sharp is not very lucid or logical in his introduction. Yet nowhere are logic and lucidity more necessary than in an attempt to make the public understand what Macpherson's 'Ossian' really is. And we may add that the influence of Macpherson's 'Ossian', turgid and windy as it is, cannot be of value to young Neo-Celtic writers, whether they 'have the good Gaelic' or no Gaelic at all. Mr Hector Maclean, quoted by Islay, says 'vagueness and obscurity abound

* Popular Tales of the West Highlands, ii. 439 ; iv. 140

everywhere, ... such lines prove to be nonsense when closely examined,' whereas, in the genuine traditional Gaelic ballads, Mr Maclean finds 'no vagueness, no mistiness, no obscurity.' Now, the essence of Macpherson's 'Ossian' is vagueness, mistiness, obscurity. To imitate this, as some Neo-Celts do, is not to Celticise, but to Macphersonise.

We next examine the whimsical Neo-Celtic endeavours to claim all that is best and rarest in English literature as due to the Celtic element. A grotesque example was lately presented by Mr George Moore, by whom Swift, the most English of men, was applauded for 'Celtic' qualities. Sir Walter Scott and Mr Louis Stevenson were denominated Scottish Celts, and Fielding was criticised in a style which demonstrated Mr Moore's ignorance of Fielding's works.

Mr Sharp is more cautious than Mr Moore, in his 'Lyra Celtica,' which is, in every way, a curious production, – a first specimen, as we learn, of an 'Anthologia Celtica,' a future rival, perhaps, of the Greek Anthology. We begin with Amergin and Taliesin, and come down to unpublished minor young poets. It is as if we ranged, in Greek, from Orpheus and Musaeus, through Marcus Argentarius and Paulus Silentiarius, to the last Romaic bard in an Athenian newspaper's Poet's Corner.[44]

To the poems we shall return after examining the editor's ideas. Like ourselves, Mr Sharp goes back to Mr Arnold's Lectures of 1867. Mr Sharp, innocently, seems to think that Islay's 'Popular Tales of the West Highlands' were unpublished when Mr Arnold lectured, yet he calls Mr Arnold 'superficial.' He goes on to meet the objectors who say that Shakespeare, Milton, Coleridge, Keats, and Shelley are English, Byron, Burns, and Sir Walter, Scotch, 'not distinctively Anglo-Celtic.' Byron's mother was a Gordon of Gight; he did not reckon himself a Scot, exactly. However, Mr Sharp talks of his 'Celtic blood.' He might as well talk of Oliver Cromwell's Celtic blood, Mrs Cromwell *mère* being a Stuart.[45] Shakespeare's Celtic blood has to be given up, as beyond proof. Milton was Welsh on the mother's side; 'Keats is a Celtic name' (compare Maquet,[46] who called himself Auguste MacKeat in 1830), and Keats's genius is convincingly Celtic. So is Wordsworth's in places, Wordsworth from whom 'a modern Anglo-Celtic poet,' unnamed, borrows the ideas in a 'haunting quatrain,' yet Wordsworth's ancestry was as English as Hereward the Wake's.[47] Coleridge and Shelley, so 'Celtic' in genius, are admitted to be of 'unmixed English blood, so far as we know,' yet Mr Sharp hankers after something atavistically Celtic in their genius. Why not in Edgar Poe's? He was of Irish origin. Meanwhile he admits the possibility, in Scotland, 'of an older race still, than even the Picts.'[48] Are these our Finnish friends? If so, why not go back to the beginning, and have a Finnish Renascence at once? It is just as cheap as a Celtic Renascence, and about as plausible. As to Burns, we presume that the Celtophiles believe in the fables of his Celtic descent from Campbell of Burnhouse (Burnus, Burnes, Burns). 'Scott, as it happens, was of the ancient stock' (Celtic?) and not 'the typical Lowlander he is so often designated.' Mr Sharp may consult the quarterings on the roof of the hall at Abbotsford. Scotts, Rutherfords, Swintons, and Haliburtons speak for themselves.[49] Sir Walter could only rake up a Campbell great-grandmother, and wore the dark-green Campbell tartan, when George IV clad his broad German acres in the tartan of the Stuarts. Let Mr Sharp claim Celtic genius for the House of Hanover! As for Mr Stevenson, 'who that has studied his genius can question the Celtic strain in him?' The old fallacy! Mr Stevenson was as purely Lowland as James Hogg, and the genius of the one was as Celtic as that of the other. The said 'genius' is found in men without a traceable drop of Celtic blood – Wordsworth, Shelley, Coleridge, Stevenson, Hogg. It is almost absent in the more or less Celtic Tom Moore (Mr Sharp admits), and wholly in the very Celtic Tom Macaulay. Indeed Mr Sharp allows that it is impossible 'to limit this charm of exquisite regret and longing to Celtic poetry.' Of course it is impossible! No more perfect and beautiful example of this 'charm' exists than in a love-song by a Red Indian squaw, who could not read, published, with a translation, by Dr Brinton.[50]

'Fleas are not lobsters, damn their souls,'

as the poet says,[51] and Algonquins are not Celts.

'They went forth to the war, but they always fell,' says Mr James Macpherson. The Celts, in this argument, always fall. They admit, what is wholly undeniable, that certain poetic qualities are not peculiar to the Celtic peoples. Then when they find, or fancy, these qualities in the work of men without a traceable drop of Celtic blood in their veins, they make the qualities, common to many literatures, a presumption in favour of the presence of Celtic blood. In the same way 'second sight' is averred to be a Celtic gift. You might as well call epilepsy a Celtic gift. Every savage – the Maori, the Red Indian, the Zulu – is as full of second sight as any man of Moidart.[52] What is called 'Celtic' in poetry or in superstition is really early human, and may become recrudescent anywhere, for good or for evil. Listen to a song of the New Hebrides, 'and you in dreams behold the Hebrides,' the Old Hebrides, so exactly identical is the wailing cadence in Gaelic and in New Hebridean minstrelsy. Comparative science dispels the Celtic illusion that anything whatever is peculiarly Celtic, or dependent on Celtic race and blood.

Turn we now to the poetry of the 'Lyra Celtica,' old or new. The translations in verse, like all translations in verse, may be neglected [...] Of course there are better passages in these old Welsh writers; we find love of nature, pensive melancholy, 'old unhappy far-off things,' but not so very much to brag of: there is less of Tennyson than of Tupper.[53]

The modern pieces are chiefly later than Mr Arnold's lectures. The young generation is Celtic enough, but that proves nothing. It has read Mr

Arnold, and Mr Sharp, and M. Renan, and Mr Grant Allen,[54] and it says, 'Go to, let us be Celtic!' The Celticism is self-conscious, *voulu*, of *malice prepense*.[55] For the real thing, in modern poetry, we must go to the peasant songs of Ireland, *Volkslieder*, published by Dr Hyde.[56] They are charming, as charming as Italian, Spanish Gipsy, or Romaic *Volkslieder*, and in a very similar way. It is not that a number of these young Neo-Celtic poets lack lyrical merits. Miss Fiona Macleod, Mr Yeats, Mrs Robertson Matheson, Miss Nora Hopper,[57] and several others, write very pleasing, delicate, winning poems. But poems just as pleasing are produced by our non-Celtic minstrels. The only marked peculiarities of these so-called Celts are consciously produced on the lines of Welsh and Irish minstrelsy. Mr Quiller Couch's delightful piece, 'The Splendid Spur,' is Caroline, a deliberate following, and an admirable one, of such verse as Shirley's 'The glories of our birth and state.' Mr Couch was not thinking of being Celtic; but most of these young poets are thinking of it, and are imitating certain features of Celtic poetry, just as, in the last century, they would have imitated Pope. Again, in her novel, 'Green Fire,' Miss Macleod 'Macphersonises': the windy, wailing, indistinct, and, oddly, *Lyttonian*[58] romance, is pertinaciously bent on being 'Ossianic.' Now vague, obscure mistiness is *not* Celtic, but the foible of James Macpherson, as we have heard Mr Hector Maclean declare.

Really Celtic, as a critic not without the necessary Celtic drop of blood ventures to think, are Mr Yeats's Tales in prose, and, above all, Mr Neil Munro's stories in 'The Lost Pibroch'.[59] In these we meet genius, as obvious and undeniable as that of Mr Kipling, if less popular in appeal. Accidentally or consciously, Mr Munro's powers are directed to old Highland life, and he does what genius alone can do – he makes it live again, and makes our imaginations share its life; his knowledge being copious, original, at first hand. That any human life was ever like that painted, with too rich a palette, by Miss Macleod in 'Green Fire,' we respectfully and hopefully take leave to doubt. *C'est de pur Jamie Macpherson, doublé de Bulwer Lytton*.[60] The young Neo-Celts, if they respect their often respectable talents, will try to be natural, to be themselves; and will avoid imitation of Taliesin, Aneurin, Irish peasants, and Rob Don. To these enthusiasts we would also recommend a study of the Jacobite poetry. Honestly, which songs are best – John Roy Stuart's, William Ross's, Alastair Macdonnell's, Rob Don's (rich as some of these are in bloodthirstiness for its own sake),* or the Jacobite songs of the Lowland Scots? [...] These are certainly by no means inferior in pathos and spirit, while as a matter of art, they are more terse, more concerned with what is essential, than the contemporary Gaelic songs of the Rising, the

* The reader may refer to Mr Craigie's most instructive essay on Gaelic Historical Songs, in the 'Scottish Review,' October 1891: 'All Gaelic poetry depends far more on its form than its matter; the thought may be as trifling or trite as possible, but if there is harmony of sound, the Gael is satisfied.' Artificial complications beyond those of the Chant Royal more and more beset Gaelic poetry, 1550–1750.

Neo-Celts compare them, if they know Gaelic, and then decide between the merits of Highlands and Lowlands. Those who know not Gaelic, and read the Gaelic songs in English prose, of course miss the form [...]

The spirit of these remarks will be greatly misconstrued by any one who supposes that we wish to decry Celtic literature and Celtic studies. Even in translations the 'Mabinogion' and the half-mythical Irish romances (such as 'Diarmaid and Grainne') deserve to be widely read. The popular tales, Gaelic, Irish, or Breton, the popular songs, the myths, many modern Gaelic poems, the old heroic ballads, are all full of interest and charm, even to a merely English reader, who necessarily misses the *form* of the originals, in which often lies their most conspicuous merit. Celtic literature was the natural expression of a poetical race, arrested (as far as literature is concerned) at certain rather early stages of development. There is no epic, no theatre; there is no Celtic vernacular poetry of men on a high level of conscious civilisation and social organisation, like that of Periclean Greece, or of Rome in the first century before our era, or of Elizabethan England. The Celtic-speaking peoples, as such, never attained to these social and political conditions. They have not only no Homer; they have no Sophocles, no Theocritus, no Virgil or Lucretius, no Horace or Catullus; no Shakespeare or Milton. Their development (if they had it in them to develop) was diverted by Christianity, and stunted by foreign conquest. Their educated classes were Anglicised, or Frenchified. They never enjoyed the chances of Greece, Rome, France, Italy, Germany, Spain, and England. Their vernacular literature has been that of old bards, sennachies,[61] peasants, medieval romancers, and ecclesiastics: it has never been that of a highly instructed and reflective literary class. For what it is, – a literature of a development arrested early, – it is rich, poetical, tender, and imaginative.

If the Neo-Celts are in earnest, let them provide us with Celtic texts and literal translations of Celtic literature, or do for Ireland, Brittany, and Wales what Mr Neil Munro has begun to do for the West Highlands. This is the path; to make large claims of the best things in English literature, or in French heroism, for 'the Celtic element' is not the path. Conscious modern imitation of poetry which the imitators, as a rule, cannot read in the original languages, is not the path. These proceedings irritate the so-called Saxon, provoke his ridicule, and keep alive his prejudices. It is foolish to call Jeanne d'Arc or Walter Scott 'Celts'; foolish to say that a poet must have Celtic blood because, in fact, you like his poetry. Let us repeat that the relations of race to poetic or other mental qualities is a mystery – that *verae causae*,[62] as of environment and historical circumstances, must be exhausted before we can claim this or that gift as a gift of race. Races have too long been mixed, and the history of race is too profoundly obscure. When we bring race into literary criticism, we dally with that unlovely fluent enchantress, Popular Science.

Introduction to Sir Walter Scott, *Waverley, Or 'Tis Sixty Years Since*

(London: Macmillan 1893)

'What is the value of a reputation that probably will not last above one or two generations?' Sir Walter Scott once asked Ballantyne. Two generations, according to the usual reckoning, have passed; ''T is Sixty Years since' the 'wondrous Potentate' of Wordsworth's sonnet[1] died, yet the reputation on which he set so little store survives. A constant tide of new editions of his novels flows from the press; his plots give materials for operas and plays; he has been criticised, praised, condemned: but his romances endure amid the changes of taste, remaining the delight of mankind, while new schools and little masters of fiction come and go.

Scott himself believed that even great works usually suffer periods of temporary occultation. His own, no doubt, have not always been in their primitive vogue. Even at first, English readers complained of the difficulty caused by his Scotch, and now many make his 'dialect' an excuse for not reading books which their taste, debauched by third-rate fiction, is incapable of enjoying. But Scott has never disappeared in one of those irregular changes of public opinion remarked on by his friend Lady Louisa Stuart.[2] In 1821 she informed him that she had tried the experiment of reading Mackenzie's 'Man of Feeling'[3] aloud: 'Nobody cried, and at some of the touches I used to think so exquisite, they laughed.'* His correspondent requested Scott to write something on such variations of taste, which actually seem to be in the air and epidemic, for they affect, as she remarked, young people who have not heard the criticisms of their elders.† Thus Rousseau's

* Abbotsford Manuscripts.

† See Scott's reply, with the anecdote about Mrs. Aphra Behn's novels, Lockhart, vi. 406 (edition of 1839).

'Nouvelle Heloise,'[4] once so fascinating to girls, and reputed so dangerous, had become tedious to the young, Lady Louisa says, even in 1821. But to the young, if they have any fancy and intelligence, Scott is not tedious even now; and probably his most devoted readers are boys, girls, and men of matured appreciation and considerable knowledge of literature. The unformed and the cultivated tastes are still at one about Scott. He holds us yet with his unpremeditated art, his natural qualities of friendliness, of humour, of sympathy. Even the carelessness with which his earliest and his kindest critics – Ellis, Erskine,[5] and Lady Louisa Stuart – reproached him has not succeeded in killing his work and diminishing his renown.

It is style, as critics remind us, it is perfection of form, no doubt, that secure the permanence of literature; but Scott did not overstate his own defects when he wrote in his Journal (April 22, 1826): 'A solecism in point of composition, like a Scotch word, is indifferent to me. I never learned grammar … I believe the bailiff in "The Goodnatured Man"[6] is not far wrong when he says: "One man has one way of expressing himself, and another another; and that is all the difference between them."' The difference between Scott and Thackeray or Flaubert among good writers, and a crowd of self-conscious and mannered 'stylists' among writers not so very good, is essential. About Shakspeare it was said that he 'never blotted a line.' The observation is almost literally true about Sir Walter. The pages of his manuscript novels show scarcely a retouch or an erasure, whether in the 'Waverley' fragment of 1805 or the unpublished 'Siege of Malta' of 1832.* The handwriting becomes closer and smaller; from thirty-eight lines to the page in 'Waverley,' he advances to between fifty and sixty in 'Ivanhoe.' The few alterations are usually additions. For example, a fresh pedantry of the Baron of Bradwardine's is occasionally set down on the opposite page. Nothing can be less like the method of Flaubert or the method of Mr. Ruskin, who tells us that 'a sentence of "Modern Painters" was often written four or five times over in my own hand, and tried in every word for perhaps an hour, – perhaps a forenoon, – before it was passed for the printer.'[7] Each writer has his method; Scott was no stippler or niggler,[8] but, as we shall see later, he often altered much in his proof-sheets.† As long as he

* A history of Scott's Manuscripts, with good facsimiles, will be found in the Catalogue of the Scott Exhibition, Edinburgh, 1872.

† While speaking of correction, it may be noted that Scott, in his 'Advertisement' prefixed to the issue of 1829, speaks of changes made in that collected edition. In 'Waverley' these emendations are very rare, and are unimportant. A few callidae juncturae [clever couplings] are added, a very few lines are deleted. The postscript of the first edition did not contain the anecdote about the hiding-place of the manuscript among the fishing tackle. The first line of Flora Macdonald's battle-song (chapter xxii.) originally ran, 'Mist darkens the mountain, night darkens the vale,' in place of 'There is mist on the mountain and mist on the vale.' For the rest, as Scott says, 'where the tree falls it must lie.'

was understood, he was almost reckless of well-constructed sentences, of the one best word for his meaning, of rounded periods. This indifference is not to be praised, but it is only a proof of his greatness that his style, never distinguished, and often lax, has not impaired the vitality of his prose. The heart which beats in his works, the knowledge of human nature, the dramatic vigour of his character, the nobility of his whole being win the day against the looseness of his manner, the negligence of his composition, against the haste of fatigue which set him, as Lady Louisa Stuart often told him, on 'huddling up a conclusion anyhow, and so kicking the book out of his way.'[9] In this matter of *dénouements*[10] he certainly was no more careful than Shakspeare or Molière.

The permanence of Sir Walter's romances is proved, as we said, by their survival among all the changes of fashion in the art of fiction. When he took up his pen to begin 'Waverley,' fiction had not absorbed, as it does to-day, almost all the best imaginative energy of English or foreign writers. Now we hear of 'art' on every side, and every novelist must give the world his opinion about schools and methods. Scott, on the other hand, lived in the greatest poetical age since that of Elizabeth. Poetry or the drama (in which, to be sure, few succeeded) occupied Wordsworth, Byron, Coleridge, Shelley, Crabbe, Campbell, and Keats. Then, as Joanna Baillie[11] hyperbolically declared, 'The Scotch novels put poetry out of fashion.'* Till they appeared, novels seem to have been left to readers like the plaintive lady's-maid whom Scott met at Dalkeith, when he beheld 'the fair one descend from the carriage with three half-bound volumes of a novel in her hand.'[12] Mr. Morritt, writing to Scott in March, 1815, hopes he will 'restore pure narrative to the dignity from which it gradually slipped before it dwindled into a manufactory for the circulating library.' 'Waverley,' he asserted, 'would prevail over people otherwise averse to blue-backed volumes.'[13] Thus it was an unconsidered art which Scott took up and revived. Half a century had passed since Fielding gave us in 'Tom Jones' his own and very different picture of life in the 'forty-five,'– of life with all the romance of the 'Race to Derby'[14] cut down to a sentence or two. Since the age of the great English novelists, Richardson and Fielding and Miss Burney, the art of fiction had been spasmodically alive in the hands of Mrs. Radcliffe, had been sentimental with Henry Mackenzie, and now was all but moribund, save for the humorous Irish sketches of Miss Edgeworth. As Scott always insisted, it was mainly 'the extended and well-merited fame of Miss Edgeworth' which induced him to try his hand on a novel containing pictures of Scottish life and character. Nothing was more remarkable in his own novels than the blending of close and humorous observation of common life with pleasure in adventurous narratives about 'what is not so, and was not so, and Heaven forbid that it ever should be so,' as the girl says in the nursery tale.[15] Through his whole

* Abbotsford Manuscripts. Hogg averred that nobody either read or wrote poetry after Sir Walter took to prose.

life he remained the dreamer of dreams and teller of wild legends, who had held the lads of the High School entranced round Luckie Brown's fireside, and had fleeted the summer days in interchange of romances with a schoolboy friend, Mr. Irving, among the hills that girdle Edinburgh. He ever had a passion for 'knights and ladies and dragons and giants,' and 'God only knows,' he says, 'how delighted I was to find myself in such society.' But with all this delight, his imagination had other pleasures than the fantastic: the humours and passions of ordinary existence were as clearly visible to him as the battles, the castles, and the giants. True, he was more fastidious in his choice of novels of real life than in his romantic reading. 'The whole Jemmy and Jessamy tribe [16] I abhorred,' he said; 'and it required the art of Burney or the feeling of Mackenzie to fix my attention upon a domestic tale.' But when the domestic tale was good and true, no man appreciated it more than he. None has more vigorously applauded Miss Austen than Scott, and it was thus that as the 'Author of "Waverley"' he addressed Miss Edgeworth, through James Ballantyne: 'If I could but hit it, Miss Edgeworth's wonderful power of vivifying all her persons, and making them live as beings in your mind, I should not be afraid.' 'Often,' Ballantyne goes on, 'has the Author of "Waverley" used such language to me; and I knew that I gratified him most when I could say, "Positively, this *is* equal to Miss Edgeworth"'.

Thus Scott's own taste was catholic: and in this he was particularly unlike the modern novelists, who proclaim, from both sides of the Atlantic, that only in their own methods, and in sharing their own exclusive tastes, is literary salvation. The prince of Romance was no one-sided *romanticiste*; his ear was open to all fiction good in its kind. His generosity made him think Miss Edgeworth's persons more alive than his own. To his own romances he preferred Mrs. Shelley's 'Frankenstein.'* As a critic, of course, he was mistaken; but his was the generous error of the heart, and it is the heart in Walter Scott, even more than the brain, that lends its own vitality to his creations. Equipped as he was with a taste truly catholic, capable in old age of admiring 'Pelham,'[17] he had the power to do what he calls 'the big bow-wow strain;'[18] yet he was not, as in his modesty he supposed, denied 'the exquisite torch which renders ordinary commonplace things and characters interesting, from the truth of the description and the sentiment.'†

---

* Scott reviewed 'Frankenstein' in 1818. Mr. Shelley had sent it with a brief note, in which he said that it was the work of a friend, and that he had only seen it through the press. Sir Walter passed the book on to Mr. Morritt, who, in reply, gave Scott a brief and not very accurate history of Shelley. Sir Walter then wrote a most favourable review of 'Frankenstein' in 'Blackwood's Magazine,' observing that it was attributed to Mr. Percy Bysshe Shelley, a son-in-law of Mr. Godwin. Mrs. Shelley presently wrote thanking him for the review, and assuring him that it was her own work. Scott had apparently taken Shelley's disclaimer as an innocent evasion; it was an age of literary superscheries. –Abbotsford Manuscripts.

† Journal. March 14, 1826.

The letter of Rose Bradwardine to Waverley is alone enough to disprove Scott's disparagement of himself, his belief that he had been denied exquisiteness of touch. Nothing human is more delicate, nothing should be more delicately handled, than the first love of a girl. What the 'analytical' modern novelist would pass over and dissect and place beneath his microscope till a student of any manliness blushes with shame and annoyance, Scott suffers Rose Bradwardine to reveal with a sensitive shyness. But Scott, of course, had even less in common with the peeper and botanizer on maidens' hearts than with the wildest romanticist. He considered that 'a want of story is always fatal to a book the first reading, and it is well if it gets a chance of a second.' From him 'Pride and Prejudice' got a chance of three readings at least. This generous universality of taste, in addition to all his other qualities of humour and poetry, enabled Scott to raise the novel from its decadence, and to make the dry bones of history live again in his tales. With Charles Edward at Holyrood, as Mr. Senior wrote in the 'Quarterly Review,'[19] 'we are in the lofty region of romance. In any other hands than those of Sir Walter Scott, the language and conduct of those great people would have been as dignified as their situations. We should have heard nothing of the hero in his new costume "majoring afore the muckle pier-glass," of his arrest by the host of the Candlestick, of his examination by the well-powdered Major Melville, or of his fears of being informed against by Mrs. Nosebag.' In short, 'while the leading persons and events are as remote from ordinary life as the inventions of Scudéry, the picture of human nature is as faithful as could have been given by Fielding or Le Sage.' Though this criticism has not the advantage of being new, it is true; and when we have added that Scott's novels are the novels of the poet who, next to Shakspeare, knew mankind most widely and well, we have the secret of his triumph.

For the first time in literature, it was a poet who held the pen of the romancer in prose. Fielding, Richardson, De Foe, Miss Burney, were none of them made by the gods poetical. Scott himself, with his habitual generosity, would have hailed his own predecessor in Mrs. Radcliffe. 'The praise may be claimed for Mrs. Radcliffe of having been the first to introduce into her prose fictions a beautiful and fanciful tone of natural description and impressive narrative, which had hitherto been exclusively applied to poetry. . . . Mrs. Radcliffe has a title to be considered the first poetess of romantic fiction.' When 'Guy Mannering' appeared, Wordsworth sneered at it as a work of the Radcliffe school. The slight difference produced by the introduction of humour could scarcely be visible to Wordsworth. But Scott would not have been hurt by his judgment. He had the literary courage to recognize merit even when obscured by extravagance, and to applaud that in which people of culture could find neither excellence nor charm. Like Thackeray, he had been thrilled by Vivaldi in the Inquisition,[20] and he was not the man to hide his gratitude because his author was now out of fashion.

Thus we see that Scott, when he began 'Waverley' in 1805, brought to his labour no hard-and-fast theory of the art of fiction, but a kindly readiness to be pleased, and to find good in everything. He brought his wide knowledge of contemporary Scottish life 'from the peer to the ploughman;' he brought his well-digested wealth of antiquarian lore, and the poetic skill which had just been busied with the 'Lay of the Last Minstrel,' and was still to be occupied, ere he finished his interrupted novel, with 'Marmion,' 'The Lady of the Lake,' 'Rokeby,' and 'The Lord of the Isles.' The comparative failure of the last-named no doubt strengthened his determination to try prose romance. He had never cared much for his own poems, he says, Byron had outdone him in popularity, and the Muse – 'the Good Demon' who once deserted Herrick[21] – came now less eagerly to his call.

[...]

The reception of 'Waverley' was enthusiastic. Large editions were sold in Edinburgh, and when Scott returned from his cruise in the northern islands he found society ringing with his unacknowledged triumph. Byron, especially, proclaimed his pleasure in 'Waverley.' It may be curious to recall some of the published reviews of the moment. Probably no author ever lived so indifferent to published criticism as Scott. Miss Edgeworth, in one of her letters, reminds him how they had both agreed that writers who cared for the dignity and serenity of their characters should abstain from 'that authors' bane-stuff.'[22] 'As to the herd of critics,' Scott wrote to Miss Seward, after publishing 'The Lay,' 'many of those gentlemen appear to me to be a set of tinkers, who, unable to *make* pots and pans, set up for *menders* of them.' It is probable, therefore, that he was quite unconcerned about the few remarks which Mr. Gifford, in the 'Quarterly Review' (vol. xl., 1814), interspersed among a multitude of extracts, in a notice of 'Waverley' manufactured with scissors and paste.

[...]

[Scott] himself, writing to Morritt, calls his hero 'a sneaking piece of imbecility;' but he probably started with loftier intentions of 'psychological analysis' than he fulfilled. He knew, and often said, in private letters, as in published works, that he was no hand at a respectable hero. Borderers, buccaneers, robbers, and humorsome people, like Dugald Dalgetty and Bailie Nicol Jarvie and Macwheeble, whom he said he preferred to any person in 'Waverley,' were the characters he delighted in. We may readily believe that Shakspeare too preferred Jacques and the Fat Knight to Orlando or the favoured lover of Anne Page. Your hero is a difficult person to make human,– unless, indeed, he has the defects of Pendennis or Tom Jones. But it is likely enough that the Waverley whom Scott had in his mind in 1805 was hardly the Waverley of 1813. His early English chapters are much in the ordinary vein of novels as they were then written; in those chapters come the 'asides' by the author which the 'Edinburgh Review' condemned. But there remains the kindly, honourable Sir Everard, while the calm atmosphere of English meadows, and the plump charms of Miss Cecilia Stubbs, are intended as foils to the hills of the North, the shy refinement of Rose, and the heroic heart of Flora Mac-Ivor. Scott wished to show the remote extremes of civilization and mental habit co-existing in the same island of Scotland and England. Yet we regret such passages as 'craving pardon for my heroics, which I am unable in certain cases to resist giving way to,' and so forth. Scott was no Thackeray, no Fielding, and failed (chiefly in 'Waverley') when he attempted the mood of banter, which one of his daughters, a lady 'of Beatrice's mind',[23] 'never got from me,' he observes.

In any serious attempt to criticise 'Waverley' as a whole, it is not easy to say whether we should try to put ourselves at the point of view of its first readers, or whether we should look at it from the vantage-ground of to-day. In 1814 the dead world of clannish loyalty was fresh in many memories. Scott's own mother had often spoken with a person who had seen Cromwell enter Edinburgh after Dunbar.[24] He himself knew heroes of the Forty-five, and his friend Lady Louisa Stuart had been well acquainted with Miss Walkinshaw, sister of the mistress of Charles Edward. To his generation those things were personal memories, which to us seem as distant as the reign of Men-ka-ra.[25] They could not but be 'carried off their feet' by such pictures of a past still so near them. Nor had they other great novelists to weaken the force of Scott's impressions. They had not to compare him with the melancholy mirth of Thackeray, and the charm, the magic of his style. Balzac was of the future; of the future was the Scott of France, – the boyish, the witty, the rapid, the brilliant, the inexhaustible Dumas. Scott's generation had no scruples about 'realism,' listened to no sermons on the glory of the commonplace; like Dr. Johnson, they admired a book which 'was amusing as a fairy-tale.'[26] But we are overwhelmed with a wealth of comparisons, and deafened by a multitude of homilies on fiction, and distracted, like the people in the Eyrbyggja Saga, by the strange rising and setting, and the wild orbits of new 'weirdmoons' of romance.[27] Before we can make up our minds on Scott, we have to remember, or forget, the scornful patronage of one critic, the over-subtlety and exaggerations of another, the more than papal infallibility of a third. Perhaps the best critic would be an intelligent school-boy, with a generous heart and an unspoiled imagination. As his remarks are not accessible, as we must try to judge 'Waverley' like readers inured to much fiction and much criticism, we must confess, no doubt, that the commencement has the faults which the first reviewers detected, and which Scott acknowledged. He is decidedly slow in getting to business, as they say; he began with more of conscious ethical purpose than he went on, and his banter is poor. But when once we enter the village of Tully-Veolan, the Magician finds his wand. Each picture of place or person tells, – the old butler, the daft Davie Gellatley, the solemn and chivalrous Baron, the pretty natural girl, the various lairds, the factor Macwheeble, – all at once become living people, and friends whom we can never lose. The creative fire of Shakspeare lives again. The Highlanders – Evan Dhu, Donald Bean Lean, his charming daughter, Callum Beg, and all the rest – are as natural as the Lowlanders. In Fergus and Flora we feel, indeed, at first, that the author has left his experience behind, and is giving us creatures of fancy. But they too become human and natural, – Fergus in his moods of anger, ambition, and final courageous resignation; Flora, in her grief. As for Waverley, his creator was no doubt too hard on him. Among the brave we hear that he was one of the bravest, though Scott always wrote his battle-pieces in a manner to suggest no discomfort, and does not give us particular details of Waverley's prowess. He has spirit enough, this 'sneaking piece of imbecility,' as he shows in his quarrel with Fergus, on the march to Derby. Waverley, that creature of romance, considered as a lover, is really not romantic enough. He loved Rose because she loved him, – which is confessed to be unheroic behaviour. Scott, in 'Waverley,' certainly does not linger over love-scenes. With Mr. Ruskin, we may say: 'Let it not be thought for an instant that the slight and sometimes scornful glance with which Scott passes over scenes which a novelist of our own day would have analyzed with the airs of a philosopher, and painted with the curiosity of a gossip, indicates any absence in his heart of sympathy with the great and sacred elements of personal happiness.'[28] But his mind entertained other themes of interest, 'loyalty, patriotism, piety.' On the other hand, it is necessary to differ from Mr. Ruskin when he says that Scott 'never knew "l'amor che move 'l sol e l'altre stelle."'[29] He whose heart was 'broken for two years,' and retained the crack till his dying day, he who, when old and tired, and near his death, was yet moved by the memory of the name which thirty years before he had cut in Runic characters on the turf at the Castle-gate of St. Andrew, knew love too well to write of it much, or to speak of it at all. He had won his ideal as alone the ideal can be won; he never lost her: she was with him always, because she had been unattainable. 'There are few,' he says, 'who have not, at one period of life, broken ties of love and friendship, secret disappointments of the heart, to mourn over, – and we know no book which recalls the memory of them more severely than "Julia de Roubigné."'[30] He could not be very eager to recall them, he who had so bitterly endured them, and because he had known and always knew 'l'amor che move 'l sol e l'altre stelle,' a seal was on his lips, a silence broken only by a caress of Di Vernon's.*

* In a letter to Lady Abercorn, written when he was busy with 'The Lady of the Lake', Scott complained that he could not draw a lover, in spite of his own experience.

This apology we may make, if an apology be needed, for what modern readers may think the meagreness of the love-passages in Scott. He does not deal in embraces and effusions, his taste is too manly; he does not dwell much on Love, because, like the shepherd in Theocritus, he has found him an inhabitant of the rocks.[31] Moreover, when Scott began novel-writing, he was as old as Thackeray when Thackeray said that while at work on a love-scene he blushed so that you would think he was going into an apoplexy. 'Waverley' stands by its pictures of manners, of character, by its humour and its tenderness, by its manly 'criticism of life,' by its touches of poetry, so various, so inspired, as in Davie Gellatley with his songs, and Charles Edward in the gallant hour of Holyrood, and Flora with her high, selfless hopes and broken heart, and the beloved Baron, bearing his lot 'with a good-humoured though serious composure.' 'To be sure, we may say with Virgilius Maro, "Fuimus Troes" and there's the end of an auld sang. But houses and families and men have a'stood lang enough when they have stood till they fall with honour.'[32] 'Waverley' ends like a fairy-tale, while real life ever ends like a Northern saga.

But among the good things that make life bearable, such fairy-tales are not the least precious, and not the least enduring.

'At the Sign of the Ship', *Longman's Magazine* 9:49
(November 1887), pp.107–9

It is not uncomplimentary to the Celtic spirit, I hope, to say that the Celtic spirit is a little impracticable. 'They don't know what they want, and they won't be satisfied till they get it,' said an Irish orator of his own countrymen.[1] This is the aspiring temper, incapable of yielding to circumstances, which Mr. Matthew Arnold calls 'Titanic' when it exhibits itself in literature.[2] The ancient Celts had a law, it appears, which punished a man who, when arrayed in line of battle, 'stuck out too much in front.' This contempt of circumstances, which made the Celts of old decline to be frightened even by earthquakes, displays itself in the whole Celtic land difficulty. Land cultivated in a certain fashion, that is in small lots, does not pay in some places. A Teuton[3] would therefore give up his farm. But the Celt won't; he just stops there.

A few weeks ago I had the chance to see a very wretched sight, a Highland eviction, which illustrated these Titanic Celtic qualities.

It was a very wet afternoon, and I was walking along Strathwhacket (let us call it), in conversation with a charming old Highlander. He carried my rod and creel (empty), but his conversation was as good as any one is likely to find anywhere. He spoke of Montrose's wars, and was not on the side of the Argyles.[4] He spoke of the *Taishtaragh* (I think he called it) or second sight.[5] 'Every man sees three sights in his lifetime they say,' he remarked, and confessed that he had not even seen one 'sight' yet. 'But there is a man at Fort William who sees everything that is going to happen.' I suggested that this gentleman might make a rapid fortune if he would turn his inspired gaze on the British Turf, but at that moment we noticed a great brown smoke hanging in the wet air. It was an eviction. The 'sight' was not of the supernatural kind which the gillie[6] spoke of, but it was fit to make a mark on the memory. Beyond the river there was a high, wooded hill, all blue in the rain. Against this the smoke arose white, and in the midst of the clear red flame the black gables of the burning cottage stood out clear. There were some sappy, green bunches of trees by the gable; on the grass near the roadside a woman was trying to cover her property – chairs, table, an old delf dinner service,[7] all very decent furniture. The old gillie was very much excited, and full of anger and pity. 'The pony saw it,' he said, 'this is what the pony saw.' He referred to a misdemeanour of our pony, which had shied violently as we drove down the road in the morning. To me it seemed that the horse was alarmed by a big sheep which had bounced up under its nose, but my friend credited the pony with the *Taishtaragh*. 'The beasts see things we can't see,' he told me. This gift is very interesting, but it would not comfort me to have my neck broken by a prophetic quadruped, because a farmer I did not know was going to be evicted. The case of the farmer, if it was correctly reported, seemed to illustrate the Titanic Celtic temper very well. He had not paid a penny of rent for four years. The rent may have been high, but he surely might have paid some of it. Yet, though he had economised in rent, he was unable to pay his other creditors, and his stock and cattle had been sold up.

An Englishman would have perhaps thought it well to leave a farm which he could not make profitable, when he had money and stock. But the Celtic tenant simply declined to leave, in spite of many requests and warnings. The burning of his house, it was said, was an example of *trop de zèle*[8] on the part of the Messenger at Arms,[9] who exceeded his instructions. It was certainly a miserable and ill-advised action. But, as we slowly climbed the hill, and saw the smoke clinging to the valley, and saw the blackened beams of an old family home, we seemed to discern the differences between our race and the Celtic peoples. We have lost the old poetical beliefs, the *Taishtaragh* and the rest of it. No English beater nor under-keeper (except Kingsley's poet of gamekeeping life[10]) could have talked as that old gillie talked, an unschooled man, to whom English was a foreign tongue, half learned. History was tradition to him, a living oral legend. But we can recognise the nature and pressure of facts, without which sad knowledge society would revert into barbarism in a fortnight.

'At the Sign of the Ship', *Longman's Magazine* 28:165

(July 1896), pp.320–2

'Dorians may talk Doric,' according to Praxinoë and Gorgo,[1] but, according to a certain kind of reviewer, Scotch novelists should not write Scotch. The remarks of the critic of Mr. Stevenson's *Weir of Hermiston* in the *Athenaeum* are typical.[2] Long ago the *Quarterly Review* discovered that *Guy Mannering* was couched in 'a darkened dialect of Anglified Erse'[3] – 'the language of Ossian,' as a recent newspaper philologist has it. 'We can scarcely have half the book before us,' says the *Athenaeum* about *Weir*, 'yet already the glossary, which is eminently necessary, deals with over a couple of hundred words. Lord Hermiston objects to "palmering about in bauchles". He talks a little "sculduddery" after dinner. We have "ettercaps" and "carlines," scraps of Scot's "ballants," and, in short, the book is not for the Southron.'

This is either gross ignorance or puerile affectation. The Scotch Ballads, the Waverley Novels, and Burns's poems are familiar to every Englishman with the slightest pretensions to literature. The words – the two hundred Scotch words used by Mr. Stevenson – are of constant occurrence in Burns, Scott, and the Ballads. If this reviewer really does not understand them, he cannot read, without a glossary, books with which every educated man is supposed to be familiar. The words themselves, as a rule, are old English surviving north of the Tweed. A critic ought to be enough of a philologist to comprehend them, especially by aid of the context. When we are told that a coarse, sensual humorist talks 'sculduddery' after dinner, we must be idiots if we fail to understand the nature of his conversation. It was 'bold bawdry,' as Ascham calls it.[4] There are scarcely any Celtic words in Scotch; the terms are old English, with a few corruptions of French. A person who does not understand most of the peculiar terms is more dull and ignorant than a critic should like to write himself down, or to write his reading fellow-countrymen down. It is ridiculous to pretend, in the face of facts, that educated 'Southrons' do not read and appreciate Scott, Burns, and the Ballads. All of these circulate, and for eighty years have circulated, very widely, south of the Tweed. People do not buy millions of copies of books which they cannot read with ease. Moreover, hundreds of thousands of Mr. Barrie's and of Mr. Crockett's novels[5] have been bought in England. These books are full of the Scots, and it is plain that they are understood; if not, they would not be so popular.

One cannot suppose that the *Athenaeum* censor is really puzzled, either by 'sculduddery' or by 'bauchles.' If he really is puzzled, he must be excessively unread and inordinately dull. He must, therefore, be posing, and, if so, for what gallery? Certainly not for the largest English novel-reading public, for that is the public of Burns, Scott, Mr. Barrie, Mr. Crockett, and Mr. Stevenson. No works of old fiction have the circulation of Sir Walter's; no new novels, as far as anybody can judge, are more largely read than those of the authors of *Kidnapped*, *A Window in Thrums*, and *The Raiders*. Assuredly the English are the chief purchasers. They are not ignorant and stupid enough to be puzzled by some few hundred words constantly recurring in fiction and poetry ever since the days of Burns, Hogg, and Scott. Nobody seems to be perplexed but learned newspaper critics. It is, perhaps, less unkind to regard them as affected than as really much more stupid than the novel-reading public at large. Why they put on this particular affectation, and strike this especial pose in the *Athenaeum* and elsewhere, is a mystery. Probably it is a survival of that English superiority which, long ago, spoke of Scotch as 'Anglified Erse,' and to-day thinks that Ossian sang Lowland Scotch. This would certainly be very superior ignorance, if it were genuine, and would indicate a real genius for not knowing things. Such stupidity is rare, and is confined to reviewers, if it exists at all. On the whole, one prefers to believe that the *Athenaeum* gentleman is not so obtuse as he takes a mistaken pride in appearing. It is rather his sense of humour that is antiquated than his education that is neglected. Now reviewers really need not affect ignorance: they have such quantities of the genuine article. However, if they will insist on averring that they review Scotch novels in ignorance of Scotch, Latin essays in ignorance of Latin, and translations from Greek in ignorance of Greek, we can only say that it is time for them to receive the homely compliment of the sack. There must, surely, be qualified men who would do the work; if not, the pretence of doing the work had better be dropped altogether.

I ought to have explained that Praxinoë and Gorgo are Syracusan, Doric-speaking women in an idyll of Theocritus, a Greek poet. They do not hail from the Saut-market. *Saut* is Scotch for *salt* and the 'Saut-market' is referred to by a character in a 'Kailyard novel'[6] named *Rob Roy* by one Walter Scott, who died in 1832, or, according to Professor Goldwin Smith,[7] in 1836. Professor Goldwin Smith makes this assertion in his *Life of Scott* but it is unsupported by contemporary evidence.

'At the Sign of the Ship', *Longman's Magazine* 28:166

(August 1896), pp. 416–22

Last month all the Scottish lion in a peaceful nature was aroused by reviewers who did not understand, or pretended not to understand, common Scots words. Since then another critic, Mr. Purcell, devotes three columns and a half of the *Academy* (June 27) to what I fear I must call incoherences about Scotland and Scotch authors and critics, all *à propos* of Mr. Stevenson's *Weir of Hermiston*. As Mr. Purcell has never crossed the Tweed (he says), his opinion of Caledonia[1] is like that about 'rich Cyrene,' which the Delphic oracle treated with contempt.[2]

Mr. Purcell says: 'Caledonia ... has ever been to each poetic child of her own, not only a fit nurse, but a most partial, indulgent, and boastful one.' If Mr. Purcell knows anything at all about literary history, he knows, on reflection, that his remark is incorrect. He must have heard of Jeffrey's reviews of 'a poetic child' named Scott.[3] Was Jeffrey – then the first of British critics – 'partial, indulgent, and boastful' as regards Sir Walter? Nonsense! In fact no man is a prophet in his own country, a Scot least of all. San Francisco, not Edinburgh, has a memorial of Mr. Stevenson. Mr. Crockett has told a tale which I may therefore repeat. It is *ben trovato*, if not *vero*.[4] When Mr. Barrie's amusing *Professor's Love Story* was played in Kirriemuir (Thrums), one of the audience was heard to remark, 'Man, this is waur nor (worse than) *Walker London*!'[5] This is the common line of Scotch criticism of 'a brither Scot.' 'Brither' is Scots for 'brother,' by the way. Yet Mr. Purcell, with fine humour, avers that the critical Caledonian 'feels that he has discovered another masterpiece "if he sees in print" but one cherished topographical name – the Brig o'Guddlepaddock, or the Kirk o'Cuddyclavers.' Alas! I have not found the Northern reviewer so complacent, and it was a Scot who trampled so noisily on what he called 'The

Kailyard School.'[6] Five or six Scotch novels have long lain unopened on the shelves of one Caledonian critic, who owns that he cannot draw paper-knife on them, for good or bad, we have, at present, too much of the *genre*. The English, it appears to me, and not the Scotch, have commonly given to Scotch writers the warmest welcome, while the severities of Scotch critics to their literary fellow-countrymen, from Jeffrey on Scott to the lowest country newspaper on Mr. Crockett, are notorious. It is quite true, as Mr. Purcell sees, that the Scot who stays at home is more severe to his countrymen than the exile.

Mr. Purcell continues thus: 'There is the grossest assurance, effrontery, downright impudence ('his mainers astonishes *me*') in the Scotch argument that you and I cannot appreciate or criticise Scotch genius because we do not exactly know what "paddocks" are, and have never gone there (in Heaven's name, where?) "to identify them." Is it, then, impudent to say that even a person so superior (to grammar) as Mr. Purcell cannot criticise an author whom he cannot translate? Mr. Purcell obviously does not know that 'paddock,' or 'padock,' is English for a frog. Though he does not know English, and thinks that English is Scots, he supposes that he can appreciate a writer of Scots. 'The padock, or frogpadock, usually keeps or breeds on the land,' says Walton, an old English writer,[7] not partial to his country's invaders. So Mr. Purcell may go 'there' – namely, to the *Compleat Angler* – for the information which he is so strangely pleased at not possessing. Probably he is not really so very ignorant; the affectation is a cryptic kind of reviewer's joke.

For my part, I think it very probable that an Englishman as ignorant as Mr. Purcell pretends to be, or is, cannot appreciate Burns or Scott, simply because he cannot translate them. Nor can he fully appreciate 'Hesiod, or Hafiz, or Dante, or Tourgenieff,' as Mr. Purcell seems to think he can, if he knows neither Greek, Persian, Italian, nor Russian. For my part, there is only one language of these four in which I can appreciate an author, and, if I knew Greek better, doubtless I could appreciate Pindar more. Perhaps Mr. Purcell reads Burns and Tourgenieff in French translations; perhaps he is a master of all the tongues. Like gifted Gilfillian, 'I hae been as far as Muscovia in my sma' trading way,'[8] and have read Russian authors in French translations. I cannot doubt that I missed much of merit, and that I must learn Italian and Spanish if I would appreciate Dante and Cervantes. In the same way exactly, a person proud of his ignorance of Scots must lose a great deal when he tries to appreciate a writer in Scots. But, cries Mr. Purcell, in his urbane tones, 'this is just disgusting conceit veiled under flimsy mysticism.' Mr. Purcell is the child of an age of popular education. Where is the conceit, and where the mysticism, in the opinion that persons ignorant of a language are not the best judges of the literature of that language?

I will go further, and say that people acquainted with a country and with a national character get more pleasure than others do from the literature of that country. Conceited and mystical as Mr. Purcell may deem me, I am convinced that if I knew Russia and knew Spain, Cervantes and Tolstoi would give me certain pleasures which, in my ignorance, I do not taste. In the same way there are certain touches in Mr. Stevenson's work which please me, I am sure, more than they can please aliens in whom they awaken no old impressions, no certainty of experience testifying to their truth. No doubt Mr. Hardy has touches which produce the same pleasure in a Wessex man. Of course only an idiot would argue that only a Scot can appreciate Mr. Stevenson, or Scott, or Hogg. Any one can do so if, unlike Mr. Purcell, he knows enough of English to understand Scots, when his author is writing Scots. Certain local touches – Breton, Welsh and New England, Irish, Scotch, or what you please – will be missed by all but local readers. *The Lost Pibroch*, Mr. Neil Munro's excellent book,[9] pleases me most where I know the scenes, and when I can fathom the Gaelic. An Anglo-Indian will get more than I do (which is abundant) out of Mr. Kipling. We can all, however, with limitations appreciate Mr. Kipling, and so any intelligent and educated Englishman can appreciate Mr. Stevenson. But an Englishman who does not know what a 'paddock' is cannot be called educated, and an Englishman who, knowing, pretends not to know, cannot be called intelligent. He cuts a very poor figure.

Mr. Purcell supposes that a Scot learns Scots by being 'born a peasant or allowed' (*proh pudor*![10]) 'to mix with the servants' or to speak with his tenantry, I would add, or by keeping a notebook. Mr. Purcell is, doubtless, unaware that there is also a not inconsiderable literature, poetical and historical, in the language which Quintin Kennedy[11] wrote, and which John Knox anglicised. Professor Blackie[12] being dead, I have ventured to lift up the voice of my testimony against the ignorance and incoherences of Mr. Purcell. What he really means, probably, is that friendship, regret, and national feeling[13] have over-praised *Weir of Hermiston*. It may be so; I have not studied the reviews elaborately. We have a Scots proverb, 'Fules and bairns' (fools and children) 'should not see half-done work.' *Weir* is scarcely half-done, and no sensible adult will offer an opinion as to what the completed romance would have been. Friends and fellow-countrymen may have been betrayed by feelings not ungenerous, but Mr. Purcell's protests are not remarkable for taste, sense, or knowledge.

As 'that Prince of Paper Lords, Lord Peter, broke the Laws of God, and Man, and Metre',[14] so a distinguished living writer objects even to the very rules of tradition in English style. I shall not name him, for his remarks have interest enough without personalities. He says: 'How often does it not happen to painstaking writers to alter such stiff "literary" English in their first draughts into the honest colloquialism; and how often do they not find the national-schoolmaster type of critic finding fault with them for their "carelessness"– which is really the effect of careful and thoughtful revision. The plain truth is that, whenever a man takes a pen in hand to write, his first instinct is to adopt a certain impossible "literary" dialect, which became obsolete as speech a hundred years ago; only by the utmost consideration of every phrase – by deliberately asking himself, "Do I ever *say* that?"– by carefully splitting his infinities (*sic*), throwing his prepositions away from his verbs to the end of his sentences, and leaving many pendent to's and at's, can he attain at last to the desired and desirable colloquialism. Any school-girl can write absolutely "correct" and academic English; it is the pure spoken English of everyday life which costs a man hard in time and trouble.'[15] This argument appears to take it for granted that colloquial English, 'as she is spoke' by every one who is not a prig, should be the model in literary composition. This doctrine I cannot accept. First, it is contrary to all tradition, which, of course, in my learned opponent's eyes, proves it to be right. But I am fond of tradition, on the whole, as it represents the sum of human experience. Thus mankind has made every sort of experiment in marriage, and all the civilised Western races have ended in monogamy. Monogamy has its drawbacks, but experience has proved these to be less unendurable than the inconveniences attendant on polygamy, polyandry, and the delightful system of 'going as you please.' In the same way, universal tradition has recognised a certain standard of accuracy in literary language which is not demanded in ordinary talk. Greeks and Romans did not speak as they wrote. We do not praise a person who 'speaks like a printed book' and it is a curious and inexplicable fact that some Americans talk more like printed books than we do. Yet I should hesitate to applaud a man who wrote, on all occasions and on all themes, as the mass of people talk, that is, loosely, incorrectly, with many an aposiopesis, and without distinction. Mr. Stevenson, who wrote with such a distinguished charm, in conversation was boyishly colloquial. I am glad he tallked as he talked, and wrote in a very different style. Dr. Johnson was an example on the other side; he talked much better English than he wrote, except when he wrote the *Lives of the Poets*.

Literature, in brief, is expected to use language as an artist uses his materials; few of us are artists in conversation, and the exceptions are subject to laws of a different kind. A sort of standard is kept up in literature; a measure of cadence, a quality of accuracy is required. If these be neglected, and if the standard of current talk be adopted by authors, that standard, through human indolence, will be constantly degraded. The advocate of the opposite theory tells writers that they should 'carefully split their infinities,' by which I doubt not that he means their *infinitives*. In place of writing 'to run rapidly,' he should write 'to rapidly run.' As a matter of fact, I am priggish enough not to split my infinitives in ordinary talk. I feel no kind of temptation to do so, nor do I think that most people are thus tempted. On the other hand, the lax, formless scribes of to-day break all the decent rules of language without an effort. Why should I do violence to my tastes and habits by imitating their slovenliness at great cost of labour? In conversation I know that I sin in 'shalls' and 'wills,' 'woulds' and 'shoulds.' This is the inborn fault of the Scot and the Hibernian. My endeavour, often futile is to be correct with the pen, at least. Apparently my labour should be given to perpetrating distasteful blunders. If I wrote, 'How often do they not find the national-schoolmaster type of critic finding fault as our author does', the two 'finds' would annoy my ear – a proof of my depravity. 'The national-schoolmaster type' again, strikes me as an ill phrase; I cannot help preferring some other 'nice derangement of epitaphs.'[16] But no doubt our authority has accumulated his sentence toilsomely, in a conscientious pursuit of the colloquial. To be colloquial, 'he is at pains to write ill,' and occasionally succeeds. At the same time, after all his trouble, he does not write in the least as any mortal talks. To oblige him, I say 'as any mortal talks,' for the colliding 'tals,' in 'mortal talks,' are annoying to my ear. Here is an example of failure to write as people speak:

> 'I do not know what authority exists for importing the ethical limitation of an "ought" into this special matter, the prohibition is probably as baseless in its way as that other famous critical prohibition, so much in vogue in the eighteenth century, against the admission of similes into the first book of an epic poem.'[17]

Does anybody, does Mr. Herbert Spencer[18] even, *talk* like that? A man would put it, 'I don't see where the ought comes in. One might as well say there shouldn't be a simile in the first book of an epic, like Boileau, or some other old Johnnie.' Do *you* talk about 'unawakened potentialities'? I don't, for one, but our author writes about them. Oh, heaven and earth, does any mortal speak like this? – 'To see these things' (some Italian peculiarities) 'aright, however, we must possess the rare gift of ethnical psychology, backed by the power of throwing ourselves outside the ethnical ethics of our own idiosyncrasy.'[19] The English for *that*, I fancy, is 'we must judge foreigners by their own standards.' This is colloquial, without being slipshod, and the maxim thus expressed loses its appearance of scientific profundity. That may, or may not, be a thing to regret. As my version is not bad in grammar, I am conceited enough to prefer it to a sentence which seems inconsistent with its author's principles. When he wrote all that about 'ethnical psychology,' and 'the ethnical ethics of our own idiosyncrasy,' I wonder if he deliberately asked himself 'Do I ever say that?' And, if he does '*say* that,' does he not 'speak like a printed book,' a printed book by George Eliot in her wildest mood? To be sure it is not so much literary English as scientific terminology. The 'dialect,' alas! is too obviously not impossible; would that, in literary discussion, it were 'obsolete'! *Enfin*, there are, and ought to be, different standards for the written and the spoken word, and these standards vary in various kinds of composition. There are rules in every game, and no game can be played without rules. Meanwhile, if any schoolgirl can write absolutely correct and academic English, what enormous pains must many writers be at before they attain their present desirable slipslop!

Introduction to J. Vyrnwy Morgan, *A Study in Nationality*

(London: Chapman & Hall, 1911)

With Dr. Morgan's permission I write a brief Introduction to that part of his work which deals with the Reformation and its results in my own country, Scotland. Dr. Morgan is a Welsh divine of Wales, and after being myself honoured with the degree of Doctor of Sacred Theology by the University of Breslau, I feel free from the reproach of a friend who dubbed me 'an amateur divine.' Both Dr. Morgan and I speak not only as D.D.'s, but as members of 'small nationalities,' each of them fertile since the Reformation in the production of schism and sects such as MacMillanites, Irvingites, 'glancing Glassites,' Auld Lichts, New Lichts, and Sandemanians.[1]

Both of us are well aware that, in Dr. Morgan's words, 'there has grown up around the Reformation ... a mass of legend from which it is difficult to disentangle the truth.' But I was hitherto unaware that among the legends 'is that the high-water mark in architecture was the direct result of the Reformation' (p. 56). Here, indeed, is a large sample of the mass of legend that hangs about the Reformation. The Reformers, in Scotland, 'hated boetry and bainting,' like George II.[2] In my own beloved country, the complete pulverisation of mediaeval architecture, save in a few examples, was the direct result of the Reformation. Mediaeval works of art were destroyed as 'monuments of idolatry,' while everywhere the development of art, whether for good or evil, was no more the result of the Reformation than of the Council of Nicea.[3]

In literature, on the other hand (at least in England), the amazing splendour of the Elizabethan literature was concomitant with, if not caused by, the Reformation; while in Scotland presbyterial government refused the drama leave to exist, and the contemporary Scottish literature, in belles lettres, was, and long remained, insignificant.

Only persons under a strong delusion will differ from Dr. Morgan when he avers that 'letters, art, architecture, painting, and music were not the distinct products of the Protestant Reformation.' As to music, the church organs were made into firewood, or, like a wicked French clock which fell into the hands of a Presbyterian forbear of my own, the works were scooped out, because, as in the case of Prince Charlie's clock, 'the heathenish timepiece played tunes on the Sabbath.'[4] So much for music: in art we had not even a portrait painter, as late as 1680, and 'letters' were busy with polemical divinity, except in the hands of a few minor poets.

Dr. Morgan can recognise that intolerance, even unto slaying, was not confined to the ancient faith. Unlike a recent Nonconformist historian, he could not write the history of the Church of Geneva without making the most distant allusion to the burning of Servetus![5] But I am not acquainted with Dr. Morgan's evidence for the statement (p. 60) that John Knox 'advised the burning of Gardiner[6] and others of the Catholic party.' As a biographer, and not a favourably prejudiced biographer of Mr. Knox,[7] I never came across authority for this charge: if it is good, I bitterly lament having over-looked it. I feel sure that, if Knox advised any penalty against Gardiner, it was not the Romish punishment of burning. That he reserved for witches, and even they, I believe, were usually strangled first and burned afterwards.

Knox had a much higher opinion of Geneva than the Geneva doctors had of Knox. He went far too far for them on some points, and it may not be universally known that Calvin's immediate successors were terribly bored by what they thought the querulous complaints of the English Puritans who consulted them, and that they even expressed a friendly opinion of the English bishops who were being inveighed against. The Church discipline of Calvin might perhaps be valuable in a small 'city state,' a 'City of God,' but it did not bear transplantation to even a small nation like Scotland. A study of the records of kirk-sessions, dealing with peccant maids and bachelors, and profane swearers, and Sunday golfers, leaves one with the impression that ordinary morality did not improve under this regime, that sinners did not become less numerous, because they were put under sackcloth.[8] True, Sunday golf was finally eradicated (happily for the links and the greens, which need a day's rest), but 'Love would still be lord of all,'[9] and as for witches, the more they were burned, the more there were to burn.

In any case, as Dr. Morgan says, the sons of Calvinism have, in many ways, been splendid characters, tough and true as steel. But I doubt if the Puritans who put down the tyrannies of Charles I. and Laud,[10] were 'almost to a man, Calvinists.' The Sectarians, the Independents, won the battle, and surely among them were many heroes of 'fancy religions'; there were scores of these queer sects. 'Not as their friend or child I speak,'[11] but they had their good points, and if Calvinism is necessarily Presbyterian, Milton and England rejected Presbyterianism, after getting all the help they could out of the Scots by a feigned acceptance of the Solemn League and Covenant.[12]

Dr. Morgan, very properly (pp. 6–7), gives prominence, with Dr. Hay Fleming, to the extreme corruption of the Catholic Churchmen in the two, if not the three, centuries preceding the Reformation. We need not force an open door; 'who's a deniging of it,'[13] of the corruption? Certainly not Mary of Guise, who tried hard to induce the Pope to reform the scandalous nuns; certainly not Archibald Hay, Principal of St. Mary's College, St Andrews (1546); certainly not good Ninian Winzet, or Quentin Kennedy,[14] or even the papal nuncio who secretly visited Queen Mary, taking his life in his hand; and certainly not Father Pollen, S.J.,[15] in our own time. Except the Observantine Friars,[16] and a few priests like Winzet and Hay, we can scarcely find ten righteous men among the clergy who are known to us in the Scotland of the middle of the sixteenth century. Almost all were ignorant, dissolute, and avaricious. But the counter-Reformation came, and, despite Presbyterian persecution, many Scots of the highest intelligence, risking punishment, went back to the ancient faith as the more reasonable and logical in their conscience and judgment.

Dr. Morgan liberally allows that the intolerance of Knox was part of the force which established presbyterial government. To be sure the nobles and gentry would not allow the death penalties to be executed on Catholics, who had only to submit to fines, imprisonment, outlawry, exile, civil disabilities, and the pillory. The intolerance of Knox (not by nature an unkind man) sprang, I think, from the doctrine on which he often harps, that Catholicism is idolatry, is high treason to God, and that 'idolaters must die the death'[17] lest God, very jealous of His glory, should punish the whole community at large for the high treason of individuals. That is Knox's doctrine, whether he invented it or picked it up in Geneva, I do not know.

As to our Protestant martyrs to the death, during the ferocious regime of the Church, I cannot find, nobody can find, more than twenty in a hundred and fifty years. They were usually 'kinless loons,'[18] of low birth, without clans or names to avenge them, though Wishart was avenged by the murder of Cardinal Beaton.[19] In the same way it was not safe for the Presbyterian preachers to punish Catholics to the death, and for these reasons there were few martyrs in Scotland under either regime; though Scottish law, in a day, converted the exercise of the old-established religion into a capital crime. It is not burnings that destroy, or all but destroy, a faith; it is the ceaseless daily grind of fines and disabilities and general injustice.

I confess that I cannot follow Dr. Morgan's historical statements (p. 79) as to why our 'Scottish nobility accepted the Protestant principles.' The nobility, in the minority of James V., were of various factions; it was not the nobility but the Douglases[20] who held the boy-king captive, and when the Douglases were driven into England, and took English pay, they cared nothing about rival creeds, but accepted whatever creed might be that of their master, Henry VIII., at the moment. The Douglas faction had political and personal reasons for backing the shifting creed of Henry VIII.

When we come to the question of Episcopacy in Scotland[21] (pp. 80, 81) we must remember that, before Knox's return in 1559, the Protestants in Scotland were introducing the English liturgy, hateful to Knox, and, as far as I am aware, had no objection to bishops save social objections. Bishops were often men of the middle classes: 'smaiks,' as the aristocrats called them. Knox himself was not a strict anti-episcopite, and James VI. was not the first to introduce Episcopacy. Twelve years after the Reformation, when James was a boy of six, the Earl of Morton, to serve his private ends, brought back bishops, and after that there were very few years in which bishops were not more or less in evidence till 1638. James VI. suffered such intolerable things from the preachers, and their claims to implicit obedience, and to the right to excommunicate men with civil penalties, that he needed bishops as a kind of police, a buffer between him and the preachers. Nobody can approve of James's methods, which were of the 'lobbying' and 'wire-pulling' order (and worse), but any one can see that the preachers were working to dominate the State.

Nobody, perhaps, who is not a fanatic can deny, when he has carefully read the history of Scotland from 1580 to 1596, that the 'sacerdotalism'[22] of the Kirk (as Lord Guthrie calls it), the more than Hildebrandine claims[23] of the preachers to 'judge Angels,' Kings and Ministers of State, and to be implicitly obeyed, in short, were absolutely intolerable and inconsistent with the freedom of the State. James had to do something to shake off this tyranny. He was hunted like a partridge on the mountains, seized in his bedroom, and insulted by wild Frank Bothwell,[24] with the approval of the Kirk. At the end of 1596 he had done all that was necessary, almost, not quite, he had not abolished the civil outlawry attending on clerical excommunication. But he went on to do the wrong thing in the worst way, to introduce bastard kinds of Bishops by pettifogging devices, and to increase their power by every unconstitutional ruse, till they excited the jealous hatred of the nobles. Charles I. went further, and reaped the whirlwind. The government of the Restoration, while despising the prelates and treating them as cavalierly as if they had been clerks in the Civil Service, made the same fatal error of restoring Episcopacy. The King 'went coldly into it,' knew his bishop-hating countrymen too well to approve of it, but indolently yielded to Middleton, a fine soldier, but no politician, and to Clarendon, whose sympathy with the Scots (like that of Charles Lamb)[25] was 'imperfect.' In the Revolution Settlement (1689–1690), the error was avoided, while the preachers, outworn by a struggle of nearly thirty years, were deftly put in their proper place, and deprived of their great weapon, excommunication with civil penalties. The Government of Cromwell had taken this sword away, had prohibited General Assemblies, and preserved peace.

After 1690 the chief of the Kirk's sorrows was the revival of lay Patronage. The Jacobites, their own religion being persecuted, left the barb of Patronage to rankle in the bosom of the Kirk, and for nearly two centuries to be one cause (there were plenty of other causes) of Secession and Schism. The Disruption of 1843 arose from the circumstance that a Church, if it be a State Church, must conform to the law of the land. If it does not like it, then it can leave it, and be a Free Kirk: so that every Scottish town or village may have, and often has, a doublette, an 'Auld Kirk' and a 'Free Kirk,' perhaps also a 'Wee Kirk,' with, of course, an 'Episcopal' Kirk and a Catholic Kirk, and a few miscellaneous Kirks. I know all of them coexisting, quite friendly, in a single Highland village. 'What for no?' But Scotland, theologically, as Dr. Morgan says, 'no longer stands where she did.' Thanks to the Higher Criticism,[26] the clergy may believe what they please, and some very queer things many of them do believe, while as to how much of the Apostles' Creed [27] they accept, it does not become me to ask impertinent questions.

I must venture to differ from my learned author when, speaking of the Covenanters, he says that they 'were engaged in a fierce struggle for liberty of conscience' (p. 83). They would have regarded this as a cruel libel. They declared that 'the vomit of toleration' must never be 'licked up,' and they resolutely bade Charles II. inflict Presbyterianism on England. (I give you my reference. Mr. Wodrow's Sufferings, vol. i. pp. 66–71.) They urged the persecution of Quakers, Catholics, persons who used our Liturgy, and so forth. This was their fight for 'liberty of conscience'! They fought like fiends, or paladins,[28] for their own liberty of conscience, but that included permission to persecute any body whose conscience was not their own. That is the pity of it, but that is the historical truth of the case. The widespread belief, found in so many modern books, that the Reformers, or the Covenanters, or the Kirk after 1688, fought for 'liberty of conscience,' is part of the mass of legend which hangs about the Reformation. From the day when, as Knox tells us, the Congregation overthrew the religious houses at Perth, and threatened death against priests who celebrated Mass (1559), to the time when the Anglican cult was decried as Baal-worship, and the day (1711) when Mr. Greenshields was imprisoned for using the Prayer Book, the Reformed was a persecuting Church. You cannot easily conceive the lengths to which hatred of prayers not extempore[29] was carried. It was an offence to say the Lord's Prayer in the service, and even for the minister to premeditate his own prayers. 'These things are very uneasy to honest old men that have seen the glory of the old Temple,' says Wodrow. In the old Temple the minister was expected to say, in prayer, whatever came into his head, by inspiration, at the moment. So vigorous a Covenanter as Brodie of Brodie,[30] after hearing the Liturgy in London, wrote in his Diary, 'I have seen, and daily, much disorder and extravagance in conceived prayers' (unpremeditated effusions) 'which does afflict me.'

I only want to shake, if I can, the belief that any of our Reformers and their successors were friends of freedom of conscience. In doing their best for education they were unconsciously opening the way to freedom of thought. But they had no more idea of what would result from education than had the Catholic bishops who founded the Scottish universities, St Andrews, Aberdeen, Glasgow, and, in origin, Edinburgh. The politicians of the Reformation, despite the noble scheme of Knox, robbed the universities. All was not ignorance even in the year of the Reformation. In the school of Linlithgow, Winzet was setting his boys Latin essays on important subjects, and probably he was not the only good schoolmaster. But to the Reformers, from Erskine of Dun to Andrew Melville,[31] Scotland owed the introduction of Greek studies, and Oriental tongues soon became more generally studied than they are at present. Scotland was far in front of England in possessing a school of considerable poets, Henryson, Dunbar,[32] and others, long before Luther's voice was heard. The school became nearly extinct, after the Reformation, in the din of war and controversy; under the Restoration the foremost man of letters 'that noble wit of Scotland,' as Dryden called him, was the persecutor of the Saints, 'the bloody Advocate,' Sir George Mackenzie.[33] He was a man of letters by nature, a persecutor only for professional reasons not a good character! The men of letters of the eighteenth century sedulously copied the English style (indeed, Knox, as far as in him lay, wrote English, not Scots), and were sceptics like Hume, or Moderates like Robertson, in opposition to the party which platonically still loved the Covenant, Calvinism, and the burning of witches, itself the baneful result of an early Act of Knox's day. These Moderates were the clerics esteemed by Robert Burns, who, to be sure, was at once a Jacobin and a Jacobite.[34]

However, I am not to follow my author in his roll-call of eminent modern Scots, though I can scarcely dare to accept the compliment, 'Scotland, within the circle of the smaller nationalities, stands, in relation to the modern world, where Greece stood in relation to the ancient.' Post-Minoan Greece, he goes on to say, was original, 'self-taught' like the minstrel of Odysseus. Her art and thought learned little from foreign contemporary peoples, while Scotland learned much from France, and, later, much from Germany and England. All Western Europe was a community, with constant inter-borrowings. The Scottish Reformation came from Geneva, with important features derived, I think, from ideas either peculiar to Knox, or by him emphasised beyond the measure of his masters and pastors. That the stern morality of the Genevan discipline greatly affected Scottish morality, I doubt. In rustic regions, before and after Knox, as the old popular songs, and many songs of Burns, attest, morality was much like that of the Sicily of Theocritus, though the Scottish priestesses of Aphrodite were firm on one point, 'Laddie, ye manna whustle on the Sabbath.'[35]

I have not ventured to comment on the greater portion of Dr. Morgan's book, dealing with subjects of which I am ignorant, the history and modern conditions of Wales. The people are Celts. The people and the dynasty of Southern Scotland were English by blood, in language, and in most institutions, before the days of Edward I.

Of them it could not be said, as about so large a proportion of the Cymry, their language they kept; and it is a curious fact that they did not, like the Welsh and the Gaelic-speaking people, keep to their prehistoric poetic legends; even of Arthur the name only lingers like a cloud in the place-names of the Lowlands. These facts differentiate from each other the small nationalities of Scotland, which I know, and of Wales, concerning which I have everything to learn from Dr. Morgan. His lucidity of style, candour, and tolerance, and his wide and minute knowledge of his native country, make him a trustworthy enlightener of Scottish and English ignorance of the Wales of the past, and of the tumultuous to-day. For we are, as a rule, very ignorant, and a Scot is apt to know as little of the Welsh, as an Englishman usually knows of the past of Scotland. If we remain in this darkness, it is not the fault of Dr. Morgan.

'History As She Ought To Be Wrote', *Blackwood's Edinburgh Magazine* 1006:166

(August 1899), pp. 266–74

'Alas!' murmured the Quaker lady, 'alas for the Bruisers of England! How are they fallen!' When one thinks of the historical writers of modern England, we sympathise with Borrow's Quaker lady.[1] 'How are they fallen!' the historical writers of England, or perhaps we should say, 'How are they risen!' out of human ken. Certain it is that, for one reason or another, our living historical writers are not much read. The world does not welcome them as it welcomed Hume, Macaulay, Froude, or even Mr J. R. Green,[2] who, but for evil fate, might still be competing with our most popular novelists. A readable historian might still hold his own, but our historians do not usually permit themselves to be read without too extreme labour.

That history, composed in our own day, is unpopular, does not seem wholly the fault of a public sunken in sloth. Many most applauded and popular novels demand, from the natural man, a laborious patience, such as is not called for even by the author of 'Feudal England,'[3] who does not aim at attracting the volatile or stooping to the herd. The style and touch of Professor Maitland, as in 'Domesday Book and Beyond,'[4] are charming and buoyantly light in comparison with those of certain authors of modern romance. The public, in short, can undertake very hard and heavy reading, where some applauded novels are concerned, yet history, as now written, is neglected. People who care for history fall back on Froude and Macaulay, though their works, in every sense, are not 'up to date,' and would benefit by *notae variorum*,[5] correcting the errors and adding new material. The truth is that the books of Macaulay and Froude, nay, even of Mommsen,[6] are literature, while the new schools of historians 'despise literature,' and insist on producing what they call 'science.' Thus, though in our universities historical study is infinitely more popular than ever it was; though our young men pore over charters, and our young women (according to Mr Frederic Harrison)[7] peruse medieval washing-bills, none the less we have scarcely a historian whom the public reads. In truth, history is in a parlous case, and the interesting thing is that historians love to have it so. This I gather from a curious, instructive, and even diverting book, 'Introduction to the Study of History,' by C. V. Langlois, and C. Seignobos, of the Sorbonne. Translated by G. G. Berry, with a preface by F. York Powell.* From this book I learn, generally, that history is not (now) for the public, that history is not literature, and that it ought to be devoid of human interest. Now, lack of human interest is the very last thing with which Mr York Powell's[8] enemies (if he has any) would charge him. His preface to this learned work is full of interest, yet he seems to believe, *contre-coeur*[9] as it were, in the theories of MM. Langlois and Seignobos. 'A history-book is not necessarily good,' he says, 'if it appears to the literary critic "readable and interesting", nor bad because it seems to him "hard or heavy reading."' 'The literary critic' is a vague quantity. But surely no book of history need be, in fact, 'hard and heavy *reading.' Mr* Maitland's books,[10] for example, are not heavy reading, even when he deals with points the most obscure in the development of institutions. They are extremely readable by persons who care to know about serfs, villeins, the origin of boroughs, and so forth. A book is bad, we think, if it is 'heavy' in manner, however 'heavy' its theme may be. Mr York Powell goes on, 'The formation and expression of ethical judgments, the approval or condemnation of Caius Julius Caesar or of Caesar Borgia, is not a thing within the historian's province.' Therefore all historians, from Herodotus to Mommsen, who deal in moral verdicts, are, so far, out of their province. A historian, it seems, must divest himself of humanity, and of human interests, while he narrates the actions of human beings. The 'portraits' of Clarendon, Thucydides, Freeman, Macaulay, Mommsen,[11] are all matter in the wrong place. Without these, however, history must inevitably be dull, and unreadable, and heavy, and a closed book to the public. In fact, as far as I can understand our authors, the public has no business with history. History is to be written by specialists for specialists. Now Mommsen, for instance, is of specialists the most distinguished. But as soon as he writes what the public can read, deserting the collection of inscriptions for exposition in narrative, he becomes little better than one of the wicked. His Caesar, his Gracchi, his Cicero,[12] are sins against history. 'We find,' say the French authors, 'specialists in critical scholarship writing general histories *in which they let their imaginations guide them in the work of construction.*' Curtius[13] and Mommsen are examples of this crime. Well, can science be pursued at all without imagination? Darwin and Newton needed, and used, imagination, as much as Homer or

* Duckworth & Co., London, 1898.

Shakespeare. Without imagination construction is impossible. Without imagination to construe them, documents are meaningless.

Again, 'Men whose information is all that could be desired, whose monographs intended for specialists are full of merit, sometimes show themselves capable, when they write for the public, of grave offences against scientific method. The Germans are habitual offenders. Consider Mommsen … ' I do consider Mommsen, – with grateful and respectful admiration. I need no more accept Mommsen's Cicero, for example, than I believe in Mr Froude's Mary Stuart, or in his Henry VIII. But I find a man of vast knowledge writing about men 'in a human kind of way,' though, of course, in a fallible way. I can read Mommsen: a part of the public can read him, and where is the use of an author who does not permit himself to be read? Mommsen, with other sinners, applies himself 'to the task of producing works of art: in this endeavour those who have no talent make themselves ridiculous, and the talent of those who have any is spoilt by their preoccupation with the effect they wish to produce.' Perhaps 'those who have no talent' are excellent hands at writing for specialists. But that the talent of Mommsen or Macaulay is 'spoilt,' who but MM. Seignobos and Langlois will declare? They have the defects of their qualities, for which every reader of sense knows how to make due allowance. We do not accept Macaulay's Claverhouse[14] or Mommsen's Caesar as the Claverhouse or Caesar who is known only to his Maker. But we learn (after due deductions) and we are entertained.

The result of these 'scientific' notions is, I think, that the public is to have no history, for men of real information are demoralised by writing for the public, while the non-specialist (the abandoned 'populariser') is a person of contemptible character. 'General history,' as I understand our authors, cannot be written at all. No man is a specialist in all the elements of a nation's history, and if such a phoenix did exist, and did write 'general history,' the odds are that he would be demoralised, like Mommsen, would become a 'habitual offender.' Thus tiny bits of knowledge are to be the special property of a small class; some owning one 'poffle or pendicle,'[15] some another. Nobody has a right in the general folkland of the past. To vary the metaphor, I venture to conceive that just as rivers exist to feed navigable canals, so monographs, and other valuable works of specialists, exist as feeders of 'general history'; of something that intelligent men and women can read, and thereby be instructed. I am not arguing that the historian ought to be a mass of prejudices, like Froude or Macaulay; still less that he ought to employ the violent rhetoric of Mr Green. But he should aim at producing a 'work of art'; he should, indeed he must, employ his constructive imagination. The defect of Macaulay's, Froude's, and Mommsen's books is not that they are works of art, but that, as works of art, they are injured by glaring colour, and want of keeping, and discordant 'values.' These are injurious to art no less than to science. The sin lies, not in the presence of the element of art, but in crimes against the canons of art. Such crimes are easily avoided by historians who, dispensing with art, are also condemned to dispense with readers.

Mr York Powell, when introducing his French friends, reinforces their argument. 'Whether we like it or not' (we like it rarely), 'history has got to be scientifically studied, and it is not a question of style, but of accuracy, of fulness of observation, and correctness of reasoning that is before the student.' But it is also, I maintain, a question of style. Without style no book will endure, as Gibbon's great work,[16] for example, does endure. But perhaps our scientific friends will carry matters so far as to deny that any historical book whatever deserves to endure – has any right to endure. For if history is science, books of science do not persist (as a rule), but in a year or two become rococo, *passés*, out of date. Where are some of the scientific articles in the 'Encyclopaedia Britannica'? Where are the snows of yesteryear?[17]

Our authors keep insisting that history must be 'up to date.' But history simply cannot be up to date. New facts are unearthed, new theories (mostly absurd) are evolved, while a new history book is passing through the press. The 'up to date' of to-day is the exploded fancy of to-morrow. The very latest notion about these exciting themes, Knights' Fees, Boroughs, Manors, *Mercheta Mulierum*,[18] to-day are, [omission in original] and to-morrow are cast into the oven. Science, in many branches, is a set of mirages. I myself, lately, was at great pains to confute a certain author's Theory of West African Religion.[19] I *did* confute it, I think; but I did not know that, in a paragraph of a more recent work, my author had already thrown his theory overboard. I was unconsciously forcing an open door. This kind of experience is eternally recurring; the mists of science are constantly, by their very nature, dissolving and taking fresh forms. Thus considered, history 'written scientifically,' and without regard to style, can never endure. It is history written as literature, and with regard to style, that does and will remain, *oere perennius*.[20] Clarendon lasts, Macaulay persists, Hume endures, Carlyle is not superannuated; though fresh facts are discovered, and old stories are disproved. These, and many other great historical writers, survive by their style. A historian, of course, ought to be accurate (as far as mere mortals may); of course he ought to reason correctly ('at least as far as he is able'); but if he wants his book to be read, and if he wants it to go on being read after he is dust, a historian must have style. It is essential. Style is the salt of literature, and history is literature.

Of course neither Mr York Powell nor his French allies instigate historians to write badly, blankly, baldly. 'Huxley, and Darwin, and Clifford have shown that a book may be good science and yet good reading.' 'I am no that sure about' Mr Huxley, always. But I am fairly sure that a book, if it is to survive a year or two, must be well written. It is not enough to be accurate, it is not enough to be up to date. In fact, I repeat, no mortal *can* be up to date. As I write (July 12, 1899, 6.30 p.m.) an example arrives. I have passed for press a chapter on Roman Scotland. I have insisted that the Romans did not invade Ireland.[21] That seemed a safe thing to say. But, lo! comes in the 'Classical Review,' July 1899. Herein I learn that Pfitzner and Gudeman hold that Agricola *did* invade Ireland. The reasons of Pfitzner 'were foolish,' but Mr Haverfield examines the reasons of Gudeman. The reasons of Gudeman are 'a straw theory set up to be demolished.' That is very satisfactory: still, no history can be 'up to date.' 'Foolish' ideas, 'straw theories,' insist on being set up, and no mortal can keep pace with them.

Now, for a last word on style. 'It is not a question of style,' we have heard Mr York Powell maintain. But, later, he cites his authors as saying that 'the historian has *not* the right to use a faulty, low, careless, or clogged style ... He has not the privilege of writing badly. But he ought *always* to write well, and not to bedizen his prose with extra finery once a-week.' Then, after all, it is a question of style, and for that I am arguing. As to 'bedizening his prose once a-week,' our prose must match our topic. We need not describe the battles of Hastings or Bannockburn in the same level manner and pedestrian fashion as we discuss Knights' Fees or the Lords of the Articles. 'Purple patches'[22] are an abomination, but he who tells the tale of a great event, or a romantic adventure, must tell it with spirit. I will go further: the historian is not compelled to lack the sense of humour. Nothing can be more comic than the attitude of Henry VIII. towards Scotland after Solway Moss.[23] Henry appears as the big, strong, vain, stupid giant of fairy tale, always baffled and mocked by his little human opponent. When Henry desires to kidnap the baby Mary Stuart, and then fears that she has already been 'changed at nurse,' and that he is stealing the wrong child, Henry is frankly an object of mirth. Why not say so; why keep up the old unscientific idea of 'the dignity of history'? The situation being humorous, it is actually 'scientific' to say, and show, that humorous it is.

While maintaining that history was, is, and must be literature, I do not, of course, deny that it also was, is, and must be 'scientific.' Science is organised common-sense, applied to inquiry. Every historian worth naming has been as scientific as his temperament, and the ideas of his age, permitted. It is not within the last fifty years alone that historians have laboriously un-earthed and consulted 'documents.' No modern historian has travelled and toiled more laboriously to gather MSS. than did honest John of Fordun, in the late fourteenth century. We do not call Fordun a scientific historian, up to the present standard, but he was as scientific as he knew how to be. He did his best, and 'the men of the Merse can do no more.'[24] Consider how Carte practised 'Heuristik,'[25] the slang word for the research of documents. Our age, most properly, is more precise, more 'pernickety,' as the Scots has it, as to evidence, but all this is matter of degree, not difference in kind. Indices, catalogues, calendars of MSS. are compiled and printed: palaeography is studied at the Universities, till the number of young experts almost constitutes a public in itself. The French, with their École des Chartes,[26] are in advance of us. We applaud their labours: we all wish history to be more and more scientific in her inquiries. But we insist that human qualities in exposition must keep pace with patience in acquisition. 'Toute trouvaille procure une jouissance,' say our mentors: 'Every new find is enjoyable.' But whatsoever is new is not, therefore, important. The modern historian is apt to make a mountain out of his mole-hill of a new discovery, or to rewrite history under the influence of a 'straw theory.' This may be strikingly original, it may be magnificent, but History it is not.

Another blunder (as our authors note) is blind devotion to the 'emendation game.' MSS. must be critically examined, as a matter of course. James I. of Scotland long suffered under a false imputation, to which he was condemned by a comma or two printed in the wrong place. The vast collections of our printed State Papers are not always to be relied upon. The old English and Scots are modernised; punctuation is muddled, by even painstaking editors; one does not always feel sure of the accuracy of the translations from old French and Spanish. To be freely scientific, a historian should be a palaeographer, capable of comparing with the MSS., and so controlling, the useful printed documents. This is well – nay, indispensable – but to make emendations for the sake of the sport is as injurious to history as to scholarship. Our authors, always judicious in detail, warn us against the violent delights of the Emendation Game. Researches into authorship, of course, they recommend. Historians were once apt to quote Matthew of Westminster, or Simeon of Durham, or I forget who of Brompton,[27] and to think that they had done enough. Now, we ask, Who was Matthew of Westminster? Too clearly his name was Harris; nor was the Brompton historian what Dr Lingard[28] supposed. We used to think that Mr Freeman's honest Winchester Chronicle was plenarily inspired. Was it not written in 'honest English'?[29] But times are altered, and the statements of the Winchester Chronicle are not always regarded as 'honest Injun.'[30] Our French mentors, however, are very much mistaken if they think that critical analysis of authorities is 'a new invented game.' I open Horace Walpole's 'Historic Doubts on the Life and Reign of King Richard the Third' (1768). On the title-page Walpole prints as his motto –

> 'History is only founded on the evidence of the authors who have transmitted it to us. It is of the highest moment, then, to know precisely who and what these authors were. On this point nothing ought to be neglected; their date, their birth, their part, if any, in affairs, their sources, their interest in these, are all essential circumstances, which we have no right to ignore. On all these things depends their measure of authority, and without knowledge of these particulars we run the risk of relying on an historian who may be unfair, or, at least, ill-informed.'

I translate the French, from 'Histoire de l'Académie des Inscriptions,' vol. x. The remarks are common-sense, and it was not left to our age to show common-sense. Even our great poet-historian, Barbour,[31] prefers and specifies the authors of his first-hand evidence (1370).

'The public at large,' say our authors, 'with its vulgar and superficial standards, has nothing but disdain for the whole of critical scholarship.' I am not arguing for the vile herd; but I do think that the public is anxious to accept the proved results of critical scholarship, if it can get them, while it does not want to have all the laboratory processes forced on its attention. But, till scientific historians write readably, what is the public to do? It reads Mr Froude, because he is so readable. From Mr Froude the public will never be won, till some scientific historian writes about his topics as agreeably, with less bias and with more accuracy. Why should not one of our scientific historians stoop to this labour? Nobody prevents him from being as scientific as he pleases, but the public insists that he shall be able to write. Surely it is possible to please, without being inaccurate and unfair. 'A complete divorce between erudition and history seems to-day almost inexplicable,' say our authors, yet it is they who, at some moments, pronounce a divorce between history and literature.

They are most entertaining when they diagnose what they call 'Froude's Disease.' Now Bright's disease[32] (I fancy) was not one from which Dr Bright personally suffered. Possibly we should say 'Freeman's Disease,' as Mr Freeman so frequently diagnosed the malady of his great contemporary, just as others now diagnose the complaint of Mr Freeman. 'Chronic inaccuracy' is the malady, however we choose to name it. The late Mr Paget, in 'Maga,'[33] studied this disease as exhibited in the case of Macaulay. Everybody has had Froude's disease, like measles, more or less severely. A conscious sufferer, I have taken pleasure in studying my own symptoms as exhibited by the most scientific historians of our day. They all (or almost all), in undergraduate phrase, 'make howlers.' The best man (as far as accuracy goes) is he who makes the minimum of 'howlers.' Mr Froude, considering his eminent industry in research, made the maximum of howlers. He was not, indeed, as our authors say, 'one of the first in England to base the study of history on that of original documents, as well unpublished as published.' Everybody did that. Florence of Worcester did it (in a way), Hemingburgh did it, Fordun did it, Carte did it, Tytler[34] did it in Mr Froude's own field. Mr Froude only broke into a virgin collection of documents, at Simancas.[35] To say that he was 'one of the first in England to use unpublished documents' is to suffer from Froude's disease, from 'chronic inaccuracy.' Our authors admit that 'everyone makes mistakes.' 'What is abnormal is to make many mistakes, to be always making them, in spite of the most persevering efforts to be exact.' In truth, the efforts of Mr Froude and of other sufferers are *not* 'the most persevering.' By real perseverance in a most disagreeable task, that of eternally repeated verification, a man must be able to get rid of, at least, many of the spots of Froude's disease. The weaker his power of meticulous attention, the stronger the activity of his subconscious imagination, the more must he persevere. I do remember getting into trouble at school from translating the Greek words that my subconscious self beheld on the printed page before me. I translated them correctly, but – the words were not there. Something else was there. Perseverance in struggling with my subconscious self was inculcated by the application of physical suffering. Perhaps imperfect sight aids the unconscious self which presented Mr Froude with so many facts that were not facts. 'Precipitancy' is another factor in the malady. Yet we are bidden, by a German, to avoid 'excessive preoccupation with little things.' Another says, 'The criticism of texts and sources has become a branch of sport: the least breach of the rules is considered unpardonable ... Scholars are mostly malevolent and discourteous to each other.' Instead of doing perfectly what Mr Froude or any other author did imperfectly, they show up their neighbours' 'howlers'! Thus 'men reach at length a state of morbid anxiety and scrupulosity which prevents them from doing anything at all, for fear of possible imperfections.'

Thus historians are between Scylla and Charybdis,[36] to use a novel phrase. They jump, like Mr Froude, into a sea of MSS. and bring up a book of absorbing interest – a pearl, but a bizarre pearl, like those so cunningly set in gold by the artists of the Renaissance. Or they pore over their work with a patent double-million magnifying pair of spectacles, and never produce anything worth looking at. Of the two maladies, give me Froude's disease. Measles is better than paralysis. And paralysis it is when, as Von Pflugk Harting[37] says, 'The highest branches of historical science are despised: all that is valued is microscopic observations and absolute accuracy in unimportant details.' Our authors, nevertheless, applaud the perpetual microscopic criticism which scholars bestow on each other. 'Barring the harshness, they are quite right.' They 'bar the door against the tribe of incapables and charlatans who once infested their profession.' But how can a scholar be doing anything worth mentioning if he eternally 'gets up and bars the door'? Time, and that promptly, will get rid of humbugs. 'In most works of historical popularisation there inevitably appear blemishes of every kind, *which the well-informed always note with pleasure.*' The well-informed always note the blunders of histories that appeal to the public 'with pleasure.' In the name of Science, why? Let me be very impertinent. In the Introduction of ten pages which so great and genial a scholar as Mr York Powell has contributed to the work of MM. Langlois and Seignobos, I remark an interesting set of – inaccuracies! In one way this is consolatory; if there is a beam in my own eye, there are motes in his organ of vision. But am I to 'note them with pleasure'? Perish the thought!

These are the joys of pedants. Let them popularise something themselves. Let them compete with and supersede our vulgar Michelets, Froudes, Macaulays, Mommsens. But, to do that, the well-informed need genius, and genius is what they do not always possess, and do not view, like other men, 'with pleasure.' It is written, 'We no longer go to history for lessons in morals, nor for good examples of conduct, nor yet for dramatic or picturesque scenes.' But we, for our part, do go to history for all these things. We go for them, and we get them abundantly.

Scotland has now, at last, Chairs of History in the Universities of Edinburgh and Glasgow, and, I believe, at Aberdeen. There is even a kind of Stool of History, a fearfully under-endowed Stool, in that centre of history, St Andrews. Let us hope that the learned Professors do not adopt the opinion that history is not literature, do not over-estimate tithes of mint and cumin,[38] but teach their pupils that history is a human, and should be a delightful, study by men and women, of what our ancestors did and endured for causes now religious, now romantic, but always deserving to be recorded not only with accuracy but with charm.

'At the Sign of the Ship', *Longman's Magazine* 28:163

(May 1896), pp. 101–5

A recent biography, that of Cardinal Manning,[1] has revived a question which can never be absolutely settled, for it is a question of degree. What is the precise duty of a Biographer? When Lockhart's Life of Scott was published, in 1837–38, a storm of abuse arose against both the historian and his hero. Lockhart was accused of blackening Scott's character. He had shown that Sir Walter was a bad man of business, in a business where he had no right to be. Everyone knew that before. He had shown that Scott associated more than need be with the Ballantynes, hardly the right mates for him. He had told the story of how the sheriff sat on the treasured wine-glass of George IV. He had given one instance of deliberate rudeness to Lord Holland, arising out of a private grudge, and one of terribly severe judgment on another's fault. He had admitted, and explained, what many thought Sir Walter's extreme deference to rank. There, in a page of letter-paper, are the examples of blackening Scott's character. More were not given, there were, practically, no more to give. In a course of study recently imposed on me, I have detected just one instance of a foible of Scott's, which Lockhart generalised; he did not reproduce the details, which were extremely unimportant.

The truth, and the whole of it, was told in this biography, and the wise world howled, as we may still read in Mr. Carlyle's essay.[2] Mr. Carlyle, on the other side, praised a courageous blow dealt at a common form of cant. A biographer must be truthful or hold his hand altogether. I am informed that Mr. Carlyle insisted on the publication, by Mr. Froude, of some unhappy details about his own married life; they were published, and most of us remember, perhaps helped to swell, the hubbub.[3] A very disagreeable theory of Mr. Carlyle became current; now, probably, that theory is fading away. He had chosen to do a sort of public penance, like Dr. Johnson at Lichfield.[4]

He had chosen it, but, if he had not, would it have been Mr. Froude's duty, as a biographer, to give such a large exhibition of blots? Did truth demand all these domestic janglings? I venture to think not, for truth of representation must always be a compromise. Details can only be introduced in such measure as will not mischievously affect the truth of the likeness as a whole. In Mr. Carlyle's case every wart was photographed,[5] as it were; even Cromwell would not have insisted on that sort of accuracy.

Mr. W. B. Scott,[6] that amiable chronicler, once (he says), when a boy, saw Sir Walter. He saw him in a passion, and heard him swear profane, an offence of which, his intimates avow, he was rarely guilty. Had Mr. W. B. Scott written his namesake's Life, he would have been on the outlook for profanity. If he found 'a swear word' in a letter, that letter he would have published, however otherwise unessential. Sir Walter would have gone down to posterity with the florid eloquence of our troops in Flanders.[7] This is only an example of the difficulties of the biographic art. A man forms, perhaps unconsciously, an idea of his subject, and that idea dominates the portrait which he draws. Quite unintentionally he selects all that bears out his theory, and he has a tendency to omit a good deal of what makes against it. This must occur in all art, and if Sir E. B. Jones[8] took to portrait painting, probably his favourite type of face would be conferred on his sitters. A blusterous genial biographer would have made Scott as noisy as Professor Wilson;[9] a sentimental biographer would have made him a man with a broken heart, badly mended. Why did Scott work so hard, and spend so much? Obviously in the endeavour to forget Lady Forbes![10] Neither portrait would have been accurate; either theory might have been plausibly supported. It is in this direction that a biographer who did not know his subject, or knew him but slightly, is most certain to err. Like jesting Pilate we ask 'What is Truth?'[11] Actual, absolute, full-bodied truth is unattainable. A letter or two, a page of a diary, may upset, in fact, our theory of a life. We can never know, in such case, that such letters or pages have not existed, though they may be inaccessible. At best we work in a twilight.

Let us take the extreme case that a biographer discovers a single action in an honourable life in which his hero 'sails near the wind.' Nothing ill came of it, or nothing any longer traceable. Does truth compel the biographer to drag this fact (of which, at most, he has only an inkling) into the central light? Must he dwell on it in a fervour of reproach? No doubt the question may be answered either way, but on the whole, as a biographer is not precisely the Recording Angel, I think he may let the matter slip by. If he does not it will be pounced upon, and made the chief topic of remark, and so, for awhile at least, the general effect of the portrait will be lost. The fault will swell blackly all over the canvas, like the genie streaming out of his vase in the *Arabian Nights*. Nothing but this fault will be visible, yet it obviously occupied no such prominent place in the life, and did not indicate the general temper and conduct of the hero.

Another limit on 'the whole truth' is placed by the feelings of other people. Your hero says in his letters this or that about the Rev. Tom, Sir Dick, my Lord Harry. His remarks illustrate his character. You have *that* excuse for bringing them in; you may also believe that his observations are accurate. But you are not writing the lives of the persons commented upon, who may have left a reputation dear to many, and descendants in the land. Undoubtedly a biographer must deny himself the pleasure of printing these entertaining passages, if he happens to be a gentleman. It may be hard on him and on the public, but the taboo ought to be observed. 'Poor, greedy, pigeoning devil,' says the hero, about an interesting person.[12] I choose an actual example. The truth does not compel a biographer to publish these comments, with the poor devil's name.

A recent biography appears to have fluttered some estimable dovecots, and stirred up a number of sleeping embers into a lively flame. This may have been demanded by the theory of 'all the truth,' but there is an easy remedy for the trouble. There is no absolute occasion for saying anything at all in a hurry. When a notable person is recently dead it is not an inevitable duty to publish all his correspondence and diaries. They can slumber comfortably in a vault of the British Museum till Time quiets passions *pulveris exigui jactu*.[13]

In support of the notion that Truth need not be too hard a task-mistress, too exacting, take Lockhart's own conduct. About Scott he told everything, for the few darker spots only increased the general brilliance of the lights, and prevented the exhibition of an impossible, impeccable statue in alabaster. But, in his life of Burns, Lockhart, in spite of theory, did *not* tell all, or nearly all, that he knew, or surmised, or had been told. He generalised, for many were living to whom the whole truth would have been a needless infliction of pain. In such cases, to generalise is quite enough. We know at least enough about Coleridge and Byron, without a note of every dose of laudanum and every amour. I even go so far as to think that we have lately been allowed to hear too much of Mr. Pepys's autobiographic babble.[14] It was easy to spare some of his confessions; I admit that I had thought Mr. Pepys a more manly libertine, and could willingly have remained in ignorance. His character, all the characters of interesting persons long ago with Tullus and Ancus,[15] are part of our stock of pleasure in life. If I discovered, *per impossibile*,[16] that Jeanne d'Arc ever did a wrong thing, my duty to the stock of human pleasure would outweigh my duty to the truth. 'Never mind the truth' would be my motto; 'perhaps there is some mistake somewhere.' Or suppose, also *per impossibile*, that one discovered a cheque forged by Burns. One would destroy it and say nothing about it. A biographer is not a detective – he is not presiding at the Day of Judgment. These ideas will be considered immoral. Many French authors try (quite in vain) to prove that Molière married the daughter of his mistress. This kind of spirit seems to be not uncommon, at present, among biographers, a class which Mr. Carlyle thought used to be so 'mealy-mouthed.' Poor Highland Mary is harried in her modest resting-place, 'washed by the western wave.'[17] One thing we do know very well about her – namely, that Burns wanted nothing to be known. She had lived and he had loved her; there he manifestly desired that information should cease, and Lockhart has actually been blamed for leaving it there. Of all the duties of a biographer, one can regard none more stringent than respect to the secrets of his subject. If he can, he should burn and obliterate; if he cannot, he should forget. Yet if a letter of Burns's to Highland Mary, clearing up all that he desired to remain concealed (if anything is left) could be found, the devotees of Burns (as a rule) would make haste to publish the epistle. Of all cant 'the public has a right to know' is the most odious. The public has not a right to know. The greater a man is, the more he has done for us, the less right have we to pry into his secrets. Byron, apparently, did not want his famous burned Memoirs to be secret, and the destruction of them was a strong measure. But, as certainly, Keats did not mean his love-letters to be published. A biographer at this distance of time might read them and give his account of the general impression which they convey as to Keats's health and mental condition.

Because a man is dead, we should not regard him as deprived of all human rights. A biographer should try to write as if he were in the sacred presence of the dead. His actions are to be criticised, his motives analysed, his faults censured, but his secrets are to be respected. 'How would you like it yourself?' we may ask the publishers of documents like the letters of Keats. One is not speaking of the secrets of dead politicians, which no longer affect the living. If we can find out Junius, if we can unearth a letter of Marlborough's to the King over the water, let us do so by all means.[18] But the love-letters of a dying poet are on a totally different level.

On the whole, these remarks, if acted upon, would leave Truth alone in her well, on occasion, and would deprive biographers of a success of scandal, and the public of 'spicy revelations.' We should practise a certain 'economy,' and Truth, in biography, is a question of degrees, and shades, and *nuances*, not a thing hard and fast, blotched and glaring.

'New Light on Mary Queen Of Scots', *Blackwood's Magazine* 182:1001

(July 1907), pp. 17–27

After all the many years since 1586,[1] the Life of Mary Queen of Scots remains to be written. The task can only be achieved by a person of genius, and no person of genius, of either sex, has attempted the adventure. Sir Walter Scott always refused, for chivalrous reasons, to write the biography of the Queen; and Mr Swinburne, his tragic poems apart, has only consecrated an essay to the topic. We thus await the coming of a genius who is not too chivalrous of heart, and who is also a laborious and untiring 'searcher of records.'[2] A newspaper editor has recently informed the world that history must not be abandoned to 'searchers of records.' Yet without exhaustive study of documents it is not easy to see how such measure of truth as is attainable can be attained. The public may be indifferent to truth, but history cannot be satisfied with less than the fullest possible measure of that unpopular commodity.

The new, easy-going way of writing history is to distil it out of printed Calendars of State Papers. These are 'one-eyed calendars,' like the three in the 'Arabian Nights.'[3] They are *summaries* of the original letters and despatches; they contain not only omissions of important matter, but actual blunders of every kind. The person of genius who is to write Queen Mary's biography must not be content with your Calendars, your Lemons, Father Stevensons, and Dr Joseph Bains,[4] but must peruse all the actual manuscripts.

This truth has been impressed on me by practical experience and by the study of certain letters written at a crisis of Mary's life. They have remained unknown to our historians, as far as I am aware, though the epistles have long been in the daylight of the Advocates' Library in Edinburgh, and in the British Museum. The letters are by that well-known diplomatist, Thomas

Randolph. The son of an English squire, Randolph was bred 'to a scholar's life,' and in France was intimate with George Buchanan.[5] In 1559 Randolph, then in Paris, is spoken of by Throckmorton, the ambassador of Queen Elizabeth, as 'my man, Barnabie.' He seems to have been 'hanging loose on the town'; he was well educated, familiar with 'the tongues,' and still young enough to tell a soft tale in the ear of a maid of honour, Mary Fleming or Mary Beaton,[6] or to draw steel if need arose among the adventures of a secret and perilous mission. Randolph was a tavern-companion, in Paris, of that good swordsman, William Kirkcaldy of Grange:[7] he was in fact, like the adventurous Tremaynes, and the accomplished Harry Killegrew,[8] the kind of man whom Elizabeth's ministers found useful. Some of these adventurers became *attachés*, or spies, some rose to be ambassadors; they were always ready to ride a couple of hundred miles at a moment's notice; to bribe the secretary of a foreign minister; to buy or steal the key to a correspondence in cipher; and generally to serve their queen without scruple, and for small reward. If they often voyaged 'at their own charges,' as Killegrew complains, rich presents of jewels from queens and kings came sometimes in their way; they dined at royal tables; they knew all the leading men, and danced with the prettiest women; while some post or monopoly might be found for them, late in life, to serve as an old-age pension.

We first hear of 'my man, Barnabie' – that is, Randolph – in the summer of 1559. He then managed to steer, from the heart of France to the Swiss frontier, an eccentric Calvinistic nobleman whom France was eager to clap in prison, while Elizabeth needed his aid in stirring the flames of the Protestant revolt in Scotland. This noble, the Earl of Arran,[9] was the heir-apparent of the Scottish crown; the Scots and some English Puritans hoped that Elizabeth would marry him, and to carry a personage so important through hostile France to Geneva was a delicate task. The cunning and courage of Randolph succeeded; the Protestant party in Scotland were grateful, and he became settled as Elizabeth's agent and informer in Edinburgh. He represented her at Edinburgh while the Reformation passed into law; and he continued to reside in attendance on the Court of Holyrood[10] during most of Queen Mary's reign. He thoroughly enjoyed the atmosphere of intrigue, political and amorous; he was especially attached to one of the Queen's Maries, – Mary Beaton, 'my dear mistress,' – and, as we shall see, he gives the strongest of extant testimonies to the beauty and charm of the fated Queen. Though a sturdy Protestant, Randolph found Knox too 'bytter,' – many a demure hint he drops of his disapproval of the preacher; and, though an eager patriot, all for England and Elizabeth, Randolph beheld, with grief and rage scarcely concealed, the 'devilish' machinations by which Elizabeth drew Mary to her doom. He was not romantic, he could not afford to change sides: 'my country, right or wrong,' was his motto. Presently we find him possessed of guilty foreknowledge of a plot directed against the life of Mary, a life inconvenient to Elizabeth, to England, and to the Protestant verity. None the less, at the moment when

Randolph wrote the letters, hitherto unpublished and unquoted, Mary enjoyed his esteem, his admiration, and even his affection; though his heart was more or less given to Mary Beaton.

The topic with which these *lettres inédits*[11] deal is the latest moment in Elizabeth's long game of cat-and-mouse in the matter of Queen Mary's proposed marriage to Lord Robert Dudley, Earl of Leicester.[12] This strange union was first mooted by Elizabeth herself to Mary's Secretary of State, Maitland of Lethington, in March 1563. Maitland did not reject the idea, but insisted that Elizabeth must first recognise Mary's right of succession to the crowns of England and Ireland. Otherwise Mary would 'seek abroad' for a husband. Elizabeth's reply was to intimate that, practically, any marriage with a foreign and Catholic prince would be regarded by her as 'an unfriendly act.' This was part of her instructions to Randolph in August 1563. He was allowed to add that Elizabeth might propose for Mary an English noble, 'perchance such an one as she would hardly think we could agree to.' These words pointed at her own favourite, Lord Robert Dudley, a man not of an old house, but of a house spotted with treason; a man 'infamed' (though doubtless unjustly) by the mysterious death of his wife, Amy Robsart;[13] finally, a man who was secretly professing his attachment to Philip of Spain and the Catholic cause, while publicly coquetting with the Puritans, and in friendly correspondence with John Knox.

There was just a chance, however, that Elizabeth's hint might refer to Mary's cousin, Darnley, who played the lute to Elizabeth, with her critical approval, and carried the sword of state when Dudley was belted earl. Darnley's religion (like that of Prince Charles in 1745) 'was still to seek,' but he was the hope of the English Catholics. Few in Scotland, according to Randolph, guessed (though Mary certainly did) that Elizabeth meant to indicate Leicester. Mary asked Randolph two questions, thus condensed: 'Who is the man your mistress means?' and 'Where do I come in?' – what compensation was she to receive for marrying so much under her rank?

The negotiations dragged on, Elizabeth's sole object being to make Mary's affairs hang in uncertainty. Of this Mary had warnings enough: for example, from Sir James Melville, her envoy to Elizabeth in September 1564, who saw Dudley made an earl, and caressed in the process, by Elizabeth. As to Leicester himself, he naturally preferred his chances of wedding Elizabeth to his chances of being presently dirked[14] in Scotland as the husband of Mary. According to a fragmentary memorandum in French, written in Mary's own hand after the events, but undated, much defaced, and less than candid, Leicester 'knew well that though his mistress had written to me in his favour, her purpose was merely to deceive me, and keep other suitors at a distance. Leicester himself made me aware of this, secretly, through Randolph. ...'*

* Bain, Calendar of State Affairs relating to Scotland, ii. 233, compared with the original draft in the British Museum.

If Mary tells truth, Randolph must have been unaware of the contents of Leicester's letters to her, and we do not know their date. Probably they were posterior to March 16, 1565, shortly after which Mary and her advisers, the Earl of Murray and Maitland of Lethington, saw and said that all hope from Elizabeth must be abandoned.

Did Mary ever seriously intend to marry Leicester, always on condition that Elizabeth recognised her place in the succession to the English crown? Mr Froude has argued that the consent which Mary gave in February 1565 was pure hypocrisy, her real object being to secure leave for Darnley to visit Scotland.* Mary did desire this, but Darnley was only her 'second string'; she preferred Leicester, with her own recognition as heiress (failing Elizabeth and her issue, if any) of the English crown. Granted that condition, she was resolved to marry Leicester. This fact is proved by Randolph's hitherto unnoticed letters.

Mary would have wedded Leicester if her claims were recognised, and she was bitterly disappointed when her conditions were waived. Mr Henderson, the latest historian of Mary, speaks of Randolph as 'a deluded simpleton,' who both believed that Elizabeth was sincere in her offer of Leicester, and that Mary meant nothing but courtesy by her friendly talks with Darnley in February–March 1565.† But Mary herself declares that she was ready to wed Leicester; she said so to Throckmorton when he came on a special mission after her betrothal to Darnley, in May 1565. 'She confessed,' writes Randolph, 'unto his Lordship' (Throckmorton), 'that she never bore better good-will unto any man than to him' (Leicester), 'before she despaired through the slowness of the Queen's' (Elizabeth's) 'resolution, that any good was intended.'‡ But Mary's word may go for nothing, – I adduce other evidence.

It is usually supposed that Mary finally despaired of Elizabeth's good faith as regards the Leicester marriage on March 16, 1565. Elizabeth then announced that she would not proceed to the examination or declaration of Mary's interest in the succession, 'until she herself had married or notified her determination never to marry,' as Mr Hay Fleming puts it.§ So Randolph writes, adding that Murray and Lethington 'could not advise their mistress to make any longer stay, or to drive any more time.'¶

We now arrive at the date, certainly, of one of Randolph's unpublished letters, March 20, 1564–65. As this letter to Leicester is verbose, I condense

* The dates in the affair destroy Mr Froude's theory. See my ' History of Scotland,' ii. 130–137.

† Mary Queen of Scots, i. 310.

‡ Foreign Calendar, Elizabeth, 1565, May 21, p. 372.

§ Citing Stevenson's Selections, pp. 134, 135. Keith, ii. 266, 330. Murdin, State Papers, p. 758. Nares's Burghley, ii. 234.

¶ Foreign Calendar, Elizabeth, 1564–65, pp. 315, 316.

it. To me it seems that Mary was certainly as bitterly disappointed as Murray and Lethington were enraged: they were not merely playing their parts, but earnestly regretted the failure of the Leicester marriage; and, finally, Mary and they tried to keep the negotiations alive. Mary 'altogether grew discontented,' says Randolph. She blamed him for 'training her so long time, and nursing her in such vain hope.' She feared that the long deceit would turn to Elizabeth's discredit. Yet 'I will not fail in any good offices towards my sister, but trust myself to her henceforth I will not.' This resolve was fatally broken! Mary then left Randolph, and Murray and Lethington met him. 'As to my Lord of Murray,' Randolph says, 'I found him almost stark mad,' from fear of the unfriendly nature of future relations between the two Queens. Lethington entered, and, on hearing the tidings, said that he was not surprised, – he knew Elizabeth too well to believe that she would 'ever resolve in that point.' He showed 'somewhat more choler than judgement.' The Queen, who had been riding, at what pace we may guess, now returned, showing more sorrow than anger, while Randolph and the two Scots renewed their debate. 'I know not of us all three who was most angry.'

Next day Lethington declined Randolph's invitation to dinner, and Randolph, with Mary, watched Darnley, Lord Robert Stewart, and others ride at the ring[15] – a very poor performance, says Randolph. Meanwhile Mary, with tears in her eyes, vowed to Randolph that she would obey Elizabeth 'almost so far as her own dear mother.' Mary's tears were ready; but Randolph mentions them sympathetically, 'with no dispraise to her Majesty.' Her sorrow was 'the dishonour and shame to be deceived,' in spite of the many warnings to which she had listened. She told Randolph that next day she would send Beaton to England, requesting a safe-conduct for Lethington to go to France.

Randolph asked Murray to prevent this move. 'Beshrew me,' said Murray, 'I have travailed over far in the matter, and fear that I shall repent it.' Beaton next came up, asking for a letter from Randolph to Bedford, then commanding at Berwick, on the frontier.

Randolph goes on – 'This Sunday, after the sermon, to which my Lord of Murray never faileth to come, though it be far from his lodgings, I asked him if his anger were digested. "The devil cumber you," said he, "our Queen doth nothing but weep and write. Amend this betimes, or all will go amiss."'

It is pleasant to find the pious Murray swearing quite like a man of this world after coming from sermon. Not less natural it is that Mary should 'do nothing but weep and write.' Her letters she probably burned when they had served as a safety valve, for none of this date occurs in Labanoff's collection of her correspondence.[16] Would that she had burned certain other letters! On Monday there was such a snowstorm that Randolph could not venture out. On Tuesday he met Murray, 'who cursed me because I can guide a Queen no better when I have her at my will, but must so handle her that she is fain to put herself in her enemies' hands.' As before, Murray cursed with unaffected freedom, and blamed Randolph for what was no fault of his.

'In cometh Lethington,' and debate was warm. 'We chafed ourselves well.' They grew cool, and '*found it good that this matter*' (the Leicester marriage) '*should not thus be given over.*' Lethington confessed that his mission to France was a mere cover for a voyage into England to renew negotiations. His mission to England, however, was delayed, for reasons to be given later, during nearly a month, in which time Mary had changed her mind irrevocably, and with good cause. 'In much gentler words we parted than we met ... There is yet no doubt that all matters between the Queen's Majesty and this Queen may very well be accorded.' Randolph then tells Leicester that he conceals Leicester's part in sending Darnley (in mid-February) to Scotland, and urges him to come instantly 'and enjoy the best place in the whole country.' Murray, though angry with Leicester, entreats him to come. The letter is sent to forestall Beaton's visit to the English Court. Thus Randolph ends on March 20, when he and Murray both hope that all may yet go well. This letter is in the British Museum, or rather a copy is there.

It appears, then, that at this date (March 20, 1564–65) Mary had not resolved to marry Darnley; but, grieved as she was by Elizabeth's conduct, meant to send Lethington with orders to renew the Leicester negotiations. She had given no sure sign of intention to wed Darnley (a resolution fatal to her, but secretly desired and intrigued for by Elizabeth) as late as March 27. On that day Randolph wrote to Cecil[17] saying that Mary's uncle, the Cardinal of Lorraine, wished her to send Lethington to France to arrange a marriage with the Duc d'Orléans. This alliance both she and her people despise. 'She desires to do what may be most to our sovereign's contentment,' under the influence of Murray, who says that Elizabeth has it in her power to give peace and contentment to Mary and to the Protestant party.*
Thus, as late as March 27, Mary was still hoping that the Leicester marriage might yet be arranged, and had not committed herself with Darnley. On this point I cannot believe that she, Murray, and Lethington were duping Randolph, who remained full of hope, and, really, was duped only by Elizabeth.

Our second unpublished letter shows Randolph, on March 31, more confident than ever that all will go well. Nothing stands in the way of the Leicester marriage but the inexplicably laggard behaviour of Leicester himself. Randolph writes to Leicester's brother-in-law, Sir Henry Sidney, who had visited the Scottish Court in July and August 1562. He had come with one of Elizabeth's usual disappointments for Mary: the English Queen would not meet her that year, as had been arranged. Mary had wept bitterly, and, doubtless, was not in her best looks. But now, says Randolph, all is

* Bain, ii. 137.

happier, and the Queen herself is a paragon of beauty. Randolph ends this sanguine letter with some Court gossip about a love affair of one of the Queen's Maries, Mary Fleming, which has not hitherto been recorded.

[...]

The more private gossip of this letter needs some explanation. It appears that when Sir Henry Sidney visited Mary's Court in 1562, he was smitten by the charms of the Queen's favourite among the four Maries, Mary Fleming. But while the Maries and their Queen were still in France, Mary Fleming, according to Randolph, gave her heart to Henry Killegrew, a gallant, gay, and accomplished English diplomatist. Lloyd, in his 'Worthies,' praises Killegrew as a master in the art of painting, then seldom practised by men of birth. He is 'a Holbein for oyl,'[18] writes Lloyd, with many other terms of applause. It is a wild conjecture; but conceivably Killegrew was the painter of the Leven and Melville portrait of Mary, in which she wears several of the jewels historically known to have been hers in 1559–1561.

Killegrew was in Scotland in 1559, but himself, in a record of his services, mentions no later visit, till he was admitted to Mary's presence in a darkened room after the murder of Darnley (1567). It seems that his passages with Mary Fleming must have occurred in France, before Queen Mary's return to Scotland in 1561. He *did* marry 'the Cook's daughter,' Catherine, fourth daughter of Sir Anthony Cooke, on November 4, 1565, leaving Mary Fleming to console herself with Lethington, to whom she was wedded in January 1566.

As to the political part of the letter, we have an unpublished, incomplete, and therefore dateless letter of Randolph's to Leicester himself. This epistle (in the British Museum) is clearly of the same date (March 31, 1565) as the letter to Sidney. It contains the same complaints of Leicester's coldness, and the same advice. Randolph has been told, in Scotland, that Leicester's indifference, silence, and even want of ordinary courtesy, are much blamed. Leicester knows how difficult it was to bring Mary, Murray, and Lethington to accept him. Randolph is 'now in better hope than ever I was, but' Leicester 'neglects the honour, the felicity which I am sure you will not deny to be great.' Leicester shows less goodwill to Mary and her ministers than he did 'before this matter was thought of.' Mary and her advisers, '*now that they assure themselves of* Elizabeth's '*intentions*, would willingly have some knowledge of your own desire.' Of that they cannot doubt, 'for what living man would refuse it if it fell to his lot,' but they want some sign from Leicester.

This suggests that Mary and her advisers were at last ready to close with Elizabeth on her own terms, but this they could not decently do while Leicester held sullenly aloof. However, Randolph adds, 'I find no obstacle except in that which' Elizabeth 'will do for you both.' To that point

Lethington was to attend at the English Court. 'If once in this point we sever, it will be hard to join us again in the same affection.' Randolph implores Leicester to come to Scotland. If not, Cecil should be sent. Scotland is only anxious for peace and friendship with England.

But Leicester did not move, and the end came thus: On the day (March 31) when Randolph wrote to Sidney and Leicester, he also wrote to Throckmorton in Paris,* with news which would have made any woman, even if spiritless, abandon Leicester. Tidings had just come to the Earl of Atholl that, in a tennis match between Norfolk[19] and Leicester, Leicester had taken Elizabeth's handkerchief from her hand and wiped his sweaty face with it. Norfolk broke into rage; Elizabeth took Leicester's part eagerly. By March 31 Mary knew of this indecent familiarity between Elizabeth and the man whom she offered as husband to a Queen.

Mary took no more thought of Leicester: what lady could have so debased herself! She turned to Darnley, she nursed him through a sickness, she delayed Lethington's journey to England, and, when he did arrive (April 18), it was not to negotiate the Leicester but to announce the Darnley marriage. Randolph had frequently and vainly found fault with the sending of Darnley to Scotland (February 1564–65) by Leicester, Cecil, and Elizabeth. He knew that they had contrived that scheme, and, when the mischief was done, he took (May 21) the ironical revenge of asking Leicester how it came about?

'To whom,' he writes to Leicester, 'this may chiefly be imputed, what crafty subtlety or devilish device hath brought this to pass, I know not; but woe worth the time that ever the Lord Darnley did set his foot in this country.'† Randolph laments for 'this poor Queen, whom ever before I esteemed so worthy, so wise, so honourable in all her doings.' Now, through the coming of Darnley, all is at hazard: honour, realm, and peace with England. The sole cause, Randolph tells Leicester, is Darnley's arrival, and 'most men are persuaded that in the sending of him' from England, 'there is other meaning than was shown.'

This is all part of Randolph's irony, for he knew who had sent Darnley, and for what end he was sent. On February 12 he had written to Cecil: 'By your letter I perceive what earnest means hath been made both by my Lord Robert (Leicester) and your honour, for my Lord Darnley's licence to come to Scotland.'

He tells Cecil not only that Darnley's arrival is likely to cause fatal mischief, but that Cecil has been duly warned of the evil that must ensue. Leicester and Cecil have procured it, and when the evil is accomplished, in May, Randolph innocently wonders, in his letter to Leicester, 'to *whom* this may chiefly be imputed'; and *whose* is 'the crafty subtlety or devilish device.'

---

* Bain, Calendar, March 31, 1565.

† Ibid., May 21, 1565.

Randolph must have taken some comfort in his irony, for he speaks of himself as one of the men who 'loved' Mary (not *par amours* of course), and who had found her 'worthy, wise, and honourable in all her doings,' before the calculated delays and treacheries of Leicester and Elizabeth drove her from her course.

There is, I think, no room for doubt. Elizabeth, her favourite, and her advisers, after trying Mary's temper unsuccessfully for two years, exasperated her by insult, and in sending Darnley deliberately lured her to her doom.

The concord between Mary and *les politiques*,[20] the sane Protestants, Lethington and Murray, was broken. The less sane Protestants were reunited with *les politiques*. The feud of Hamiltons and Stewarts broke out afresh; Murray took up arms. The wars of the Congregation were renewed, and Elizabeth had what she desired – a disunited Scotland as a field for intrigue.

The interesting letter of Randolph to Sidney (March 31, 1564–65) is in the Advocates' Library.* I owe my knowledge of it to the kindness of the librarian, Mr W. K. Dickson. I have modernised the spelling, and omitted some unessential passages, and a passage which is too incoherent to be construed. The letter to Leicester, of March 20, 1564–65, is from a copy in the Egerton MSS., British Museum. To this letter I was directed by the kindness of Father Pollen, S. J. In the same collection Miss E. M. Thompson found the fragmentary letter to Leicester, which must be of the same date as the epistle to Sidney of March 31, 1564–65. There is also an earlier letter by Randolph on an illness of Mary Beaton.

The letters which have been cited prove, I think, contrary to Mr Henderson's opinion and that of many critics, that in her clever trickery Elizabeth was not 'playing exactly the game that Mary desired.' By the evidence of Lethington and Murray, given to Randolph, Mary was reduced by Elizabeth's delays to a passion of angry disappointment, and could only weep and write letters of complaint to her friends. Then she was calmed, and, with her advisers, was about to renew negotiations for the marriage with Leicester. And then came the story of Queen Elizabeth's handkerchief, and the end of possibility of hope.

---

* The letter of Randolph to Sir Henry Sidney has been in the Advocates' Library, as I understand, for eighty years. Circumstances have hitherto prevented me from studying the mass of important papers of Mary's period in that collection: they seem to have been overlooked by our historians. The letters cited in the British Museum appear to be transcripts from originals once among the Lauderdale papers: it looks as if Maitland or Lethington had somehow acquired them.

'M. Anatole France on Jeanne d'Arc',* *Scottish Historical Review* 5:2

(1908), pp. 411–39

France has at this hour no more distinguished man of letters than M. Anatole France. Before he became a novelist and essayist, and a moralist in his own way, he had been, I believe, a trained student of history.[1] When a man of his great qualities and exquisite style devotes years to the study of Jeanne d'Arc, we expect much from him, and much for her. These expectations are not fulfilled to the heart's desire. M. France has been industrious; perhaps no works and documents relative to Jeanne, nothing that illustrates her environment – political, social, religious, legendary, and biographical – has escaped his research. But his inaccuracies are a constant marvel; and his inconsistencies are no less surprising. While in a few passages he recognises the noble character of the Maid, as a rule he finds, often he unconsciously invents, pretexts for pointless sneers at herself and her inspiration. Why he adopts this line I can only guess, but why he fails all along the line it is easy to understand. M. France, for all that I know, may dislike Jeanne because she is a favourite of the clergy (though the Church is in no hurry to canonise her),[2] or because she is dear to all patriots (and patriotism is apt to be military). But he fails, because in the character and career of the Maid there is no act or word which deserves a sneer unless she is despicable because she shared the religious beliefs of her age.

Of M. France's inconsistencies let us take a typical example from the second and third pages of his preface. 'We all know the value of the replies of the Maid' (at her trial in 1431). 'They are heroic in their sincerity, and, *le plus souvent*, are translucently clear' (p. ii).[3]

---

* Vie de Jeanne d'Arc, vol. i. Calmann Lévy, Paris.

That is true. Turn to page iii. 'It is certain that but a year after date she had only a confused memory of important facts in her career. *Enfin*, her perpetual hallucinations made her, *le plus souvent*, incapable of distinguishing between the true and the false.'

Were ever two such statements offered in two consecutive pages? The Maid is heroically sincere, and cannot distinguish between truth and error. Her replies are as clear as crystal, and as obscure as her incapacity to discern the truth can make them! This is an early but a fairly adequate specimen of the mental bewilderment of Jeanne's historian.

M. France ends the last chapter of his first volume with the words, 'Behold her, from the beginning, and perhaps for ever, a prisoner within the blossomed wood of legends'! This is the keynote of his book; Jeanne is a legendary personage.

From his opinion I venture to differ absolutely. It appears to me that concerning scarcely a human being, dead for nearly five centuries, do we know so much, and know that much so certainly, as about Jeanne. The contemporary myths concerning a person so wonderful are wonderfully few, and their flowers have long ago withered and fallen into dust. What remains, and will remain, is her genius, her character, her imperishable achievement. These are easily to be discerned in her own replies to her judges between February 22 and the day of her martyrdom, at the end of May, 1431. Her words are recorded by the clerks of her enemies, and they bear witness to her courage, her faith, her purity of heart, her untaught sagacity, even to her sense of humour. *Hilarem vultum gerit*,[4] as was said in her happy days by one who saw her. If we had no other evidence than the authentic record,* written day by day, of her replies, we could not but confess that this illiterate girl of nineteen (or of twenty-one, she was born in 1410, 1411, or 1412) was a paragon.

Again, the evidence of scores of witnesses of all ranks, from priests and peasants to princes, who knew her in most stages of her existence, evidence taken on oath in 1450–1456, is, as to her character, precisely in accord with her own replies to her judges. She was brave, they say, devout, pure, her manners were noble, she was charitable, kind, as loyal as Montrose, and gifted with extraordinary enthusiasm and energy. The evidence of 1450–56 is late, indeed, it was taken a quarter of a century after her death, and it was given at an inquiry intended to clear her character, and to prove that her king, Charles V., had not been beguiled by an impostor, had not tampered with a sorceress or daemoniac. Allowing for these facts, none the less all the witnesses are consistently in accord with the words of Jeanne herself. Indeed, nobody, it may be presumed, doubts that she was chaste, pious, generous, the soul of honour, brave, and (as M. France now and then acknowledges) practically sagacious and well advised.

* The record is not always fair, when we can compare the original French with the official Latin translation.

When we know all this, in copious detail, about a girl who was burned alive at Rouen three hundred and seventy years ago, how can it be said that the Maid is 'from the first, and perhaps for ever, a prisoner in the flowery forest of legend'?

If people of various factions, at various times, have conceived of Jeanne as 'a warrior Maid, yet a peaceful one, a *béguine*, a prophetess, a sorceress, an Angel of the Lord, and an ogress,' what does that matter to us or to her? The legends of Jeanne as a 'witch' and an 'ogress' have long gone the way of such hostile contemporary scandals about all distinguished persons, from Sir William Wallace to Bonaparte, 'the Corsican ogre.'[5]

It seems, then, to be the aim of M. France to prove that Jeanne is an inscrutable legendary being, that she was moved like a puppet by priests, that she was a cheat, and a very honest girl, and that we cannot know her as she was in fact.

Following Jeanne from her infancy in her father's house at Domremy, separated only by the churchyard from the church, what did legend do for her success, which M. France regards as based on legend? Again, did the prompting of priests, as her biographer supposes, start her on her mission? In March–April, 1429, when Jeanne had reached the Dauphin, and was being examined for three weeks before the clerical legists at Poitiers, people were sent to her own country to collect information. Probably through them such tales were gathered as Perceval de Boulainvilliers wrote (June 21, 1429) to some foreign prince.* On the night of her birth, the Epiphany (1410?–1412?) the villagers felt strangely joyful, they knew not why, and the cocks crowed all night. At that season, in fact,

> 'The lusty bird takes every hour for dawn,'[6]

and crows accordingly.

The wolves did not touch the sheep that she shepherded; foes did not attack Domremy, which suffered, in fact, but seldom, though there was constant anxiety. Then comes the tale of how, after a victory in a foot race, Jeanne heard a Voice, and saw a brilliant cloud. The voice bade her go on her mission. This, save for the foot race, is very much what Jeanne told her judges in 1431. But Boulainvilliers says nothing of her visions of her three Saints, nor are they ever mentioned in any records till Jeanne confessed them, refusing to give all details, to her judges at Rouen. They were unknown in France, except apparently to the Dauphin. I think that M. France does not remark on this sacred reticence of the Maid. Boulainvilliers says that she spoke of the Voices to her curate in confession. She denied this at her trial, though it was in her interest to say that she had confessed. If she did not, the inference was that she knew her Saints to be fiends in disguise. Could she have said truthfully that she consulted her director, she would have done so.

* Procès, v. 11–21.

Thus legend fell far below the facts, as Jeanne understood them.

M. France says that, in legend, she was born 'on the night of Christmas day,' 'and in her cradle had her adoration of the shepherds' (p. 542). The shepherds, says Boulainvilliers, were '*ignari nativitatis puellae*,' did not know of her birth and Twelfth Night is not Christmas day! M. France is perpetually mythopoeic; he keeps on inventing legends not to be found in his authorities. Wild birds fed from her lap, says Boulainvilliers. And why not? Thoreau was not singular in the intimacy of his acquaintance with wild birds;[7] I myself have been oddly favoured by their familiarity. Jeanne was said to have averred (she denied it) that she would find a lost pair of gloves, was said to have found a stolen cup, to have known that a priest was an immoral man, to have noticed that a priest was deliberately offering her an unconsecrated wafer. Even her judges hardly touched on these prodigies in their questions. Most of these legends, and all the most puerile or extraordinary, are found in Morosini's reports,[8] and not in authentic records. Such trash was current about every one who roused the popular fancy. The influence of Jeanne was not based on such fables, but such fables gather round persons of influence, as round Montrose.*

If you scrape together all the popular legends about Jeanne, you are surprised by their scarcity when compared with the miraculous healings, flights in the air, and conflicts with the devil, of the contemporary St. Colette, of St. Theresa, of St. Joseph of Cupertino.† Jeanne performed no miracles, and claimed to perform none. She healed nobody, nor tried to heal any; she was not 'levitated,' the devil did not jerk her chair, like the chair of St. Colette, from under her!

The childhood of Jeanne, in fact, was that of a good, charitable, devout, industrious peasant girl, in a village sometimes as much in danger of attack as every farmer's house was, from Liddel to Tyne, during four hundred years. She was ardently patriotic, a listener to sermons, which then often dealt with saints, with ghosts, with prophecies, with the distress of the country, the cruelty of the English, the sorrows of the Dauphin, who had never been anointed with the sacred oil from the miraculous ampulla of St. Remigius at Reims. All this was the soil of the flower of her inspiration.

To her judges in 1431 she said that when she was about thirteen she 'had a Voice to direct her.' It came from the right when she was in her father's garden, from the side of the church, separated, as we saw, from the house only by the churchyard. She also saw a bright light (the 'shining cloud' of Boulainvilliers). At first she was in doubt and fear, finally she recognised that the speaker was St. Michael, later accompanied by the two lady saints, Katherine and Margaret.

---

* See the prodigies attending him recorded by Patrick Gordon, Britain's Distemper.

† See France, La Légende de la Première Heure, pp. 53–53.

On this subject the spirit of myth has taken possession of the critical M. France. He writes, 'She saw St. Michael sometimes by some pillar of a church or a chapel, in the guise of a fair knight, with coroneted helm, shield, and coat of arms, piercing the demon with his lance … She knew the angel by his arms, his courtesy, and his noble maxims.'*

In the pages of the *Procès* quoted Jeanne *refuses to answer* any question on the aspect of St. Michael, nor can I find any description by her of the angel.[9] She refused on seven later occasions to gratify the curiosity of her judges. Yet M. France knows in what shape and costume she saw the angel.† He also knows that nobody knows! He writes, 'Whether she would not or whether she could not, she never gave her judges at Rouen a clear and precise description.'‡

The counsel of the Voice, in the statement of Jeanne, 'bade her govern herself well, go often to Church,' and said 'it was necessary that she should go into France.' This command was given two or three times weekly. M. France says that she 'was *perpetually* hallucinated.' She concealed her visions from her curate and all other ecclesiastics,§ and revealed some only to Robert de Baudricourt, captain of the neighbouring town of Vaucouleurs, and to the King.

We see that the visits of the Saints lasted from Jeanne's thirteenth year, probably 1424, or 1425, till, unable to resist their importunities, she began, in the spring of 1428, to proclaim her mission, without plainly revealing her experiences.

M. France explains the origin of her idea of 'going into France' thus: 'She was in relation with a number of ecclesiastics, very capable of recognising her singular piety' (which all witnesses attest), 'and her gift of seeing things invisible to the common run of Christians. Their talk with her, if it had been recorded, would no doubt reveal to us one of the sources of this extraordinary vocation of hers. One of them, whose name will never be known, prepared for the King and Kingdom of France an angelic defender.'¶

To reach this conclusion, M. France had to leap over the fact cited by himself (p. 50), that Jeanne concealed from all ecclesiastics her gift of 'seeing things invisible to the common run of Christians.' Consequently M. France is not justified in saying that a number of ecclesiastics knew of her visions, and that one of them 'initiated' her into her mission. The ecclesiastics knew

* For the first of these strange statements M. France quotes (pp. 34, 35) modern authors; for the last he cites Procès, pp. 72, 73.

† France, pp. 34, 35.

‡ France, p. xxxiii.

§ Procès, i. 128, and note I.

¶ France, p. 54.

nothing about her visions, but, in 1428, three or four years after the visions and voices began, they, and all her neighbours, knew that she was determined 'to go into France.'

M. France proves his theory of a clerical inspirer of her mission thus:

> Two witnesses, more than twenty years later, averred that, in 1429, when Jeanne was at Burey, a village near Vaucouleurs, she said to one of them (a kinsman of hers, Durand Laxart or Lassois), 'is it not said of old that France shall be ruined by a woman and restored by a maid?'*

In another version, from a woman of Vaucouleurs, Jeanne said in her hearing, 'Have ye not heard the prophecy that France is to be ruined by a woman, and restored by a maid *from the marches of Lorraine*?'† (February, 1429.)

M. France, not, perhaps, observing that Jeanne's words (the woman's version) were spoken in February, 1429 whereas the visions, unknown to the clergy, began in 1424, or 1425 argues that Jeanne heard of this prophecy, itself 'a forged prophecy,' from one of his clerical suspects. It was the origin, or one of the origins, of her mission. For no peasant, he reasons, was likely to know about the prophecy, much less would a peasant add to it the words 'from the marches of Lorraine.'‡ 'This *addition topique*,' says our author, 'cannot be the work of a ploughman, and reveals an intelligence skilled in governing minds and directing actions. The prophecy thus completed and thus pointed, comes from a cleric, whose intentions are obvious. Doubt is no longer possible' on that head (p. 52).

Aimable sceptique! The witness '*remembered having heard the saying before!*' It was 'the clash of the country side.'

One of the clerical judges in the examination of 145–456, a divine and legist of note named Jean Brehal, speaks of the oak wood, near Domremy (*bois chesnu*) 'of old styled *nemus canutum*.' He then seizes the opportunity not to verify his references, and quotes from the *Historia Bruti*, that is, *Le Roman de Brut*,[10] a prophecy really attributed to Merlin by Geoffrey of Monmouth, in his *De Prophetiis Merlini*. 'From the *Nemus Canutum* will come a maid for the healing of evil.' But the point is that, according to Brehal, the prophecy won its way into *folk lore*, like the other predictions of Merlin, Nostradamus, Thomas of Ercildoune, 'the red-faced Nixon,' the Brahan seer,[11] and a host of mediaeval visionaries, lay or ecclesiastical. In

* M. France, pp. 67, 68, dates this remark before Jeanne went for the first time to Vaucouleurs, in May, 1428. On reading the testimony of Lassois carefully (Procès, ii. p. 444) it seems to me that he is speaking of her second visit to Vaucouleurs, in January and February, 1429. Lassois goes on to tell how Jeanne got clothes from him, and went to a shrine of St. Nicholas, and proceeded to visit the Due de Lorraine; all this was in 1429.

† Procès, vol. ii. p. 447.

‡ France, pp. 5–5.

Brehal's words, *vulgaris ex antiqua percrebuit fama*, 'an old popular rumour arose' about a marvellous maid who should come from the oak wood of Domremy, 'which the prophecy of Merlin not a little confirms.'*

In my opinion the prophecy of Merlin filtered down into folk lore, and so became known, by 1428–1429, to Jeanne.

Now, as to the prophecy, there is no proof that Jeanne knew of it before she came to Vaucouleurs and Burey in 1429. Nor is it possible for any one who knows the popular vogue of prophecies, in England, Scotland, and France – those of various nuns and monks, of Merlin, of Thomas the Rhymer, and so forth – to be certain that such predictions did not reach the populace, in sermons, in sayings, in popular rhymes. The battle of Prestonpans, in 1745, was called the battle of Gledsmuir, to fit a prediction of Thomas the Rhymer.[12]

As to the prediction about a Maid from the marches of Lorraine, it seems to be a combination of two predictions. One is that attributed to a female visionary, Marie d'Avignon, whose prophecies, says Quicherat,[13] 'made a great noise at the beginning of the fifteenth century.'†

She told Charles VI. that France would suffer much sorrow, that in visions arms and armour were shown to her, that she, in terror, refused to accept them, that she was told not to be afraid, they were not meant for her wearing, but for a Maid who would come after her, bear the arms, and free France. At Poitiers, in March-April, 1429, a professor of theology, Jean Erault, mentioned this story to Jean Barbin.‡

The prophecies of Marie d'Avignon were widely known, 'firent grand bruit.'[14]

As to 'the marches of Lorraine,' a Latin prophecy of Merlin, about a victorious Maid *ex nemore canuto*, made much stir after the first successes of Jeanne.§

Near Domremy was the *Bois Chesnu* (oak wood), visible from Jeanne's garden, translated *nemus canutum* by her accusers. The real name, given by Jeanne, was *bois chesnu*, 'oak wood.' When Jeanne went, in March, 1429, before her King, 'some asked her whether there was not a *nemus canutum* near her home, because prophecies said that a marvellous Maid was to come thence, but she had no faith in this prophecy.'¶ If we believe the witness, who, more than twenty years after date, said that Jeanne, in 1429, spoke of a prophecy of a martial Maid 'from the marches of Lorraine,' then, by 1429, she had heard a mixture of the prediction of Marie d'Avignon with that of

* Procès, iii. 339, 340.

† Ib. iii. 83 note 2.

‡ Ib. iii. 83, 84.

§ Ib. iii. 341, 342.

¶ Ib. i. 68,213.

Merlin about *nemus canutum*. After so long a space of time, the witness's memory may have been erroneous. But suppose it correct, we learn no more than that, from somebody, lay or cleric, *after Jeanne had announced her mission*, she heard of the prophecy. This might confirm her belief in herself, or she might quote the prophecy to convince others, but the prophecy was not the origin of her mission. That arose in her visions, which, by 1429, had attended her for four or five years. Nor did a cleric forge the prophecy, and tell her of it to make her start on her course, because he knew she was a visionary; for she had, as she says, kept secret from all the appearances and voices of the Saints, nor are the saintly apparitions ever alluded to till she confesses them to her judges in 1431.

At most, we can say that, after Jeanne had announced her mission to France, she heard of a confirmatory prediction. As for the clergy, one of them had exorcised her, lest she might prove a daemoniac, and this man had been her confessor.*

M. France, believing that a fraudulent priest was her 'initiator,' writes: 'Meanwhile Jeanne lived in the full tide of illusion. Ignorant of the influences' (clerical) 'which beset her, incapable of recognising in her Voices the echo of a human voice, or the *voice of her own heart*, she answered timorously to her Saints, "I am a poor girl who can neither ride nor fight."'†

It was to 'the voice of her own heart,' or rather of her own subconscious genius, manifesting itself in the 'automatisms' of Voices and forms of the heavenly counsellors, that Jeanne listened recalcitrant, disobedient, till they overcame her. The clergy knew nothing about them.

[...]

M. France himself now enters 'the blossomed forest of legend,' and culls a flower of his own finding. He tells us that when Jeanne, in March, 1429, came to Chinon, bearing that aid which she had promised in May, 1428, she was interviewed by some clerics. She would only say that she was to relieve Orleans (the siege had begun in September, 1428), and to lead the Dauphin to be crowned at Reims. 'Before these churchmen, as before Baudricourt at Orleans, she repeated, word for word, the message of the *vavasseur* of Champagne, sent to King John just as she was sent to the Dauphin Charles.' Then M. France gives again, at full length, the story of the tiresome peasant (pp. 18–89). His authority for Jeanne's repetition, at Chinon, of what the peasant had said, is *Procès*, vol. iii. p. 115, and he repeats the story which he abridged on p. 72. There is not, in *Procès*, iii. 115 (evidence of Simon Charles), a single word about Jeanne's warning the King not to hazard a battle! It would be odd if there were, as she had come

* Procès, ii. 446, 447.

† France, p. 541; Procès, i. 52, 53.

expressly to demand that he should hazard a fresh force in an attack on the English besiegers of Orleans.

M. France has added a myth to the myths which he condemns. When M. France thinks that he has discovered a blunder committed by Jeanne, he seems to chuckle inwardly, and he likes to repeat the story of his discovery again and again. Meanwhile, as the advocate of Jeanne, I also smile when M. France's valuable trouvaille is an illusion of his own, an illusion rather apt to be recurrent in his work, unless my eyes deceive me.

Hunting always for the mysterious cleric who prompted Jeanne, M. France finds another proof of his agency in Bertrand de Poulengy's report, already cited, of her first conversation with Baudricourt (May, 1428): 'Jeanne said that the Kingdom of France is not the Dauphin's' (*non spectabat Delphino*), 'but her Lord's, yet her Lord wished the Dauphin to be [crowned] King, and hold that Kingdom in trust' (*in commendam*). The Dauphin, as Andrew Melville said to James VI., 'was Christ's silly vassal.'[15]

All this, says M. France, '*donne à penser.* These ideas were the ideas of the most pious men in the kingdom, as to the government of realms by our Lord. Jeanne could not have found, by herself, either the word or the fact; she was visibly primed (*endoctrinée*) by one of those churchmen whose influence we have detected in the affair of a Lor[r]aine prophecy, and whose trace is totally lost' (p. 74).

Now Poulengy's evidence is given in a Latin translation, hence the appearance of the *words in commendam.* We have no reason to suppose that either he or Jeanne said *in commendam.* Grant that she said *en commande*, that is, 'in trust,' since the doctrine that God is 'King of Kings' was current in Catholic Europe as later in Presbyterian Scotland, did Jeanne need a furtive clerical private tutor to instruct her on the point? Even if she used as *technical* the term *en commande*, what prevented her, a church-frequenting girl as she was, from hearing the phrase in a public sermon?

The clergy knew nothing, we repeat, of her visions; when she came to Vaucouleurs and was exorcised as perhaps a daemoniac; they then knew her errand, but they did not suggest her mission.

M. France decides (p. 207) that the 'false prophecies' about the Maid from Lorraine were 'the means by which they set the young inspired girl at work … Do not let us be too much moved by the discovery of these pious frauds without which the miracles of the Maid would not have been produced.'

We are not moved at all!

The Maid may, conceivably, have heard it said, in a sermon, or in conversation, that there would come a conquering virgin from the marches of Lorraine. Yet the statement might arise, not from fraud, but from the mediaeval habit (with which M. France should sympathise) of not verifying references. We have a case in point. A friar of Longueville Caux, Migiet, was one of Joan's judges, though a friendly judge, in 1431. Some twenty years later he deponed that, 'some time or other, he had read in some old book or other the prophecy of Merlin that a virgin was to come from some *nemus canutum* or other, *in Lorraine*.'*

In this vague way the *nemus canutum* of Merlin was identified with the *bois chesnu* of the marches of Lorraine, and men thought that they had read, 'in some old book,' what was not and could not be in any book of Merlin's prophecies. There was no need of 'pious frauds.' The habit of not verifying references leads all who cultivate it into erroneous ways.

[. . .]

When Jeanne reaches Orleans, with an army and a great convoy (April 29), M. France's treatment of his theme becomes unintelligible to me. He is confused between his two perspectives. On one hand he wishes to reduce Jeanne and her achievements to the lowest possible or impossible dimensions. On the other he has glimpses of her greatness. 'It was supposed that all was done by her, that the King had consulted her in everything, whereas, in reality, the advisers of the King and the leaders hardly ever asked her advice, scarcely listened to her, and exhibited her when it seemed *à propos*' (p. 536).

M. France keeps harping on this string, but the evidence which he cites contradicts him at every turn, and the testimony is that of the leaders themselves, Dunois and the Duc d'Alençon. I shall cite the evidence as occasion arises.

He tells us that, at Orleans, in a moment when the excited townsfolk, 'in the absence of captains and men at arms, waited only a sign from her to charge and break themselves against the English forts, despite her warlike visions she made no sign. Child as she was, ignorant of war and of everything, she had the power and the goodness to prevent the disaster. She led the crowd of men, not against the forts, but to the holy places of the city' (p. 323). 'It was then that she showed herself, good, wise, equal to her mission, and truly born for the salvation of all.'

M. France has elsewhere said that Jeanne understood fighting in another fashion than the chivalry of France. We see how she understood it: to strike swiftly, to strike hard, to hold on with unabated tenacity, to abstain from battle when battle meant disaster – that is how the Maid understood fighting. Jeanne brought to a demoralised country and city the first principles of the art of war.

M. France, in one page and in one mood, acknowledges the military merits of the Maid, in another mood and another page avers that the Captains did not consult her, but led her about because she was reckoned 'lucky' (*chanceuse*).

---

* Procès, iii. 133.

He says, rightly or wrongly, as to the strong English fort of St. Loup, that no serious attack was intended by Dunois and the French tacticians. The forces were to make a diversion, and contain the English in St. Loup while a convoy from Blois was ferried across the river. Jeanne was not told of this purpose, 'of this Dunois did not breathe a word to the Maid' (p. 331), and she lay down to sleep beside her hostess in a room where her equerry was also slumbering. He was awakened by the noise she made as she leaped up from her rest. 'My Voices tell me that I must go against the English, but not *where*.'

'Her Saints had only told her what she knew herself,' says M. France. They *did* know while she slept that there was fighting to be done, and she, M. France has said, did not know.* She galloped with d'Aulon to the fort of St. Loup. Thanks to the energy and courage of Jeanne, now for the first time under fire, 'what was meant for a diversion became an attack, and was driven home.' The attack succeeded; St. Loup with all its defenders was taken. This was, M. France says, entirely due to the conduct of Jeanne (p. 336).

As for the great fort of the English on the further bank of the Loire, the Tourelles, some of the French, on approaching that hold, said, 'A month would not suffice for the taking of it' (p. 350). But Jeanne prophesied that the French would take it in a day, and would return to Orleans *by the bridge*, of which two arches had been destroyed. Jeanne did lead the attack, and was seriously wounded; the arrow-shaft stood a handbreadth out behind her shoulder. Later in the day, when Dunois had actually sounded the retreat, she induced him to command a last charge. So they did listen to her. She seized her banner beside the fosse, she bade the men charge once more, when her banner touched the wall, and they carried the position, returning to Orleans by the bridge, which they repaired. So says Dunois.†

M. France says (p. 366), 'Even so were fulfilled all her prophecies, when their accomplishment depended on her own courage and good will.' This being so, why does M. France keep denying it? There was no miracle, of course; there was only a military miracle. Dunois had abandoned all hope of accomplishing the task, but Jeanne caused it to be accomplished. Jeanne knew, as he has shown us, how to turn a mere diversion into a successful assault, how to lead men to a final attack on a strong fortress; and she knew, as M. France has told us, when to abstain from fighting and avoid disaster. Verily she was no mere *porte-bonheur*, but an invaluable leader.

When Talbot retired from Orleans, on May 8, the day after the fall of the Tourelles, he drew up his army in array, and offered battle. The Maid declined the offer (the leaders obeying her), whether from aversion to bloodshed, or because, in the open field, the archers and men-at-arms of England were still, in her opinion, too strong for French forces greatly superior in

* D'Aulon, Procès, iii. 212

† Procès, iii. 8.

numbers. The Captains 'who scarcely ever took Jeanne's advice' were probably wise when they did take it on this occasion. Few weeks passed before the great Dunois again refused to fight Talbot's force, in battle array, on a fair field, though Jeanne wished to charge.

The Dauphin, in his letters to the towns, declared that the Maid 'had always been personally present at the achievement of all these successes.' M. France says, in his grudging manner, 'her part in the victory was in nowise that of a captain; she had no command.' None the less she played the part of a captain, of a staff officer, and of a leader; nay, of commander-in-chief. *She* decided that Talbot should not be met on May 8. Sometimes M. France acknowledges all this, again he withdraws his acknowledgment (p. 372). His book is thus a tissue of incoherencies; his portrait of the Maid is an unintelligible blur.

[...]

As all these things were so, what is it that ails M. France against the little saint? Her ideas being correct, or as good as any others in the circumstances, why does he gird at the Maid? He seems to seize in haste at every opportunity to sneer, and then, as he goes on writing, he finds that there was nothing to sneer at. But he leaves his gibe in its position.

[...]

M. France has his defence, as to his many fatal inaccuracies. In his preface he tells an amusing tale of a fiend named Titivillus, who daily took to Satan the changed or omitted letters in the work of copyists, to be charged against the salvation of the blunderers. I have played the part of Titivillus, collecting some of the errors in a book which 'pretend à l'exactitude.' The printer's devil will have a hand in all books; but citations of authorities which do not contain the evidence attributed to them, evidence essential to the author's arguments, cannot be fairly charged on that scape goat, the compositor. I have only noted a few of the inaccuracies of M. France. Let any reader compare his pages about the Maid's breach of promise of marriage case with the pages in the *Procès* which M. France cites. Let any one compare his pages 116, 117 with his authorities; and his pages 316, 317 with his authorities. New legends are invented by M. France at every turn, because he reads the authorities incorrectly, or gives the wrong references for facts which I can nowhere find.

M. France tells us how difficult it is for the historian to inhabit two worlds at once, that of 142–431, and that of the twentieth century. Perhaps he dwells too much in our own age, is too deficient in chivalrous generosity, and, so far, fails to understand the candour of the Maid, who was no fraudulent medium, but, in character and genius, a world's wonder, while her apparently supranormal faculties are a problem not to be solved by a gibe. For my own part, I confess that I see the Maid, not as M. France does (in some passages, in others he gives her due praise), but as did the young, brave, and generous Guy de Laval, the kind and courteous son, the tennis player, the knight who beheld the Maid with the eyes of youth and loyalty.

Elle semble chose toute divine de son faict, et de la voir et de l'ouïr.[*16]

---

* Hilarem gerit vultum, 'her face was glad,' says Perceval de Boulainvilliers. She had 'a sweet low voice, an excellent thing in woman.' 'Elle parlait en assès voix de femme' (Guy de Laval). 'Vocem mulieris ad instar habet gracilem' (Perceval de Boulainvilliers, Procès, v. 108, 120).

From *The Maid of France: Being the Story of the Life and Death of Jeanne d'Arc*

(London: Longmans, Green and Co., 1908)

Preface

Jeanne d'Arc, during her nineteen years of life, was a cause of contention among her own countrymen, and her memory divides them to the present day. In her life she was of course detested as a witch and heretic by the French of the Burgundian faction. After her death, her memory was distasteful to all writers who disbelieved in her supernormal faculties, and in her inspiration. She had no business to possess faculties for which science could not account, and which common sense could not accept.

To-day, the quarrel over her character and career is especially bitter. If the Church canonises her, the Church is said, by the 'Anticlericals,' to 'confiscate' her, and to stultify itself.[1] Her courage and her goodness of heart are denied by no man, but, as a set-off against the praises of the 'clericals,' and even of historians far from orthodox, her genius is denied, or is minimised; she is represented as a martyr, a heroine, a puzzle-pated hallucinated lass, a perplexed wanderer in a realm of dreams; the unconscious tool of fraudulent priests, herself once doubtfully honest, apt to tell great palpable myths to her own glorification, never a leader in war, but only a kind of *mascotte*, a 'little saint,' and a beguine – in breeches!

It has appeared to me that all these inconsistent views of the Maid, and several charges against her best friends, are mainly based on erroneous readings of the copious evidence concerning her; on mistakes in the translating of the very bad Latin of the documents, and, generally, are distorted by a false historical perspective, if not by an unconscious hostility, into the grounds of which we need not inquire.[2] I have therefore written this book in the hope that grave errors, as I deem them, may be corrected; and also because, as far as I am aware, no British author has yet attempted to write a critical biography of the Maid. Of course, there no longer remains, in England, a shadow of prejudice against the stainless heroine and martyr. It has pleased the Chanoine Dunand, however, in his long biography of *La Vraie Jeanne d'Arc*, and in his learned but prolix series of *Études Critiques*, to speak of 'the English,' and the 'Franco-English' schools of History.[3] Masters and disciples in these schools, it appears, are apt to defend the regularity and the legality of her trial in 1431, and to deny to her the possession of 'heroic' virtues.

The English masters of history who do this thing are not named by the Chanoine Dunand. It is, indeed, easy to show that, in the age of the Maid, and later, England had practically no historian, no contemporary chronicler. When Fabyan, Holinshed, and Polydore Virgil,[4] a century later, wrote concerning Jeanne d'Arc, they drew their information, not from our archives (which are mute, save for one allusion to Jeanne), nor from English chroniclers contemporary with the Maid (for there is but a page of Caxton,[5] written fifty years after date), not from the *Procés* of the Trial of Condemnation and the Trial of Rehabilitation, but from the French chroniclers of the Burgundian party, such as Monstrelet; and from later antipathetic French historians, like du Haillan.[6] The Elizabethan historians were, of course, full of hostile national prejudice, they neglected the French chroniclers of her own party – if these were accessible to them – and the result was the perplexity, the chaotic uncertainty about the Maid, which is so conspicuous in the dubiously Shakespearean play, *Henry VI*, Part I, and is confessed in the remarks of the jocular Thomas Fuller, as late as 1642.[7]

But, in the middle of the eighteenth century, David Hume, in the spirit of the Scottish chroniclers who were contemporaries of the Maid, fully recognised the nobility of her character, and the iniquity of her condemnation. Though Hume was no Englishman, his History was widely read in England, and from his day onwards, perhaps Dr. Lingard, a Catholic, has been alone in taking an unworthy view of Jeanne d'Arc.[8]

In 1790 appeared the books of François de L'Averdy on the manuscript records of the two trials.[9] Henceforth the facts were accessible, and Jeanne d'Arc inspired both Coleridge and Southey with poems in her honour;[10] to be sure the inspiration did not result in anything worthy of her greatness. From that period it would be difficult to find any English historian who has applauded the regularity, or palliated the illegalities, of her condemnation, or who, save Lingard, has failed to recognise her heroism. But authors of general histories of England can give but limited space to the glorious Maid who emancipated France; and while America has a critical and valuable *Life of Joan of Arc* – that by Mr. Francis Lowell, – England has none that is critical and complete, and informed by documents brought to light since the time when Jules Quicherat published the five volumes entitled *Procès de Jeanne d'Arc* (1840–1850).[11] We have, indeed, the short but good monograph of Miss Tuckey, and a book by Lord Ronald Leveson-Gower, with a recent translation of the *Procès*, while brief stories of the life of the Maid for children are common, and excite the enthusiasm and the pity of little boys and girls.[12] But a work based on a study of all the documents, and equipped with full references, has been still to seek. I have therefore tried to fill this empty place in our bookshelves, and to depict, however feebly, this glory of her sex, 'a Star of ancient France.'

There is no Englishman alive who, from obsolete national prejudice, would try to diminish her greatness, or to palliate the shameful iniquity of his ancestors in all their relations with her. But a Scot is especially devoid of temptation to defend Cauchon, Warwick, Bedford, and the rest of 'our old enemies of England.' The Scots did not buy or sell, or try, or condemn, or persecute, or burn, or – most shameful of all – bear witness against and desert the Maid. The Scots stood for her always, with pen as with sword.[13]

The historical evidence for the career of the Maid is rich, multifarious, and of many degrees of comparative excellence. In the front stands the official record of her trial at Rouen in 1431. On each day of her trial, the clerks of the Court took down in French her replies to the questions of the judges and assessors. The French version was, later, officially rendered into Latin, with all the other proceedings: and certain posthumous documents were added. The whole book is official, the work of her enemies. How far it is fair and honest is a question to be discussed in the text. At all events we have here a version of what Jeanne herself told her judges, as to her own life, and as to future events. Next we have letters dictated by her, and letters written about her, during her active career, from April 1429 to May 1430. These are of varying value: the News Letters of the age, French, Italian, and German, answer to the letters of Foreign Correspondents in our newspaper press. Some are full of false gossip.

As to the politics of the period we have diplomatic documents, treaties, memoirs, and despatches. We also possess notes in the contemporary account books of various towns, and the jottings of contemporary diarists, well or ill informed, as the case may be.

The historical chronicles concerning the Maid date from 1430 to 1470: some are by friendly French, some by hostile Burgundian hands. Their evidence needs to be studied critically, with an eye on the probable sources of information of each chronicler. The mystery play, *Mistère du Siège d'Orléans*, is a late poetical chronicle (*circ.* 1470?). A few facts may be gleaned from works even later than 1470, when the writer's sources of information are mentioned and seem to be good.

Finally we have the records of the Trial of Rehabilitation (1450–1456), with the sworn evidence of more than a hundred and forty eye-witnesses, who knew the Maid at various periods from her infancy to her martyrdom. In judging their depositions, we must make careful allowance for errors of bias, for illusions of memory, and for the natural desire of persons who took part in her trial to shield themselves, and to throw blame on her judges and their assessors who were by that time dead, or for any reason were not able to speak for themselves.

The main defect of the Trial of Rehabilitation is the singular fact that only two witnesses testified to any event in the life of the Maid between the failure at Paris, in September 1429, and her capture in May 1430. No questions on this period were put, for example, to her confessor, Pasquerel, and her equerry, d'Aulon, an omission which cannot be defended, even if it was caused by a desire to spare the feelings of the King, Charles V. His conduct, and his diplomacy, from his Coronation to the capture of the Maid, must for him have been full of tormenting memories. I have also suggested in the text, that as the Maid, like any other leader, certainly assured her men of success, 'fight on, you will have them!' on occasions when they were not successful, the inquirers in 1450–1456 may have shrunk from asking 'Did Jeanne utter these promises as the predictions of her Saints?' We have only her own denial.

The evidence of the cloud of witnesses in 1450–1456 is commonly disparaged by the scientific spirit. Even Quicherat wrote: 'The depositions of the witnesses have the air, for the most part, of having undergone numerous retrenchments,' of having been 'cut,' as we say, or garbled. Quicherat gives no proof of this; and none is visible to me. On certain important points, such as 'What did Jeanne do at Paris, La Charité, Lagny, Melun, and Compiègne?' no questions were asked, though her judges in 1431 had accused her of several misdeeds at these places. Nothing was asked as to her leap from the tower (or her attempt to let herself down from a window of the tower) at Beaurevoir. These omissions are a great blot on the Trial of Rehabilitation, but that the judges cut and garbled the replies to questions actually put is a mere baseless assertion.*

Quicherat had said, 'The judges at the Rehabilitation were probity itself.' Yet he also says that they seem to have garbled 'the majority of the depositions'!

M. Anatole France is specially severe on the Trial of Rehabilitation, though he freely quotes the depositions.

In the first place, the witnesses merely answered the questions put to them 'in the course of ecclesiastical justice.' Certainly we now should put many other questions.

Secondly, 'the majority of the witnesses are excessively simple and lacking in discernment.' They were men and women of their own time, not savants of our time – that is undeniable!

Again, Pasquerel misplaces the sequence of certain events, it is true, but so does M. Anatole France on several occasions, as we shall try to show.

The deposition of Dunois 'must have been mishandled by the translator and the scribes,' as when he speaks of 'the strong force of the enemy.' But

* See Dunand, La Sociètè de l'Histoire de France, Jules Quicherat, et Jeanne d'Arc, pp. 15–68, 1908, and Quicherat, Aperçus Nouveaux, 1850.

Bedford, the English commander-in-chief, also says that the English at Orleans were numerous, before the men began to desert. Their numbers were reduced by desertions, but if Dunois overestimated them, how often, in the South African war, did our leaders make the same mistake as to the enemy! The other sins of Dunois are either no sins at all, or are easily pardonable, and the burden of them need not be thrown on translator or scribe.

As to the witnesses who had been assessors, scribes, or officers of the Court in 1431, 'all these ink-pots of the Church who had fashioned the documents for the death of the Maid, showed as much zeal in destroying it,' in 1450–1456. Let that be granted; it does not follow that the evidence, for example, of Manchon is false. The witnesses say that they were terrorised by Cauchon and the English, and perhaps nobody doubts that they did go in fear. Poor clerks and officials, it is part of the injustice of the trial of 1431 that they were threatened and bullied. 'They denounced the cruel iniquity which they had themselves put in good and proper form.' The form, in fact, is not so good and proper: one document the scribes refused to sign, and unsigned it remains.

Probably few penmen, even now, would have the courage to throw up their duties and their livelihood, and incur a fair chance of being cast into dungeons, or into the river, because they disliked their work. The scribes did their task: they were not heroes. Had they been heroes, we should not have had their evidence.

> 'A pair of lamentable monks, Brother Martin Ladvenu and Brother Isambart de la Pierre, wept bitterly while they told of the pious death of the poor Maid whom they had declared heretic, then relapsed, and had burned alive.'

There is no evidence that the two monks wept while they gave their testimony; at the last, they did not – unconditionally – declare Jeanne heretic; to burn her or to save her they had no more power than I who write. That power was in the hands of Cauchon, Bishop of Beauvais. At the same time I regard with suspicion several parts of the evidence of these two lamentable monks, and 'the ink-pots of the Church.'

> 'The captains said that Jeanne was expert in placing guns, when they knew that it was untrue.'

One captain, d'Alençon, swore to her skill in artillery, and M. Anatole France knows that this witness deliberately perjured himself. Less omniscient, I know not how he knows; or what his acquaintance with mediaeval artillery may be; but I suspect, from examination of a contemporary breech-loading field-piece, that any one with a good eye and a little practice could do what was needed. Many women are good shots.

'The effort was made to prove that Jeanne was destitute of intelligence, to show that the Holy Spirit was more manifest in her.' M. Anatole France himself does not credit the Maid with much intelligence (esprit) but many of the witnesses did. 'The examiners led the witnesses to keep repeating that the Maid was simple, very simple.' He himself gives the same opinion: often.

Many said that she was chaste. Does any mortal deny it? Some of her companions vowed that she did not excite their passions. Is that, considering their deep reverence and regard for the Maid, a thing incredible? Naturally her enemies were not affected in the same way.

'Sometimes the clerks content themselves with saying that one witness deposed like the preceding witness.' Nothing was more usual in the records of *secular* trials one hundred and forty years later, as in the trial of the accomplices of Bothwell in Darnley's murder.* 14

It is proper to notice these objections to the evidence of 1450–1456. We shall use it with the warning that, in twenty-five years, human memories are apt to be fallacious; that the bias of the witnesses was favourable to the Maid; and that some witnesses had to excuse their own share in the trial of 1431, and to exhibit the judges, mainly Cauchon and the accuser, in the most unfavourable light. But we shall not accuse the captains of deliberate perjury, out of our own will and fantasy.

Mr. Frederick Myers, when studying the Maid in the light of psychical research,† spoke of the records of the Trial of Rehabilitation as practically worthless. The events were too 'remote' for evidence given twenty-five years later to be trustworthy. I venture to think that he rated the powers of memory too low, when he thought that, in a quarter of a century, all witnesses would necessarily err as to the most impressive experience of their lives, their acquaintance with Jeanne d'Arc. The psychical researcher feels bound to take it for granted that strange affairs will be unconsciously exaggerated by memory, after twenty-five years. There are, in fact, two tendencies; one man exaggerates, another begins to doubt, when the first freshness of his impression has been worn off, and he minimises. But every reader of the Trial of Rehabilitation must see that the witnesses, in 1450–1456, are usually sparing in marvels, except Pasquerel and Dunois. We hear from them of no miracles attributed to Jeanne, though Dunois obviously regarded the fortunate change of the wind on the Loire, on April 28, 1429, as verging on miracle. Pasquerel exaggerated its effects; and also said that, on May 6, Jeanne named the day and the place of her arrow-wound. Very possibly his memory deceived him. But witnesses say nothing of the clairvoyance about Rouvray fight, or about the sword at Fierbois; about the Maid's knowledge of the King's secret they could not, of course, say anything definite. They never mention her saintly visitors. The only hagiographic marvels are negligible; and are connected with the martyrdom. The

* Cf. Anatole France, Vie de Jeanne d'Arc, vol. i. pp. xx.–xxz., vol. ii. pp. 445–452.

† Human Personality. Cf. Index, Jeanne d'Arc.

contemporary tales (1429) about marvels at the time of the birth of Jeanne, are not repeated by the witnesses from Domremy: about these marvels no questions were asked.

[…]

Introduction: The Maid and Theories About Her

[…]

The similar opinion, that she was known by the clergy of her native place to be a visionary, and that they invented her military mission and imposed it on her through her Voices, while Brother Richard took her in hand later, has been put forward by M. Anatole France.* Dr. Dumas of the Sorbonne has hailed M. France's revival of the old system of 'indoctrination' as the last word of Science on the subject.†

If I stated the scientific theory in my own words, I might readily be suspected of maliciously distorting it. I translate, therefore, the scientific formula as given by Dr. Dumas. 'It is outside of the Maid that M. Anatole France resolutely seeks the source of her political inspirations and Messianic ideas. Thus, behind her first visions, he already detects the influence of some unknown clerical person who wished to turn these visions to the good of the kingdom, and to the conclusion of peace. Jeannette brought, for her part, her piety, her horror of war, her love of the unhappy and afflicted, her memories of her nights of anguish, and of her frightful dreams. The clerical person contributed the Mission; and out of the Voices which at first only said, "Jeannette, be a good girl," he made the Voices which said, "Daughter of God, leave thy village and go into France to let consecrate the Dauphin."'‡

How the priest came to know that Jeanne (who confided the facts to no churchman) saw Angels and Saints, Dr. Dumas does not tell us. How, when the priest did know, he 'made the Voices urge Jeanne to go to France, despite her remonstrances – "I cannot ride and fight",'§ Dr. Dumas does not inform us. He even drops the fact that the mission was *military*; probably because he sees that no priest could be so mad as to advise a peasant girl to ride in the van of armies. The mission, however, was 'holy and *warlike*'

* Vie de Jeanne d'Arc, 1908. Vol. i. p. 54, and passim.

† Revue du Mois, May 10, 1908.

‡ Ibid., May 10, 1908.

§ Procès, vol. i. p. 53.

says M. France himself, with truth.* His neuropathological disciple, in the interests of the scientific theory, is obliged to ignore that essential circumstance.

It cannot be ignored by the historian! Again, Jeanne had no 'horror of war' in a just cause. She did not want to fight, and as soon as her Voices bade her go into France, and lead her King to Reims through a country full of hostile garrisons, she perceived that her mission must be military, and replied that she could not fight and lead men-at-arms. But, yielding to the monitions of her Voices, she took up a mission professedly warlike. When she left Vaucouleurs on February 23, 1429, to rescue France, she was girt with a sword: she carried sword, lance, steel sperth, and dagger – or such of these weapons as she found appropriate – till the hour of her capture. 'Her nights of terror and fearful dreams' are as destitute of evidence as her clerical tutors. She was not timid!

When we refuse to ignore, with Dr. Dumas, the fact that the mission of the Maid, from the first, was *military*; when we agree, with M. France, and all the evidence, that the mission was *warlike* the scientific theory ceases to exist.

No priest could possibly have taught her, through her Voices, that only an ignorant peaceful peasant girl, herself, in male costume, could drive the English out of France. Much less could a supposed series of clerical impostors have, through all her career, unanimously insisted on a course which, to human common sense, seemed the quintessence of crazy folly.

This theory is unthinkable. First, it cannot be thought that even if one mad curé bade the girl to make peace by restoring France with the sword in her own hand, Jeanne's other clerical tutors would all follow him. If they thought that they had got hold of a useful saintly visionary, – to such a person, princes, popes, the English Government, and the Duke of Burgundy were, in that age, apt to listen, – they would employ her as a messenger of peace, not of war. Popes and princes and cities had listened to St Catherine of Siena: the English Government and the Duke of Bedford listened to the devout Dame Eleanor Raughton, All Hallows, North Street, York.† [15]

But the priests of the theory sent their visionary to ride in man's dress, armed, and to bid the English depart at the point of the lance! The only named director whom Jeanne's enemies accused of 'indoctrinating' her, Brother Richard, found that she spurned his peaceful methods of negotiating through a visionary.

The scientific hypothesis, then, cannot be accepted by the historian. Moreover, the hypothesis is self-contradictory, if that be any objection in modern logic. It is distinctly and frequently, and correctly maintained, by

* France, vol. i. p. 51.

† Pageants of Richard Beauchamp, Earl of Warwick, p. iii. Roxburghe Club, 1908.

the advocate of the theory of clerical 'indoctrination,' that no priest knew anything from Jeanne of her psychical experiences, *that Jeanne never told about her 'revelations' to her curé or any churchman.*‡ That she did not do so is very extraordinary; and the fact, to this day, afflicts her clerical defenders, Father Ayroles, S.J., and the Chanoine Dunand.[16] But that Jeanne was thus secretive, that she never took a priest into her confidence as concerning her visions and Voices, was a point urged against her claims to canonisation in 1903. The *Advocatus Diabolic* Monsignor Caprara (*Promoteur de la Foi*), dwelt severely on the conduct of Jeanne in not consulting her spiritual director about her revelations.§

That she confided the facts of her visions and Voices to no churchman is thus maintained by the friends of the theory that, apparently because she *did* confide them, the churchmen knew about them, and 'indoctrinated' her; taught her the nature of her warlike mission; and used her as their mouthpiece and puppet. The theory of 'indoctrination' rests on a contradiction in terms.

Thus the logic of the case proves that there was no less of truth than of loyalty in the dying declaration of the Maid; that what she had done, be it good or bad, was entirely of her own doing without counsel from any man.

The theory that she was 'indoctrinated' has no historical basis, and less than no logical basis. She was not – save in accepting the contemporary ideas, expressed even on the coinage, about kings being the lieutenants of God, and about the need of consecration and coronation – the pupil of priests or politicians.

As a proof that her mission was suggested by fraudulent priests, we are told that it was initiated and advertised by means of forged prophecies, chiefly by a special version of a prophecy of Merlin, fraudulently constructed to these ends. But we shall demonstrate, by unimpeachable evidence, that this prediction was a thing already current in folklore on the marches of Lorraine.

The author who presents us with these ideas adds that, in her lifetime, Jeanne was only known to men in a radiant mist of childish and incredible legends, reported by the press, so to speak, of the period, the news letters sent to foreign countries. If this were true, it is not easy to guess where the critic obtained the materials for his portrait of the Maid. Of course, in her lifetime Jeanne was well known to hundreds of persons.

It should be superfluous to remark that the materials for an historical portrait cannot be disengaged out of the ephemeral legends which, in all ages, gather round every important personage. Lord Morley's *Life of William Ewart Gladstone* would have been much more lively, but much less edifying, had he made use of the contemporary legends concerning the famous pol-

‡ France, vol. i. p. 50, ii. p. 307.

§ Langogne, Jeanne d'Arc devant la Congrégation des Rites, 1894, p. 174.

itician.[17] We do not take our ideas of Montrose, Claverhouse, or Mary of Guise from the contemporary legends of the Covenanters or the myths of John Knox.[18]

In the same way the tattle of contemporary writers of news letters, who in 1429–1431 sent to Germany and Italy, 'under all reserves,' the fables about Jeanne d'Arc which reached them, does not make her a legendary personage. The romances of victories and defeats that never occurred, in the South African war, did not outlive three days' life of the British and foreign newspapers which circulated them; and scarcely one of the fables about Jeanne, published in the news letters of 1429–1430, found its way into the Chronicles of 1430–1470. A few of the myths were made the subjects of questions put to Jeanne by her judges in 1431. Of some she had never so much as heard; the truth of others she denied.

To say that 'the history of Jeanne d'Arc is a religious history just like that of Colette de Corbie,' is an error in criticism.* In the case of Jeanne we have, in the case of St Colette we have not, an enormous body of historical materials, – almost destitute of 'hagiography,' wholly destitute of imputed miracles, – unless a few cases of premonition and clairvoyance are to be held 'miraculous.' In Jeanne we see the warrior and the politician, not the ecstatic and the thaumaturge. Miracle-working she again and again, in freedom and in prison, disclaimed. If she occasionally exhibited such faculties as 'second sight' and telepathy, Thackeray, Nelson, and Catherine de Medici have been credited with similar powers.

To reject abundance of sworn evidence because it conflicts with a critic's personal idea of what is probable or possible is not the method of History, and will not be adopted in this book. Much less will I reject, for instance, the evidence of Jeanne herself on any point, and give a fanciful theory of my own as to what really occurred. If there are incidents in her career which Science, so far, cannot explain, I shall not therefore regard them as false. Science may be able to explain them on some future day; at present she is not omniscient.

The mournful truth is that the historian has a much better chance of being read if he gives free play to his fancy than if he is strictly accurate. But to add the figments of fancy to the facts on record, to cite documents as if they were warrants for the statements which they do not support, is to wander from history into the enchanted forest of romance.

---

* France, vol. i. p. lxxx.

5

THE BUSINESS AND INSTITUTIONS OF LITERARY LIFE

Much of Lang's journalism, especially in his regular 'At the Sign of the Ship' column in *Longman's Magazine*, is concerned with the business of writing. He is conscious of the differentiation made between 'hack' writers in the trade for an income and the grander authors of 'Literature' and is uncertain about where he identifies himself. His pieces on these topics show his familiarity with the business of writing and the problems facing both aspiring and successful writers. There were several issues that concerned professional writers of the time, such as copyright, on which he comments in the piece selected here, first published in *Longman's Magazine* 7:41 (March 1886), pp. 551–3.

He writes also on the subject of authors' pay and the iniquities of the market in two further 'Sign of the Ship' columns extracted here (*Longman's Magazine* 8:46 (August 1886), pp. 455–8 and *Longman's Magazine* 22:129 (July 1893), pp. 273–80), as well as frequently elsewhere, for example: *Longman's Magazine* 23:134 (December 1893), pp. 210–18; 'What is a Hack?', *Illustrated London News* 108:2963 (1 February 1896), p. 134; 'Literature as a Trade', *St. James's Gazette* (22 October 1890), p. 5 and 'A Literary Mystery', *The Pilot* (20 April 1901), pp. 498–9. Despite his consciousness of the problems of literature as a trade he was not sympathetic to the aims of those like Walter Besant who attempted to form a kind of trade union for writers, the Society of Authors, to take collective action to redress those problems. When Besant attended the Congress of Authors in Chicago in 1893, Lang writes scathingly of the event and Besant's efforts in, for example, the 'Sign of the Ship' column for December (see above) and 'Chicagomania', *Illustrated London News* 102:2820 (6 May 1893), p. 546.

The long essay *How To Fail In Literature* was first delivered as a lecture at the South Kensington Museum on 28 November 1889, held in order to raise funds for a working men's college. It was published in the following year (London: Field & Tuer, The Leadenhall Press, 1890). It is revealing of Lang's attitude to his own success as well as of the difficult world of 'Grub Street' in the late Victorian period. 'To A Young Journalist' (first published in *Essays in Little*, London: Henry and Co., 1891, pp. 191–7) shows that the problems were still very present to him after nearly two decades in the business.

'The Teaching of English Literature' was first published in the *Illustrated London News* 909: 2749 (26 December 1891), p. 834. It is a response to John Churton Collins' book, *The Study of English Literature* (London: Macmillan, 1891) but also to the wider debate about the study of English at university and whether writing can be taught or the appreciation of literature learned. Collins (1848–1908) was an energetic campaigner for the establishment of English as a university subject, eventually becoming Professor at Birmingham in 1904. In the 1890s there was a difficult struggle at Oxford to separate literary study from philology and history and although several Professors of Literature had been appointed at universities by the time of Lang's death, including at Oxford, Lang never supported the subject and never lectured on literature in a university as he did on anthropology. Lang returns to the topic of teaching English on several occasions, see for example, 'A School of Fiction', *Longman's Magazine* 18:104 (June 1891), pp. 215–18; 'At the Sign of the Ship', *Longman's Magazine* 21:122 (December 1892), pp. 214–20; 'The Science of Novels', *Illustrated London News* 105:2899 (10 November 1894), p. 598; 'Examinations in Fiction', *Cornhill Magazine* 83 (January 1901), pp. 80–9; 'The Teaching of Literature', *The Pilot* (13 April 1901), pp. 466–7 (reproduced here) and 'Can Literature Be Taught?' *The Pilot* (29 June 1901), pp. 805–6.

'At the Sign of the Ship', *Longman's Magazine* 7:41

(March 1886), pp. 551–3

One of Henri Murger's heroes[1] hired a man to waken him every morning, tell him what the weather was like, and 'what Government we are living under.' Without being a prophet, no man can tell what Government we shall be under when this talk is published, but it is certain that Lord Salisbury[2] wished to do something for International Copyright. Matters cannot be much worse than they are. The Americans can get our books, and do get them, and republish them and give us nothing – that awful minus quantity, 'nuppence'! And then a critic in the *Nation* (a very good New York paper, though somewhat harsh and crabbed) accuses many of our novelists of 'getting money under false pretences.' He does not care for our recent romances, this courteous reviewer in the *Nation* and he cries out that he is being defrauded. I make him my compliments, and am reminded of the fable of the Wolf and the Lamb.[3] 'You trouble the stream from which I drink!' says the Wolf; and the Lamb in vain replied that he himself drank lower down the water.

Conceive a buccaneer of the old sort, Captain Kidd, or honest John Silver,[4] making prize of a British barque and then finding the cargo, cottons or cutlery, not to his taste; he calls the luckless skipper to the quarter-deck, and preaches him a sermon on his commercial dishonesty, and gives him a dozen, and makes him walk the plank, and then sails away with his disappointing prize. The critic's conduct is like that of Captain Kidd, and we may reply, 'Sir, if we obtain money on false pretences it is British specie, none of your dollars.' The American author, too, does not enjoy the easy stratagem by which our books are pilfered (by the Western or Eastern robber) ready made. Not many of his countrymen will buy his expensive novel, 'The

Philadelphians,' when they can get Mr. Besant's books, or Mr. Stevenson's, for next to nothing. So the American authors have published a Round Robin, denouncing the pirates' industry, in the most feeling and masculine language, as a national and personal disgrace. The Round Robin is signed with facsimiles of their autographs, and it is pleasant to learn that our brethren of the pen over-seas are of our mind, and give a piece of that mind, with the frankest generosity, to their country's Legislature. We don't steal their books '– much,' as the Russian Prince says in the 'Great Pink Pearl,'[5] and it neither suits the British nor the American author that our books should be stolen. How it suits the American consumer is another question. Perhaps he does not feel the national and personal disgrace quite so keenly.

As a contribution to this discussion comes a pamphlet by an American author[6] whose books 'have a large circulation in England, and in several Continental languages.' I cannot analyse all his argument here, but he thinks he has a new plan to propose. The plan is 'Protected Author's Copyright, with Free Trade Competition.' A combination of Free Trade and Protection should win every vote. The object is to keep books cheap, and yet give the writers liberal payment. Americans would not relish paying whatever it is that people do pay for novels, which nominally cost a guinea and a half. Yet, if British copyright were simply extended to America, I presume that the denizens of the States would be victims of this cruel necessity. At present American publishers find it pays them to publish a book like Farrar's 'Life of Christ'[7] for twenty pence. No doubt it pays them, if they don't pay the learned divine who wrote the book, nor his English publishers. Well, the new dodge is that an author's books shall all be stamped with a trade mark, say the Lion and the Eagle[8] fondly embracing. Anyone who bought or sold a book without the stamp would be liable to prosecution and fine. The American publisher who wanted some of Mr. Froude's works, let us say, would buy 10,000 stamps from Mr. Froude, each stamp bearing the retail price per volume legibly printed. I understand that the publisher might buy 9,000 shilling stamps for a cheap edition, and 1,000 ten shilling stamps for a handsome edition, and so on. Perhaps the reader understands this scheme which, apparently, permits half a dozen publishers, if they choose, to put forth the same author's works, while he (as I take it) receives a royalty of about an eighth on the retail price. I don't see where the English publisher's share comes in, and he will probably examine the project with a keen eye on that part of its details. Perhaps he and the English author split the eighth, or toss for it.

Probably the most diverting of the comments by American authors on copyright were Mark Twain's endeavours to prove that cheap foreign books are bad for American manners and American morals. Our novels establish a false ideal in the American imagination, and the result is that mysterious being 'The Dude.'[9] Yet our books must have taught Americans a good deal, too, for it can never be well for a great people to remain in ignorance of the rest of the civilised world. Dickens's 'American Notes' must have been quite educational (as, perhaps, Mr. W, D. Howells would allow), but there is no reason why free education should be extended by the transfer of England's books, for nothing, to America. That arrangement has always been, on our side, as Aristotle says about robbery, 'an involuntary exchange.'

'At the Sign of the Ship', *Longman's Magazine* 8:46

(August 1886), pp. 455–8

After a month nearly vitrified by the heat of the weather and the ardour of politics,[1] an inconsecutive writer naturally looks about for some questions that are not blazing. [...] A cool unexciting topic, especially in August, seemed to be the future of the British Novel. Mr. Shand[2] has been discoursing of this in the *Fortnightly Review*. One need not accept all his facts and all his conclusions: for example, there is not a definite, certain twopence of profit on a shilling novel. One shilling novel differs from another in magnitude. One may contain a hundred and seventy widely printed pages, another may hold two hundred and thirty pages of closely printed matter. It is evident that the expenses of the former will be much smaller, and the profits, supposing sales equal, proportionally greater.

Without accepting all Mr. Shand's views, then, it may be granted that 'the novel business' is not in the best possible condition. To the young gentleman or lady about to commence novelist one would whisper 'Beware!' and counsel some attention to statistics. In the first place, Sir or Madam, do you propose to use novel writing as a staff or a crutch? Can you live even if your books be a failure? According to the Old Man, even Nicholas,[3] 'literature is only respectable when combined with some other avocation, such as not being employed at the bar.'

A glance at the weekly advertising columns of the literary papers will show that perhaps one novel out of fifty is even moderately successful. In the last ten years any one of mature age can remember some five great 'hits,' and perhaps twenty stories which paid their authors about half or a quarter as well as they would have been paid for equivalent success at the Bar, in Medicine, in Business, and about an eighth as well as if the triumph had been won on the stage. Compare the pecuniary profits of *Called Back*, or

John Inglesant, or even, in better days, of *Romola*, with those of *Our Boys* or *The Private Secretary*.[4] Again, without going into figures too invidiously, contrast the probable income of the most successful living novelist with the income of a dull, plodding man who is in good practice at the Bar. The money balance is all against the bright romanticist, even at his best. The chances that any beginner will ever reach the foremost rank are almost incalculably adverse. And even in the foremost rank the profits are scanty, in comparison with the rewards of other professions. Why, in fiction, there are not half a dozen such good things as a county court judgeship or an inspectorship of schools.

As the human demand for instruction is less ardent than the demand for amusement, the pecuniary reward of even the luckiest novelist seems slight. We hear of fortunes made in France by novelists like M. Zola and M. Daudet. Why is similar luck so very, very rare in England? Why do M. Zola and M. Daudet do so much better than our Englishman of letters, like Mr. Trollope, who was also a man of business? This is a mystery. No economist has fathomed it. Certainly the French system of publishing novels is infinitely more simple than the English system. Novels are usually sold in one volume, at a price rather over half-a-crown, say three-and-sixpence, adding the expense for a plain binding. Of this half-crown the author receives a royalty – fourpence, or fivepence, or only twopence, according to his popularity and the demand for his books. Say he sells eighty thousand copies of a novel (and M. Ohnet,[5] M. Zola, M. Daudet, often sell far more), and he makes about 1,400*l.* at a royalty of fourpence. This is exclusive of the price paid for the serial publication of the tale as the *feuilleton* of a newspaper.[6] Most French newspapers have their novel running, and, on the whole, it will appear that a successful French novelist has rather a profitable business, especially as he often dramatises his tale, and reaps the rich rewards of the theatre. But though the facts are patent, no one has yet discovered *who* buy the eighty thousand or one hundred and twenty thousand copies of 'Sappho' or 'Serge Panine.'[7] I never saw a Frenchman buy a novel at a railway station, or read anything but a newspaper. This, then, is the great mystery. But it is certain that their half-crown books do sell, somehow, and it is certain that the British novel's sale is limited to the brief and accidental demand of the circulating libraries. Mr. Mudie[8] is at the bottom of our English woes – Mr. Mudie and the conventional price of thirty-one shillings and sixpence for the conventional three volumes. Mr. Shand thinks that, if publishers could agree and combine, and, above all, if fictitious trash were not published at the author's expense, then we might have a system of cheap novels like the French, of novels with a large sale. I doubt it, and I am sure, whatever Mr. Shand may think, that Victor Hugo's tales were never published 'in folios.' Both his and Flaubert's saw the light in large octavos.[9] But a novel in folio! It is incredible.

There remains one important reason why novels as a rule do not sell very well, either in three volumes, or at a shilling, or in the French form. As a rule, novels are not very well worth buying. A good book, and a book that takes the public, will do excellently in any shape, just as a good horse never yet was of a bad colour. Unless the commencing novelist feels with the intuition of genius that he can do something immensely better than the average, he had better leave the business alone. The earnings are small, the mortifications numberless, and the neophyte must not even dream of fame, or expect pleasant society to welcome him as the author of half a dozen romances of the usual type. A certain place, paved with good intentions, is full of such romances.

Successes are very rare indeed, and we all envy them, but 'Bre'r Fox', in a modern literary fable, might 'allow' with some truth that the grapes are often sour.[10] It would be easy to write a lament on the Sorrows of a Success. A young man makes a hit in literature, and his name, yesterday unknown, is to-day in every one's mouth, and in the *Morning Post* among those who attend the banquets and participate in the caresses of the Great. How very jolly we think; all we toilers and spinners, hewers of wood and drawers of water, the Children of Gibeon of literature![11] But it is not all jollity. To be envied, and begrudged, and censured, to have a hundred people declaring that you went up like a rocket and will come down like the stick, is exceedingly irksome. I can conceive no position more anxious than that of the author who, having once scaled the peaks of success, is attempting a second flight. *He* knows very well what is being prophesied about him by his rivals, and he knows that those predictions, like the threats and ill words of witches, have a trick of seeming their own fulfilment. This consciousness interferes with the freedom of his powers in working. In an amusing little tract, 'Hints on Golf,' Mr. Horace Hutchinson[12] mentions that you can put a player off his play by remarking, 'How very unusually well you are making your iron strokes just now! Can you account for it in any way?' This causes your opponent to feel a certain trepidation when he takes his iron in hand – the spontaneity of his action is checked, and perhaps he loses the game. Now, the consciousness of unfriendly, jealous watchers may, or must, affect the writing of a successful beginner, still all in a flutter at the march of his own triumph. He knows what people are saying. They say that his book was a 'fluke,' that he hit on a happy thought and cannot recover such another, that he just happened to seize a topic which was coming into fashion; they say he is overrated, they speak about a *tour de force*[13] and forget that *ne faict ce tour qui veult*.[14] They also insinuate that the whole story, or the best of it, was old, and has been stolen, or borrowed, and they imply that *they* could do as well were they not too honest to borrow. I hardly remember a recent success which has not been denounced as a tissue of borrowings. It is odd that when borrowing is so easy and profitable we do not all convert ourselves from jays into peacocks.

'At the Sign of the Ship'
Longman's Magazine 22:129
(July 1893), pp. 273–80

In the June 'National Review' in addition to Mr. Toole's essay on 'New Humour and Non Humour' (write on, write ever thus, Mr. Toole!) there is a very pleasing study of 'The New Literary Era,' by Mr. Arthur Waugh. The professional aspect of literature engages Mr. Waugh's attention. He 'says what he ought to have said,' and is very polite to professionalism, but one fancies that he is not in love with it. 'We have left behind all the possibilities of literary sweating' he says. Perhaps Mr. Besant is not entirely of this opinion.[1] The *sommités*[2] of literature are not 'sweated,' but the persons who produce 'novelettes,' and many translations, are still paid at rates probably much out of proportion to the profits. The reason, as in all cases of 'sweating,' is that almost anybody can do the kind of thing – the empty novelettes, the artless renderings from the French. This labour market is overstocked. If Miss Jones refuses to write two hundred pages for thirty pounds, why Miss Smith will do it, and no mortal can distinguish between the work of Miss Smith and the work of Miss Jones. It is all writing, but none of it is literature: it is hardly to be called skilled labour. Therefore dealers in these wares will pay the lowest prices, and what is that but sweating, and how are you to cure it, as the victims cannot strike and howl in the streets? How can you cure it, for the world can wag on without halfpenny novelettes and bad translations? There is no competition among purchasers for the novelettes and the perversions from the French. As far as literature is concerned, people who write these, generally speaking, should not be writing at all; these things should not be done.

Turning to authors more fortunate, by dint of luck or merit, one doubts if *they* ever were much sweated. True, Ronsard complains that publishers 'take everything and give nothing,' but the Prince of Poets lived on ecclesiastical revenues,[3] and probably there was no great purchasing public for the Prince of Poets. Rabelais, one feels sure, never heard of royalties; his would have been immense. We do not learn that he was opulent, or that his publishers made fortunes. In the last century, the century of Grub Street,[4] what amazes me is the open hand and credulous trust of the booksellers. They were always paying Collins,[5] and people like him, a good deal of money for an unwritten book, which remained unwritten. Johnson's virtue was not proof against this easy-going arrangement: it was hard work for the booksellers to get his various compositions out of the doctor, who had received the price. The doctor 'uniformly expressed much regard for the booksellers of London,' says Mr. Boswell.[6] Not quite uniformly; in his 'Life of Savage,'[7] he speaks of 'the avarice by which the booksellers are frequently incited to oppress that genius by which they are supported.' But 'Millar, the bookseller, has done very generously by Fielding; finding "Tom Jones", for which he had given him 600*l.*, sell so greatly, he has since given him another hundred,' writes Horace Walpole.[8] Do you know any other trade in which such things are done? Boswell once said to Johnson that he was 'sorry he did not get more for his dictionary.' 'I am sorry, too,' said the doctor, 'but it was very well. The booksellers are generous, liberal-minded men.'[9] The chances of profit on a book he regarded as very uncertain. Now if Dr. Johnson was 'satisfied,' as he declared himself to be, in a letter read aloud in the House of Commons (1774), one may doubt whether the booksellers were so very bad, after all.

After rejoicing over the prosperity of the modern author, Mr. Waugh remarks that 'the ubiquity of the pecuniary estimate' is not a pretty trait in our generation. And, after decrying 'the City of Prague,' and announcing that 'to mourn over the collapse of Bohemia[10] is sheer affectation,' in the very next page he is pleased to find that 'among men of letters there is a strong tincture of gracious Bohemianism still.' Clearly that article was written by two people at least; there is the original Waugh, of p. 11, and the unscrupulous *diaskeuast,* or interpolator, of p. 12. So the Higher Criticism would decide,[11] but, in fact, Mr. Waugh wishes both to share

> 'The song of them that triumph.
> The shout of them that feast –'[12]

the representatives of the Incorporated Authors' Society, at Chicago;[13] and he also wishes to show his natural disgust at the endless talk of royalties and of prices. The natural Mr. Waugh is on this side, the Mr. Waugh who wants to be modern, sensible, practical, is on the other, 'over the water' at Chicago. 'Too much thought and too much reliance are bestowed on the remuneration. In the case of tried authors, this is only as it should be.' Why on earth should the well-tried author bestow '*too much* thought' on anything? Mr. Waugh gives a case: 'The author leaves the publisher's office in careless opulence, and forgets his undertaking, for which he has been paid in advance. This brings the well-tried author to grief, so, it seems, he *does* bestow 'too much thought on remuneration,' and not enough on anything else. He has to pay forfeit, or to hand in hasty trash. This way of paying for work unbegun was a curse of letters in the last century; one is sorry to hear from Mr. Waugh that the habit is reviving. Nothing but mischief can come of it; but it is not new, it is not a glorious result of the Authors' Society; nay, I doubt not that the society sets its face against such arrangements. But why the giving of too much thought to remuneration is 'only as it should be,' in the case of a 'well-tried author,' remains a mystery. As to 'gracious Bohemianism,' about which Mr. Waugh seems to be in two minds, the phrase probably means this: an artist of any kind, even a writer, works primarily for love. In the stress of his final fatal labours, Scott said that, were he out of debt and happy, he still would do the same things, but not so sedulously. A carpenter, of course, would not work at his craft were there no pay, but an author will write, even if he gets little or nothing by it. Hence he naturally gives less thought to his wages than those who work for wages alone. Wages are not his chief preoccupation. This is the 'gracious Bohemianism,' which Mr. Waugh seems to applaud on p. 512, after declaring that to mourn over the fallen capital of Bohemia is 'affectation' on p. 511.

Here I must seem inconsistent with these noble ideas, and defend a *bête noire*[14] of Mr. Waugh's, the man who 're-collects everything he has scribbled, and tries to make a double income by a double publication. He is foolish for his pains as well; he only fills the public with distrust, and his editors with amusement.' Well, perhaps no mortal collects '*everything* he has scribbled;' the whole world would not contain the books that should be made. But many men, this most impenitent sinner among them, collect a good deal. I don't know about editors laughing; contrariwise, in asking for a set of articles, they recommend their later collection. Of course, when the public is full of distrust, it does not purchase; then, indeed, it is time to desist. But while 'our kind friends' absorb the article, why should the article be refused to them? Why should 'a double income' *not* be made, if there is a double market? The income is not so very much calculated to excite envy, when all is said. In brief I have never been able to understand this wrath against collecting scattered efforts; as long as they are thought not unworthy by their readers. We are not like the mighty men of old: Lamb, Hazlitt, Leigh Hunt, and so forth. But their example justifies us in placing between the boards of a book essays or tales previously scattered. There is no arbiter here but the general taste; if people do not want a thing they will not buy it, as a general rule.

Mr. Waugh next assails a practice rather contemptible. It has happened, now and then, that a book of poems, say, was published in a small edition, because there was no demand for a big one. Time goes on, the author is appreciated, the curious pay large sums, comparatively, for a specimen of this little old edition, as of 'Omar Khayyam,' 'The Strayed Reveller,' 'Empedocles on Etna,' the Tennysons of 1830 and 1833, the original Keatses.[15] But now, Mr. Waugh says, 'a kind of false reputation is started,' by purposely announcing that an edition, perhaps of an author quite untried, is to be a very tiny edition. Then it is advertised that all the three hundred copies are already sold, probably to speculators in rarities, that a new edition is ready, and so on. This ground-bait takes, and a bard is 'boomed.' This 'would be laughable if it were not undignified,' as if undignified things were, essentially, *not* laughable. There are just reasons, in some cases, for publishing small editions of books with a merely antiquarian or historical interest, for example. The people who can really enjoy and make use of these are very rare, so that there is no chance of selling a large edition. But there are also people who will buy, merely because the edition is small, and these amateurs are useful: they make the publication of such books possible. This is the principle of the Bookish clubs – Roxburghe, Bannatyne, Maitland, Abbotsford, Wodrow,[16] and so forth. Many members read none of the books, but their *abonnements*[17] enable the book to exist, and exist usefully for the right readers. But this is a very different thing from the speculations denounced by Mr. Waugh, where the poet makes 'a corner' in his own work, holds on till it rises in price, and 'doubles the parts of poets and retail dealer.' But this story is based on 'whispers,' which have not reached me, and may be inventions of the enemy. To act thus would really be too troublesome: risky also, for there may be a ruinous fall in these poetic stocks.

Transactions of this kind, if they exist at all, are a result of the commercial spirit in literature. There is, of course, such a thing as literary property; that is not exactly a new discovery. But there is also such a thing as making far too much noise about literary property, till the evening papers simply chink with a noise of money earned by Mr. Jones and Mrs. Brown. The sound of silver and gold, one fears, is often a mere empty jingle, like the noise of scattered money which Jeffrey, that joyous goblin, used to cause in the rectory of Mr. Samuel Wesley at Epworth.[18] The hungry paragraph maker invents mountains and miracles of literary wealth. But this kind of talk goes on increasing, till at last poets are said to make 'corners' in their own limited editions. It is in much better taste not to talk so much about the circulating medium.

This was the chief of what I meant by some recent remarks on a Congress of Authors at Chicago. All Congresses and crowds are things to keep out of, and I ventured to add that I failed to see what Authors wanted with a Congress. 'We write, and sell our writings as well as we can, or as well as we can take trouble about selling them, or we employ an agent, and there, surely, should be an end of the matter.' Well, I hold by these opinions, *we write*; that is the main thing; that is our art, so to speak; we sell our writings as well as we can, that is the commercial aspect of the profession, and a Congress seems a luxury rather than a necessary. To all this an anonymous writer in *The Author* replies at some length, and not in a very lucid manner. There are two classes of literary men, he says, 'the one which understands the existence of literary property, and the other which cannot believe or understand that literature is, or can be, concerned with a material side, that there exists such a thing as literary property.' Well, I don't believe in the existence of this second class of literary men; I never met one of them, never read of one in books; though I have both met and read of literary men who did not dwell on this question of property. Burns would not be paid for his songs, but he was paid for his earlier poems, and, apparently, gave away most of the money. He knew his property was property, but his heart was with another kind of treasure. No, never did I meet the author who said that literary property does not exist. Never did I meet an author who 'pretended that no man of genius ever paid the least attention to literary property,' as my critic in *The Author* asserts that some men pretend. 'Scott' – well, I know what a mess he made of his literary property; 'Byron,' he began by disdaining it; see 'Life of Mr. Murray,' the publisher. And so of the rest; they did what they could for their material interests. 'Who's deniging of it, Betsy Prig? Betsy Prig, who's deniging of it?'[19] My critic rambles on, 'In spite of those names and examples, they hold up their hands and point to the sordidness of looking after literary property. "We sell our wares and there's an end," says Mr. Andrew Lang. But suppose we do not sell our wares; suppose we retain our property and either do not sell it at all but keep it, as some men keep house property, or sell it only after carefully ascertaining that we get a proper equivalent for it?'

Suppose we do let our property, instead of selling it out and out; by 'sell,' I meant dispose of it to an advantage; make what we can of it; we need not fight about a word. After some comments very true and obvious, *The Author* says, 'There are more things about literature than the selling of wares for what they will fetch.' Precisely, there is the making of it, as I said, and this is really the important thing. But *The Author* wanders on: 'Literature is not all standing, hat in hand, with bending knees and bowing back, entreating the generosity of the man with the bag.' What in the world has this to do with the matter? When an author has written a book, he sends it to his friend the publisher. The publisher replies, 'Dear Smith, thanks for your MS. We are prepared to produce it in such and such a shape, on such and such terms.' Then the author either says, 'All right,' or he says, 'You offer too much, I'll take so and so,' or he says he would rather have better terms, and the pair agree or disagree, in the latter case the author tries somebody else. But where are 'The bending knees and bowing back'? The critic in *The Author* decides that there is a prejudice against literary men, 'as a set of needy mendicants ... whose only business, as Mr. Andrew Lang says, is to sell their wares, and there's an end.' I did not say anything of the sort. I said, 'We write' (that is really our business), 'and sell our writings as well as we can.' A needy mendicant does not sell wares at all, except matches occasionally; wares, heaven help you, he has none to sell, sir. A tailor, a painter, a billiard-cue maker, a hatter, a dresser of artificial flies, a plumber, makes his wares, and sells them as well as he can. This does not constitute him a mendicant (as *The Author* appears to think), nay, this is exactly what differentiates him from a mendicant. What can *The Author* mean; why all this talk about mendicants? The whole statement is like the proposition that 'Humpty Dumpty is Abracadabra.'[20] I say that an author's affair is to do his work and dispose of his work; and *The Author* seems to think that this is equivalent to advice that authors should go begging.

I have a month's mind[21] to sail to Chicago, and try to explain the difference between art and trade, on one hand, and mendicancy on the other. But probably the American understands this obscure point. Authors really do need a Congress, if many of them are bemused in these perplexities, and if the hospitalities of Chicago are likely to clear the brain. 'The relations of authors and publishers' are to be discussed, and one might possibly succeed in demonstrating that for two men to sell and buy is not exactly the same thing as for one man to beg and for another to give. The Congress, I gather, is to 'assist literature by promoting the independence of those who write.' But are we who write 'dependent' at this hour? In what sense are we 'dependent,' except as painters, sculptors, hatters, actors, are dependent? We are dependent on the public taste, dependent for our commercial profits, but we are dependent on no other thing under heaven. 'The finest work that the world has ever seen has been produced under circumstances of physical and material well being, with a reasonable amount of self-respect. All the writers mentioned above, to whom must be added such names as Southey, Wordsworth, Lamb, Keats, Tennyson, Browning, have written under conditions of comparative independence.' Assuredly, but how can a hundred Congresses at Chicago secure those conditions? Scott had a patrimony, he was an official in Edinburgh, he was Sheriff of the Forest. Byron had originally property in land. Dickens was a reporter, then an author. Thackeray had a patrimony, then he wrote in *Punch* and elsewhere. Lord Lytton had lands and gear. Of George Eliot, and Charles Reade, and Wilkie Collins,[22] I know less. Mr. Reade had a fellowship at Magdalene. Southey lived by histories, and articles in the *Quarterly*. Wordsworth chose to be poor, till he got a stamp collectorship. Lamb was a clerk in the India Office. Keats, I presume, had a small patrimony, and was helped by friends and strangers. Now, how can Congresses of Authors get men patrimonies, sheriffships, stamp collectorships? As to literary earnings, they only come to those whom the public will read; and to them they come, Congress or no Congress. Authors whose books the world buys in sufficient quantities are not 'cheated, starved, dependent, humiliated,' unless as a result of some vice (as in the case of Savage),[23] say drink, or some irremediable weakness of character which no Congress can cure. No, it is very natural that some authors should like to meet, and talk about copyright, and 'various modes of publishing,' and 'syndicate publishing.' But I fail to see that we are more 'dependent, cheated, starved, humiliated,' than painters, or actors, or professional bowlers, or are more than they in the position of mendicants. Perhaps a failure to observe facts so obvious means an inability to understand that there is such a thing as literary property, and I may not be thought to understand that, till I see no difference between trade and mendicancy.

How to Fail in Literature

(London: Field & Tuer, The Leadenhall Press, 1890)

Preface. *This lecture was delivered at the South Kensington Museum, in aid of the College for Working Men and Women.*[1] *As the Publishers, perhaps erroneously, believe that some of the few authors who were not present may be glad to study the advice here proffered, the Lecture is now printed. It has been practically re-written, and, like the kiss which the Lady returned to Rudolphe, is* revu, corrigé, et considerablement augmenté.[2]

What should be a man's or a woman's reason for taking literature as a vocation, what sort of success ought they to desire, what sort of ambition should possess them? These are natural questions, now that so many readers exist in the world, all asking for something new, now that so many writers are making their pens 'in running to devour the way'[3] over so many acres of foolscap. The legitimate reasons for enlisting (too often without receiving the shilling[4]) in this army of writers are not far to seek. A man may be convinced that he has useful, or beautiful, or entertaining ideas within him, he may hold that he can express them in fresh and charming language. He may, in short, have a 'vocation,' or feel conscious of a vocation, which is not exactly the same thing. There are 'many thyrsus bearers, few mystics,' many are called, few chosen.[5] Still, to be sensible of a vocation is something, nay, is much, for most of us drift without any particular aim or predominant purpose. Nobody can justly censure people whose chief interest is in letters, whose chief pleasure is in study or composition, who rejoice in a fine sentence as others do in a well modelled limb, or a delicately touched landscape, nobody can censure them for trying their fortunes in literature. Most of them will fail, for, as the bookseller's young man told an author once, they have the poetic temperament, without the poetic power.

Still among these whom Pendennis[6] has tempted, in boyhood, to run away from school to literature as Marryat has tempted others to run away to sea,[7] there must be some who will succeed. But an early and intense ambition is not everything, any more than a capacity for taking pains is everything in literature or in any art.

Some have the gift, the natural incommunicable power, without the ambition, others have the ambition but no other gift from any Muse. This class is the more numerous, but the smallest class of all has both the power and the will to excel in letters. The desire to write, the love of letters may shew itself in childhood, in boyhood, or youth, and mean nothing at all, a mere harvest of barren blossom without fragrance or fruit. Or, again, the concern about letters may come suddenly, when a youth that cared for none of those things is waning, it may come when a man suddenly finds that he has something which he really must tell. Then he probably fumbles about for a style, and his first fresh impulses are more or less marred by his inexperience of an art which beguiles and fascinates others even in their school-days.

It is impossible to prophesy the success of a man of letters from his early promise, his early tastes; as impossible as it is to predict, from her childish grace, the beauty of a woman.

But the following remarks on How to Fail in Literature are certainly meant to discourage nobody who loves books, and has an impulse to tell a story, or to try a song or a sermon. Discouragements enough exist in the pursuit of this, as of all arts, crafts, and professions, without my adding to them. Famine and Fear crouch by the portals of literature as they crouch at the gates of the Virgilian Hades.[8] There is no more frequent cause of failure than doubt and dread; a beginner can scarcely put his heart and strength into a work when he knows how long are the odds against his victory, how difficult it is for a new man to win a hearing, even though all editors and publishers are ever pining for a new man. The young fellow, unknown and unwelcomed, who can sit down and give all his best of knowledge, observation, humour, care, and fancy to a considerable work has got courage in no common portion; he deserves to triumph, and certainly should not be disheartened by our old experience. But there be few beginners of this mark, most begin so feebly because they begin so fearfully. They are already too discouraged, and can scarce do themselves justice. It is easier to write more or less well and agreeably when you are certain of being published and paid, at least, than to write well when a dozen rejected manuscripts are cowering (as Theocritus says) in your chest, bowing their pale faces over their chilly knees, outcast, hungry, repulsed from many a door. To write excellently, brightly, powerfully, with these poor unwelcomed wanderers, returned MSS., in your possession, is difficult indeed. It might be wiser to do as M. Guy de Maupassant is rumoured to have done, to write for seven years, and shew your essays to none but a mentor as friendly severe as M.

Flaubert.[9] But all men cannot have such mentors, nor can all afford so long an unremunerative apprenticeship. For some the better plan is *not* to linger on the bank, and take tea and good advice, as Keats said,[10] but to plunge at once in mid-stream, and learn swimming of necessity.

One thing, perhaps, most people who succeed in letters so far as to keep themselves alive and clothed by their pens will admit, namely, that their early rejected MSS. *deserved to be rejected*. A few days ago there came to the writer an old forgotten beginner's attempt by himself. Whence it came, who sent it, he knows not; he had forgotten its very existence. He read it with curiosity; it was written in a very much better hand than his present scrawl, and was perfectly legible. But *readable* it was not. There was a great deal of work in it, on an out of the way topic, and the ideas were, perhaps, not quite without novelty at the time of its composition. But it was cramped and thin, and hesitating between several manners; above all it was uncommonly dull. If it ever was sent to an editor, as I presume it must have been, that editor was trebly justified in declining it. On the other hand, to be egotistic, I have known editors reject the attempts of those old days, and afterwards express lively delight in them when they struggled into print, somehow, somewhere. These worthy men did not even know that they had despised and refused what they came afterwards rather to enjoy.

Editors and publishers, these keepers of the gates of success, are not infallible, but their opinion of a beginner's work is far more correct than his own can ever be. They should not depress him quite, but if they are long unanimous in holding him cheap, he is warned, and had better withdraw from the struggle. He is either incompetent, or he has the makings of a Browning. He is a genius born too soon. He may readily calculate the chances in favour of either alternative.

So much by way of not damping all neophytes equally: so much we may say about success before talking of the easy ways that lead to failure. And by success here is meant no glorious triumph; the laurels are not in our thoughts, nor the enormous opulence (about a fourth of a fortunate barrister's gains) which falls in the lap of a Dickens or a Trollope. Faint and fleeting praise, a crown with as many prickles as roses, a modest hardly-gained competence, a good deal of envy, a great deal of gossip – these are the rewards of genius which constitute a modern literary success. Not to reach the moderate competence in literature is, for a professional man of letters of all work, something like failure. But in poetry to-day a man may succeed, as far as his art goes, and yet may be unread, and may publish at his own expense, or not publish at all. He pleases himself, and a very tiny audience: I do not call that failure. I regard failure as the goal of ignorance, incompetence, lack of common sense, conceited dullness, and certain practical blunders now to be explained and defined.

The most ambitious may accept, without distrust, the following advice as to How to Fail in Literature. The advice is offered by a mere critic, and it is an axiom of the Arts that the critics 'are the fellows who have failed,' or have not succeeded. The persons who really can paint, or play, or compose seldom tell us how it is done, still less do they review the performances of their contemporaries. That invidious task they leave to the unsuccessful novelists. The instruction, the advice are offered by the persons who cannot achieve performance. It is thus that all things work together in favour of failure, which, indeed, may well appear so easy that special instruction, however competent, is a luxury rather than a necessary. But when we look round on the vast multitude of writers who, to all seeming, deliberately aim at failure, who take every precaution in favour of failure that untutored inexperience can suggest, it becomes plain that education in ill-success, is really a popular want. In the following remarks some broad general principles, making disaster almost inevitable, will first be offered, and then special methods of failing in all special departments of letters will be ungrudgingly communicated. It is not enough to attain failure, we should deserve it. The writer, by way of insuring complete confidence, would modestly mention that he has had ample opportunities of study in this branch of knowledge. While sifting for five or six years the volunteered contributions to a popular periodical, he has received and considered some hundredweights of manuscript. In all these myriad contributions he has not found thirty pieces which rose even to the ordinary dead level of magazine work. He has thus enjoyed unrivalled chances of examining such modes of missing success as spontaneously occur to the human intellect, to the unaided ingenuity of men, women, and children.*

He who would fail in literature cannot begin too early to neglect his education, and to adopt every opportunity of not observing life and character. None of us is so young but that he may make himself perfect in writing an illegible hand. This method, I am bound to say, is too frequently overlooked. Most manuscripts by ardent literary volunteers are fairly legible. On the other hand there are novelists, especially ladies, who not only write a hand wholly declining to let itself be deciphered, but who fill up the margins with interpolations, who write between the lines, and who cover the page with scratches running this way and that, intended to direct the attention to after-thoughts inserted here and there in corners and on the backs of sheets. To pin in scraps of closely written paper and backs of envelopes adds to the security for failure, and produces a rich anger in the publisher's reader or the editor.

The cultivation of a bad handwriting is an elementary precaution, often overlooked. Few need to be warned against having their MSS. typewritten, this gives them a chance of being read with ease and interest, and this must

* As the writer has ceased to sift, editorially, the contributions of the age, he does hope that authors will not instantly send him their MSS. But if they do, after this warning, they will take the most direct and certain road to the waste paper basket. No MSS. will be returned, even when accompanied by postage stamps.

be neglected by all who have really set their hearts on failure. In the higher matters of education it is well to be as ignorant as possible. No knowledge comes amiss to the true man of letters, so they who court disaster should know as little as may be.

Mr. Stevenson has told the attentive world how, in boyhood, he practiced himself in studying and imitating the styles of famous authors of every age. He who aims at failure must never think of style, and should sedulously abstain from reading Shakespeare, Bacon, Hooker, Walton, Gibbon,[11] and other English and foreign classics. He can hardly be too reckless of grammar, and should always place adverbs and other words between 'to' and the infinitive, thus: 'Hubert was determined to energetically and on all possible occasions, oppose any attempt to entangle him with such.' Here, it will be noticed, 'such' is used as a pronoun, a delightful flower of speech not to be disregarded by authors who would fail. But some one may reply that several of our most popular novelists revel in the kind of grammar which I am recommending. This is undeniable, but certain people manage to succeed in spite of their own earnest endeavours and startling demerits. There is no royal road to failure. There is no rule without its exception, and it may be urged that the works of the gentlemen and ladies who 'break Priscian's head'[12] – as they would say themselves – may be successful, but are not literature. Now it is about literature that we are speaking.

In the matter of style, there is another excellent way. You need not neglect it, but you may study it wrongly. You may be affectedly self-conscious, you may imitate the ingenious persons who carefully avoid the natural word, the spontaneous phrase, and employ some other set of terms which can hardly be construed. You may use, like a young essayist whom I have lovingly observed, a proportion of eighty adjectives to every sixty-five other words of all denominations. You may hunt for odd words, and thrust them into the wrong places, as where you say that a man's nose is 'beetling,' that the sun sank in 'a cauldron of daffodil chaos,' and the like.* You may use common words in an unwonted sense, keeping some private interpretation clearly before you. Thus you may speak, if you like to write partly in the tongue of Hellas, about 'assimilating the *êthos*' of a work of art, and so write that people shall think of the processes of digestion. You may speak of 'exhausting the beauty' of a landscape, and, somehow, convey the notion of sucking an orange dry. Or you may wildly mix your metaphors, as when a critic accuses Mr. Browning of 'giving the irridescence of the poetic afflatus,'[13] as if the poetic afflatus were blown through a pipe, into soap, and produced soap bubbles. This is a more troublesome method than the mere

* I have made a rich selection of examples from the works of living English and American authors. From the inextensive volumes of an eminent and fastidious critic I have culled a dear phrase about an oasis of style in 'a desert of literary limpness.' But it were hardly courteous, and might be dangerous, to publish these exotic blossoms of art.

picking up of every newspaper commonplace that floats into your mind, but it is equally certain to lead – where you want to go. By combining the two fashions a great deal may be done. Thus you want to describe a fire at sea, and you say, 'the devouring element lapped the quivering spars, the mast, and the sea-shouldering keel of the doomed Mary Jane in one coruscating catastrophe. The sea deeps were incarnadined to an alarming extent by the flames, and to escape from such many plunged headlong in their watery bier.'

As a rule, authors who would fail stick to one bad sort of writing; either to the newspaper commonplace, or to the out of the way and inappropriate epithets, or to the common word with a twist on it. But there are examples of the combined method, as when we call the trees round a man's house his 'domestic boscage.' This combination is difficult, but perfect for its purpose. You cannot write worse than 'such.' To attain perfection the young aspirant should confine his reading to the newspapers (carefully selecting his newspapers, for many of them will not help him to write ill) and to those modern authors who are most praised for their style by the people who know least about the matter. Words like 'fictional' and 'fictive' are distinctly to be recommended, and there are epithets such as 'weird,' 'strange,' 'wild,' 'intimate,' and the rest, which blend pleasantly with 'all the time' for 'always'; 'back of' for 'behind'; 'belong with' for 'belong to'; 'live like I do' for 'as I do.' The authors who combine those charms are rare, but we can strive to be among them.

In short, he who would fail must avoid simplicity like a sunken reef, and must earnestly seek either the commonplace or the *bizarre,* the slipshod or the affected, the new-fangled or the obsolete, the flippant or the sepulchral. I need not specially recommend you to write in 'Wardour-street English,'[14] the sham archaic, a lingo never spoken by mortal man, and composed of patches borrowed from authors between Piers Plowman and Gabriel Harvey.[15] A few literal translations of Icelandic phrases may be thrown in; the result, as furniture-dealers say, is a 'made-up article.'[16]

On the subject of style another hint may be offered. Style may be good in itself, but inappropriate to the subject. For example, style which may be excellently adapted to a theological essay may be but ill-suited for a dialogue in a novel. There are subjects of which the poet says *Ornari res ipsa vetat, contenta doceri.*[17]

The matter declines to be adorned, and is content with being clearly stated. I do not know what would occur if the writer of the Money Article in the *Times* treated his topic with reckless gaiety. Probably that number of the journal in which the essay appeared would have a large sale, but the author might achieve professional failure in the office. On the whole it may not be the wiser plan to write about the Origins of Religion in the style which might suit a study of the life of ballet dancers; the two MM. Halévy,[18] the learned and the popular, would make a blunder if they exchanged styles.

Yet Gibbon never denies himself a jest, and Montesquieu's *Esprit des Lois* was called *L'Esprit sur les Lois*. M. Renan's *Histoire d' Israel*[19] may almost be called skittish. The French are more tolerant of those excesses than the English. It is a digression, but he who would fail can reach his end by not taking himself seriously. If he gives himself no important airs, whether out of a freakish humour, or real humility, depend upon it the public and the critics will take him at something under his own estimate. On the other hand, by copying the gravity of demeanour admired by Mr. Shandy in a celebrated parochial animal,[20] even a very dull person may succeed in winning no inconsiderable reputation. To return to style, and its appropriateness: all depends on the work in hand, and the audience addressed. Thus, in his valuable Essay on Style, Mr. Pater says, with perfect truth:* 'The otiose, the facile, surplusage: why are these abhorrent to the true literary artist, except because, in literary as in all other arts, structure is all important, felt or painfully missed, everywhere? – that architectural conception of work, which foresees the end in the beginning, and never loses sight of it, and in every part is conscious of all the rest, till the last sentence does but, with undiminished vigour, unfold and justify the first – a condition of literary art, which, in contradistinction to another quality of the artist himself, to be spoken of later, I shall call the necessity of *mind* in style.'

These are words which the writer should have always present to his memory, if he has something serious that he wants to say, or if he wishes to express himself in the classic and perfect manner. But if it is his fate merely to be obliged to say something, in the course of his profession, or if he is bid to discourse for the pleasure of readers in the Underground Railway, I fear he will often have to forget Mr. Pater. It may not be literature, the writing of *causeries*,[21] of Roundabout Papers,[22] of rambling articles 'on a broomstick,' and yet again, it *may* be literature! 'Parallel, allusion, the allusive way generally, the flowers in the garden' – Mr. Pater charges heavily against these. The true artist 'knows the narcotic force of these upon the negligent intelligence to which any *diversion* literally, is welcome, any vagrant intruder, because one can go wandering away with it from the immediate subject. ... In truth all art does but consist in the removal of surplusage, from the last finish of the gem engraver blowing away the last particle of invisible dust, back to the earliest divination of the finished work to be lying somewhere, according to Michel Angelo's fancy, in the rough-hewn block of stone.'

Excellent, but does this apply to every kind of literary art? What would become of Montaigne[23] if you blew away his allusions, and drove him out of 'the allusive way,' where he gathers and binds so many flowers from all the gardens and all the rose-hung lanes of literature? Montaigne sets forth to write an Essay on Coaches. He begins with a few remarks on sea-sickness in the common pig; some notes on the Pont Neuf at Paris follow, and a

* Appreciations, p. 18

theory of why tyrants are detested by men whom they have obliged; a glance at Coaches is then given, next a study of Montezuma's gardens, presently a brief account of the Spanish cruelties in Mexico and Peru, last – *retombons à nos coches*[24] – he tells a tale of the Inca, and the devotion of his Guard: *Another for Hector*!

The allusive style has its proper place, like another, if it is used by the right man, and the concentrated and structural style has also its higher province. It would not do to employ either style in the wrong place. In a rambling discursive essay, for example, a mere straying after the bird in the branches, or the thorn in the way, he might not take the safest road who imitated Mr. Pater's style in what follows: 'In this way, according to the well-known saying, "The style is the man," complex or simple, in his individuality, his plenary sense of what he really has to say, his sense of the world: all cautions regarding style arising out of so many natural scruples as to the medium through which alone he can expose that inward sense of things, the purity of this medium, its laws or tricks of refraction: nothing is to be left there which might give conveyance to any matter save that.'[25] Clearly the author who has to write so that the man may read who runs will fail if he wrests this manner from its proper place, and uses it for casual articles: he will fail to hold the vagrom[26] attention!

Thus a great deal may be done by studying inappropriateness of style, by adopting a style alien to our matter and to our audience. If we 'haver' discursively about serious, and difficult, and intricate topics, we fail; and we fail if we write on happy, pleasant, and popular topics in an abstruse and intent, and analytic style. We fail, too, if in style we go outside our natural selves. 'The style is the man,' and the man will be nothing, and nobody, if he tries for an incongruous manner, not naturally his own, for example if Miss Yonge were suddenly to emulate the manner of Lever, or if Mr. John Morley were to strive to shine in the fashion of Uncle Remus, or if Mr. Rider Haggard were to be allured into imitation by the example, so admirable in itself, of the Master of Balliol.[27] It is ourselves we must try to improve, our attentiveness, our interest in life, our seriousness of purpose, and then the style will improve with the self. Or perhaps, to be perfectly frank, we shall thus convert ourselves into prigs, throw ourselves out of our stride, lapse into self-consciousness, lose all that is natural, *naif* and instinctive within us. Verily there are many dangers, and the paths to failure are infinite.

So much for style, of which it may generally be said that you cannot be too obscure, unnatural, involved, vulgar, slipshod, and metaphorical. See to it that your metaphors are mixed, though, perhaps, this attention is hardly needed. The free use of parentheses, in which a reader gets lost, and of unintelligible allusions, and of references to unread authors – the *Kalevala* and Lycophron, and the Scholiast on Apollonius Rhodius,[28] is invaluable to this end. So much for manner, and now for matter.

The young author generally writes because he wants to write, either for money, from vanity, or in mere weariness of empty hours and anxiety to astonish his relations. This is well, he who would fail cannot begin better than by having nothing to say. The less you observe, the less you reflect, the less you put yourself in the paths of adventure and experience, the less you will have to say, and the more impossible will it be to read your work. Never notice people's manner, conduct, nor even dress, in real life. Walk through the world with your eyes and ears closed, and embody the negative results in a story or a poem. As to Poetry, with a fine instinct we generally begin by writing verse, because verse is the last thing that the public want to read. The young writer has usually read a great deal of verse, however, and most of it bad. His favourite authors are the bright lyrists who sing of broken hearts, wasted lives, early deaths, disappointment, gloom. Without having even had an unlucky flirtation, or without knowing what it is to lose a favourite cat, the early author pours forth laments, just like the laments he has been reading. He has too a favourite manner, the old consumptive manner, about the hectic flush, the fatal rose on the pallid cheek, about the ruined roof tree, the empty chair, the rest in the village churchyard. This is now a little rococo and forlorn, but failure may be assured by travelling in this direction. If you are ambitious to disgust an editor at once, begin your poem with 'Only'. [...] Another good way is to be very economical in your rhymes, only two to the four lines, and regretfully vague. [...]

If you are not satisfied with these simple ways of not succeeding, please try the Grosvenor Gallery[29] style. Here the great point is to make the rhyme arrive at the end of a very long word, you should also be free with your alliterations. [...]

Alliteration is a splendid source of failure in this sort of poetry, and adjectives like lissom, filmy, weary, weird, strange, make, or ought to make, the rejection of your manuscript a certainty. The poem should, as a rule, seem to be addressed to an unknown person, and should express regret and despair for circumstances in the past with which the reader is totally unacquainted. [...] Every form of imitation (imitating of course only the faults of a favourite writer) is to be recommended.

Imitation does a double service, it secures the failure of the imitator and also aids that of the unlucky author who is imitated. As soon as a new thing appears in literature, many people hurry off to attempt something of the same sort. It may be a particular trait and accent in poetry, and the public, weary of the mimicries, begin to dislike the original.

> 'Most can grow the flowers now,
> For all have got the seed;
> And once again the people
> Call it but a weed.'[30]

In fiction, if somebody brings in a curious kind of murder, or a study of religious problems, or a treasure hunt, or what you will, others imitate till the world is weary of murders, or theological flirtations, or the search for buried specie, and the original authors themselves will fail, unless they fish out something new, to be vulgarized afresh. Therefore, imitation is distinctly to be urged on the young author.

As a rule, his method is this, he reads very little, but all that he reads is *bad*. The feeblest articles in the weakliest magazines, the very mildest and most conventional novels appear to be the only studies of the majority. Apparently the would-be contributor says to himself, or herself, 'well, *I* can do something almost on the level of this or that maudlin and invertebrate novel.' Then he deliberately sits down to rival the most tame, dull, and illiterate compositions that get into print. In this way bad authors become the literary parents of worse authors. Nobody but a reader of MSS. knows what myriads of fiction are written without one single new situation, original character, or fresh thoughts The most out-worn ideas: sudden loss of fortune; struggles; faithlessness of First Lover; noble conduct of Second Lover: frivolity of younger sister; excellence of mother: naughtiness of one son, virtue of another, these are habitually served up again and again. On the sprained ankles, the mad bulls, the fires, and other simple devices for doing without an introduction between hero and heroine I need not dwell. The very youngest of us is acquainted with these expedients, which, by this time of day, will spell failure.

The common novels of Governess life, the daughters and grand-daughters of *Jane Eyre*, still run riot among the rejected manuscripts. The lively large family, all very untidy and humorous, all wearing each other's boots and gloves, and making their dresses out of bedroom curtains and marrying rich men, still rushes down the easy descent to failure. The sceptical curate is at large, and is disbelieving in everything except the virtues of the young woman who 'has a history.' Mr. Swinburne hopes that one day the last unbelieving clergyman will disappear in the embrace of the last immaculate Magdalen, as the Princess and the Geni burn each other to nothingness, in the *Arabian Nights*. On that happy day there will be one less of the roads leading to failure. If the pair can carry with them the self-sacrificing characters who take the blame of all the felonies that they did not do, and the nice girl who is jilted by the poet, and finds that the squire was the person whom she *really* loved, so much the better. If not only Monte Carlo, but the inevitable scene in the Rooms there can be abolished; if the Riviera, and Italy can be removed from the map of Europe as used by novelists, so much the better. But failure will always be secured, while the huge majority of authors do not aim high, but aim at being a little lower than the last domestic drivel which came out in three volumes, or the last analysis of the inmost self of some introspective young girl which crossed the water from the States.

These are general counsels, and apply to the production of books. But, when you have done your book, you may play a number of silly tricks with your manuscript. I have already advised you to make only one copy, a rough one, as that secures negligence in your work, and also disgusts an editor or reader. It has another advantage, you may lose your copy altogether, and, as you have not another, no failure can be more complete. The best way of losing it, I think and the safest, is to give it to somebody you know who has once met some man or woman of letters. This somebody must be instructed to ask that busy and perhaps casual and untidy person to read your manuscript, and 'place' it, that is, induce some poor publisher or editor to pay for and publish it. Now the man, or woman of letters, will use violent language on receiving your clumsy brown paper parcel of illegible wares, because he or she has no more to do with the matter than the crossing sweeper. The MS. will either be put away so carefully that it can never be found again, or will be left lying about so that the housemaid may use it for her own domestic purposes, like Betty Barnes, the cook of Mr. Warburton, who seems to have burned several plays of Shakespeare.[31]

Not only can you secure failure thus yourself, but you can so worry and badger your luckless victim, that he too will be unable to write well till he has forgotten you and your novel, and all the annoyance and anxiety you have given him. Much may be done by asking him for 'introductions' to an editor or publisher. These gentry don't want introductions, they want good books, and very seldom get them. If you behave thus, the man whom you are boring will write to his publisher:

> Dear Brown,
> A wretched creature, who knows my great aunt, asks me to recommend his rubbish to you. I send it by to-day's post, and I wish you joy of it.

This kind of introduction will do you excellent service in smoothing the path to failure. You can arrive at similar results by sending your MS. *not* to the editor of this or that magazine, but to someone who, as you have been told by some nincompoop, is the editor, and who is *not*.[32] He *may* lose your book, or he may let it lie about for months, or he may send it on at once to the real editor with his bitter malison. The utmost possible vexation is thus inflicted on every hand, and a prejudice is established against you which the nature of your work is very unlikely to overcome. By all means bore many literary strangers with correspondence, this will give them a lively recollection of your name, and an intense desire to do you a bad turn if opportunity arises.*

---

* It is a teachable public: since this lecture was delivered the author has received many MSS. from people who said they had heard the discourse, 'and enjoyed it so much.'

If your book does, in spite of all, get itself published, send it with your compliments to critics and ask them for favourable reviews. It is the publisher's business to send out books to the editors of critical papers, but never mind *that.* Go on telling critics that you know praise is only given by favour, that they are all more or less venal and corrupt and members of the Something Club, add that *you* are no member of a *côterie* nor clique, but that you hope an exception will be made, and that your volume will be applauded on its merits. You will thus have done what in you lies to secure silence from reviewers, and to make them request that your story may be sent to some other critic. This, again, gives trouble, and makes people detest you and your performance, and contributes to the end which you have steadily in view.

I do not think it is necessary to warn young lady novelists, who possess beauty, wealth, and titles, against asking Reviewers to dine, and treating them as kindly, almost, as the Fairy Paribanou treated Prince Ahmed.[33] They only act thus, I fear, in Mr. William Black's novels.[34]

Much may be done by re-writing your book on the proof sheets, correcting everything there which you should have corrected in manuscript. This is an expensive process, and will greatly diminish your pecuniary gains, or rather will add to your publisher's bill, for the odds are that you will have to publish at your own expense. By the way, an author can make almost a certainty of disastrous failure, by carrying to some small obscure publisher a work which has been rejected by the best people in the trade. Their rejections all but demonstrate that your book is worthless. If you think you are likely to make a good thing by employing an obscure publisher, with little or no capital, then, as someone in Thucydides remarks, congratulating you on your simplicity, I do not envy your want of common sense.[35] Be very careful to enter into a perfectly preposterous agreement. For example, accept 'half profits,' but forget to observe that, before these are reckoned, it is distinctly stated in your 'agreement' that the publisher is to pay *himself* some twenty per cent, on the price of each copy sold before you get your share.

Here is 'another way,' as the cookery books have it. In your gratitude to your first publisher, covenant with him to let him have all the cheap editions of all your novels for the next five years, at his own terms. If, in spite of the advice I have given you, you somehow manage to succeed, to become wildly popular, you will still have reserved to yourself, by this ingenious clause, a chance of ineffable pecuniary failure. A plan generally approved of is to sell your entire copyright in your book for a very small sum. You want the ready money, and perhaps you are not very hopeful. But, when your book is in all men's hands, when you are daily reviled by the small fry of paragraphers, when the publisher is clearing a thousand a year by it, while you only got a hundred down, then you will thank me, and will acknowledge that, in spite of apparent success, you are a failure after all. There are publishers, however, so inconsiderate that they will not leave you even this consolation. Finding that the book they bought cheap is really valuable, they will insist on sharing the profits with the author, or on making him great presents of money to which he has no legal claim. Some persons, some authors, cannot fail if they would, so wayward is fortune, and such a Quixotic idea of honesty have some middlemen of literature. But, of course, you *may* light on a publisher who will not give you *more* than you covenanted for, and then you can go about denouncing the whole profession as a congregation of robbers and clerks of St. Nicholas.[36]

The ways of failure are infinite, and of course are not nearly exhausted. One good plan is never to be yourself when you write, to put in nothing of your own temperament, manner, character – or to have none, which does as well. Another favourite method is to offer the wrong kind of article, to send to the *Cornhill* an essay on the evolution of the Hittite syllabary, (for only one author could make that popular;) or a sketch of cock fighting among the ancients to the *Monthly Record;* or an essay on *Ayahs in India* to an American magazine; or a biography of Washington or Lincoln to any English magazine whatever. We have them every month in some American periodicals, and our poor insular serials can get on without them: 'have no use for them.'[37]

It is a minor, though valuable scheme, to send poems on Christmas to magazines about the beginning of December, because, in fact, the editors have laid in their stock of that kind of thing earlier. Always insist on *seeing* an editor, instead of writing to him. There is nothing he hates so much, unless you are very young and beautiful indeed, when, perhaps, if you wish to fail you had better *not* pay him a visit at the office. Even if you do, even if you were as fair as the Golden Helen,[38] he is not likely to put in your compositions if, as is probable, they fall *much* below the level of his magazine.

A good way of making yourself a dead failure is to go about accusing successful people of plagiarising from books or articles of yours which did not succeed, and, perhaps, were never published at all. By encouraging this kind of vanity and spite you may entirely destroy any small powers you once happened to possess, you will, besides, become a person with a grievance, and, in the long run, will be shunned even by your fellow failures. Again, you may plagiarise yourself, if you can, it is not easy, but it is a safe way to fail if you can manage it. No successful person, perhaps, was ever, in the strict sense, a plagiarist, though charges of plagiary are always brought against everybody, from Virgil to Milton, from Scott to Molière, who attains success. When you are accused of being a plagiarist, and shewn up in double columns, you may be pretty sure that all this counsel has been wasted on you, and that you have failed to fail, after all. Otherwise nobody would envy and malign you, and garble your book, and print quotations from it which you did not write, all in the sacred cause of morality.

Advice on how to secure the reverse of success should not be given to young authors alone. Their kinsfolk and friends, also, can do much for their aid. A lady who feels a taste for writing is very seldom allowed to have a quiet room, a quiet study. If she retreats to her chill and fireless bed chamber, even there she may be chevied by her brothers, sisters, and mother. It is noticed that cousins, and aunts, especially aunts, are of high service in this regard. They never give an intelligent woman an hour to herself. 'Is Miss Mary in?' 'Yes, ma'am, but she is very busy.' 'Oh, she won't mind me, I don't mean to stay long.' Then in rushes the aunt. 'Over your books again: my dear! You really should not overwork yourself. Writing something'; here the aunt clutches the manuscript, and looks at it vaguely. 'Well, I dare say it's very clever, but I don't care for this kind of thing myself. Where's your mother? Is Jane better? Now, do tell me, do you get much for writing all that? Do you send it to the printers, or where? How interesting, and that reminds me, you that are a novelist, have you heard how shamefully Miss Baxter was treated by Captain Smith? No, well you might make something out of it.' Here follows the anecdote, at prodigious length, and perfectly incoherent. […]

Fathers never take any interest in the business at all: they do not count. The sympathy of a mother may be reckoned on, but not her judgement, for she is either wildly favourable, or, mistrusting her own tendencies, is more diffident than need be. The most that relations can do for the end before us is to worry, interrupt, deride, and tease the literary member of the family. They seldom fail in these duties, and not even success, as a rule, can persuade them that there is anything in it but 'luck.'

Perhaps reviewing is not exactly a form of literature. But it has this merit that people who review badly, not only fail themselves, but help others to fail, by giving a bad idea of their works. You will, of course, never read the books you review, and you will be exhaustively ignorant of the subjects which they treat. But you can always find fault with the *title* of the story which comes into your hands, a stupid reviewer never fails to do this. You can also copy out as much of the preface as will fill your eighth of a column, and add, that the performance is not equal to the promise. You must never feel nor shew the faintest interest in the work reviewed, that would be fatal. Never praise heartily, that is the sign of an intelligence not mediocre. Be vague, colourless, and languid, this deters readers from approaching the book. If you have glanced at it, blame it for not being what it never professed to be; if it is a treatise on Greek Prosody, censure the lack of humour; if it is a volume of gay verses, lament the author's indifference to the sorrows of the poor or the wrongs of the Armenians.[39] If it has humour, deplore its lack of thoughtfulness; if it is grave, carp at its lack of gaiety. I have known a reviewer of half a dozen novels denounce half a dozen *kinds* of novels in the course of his two columns; the romance of adventure, the domestic tale, the psychological analysis, the theological story, the detective's story, the story of 'Society,' he blamed them all in general, and the books before him in particular, also the historical novel. This can easily be done, by dint of practice, after dipping into three or four pages of your author. Many reviewers have special aversions, authors they detest. Whatever they are criticising, novels, poems, plays, they begin by an attack on their pet aversion, who has nothing to do with the matter in hand. They cannot praise A, B, C, and D, without first assailing E. It will generally be found that E is a popular author. But the great virtue of a reviewer, who would be unreadable and make others unread, is a languid ignorant lack of interest in all things, a habit of regarding his work as a tedious task, to be scamped as rapidly and stupidly as possible.

You might think that these qualities would displease the reviewer's editor. Not at all, look at any column of short notices, and you will occasionally find that the critic has anticipated my advice. There is no topic in which the men who write about it are so little interested as contemporary literature. Perhaps this is no matter to marvel at. By the way, a capital plan is not to write your review till the book has been out for two years. This is the favourite dodge of the —, that distinguished journal.

If any one has kindly attended to this discourse, without desiring to be a failure, he has only to turn the advice outside in. He has only to be studious of the very best literature, observant, careful, original, he has only to be himself and not an imitator, to aim at excellence, and not be content with falling a little lower than mediocrity. He needs but bestow the same attention on this art as others give to the other arts and other professions. With these efforts, and with a native and natural gift, which can never be taught, never communicated, and with his mind set not on his reward, but on excellence, on style, on matter, and even on the not wholly unimportant virtue of vivacity, a man will succeed, or will deserve success. First, of course, he will have to 'find' himself, as the French say, and if he does *not* find an ass, then, like Saul the son of Kish, he may discover a kingdom.[40] One success he can hardly miss, the happiness of living, not with trash, but among good books, and 'the mighty minds of old.' In an unpublished letter of Mr. Thackeray's, written before he was famous, and a novelist, he says how much he likes writing on historical subjects, and how he enjoys historical research. *The work is so gentlemanly* he remarks. Often and often, after the daily dreadful lines, the bread and butter winning lines on some contemporary folly or frivolity, does a man take up some piece of work hopelessly unremunerative, foredoomed to failure as far as money or fame go, some dealing with the classics of the world: Homer or Aristotle, Lucian or Molière. It is like a bath after a day's toil, it is tonic and clean; and such studies, if not necessary to success, are, at least, conducive to mental health and self-respect in literature.

To the enormous majority of persons who risk themselves in literature, not even the smallest measure of success can fall. They had better take to some other profession as quickly as may be, they are only making a sure thing of disappointment, only crowding the narrow gates of fortune and fame. Yet there are others to whom success, though easily within their reach, does not seem a thing to be grasped at. Of two such, the pathetic story may be read, in the Memoir of *A Scotch Probationer*,[41] Mr. Thomas Davidson, who died young, an unplaced Minister of the United Presbyterian Church, in 1869. He died young, unaccepted by the world, unheard of, uncomplaining, soon after writing his latest song on the first grey hairs of the lady whom he loved. And she, Miss Alison Dunlop, died also, a year ago, leaving a little work newly published, *Ancient Old Edinburgh* in which is briefly told the story of her life. There can hardly be a true tale more brave and honourable, for those two were eminently qualified to shine, with a clear and modest radiance, in letters. Both had a touch of poetry, Mr. Davidson left a few genuine poems, both had humour, knowledge, patience, industry, and literary conscientiousness. No success came to them, they did not even seek it, though it was easily within the reach of their powers. Yet none can call them failures, leaving, as they did, the fragrance of honourable and uncomplaining lives, and such brief records of these as to delight, and console and encourage us all. They bequeath to us the spectacle of a real triumph far beyond the petty gains of money or of applause, the spectacle of lives made happy by literature, unvexed by notoriety, unfretted by envy. What we call success could never have yielded them so much, for the ways of authorship are dusty and stony, and the stones are only too handy for throwing at the few that, deservedly or undeservedly, make a name, and therewith about one-tenth of the wealth which is ungrudged to physicians, or barristers, or stock-brokers, or dentists, or electricians. If literature and occupation with letters were not its own reward, truly they who seem to succeed might envy those who fail. It is not wealth that they win, as fortunate men in other professions count wealth; it is not rank nor fashion that come to their call nor come to call on them. Their success is to be let dwell with their own fancies, or with the imaginations of others far greater than themselves; their success is this living in fantasy, a little remote from the hubbub and the contests of the world. At the best they will be vexed by curious eyes and idle tongues, at the best they will die not rich in this world's goods, yet not unconsoled by the friendships which they win among men and women whose faces they will never see. They may well be content, and thrice content, with their lot, yet it is not a lot which should provoke envy, nor be coveted by ambition.

It is not an easy goal to attain, as the crowd of aspirants dream, nor is the reward luxurious when it is attained. A garland, usually fading and not immortal, has to be run for, not without dust and heat.

'To a Young Journalist', *Essays in Little*

(London: Henry and Co., 1891)

Dear Smith,

You inform me that you desire to be a journalist, and you are kind enough to ask my advice. Well, be a journalist, by all means, in any honest and honourable branch of the profession. But do not be an eaves-dropper and a spy. You may fly into a passion when you receive this very plainly worded advice. I hope you will; but, for several reasons, which I now go on to state, I fear that you won't. I fear that, either by natural gift or by acquired habit, you already possess the imperturbable temper which will be so useful to you if you do join the army of spies and eavesdroppers. If I am right, you have made up your mind to refuse to take offence, as long as by not taking offence you can wriggle yourself forward in the band of journalistic reptiles. You will be revenged on me, in that case, some day; you will lie in wait for me with a dirty bludgeon, and steal on me out of a sewer. If you do, permit me to assure you that I don't care. But if you are already in a rage, if you are about tearing up this epistle, and are starting to assault me personally, or at least to answer me furiously, then there is every hope for you and for your future. I therefore venture to state my reasons for supposing that you are inclined to begin a course which your father, if he were alive, would deplore, as all honourable men in their hearts must deplore it. When you were at the University (let me congratulate you on your degree) you edited, or helped to edit, *The Bull-dog*.[1] It was not a very brilliant nor a very witty, but it was an extremely 'racy' periodical. It spoke of all men and dons by their nicknames. It was full of second-hand slang. It contained many personal anecdotes, to the detriment of many people. It printed garbled and spiteful versions of private conversations on private affairs. It did not even spare to make comments on ladies, and on the details of domestic life in the town and in the University. The copies which you sent me I glanced at with extreme disgust.

In my time, more than a score of years ago, a similar periodical, but a much more clever periodical, was put forth by members of the University.[2] It contained a novel which, even now, would be worth several ill-gotten guineas to the makers of the *chronique scandaleuse*.[3] But nobody bought it, and it died an early death. Times have altered, I am a fogey; but the ideas of honour and decency which fogies hold now were held by young men in the sixties of our century. I know very well that these ideas are obsolete. I am not preaching to the world, nor hoping to convert society, but to *you* and purely in your own private, spiritual interest. If you enter on this path of tattle, mendacity, and malice, and if, with your cleverness and light hand, you are successful, society will not turn its back on you. You will be feared in many quarters, and welcomed in others. Of your paragraphs people will say that 'it is a shame, of course, but it is very amusing.' There are so many shames in the world, shames not at all amusing, that you may see no harm in adding to the number. 'If I don't do it,' you may argue, 'some one else will.' Undoubtedly; but *why should you do it?*

You are not a starving scribbler; if you determine to write, you can write well, though not so easily, on many topics. You have not that last sad excuse of hunger, which drives poor women to the streets, and makes unhappy men act as public blabs and spies. If *you* take to this *métier*,[4] it must be because you like it, which means that you enjoy being a listener to and reporter of talk that was never meant for any ears except those in which it was uttered. It means that the hospitable board is not sacred for you; it means that, with you, friendship, honour, all that makes human life better than a low smoking-room, are only valuable for what their betrayal will bring. It means that not even the welfare of your country will prevent you from running to the Press with any secret which you may have been entrusted with, or which you may have surprised. It means, this peculiar kind of profession, that all things open and excellent, and conspicuous to all men, are with you of no account. Art, literature, politics, are to cease to interest you. You are to scheme to surprise gossip about the private lives, dress, and talk of artists, men of letters, politicians. Your professional work will sink below the level of servants' gossip in a public-house parlour. If you happen to meet a man of known name, you will watch him, will listen to him, will try to sneak into his confidence, and you will blab, for money, about him, and your blab will inevitably be mendacious. In short, like the most pitiable outcasts of womankind, and, without their excuse, you will live by selling your honour. You will not suffer much, nor suffer long. Your conscience will very speedily be seared with a red-hot iron. You will be on the road which leads from mere dishonour to crime; and you may find yourself actually practising *chantage*[5] and extorting money as the price of your silence. This is the lowest deep: the vast majority, even of social *mouchards*,[6] do not sink so low as this.

The profession of the critic, even in honourable and open criticism, is beset with dangers. It is often hard to avoid saying an unkind thing, a cruel thing, which smart, and which may even be deserved. Who can say that he has escaped this temptation, and what man of heart can think of his own fall without a sense of shame? There are, I admit, authors so antipathetic to me, that I cannot trust myself to review them. Would that I had never reviewed them! They cannot be so bad as they seem to me: they must have qualities which escape my observation. Then there is the temptation to hit back. Some one writes, unjustly or unkindly as you think, of you or of your friends. You wait till your enemy has written a book, and then you have your innings. It is not in nature that your review should be fair: you must inevitably be more on the look-out for faults than merits. The *éreintage*,[7] the 'smashing' of a literary foe is very delightful at the moment, but it does not look well in the light of reflection. But these deeds are mere peccadilloes compared with the confirmed habit of regarding all men and women as fair game for personal tattle and the sating of private spite. Nobody, perhaps, begins with this intention. Most men and women can find ready sophistries. If a report about any one reaches their ears, they say that they are doing him a service by publishing it and enabling him to contradict it. As if any mortal ever listened to a contradiction! And there are charges – that of plagiarism, for example –which can never be disproved, even if contradictions were listened to by the public. The accusation goes everywhere, is copied into every printed rag; the contradiction dies with the daily death of a single newspaper. You may reply that a man of sense will be indifferent to false accusations. He may, or may not be, – that is not the question for you; the question for you is whether you will circulate news that is false, probably, and spiteful, certainly.

In short the whole affair regards yourself more than it regards the world. Plenty of poison is sold: is it well for you to be one of the merchants? Is it the business of an educated gentleman to live by the trade of an eavesdropper and a blab? In the Memoirs of M. Blowitz[8] he tells you how he began his illustrious career by procuring the publication of remarks which M. Thiers[9] had made to him. He then 'went to see M. Thiers, not without some apprehension.' Is that the kind of emotion which you wish to be habitual in your experience? Do you think it agreeable to become shame-faced when you meet people who have conversed with you frankly? Do you enjoy being a sneak, and feeling like a sneak? Do you find blushing pleasant? Of course you will soon lose the power of blushing; but is that an agreeable prospect? Depend on it, there are discomforts in the progress to the brazen, in the journey to the shameless. You may, if your tattle is political, become serviceable to men engaged in great affairs. They may even ask you to their houses, if that is your ambition. You may urge that they condone your deeds, and are even art and part in them. But you must also be aware that they call you, and think you, a reptile. You are not one of those who will do the devil's work without the devil's wages; but do you seriously think that the wages are worth the degradation?

Many men think so, and are not in other respects bad men. They may even be kindly and genial. Gentlemen they cannot be, nor men of delicacy, nor men of honour. They have sold themselves and their self-respect, some with ease (they are the least blamable), some with a struggle. They have seen better things, and perhaps vainly long to return to them. These are 'St. Satan's Penitents,'[10] and their remorse is vain: *Virtutem videant, intabescantque relicta.*[11] If you don't wish to be of this dismal company, there is only one course open to you. Never write for publication one line of personal tattle. Let all men's persons and private lives be as sacred to you as your father's, – though there are tattlers who would sell paragraphs about their own mothers if there were a market for the ware. There is no half-way house on this road. Once begin to print private conversation, and you are lost – lost, that is, to delicacy and gradually, to many other things excellent and of good report. The whole question for you is, Do you mind incurring this damnation? If there is nothing in it which appals and revolts you, if your conscience is satisfied with a few ready sophisms, or if you don't care a pin for your conscience, fall to!

Vous irez loin?[12] You will prattle about men's private lives, their hidden motives, their waistcoats, their wives, their boots, their businesses, their incomes. Most of your prattle will inevitably be lies. But go on! nobody will kick you, I deeply regret to say. You will earn money. You will be welcomed in society. You will live and die content, and without remorse. I do not suppose that any particular *inferno* will await you in the future life. Whoever watches this world 'with larger other eyes than ours'[13] will doubtless make allowance for you, as for us all. I am not pretending to be a whit better than you; probably I am worse in many ways, but not in your way. Putting it merely as a matter of taste, I don't like the way. It makes me sick – that is all. It is a sin which I can comfortably damn, as I am not inclined to it. You may put it in that light; and I have no way of converting you, nor, if I have not dissuaded you, of dissuading you, from continuing, on a larger scale, your practices in *The Bull-dog*.

'The Science of Novels', *Illustrated London News* 105:2899

(10 November 1894), p. 598

The merits and demerits of University Extension[1] are a theme of which I have no knowledge. I have been invited to lecture to University Extensionists in the Feast of Reason, and, I hope, of other wares, which they hold at Oxford, but modesty compelled me to decline. A volume of a series of University Extension Manuals, a volume on the English Novel, lies before me, published by Mr. Murray, and written by Mr. Walter Raleigh.[2] Before the University was extended, we had no manuals of the English Novel, and no lectures or examinations therein. That kind of topic was supposed to be discussed in Essay Societies, but nobody, or next to nobody, ever wrote essays for them. Such themes were occasionally set for Balliol Essays,[3] a form of composition not taken seriously by the victims. And now, what is the use of a Manual about English novels? Do the readers of it read the novels with which it deals rather in a hurry? DO they read Mrs. Behn, Mrs. Haywood, Bluidy Mackenzie, Henry Mackenzie,[4] and the rest? If they do not study, say, Miss Jane Porter,[5] where is the use in their perusing a page about Miss Porter? Really her performances, and Mrs. Haywood's, and even Bluidy Mackenzie's, still more the gallant Aphra's, are no essential parts of education. I have a slight acquaintance with the authors, and say, without hesitation, that they may be dropped, though Aphra gets a laugh now and then. We had manuals of this kind, before the Universities were extended, on the History of Philosophy. Schwegler hurried us from Heraclitus to Hegel.[6] But then we verily had to read Heraclitus, and all that 'gallant company of gentlemen' in whom Sidney Smith took no interest[7] – we had to read them in the original Greek. So of the other philosophers (except the modern foreign thinkers); we read their books, we did not only read *about* them. If the Extension people also read 'Euphues,' 'Urania,' 'Parthenissa,' 'David Simple,' 'Sukey Shandy,'[8] and the rest, well, so be it. For pleasure, I may prefer Empedocles.[9] I do not see exactly what education gains by the study of dull dead novels, and certainly education gains nothing by a flight through a manual about them, and about them. It is a good manual in its way, and contains some pleasant observations, as the remark that Mrs. Radcliffe's heroes are the kind of people that Byron's heroes want to be. Scott's remarks on Mrs. Radcliffe, however, are still more interesting that Mr. Raleigh's. On De Foe's Mrs. Veal,[10] again, Mr. Raleigh is good, but everybody knows what is the right thing to say about Mrs.Veal. She was a very fair ghost for the time, but she talked too much. A genuine ghost, as a rule, is silent. In short, to a person well acquainted with the British novel, from Malory to Scott, Mr. Raleigh's manual is agreeable company. But, if people are going to feed their intellects on the manual alone, they might as well do without the manual.

At the back of all novel-writing lies the oral story, which does not enter into Mr. Raleigh's plan at all. Before there were novelists there were story-tellers, amateur or professional. These nameless artists, long before writing was used for literary purposes, had exhausted most of the *genres* of fiction. They had established romance in the tales of which are the basis of the 'Odyssey.' They had done the historical novel in stories about the Siege of Troy. The apologue, with its moral purpose, had preceded Miss Edgeworth, and Richardson, and all the narrators who aim at edification. 'Little Red Riding Hood' and 'Cinderella' are tales with a moral purpose. Love, war, the supernatural, had all been illustrated in oral fiction when the ancestors of Dumas and Scott wore paint and the skins of wild beasts. Only the novel of psychological analysis remained to be attempted in pen and ink.

As far as I can see, novels should be read 'for human pleasure,' without any hankering after education. If they must be made matter of education, the process should be historical. We may read a period of history and take in the novels of that period as expressions of the taste and ideals of the age, or of some people in that age. We see how 'Beowulf' fits the early Christianised English, and how Malory suits the English of Edward I., and how the long chivalrous romances exactly answer to the sham chivalry and sham classicism of the age of Louis XIII. In Richardson we see the dawn of Sensibility and Virtue, in Fielding we have the very blood and brain of Georgian England; in Scott we have the historical imagination become self-conscious, become aware that the dead generations were men of like passions with ourselves. In this way, if we insist on being educational, we may regard novels as elements in the vast and eternally changing, eternally entertaining pageant of life. Novels illustrate the varying tastes, dreams, ideals of successive periods, and are part of history, as the different arts and styles and costumes and manners are parts thereof. These things all hang together, and, educationally, may be studied together, but I see no other way of making the examination of dead novels educational.

Of novels very few have real life in them. Malory lives because he entertains; can we honestly say that 'Euphues' or the 'Arcadia' is entertaining? 'Parthenissa,' I understand, is not amusing; why should we trouble the memory with remarks on 'Parthenissa'? Are University Extension students examined in their knowledge of these remarks, or in their knowledge of Lord Orrery's masterpiece?[11] And, if so, is there not here a great waste of energy? Nobody is the better educated for knowing what Mr. Raleigh, or any man, thinks about Miss Reeve's 'Champion of Virtue, a Gothic Story' (1777). Now, Dunlop's 'History of Fiction'[12] is a *book*, an entertaining book, but perhaps it is too long for the pupils of University Extension. As had been said, I am not acquainted with the methods and merits of University Extension. Perhaps it only tells its pupils what books exist, and bids them fall to – a very useful programme. Perhaps it really makes them study fiction historically, in the manner suggested; but any such thorough pursuit of knowledge demands almost of the leisure of the professional student. And even *he* might neglect, unharmed, Miss Reeve's Gothic story. Are generations yet unborn to have manuals about Ouida, and 'Bootles' Baby,' and Mr. Hawley Smart?[13]

'The Teaching of English Literature', *Illustrated London News* 909: 2749

(December 1891), p. 834

Can English literature be made, and should it be made, the subject of teaching and of examination in the Universities? That is really the topic of Mr. Churton Collins's book 'The Study of English Literature' (Macmillan).[1] In considering a question of this kind, every person of mature years will be swayed by his own experience. Mine rather turns me against Mr. Collins's enthusiasm for teaching our literature at Oxford and Cambridge. I went to school with, perhaps, rather a wide knowledge of books for a boy, and at school they tried to teach us English literature. We possessed 'Paradise Lost,' Cowper's 'Task,' and an historical manual of the literature of England; but I do not suppose that I ever prepared one single lesson in these books or ever answered more than one question. Yet, wherein am I the worse, or wherein are the hundred of other contemporary boys who were in the same or similar classes the better? As to one's school experience, then the teaching of English literature was an arid waste of time, although, or because, one was never without a book in one's hand or one's pocket. At college nobody pretended to teach English literature, yet Mr. Collins, at college, knew plenty of it. I am concerned to believe that, had they been part of the curriculum, Mr. Collins might have been less devoted to the poetry and prose of our dear century. The truth is, as Mr. Collins perceives (p. 125, note), that young men who are inclined to be literary 'have generally preferred, and, in all probability, will continue to prefer, to take their education into their own hands.' Nothing can be more true: from the rare geniuses, like Shelley, Mr. Matthew Arnold, Gibbon, and so forth, who have been at Oxford, down to the mere literary trifler, all students whose main interest is literature have taken, and will take, the chief of their education into their own hands. There is no need to educate in English literature those 'who wish and will know everything,' as the infant Scott defined the virtuoso.[2]

And where is the use of educating the others at all? What have *they* to do with English literature? The newspapers and a few novels serve their turn. You cannot teach them taste; you cannot inspire those whom the Muse has not inspired, and the knowledge with which you cram them they promptly forget. I have examined young men in English literature. Eight out of ten returned mere mechanical answers with which they have been 'crammed.' Mr. Collins will say, 'This they did because they had been badly instructed.' But no lads who possessed a grain of literary taste, none who had the power of taking pleasure in books, could have answered so baldly and with such dismal dulness as these poor young men. There was no use in teaching them English literature. You might as well try to teach me the piano. They could read the papers, and a novel when they have exhausted the news, but of literature as an art, with laws, with an evolution of its own, with a charm and a delicacy unspeakable, they had, and could have, no conception. They were born without a literary taste, as another man is born without an ear for music. Most people have an ear for music; few have a taste for letters, and those few, as Mr. Collins says, will take their education 'into their own hands.' 'The rest, they may live, and *not* learn.'

To this doctrine Mr. Collins may urge two replies. He may say, 'But most people have no more taste for philosophy and history than for literature, yet history and philosophy are taught.' Here I dispute the assertion that philosophy and history are quite as painfully distasteful as literature to most people. History can be hitched into politics, philosophy can be tacked on to religion, and neither history nor philosophy is, like literature, an *art*. Consequently, plenty of persons can take quite heartily to learning philosophy and history. As an example, in the *Contemporary Review* we find Mrs. Sutherland Orr trying to define Mr. Robert Browning's religious beliefs. She speaks of 'large groups of men and women whose faith in Mr. Browning was bound up with his supposed allegiance to the literal forms of Christianity.'[3] These large groups went round talking about Mr. Browning, and the careless observer thought that they were taking an interest in literature. What had they to do with literature? It was religion that concerned *them*. Now, to a lover of letters, Mr. Browning's beliefs are neither here nor there. Mr. Browning's own happiness would be affected by his beliefs, and, as a religious matter, we are all deeply interested in learning how faith appealed to his energetic mind. But, as matter of literature, his beliefs are no more important than Shakspere's, of which we know nothing at all. Our 'faith' in Shakspere is not 'bound up with his allegiance' to any dogma, nor is our literary faith in Mr. Browning, nor in Paulus Silentiarius,[4] nor in anybody. Thus, one remains of the opinion that the chosen of literature are few, though they seem to be many, because Mr. Browning, for example, produced literature, and many excellent persons had faith in him. It was not his literature they cared about, it was his theology. Not literature, but religious discussion, makes theological romances popular. So far, then, I maintain that literature is not on a footing with history or philosophy. Literature is a source of pleasure. History teaches politics, philosophy teaches conduct and is mixed up with religion. The many cannot be taught literature; the few do not need teaching, if once they can read – read Greek, Latin, English, French, Italian, German. Their literary education they will 'take in their own hands.'

Mr. Collins may next reply unto me: 'But literature *is* taught all over the country, and taught very badly. Much of the teaching is merely philological; much is only cram of names and dates. If literature were taught in the Universities, the general level all over the land would be raised.' To this I must reply that the public cannot be taught literature. But, under the delusion that they are learning literature, they can be made to puzzle out the 'skews'[5] in Shakspere, to understand the hard words and odd constructions, and to get by heart a few pieces of general information: the date of Chaucer, the names of Pope's books, and so on. All that kind of thing they can be got to remember long enough for purposes of examination. Mr. Collins supplies questions which he thinks might be set in real valuable literary teaching. Alas! I fear any crammer could prepare his pupils with answers that must receive marks. Let me try a question myself: 'Discuss "prose poetry," illustrate from Aristotle.' The crammer could put his pupils up to that 'tip' in a quarter of an hour. The crammer will always beat the examiner, and in literature the pupils not born literary will always give parrot answers. Mr. Collins provides ten pages of questions for the new school. Many, I think, are just such questions as were set in 'General Papers' when I was an undergraduate.

Many other questions here might be, and may be, set in the modern history schools. Others might be set in a Taylorian scholarship.[6] All the questions deal with matters which a man of literary taste will study unurged by examinations. For example, Mr. Collins probably would have rejoiced to find many of those questions set in 'Greats'[7] or a Fellowship examination. Yet he had never been told to 'get them up'; they came by nature. People to whom they do not come by nature will merely cram replies, and be nothing the better. It may be said that the student needs instruction, advice, the pointing out to him of books. Not he! To discover the books is as natural to him as to 'see the hare first' is natural to another kind of sportsman.

Thus, to myself, 'the higher' kind of literary teaching seems either superfluous for the few or useless waste of time and trouble for the many. Mr. Collins, however, is backed up by a multitude of allies, from Mr. Huxley to Canon Farrar,[8] from Mr. Pater to the Archbishop of Canterbury. What am I against so many! Moreover, Mr. Collins's arguments are so numerous and serried that he who would understand them all must read them for himself. I do not presume to suppose that I have confuted Mr. Collins: I only try to explain why I do not believe in the teaching of literature. It is not that English literature should *not* be studied in company with the ancient classics. English literature is already so studied, probably, by every undergraduate of taste: the others will never make anything of literature, whether there be a school of literature or not. Here followeth an anecdote: In my freshman's year 'Atalanta in Calydon'[9] came out, and I purchased a copy – a good investment too, as the first edition is now rare. To me enter another undergraduate, justly distinguished in all ways and a scholar of the first mark. He borrowed my 'Atalanta,' and brought it back in a week, saying, with considerable vigour, that he could make neither head nor tail of the stuff. This gentleman had endless accomplishments, excellent abilities, but he did not happen to be literary. The majority is like him, without his qualities: the majority cannot be taught literature, and the minority need no teaching.

'The Teaching of Literature', *The Pilot*

(13 April 1901), pp. 446–7

I am old-fashioned and prejudiced enough to believe that literature cannot be taught; that there is no earthly use in schools and classes, and, if I may say so in a purely Pickwickian sense, no use in professors of literature, as professors. As a man and a man of letters, the professor may be both useful and beautiful, and I rejoice to think that chairs (far too few) have been founded for the repose of these good beings. Had every man of letters a chair of literature wherein to sit and be instructive, what a good-Humoured set of mortals we should be! But adequate provision has not been made, and though, as a thinker, I deprecate the 'teaching of literature,' as a philanthropist, I wish that all my brethren were paid to teach it. Had pious founders taken this vision, our *genus*[1] would not be irritable, and the 'Ephemera Critica' of Mr. Churton Collins[2] would be a book with which a child might play. As things stand, it is perhaps deficient in mansuetude,[3] though it deals with the teaching of ingenuous arts; too often by 'careless professors.'

On *a priori* grounds, and also by virtue of personal experience, I do not believe in the teaching of literature. When at school I must have been one of the most literary of my young companions; indeed, as Scott said when a boy, 'You can't think how ignorant these boys were.' Like the rest, I went to an English class till I was fourteen, after which we were supposed to know all about English literature, and turned to higher things. Dismal hand-books about Gower and Lydgate were placed in our reluctant and grubby little fists. My memory is not soiled with any recollection of the contents of these manuals. We were expected to read 'The Task,' by the ingenious Mr. Cowper; but I read 'Tirocinium,' a poem about the very worst boys, except those in 'Stalky and Co.,'[4] who are yet more odious. And that is all the teaching in English literature that I and my contemporaries ever received. Now, Shakespeare had not even so much as a manual about Lydgate and Gower, nor had Spencer, or Milton, or Herrick, or Shelley, or Thackeray, or Tennyson. Yet they made very good literature, as did and do, many other gentlemen who never even attended an University Extension lecture nor the discourse of a professor. Literature is not made as a result of teaching, nor is it appreciated as a result of teaching. A man is born to be so, to appreciate literature or to detest it exceedingly, which I take to be human nature, in the general. Have we better poets since English was taught? Perhaps we have, if Mr. A., Mr. B., and Mr. C. are as great as their young friends do report of them, but it is 'early days' to decide. If Shakespeare had enjoyed the advantages of Mr. Stephen Phillips and Mr. Laurence Binyon,[5] I doubt if 'Macbeth,' and 'As You Like It,' would be much better than they are. Speaking for myself, I would be neither a worse nor a better scribbler if I had been taught and examined in the works of Huchown[6] (or however he spells his name), and Pecock,[7] his 'Repression of Overmuch Blaming of the Clergy.' We ought not to blame anybody overmuch, but one cannot read every thing, and if I must choose between Pecock and Mr. Guy Boothby,[8] my choice is made. A man who loves books naturally finds out those which suit his taste; public rumour directs him, from his childhood, to the great names; he tries their works, and rejoices in the same (if he has taste, and if he has not, nobody can impart it). At school we opened Homer, to read was to rejoice. Nobody was needed to say 'Observe, this is very fine,' or 'remark the pathos of those observations of Helen. Virgil has imitated the passage, and Pope's translation is much admired.' Nobody was needed to say these instructive things, and nobody was so fatuous as to do so. It is literature that teaches literature.

The history of literature is quite another affair. It can be taught like any other history. But what, comparatively speaking, is the history of literature? A man might know Homer by heart, and have Shakespeare at his fingers' ends, and so be happy and educated, and yet might never have heard of Wolf or Fick, or Mr. Walter Leaf;[9] or cared about 'A Shakespeare's Dark Lady,' her name and address, or about Nash, or Greene, or Adrian Quiney, or Mr. Sidney Lee.[10] Any history almost, or any biography of a literary character, I rather like to read, and many persons share the harmless curiosity. The thing can be taught. You can show how France influenced Scottish poetry, and the sources of Burns's metres, and the effect of the revival of classical learning on Chettle[11] and his work, and you can easily prove that Boileau did not know much about Aristotle. You might pass a lifetime is grubbing up the source of 'The High History of the Holy Graal,' but that kind of study is not literature, whereas the 'High History' is. These historical and antiquarian studies can be taught, and are taught by professors and lecturers. Examinations are held; industry is rewarded with marks. But literature is a light and sacred thing; her wings outsoar the professors, while a child in a nook with a book captures the divine butterfly.

It appears that the English universities, Oxford at least, are of my opinion. In Mr. Collins's Index we read, 'Universities, their indifference to the interests of literature.' One example is 'so scandalous that it must be specified.' The Cambridge Press, in fact, is so lost as to circulate a volume of Cambridge Lectures which a writer in a review proved to 'swarm with blunders.'

In some respects, I find myself agreeing with Mr. Collins. We cannot teach literature, I think, but if we teach the history of literature we ought to teach it right. Many years ago there was a vacant ecclesiastical chair in a Scottish university. The justly successful candidate was, of course, assailed with abuse. That is often the way. It is safer to stand for a constituency than for a chair – at least, if you win. Somebody who had read the attacks on the successful candidate said plaintively, 'If we must have a professor of theology (for which I see no occasion), why elect a deaf and dumb Atheist?' In the same way, if we must have manuals of literary history, if we must give a hundred pages of notes to a short poem, why should we have the work done without knowledge? Mr. Collins takes an edition of the 'Adonais,' published by the Oxford Press. This work appears to illustrate both his contention and mine. 'Adonais' is excellent literature, and it is very literary literature, full of literary allusions. But its author never attended a lecture on literature, and, indeed, probably 'cut' lectures at large, as well as chapels. Therefore the teaching of literature is a vain superfluity. We can do without it. But the untaught Shelley was full of Greek (though not technically a scholar), and his editor, it seems 'in Greek was sadly to seek.'[12] He did not know 'what any schoolboy could have told him, that the allusion is a technical one to the platonic "forms" or archetypes.' The schoolboys of my acquaintance never heard of *these* 'forms'; still, the editor ought to have prosed about them. He ought to have known all about 'the *scutum crystallinum* of Pallas Athene,'[13] as any well-informed fourth form schoolboy would know. Alas, I am not so well informed, but then I am not editing the 'Adonais.' The editor ought to have known, not a doubt of it, and Mr. Collins is quite right. These instructive editions of the poets may be the abomination of desolation, but if we must have them, their editors ought to be instructed.

'We don't learn Shakespeare,' a young friend said to me lately; 'we learn Clarendon Press notes.' Mr. Collins has a fling at these notes, and again my theory is illustrated. The notes do not teach literature, for that is impossible; they recognise the impossibility, and they teach philology. What can you teach about the madness of Hamlet? The editor probably knew that you can teach nothing; so he wrote, 'Hamlet's madness has formed the subject of special investigation by several writers, among others by Dr. Conolly and Sir Edward Strachey.' That is not a valuable note, but what was the poor gentleman to do? Was he to add another essay on points in Hamlet's soul? We should read Hamlet 'for human pleasure,' and, perhaps, like Mr. Zangwill's barber, our simple comment may be that 'Hamlet is too thick.'[14] In any case, the hero's madness, real or feigned, like that of David, will produce in us its own impression. We may or may not be curious about the impression which it has produced on Dr. Conolly. The impression of Dr. Johnson was that we should read Shakespeare himself uncommented on, and only look at notes if we really could not help it, as when he uses words that we do not understand. An elder contemporary of his writes that one of the Queen's Maries, Mary Beaton, 'is both darimpus and skelenbrunit.' If Shakespeare had said so about Ophelia, what reams of notes would the editors have contributed; also on the statement that Thomas Randolph is 'without contrebaxion or kylteperante.' *Periculo meo*, 'Kittlerumpit.'[15] Yet the notes would not have told us what we want to know, or they would have been very unlike notes in general. Nobody but an idiot can help knowing what Shakespeare meant about the engineer and his own petard, or petar. But a vast note is given about 'petar' and 'petard,' and 'hoise' or 'hoist,' while the Sledded Polacks are treated in the same way, without reference to the name Pollock, whether as indicating Polish descent or as connected with Pollockshiels and the house of Maxwell. All this has no more to do with literature than with conic sections, but an editor must be editing, and, as he cannot teach literature, must try to teach something else, on which young men and maidens may veritably be examined and get marks. The Ghost, in the quarto of 1603, 'enters in his nightgowne.' We ought to ask in examinations, 'What *is* a nightgown?' Probably the boys do not know that it was a dressing-gown. Darnley's 'nightgown' was of violet velvet, furred with sables. As it was bitter cold, the nightgown of Hamlet's father may have been of the same sort. But how would glowworms be 'out and around,' if it was 'bitter cold,' and is the glowworm indigenous to Denmark? These are points on which questions may be set. I know that boys read the notes and do not read the plays. Why should they? It is in the notes that they are examined.

'What is likely,' Mr. Collins asks, 'to be the fate of English literature as a subject of teaching,' while this kind of thing is done? Of course, every bored pupil must hate Shakespeare as much as Mr. Darwin hated him.[16] Untaught in literature, the pupils would leave Shakespeare alone. They would suppose (like a gallant captain at the play) that Shakespeare wrote 'Charles I.,' which is by another author. People at Oxford, compelled by the public to teach literature, and not caring for literature, knowing too that literature cannot be taught, teach some literary history, some philology, and prose about Polacks and Petards. What is learned of literature, at Oxford, is learned from reading the best literature, that of Greece and Rome, and from reading for human pleasure. Mr. Collins, himself learned literature in no other way – there *is* no other way. Schools of literature, examinations, and all, ought to be abolished. It is the general public that demands literary teaching, and Mr. Augustine Birrell, I think, has asked, 'What, in the name of the Bodleian, has the general public to do with literature?'[17]

APPENDIX:
Names frequently cited by Lang

Aristotle (384 BCE–322 BCE). Greek philosopher and student of Plato. His work is fundamental to Western philosophy, covering logic, physical science, biology, ethics, politics, metaphysics and rhetoric.

Arnold, Matthew (1822–88). British poet and critic whose writings were deeply influential on literary, social and educational issues. *Culture and Anarchy* (1869) is one of the major works of Victorian prose and its proposition of the definition and function of culture in society shaped intellectual life in the twentieth century. Arnold was Professor of Poetry at Oxford during Lang's undergraduate years and had a formative effect on him.

Austen, Jane (1775–1817). Novelist, now very well-known and whose works have frequently been adapted for film and television. Although fairly popular in the early nineteenth century, when Walter Scott reviewed her work enthusiastically, she was not the focus of admiration that she later became. Charlotte Brontë and Elizabeth Barrett Browning, for example, were both critical of her narrow range. Lang, perhaps influenced by Scott's appreciation, liked her work.

Ballantyne, James (1772–1833) was a printer who printed the work of Walter Scott. His brother John (1774–1821) started, with Scott, a publishing firm based in Edinburgh in which James also had a small share. The printing business was more successful than the publishing, but both brothers were financially ruined in the 1820s. James particularly was a friend of Scott's and offered editorial advice on many of Scott's works.

Balzac, Honoré de (1799–1850). French novelist and playwright, author of the enormous series of 91 separate works that make up the *Comédie Humaine*. He aimed to imitate the methods of history and natural science in fiction, in order to give a comprehensive representation of contemporary French society. His Realist practice was influential on French and other European literature, though less immediately on English writing. Lang found Balzac's Realism more congenial than Émile Zola's later work in similar 'scientific' style.

Besant, Walter (1836–1901). Writer and social critic, he was the author of several novels including *All Sorts and Conditions of Men* (1882) and *Children of Gibeon* (1886) which drew attention to the appalling conditions of poor industrial workers in the East End of London. His work prompted the foundation of the People's Palace in that area in 1887, intended for the intellectual improvement and educational entertainment of local people. He also founded the Society of Authors in 1884 to promote the business interests and rights of authors.

Boileau-Despréaux, Nicolas (1636–1711). Poet and critic who revolutionised French poetry by introducing a new emphasis on strictness and regularity of verse structure. His 1674 book *L'Art poétique*, written in imitation of Horace's *Ars Poetica*, sought to set out a new code for poetic composition, and, through Dryden's revised translation, had a considerable influence on English literature, particularly Alexander Pope's *Essay on Criticism* (1711).

Boisgobey, Fortuné du (1821–91). Pen-name of French novelist Fortuné Hippolyte Auguste Castille. He wrote a number of popular and sensational novels, some published in *feuilleton*, the supplements to French newspapers, and mostly concerned with Parisian crime and the police. Du Boisgobey is often associated with another French crime novelist, Émile Gaboriau, and Lang liked the work of both writers.

Bothwell, Earl of (*c.*1534–78). James Hepburn, fourth Earl of Bothwell was the third husband of Mary, Queen of Scots. In 1567, Bothwell was one of those accused of having murdered the Queen's second husband Lord Darnley, but Mary married him in May of that year after his acquittal. The marriage was unpopular with other powerful Scottish nobles; Bothwell fled in June. He was taken prisoner by the King of Denmark and died in that prison ten years later. It remains unclear whether Mary was an accomplice in the murder or the apparently forced marriage, and the accusation of Mary's complicity is one of the central points of the argument about her character that Lang took part in.

Bridges, Robert (1844–1930). Originally a doctor, he became a poet and literary critic and was elected Poet Laureate in 1913. He also wrote and translated hymns.

Brontë, Charlotte (1816–55). The longest-surviving of the three Brontë sisters who were well-known for their writing. Emily, Anne and their brother Branwell all died within eight months between 1848 and 1849. The women all originally published under pseudonyms although were soon known to be the authors. As with her sisters' novels, Charlotte's work, especially *Jane Eyre* (1848) was thought by some to be coarse and improper, though Elizabeth Gaskell's biography of her friend, published in 1855, began a defence against those charges. Lang too makes a strong defence of Brontë's writing and appreciated it at a time when it was unfashionable.

Browning, Robert (1812–89). English poet and playwright whose work is best known for the development of the dramatic monologue in verse form. His early poetry was well received but the hostile reception of *Sordello* (1840) put his growing reputation into the shade until twenty years later when his long narrative poem *The Ring and the Book* (1868–69) was very successful. He married the poet Elizabeth Barrett after eloping with her to Italy in 1846.

Bulwer-Lytton, Edward (1803–73). English politician who began as a Liberal and then became a Tory. He wrote many novels in a variety of genres including historical fiction, mystery and romance. His *The Last Days of Pompeii* (1834) amplified popular enthusiasm for the archaeological discoveries made at Pompeii and Herculaneum and contributed to the craze for art and craft in the style of those discoveries. His colourful personal life and the extravagance of his writing made him the butt of jokes, especially for J. G. Lockhart (of whom Lang wrote a biography) and William Thackeray, but he was admired by other influential people including Dickens and Disraeli.

Bunyan, John (1628–88). Bunyan was a village artisan with a rudimentary education who became a Puritan preacher after the English Civil War. His message, which placed the poor and simple above the wealthy and educated, alarmed the Restoration authorities and he was arrested. In his twelve-year imprisonment he wrote a number of books, including part of his most famous work *The Pilgrim's Progress*, which he completed during his shorter second imprisonment in 1677. *The Pilgrim's Progress* is a long religious allegory, telling the story of the journey of Christian through the toils of the world to Heaven.

Burney, Fanny (1752–1840). Frances Burney was a society lady who published her first novel, *Evelina* in 1778. Although anonymous, her authorship was soon known and she became famous as a writer of letters and journals as well as further novels. Her work was admired by Jane Austen.

Burns, Robert (1759–96). Scottish poet and lyricist. He wrote in both English and Scots and also collected and amended many old Scottish songs and ballads, including 'Auld Lang Syne'. He was very popular in his homeland and his birthday, 'Burns Night', is still celebrated. Lang was not a great admirer of Burns' poetry and believed that that he altered too much in the ballads that he gathered and published.

Byron, Lord (1788–1824). English poet and leading figure in the Romantic movement, he was as well-known for his scandalous lifestyle as for his long narrative poems and short lyrics. Despite bitter attacks by critics, he was popular in England, and was even more celebrated in Europe where he lived in several countries after leaving England in 1816. He favoured revolutionary causes and died in Greece, having gone there to support the insurgency.

Calvin, John (1509–64). French theologian, one of the most important figures in the Reformation. His vision for the reformed church was austere and in practice it imposed a strict morality that was sometimes enforced by persecution and even torture. In Scotland John Knox, influenced by Calvin and Luther, was a powerful force in the Protestant Reformation and a predominately Calvinist national church emerged which retained a strong hold in subsequent centuries.

Carlyle, Thomas (1795–1881). Scottish historian, essayist and social commentator. Regarded as one of the Victorian 'sages', his writings on current conditions had a significant impact on contemporary ideas. In *Chartism* (1839) and *Past and Present* (1843) he reflected on what he called 'the Condition of England Question', evincing a sympathy for the industrial poor that is then apparent in the 'social question' novels of writers like Elizabeth Gaskell. He left his own and his wife Jane Welsh's papers to the historian J. A. Froude, who published them to great controversy after Carlyle's death.

Chaucer, Geoffrey (*c.*1343–1400). English poet who also served in several positions at court, including undertaking diplomatic missions. He wrote in vernacular Middle English rather than the scholarly or courtly languages of French or Latin. His great work, *The Canterbury Tales,* is a series of linked stories told in prose and verse and was probably designed in about 1387.

Coleridge, Samuel Taylor (1772–1834). Romantic poet, philosopher, critic and essayist. He worked closely with the poet Southey and, later, Wordsworth. Initially enthusiastic about the French Revolution, he became disenchanted and turned to Germany and German philosophy from which came his critical ideas about poetry and the imagination. His long addiction to opium contributed to the visionary quality of some of his works.

Cowper, William (1731–1800). English poet and writer of hymns. Cowper had a profound effect upon nature poetry through his focus on everyday rural life, which was to be a major influence on English Romanticism. Sent to a mental asylum for three years in 1763 following a nervous breakdown, he subsequently became a devout evangelical Christian.

Dante (1265–1321). Dante Alighieri was born and worked in Florence, until obliged to leave in 1301 when the political regime of the city state changed. The dates of composition of his long poems *Vita Nuova* and *Divina Commedia* are uncertain, but in both form and content had a profound influence on subsequent writers in Europe and in England.

Darnley, Lord (1545–67). Henry Stewart or Stuart was a Scottish aristocrat whose grandmother was Margaret Tudor, daughter of Henry VII of England, and widow of James IV of Scotland. He was the cousin of Mary, Queen of Scots and they were married in 1565, presenting a strong claim to the English throne. The marriage was unhappy, Darnley was unpopular and also accused of involvement in the murder of one of the Queen's favourites. In 1567, the year after the birth of their son, Darnley was murdered. Mary subsequently married one of the men accused of his murder and the question of her complicity in the matter has never been resolved. Lang was a vocal participant in the debate about Mary's character. Darnley's son James succeeded Elizabeth I to the English throne and united the crowns of the two kingdoms as James I of England and VI of Scotland.

Darwin, Charles (1809–82). English naturalist and the most important scientist of his era whose 1859 book *The Origin of Species* is credited with providing the first proper scientific evidence for the theory of evolution. Although Darwin himself largely avoided public life, he was a controversial figure for much of the nineteenth century by virtue of the apparent threat posed to orthodox Christian theology by his ideas, as well as the extension of his theory of natural selection to modern human societies in so-called 'Social Darwinist' philosophy.

Daudet, Alphonse (1840–97). Prolific French novelist whose works were being translated into English during the 1880s and 1890s, though Lang would also have been able to read them in French. Daudet was a monarchist and thus an opponent of the French Republic. He was also anti-Jewish. His novel *L'Immortel* (1888), published in English as *One of the Forty* (1888), is a trenchant attack on the Académie française and although Lang might have sympathised with the anti-Academy stance, he regarded Daudet in the same way as he did Zola, as a 'realist' with an unnecessary focus on low life.

Defoe, Daniel (1660–1731). Writer, journalist and pamphleteer who produced over 500 works. His prose narratives represent some of the earliest novels written in English and his most famous, *Robinson Crusoe* (1719), has been popular since its first publication.

Dickens, Charles (1812–70). The most popular of Victorian novelists, Dickens was also a prolific writer of stories and non-fiction and was an energetic editor of the periodicals *Household Words* and *All The Year Round.* Although immensely admired by the general reading public, the literary elite did not regard him highly and by the end of the nineteenth century his reputation was not high. Lang was somewhat against critical opinion in his appreciation of Dickens.

Dostoievsky, Fyodor (1821–81). Influential Russian novelist and writer of short stories. His best known novel is *Crime and Punishment* (1866) which, like his other fiction, explores human psychology in the turbulent society of contemporary Russia. Lang found his novels, as he did those of Tolstoy, dismal and depressing.

Dryden, John (1631–1700). Poet, playwright and critic, he dominated the literary life of Restoration England. He was fiercely Tory in his politics and also a Jacobite sympathiser. He was made Poet Laureate in 1868 and Historiographer Royal in 1670.

Dumas, Alexandre. Dumas (1802–70) and his son (1824–90), also called Alexandre, were equally popular French writers. The elder Dumas wrote plays, travel books, memoirs and children's stories but also and most famously *Les Trois Mousquetaires* (1844), the first of several historical novels featuring D'Artagnan and the three muskeeters. Other works, such as *The Count of Monte Cristo* (1844) and *The Corsican Brothers* (1844) were also very popular in England. He is the Dumas to whom Lang refers frequently and appreciatively; the work of his son, such as his novel about a courtesan *La Dame Aux Camélias* (1852), was less to Lang's taste. Lang wrote introductions to the collected works of Dumas *pére*.

Edgeworth, Maria (1768–1849). Irish writer who produced moral novels for children and both historical and contemporary fiction for adults. Her treatise *Practical Education* (1798) encouraged independence and moral responsibility and her children's fiction followed similar principles. She was a celebrated literary figure who was visited by Walter Scott and admired by Jane Austen.

Eliot, George (1819–80). Pen name of Mary Ann (Marian) Evans. Eliot was a leading novelist of the period, but also a translator of important works of theological 'higher' criticism, such as Strauss' *Life of Jesus* (1846). Although she lived with George Henry Lewes to whom she was not married, she was widely celebrated and admired by a diverse readership that included Queen Victoria and Henry James. Lang too regarded her as one of the 'great masters' of the English novel.

Fielding, Henry (1707–54). Writer and dramatist who, breaking away from the epistolary form in fiction, coined the term 'comic epics in prose' and produced some of the earliest English novels, such as *Tom Jones* (1749). Lang thought Fielding's writing style was of the highest order, often commented appreciatively its comic quality and seems to have regarded Fielding as the best of all English novelists.

Flaubert, Gustave (1821–80). French writer whose first novel *Madame Bovary* (1857) led to his prosecution, along with his publisher and printer, for offence to public morals. He was acquitted. He undertook detailed research for his novels which he reproduced with accuracy in his writing. Lang regarded him as a great prose stylist and admired his precision.

Froude, James Anthony (1818–94). Historian and essayist who was also the editor of *Fraser's Magazine* between 1860 and 1874). He was a friend of Carlyle, the poet Arthur Hugh Clough and the novelist Charles Kingsley and a highly successful writer on history, particularly on the Tudors and Elizabethan sea-faring. Later in his career he was accused of inaccuracy by fellow historian E. A. Freeman, and Lang too is critical of his handling of facts. His frank memoirs of Carlyle and his wife, published after their deaths and on Carlyle's instruction, caused great controversy, but he became Regius Professor of Modern History at Oxford in 1892.

Gautier, Théophile (1811–72). French poet, dramatist, novelist, journalist, and critic of art, music, ballet and literature. Prominent in the Romantic movement he also became associated with the latrer doctrine of 'l'art pour l'art' or 'art for art's sake' that was influential on such writers as Oscar Wilde.

Gibbon, Edward (1737–94). English historian and politician. His multi-volume work *The History of the Decline and Fall of the Roman Empire* (1776, 1781 and 1788) covers thirteen centuries and decisively shaped the historiography of the Roman Empire. His conclusions were often taken in considerations of Britain's own empire during the later nineteenth century. His memoirs give a very poor account of Oxford University.

Gladstone, William Ewart (1809–98). One of the most important statesmen of the nineteenth century. Though first entering Parliament as a Tory in 1832, it was as a Liberal that he was four times Chancellor of the Exchequer and four times Prime Minister. He took up his last ministry at the age of 82 in 1892, partly from his commitment to bringing Home Rule in Ireland. Gladstone had studied classics and he published a book *Studies on Homer and the Homeric Age* (1858) that Lang certainly knew.

Godwin, William (1756–1836). English radical philosopher and writer, husband of the feminist Mary Wollstonecraft and father of the novelist Mary Shelley. He wrote some novels and biographies but his essays on political philosophy are better known.

Goethe, Johann Wolfgang von (1749–1832). Author, essayist, scientist and politician who is regarded by many as the most important single figure in German literature. His many works include the epic poem *Hermann and*

Dorothea (1796–97), and the two-part closet drama *Faust* (1808–31), as well as the scientific works *The Metamorphosis of Plants* (1790) and *Theory of Colours* (1810). His first two novels *The Sorrows of Young Werther* (1775) and *Wilhelm Meister's Apprenticeship* (1795–6) had a huge influence upon, respectively, the Sturm und Drang movement, as well as later Romanticism, and the Bildungsroman or 'novel of formation'.

Haggard, Henry Rider (185–925). Haggard worked in colonial administration in South Africa during the 1870s and on his return to England began to write adventure novels set in Africa. The manuscript one of these, *King Solomon's Mines*, came to Lang's attention and he strongly encouraged its publication in 1885. The two men became close friends and Lang was instrumental in Haggard's success. Haggard wrote sequels to *King Solomon's Mines* and a number of other adventure novels set in imperial locations and 'lost worlds'. He was knighted in 1912.

Hardy, Thomas (1840–1928). Important English novelist, poet and short story writer. Some of his works were controversial, and he gave up writing novels after the hostile reception of *Jude the Obscure* (1895). Hardy and Lang knew one another: it was Lang's unsympathetic review of *Tess of the d'Urbervilles* and Hardy's response in the preface to the fifth edition of the novel that contributed to an image of Lang as a critic unable to recognise important new literary talent.

Hogg, James (1770–1835). Scottish writer acquainted with Walter Scott and the English Romantic poets. He worked on the collection of ballads for Scott, but first became famous for his work in *Blackwood's Edinburgh Magazine*. He wrote fiction and non-fiction, both in Scots and in English, and is now best known for his novel *The Private Memoirs and Confessions of a Justified Sinner* (1824).

Homer Name conventionally given to the poet of the *Iliad* and the *Odyssey*, although his date, authorship and even his existence are still debated. The poems are usually thought to date from the eighth century BCE, though perhaps existing in oral form from considerably earlier. No evidence of Homer exists, though many versions of his life have been proposed since times of antiquity. A consensus that Homer was the single author of the poems first emerged in about 350 BCE, but this has been continually under question since then. During the nineteenth century the general view was that the poems were works of multiple authorship produced over an extended period of time, so Lang's position that Homer was one person and the author of both epics was unusual.

Horace (*c*.65 BCE–*c*.8 BCE). Latin poet and friend of Virgil. Writer of odes that imitated the lyric poets of early Greece and ranged in theme from pleasure and love to political comment. His *Satires* and *Epistles* were in an ironic style, mocking the satirists as well as his targets.

Howells, William Dean (1837–1920). American writer of novels, drama, travelogues and criticism. He was an influential journalist, editor of the *Atlantic Monthly* from 1871 to 1881 and columnist on *Harper's Magazine* from 1886 to 1892. In *Harper's* his column began in the same month as Lang's 'At the Sign of the Ship' started in *Longman's*, and Howells was Lang's principal adversary in the Realism vs. Romance debate conducted in the literary periodicals. Howells championed contemporary Realist writers and his own novels were written in that style.

Hugo, Victor (1802–85). French poet, novelist and essayist. A popular writer, but also a politician whose strong opposition to Louis Napoleon obliged him to go into exile for twenty years. He published many works of poetry and prose, including *Notre Dame de Paris* (1831), in which he created the character of the 'Hunchback of Notre Dame', and *Les Misérables* (1862).

Hume, David (1711–76). Scottish philosopher, historian, economist, and essayist. He is a significant figure in the history of Western philosophy and the major thinker of the Scottish Enlightenment. His philosophy of empiricism is based in the idea that experience is the condition of knowledge. Lang was more interested in Hume as an historian and in his huge work *The History of England* (1754–62) that was long regarded as the standard work on the subject.

Hunt, Leigh (1784–1859). English writer and journalist who was a friend and supporter of both Keats and Shelley. With his brother John (1775–1848) he founded the *Examiner*, a paper espousing liberal and reforming causes that was frequently threatened with legal action for libel. In 1813 both brothers were imprisoned for two years for a libel on the Prince Regent. He founded a number of other publications that printed work by Keats, Byron, Percy Shelley, Hazlitt, Hogg and many others of the Romantics.

Huxley, Thomas Henry (1825–95). Biologist and at the time the most famous scientist in Britain. He was known as 'Darwin's bulldog' for his powerful defence of the theory of evolution, and he coined the term 'agnostic'. He was Professor of Natural History at the Royal School of Mines, later President of the British Association for the Advancement of Science and President of the Royal Society. His collection of essays, *Science and the Christian Tradition*, was first published in 1894. These essays, and those in *Science and the Hebrew Tradition* (1893), were the result of his very public debate, between 1885 and 1891, with W. E. Gladstone in the pages of the *Nineteenth Century* over evolutionary science and its implications for the status of biblical truth. He taught H. G. Wells, who credited the idea of the Eloi and the Morlocks in his novel *The Time Machine* (1895) to Huxley's lecture on evolution and degeneration.

James, Henry (1843–1916). American-born writer who lived in Europe, mainly London, from 1875. W. D. Howells was instrumental in the early part of James's career, which began with reviews and short stories. He continued to write short stories, publishing more than a hundred, and his novels were critically admired, though considered 'difficult'. His essays on the nature and function of fiction and criticism were important and influential in the development of literary studies. James and Lang knew one another well and although Lang appreciated James's early novels they differed in their opinions on fiction and it is James's withering description in a letter to Edmund Gosse that has long stood as the summary account of Lang's work.

Johnson, Samuel (1709–84). Prolific writer in a variety of genres, founder of the *Gentleman's Magazine* and the *Rambler*, he was a dominating figure in eighteenth-century literary life. His own life was chronicled in detail by his friend James Boswell and Bowell's accounts of Johnson's wit, erudition and eccentricities shaped his reputation.

Keats, John (1795–1821). Important English poet of the second generation of Romantic writers, along with Percy Shelley and Byron. He was qualified to practise as an apothecary, but turned to writing instead, publishing his first work in 1816. He was attacked by J. G. Lockhart in *Blackwood's Edinburgh Magazine*, with Lockhart calling Keats, Hazlitt and Leigh Hunt the 'Cockney School' of writers. Keats' work was, however, admired during his short lifetime and after his death other poets such as Tennyson and Matthew Arnold contributed much to his lasting reputation.

Kingsley, Charles (1819–75). A clergyman in the Church of England, who was appointed canon of Westminster Abbey two years before his death, Kingsley was also a Professor of Modern History at Cambridge University. He published a number of historical novels, including *Hypatia* (1853) and *Westward Ho!* (1855), but is best known for his 1863 children's novel *The Water-Babies* about a young chimney sweep. A friend of Charles Darwin, whose work influenced *The Water-Babies*, Kingsley was a vociferous critic of Roman Catholicism and engaged in a public argument with John Henry Newman that prompted the latter's *Apologia Pro Vita Sua* (1864) in defence of his religious convictions.

Kipling, Rudyard (1865–1936). Novelist, poet and writer of short stories who was born in India and spent much time travelling, especially in South Africa. He is often represented as jingoistic and uncritical in his celebration of the British Empire but his work is more complex in its treatment of race, class and the British Raj than this would suggest. His output was vast, including many stories for children, *The Jungle Book* (1894) and *Just So Stories* (1902) among them. Lang was one of the first to note Kipling's work and was important in gaining recognition for him.

Knox, John (*c*.1514–72). Leader of the Protestant Reformation and among the founders of the Presbyterianism in Scotland. Involved in events around the murder of Cardinal Beaton in 1546 he was exiled to England and also spent some time in Geneva where he was influenced by the Protestant reformer John Calvin. On his return to Scotland he led the Protestant Reformation of the church, and the creation of the Kirk. The religious revolution was also deeply political, leading to the deposing of Mary of Guise, who was governing as regent in the name of her daughter Mary, Queen of Scots. When Mary was later imprisoned for her alleged role in the murder of her husband Knox advocated her execution. Lang recognised Knox's importance in Scottish history, but regarded him as violent and unscrupulous. His biography of Knox appeared in 1905.

Lamb, Charles (1775–1834). Essayist, best known for the children's book *Tales from Shakespeare* (1807), which he produced with his sister, Mary (1764–1847). He wrote for Leigh Hunt's publications and was part of the circle of Romantic poets and critics. He was a regular contributor to the *London Magazine* and his critical writings were well-regarded in their time.

Lockhart, John Gibson (1794–1854). Scottish lawyer who became an important critic and translator. He was one of the main contributors to *Blackwood's Edinburgh Magazine*, where he published his attacks on the 'Cockney School': Keats, Hazlitt and Leigh Hunt. His translations of German Romantic theory were influential, as were his essays on German literature. His reputation as a fierce critic was cemented during his long editorship of the *Quarterly Review* (1825–53). Lang became interested in him through Lockhart's biography of Walter Scott, and he declared his own biography *The Life and Letters of John Gibson Lockhart* (2 vols, 1896) a defence of Lockhart's character and reputation.

Longinus Name given to the first-century Greek author of the critical treatise 'On the Sublime'. It identifies the source of poetic greatness in the emotions of the poet. Translated into English in 1652 and into French in 1674, the French version was influential on John Dryden and through him it became a key text in eighteenth-century aesthetics.

Macaulay, Thomas Babington (1800–59). Politician, historian, essayist and reviewer. A 'Whig' historian he presented contemporary British society as the culmination of the natural advance of constitutional government, personal freedom and scientific progress. His *History of England* (1849 and 1855) was a best-seller, bringing him wealth and a peerage. Intended to cover up to 1830, the four volumes had only reached the year1697 when he died.

Mackenzie, Henry (1745–1831). Scottish novelist, playwright, poet and editor who was a strong Tory and fiercely critical of the French Revolution. His popular best-seller was *The Man of Feeling* (1771) a series of sentimental moral scenes depicting the exploitation of a gentle and innocent man in the city. His epistolary novel *Julia de Roubigné* was published, again with some success, in 1777.

Macpherson, James (1736–96). Scottish poet who produced works that appeared to be translations of the work of a previously lost Gaelic epic poet 'Ossian'. Interest in early epic works was high all over Europe at this time and 'Ossian's' work was enthusiastically received by Schiller, Goethe and Napoleon, among others. The authenticity of the poems was questioned almost immediately, most notably by Samuel Johnson, and after Macpherson's death they were found to contain liberal editing of original material gathered in the Highlands and large sections of Macpherson's own invention. The discovery did not diminish their popularity.

Milton, John (1608–74). Poet and political radical. Living during the English Civil War, he was a supporter of republicanism, though he retained a government office (as Latin Secretary) after the restoration of the monarchy. His great work *Paradise Lost* narrates the fall of Satan and of humankind and emphasises the role of free will. It was published in 1667 and is regarded as one of the most important works of English literature.

Moliére (1622–3). Pseudonym of Jean-Baptiste Poquelin, French dramatist and the creator of classical French comedy. His plays courted controversy, receiving adulation from the court and Parisian society and criticism from the Church, secular moralists and professional rivals.

Moore, George (1852–1933). Irish novelist and man of letters. A prolific writer with more than sixty novels to his name, he brought a Naturalist style to his work that he had learned from French authors such as Balzac and Zola. He stood against what he saw as prudery and censorship in literature.

Morris, William (1834–96). Better remembered now as a designer and for his socialist views, he was also a poet and novelist. His literary work drew strongly on the old epics of Northern Europe and, like others of the Pre-Raphaelites, on the romantic version of mediaevalism. While at Oxford Lang admired his work greatly, but his enthusiasm later dimmed.

Pater, Walter (1839–94). Essayist and critic. His theories of art and its relation to life were influential in the development of the Aesthetic movement and on writers like Oscar Wilde. Lang knew Pater at Oxford and received a copy of *Studies in the History of the Renaissance* from him on its publication in 1873.

Poe, Edgar Allan (1809–49). American short story writer, poet and critic, he is best known for his tales of mystery and suspense, as well as for his major contribution to the emergence of both science fiction and the detective story. His 1845 poem 'The Raven' bought him literary celebrity, but financial problems and heavy drinking affected his health and he died in Baltimore at the age of 40. Lang wrote an introduction to *The Poems of Edgar Allen Poe* in 1881.

Pope, Alexander (1688–1744). Largely self-educated son of a Catholic draper, Pope became an important part of eighteenth-century London literary life, collaborating with many other writers and dramatists. His translations of the *Iliad* and the *Odyssey* were much admired and his own poetry drew on classical models. His biting satires on contemporary writers and culture, such as the *Dunciad* (1728) and the *Epistle to Dr Arbuthnot* (1735) involved him in a number of sharp public disputes.

Rabelais François (*c.*1494–*c.*1553). French physician and satirist. He published works on medicine and antiquarianism in Latin, but his comic masterpieces *Gargantua* (1534) and *Pantagruel* (1532) were written in French. The two eponymous giants are exuberant in their appetites and their burlesque adventures mock classical learning and ecclesiastical authority.

Racine, Jean (1639–99). French tragic dramatist whose plays explore the folly of human passions. The English translations of the dramas were in wide circulation but were notoriously poor versions of the originals.

Radcliffe, Ann (1764–1823). More usually referred to by her contemporaries as Mrs Radcliffe, she was one of the early Gothic novelists. Her works, including *A Sicilian Romance* (1790) and *The Mysteries of Udolpho* (1794), were extremely popular and highly remunerative.

Reade, Charles (1814–84). Very well-known and highly regarded novelist in his time, Henry James thought his work better than that of George Eliot. He had a controversial career because of his defence of the frank discussion of social and sexual problems in his novels, such as *The Cloister and the Hearth* (1861) and *Hard Cash* (1863) which were minutely researched in the manner of Zola. He was also accused of plagiarism in his work, especially in *The Wandering Heir* (1875), but his defence was much like Lang's position, that originality was not necessarily a good test, whereas treatment of the material was.

Renan, Joseph Ernst (1823–92). French scholar of ancient Middle Eastern languages and civilisations, he also wrote on other topics and is best known for his influential historical works on early Christianity and his political theories of nationalism and national identity.

Richardson, Samuel (1689–1761). Beginning as a printer and publisher, success in his own writing only came at the age of 51 with *Pamela: Or, Virtue Rewarded* (1740), after which he continued as a novelist with some less successful sequels to *Pamela* and then the better-received *Clarissa: Or the History of a Young Lady* (1748) and *The History of Sir Charles Grandison* (1753). He and his rival writer Henry Fielding are crucial figures in the emergence of the English novel.

Rossetti, Dante Gabriel (1828–82). Painter and one of the founders of the Pre-Raphaelite Brotherhood in 1848. Although more famous for his paintings he was also a poet, notoriously attacked as leader of the 'Fleshly School of Poetry' by the irascible critic Robert Buchanan. Lang was a great admirer of Rossetti's poetry though he also says that this enthusiasm waned later in his life.

Rousseau, Jean-Jacques (1712–78). Swiss-born writer and philosopher. His political philosophy influenced the French Revolution and was highly significant for Romantic poets and novelists. His novel *Émile* (1762) set out the ideal education for children and was formative of Romantic ideas of childhood as a natural and ideal state corrupted by faulty civilisation. His sentimental novel *Julie, or the New Heloise* (1761) was also important and both books were the source of considerable controversy when published.

Ruskin, John (1819–1900). The most powerful and influential writer on art and architecture in the Victorian period, Ruskin was a champion of the Pre-Raphaelites. He also wrote on politics, economics and social issues, strongly advocating heroic, feudal and Christian ideals against what he saw as the soulless false progress of his times. After his odd and controversial lectures as Professor of Art at Oxford in the 1880s he became isolated and disappeared from public life.

Sainte-Beuve, Charles Augustin (1804–69). French literary historian and critic, his articles 'Causeries du lundi' published every week in Parisian newspapers between 1849 and 1869 were the model for Lang's 'At the Sign of the Ship' column in *Longman's Magazine*. They were a mixture of literary criticism, biographical notes, social comment and wider interests. He held a seat in Napoleon III's senate, but continued to defend ideas of free speech.

Scott, Walter (1771–1832). Scott wrote in different genres but is generally regarded as having established the historical novel as a form. He was deeply interested in traditional Scottish culture and was important in collecting and preserving old ballads and stories of the Border country, many of which feature in his works. He was a prolific writer, beginning with verse and then publishing the first of his many novels, *Waverley*, in 1817. Lang was devoted to Scott's work and shared his conservative and Jacobite views as well as claiming a common ancestor with him from his own Border lineage.

Shakespeare, William (1564–1616). Playwright and poet who has, since the late eighteenth century, been almost universally regarded as the greatest and most important writer in the history of English literature. Lang persisted in spelling his name 'Shakspeare', which is one of the variants found in contemporary references to him, and wrote a series of fourteen essays on the Comedies for *Harper's* magazine. During the nineteenth century, as the adulation of Shakespeare grew, a question as to whether he was the author of the plays also arose. Although only a few people persisted in the speculation and the general consensus was then, as now, that Shakespeare existed and was the author of the works, the 'authorship question' produced a huge amount of literature. Lang's contribution, as well as in shorter pieces, was *Shakespeare, Bacon and the Great Unknown* (Longmans, Green and Co., 1912), where he is firmly against the sceptics.

Shelley, Mary (1797–1851). Daughter of the political radicals William Godwin and Mary Wollstonecraft and wife of the poet Percy Bysshe Shelley, Mary was also a writer. By far her most well-known work is *Frankenstein* (1818), but she also produced other novels, short stories, biographies and travel writing as well as editions of her husband's work.

Shelley, Percy Bysshe (1792–1822). Poet and husband of the writer Mary Shelley, he is now regarded as being among the most important English poets but during his short lifetime, while appreciated by some critics, he was more widely thought a dangerous radical in both style and political views. His poetry varies in form, length and subject matter though often represents oppression and injustice and embraces freedom and liberty.

Smollet, Tobias (1721–71). Scottish, originally in the medical profession, he travelled widely including a period in the navy in the West Indies. Financially insecure, he became a surgeon in London, where he then became involved in literary circles, publishing his first novel *The Adventures of Roderick Random* in 1748. This, like his subsequent works, was successful but his caustic and often libellious writings involved him in many public feuds, notably with the writer Henry Fielding. Editor of the *Critical Review* from 1756 to 1763, he carried on his assaults and was actually imprisoned for libel in 1760. Lang enjoyed the picaresque style and humour of Smollet's novels.

Sophocles (496 BCE–406 BCE). Greek playwright of whose plays only seven survive, but which are regarded among the great works of Western literature. The 'Theban Plays', *Oedipus Rex*, *Oedipus at Colonus* and *Antigone* have long been the source of inspiration, imitation and analysis for writers and commentators, not least Sigmund Freud who derived his description of the Oedipus Complex from Sophocles' work.

Southey, Robert (1774–1843). Romantic poet and writer, a contemporary of Wordsworth and Coleridge but never as celebrated, despite being Poet Laureate for thirty years. He was a prolific writer, producing letters, essays, translations, biographies, histories and a version of the Goldilocks story.

Sterne, Laurence (1713–68). Vicar of a Yorkshire parish, he passed his duties over to his curate after the hostile reception of an ecclesiastical satire he had written. He published the first volumes of *The Life and Opinions of Tristram Shandy, Gentleman* in 1759 and then moved to London where he was celebrated in society though unpopular with other writers. The style of his novel, which parodies the conventions of the form even as they are emerging, has made him much admired by later experimental writers. Lang liked Sterne's work, as he did that of Fielding and Smollett, often discussing them together.

Stevenson, Robert Louis (1850–94). Born in Edinburgh and trained for the profession of law, Stevenson was drawn to writing from an early age. He wrote some plays including *Deacon Brodie* (1880) the story of which would become part of the inspiration for his best-known work *The Strange Case of Dr Jekyll and Mr Hyde* (1886). His first novel, *Treasure Island* (1883) made him famous and those that followed, such as *Kidnapped* (1886) and *The Master of Ballantrae* (1889) were equally popular. He and Lang knew each other and when Stevenson left Britain to live in the South Seas to improve his health, Lang continued to send him ideas and material for novels.

Stuart, Charles Edward (1720–88). More often called Bonnie Prince Charlie or The Young Pretender, Charles Edward Stuart was the second Jacobite claimant to the thrones of England, Scotland, and Ireland. He was the eldest son of James Stuart, himself the son of King James VII and II. Charles was the instigator of the unsuccessful Jacobite uprising of 1745 (the 'Forty Five), an attempt to restore his family to the throne of the Kingdom of Great Britain. It ended in defeat at the Battle of Culloden and Charles fled into exile and remained there until his death, although he continued to be involved in plans for the invasion of Britain. The dramatic circumstances of his escape after Culloden contributed much to the romantic and heroic image of him that persisted despite his later decline. Lang's biography of Charles discusses the myth of Bonnie Prince Charlie and Lang, a Jacobite by inclination, often expressed his disappointment in Charles' personal failings.

Stuart, Mary (1542–87). More often called Mary, Queen of Scots, Mary Stuart was Mary I of Scotland from December 1542 to July 1567. She was also queen consort of France from July 1559 to December 1560 during her brief first marriage to the Dauphin, later King Francis II. As the only surviving legitimate child of King James V of Scotland, she became queen at only 6 days old, but spent most of her childhood in France, returning to Scotland in 1561. She married her cousin, Henry Stuart, Lord Darnley, with whom she had a son, but when Darnley was murdered she was suspected of involvement in his death and later married James Hepburn, 4th Earl of Bothwell, who had been tried for the murder. Their marriage was unpopular with the Scottish nobility and after an uprising Mary was forced to abdicate in favour of her son James, then one year old. She fled to England hoping for the protection of her cousin Elizabeth I but as she represented a challenge to Elizabeth's rule though her own claim to Elizabeth's throne she was not allowed liberty. Kept in various houses and castles for eighteen years, Mary was the focus of a number of plots to overthrow Elizabeth and was eventually found guilty of plotting her assassination and executed. The questions about Mary's involvement in Darnley's murder and plots against Elizabeth have never been resolved and Lang spent much time pursuing possible evidence during the writing of his biography of her.

Swift, Jonathan (1667–1745). Irish writer, sometimes referred to as Dean Swift because of his position as Dean of St Patrick's, Dublin. His most famous work is *Gulliver's Travels* (1726), but he was a prolific writer of both fiction and non-fiction. He was vigorous in his political opinions, publishing many treatises and pamphlets, especially on Irish issues. His *A Modest Proposal* (1729) satirically suggested that children of the poor should be fattened up to feed the rich as a solution to Irish poverty. He often visited London and was friendly with writers such as Pope and John Gay.

Swinburne, Charles Algernon (1837–1909). Poet, and also a writer of drama and criticism. He was celebrated, by Tennyson among others, as a gifted poet, but he began to be perceived as a writer of dubious morality, a reputation not helped by his alcoholic and other excesses. At Oxford he was associated with Rossetti and the Pre-Raphaelites and Lang was a devoted admirer of Swinburne's work while at a student there though, as it did with Rossetti, his enthusiasm somewhat waned in later years.

Tennyson, Alfred (1809–92). The most celebrated of Victorian poets, he succeeded Worsdworth as Poet Laureate in 1850. His long poem *In Memoriam* was published in the same year; in it he struggles with despair and religious doubt after the death of his friend. Queen Victoria described it and the Bible as her only comforts after the death of Prince Albert. Tennyson wrote on contemporary subject matter, most famously in 'The Charge of the Light Brigade' (1854) but more often drew on Arthurian legend and classical myth in his poetry. He was elevated to the peerage in 1884, but his great reputation was beginning to wane by that time and was at a low ebb at his death. Lang regarded Tennyson as the greatest poet of the century.

Thackeray, William Makepeace (1811–63). Trained for the law, he never practiced but became a journalist instead, working in London and in Paris. From the 1830s he was a regular contributor to periodicals; his novel *Vanity Fair* was published in serial form 1847–8 and followed by many others. Becky Sharp, the vivacious but unprincipled heroine of V*anity Fair*, was a favourite character of Lang's, who also liked Thackeray's other novels and his depictions of journalism and journalists.

Theocritus (*c.*300 BCE–*c.*260 BCE) Greek poet, important in the creation of the characteristics of pastoral poetry. Because he wrote in a dialect of Greek he was relatively neglected until the eighteenth century and even then poets tended to take Virgil as their model in writing works in the pastoral style.

Tolstoy, Lev Nikolayevich (1828–1910). A Russian author, he is best known as one of the greatest exponents of the nineteenth-century realist novel, chiefly on the basis of his two longest works *War and Peace* (1869) and *Anna Karenina* (1877). Influenced by Schopenhauer's writings, he also came to espouse a Christian asceticism and anarchistic philosophy of non-violence that was to have some influence on a number of twentieth-century political thinkers including Mahatma Gandhi. Lang did not like his work.

Trollope, Anthony (1815–82). Trollope worked as a civil servant in the Post Office for many years, and continued to do so even after his novels became successful. *The Warden* (1850) was the first of the 'Barsetshire' series. That, and the 'Palliser' series that followed, dealt with the professional middle classes, the church, the aristocracy and their concerns in sweeping depictions of political and social life. Methodically writing every day Trollope was prolific, producing more than forty novels as well as stories, biography and travel books.

Virgil (70 BCE–19 BCE). Regarded by the Romans as their greatest poet, mainly for his epic the *Aeneid* which recounts Rome's legendary foundation. The *Aeneid* became one of the central texts of a classical education after the Renaissance.Virgil also wrote the pastoral *Eclogues* and the *Georgics*, which mixes instructions for running a farm with mythological elements.

Walpole, Horace (1717–97). Fourth Earl of Orford and son of the politician Sir Robert Walpole. An MP himself for many years, he also rebuilt his family's house at Strawberry Hill in south London as an imitation Gothic castle. Writing in various genres, he is most well known for the authorship of the first Gothic novel *The Castle of Otranto* (1764) and for having been involved with Thomas Chatterton's forgeries.

Wordsworth, William (1770–1850). With Coleridge, Wordsworth produced *Lyrical Ballads* (1798), a landmark in English Romanticism and in English poetry in general. The early friendship of the two poets was productive, though they later became estranged as Coleridge's health deteriorated. Wordsworth's early revolutionary idealism also waned and he became increasingly conservative and more simplistically patriotic, attacked as dull by Byron and Shelley and later by Browning whose poem 'The Lost Leader' laments Wordsworth's loss of ideals.

Zola, Émile (1840–1902). French writer, the leading figure in the development of Naturalism, a style which emphasised fidelity to the details of human existence, however unpalatable, in novels. Zola prepared his novels through minute research, his 'documents', and regarded his method as scientific. His huge Rougon-Macquart series employs theories of heredity and degeneration in tracing the fortunes of several generations of one family in modern France. Though he had many admirers and imitators both in France and the rest of Europe, his work was controversial and in England his publisher was imprisoned for obscenity. Zola was the author of the famous 'J'accuse' letter in the French press that defended Alfred Dreyfus against the miscarriage of justice that had taken place and was obliged to spend a year in London to avoid imprisonment for libel. Lang regarded Zola's work as emblematic of everything that he disliked in a novel, though he engaged with it seriously and frequently in such a way as to suggest that he realised its importance.

EXPLANATORY NOTES

General Introduction

1 Henry James to Edmund Gosse, 19 November 1912. *Selected Letters of Henry James to Edmund Gosse 1882–1915*, ed. Rayburn S. Moore (Baton Rouge: Louisiana State University Press, 1988), p. 284.

2 The lectures in his name at St Andrews were stipulated in the will of a Professor of Mathematics at St Salvator and St Leonard, Sir Peter Redford Scott Lang, a friend of Lang's but no relation. They were annual from 1927 until 1934, then more intermittent, given in 1937 and 1939 (which was J. R. R. Tolkein's lecture on fairy stories), 1947–51, 1955, 1956, 1978, 1988, 2004 and revived again for the centenary of Lang's death in 2012.

3 A. Blyth Webster, 'Introduction', *Concerning Andrew Lang: Being the Andrew Lang Lectures Delivered Before the University of St. Andrews 1927–1937, with a Preface by J. B. Salmond and an introduction by A. Blyth Webster* (Oxford: Clarendon Press, 1949), p. xi.

4 George Saintsbury, 'Andrew Lang in the 'Seventies – and After', in Harley Granville-Barker (ed.), *The Eighteen-Seventies: Essays by Fellows of the Royal Society of Literature* (London: Cambridge University Press, 1929). p. 94.

5 Ibid., p. 95.

6 Roger Lancelyn Green calculates that Lang wrote eighty-six reviews for *The Academy* alone between 10 January 1870 and 11 June 1887. Roger Lancelyn Green, *Andrew Lang: A Critical Biography with a Short-title Bibliography of the Works of Andrew Lang* (Leicester: Edmund Ward, 1946), p. 254.

7 The only other attempt at a bibliography seems to have been C. M. Falconer, *The Writings of Andrew Lang M.A., LL.D. Arranged in the Form of a Bibliography with Notes by C.M. Falconer* (Dundee: 1894). A hundred copies were privately printed by Winter, Duncan & Co. Falconer was a Dundee man (Green describes him as a rope-spinner) who had probably a complete collection of Lang's work from 1863 to 1906 when he died in 1907. The collection was sold in one lot, but even the indefatigable Green was not able to locate it. See Green, *Andrew Lang*, p. 196.

8 Written by Douglas Young, recorded on 12 September 1962 and broadcast at 8.45pm on 13 September 1962. The script is in the Roger Lancelyn Green collection in St Andrews University Library. PR4877. ms38257.

9 John Gross, *The Rise and Fall of the Man of Letters* (London: Weidenfeld & Nicolson, 1969), p. 139.

10 Harold Orel, *Victorian Literary Critics* (London: Macmillan, 1984), p. 150.

11 Despite his frequently repeated exhortations to his correspondents to destroy his letters, a very large number remain, mostly in the archives of those correspondents. Demoor's PhD thesis 'Andrew Lang (1844–1912): Late Victorian Humanist and Journalistic Critic: with a Descriptive Checklist of the Lang Letters' (Ghent University, 1983) is in two volumes, the second being a catalogue of the letters. There are discussions of groups of the letters in Demoor, 'Andrew Lang on Gissing: A Late Victorian Point of View', *Gissing Newsletter* 20:2 (April 1984), pp. 23–8; Demoor, 'Andrew Lang's Letters to Edmund Gosse: The Record of a Fruitful Collaboration as Poets, Critics and Biographers', *Review of English Studies* 38:152 (1987), pp. 492–509; Demoor, 'Andrew Lang versus W. D. Howells: A Late Victorian Literary Duel', *Journal of American Studies* 21:3 (December 1987), pp. 416–22; Demoor, 'Andrew Lang's Letters to H. Rider Haggard: the Record of a Harmonious Friendship', *Etudes*

Anglaises 40:3 (1987), pp. 313–22; Demoor, 'Andrew Lang's Causeries 1874–1912', *Victorian Periodicals Review* 21:1 (Spring 1988), pp. 15–22 and Demoor, *Friends Over the Ocean: Andrew Lang's American Correspondents, 1881–1912* (Ghent: Rijksuniversiteit Gent, 1989).

12 This includes the PhD thesis by Antonius De Cocq, 'Andrew Lang: A Nineteenth Century Anthropologist' (University of Utrecht, 1968) and Louise McKinnell's PhD thesis 'Andrew Lang: Anthropologist, Classicist, Folklorist and Victorian Critic' (Toronto, 1993).

13 The only full-length book on Lang other than Green's critical biography is *Andrew Lang* by Eleanor de Selms Langstaff (Boston: Twayne, 1978). It is quite poorly researched and contains many inaccuracies. A special issue of *Romanticism and Victorianism on the Net* 64 (October 2013) http://ravonjournal.org/ appeared in April 2014 containing six articles on Lang.

14 George Gordon, *Andrew Lang* (Oxford: Oxford University Press, 1928), p. 12.

15 James to Edmund Gosse, 19 November 1912. *Selected Letters of Henry James to Edmund Gosse*, p. 285.

16 Margaret Beetham, '"The Agony Aunt, the Romancing Uncle and the Family of Empire": Defining the Sixpenny Reading Public in the 1890s', in Laurel Brake, Bill Bell and David Finkelstein (eds), *Nineteenth-century Media and the Construction of Identities* (Basingstoke: Palgrave, 2000), p. 266.

17 'Introduction' to J. Vyrnwy Morgan, *A Study in Nationality*, see Volume 2, pp. 207–213.

18 This was published in *St Andrews University Magazine* in April 1863.

19 Demoor, 'Andrew Lang', vol. 1, p. 79.

20 Lang never discusses why he chose to give up his Fellowship beyond a single reference where he says 'Things go wrong somehow' in *Adventures Among Books* (London:, Green and Co., 1905), p. 34. He married, but Merton allowed married Fellows to remain in college so this could not have been the reason. For further discussion see Green, *Andrew Lang*, pp. 39–41.

21 Green, *Andrew Lang*, p. 202.

22 This claim is made by J. B. Salmond in *Andrew Lang and Journalism* (Edinburgh: Thomas Nelson, 1951), p. 17.

23 For more detailed discussion see the Introduction to Volume 2.

24 See recollections in for example: H. Rider Haggard, *The Days of My Life: An Autobiography* (London: Longmans, Green and Co., 1926); Max Beerbohm, 'Two Glimpses of Andrew Lang', *Life and Letters* 1:1 (June 1928), pp. 2–13; Richard le Gallienne, *The Romantic Nineties* (London: G. P. Putnam's Sons, 1925); Edmund Gosse, *Portraits and Sketches* (London: William Heinemann, 1912); Rudyard Kipling, *Something of Myself* (London: Macmillan, 1937).

25 Letter to E. H. Coleridge (no year) cited in Demoor, 'Andrew Lang', vol. 1, p. v.

26 Green, *Andrew Lang*, p. ix.

27 Lang to Henry Rider Haggard, 26 April 1892. Roger Lancelyn Green Collection, St Andrews University Library. PR4877. ms38260.

28 Lang to Anna Hills, 31 December [1891]. Roger Lancelyn Green Collection, St Andrews University Library. PR4876. C7.ms3286.

29 See Philip Waller, *Writers, Readers and Reputations: Literary Life in Britain 1870–1918* (Oxford: Oxford University Press, 2006), pp. 456–63 on its formation.

30 Lang to Clement K. Shorter, 13 September [no year is given but from internal evidence it is certainly later than 1897]. Roger Lancelyn Green Collection, St Andrews University Library. PR4867.C7 ms1557.

31 Lang to Haggard, 26 December 1907. Roger Lancelyn Green Collection, St Andrews University Library. PR4877. ms38260.

32 Lang to Sir Oliver Lodge, 12 January [no year], in the archive of the Society for Psychical Research, Manuscripts Collection, University of Cambridge Library. SPR. MS 35/1022.

33 Demoor, *Friends Over the Ocean*, p. 17–18.

34 Green, *Andrew Lang*, p. 206.

35 Ibid., p. 207

36 Lang to Haggard, 2 June 1902, in the Roger Lancelyn Green Collection, St Andrews University Library. PR4877. ms38260.

Introduction to Volume 2

1 A.B.C.D [George Street], 'Some Opinions', *Blackwood's Edinburgh Magazine* 164 (November 1898), p. 593.

2 John Gross, *The Rise and Fall of the Man of Letters* (London: Weidenfeld & Nicolson, 1969), pp. 136, 139.

3 Henry James to Edmund Gosse, 19 November 1912. *Selected Letters of Henry James to Edmund Gosse 1882–1915*, ed. Rayburn S. Moore (Baton Rouge: Louisiana State University Press, 1988), p. 284.

4 Grant Allen, 'The Decay of Criticism', *Fortnightly Review* 31:183 (March 1882), p. 339.

5 Andrew Lang, 'The Art of Fiction', *Pall Mall Gazette* 39:5973 (30 April 1884), p. 1; Robert Louis Stevenson, 'A Humble Remonstrance', *Longman's Magazine* 5:26 (December 1884), pp. 139–47; Henry James, 'The Art of Fiction', *Longman's Magazine* 4:23 (September 1884), pp. 502–21.

6 An anthology of many of these and other essays on the topic can be found in John Charles Olmstead, *The Victorian Art of Fiction: Essays on the Novel in British Periodicals 1870–1900* (New York and London: Garland 1979).

7 James, 'Art of Fiction', p. 502.

8 Andrew Lang, 'The Science of Criticism', this volume, p. 82.

9 Ibid.

10 See for example, 'The Science of Criticism', this volume, p. 82 and 'Of Modern English Poetry', this volume, p. 146.

11 Roger Lancelyn Green, *Andrew Lang; A Critical Biography with a Short-title Bibliography of the Works of Andrew Lang* (Leicester: Edmund Ward, 1946), p. 34.

12 Andrew Lang, *Homer and the Epic* (London and New York: Longmans, Green and Co., 1893), p. 2.

13 Ibid.

14 Matthew Arnold, 'The Function of Criticism at the Present Time', *Essays in Criticism*, (London: Macmillan, 1896), p. 40.

15 Ibid., p. 36.

16 Andrew Lang, 'Poetry and Politics', this volume, p. 56.

17 Andrew Lang, 'At the Sign of the Ship', *Longman's Magazine* 20:119 (September 1892), pp. 545–6.

18 C. A. Sainte-Beuve, *Causeries du Lundi* ii:463 ('Balzac', 2 September 1850). Cited in Chris Baldick, *The Social Mission of English Criticism 1848–1932* (Oxford: Clarendon 1987), p. 11

19 Andrew Lang, 'Politics and Men of Letters', this volume, p. 88.

20 Andrew Lang, 'At the Sign of the Ship', *Longman's Magazine* 7:42 (April 1886), pp. 58–9.

21 Ibid., p. 666.

22 Andrew Lang, 'At the Sign of the Ship', *Longman's Magazine* 9:50 (December 1886), p. 447.

23 Andrew Lang, 'At the Sign of the Ship', *Longman's Magazine* 8:45 (July1886), p. 330–1.

24 Andrew Lang, 'At the Sign of the Ship', *Longman's Magazine* 8:43 (May 1886), p. 106.

25 See discussion in General Introduction, p. 14.

26 Marysa Demoor, *Friends Over the Ocean: Andrew Lang's American Correspondents 188–912* (Ghent: Ruksuniversiteit Gent, 1989), pp. 17–18.

27 Ibid., p. 97.

28 Ibid., p. 102.

29 Lang, 'Poetry and Politics', this volume, p. 60.

30 Ibid., this volume, p. 59.

31 Rudyard Kipling, *Something of Myself* (London: Macmillan, 1937), p. 85.

32 Green, *Andrew Lang*, p. 38.

33 Henry Rider Haggard, 'Two Glimpses of Andrew Lang', *Life and Letters* 1:1 (June 1928), p. 2.

34 Green, *Andrew Lang*, p. ix.

35 Lang to Haggard, 11 February 1891. Roger Lancelyn Green Collection, St Andrews University Library. PR4877. ms38260.

36 Lang to Haggard, 2 June 1902. Roger Lancelyn Green Collection, St Andrews University Library. PR4877. ms38260.

37 Andrew Lang, 'Alfred, Lord Tennyson', *Longman's Magazine* 31:181 (November 1897), p. 30.

38 Lang to Brander Matthews, 7 January1897. Cited in Demoor, *Friends over the Ocean*, p. 133.

39 See also his discussion of biography in 'At the Sign of the Ship', *Longman's Magazine* 28:163 (May 1896), pp. 101–5

40 Andrew Lang, review of Robert Louis Stevenson's *Catriona* in 'At the Sign of the Ship', *Longman's Magazine* 23:133 (November 1893), p. 104.

41 Lang to Anna Hills, 23 March 1893. Andrew Lang Collection in St Andrews University Library. PR 4876.C7. ms3301.

42 Hamilton Clayton, 'On the Trail of Stevenson', *The Bookman* 40 (1914–15), p. 504.

43 There are two brief references to Wilde in letters to Brander Matthews. In one he refers to him in passing as a minor writer, and in the other suggests that Matthews keep Wilde in America, fatten him up and sacrifice him to a recently disgraced politician. See Demoor, *Friends over the Ocean*, pp. 34, 120.

44 Hood sent Wilde a copy of Lang's *Aucassin and Nicolette* (1887) in 1888, which Hood had illustrated. Hood then illustrated Wilde's *The Happy Prince*. See Wilde to Hood, 20 January 1888. *The Complete Letters of Oscar Wilde*, eds Merlin Holland and Rupert Hart-Davis (London: Fourth Estate, 2000), p. 340.

45 Robert Buchanan, 'The Modern Young Man as Critic', *Universal Review* 13 (March 1889), pp. 353–72 Lang's response is 'Mr Buchanan's Young Man', *St. James's Gazette* (10 April 1889), pp. 3–4 and later, 'The Young Men', *Contemporary Review* 65 (February 1894), pp. 177–88.

46 Lionel Trilling, *Matthew Arnold* (New York, W. W. Norton, 1939), p. 90.

47 He refers to Hegel extensively in relation to science in *The Making of Religion* (London: Longmans, Green and Co., 1898) and in *Adventures Among Books* he says 'Hegel we knew in lectures and translations.' (London: Longmans, Green and Co., 1905), p. 39.

48 Andrew Lang, 'The Influence of Mr Jowett', *Illustrated London News* 107:2938 (10 August 1895), p. 175.

49 Lang remarks on Hegel and evolution in *Adventures Among Books*, p. 39 and on Green's lectures on Hegel at Oxford in 'Human Personality After Death', vol. 1, p. 302.

50 Among them: 'Homer and His Recent Critics', *Fortnightly Review* 1:00 (April 1875), pp. 575–89, 'Prof. Max Müller on Homer', *The Academy* 309 (6 April 1878), p. 302, 'Mr Mahaffy, Mr Paley and The Age of Homer', *The Academy* 357 (8 March 1879), pp. 216–17, 'Anthropology and Ancient Literature', *The Academy* 566 (10 March 1883) see Volume 1, pp. 168–9,'Life in Homer's Time', *Good Words* 326 (January 1891), pp. 529–35, and 'Homer and the Higher Criticism', *National Review* 18:108 (February 1892), pp. 758–70.

51 Andrew Lang, *Homer and his Age* (London: Longmans, Green and Co., 1906), p. 51.

52 Andrew Lang, *Homer and the Epic* (London and New York: Longmans, Green and Co., 1893), p. vii. He remarked that he did not re-publish the earlier volumes as the state of the scholarship had moved on, see Lang, *Homer and his Age*, p. xii.

53 G. W. F. Hegel, *Hegel's Aesthetics*, trans T. M. Knox, 2 vols (Oxford: Clarendon, 1973), vol. II, p. 1049.

54 Ibid., vol. II p. 1050.

55 Ibid., vol. II, p. 1110.

56 Ibid,, vol. II, p. 1092.

57 Andrew Lang, 'Literary Anodynes', this volume, p. 104

58 Lang, *Homer and the Epic*, p. 7.

59 See for example, Margaret Beetham, 'The Agony Aunt, the Romancing Uncle and the Family of Empire: Defining the Sixpenny Reading Public in the 1890s', in Laurel Brake, Bill Bell and David Finkelstein (eds), *Nineteenth-century Media and the Construction of Identities* (Basingstoke: Palgrave, 2000), p. 266.

60 Hegel, *Aesthetics*, vol. II, p. 1045.

61 Andrew Lang, 'Romance and the Reverse', this volume, p. 113.

62 George W. Stocking, *After Tylor: British Social Anthropology 1888–1951* (London: Athlone 1996), p. 52.

63 Hegel, *Aesthetics*, vol. II, p. 1093.

64 Andrew Lang, *The Author* 2 (July 1891). Cited in Demoor, 'Andrew Lang', vol. 1, p. 281.

65 Lang, 'Literary Anodynes', this volume, p. 105.

66 Andrew Lang, 'Émile Zola', this volume, p. 136.

67 Andrew Lang, 'An Apology for M. Zola', *Illustrated London News* 104:2864 (10 March 1894), p. 294.

68 Andrew Lang, 'At the Sign of the Ship', *Longman's Magazine* 41:241 (November 1902), p. 93.

69 Ibid.

70 Lang, 'Émile Zola', this volume, p. 138.

71 Ibid., this volume, p. 141.

72 Stevenson in 'A Gossip on Romance' in *Longman's Magazine* 1:1 (November 1882), pp. 69–79 and Haggard in 'About Fiction' *Contemporary Review* 51 (February 1887), pp. 172–80. For further discussion of the plagiarism dispute, and for Corelli's part in it, see Nathan K. Hensley, 'What is a Network (and Who is Andrew Lang?)', *Romanticism and Victorianism on the Net* 64 (October 20130 http://ravonjournal.files.wordpress.com /2011 /11/ravon64art04henville4.pdf .

73 W. D. Howells, *Criticism and Fiction*, ed. C. M and R. Kirk, (New York: New York University Press, 1959), p. 381. For a longer account of the contest with Howells see Marysa Demoor,'Andrew Lang versus W. D. Howells: A Late-Victorian Literary Duel', *Journal of American Studies* 21:3 (December 1987), pp. 416–22.

74 Andrew Lang, 'Science and Superstition', see Volume 1, p. 207.

75 Andrew Lang, 'Anthropology and Religion' II, see Volume 1, p. 246.

76 Andrew Lang, 'On A Certain Condescension in Scientific Men', *Illustrated London News* 106:2917 (16 March 1895).

77 Andrew Lang, 'Ghosts Up To Date', see Volume 1, p. 259.

78 Andrew Lang, 'M. Zola on Lourdes', *Illustrated London News* 105:2893 (29 September 1894), p. 407.

79 Andrew Lang, 'Behind the Novelist's Scenes', this volume, p. 167.

80 Andrew Lang, 'The Mystery of Style', this volume, p. 170.

81 Andrew Lang, 'The Evolution of Literary Decency', this volume, p. 116.

82 Ibid., this volume, p. 120.

83 Andrew Lang, 'Realism and Romance', this volume, p. 97.

84 Andrew Lang, 'At the Sign of the Ship', *Longman's Magazine* 27:160 (February 1896), p. 83.

85 Andrew Lang, *Letters to Dead Authors* (London; Longmans, Green and Co., 1886), p. 83.

86 R. S. Rait, 'Andrew Lang', *Quarterly Review* 218:435 (April 1913), p. 299.

87 Lang to Haggard [undated but from internal evidence probably from 1892]. Roger Lancelyn Green Collection, St Andrews University Library. PR4877. ms38260.

88 Andrew Lang, 'As You Like It', *Harper's New Monthly Magazine* 82:487 (December 1890), p. 4.

89 Andrew Lang, 'Mr Robert Browning', *Contemporary Review* 60 (July 1891), p. 71.

90 Lang's review appeared in the *New Review*'s 'Literature' column. Several other books are noted by Lang before *Tess* and his review is quite short, see *New Review* 6:3 (February 1892), pp. 247–9.

91 Hardy to Edward Clodd, 4 February 1892. *The Collected Letters of Thomas Hardy*, ed. Richard Little Purdy and Michael Milgate (Oxford: Clarendon, 1978), vol. 1, p. 257.

92 Green, *Andrew Lang*, p. 170.

93 Lang to Stevenson, 28 November [1892]. Yale University, Beinecke Library, PR4877 A47 1990.

94 Andrew Lang, 'At the Sign of the Ship', *Longman's Magazine* 21:121, (November 1892), pp. 100–6.

95 Andrew Lang, 'Notes on Fiction', this volume, p. 160.

96 Ibid., this volume, p. 164.

97 Lang, 'Realism and Romance', this volume, p. 100.

98 Henry Rider Haggard, *King Solomon's Mines* (Oxford: Oxford University Press, 1989), p. 9.

99 Cited in Green, *Andrew Lang*, p. 115.

100 Lang, 'High Gods of Low Races' from 'On Religion', see Volume 1, p. 197.

101 Cyprian Blagden, 'Longman's Magazine', *A Review of English Literature* 4:2 (April 1963), p. 10.

102 Julia Reid. '"King Romance" in *Longman's Magazine*: Andrew Lang and Literary Populism', *Victorian Periodicals Review* 44:4 (Winter 2011), p. 361.

103 Beetham, 'The Agony Aunt', p. 266.

104 Andrew Lang, 'Mr Buchanan's Young Man', *St. James's Gazette* (10 April 1889), pp. 3–.4

105 Andrew Lang, 'A Note on Footnotes', *The Pilot* 23 (February 1901), p. 244.

106 Andrew Lang, 'At the Sign of the Ship', *Longman's Magazine* 38:223 (May 1901), p. 95.

107 Beetham, 'Agony Aunt', p. 264.

108 See Lang's chapter 'The Old Degeneration Theory' in *The Making of Religion* (London: Longmans, Green and Co., 1898), pp. 278–93. For discussion of Lang's valuing of 'primitive' culture, see also Roger Luckhurst, 'Knowledge, Belief and the Supernatural at the Imperial Margin', in Nicola Bown, Carolyn Burdett and Pamela Thurschwell (eds), *The Victorian Supernatural* (Cambridge: Cambridge University Press, 2004), pp. 197–216.

109 See for example, Andrew Lang, 'At the Sign of the Ship', *Longman's Magazine* 15:85 (November 1889), pp. 106–12.

110 Lang, 'The Science of Criticism', this volume, p. 81.

111 Andrew Lang, 'Literature as a Trade,' *St. James's Gazette* (22 October 1890), p. 5.

112 Andrew Lang, *How to Fail in Literature*, this volume, p. 276.

113 Ibid., this volume, p. 277.

114 Andrew Lang, 'At the Sign of the Ship', *Longmans Magazine* 31:183 (December 1897), p. 275.

115 See Philip Waller, *Writers, Readers and Reputations: Literary Life in Britain 1870–1918* (Oxford: Oxford University Press, 2006), pp. 456–63 on its formation.

116 Lang to James Donaldson, 3 July 1889 and 23 July 1889. Roger Lancelyn Green Collection, St Andrews University Library. PR4867.C7 ms 1684.

117 Andrew Lang, 'The Merton Professorship', *The Academy* 685 (20 June 1885), pp. 438–9.

118 Green, *Andrew Lang*, p. 202.

119 Waller, *Writers, Readers and Reputations*, p. 475.

120 John Churton Collins, *The Study of English Literature* (London: Macmillan, 1891). Lang's response is 'The Teaching of English Literature', this volume, pp. 298–301.

121 Baldick, *Social Mission*, p. 74.

122 Ibid., p. 80.

123 Ibid., p. 81.

124 Quiller Couch certainly admired Lang; in his own causerie in the *Pall Mall Magazine* he wrote that Lang was the finest prose stylist of the decade. A. T. Quiller Couch, 'From a Cornish Window', *Pall Mall Magazine* 12 (July 1897), p. 424.

125 Andrew Lang, 'The Teaching of English Literature', this volume, p. 301.

126 Andrew Lang, 'Examinations in Fiction', *Cornhill Magazine* 83 (January 1901), pp. 80–9.

127 John Hill Burton, *History of Scotland,* 8 vols (Edinburgh: William Blackwood, 1853), vol. 3, p. 433.

128 Andrew Lang, *A Short History of Scotland* (London and Edinburgh: William Blackwood and Sons, 1911), p. 294.

129 Andrew Lang, 'The Celtic Renascence', this volume, p. 188.

130 Andrew Lang, *A History of Scotland: From the Roman Occupation*, 4 vols (Edinburgh: William Blackwood, vol. 1, 1900; vol. 2, 1902, vol. 3, 1904; vol. 4, 1907), vol. 1, p. 18.

131 Lang to Henry Newbolt, 29 December [1903]. Roger Lancelyn Green collection, St Andrews University Library. PR4877. ms38239/3/22.

132 John Buchan, *Andrew Lang and the Border* (Oxford: Oxford University Press, 1933), p. 19.

133 R. S. Rait, *Andrew Lang as Historian* (Oxford: Oxford University Press, 1930), p. 19.

134 Andrew Lang, *Prince Charles Edward Stuart* (London, New York and Bombay: Longmans, Green and Co., 1903), p. 4.

135 Lang to Herbert Maxwell, 13 March [no year]. National Library of Scotland. Acc 7043/HEM 30.

136 Lang to Mary Maxwell-Scott, Nov 14 [1897]. National Library of Scotland. mss 1632–3.

137 Marysa Demoor, 'Andrew Lang (1844–1912): Late Victorian Humanist and Journalistic Critic: with a Descriptive Checklist of the Lang Letters', unpublished PhD thesis, 2 vols (Ghent: Ghent University, 1983), vol. 1., p. 58.

138 William Croft Dickinson, *Andrew Lang, John Knox and Scottish Presbyterianism* (Edinburgh: Thomas Nelson, 1952), p. 29.

139 Lang to Herbert Maxwell, June 3 [1900]. National Library of Scotland. Acc 7043/ HEM30.

140 Lang to Maxwell, May [2? no year]. National Library of Scotland. Acc 7043/HEM30.

141 Robert S. Rait, *Andrew Lang as Historian* (London: Oxford University Press, 1930), p. 13.

142 Andrew Lang, 'The Voices of Jeanne d'Arc', *Proceedings of the Society for Psychical Research* 11(1895), pp. 198–212.

143 Andrew Lang, 'The Three Seeresses (1880–1900, 1424–1431)', see Volume 1, pp. 284–91.

144 Andrew Lang, 'M. Anatole France on Jeanne d'Arc', this volume, p. 239.

145 The others are 'How the Maid Marched to Blois' and 'Jeanne d'Arc', both in *New Collected Rhymes* (London: Longmans, Green and Co., 1904).

146 Andrew Lang, *Ban and Arrière Ban: A Rally of Fugitive Rhymes* (London: Longmans, Green and Co., 1894), p. 118.

147 Andrew Lang, *The Story of Joan of Arc* (London: T. C and E. C. Jack, 1906), p. 1.

148 Andrew Lang, *The Maid of France: Being the Story of the Life and Death of Jeane D'Arc*, this volume, p. 258.

149 Andrew Lang, 'A Scot to Jeanne d'Arc' in *Ban and Arrière Ban*, p. 1.

1 CRITICS AND CRITICISM

'Poetry and Politics', *Macmillan's Magazine* (December 1885)

1 *Paul de Saint Victor forgives him*: Victor Hugo supported the revolution of the Paris Commune in 1871; Paul de St. Victor (1827–81), Hugo's contemporary and fellow-countryman, published a book on the Commune *Barbares et Bandites* in 1871, a work whose title indicates his disapproval.

2 *Jeffrey's*: Francis, later Lord, Jeffrey, (1773–1850), Scottish judge and literary critic, editor of the *Edinburgh Review,* an important journal of political and literary criticism in the early nineteenth century.

3 *'The Liberal Movement in English Literature'*: William John Courthope, *The Liberal Movement in English Literature* (London: John Murray, 1885). Courthope (1842–1917) was a poet and critic, later Professor of Poetry at Oxford, so in these fields he was a direct contemporary and competitor of Lang's. His poetry was well received, especially the work that Lang later mentions, *The Paradise of Birds* (1870).

4 *'no language but a Cry'*: quotation from Alfred Tennyson's poem, *In Memoriam* (poem LIV, line 20), though Lang capitalises 'Cry' where Tennyson's original does not.

5 *Cardinal Newman*: John Henry Newman (1801–90). A leading figure in the Oxford Movement, dedicated to the restoration of Catholic elements of worship in the Church of England, Newman converted to Catholicism in 1845 and was later appointed a Cardinal by Pope Leo XIII. His religious writings were central to countering English anti-Catholicism during the nineteenth century.

6 *'Life … imagination'*: Courthope, *Liberal Movement*, p. 38.

7 *Mr Burke's*: Edmund Burke (1729–97). Irish philosopher, political theorist and Whig politician. Politically, he is best known for his opposition to the French Revolution, set out in his 1790 *Reflections on the Revolution in France*, which, in its defence of tradition over abstract rights, became a major influence on British Conservatism

8 *How many leagues … of the Legislature?*: Courthope, *Liberal Movement* pp. 52–3.

9 *deceased wife's … three acres.'*: 'Three acres and a cow' was a slogan used by land reform campaigners of the 1880s; the deceased wife's sister is one of the list of relatives to whom marriage was forbidden (the 'prohibited degrees'). Late nineteenth-century campaigns around the latter led to the allowing of such marriages by the Deceased Wife's Sister's Marriage Act of 1907. Lang means to suggest prosaic and legalistic language.

10 *Black Prince and General Gordon*: Edward 'The Black Prince' (1330–76) was a renowned military leader who died before ascending to the throne of his father, Edward III. Charles George Gordon (1833–85) was a British army officer who died in the siege of Khartoum and who became a popular figure of Victorian imperial heroism.

11 *Donne … the rest*: John Donne (1572–1631), Richard Crashaw (1612/3–49), and Abraham Cowley (1618–67) were all 'Metaphysical' poets. By 'the rest' Lang presumably means others associated with this style such as George Herbert (1593–1633) and Andrew Marvell (1621–78). They were regarded as lacking feeling in their work, concentrating rather on 'nice speculations of philosophy' as Dryden described it, and hence Lang's opposing their style to the romantic.

12 *Mr. Chamberlain*: Joseph Chamberlain (1836–1914) was a prominent Liberal politician. At the time of Lang's writing he was President of the Board of Trade in William

Gladstone's government, though he resigned in the following year (1886) because of his opposition to Gladstone's policy of support for Irish Home Rule.

13 *'revival...in our literature'*: Courthope, *Liberal Movement*, p. 238.

14 *Marcus Aurelius:* (121 CE–180 CE), Emperor of Rome 161 to 180 and considered one of the most important Stoic philosophers. His book *Meditations*, written between 170 and 180, is a series of short philosophical reflections.

15 *'kind Hunt's'*: referring to James Leigh Hunt. The phrase comes from the second line of Keats' poem, 'Written on the day that Mr. Leigh Hunt left Prison' (1817).

16 *Jesse Collings*: Jesse Collings (1831–1920), a Liberal MP and advocate of educational and land reform.

17 *Pharisaical*: meaning narrow-minded and hypocritical, derived from reference to the Pharisees, a Jewish sect criticised by Jesus in biblical accounts.

18 *amused the people*: Courthope, *Liberal Movement*, p. 122.

19 *Prometheus ... cave*: reference to act 3 of Shelley's long poetic drama *Prometheus Unbound* (1820) in which Prometheus has been reunited with his beloved Asia after his liberation from eternal punishment.

20 *'the abysmal depths of personality'*: the phrase appears to come originally from St Augustine's *City of God*, written in the fifth century, where he writes of 'abyssus humanae conscientiae', which is variously translated, but frequently as 'the abysmal (sometimes spelt 'abyssmal') depths of personality' (*Confessions* 2, 2). It is often used without reference to Augustine. Tennyson, for example, in *The Palace of Art* (1842) refers to the 'absymal deeps of personality' and it is a phrase that Lang frequently repeats.

21 *many mansions*: 'In my father's house there are many mansions' (John 14:2). This biblical quotation is often used, as Lang does here, to suggest that many different views or opinions can be accommodated.

22 Stet pro ratione voluntas: Latin, a partial and slightly inaccurate quotation from the Roman satirist Juvenal: '*Hoc volo, sic jubeo, sit pro ratione voluntas*', which translates as 'I will it, I insist on it. Let my will stand rather than reason'.

23 *'The matter... perception'*: Courthope, *Liberal Movement*, p. 93.

24 *'the test ... the first water'*: from Charles Algernon Swinburne's essay, 'Byron and Wordsworth', which was published in *Nineteenth Century* in April 1884, but Lang is repeating here Courthope's quotation of Swinburne on p. 15 of *The Liberal Movement in English Literature.*

25 *'the most sublime passages ... elements.'*: Courthope, *Liberal Movement*, p. 18.

26 *'only proves ... the poetry of the two latter'*: Courthope, *Liberal Movement*, p. 204.

27 quod semper, quod ubique, quod ab omnibus: Latin, translates as 'that which has always been believed, everywhere and by everyone'.

28 Kalevala: an epic Finnish poem based upon traditional Karelian songs published by Elias Lönrot in two versions in 1835 and (substantially expanded) 1849. The Finnish title Kalewala is now commonly rendered in English as Kalevala. Lang's notes in *Myth, Ritual and Religion,* 2 vols (2nd edition, London: Longmans, Green and Co., 1899), vol. 1, p. 59 suggest that he was working from a French translation (titled

Kalewala) made by Léouzon le Duc in *La Finlande* (Paris: Jules Labitte, 1845). The first complete translation of the Kalevala into English was published by John Martin Crawford in 1888, four years after Lang wrote this introduction.

29 *Runoia*: a bard in the Finnish epic *The Kalevala*. See note 28 above.

30 volkslieder: German, 'folk-songs'.

31 *Ronsard and Joachim du Bellay*: Pierre de Ronsard (1524–85) and Joachim du Bellay (*c.*1522–60) were French Renaissance poets, together regarded as having founded a revival of poetry in the French language.

32 *Cowper and Gray:* William Cowper (1731–1800) and Thomas Gray (1716–71), poets whose work moved away from the prevailing neo-classical style towards concerns with emotion and the sublime that presage Romanticism.

33 *Heine*: Heinrich Heine (1797–1830). German poet, literary critic and journalist. One of the most important and radical German poets of the nineteenth century.

34 *Edda*: collection of poems and prose from the Icelandic oral tradition, first written down in the thirteenth century. The Eddas (the Poetic Edda and the Prose Edda) are the main source of knowledge of Norse mythology. Lang would have been familiar with them from his studies of folklore.

35 quod semper, quod ubique, quod ab omnibus: see note 27, above.

36 *late Rector of Lincoln College*: Mark Pattison, who died in 1884, had been a literary scholar. Lang may have known him from his own career at Oxford.

37 '*the element ... styled poets*': quotations not identified.

38 *Chapelain, according to Théophile Gautier*: Jean Chapelain (1595–1674, French critic, poet and a founding member of the Académie française. Gautier wrote a newspaper article on Chapelain in 1835, later collected as part of his book *Les Grotesques* (1856). Chapelain would have been of interest to Lang as his works include *La Pucelle* (1656), an epic poem about Joan of Arc.

39 *Chapman:* George Chapman (?1559–1634), poet, dramatist and translator of the *Iliad* and *Odyssey*. Keats's sonnet 'On First Looking into Chapman's Homer' celebrates the poetic quality of the translations.

40 '*idea of external nature*': Courthope, *Liberal Movement*, p. 239.

41 '*faced nature boldly ... as they felt it*': Courthope, *Liberal Movement*, p. 233.

42 *Fight of Brunanburh ... Thread of Honour*: the Battle of Brunanburh was an English victory in 937 by the army of Æthelstan over the combined armies of Irish and Scottish leaders. Lang is probably referring to the account found in 'The Battle of Brunanburh' in the *Anglo-Saxon Chronicle*. The poem by Michael Drayton (1563–1631) celebrates Henry V's victory over the French in 1415. The 'Revenge' was an English warship involved in an heroic, though doomed, action against the Spanish in 1591, described by Tennyson in his poem. Francis Doyle (1810–88) was Professor of Poetry at Oxford and his work concerns another incident of doomed heroism, this one by a British infantry brigade in1845 after the first Afghan War.

43 *Cavalier poets*: a group of poets who were supporters of Charles I during the English Civil War (1642–51). The best known are Ben Jonson, Robert Herrick, Richard Lovelace, Thomas Carew and Sir John Suckling.

44 *'Chevy Chase,' or 'Kinmont Willie'*: the poem by Thomas Macaulay celebrates the British repulsion of the fleet of the Spanish Armada in1588. 'Chevy Chase' is a traditional English ballad existing in several written versions which describes a skirmish between English and Scottish forces, possibly based on the Battle of Otterburn in 1388. 'Kinmont Willie' is another traditional ballad, telling of a sixteenth-century Scottish border outlaw who made daring raids on English outposts. In the latter two examples, Lang is implying Scottish, rather than British, national pride.

45 *'Battle of the Baltic' ... 'Mariners of England'*: both are patriotic poems published in 1801by Thomas Campbell (1777–1844), who was actually Scottish.

46 *'Loss of the Royal George'*: the ship was lost in an accident in 1782 with more than 800 people killed. William Cowper (1731–1800), the poet also known for his hymn-writing, produced the poem at the time of the accident.

47 *'Lucknow ... Light Brigade'*: poems by Tennyson on British military engagements. Though both describe contemporary battles, 'The Defence of Lucknow' (1879), about the British under siege during the Indian Rebellion of 1857, is markedly more patriotic than 'The Charge of the Light Brigade' (1854), which offers criticism of strategic mistakes made in the engagement during the Crimean War.

48 *'on their border stands'*: Joseph Addison, *The Campaign*, published in 1704 on the Battle of Blenheim which had taken place earlier that year.

49 *stubborn spearsmen still made good*: Sir Walter Scott, *Marmion* (1808), set around the battle of Flodden Field in 1513. The battle was one of the many conflicts between the kingdoms of England and Scotland, but particularly significant because the Scots king, James IV, was killed.

50 *glorious deeds of men*: from Homer, the *Iliad*.

51 *Dieyries and Narrinyeries*: native peoples of Australia.

52 *karakias*: Maori incantations.

53 *Ojibbeways and Malagasies*: respectively, First Nation peoples of Canada and native peoples of Madagascar.

54 *'civilisation ... declines'*: from Thomas Macaulay's *Essay on Milton*, but repeated here from Courthope's quotation, *Liberal Movement*, p. 38.

55 *his capacity ... may be*: Courthope, *Liberal Movement*, p. 31.

56 *Waller*: Edmund Waller (1606–87), poet and politician. He rejected the style of Metaphysical poets and moved towards the more straightforward style, especially heroic couplets, later espoused by poets like Pope.

57 *'rather seem his healing son'*: quotation not identified. Apollo was the god of a number of things for the ancient Greeks, including healing (and plague), music and poetry. He is often depicted with a bow and is the god of archery. Asclepius, one of Apollo's sons, is more narrowly associated with healing and medicine.

58 *anapaests*: technical term for poetic rhythmic device, a metrical foot of two short syllables followed by a long syllable.

'Literary Plagiarism', *Contemporary Review* (June 1887)

1 *Of all forms … society'*: Voltaire (1694–1778) was a French writer of the Enlightenment whose work spoke out against injustice and intolerance and who was imprisoned and exiled for his views. His *Philosophical Dictionary* (1764) has an entry on plagiarism, from which this quotation comes.

2 Pausanias: (*c.*110 CE–180 CE), Greek writer whose long *Description of Greece* apparently describes ancient Greece from personal observations.

3 advocatus Diaboli: Latin, devil's advocate, meaning someone who deliberately argues the opposite point of view without necessarily espousing it.

4 *Homer… Maevius*: Lang lists a number of classical writers, both Greek and Roman, to indicate that literary borrowing is not new. Bavius and Maevius are reputed to be two critics in the time of Augustus Caesar who enviously attacked the achievements of greater writers. There is little known about their real existence but writers like Alexander Pope, and Lang in this instance, use them as emblematic figures of envious spite.

5 *Varro*: There are two Roman writers by this name: Publius Terentius Varro Atacinus (82 BCE–*c.*35 BCE) and Marcus Terentius Varro (116 BCE–27 BCE), sometimes called Varro Reatinus. It is hard to know which Lang means, though Varro Atacinus was better known as a poet and may have been the more familiar.

6 *Gibbon … to prove*: quotation not identified. Lang, who wrote quickly and revised little, sometimes mis-remembers quotations.

7 *'brooms ready-made'*: the origin of the story is difficult to locate, but the most likely source for Lang is Francis Palgrave, whose *Truths and Fictions of the Middle Ages* (London: John Parker, 1837) is concerned with relationship between learning and commerce. The section where the remark appears (p. 113) is about copyright, a topic of great interest to Lang. The next line is an English version of the 'hawk' proverb that Lang uses elsewhere.

8 *Cicero and Seneca*: Marcus Tullius Cicero (106 BCE–43 BCE), Roman politician and orator. Regarded as one of Rome's greatest orators and prose writers, his influence on the Latin language was great, in turn influencing language and prose style after the Renaissance in Europe. Seneca (*c.*4 BCE–65 CE) was also a Roman Stoic writer and statesman, tutor to emperor Nero. He was obliged to commit suicide after being accused of involvement in Nero's murder.

9 *confusion on the thief*: Marcus Valerius Martialis (40 CE–*c.*103 CE), poet known in English as Martial, published his twelve books of *Epigrams* between CE 86 and 103. This, as Lang notes, is number 52 from Book 1.

10 *Tichborne pretender*: the Tichborne case was a Victorian sensation. The heir to the Tichborne title and estates had been lost in a shipwreck in 1854 but in 1866 an Australian butcher claimed to be the missing heir and was accepted as such by Tichborne's mother. Other family members contested him, and after a long series of legal actions, the claimant was imprisoned for fraud 1874. He had been released in 1884, shortly before the publication of this article.

11 *'The Girl of the Period'*: it was written by Eliza Lynn Linton and appeared in March 1868.

12 nom de guerre: pseudonym, from the French 'war name' and derived from the practice of giving new recruits to the army an identifying name other than their own.

13 *retaria*: a retarius was a Roman gladiator who fought armed only with a net, rete being another Latin word for net. Retaria is a feminised form.

14 *Evan Harrington' and 'Richard Feverel'*: both were written by George Meredith (1828–1909), a well-known novelist and man of letters.

15 *literary Perkin Warbeck*: Warbeck (1474–99) claimed to be Richard, Duke of York, son of Edward IV and one of the 'Princes in the Tower' supposedly murdered on the orders of Richard III. Warbeck laid claim to the throne then occupied by Henry VII.

16 *novelist ....Crimean War*: Alexander William Kinglake (1809–91) published his eight-volume *Invasion of the Crimea*, between 1863 and 1887.

17 *Mr. Disraeli's raid ... Saint-Cyr*: Disraeli was found to have 'borrowed' much of his oration at Wellington's funeral in 1852 from the French politician Adolphe Thiers' 1829 eulogy for Marshal Gouvion de Saint-Cyr.

18 curari: now more usually spelt 'curare', a paralysing poison used by native peoples in the Americas on arrows and blow-pipe darts. It became the popular notion of that detective story favourite, the 'untraceable poison'.

19 *Mr. Payn's 'By Proxy'*: James Payn (1830–98), writer and novelist who became editor of the *Cornhill Magazine*. He was a childhood friend of Lang's. His novel *By Proxy* appeared in 1878.

20 *Bekker's 'Charicles'*: Wilhelm Becker (1796–1846) was a German classical scholar and the author of the novel *Charicles* (1840) set in ancient Greece and containing explanatory notes and appendices.

21 *Mr. Thomas Moore*: (1779–1852), Irish poet and writer best remembered for burning Byron's memoirs after his death, but also the author of some briefly popular novels, including *The Epicurean* (1827).

22 *Maspero and Mariette*: Gaston Maspero (1846–1916) was a French archaeologist who succeeded Auguste Mariette (1821–81) as director-general of excavations in Egypt. Lang was deeply interested in archaeology and would have been aware of the most recent discoveries in the field.

23 *Thackeray ... fairy tales*: Anne Isabella Thackeray Ritchie (1837–1919), eldest daughter of William Makepeace Thackeray, published five reworked fairy tales and a fairy-tale inspired story in her collection *Five Old Friends, and a Young Prince* (London: Smith and Elder, 1868).

24 *'Ferdinand's Folly'*: this does not appear to be a real publication.

25 sub luminis oras: Latin 'from the shores of light'. Used in classical literature as an expression meaning to come into being, perhaps Lang is also that suggesting the book has come from America.

26 *'"Daisy's Dream" ... "Psamathöe"'*: neither of these titles appear to refer to real books, but are generic types.

27 *Pisistratus*: the line comes from Ben Jonson's poem 'Song. To Celia' (1616). Pisistratus was a sixth-century BCE Athenian tyrant, whose efforts in poetry were directed towards producing definitive versions of Homer.

28 *Hawthorne's 'Scarlet Letter'*: in Nathaniel Hawthorne's novel, *The Scarlet Letter* (1850) the preacher in a small community finally confesses publically to being the father of the child of the outcast unmarried woman. Hawthorne (1804–64) was an American novelist and short story writer whose works were often set in New England. He was the subject of a book-length critical study by Henry James in 1879.

29 *Gautier and Poe and Eugène Sue*: Théophile Gautier in 'Le Chevalier de Double' in 1863, Edgar Allan Poe in 'William Wilson' (1839) and Eugène Sue in *The Mysteries of Paris* (1842–3).

30 *recent Jubilee Ode*: Lewis Morris, 'A Song of Empire', *Murray's Magazine*, 20 June 1887.

31 *Laureate's verse*: Alfred Tennyson, 'On the Jubilee of Queen Victoria' (1887).

32 *Newdigate*: a poetry prize competition for undergraduates at Oxford University.

33 *Mr. Weller*: Sam Weller, character in Charles Dickens, *The Pickwick Papers* (1837). As Mr Pickwick's servant he becomes involved in the misunderstanding about marriage between Pickwick and his housekeeper.

34 *'Chastelard'*: Swinburne's poem, published in 1865, was about Mary, Queen of Scots.

35 malice prepense*:* French legal term, more usually rendered in English as 'malice aforethought' and meaning planned misdemeanour, as opposed to impulsive action.

36 *Somaise … Chapuzeau*: Lang refers to the reception of Molière's satiric play, *Les Précieuses Ridicules* (1659) and the criticism of it led by Antoine Baudeau de Somaise. Lang edited and wrote an introduction to an edition of Molière's play that was published in 1884.

37 fanfaron: French, meaning braggart or boaster.

38 *Life of Pope*: Robert Carruthers (1799–1878) published several editions of Pope's work and letters. His *Life of Alexander Pope* was published in 1857.

'At the Sign of the Ship', *Longman's Magazine* (July 1887)

1 *'They say … Nicholas of ancient days'*: quotation not identified.

2 *Married Beneath Him:* James Payn, 1876. See this volume, p. 342, n. 19.

3 *Sister Anne* … verdoye: Lang is referring to Charles Perrault's version of the tale of Bluebeard, in which Bluebeard's seventh wife is saved from the fate of the earlier six by the arrival of her brothers, for whom her sister Anne has been watching. The conversation translates thus: 'Anne, my sister Anne, do you see nothing coming?' and the response 'I see nothing but the dappling sun and the grass growing green'.

4 *Woodlanders … Greenwood Tree*: this is a reference to Thomas Hardy and his novels *The Woodlanders* (1887) and *Under the Greenwood Tree* (1872). Lang liked Hardy's early work and the painful disagreement over the review of *Tess of the D'Ubervilles* was still some years away.

5 *Inkosi-kaas*: the name of Umslopogas's axe in Henry Rider Haggard's *Allan Quartermain* (1887).

6 *boy travelling … Rodwell Regis*: all three are relatively recently published books: Sir Charles Wentworth Dilke's *The Fall of Prince Florestan of Monaco* (1874); Thomas Anstey Guthrie (1856–1934), who wrote under the name F. Anstey published *Vice Versa:*

A Lesson to Fathers in 1882 and the boy with the donkey is probably a reference to one of Robert Louis Stevenson's earliest published works, *Travels with a Donkey in the Cévennes* (1879).

7 *Dragoon … d'Artagnan's company*: see this volume, p. 354, n. 36.

8 *watchman … across the isles*: in the opening scene of Aeschylus's play *Agamemnon* the Watchman is waiting to see the beacon that signals Agamemnon's return from the Trojan War.

'At the Sign of the Ship', *Longman's Magazine* (September 1890)

1 *Custer's last fight:* George Armstrong Custer (1839–76), US army officer during the Civil War and the Indian Wars. He was killed at the Battle of the Little Bighorn in a fight against Native American tribes in what has come to be known as Custer's Last Stand.

2 *'senselessly ceevil'*: the origin of this expression is difficult to trace, though it appears in many anecdotes, most of them Scottish, during the nineteenth and early twentieth centuries, and sometimes ascribed to a male speaker. It means unnecessarily polite, even to the point of one's own detriment. It is also an example of the 'extraordinary *voulou* Scots provincialism' that Henry James accused Lang of affecting. (Letter to Edmund Gosse, 19 November 1912 in R. S. Moore (ed.) *Selected Letters of Henry James to Edmund Gosse*, Baton Rouge: Louisiana State University Press, 1988, p. 285.)

3 *'honest enmity … bad reasons'*: William Thackeray, 'Hogarth, Smollet and Fielding', *The English Humourists of the Eighteenth Century* (Chicago: Scott, Forseman and Co., 1912), p. 178.

4 *Marie Bashkirtseff*: painter and writer (1858–84). She was best known for her voluminous diary, entitled in English *I am the Most Interesting Book of All* and published in many volumes during the 1870s.

5 *Scots Thistle* or the *Bungay Beacon:* fictional publications (the latter invented by Thackeray) suggesting provincial newspapers.

6 *Villemain … Halicarnassus:* Abel-François Villemain (1790–1870) was a French politician and writer. Dionysius of Halicarnassus lived in the first century BCE and was a teacher and rhetorician. Lang includes them as very little known authors.

7 *Canon Farrar*: Frederic William Farrar (1831–1903), an Anglican cleric and schoolmaster. His novel *Eric, Or Little By Little* (1858) was recommended as an improving work for children and his *Life of Christ* (1874) was very widely read.

8 *Mr. Gladstone … Wellhausen's*: Julius Wellhausen (1844–1918), was an important German biblical scholar and commentator. The location of Gladstone's remark has not been identified.

'The Science of Criticism', *The New Review* (May 1891)

1 *Homer's works … different authors*: this was an issue of importance to Lang. He argued strongly that Homer was a single author and the writer of all of the *Odyssey* and the *Iliad*. See, for example *Homer and His Age* (London: Longman's, Green and Co., 1906).

2 *Bishop Berkeley or Thomas Moore*: George Berkeley (1685–1753), philosopher, and Thomas Moore (1779–1852), minor poet and entertainer. Lang chooses these two figures to represent opposite ends of the cultural spectrum.

3 *Higher Criticism*: this term originally refers to the work of a group of German biblical scholars including David Friedrich Strauss (1808–74) and Ludwig Feuerbach (1804–72), who began to compare the historical records of the Middle East with the text of the Bible in search of independent confirmation of the events related. It was a somewhat shocking practice as it treated the Bible as if it were a text like any other, rather than the divine word of God. The phrase was also more widely used to mean critical work carried out in the same fashion of testing historical veracity.

4 *George Dandin*: title character in the play *George Dandin ou le Mari confondu* (1668) by Molière. Dandin marries above his rank and is obliged to endure the whims of his wife. Lang is suggesting that the public encourages poor literature and therefore has to endure bad reviews.

5 *M. Jules Lemaître*: French writer and critic (1853–1914). His impressionistic style of criticism was like Lang's own, and he too published collections of fairy tales.

6 *Lessing's* Laocoon: Gotthold Ephraim Lessing (1729–81), a German writer, philosopher, dramatist and art critic. His work 'Laocoon: An Essay on the Limits of Painting and Poetry' is regarded as an important piece of early literary criticism for its arguments about the character of poetry.

7 *Hazlitt*: William Hazlitt (1778–1830), literary critic and essayist. He wrote for periodicals on a variety of subjects including politics, philosophy and studies of great literary figures.

8 *It is an ill bird*: old proverb of unknown origin appearing in many different languages, first recorded in English in 1250. It condemns the person who does not respect the family, nation or group to which he belongs.

9 *Archdeacon Farrar*: see this volume, p. 344, n. 7. Farrar's comment on criticism has not been further identified, though his remarks on the Higher Criticism in his essay in *The Bible and the Child* (London: James Clarke, 1897, pp. 1–28) might be regarded as Lang suggests.

10 *Grub Street*: a London street at one time 'much inhabited by writers of small histories, dictionaries, and temporary poems: whence any mean production is called *grub street*'. (Samuel Johnson, *Dictionary of the English Language*, 1755).

11 *Torture Stake*: the term is more usually used in the debate about whether Jesus died on a cross or an upright pole, though Lang's subsequent reference here to 'braves' and 'squaws' suggests that he is associating it with Native American practices.

12 *'indifferent honest'*: from Hamlet's speech in Act 3, scene 1 of Shakespeare's play, suggesting that one should speak the truth regardless of one's own failings.

13 *Mrs. Carter*: Elizabeth Carter (1717–1806), writer and translator, part of the 'Bluestocking' circle of women writers and intellectuals.

14 *'It really does not seem … the* Odyssey*'*: Montagu Pennington, *A Series of Letters Between Miss Elizabeth Carter and Miss Catherine Talbot 1741–1770* (London: F. C. Rivington, 1809), vol. 1, pp. 166–7.

15 *'Mrs. Carter's criticism … public'*: this is not a direct quotation from Pennington's introduction to the letters (see note 14 above), but Lang's extrapolation of

Pennington's general defence of publishing Carter's private letters. See his editor's introduction in Montagu Pennington, *A Series of Letters Between Miss Elizabeth Carter and Miss Catherine Talbot 1741–1770* (London: F. C. Rivington, 1809), vol. 1, pp. iii–xxi.

16 *'He had not yet … despised'*: Matthew Arnold, *On Translating Homer* (London: Longman, Green, Longman and Roberts, 1861), p. 80. Arnold and Arthur Hugh Clough (1819–61) had been close friends at university. Clough published some poetry and prose and was candid in his assessments of literary work.

17 *Boileau … Quintillian*: Nicolas Boileau-Despréaux (1636–1711) was a French poet and critic and Marcus Fabius Quintilianus (*c.*35 CE–*c.*100 CE) was a Roman rhetorician. Lang uses these examples to indicate critics whose work was once much admired and imitated but is no longer fashionable.

18 *Pinero … confide in'*: Sir Arthur Wing Pinero (1855–1934) was an actor and director, but also the author of some sixty plays, mostly comedies. He was successful at the time of Lang's writing. The quotation is from Jonathan Swift's satiric poem 'On Poetry' (1733), but Lang is only using it here to suggest that, as in earlier examples, figures once regarded as important authorities pass out fashion.

19 *Burke on the Sublime*: Edmund Burke (1729–97). Irish philosopher, political theorist and Whig politician. In aesthetics, Burke's *A Philosophical Enquiry into the Origin of Our Ideas of the Sublime and Beautiful* (1756) was the first to argue that the beautiful and the sublime designated fundamentally different forms of aesthetic experience, and was a major influence on Immanuel Kant and both British and German Romanticism.

20 *Burke … same author*: as in previous examples Lang takes three once important critical works: Edmund Burke's *A Philosophical Enquiry into the Origins of our Ideas on the Sublime and the Beautiful* (1756), John Morritt's *Vindication of Homer and of the Ancient Poets and Historians, who Have Recorded the Siege and Fall of Troy* (1798) and Thomas Blackwell's *An Enquiry into the Life and Writings of Homer* (1735), to suggest the passing of critical fashion.

21 *Saintsbury*: George Edward Saintsbury (1845–1933), was an English writer, critic and journalist. He and Lang began their careers as journalists together in London in the 1870s, both contributing to the *Daily News* and the *Saturday Review* and Saintsbury became an important figure in the literary world of the 1880s and 1890s. After becoming Professor of Rhetoric and English Literature at the University of Edinburgh in 1895 he was an influential historian of both English and French literature. They remained friends throughout Lang's life, despite differences of opinion about the role of the critic. Some of Saintsbury's critical essays were collected in his *Essays in English Literature, 1780–1860* (2 vols, 1890–5).

'Politics and Men of Letters', *The Pilot* (April 1900)

1 *Mon âne … parle bien*: French 'my donkey speaks, and it speaks well'. The prophet to whom a donkey speaks is Balaam in Numbers 22:28, but the French story 'Peau d'Âne', which doesn't have a prophet, is one that Lang included in *The Lilac Fairy Book* (1912).

2 *motives of the Boers*: the Boer Wars were fought during 1880–1 and 1899–1902 by the British Empire against the Dutch settlers of two independent Boer republics, the Orange Free State and the Transvaal Republic.

3 *Gladstone ... to be free*: Gladstone had been Prime Minister at the time of the siege of Khartoum, in the Sudan, in 1884, where General Gordon was killed and became a hero in the eyes of the Victorian public. Gladstone had been against involvement with the Sudanese rebels fighting against Egyptian occupation.

4 *Greeks ... Kosciusko*: Lang names well-known independence movements and figures. Greece became independent in 1832, Hungary in 1848, William Tell is a legendary figure in Swiss national mythology and Andrzej Kosciuszko (1746–1817) was a national hero in Polish struggles against Russian dominance.

5 *Amos and Jeremiah*: prophets in the Old Testament.

6 *Gladstone ... Homeric Controversy*: Gladstone also published in the debate on the existence and authorship of Homer, *Studies on Homer and the Homeric Age* (1858).

7 *Brer Wolf, 'keep on a saying nuffin'*: Brer Wolf is a character in the 'Uncle Remus' collection of African American stories assembled by Joel Chandler Harris, published in several volumes, the first in 1880.

8 *brick-bats ... dead rats*: from Thackeray's poem 'The Battle of Limerick' describing a political affray in Ireland in 1848.

9 *Erasmus*: Desiderius Erasmus Roterodamus (1466 –1536), known as Erasmus of Rotterdam, or simply Erasmus, was a Dutch priest, theologian and teacher and an important humanist thinker, whose work emphasised religious tolerance and moderation.

10 *Decalogue*: the Ten Commandments found in the Bible.

11 *Kronos*: one of the Titans in Greek mythology, father of Zeus and other gods, who attempted to eat his children because it was foretold that they would supplant him.

12 *Jacobite ... Toryism*: Lang lists a number of opposed political positions. Jacobite, see this volume, p. 425, n. 34. The Divine Right of Kings was the belief that the monarch ruled by the providence of God, whereas the Rights of Man is the title of a book by the radical and revolutionary democrat Thomas Paine (1737–1809). Pantisocracy was a utopian scheme for an egalitarian community devised in 1794 by the poets Samuel Taylor Coleridge and Robert Southey and Tory is the nickname of those politicians who defended the hierarchies of aristocracy and land ownership.

13 *Mr Robert Buchanan*: Robert Williams Buchanan (1841–1901) was a Scottish poet, dramatist and critic who published a number of attacks on contemporary writers, most notably his essay 'The Fleshly School of Poetry' in the *Contemporary Review* (October 1871), pp. 334–50 which drew vigorous responses from those attacked, especially Swinburne. Lang engaged in other defences against Buchanan's outspoken assaults, see for example Robert Buchanan, 'The Modern Young Man as Critic', *Universal Review* 13 (March 1889), pp. 353–72. Lang's response is 'Mr Buchanan's Young Man', *St. James's Gazette*, (10 April 1889), pp. 3–4 and later, 'The Young Men', *Contemporary Review* 65 (February 1894), pp. 177–88.

2 REALISM, ROMANCE AND THE READING PUBLIC

'Realism and Romance', *Contemporary Review* (November 1887)

1 *'Whither hast thou come?'*: this is an odd choice of reference on Lang's part and possibly he again mis-remembers his source. Although the phrase appears in the Bible (John

14:5 and Judges 19:17), St Bernard's statement in one of his letters is not a question at all. 'I am horrified when I think whence thou comest, whither thou goest, and what a short penance thou hast put between thy sins and thy ordination, (Epistle 8) Bernard of Clairvaux, (1090–1153), later canonised, was the founder of the Cistercian order.

2 *Battle of the Books*: satire by Jonathan Swift, published as part of his *A Tale of a Tub* in 1704. It describes a fight between books representing different ideas. The title became a term to describe the dispute, originating in France in the late seventeenth century, about whether classical or contemporary texts ('the Ancients and the Moderns') were the most important models of writing.

3 *dispute about State Rights*: contestation of which legal and political powers belong to the separate states of the United States of America and which to the federal government.

4 *Harry Blount at Flodden*: see this volume, p. 340, n. 49.

5 *Mrs. Partington with her broom*: figure from a much-reported speech by Sydney Smith (1771–1845), an Anglican cleric and supporter of Parliamentary Reform. In a speech made in 1831 at the time of the Reform Bill he compared the House of Lords to Mrs. Partington setting out with a mop to deal with the Atlantic during a storm.

6 *Mr. Marion Crawford*: Francis Marion Crawford (1854–1909) was American writer of magazine short stories, many set in Italy (where he was born) and many having strange or supernatural themes.

7 *'Tom Jones' ... and 'Pickwick'* Henry Fielding, *Tom Jones* (1749), Walter Scott, *The Bride of Lammermoor* (1819), William Thackeray, *The History of Henry Esmond* (1852), Charles Dickens, *The Pickwick Papers* (1837).

8 *Pope translates it*: Alexander Pope's translation of Homer's *Odyssey* (1726).

9 *author of 'Phyllis'*: *Joseph Andrews* is by Henry Fielding and the other two novels by Margaret Hungerford (1855–1897). *Phyllis* (1877) was her first novel and immediately popular. Lang is contrasting what he considers a great novel with flimsier works.

10 *'Hypocrite lecteur, mon sembable, mon frère!'*: French, translates as 'hypocrite reader, my likeness, my brother'. The line is from Charles Baudelaire's poem' Au Lecteur' which appeared in his collection *Les Fleurs du Mal* (1857) and shows Lang's knowledge of French literature. The line is perhaps now better known from T. S. Eliot's later use of it in *The Waste Land* (1922).

11 *Malory's men ... marvellously'*: Thomas Malory's *Le Morte d'Arthur* (1485) is a compilation of the legends of King Arthur and the Knights of the Round Table. The quotation has not been further identified, but Lang's use of Malory seems deliberate in the context of the discussion of romance, as *Le Morte d'Arthur* is the best-known romance text in English.

12 *critical shoeblack says*: Bret Harte (1836–1902), American author and poet. In Harte's parody of the novels of Edward Bulwer Lytton ('The Dweller on the Threshold', *Condensed Novels,* 1867) the protagonist discusses literature and philosophy with a boy who polishes shoes in the street. The boy refers to the German writer Schiller as *ausgespielt,* 'played out'.

13 *in fairy lands forlorn*: the line was originally written 'in faery lands forlorn' and is from the penultimate stanza of Keats's 'Ode to a Nightingale' (1819).

14 *with the pale cast*: the line from Shakespeare's *Hamlet,* act 3, scene 1 actually reads 'And thus the native hue of resolution is sicklied o'er with the pale cast of thought'. Lang is

meaning to suggest something of the original sense of Hamlet's soliloquy which implies that thought is the enemy of action.

15 *Daisy Miller ... Ayesha*: Lang names a number of fictional characters, these latter two, from Henry James' novel *Daisy Miller* (1879) and Rider Haggard's *King Solomon's Mines* (1886) and *She* (1887), might be thought opposites, but Lang admired James's early heroines.

16 *Dear Dugold Dalgetty ... Sophia Western*: all fictional characters from works that Lang liked.

17 *'And Porthos may welcome us* there': the last line of May Kendall's poem 'A Pious Opinion' from her 1887 collection *Dreams to Sell*. The poem is a defence of fairy tales, and the collection was published by Longmans in the same year as Lang's article here. Lang collaborated with Kendall in writing *That Very Mab* in 1885 and encouraged her throughout her career.

18 *Le Crime et le Châtiment*: better known by its English title, *Crime and Punishment*.

19 *freshman's wine*: *The Adventures of Mr. Verdant Green* is a novel by Cuthbert M. Bede, a pseudonym of Edward Bradley (1827–89). It tells of the exploits of a sheltered young man as an undergraduate at Oxford University. The previously non-smoking Verdant Green is persuaded to take a large cigar at a party.

20 *Mrs. Woods*: Margaret Louisa Woods (1856–1945) wrote several novels and collections of poetry, this one was newly published at the time of Lang's writing.

21 *'ower-true tales'*: the phrase comes from Walter Scott, used to mean stories based on real events.

22 *'A Modern Instance' ... 'The Bostonian's*: these three novels are by W. D. Howells (1882), Fyodor Dostoevsky (1866) and Henry James (1886), respectively.

23 *Miss Laphams*: from William Dean Howells' novel *The Rise of Silas Lapham* (1885). Howells and Lang were involved in a long-running debate about Realism and romance, and Lang disliked Howells's novels.

24 *The Lady of the Aroostook*: from William Dean Howells' novel of that name (1879). See this volume, p. 27.

25 *'a leear'*: reference not identified, but the word means 'liar' in Scottish dialect.

26 *to grieve at their own*: the Invocation at the beginning of book 8 of Fielding's *The History of Tom Jones* (1749).

27 *tuft-hunters*: people who try to associate themselves with members of the upper classes or aristocracy. The slang term supposedly comes from titled undergraduates being permitted to wear gold, rather than plain black, tassels on their mortar-boards.

28 *corpore vili:* Latin, from the phrase 'fiat experimentum in corpore vili', meaning 'Let the experiment be carried out on a worthless body', found in Lucretius. The title of Evelyn Waugh's novel *Vile Bodies* (1930) is also derived from this phrase.

29 *Cousines Bettes*: title character of *La Cousine Bette* (1846) by Honoré de Balzac. A Realist novel set in contemporary Paris, it tells the story of an unmarried middle-aged woman who engineers the destruction of her family.

30 *Mr Christie Murray*: David Christie Murray (1847–1907) was journalist and writer who published several dozen novels, beginning in the 1870s.

31 *M. E. de Goncourt's*: this could be a reference to any of the novels of Edmond de Goncourt (1822–96), all of which are in the Naturalist style that Lang found distasteful and all of which have a woman as title character.

32 *'nice derangement of epitaphs'*: from a speech by Mrs Malprop in Richard Sheridan's play *The Rivals* (1775): 'If I reprehend anything in this world, it is the use of my oracular tongue, and a nice derangement of epitaphs' (act 3, scene 3). 'Malapropism' has become the term to describe the comic confusion of words that sound similar but have very different meanings.

33 *Sir Thomas Browne*: Lamb and Thomas Browne (1605–82) were both essayists admired for their style, even though neither wrote in a plain or unembellished fashion.

34 *Mr. and Mrs. Bartley Hubbard*: characters in William Dean Howells' novel *A Modern Instance* (1882), they also appear in *The Rise of Silas Lapham* (1885). See this volume, p. 27.

35 *The Coming Man*: this term was widely used in different contexts to mean 'the person of the future'. Most frequently, however, it was used in evolutionary terms, as Lang does here, to suggest the more highly evolved being.

36 *feed bearsomely*: John Payne (1842–1916) was a prolific poet and translator of, among other things, *The Book of the Thousand Nights and One Nights* in nine volumes (1882–4). This may be the source of the quotation, given Lang's interests, but Payne also translated many other works of folk and fairy tales. The line does not come from Payne's poem about a vampire, 'Lautrec' (1878).

37 *'Through One Administration'*: in Lang's time Frances Hodgson Burnett (1849–1924) was better known for her novel *Little Lord Fauntleroy* (1885–6), though she is now remembered as the author of the children's book *The Secret Garden* (1911). *Through One Administration* was published in 1883.

38 *nothing for to hurt her'*: 'The Sorrows of Werther' by Thackeray, a comic poem parodying Goethe's novel *The Sorrows of Young Werther* (1774) in which the hero, Werther, is in love with a woman called Charlotte.

39 *coram populo*: Latin, 'in the presence of the public'.

40 *'John Inglesant'*: popular historical novel of religious ideas set in the English Civil War, by Joseph Shorthouse (1834–1903).

41 *Buffalo Bill's Exhibition*: William Cody (1846–1917) was an American soldier and hunter who then began to organise stage shows with cowboy and Indian themes, which he toured in Great Britain and Europe as well as the United States. The show to which Lang refers was the first, and highly successful, London show in 1887. The show returned several times in subsequent years.

42 *Paulus Silentiarius and admire Rufinus*: used as examples of more obscure classical writers.

43 *other Allan*: Allan Quartermain, hero of several of Henry Rider Haggard's novels appearing first in *King Solomon's Mines* (1885).

44 *Shakespeare says of Cleopatra*: in *Anthony and Cleopatra,* act 2, scene 2. Shakespeare means that Cleopatra is so charming that even religious men bless her overt sexuality, and Lang is making a comparison with Haggard's character Ayesha.

45 *George Meredith*: Meredith (1828–1909) was a novelist and poet. He was also the model for *The Death of Chatterton*, a painting of the suicide of the literary forger by Henry

Wallis. Meredith's first wife subsequently ran away with Wallis in 1858; she died three years later. The collection of poems *Modern Love* (1862) and his novel *The Ordeal of Richard Feverel*, (1859) both draw on this experience. He and his work were highly respected and he became President of the Society of Authors.

46 *bloweth where she listeth*: 'the wind bloweth where it listeth'(the wind blows where it likes, and cannot be directed) is the line from the Bible (John 3:8) which Lang adapts.

47 *'breathed softly as through the flutes of the Grecians,'*: the reference to the flutes of the Grecians is probably taken from Francis Bacon's essay 'of Poetry', as Lang refers to it (though he misquotes) in *Letters on Literature* (London: Longmans, Green and Co., 1892), p. 11. He uses it many times and varies the misquotation each time, for example in essays on Tennyson and on William Morris, and in *Custom and Myth* (London: Longmans, Green and Co., 1884).

48 *venturous maid … man of Chios*: Mount Helicon is the home of the Muses in Greek mythology. Calliope, the muse of epic poetry, is supposed to have inspired Homer (the man of Chios) to write the *Odyssey*.

49 *Volsungs and Niflungs*: The *Völsungasaga* is a late thirteenth-century Icelandic text, telling of the origin and decline of the Völsung clan, including their destruction of the Niflungs or Burgundians.

50 *'M. Lecoq' … 'Le Crime de l'Opéra'*: Lang here mentions a selection of French novels and characters of differing types. Monsieur Lecoq is the fictional detective created by Émile Gaboriau; *Manon Lescaut* is a short, rather scandalous, novel by French author Abbé Prévost, published in 1731, *Madame Bovary* (1856) is Gustave Flaubert's first published novel, the Cardinal features in Dumas' Three Musketeers novels, and *Le Crime de l'Opéra* is by du Boisgobey (1879).

51 *Mark Twain*: pen-name of Samuel Langhorne Clemens (1835–1910), American writer and journalist and the author of *The Adventures of Tom Sawyer* (1876) and its sequel *The Adventures of Huckleberry Finn* (1885).

52 *'Prophets of the Great Smoky Mountain'*: *The Prophet of the Great Smoky Mountains* (1885) by Charles Egbert Craddock, the pen-name of a woman writer Mary Noailles (1850–1922), is an adventure novel set in the mountains of Tennessee. It has a female central character.

53 *Proteus*: figure from Greek mythology, a sea-god who was able to assume any form.

54 Homo Calvus*:* Latin, 'the bald man'.

55 modus vivendi: Latin, literally 'way of living', meaning an arrangement of a peaceful co-existence between opposing people or ideas.

56 *catawampus*: in American regional usage this word means 'crooked' or 'awry', but it also seems to be used to suggest a fierce imaginary creature, which is obviously the way in which Lang is employing it here.

57 *Ragnarôk*: the Twilight of the Gods (*Götterdämmerung*) in Norse mythology, the last battle at the end of the world.

'Literary Anodynes', *New Princeton Review* (September 1888)

1 Novum Organon: The *Novum Organum Scientiarum* (1620) is a philosophical work by Francis Bacon. The title translates as 'new instrument', meaning new method, and refers to Aristotle's work *Organon*, which was his treatise on logic. In *Novum Organum*, Bacon details a new system of logic he believes to be superior. Lang mixes the Latin and Greek of the two titles.

2 *Mr. Mudie's*: Charles Mudie (1818–90), established the first lending library in 1842. Initially lending to students in Bloomsbury, his business expanded rapidly in London and other major cities. Borrowers paid a subscription and because novels were costly items if purchased, the lending library was very successful. The library also lent boxes of books to rural readers, with librarians often choosing the contents. Mudie had great influence over publishers and writers because he could guarantee to buy large numbers of books. He also influenced the reading public by refusing to stock books of which he disapproved.

3 The Rapture: the poem by Thomas Carew (1595–1640) is the speech of a lover attempting to persuade his mistress to sleep with him.

4 *box from the circulating library*: see note 2 above.

5 *Mr. Matthew Arnold admitted*: this is not a quotation from Arnold, or anyone else, but a paraphrase of Arnold's position.

6 *wife of Thon … nepenthe*: in Homer's *Odyssey,* Polydamna, the wife of Thon, gives Helen a herb that banishes worry and sorrow. Helen uses it later to console those lamenting the absence of Odysseus.

7 *sweating system … and a stunted army*: political issues current at the time.

8 *'Ye have that lady for your wife'*: Scottish ballad, found in the first volume of Francis Child's large collection that was published in parts between 1882 and 1898. (London: Houghton, Mifflin, 1882), vol. 1, pp. 79–80.

9 *that 'god who loveth lovers'*: referring to *Aucassin et Nicolette,* the anonymous medieval French tale that Lang translated and published in 1887 (London: David Nutt, 1887).

10 *Baron of Bradwardine's Bear*: found in Scott's *Waverley* (1814), it is a large wine goblet presented to the Baron for his defence of a monastery.

11 *'cup of Hercules' of Théophile Gautier*: a very large tankard, referred to in Gautier's preface to his novel *Mademoiselle de Maupin* (1835).

12 *Montépin's*: Xavier Perrin, Comte de Montépin (1823–1902) was a popular French author of serialised novels, feuilletons and plays. His 1855 *The Daughters of the Plasterer* was condemned as obscene and resulted in Perrin being sentenced to three months in jail.

13 *Mayne Reid's*: Thomas Mayne Reid (1818–83), prolific writer of adventure stories from the 1830s until his death.

14 *M. Henri Rochefort*: Victor Henri Rochefort (1830–1913) was a combative and controversial French writer, journalist and politician. *Mademoiselle Bismarck* was published in 1881.

15 *'The world is too much with us'*: from Wordsworth's sonnet, usually given the same title as the line, published 1807.

16 monde: French, 'world' but often used to mean society or social group.

17 *First Crusade … Edict of Nantes*: in 1096 and 1685 respectively. Lang is just suggesting a long time ago.

18 *nine times 'widdershins'*: version of ideas from folklore; 'widdershins' is anti-clockwise, and nine is three multiplied by three, both thought to have special power or significance.

19 *she borrowed Tamlane*: a story with many variations. In this Scottish ballad version, Tamlane (or Tam Lin, or other variants) has been abducted by the Fairy Queen, but is rescued by his true love.

20 *dread Persephone*: in Greek mythology Persephone was the wife of Hades and queen of the underworld. Lang is suggesting that the fairy queen is simply a later version of this figure, though he does not mention that in the myth Persephone herself is initially abducted to the underworld, so it would not seem a very good comparison.

21 *Lovelace … Lucasta*: Richard Lovelace's poem 'Clitophon and Lucippe Translated' is not one of those addressed to Lucasta, but generally 'to the Ladies'. He recommends reading the long pastoral poem by the poet and courtier Sir Philip Sidney (1554–86).

22 *Marryat's novels*: Frederick Marryat (1792–1848) was a naval officer, the majority of whose popular novels featured adventures at sea.

23 *stormy petrels*: small sea birds that seem to be able to fly in storms. The term is used figuratively to suggest a person whose coming signifies trouble, though Lang's sense here is more like a person who enjoys turbulence.

24 Mystery of the Hansom Cab: *The Mystery of a Hansom Cab* is the first novel by Fergus Hume (1859–1932), who went on to write very many more. First published in Australia in 1886, it was an instant success and was published in Britain in the following year, also very successfully and considerably out-selling Arthur Conan Doyle's first Sherlock Holmes novel, *A Study in Scarlet*, also published in 1887.

25 Mr. Barnes of New York: *Mr. Barnes of New York* is a novel published in 1887 by American author Archibald Gunter (1847–1907). It was also adapted into a play (1888) and contains a number of implausible adventures on the part of Mr Barnes, including a fight with Corsican bandits.

26 *'in fairy lands forlorn'*: see this volume, p. 348, n. 13.

27 demi-monde*:* French, literally 'half world' but meaning those beyond the fringes of respectable society.

28 ingénue: French, literally 'naïve' but meaning a young and innocent female character.

29 *baccarat*: a card game.

30 nugae *and* totus in illis*:* Latin, 'frivolities' and 'completely within them'. The complete line is from Horace, *Satires* 1.9:2, and can be translated as 'I was strolling along the Sacred Way, musing on some nonsense, and completely absorbed in it.'

31 ouvriers: French, 'workers'.

32 *Alexandre the Great*: Lang means the author Alexandre Dumas, elder of the two with the same name.

33 feuilleton: a newspaper supplement, first produced in France, consisting of gossip and features, similar to the magazines that contemporary newspapers now often carry.

34 *Venus sent Psyche*: Venus, jealous of her son Cupid's love for Psyche, sets her four impossible tasks, one of which is to bring water from the source of the River Styx in the underworld. The tale is first told in Apuleius' work, *The Golden Ass*, written in the second century CE.

35 *Quentin Durward*: Walter Scott's 1823 novel of that title, which Lang is comparing to his later work, *Count Robert of Paris* (1832).

36 *D'Artagnan and Athos*: along with Porthos and Aramis, the main characters introduced in Dumas' novel *The Three Musketeers* (*Les Trois Mousquetaires*) first serialised in March–July 1844, and set in the seventeenth century. Athos, Porthos and Aramis are actually the musketeers, D'Artganan is not.

37 *House of the Seven Gables*: gothic novel published in 1851 by Nathaniel Hawthorne.

38 *Old Manse of many Mosses*: *Mosses from an Old Manse* is a collection of short stories on dark and supernatural topics by Nathaniel Hawthorne, first published in 1846.

39 *Leather-stocking, Dugald Dalgetty and Locksley*: The Leatherstocking Tales is a series of novels by James Fenimore Cooper, including *The Last of the Mohicans* (1826) all featuring the hero Natty Bumppo, a child of white parents raised by Native Americans and known as Leatherstocking. Dalgetty is a mercenary fighting in Scotland in the 1640s from Scott's novel *A Legend of Montrose* (1819); Robin of Locksley is better known as Robin Hood and appears in ballads and tales from the fifteenth century onwards.

40 *Aristotle says*: quotation not identified.

41 Figaro *or* Gil Blas*: Le Figaro* is a daily newspaper in France, founded in 1826. *Le Gil Blas* was a Parisian literary periodical that ran from1879 to 1914 and serialised several novels of the Naturalist type that Lang disliked, such as Émile Zola's *Germinal* in1884.

42 *'indignation makes verses'*: Juvenal, *Satires* 1.79.

43 *the Academy*: there are five 'academies' in France, divisions of the Institut de France, all but one founded in the seventeenth century and functioning as the highest authorities in their fields of art, culture, science and language. Lang is probably referring to the Académie des Beaux-Arts which, like the others, was regarded by experimental or avant-garde artists as stifling and conservative.

44 Cervantes: Miguel de Cervantes Saaverdra (1547–1616), Spanish writer of plays, poetry and prose. His long narrative work *Don Quixote* was published in two parts in 1605 and 1615 and is usually regarded as the first novel to be published in Europe.

45 The Leavenworth Case: Anna Green (1846–1935) was one of the first writers of detective fiction in America, and she also introduced several female detectives into her work. *The Leavenworth Case* was published in 1878.

46 *Daudet … Chasles*: Alphonse Daudet's 1888 novel *L'Immortel* is based on the real case of Michel Chasles, a member of the French Academy of Sciences who, in 1869, attempted by means of forged letters to convince fellow Academicians that he had formulated the theory of gravity before Isaac Newton.

47 *'Not here,' … meet for thee.'*: 'Not here, O Apollo, are haunts meet for thee' is from the third part of Matthew Arnold's *Empedocles on Etna,* where Callicles is telling Apollo that Etna is not an appropriate place for him. Lang substitutes the name of the central character of Daudet's 1872 novel *Tartarin de Tarascon* to suggest that French Naturalism is unwelcome in his reading.

'Romance and the Reverse', *St. James's Gazette* (November 1888)

1 *'M. Zola on the Side of the Angels'*: article published in the *St. James's Gazette,* 2 November 1888. Reprinted as 'Le Rêve' in *Impressions and Opinions* (London: David Nutt, 1891), pp. 122–9.

2 *picture by Mr. Holman Hunt*: referring to William Holman Hunt's painting *The Light of the World* (1853–4) in which Christ, carrying a lantern, is preparing to knock at an ivy-covered door.

3 *lone sitting by the shores of old Romance'*: quotation attributed to Wordsworth by Walter Scott who uses it as the epigraph to chapter 20 of *The Bride of Lammermoor* (1819).

4 *Porthos and Monte Cristo*: Porthos, see this volume, p. 354, n. 36. Monte Cristo is the title character in Alexandre Dumas, *The Count of Monte Cristo* (1844).

5 *Romuald ... 'La Morte Amoureuse'*: from Gautier's short story (1836). Romuald is a priest who falls in love with Clarimonde, a beautiful woman who turns out to be a kind of vampire.

6 impossibilium cupitor: Latin, 'longing for the impossible'. Lang may be recalling this phrase because it is used in chapter 63 of *The Count of Monte Cristo,* which he has just mentioned.

7 *Endymion ... Latmian*: Endymion is a figure of Greek mythology, sleeping in a cave in Latmia and meeting a moon-goddess in his dream. Versions of the story are mentioned by a number of ancient authors, including Theocritus, but more recently by Keats in his poem *Endymion* (1818).

8 *moonlit terrace of Belmont*: the setting of act 5, scene 1 of *The Merchant of Venice* where Portia and Bassanio affirm their love for one another.

9 *'Silas Lapham' ... Gunnar in his grave*: Silas Lapham, see this volume, p. 349, n. 23. Gunnar is a figure in the Volsung saga, see this volume, p. 351, n. 49.

10 *She was but a vestment maker, And a stained-glass painter he*: quotation not identified, if indeed it is a quotation and not Lang's own verse. He is referring to Zola's novel *Le Rêve* (1888).

11 *King Cophetua*: figure of legend, Cophetua falls in love with a beggar-girl and they are eventually married. The story is mentioned in several plays by Shakespeare, and is the subject of a poem by Tennyson, *The Beggar Maid* (1842) and a painting by Edward Burne-Jones, *King Cophetua and the Beggar Maid* (1884).

12 *'Aucassin et Nicolette'*: see this volume, p. 352, n. 9.

13 *Apuleius*: (*c.*125 CE–*c.*180 CE). Latin writer best known as the author of the satirical prose romance, *Metamorphoses*, generally referred to as *The Golden Ass*, in which the protagonist undergoes a series of picaresque adventures after having accidentally transformed himself into a donkey through the practice of witchcraft.

14 *'Athalie'*: play by Jean Racine (1641), a tragedy with a Biblical setting.

15 *'Consuelo'*: novel by Georges Sand (serialised 1842–3), describing the life of a gypsy singer and set in Venice.

'The Evolution of Literary Decency', *Blackwood's Edinburgh Magazine* (March 1900)

1 *Afra Behn*: (1640–89). Aphra Behn, English dramatist, poet and writer of fiction, who also worked as spy for Charles II during the Dutch war in 1666. Her plays were very popular and she was one of the first women to earn a living by writing, although even during her lifetime she and her work were regarded by some as unacceptably lewd. With the different public moral values of the Victorian period her reputation declined sharply.

2 *'Astraea'*: the name under which Aphra Behn published many of her writings.

3 *hero in one novel*: Harriet Beecher Stowe (1811–96) was an American writer and supporter of the abolition of slavery. Her novel *Uncle Tom's Cabin* (1852) contributed to revulsion against slavery before the American Civil War. Aphra Behn's prose work, *Oroonoko* (1688) takes an enslaved African prince as its hero.

4 *'pudibund'*: modest, ashamed.

5 *Mr Guy Boothby*: (1867–1905). Australian-born writer who began his career with novels of Australian life, moving on to publish a great number of crime and sensation fictions. His series featuring the criminal mastermind Dr Nikola was very popular, the first being published in the *Windsor Magazine*, which was set up to challenge the dominance of the *Strand* in genre fiction.

6 *Mr Henty … Marryat*: G. A. Henty (1832–1902), novelist and war correspondent, the author of many historical adventure stories for boys. He edited the patriotic magazine for boys, the *Union Jack*. For Marryat see this volume p. 353, n. 22.

7 *Suckling's ballad of a marriage*: Sir John Suckling (1609–42), 'A Ballad Upon a Wedding'. It is, as Lang argues, a far from indecent poem.

8 *Bowdler*: Thomas Bowdler (1754–1825) who published his *Family Shakespeare* in 1818, an edition that cut all the material that he thought indecent, which was a substantial amount. The edition was popular and the word 'bowdlerise' meaning to censor texts in that way, is derived from his name.

9 *Mr Lecky … that revolution*: in *A History of the Rise and Influence of Rationalism in Europe* (1865).

10 *Wilkes*: John Wilkes (1725–97) was an English radical, journalist, and politician, and the co-author of a pornographic poem, *An Essay on Woman* (1763) which caused a scandal in Parliament and led to him being charged with obscenity.

11 *Galt*: John Galt (1779–1839), Scottish writer who produced fiction and non-fiction and though better known for stories of country life was one of the first to write a novel dealing with the effects of the industrial revolution.

12 *dared to draw a man*: Thackeray makes the remark in his novel *Pendennis*, (1848–50) in which the eponymous character goes to London to make his fortune. He initially becomes a journalist, and marries late in the novel to his first love, who is also his foster-sister.

13 *Petronius … Lord Strutwell*: Strutwell is a dissolute character in Smollett's *Roderick Random* (1748) who endeavours to corrupt Roderick by giving him a copy of the *Satyricon*, a work containing many licentious scenes and supposed to have been written in the first century by Petronius.

14 *'Spectator'*: periodical produced by Joseph Addison and Richard Steele between March 1711 and December 1712. Addison produced an additional run in 1714. Published daily, it was very popular and took an explicitly moral stance.

15 *Diderot, Crébillon* fils: Denis Diderot (1713–84) was a French philosopher and writer, best known for his massive L'*Encyclopédie,* (1750–65); Claude de Crébillon (1707–77). Both wrote novels that powerfully questioned contemporary moral and religious positions.

16 *Philosophes*: not necessarily philosophers, but the intellectuals of the eighteenth-century French Enlightenment.

17 *Voltaire's unspeakable 'Pucelle'*: *La Pucelle d'Orléans* is a scandalous satirical poem on Joan of Arc by Voltaire. Never fully completed, it was circulating from about 1730. Lang, with his rather chivalrous admiration of Joan, was disgusted by it.

18 *'more for edification than for effect'*: Walter Scott, 'Samuel Richardson', *Miscellaneous Prose Works* (London: Longman and Green, 1827), vol. 1, p. 9.

19 *Miss Corelli and Mr Hall Caine*: Marie Corelli (1855–1924) was a novelist whose works were popular with the public but critically derided. She was a lively antagonist on a number of issues and was involved a public feud with Thomas Hall Caine (1853–1931), a novelist and journalist who rejected her first novel for publication. Corelli also accused Lang of bias in his support of some authors over others. See also this volume, p. 54.

20 *Dr Sherlock … twenty sermons*: Walter Scott, 'Samuel Richardson', *Miscellaneous Prose Works* (London: Longman and Green, 1827), vol. 1, p. 34.

21 *Montagu … Rochester*: Lady Mary Wortley (1689–1762) writer, poet and traveller who was one of the first Europeans to write about life in Muslim countries. John Wilmot, Earl of Rochester (1647–80) was a poet and satirist who lived a scandalising life and wrote very frankly and wittily about sex.

22 *'virtuous resistance'*: Walter Scott, 'Samuel Richardson', *Miscellaneous Prose Works* (London: Longman and Green, 1827), vol. 1, p. 35.

23 *wife of Mr Arthur Pendennis*: see note 12 above.

24 *as Horace Walpole declares*: source not identified. Another reference to this statement has Walpole making it about Richardson's novel *Sir Charles Grandison,* rather than *Pamela.* See Edith Kimpton, *Book Ways* (London: Ralph, Holland & Co., 1913), p. 153.

25 *Gyp*: Sibylle de Mirabeau, Comtesse de Martel de Janville (1849–1932) wrote under the pseudonym Gyp. Her humorous sketches and novels denounced her own fashionable society as well as the French republic's political class.

26 *James Ballantyne … 'Dombey and Son'*: Ballantyne disagreed with Scott over the ending of his novel *Saint Ronan's Well* (1824) but the changes suggested by Ballantyne weakened the plot. Lang would have known this from his work on James Gibson Lockhart, who gives an account of it in his *Memoirs of the Life of Walter Scott, Bart.* (1827). Dickens's friend, Francis Jeffrey, made a number of suggestions about *Dombey and Son,* including altering Dickens's intention of making Mrs Dombey an adulteress.

27 vile damnum: Latin, 'a cheap loss'.

28 *Matthew Bramble*: one of the six correspondents whose letters make up Smollett's novel *The Expedition of Humphry Clinker* (1771). It also transpires that Humphry is Bramble's illegitimate son.

29 *Guy de Maupassant*: (1850–93). French short story writer and novelist who was part of the group of young authors that formed around Zola.

30 *author of 'Tom and Jerry'*: Pierce Egan (1772–1849) was a journalist who produced *Life in London or, the Day and Night Scenes of Jerry Hawthorn, esq., and his elegant friend, Corinthian Tom, accompanied by Bob Logic, the Oxonian, in their rambles and Sprees through the Metropolis*. It was a series that ran from 1821–8 and was hugely popular.

31 *M. Armande Silvestre*: Paul-Armand Silvestre (1837–1901) was a serious poet, but as a novelist and contributor to *Gil Blas* (see this volume, p. 354, n. 41) he produced work of a more licentious nature.

32 *Mrs Manley, Mrs Heywood*: Mary Delarivier Manley (*c.*1670–1724) and Eliza Haywood (*c.*1693–1756), along with Aphra Behn (see n. 1 above), were highly successful writers of the Restoration period, producing plays, poetry and prose. Their work was in the style of the time, with a broader wit and greater sexual licence than allowed to women writers of the early and mid-nineteenth century.

33 *Rowlandson … Hogarth*: Thomas Rowlandson (1756–1827) was a caricaturist, rather less savage than some of his contemporaries, such as James Gillray, and more restrained than his predecessor, William Hogarth (1697–1764).

34 *'Memoirs of a Lady of Quality'*: written by Frances Vane and published in Smollett's novel *The Adventures of Peregrine Pickle* (1751).

35 *Jeremy Collier… Addison*: Jeremy Collier (1650–1726) was a theologian and pamphleteer who strongly opposed profanity and immorality on the stage, during the Restoration period. Joseph Addison (with Richard Steele) was the editor of the *Spectator*, a periodical that sought to unite wit and morality.

36 *Primrose Hill*: the essayist Charles Lamb recalls a woman of his acquaintance coming across him reading *Pamela* on Primrose Hill, a park in London, and reading a few pages. Though he says there is nothing in the novel 'to make a man seriously ashamed', he asks the reader to imagine who was the more embarrassed – he or the woman. Charles Lamb, 'Detached Thoughts on Books and Reading', *London Magazine* 6 (July 1822), pp. 33–6.

37 *far-reaching influences of the Wesleyan movement*: the Wesleyan, or Methodist, movement aimed to revivify the Church and make it more active in faith and worship. Although many break-away churches were founded, the established Church did also reform in response to the challenge of the movement. The movement was named after its founder, John Wesley.

38 *Parson Trullibers*: Trulliber is a character in Fielding's novel *Joseph Andrews* (1742), an ill-educated, hypocritical parson more fond of food, drink and merriment than religious observance or good works.

39 *Henry Tilneys*: Tilney is the clever, sophisticated young clergyman who marries the heroine, Catherine Morland, in Jane Austen's *Northanger Abbey* (1817).

40 *Clara Reeve*: (1729–1807). Amongst the early writers of gothic fiction, her book *The Old English Baron* (1777) is sometimes identified as the first gothic novel.

41 *Miss Catherine Morland*: the heroine of Jane Austen's *Northanger Abbey* (1817) who is fond of gothic romances.

42 '*senselessly decent*': see this volume, p. 344, n. 2. Here Lang renders the saying without the Scottish dialect.

43 '*the maiden passion for a maid*': the loose attitudes of Strap, Roderick's companion in *Roderick Random* and Partridge, Tom's attendant in *Tom Jones* are contrasted with the chivalric regard embodied in the quotation from Tennyson's *Idylls of the King* (1859), 1, line 479.

44 *Dr Oliver Wendell Holmes*: Holmes (1809–94) was an American doctor and medical reformer, but also a respected author whose wholesome poetry was often set for recital by schoolchildren. This led to his being called one of the 'Fireside' or 'Schoolroom' poets.

45 *had transgressed from the path of Dian*: in Roman mythology Diana is the virgin goddess. Lang's euphemism simply means to have lost her virginity.

46 *Mr Rochester … Captain Booth*: the main male characters in Charlotte Brontë's *Jane Eyre* (1847), George Meredith's *The Ordeal of Richard Feverel* (1859) and Henry Fielding's *Amelia* (1751) respectively. All three heroes have relationships with mistresses before or after their meetings with the heroines.

47 strugforlifeur*:* 'struggler for life', an expression derived from the work of the naturalist Charles Darwin in which he describes evolution through natural selection as the 'struggle for existence'.

48 *Lord Quex*: *The Gay Lord Quex* (1899) is a comedy by Arthur Wing Pinero in which the friends of a newly-engaged young man attempt to persuade him to be unfaithful.

'The Reading Public', *Cornhill Magazine* (December 1901)

1 *Christabel … in the matter*: Coleridge's long, unfinished narrative poem *Christabel* was probably written in about 1797, but not published until 1816. Christabel meets a mysterious woman, Geraldine, in the woods. They spend the night together and Geraldine is seen to have a strange mark on her body

2 *White Doe of Rylstone*: poem by William Wordsworth (1815), the story of the surviving daughter of a family of Catholic rebels and their deaths in battle.

3 '*sold like hot cakes … Mr. Kipling's*: simply meaning that they sold quickly. Rudyard Kipling supplied some lines of praise for Boothby: 'Mr. Guy Boothby has come to great honours now. His name is large upon hoardings, his books sell like hot cakes, and he keeps a level head through it all' which were used for large advertisements found in the end papers of a number of new novels. See for example Boothby's own 1901 novel *Farewell, Nikola* (London: Ward Lock).

4 *Parliamentary Committee about 1834*: the most likely is the Select Committee on the State of Education.

5 *Mark Twain … 'Immortality of the Soul'*: reference not identified.

6 *booms*: advertising, promoting.

7 '*Happy Thoughts*': reference not identified.

8 *Mr. Horace Round*: (John) Horace Round (1854–1928) was a historian whose works concentrated on the peerage and genealogy in the English medieval period.

9 *Knight's Fees, or Glamorgan's Treaty*: an old land measurement and a treaty negotiated during the English Civil War. Lang uses these as examples of obscure topics.

10 *Mr. Max Müller*: Friedrich Max Müller, (1823–1900), German philologist who was instrumental in founding the study of India and of comparative religion. He was also one of Lang's principal targets of criticism in his work on mythology, see in particular, 'Household Tales: Their Origin, Diffusion and Relations to the Higher Myths', Volume 1, pp. 88–121, 'Cupid, Psyche and the "Sun Frog"', Volume 1, pp. 66–77 and 'Fetichism and the Infinite', Volume 1, pp. 170–176.

11 *regretted Mr.David Carnegie*: David Carnegie (1871–1900), son of an aristocratic family who explored Australia, partly motivated by the possibility of finding gold. He was eventually posted to Nigeria, but died there aged only 29, after being shot with a poisoned arrow.

12 *The late master of Balliol*: Benjamin Jowett (1817–93). Influential reforming tutor and then Master (from 1870) of Balliol College Oxford. He was also an important scholar of Greek. He taught Lang and was a friend.

13 *chooses to put into their boxes*: see this volume, p. 352, n. 2.

14 *Folios … duodecimos*: see this volume, p. 393, n. 9.

15 *Mr Pepys*: Samuel Pepys (1633–1703) was an English naval administrator and Member of Parliament. He is better remembered for his diary, which contains frank accounts (though in code) of sexual encounters. See also this volume, p. 386, n. 14 for editions of the diary in Lang's lifetime.

16 *'The Rivals'*: Richard Sheridan's play (1775).

17 *Prince Bismarck*: Otto von Bismarck (1815–98), statesman, often credited with the unification of Germany in 1871, and a dominant figure in European politics for more than thirty years.

18 grandes dames de par le monde: French, 'women of the world' not meaning all women, but those with some experience of life.

19 Cornhill Magazine *on 'Examinations in Fiction'*: published in vol. 83 (January 1901), pp. 80–9.

20 *Oxford tract …* Literae Fictitiae: the predecessor of the university English department, where literature was studied more generally and regarded as inferior to the study of Classics.

21 *Spiritualist and a Freethinker*: spiritualism, the contacting of the dead via a medium, was highly developed by the end of the nineteenth century and ranged from casual participants to fully formed Spiritualist Churches. Freethinkers held to a strictly rationalist philosophy and depended on evidence for any matter. These two speakers would have been firmly opposed in their views.

22 *Donelly … Shakespeare's work*: Ignatius Donnelly (1831–1901) was a US Congressman and amateur scientist who espoused a range of fringe beliefs, such as the existence of Atlantis. In 1888, he published *The Great Cryptogram* in which he proposed that Shakespeare's plays had been written by Francis Bacon. Lang was much involved in the

debate and eventually published his own refutation of the arguments in *Shakespeare, Bacon and the Great Unknown* (London: Longmans,1912).

23 *'Artemus Ward his Book'*: Artemus Ward was the pen-name of Charles Farrar Browne (1834–67) an American humourist. After the success of *Artemus Ward his Book* (1862) he published three further volumes with similar titles and content.

24 *Eliza Cook*: poet, (1818–89). Working-class and largely self-educated, her work reflected her beliefs in social equality and was popular with working-class readers.

25 *'History of the Jews … the English People'*: Henry Hart Milman (1791–1868), *The History of the Jews* (1829); William Nassau Molesworth (1816–90), *The History of England from the Year1830–74* (1874); John Richard Green (1837–83), *A Short History of the English People* (1874)

26 *'Life of Wellington'*: there were numerous biographies of Wellington; the edition mentioned could be any one of them.

27 *Smiles's 'Lives of the Engineers'*: Samuel Smiles (1812–1904) was a writer best known for his book *Self-Help* (1859) which recommended self-reliance as the means to success. His *Lives of the Engineers* in four volumes (1862) a collection of biographies also designed to promote the values of self-help.

28 *Robert Stephenson*: (1803–59). Son of another great engineer, Robert Stephenson, with whom he worked on a range of projects, including railway and bridge building.

29 *'Lives of British Reformers'*: this is likely to be George Stokes, *Lives of the British Reformers* (London: London Tract Society, 1844).

30 *'Industrial Biography'*: another work by Samuel Smiles (see note 27, above), published in 1863.

31 *'Elements of Geology'… and 'Experiments in Steel'*: Charles Lyell's *Principles of Geology* was first published between 1830 and 1833, of the other texts only Professor O. M. Mitchell, *The Planetary and Stellar Worlds* (London: T. Nelson, 1859) can be identified.

32 *Henry Cockton's 'Valentine Fox'*: Henry Cockton (1807–53) was an English novelist. His book is actually called *The Life and Adventures of Valentine Vox, the Ventriloquist* (1840) and not Fox as printed in the article.

33 *Mrs Henry Wood*: Ellen Wood (1814–87), was a prolific novelist who published under her married name, Mrs. Henry Wood. Her works were very popular, especially the best-seller *East Lynne* (1861), a sensation novel with a tangled plot of double identities. See also note 35 below.

34 *Sir William Richmond*: Richmond (1842–1921) was at this time Professor of Painting at the Royal Academy, London.

35 *Dean Stanley … 'East Lynne.'*: Arthur Penrhyn Stanley (1815–81) eventually became Dean of Westminster, but as a younger man had been engaged as a tutor to the Prince of Wales. He describes a boat trip on the Nile with the Prince and his companions, all of whom read Mrs. Henry Wood's best-selling novel and the quiz that they afterwards set each other on the story. See R. E. Prothero and G. G. Bradley, *The Life and Correspondence of Arthur Penrhyn Stanley* (London: John Murray, 1893), vol. 2, pp. 67–9.

36 *most refined vintages*: source not identified.

37 *Dieri*: aboriginal people of south Australia.

38 *Philosophy of the Unconscious*: book by Eduard von Hartmann which appeared in German in 1869). A major work, the three-volume English translation by W. C. Coupland had appeared in 1884.

39 *mediaeval Cnichtengild*: discussed in the essays of Horace Round. See this volume, p. 401, n. 8.

40 *Opera on the subject*: George Frederick Handel's *Israel in Egypt* (1739) is not really an opera but an oratorio.

41 *'vortices' … Montesquieu'*: Lang lists a number of topics and writers to indicate the range and elevated taste of past ages.

42 *'Tit-Bits'*: the weekly magazine *Tit-Bits from all the Interesting Books, Periodicals, and Newspapers of the World* was founded in 1881, aimed a mass audience with its edited pieces which were often of sentimental or sensational character. It did publish original fiction too, including some of Haggard's.

3 ON WRITERS AND WRITING

'Émile Zola', *The Fortnightly Review* (April 1882)

1 *'sandwich men'*: a form of advertising in which a person is paid to walk about the streets wearing a 'sandwich board': two pieces of wood or card carrying the advertisement, joined by straps worn over the shoulder. This was a common type of advertising during the later nineteenth century.

2 Lisez: French, 'Read!'

3 *puff preliminary*: Lang invents this term and variations upon it (such as the 'puff mutual'), based on Touchstone's speech in act 5, scene 4 of *As You Like It*, where Touchstone speaks of the 'Quip Modest', the 'Lie Circumstantial' and the 'Lie Direct.' Lang discusses 'puffing' and 'log-rolling' further in 'At the Sign of the Ship', *Longman's Magazine*, 9:50 (December 1886), pp. 216–20.

4 *biography of M. Zola*: Paul Alexis (1847–1901) was a French writer. He is best remembered today as the friend and biographer of Émile Zola and for Paul Cézanne's painting of Alexis reading to Zola. His biography was published in 1882, which may have prompted Lang's article.

5 de Sanctis at Naples: Francesco de Sanctis (1817–83) was an Italian scholar, literary critic, and Zola enthusiast The proceedings of his conference were published as *Zola and Assommoir: conference held at the Club of Naples Philological June 15, 1879* (Milan: Fratelli Treves, 1879).

6 naturalisme: literary style that endeavoured to reveal the truth of contemporary society through accurate and unflinching description of everyday life. Zola particularly drew analogies between scientific method and the novelist's work, and further believed that humans were simply higher animals, entirely determined by heredity and environment.

7 *positivement malade!'*: French, 'I am ill! This Zola makes me positively sick.'

8 *M. Sarcey*: Francisque Sarcey (1827–99) was a French journalist and drama critic who often expressed ill-tempered views on modern plays.

9 les illustres inconnnus: French, 'the illustrious unknowns'.

10 documents: research notebooks which were central to Zola's Naturalist method. His novels were based on dossiers of detailed information and observations of people, things and places.

11 *M. Hachette's establishment*: Zola's first literary employer, Louis Hachette (1800–64) was a publisher. Zola was initially a salesman before producing his own writing.

12 *the Salon*: the annual exhibition of art at the Académie des Beaux Arts in Paris. The Académie was the dominant, and conservative, authority on art and during the nineteenth century the show was the most important Europe.

13 Comme ... naturalisme: French, 'like the Messiah of the great school of Naturalism'.

14 *'delivered from the body of this death'*: Romans 7:4. This chapter of Romans is concerned with the disparity between body and mind and the tendency of the body to sin, despite the faith of the mind. Delivery from the body is release from sin.

15 *Gaboriau in* Le Crime d'Orcival: Emile Gaboriau, (1832–73). French novelist and journalist, and an important figure in the development of crime fiction, particularly in his series of novels featuring the detective Monsieur Lecoq, of which *Le Crime d'Orcival* (1867) is one.

16 *Paul and Virginia*: *Paul et Virginie*, novel by Jacques-Henri Bernardin de Saint-Pierre, first published in 1787. The title characters are a devoted couple who live an ideal life of harmony and equality on an island, uncorrupted by society or technology.

17 *alarmed Mr. Pickwick*: Ben Allen and Bob Sawyer are rather drunken and dissolute medical students in Charles Dickens's *The Pickwick Papers*. Mr Pickwick is alarmed by the freedom of their conversation about medical matters on a number of occasions.

18 *Claude Bernard*: French physiologist (1813–78) and author of a number of scientific works including *An Introduction to the Study of Experimental Medicine* (1865). He was a great advocate of objectivity in method and his principal experiments were in vivisection. He claimed that the scientist should be possessed by the pure intellectual idea and be able not to hear cries of pain from the animal.

19 *George Sand's*: Pseudonym of the French writer Armandine-Aurore-Lucie Dudevant (1804–76). Extremely successful, she produced Romantic novels of rustic life with a socialist tone as well as a good deal of literary criticism, theatrical work, political commentary and biographical pieces.

20 *By Proxy*: see this volume, p. 342, n. 19.

21 *Pinero*: see this volume, p. 346, n. 18.

22 Daudi: It is not clear to whom Lang is referring. It may be the French novelist Alphonse Daudet who Lang certainly regarded as being like Zola in his approach, However, Lang was very familiar with Daudet's work so it seems unlikely that he would misspell his name.

23 *Mr. Casaubon*... Mythologies: Casaubon is the scholar in George Eliot's *Middlemarch* (1871–2) and the first husband of the one of the central characters, Dorothea. He has spent his life making notes for his great work at the cost of experiencing life and feeling for other people. He dies with the work unfinished. The title has come to mean any great work doomed by the impossibility of its being completed.

24 *'un livre très documenté*, Souvenirs d'un valet de chambre: French, 'A well-researched book, *Memoirs of a Manservant*'.

25 *'loves without stain'*: from Swinburne's poem, 'Dedication, 1865', lines 63–4.

26 *lovely and of good report*: Philippians 4:8. The full line is 'whatsoever things are true, whatsoever things *are* honest, whatsoever things *are* just, whatsoever things *are* pure, whatsoever things *are* lovely, whatsoever things *are* of good report; if *there be* any virtue, and if *there be* any praise, think on these things.'

27 *'practical sociology'*: Zola refers to his work in this way in his 1880 essay 'The Experimental Novel'.

28 *physico-chemical laws*: Lang is translating here from Zola's essay 'The Experimental Novel, (1880).

29 *Lucas's* Traité de l'Hérédité Naturelle*:* Prosper Lucas (1805–85), a French biologist whose book referred to here was a long study of heredity, published in two parts in 1847 and 1850. Darwin also refers to it in his *Origin of Species* (1859).

30 *House of Atreus*: the family around which the Greek tragedies of Aeschylus's Orestia are centred. The four generations begin with Tantalus who is condemned forever to suffer hunger and thirst as fruit and water recede from his reach. He is the grandfather of Agamemnon and his cousin, Aegisthus. Aegisthus becomes the lover of Agamemnon's wife while the latter is away at the siege of Troy and they murder him on his return. Agamemnon had sacrificed his and Clytemnestra's eldest daughter to ensure a wind to propel the Greek fleet, and their remaining children Orestes and Electra play out the rest of the tragedy.

31 *awful Atê... Mycenae*: Atê is the Greek goddess of delusion and folly and is the force of hubris which brings about the downfall of heroes. Tiryns and Mycenae were the two cities ruled by the members of the tragic House of Atreus.

32 *Miss Yonge*: Charlotte Yonge (1823–1901). Beginning her writing career in 1848, Yonge became one of the most prolific English writers of the nineteenth century, producing around 160 works, mostly novels. A very commercially successful novelist, she was also much admired in the Victorian era, including by Trollope, Eliot, Tennyson and the Pre-Raphaelites. However, her works fell out of favour during the early twentieth century.

33 *bats to smite*: Francis Villon (1431–64) 'Double Ballad of the Like Report', stanza 5. It is a poem about the 'light loves' of casual sexual relationships. Villon's own life was a dramatic one, he killed a man in a fight, was arrested and tortured on suspicion of theft and twice had the death penalty passed on him and then reduced to banishment.

34 *'Être maître ... du travail humain*?' French 'Being master of good and evil, arrange life ... isn't the life of the workers the most useful and moral of human labour ?'
The quotation is from Zola's essay 'The Experimental Novel.'

35 *Special Reporter's*: special reporters were usually those who covered the criminal courts and the divorce courts. Their reports were typically sensational and formed a good part of the contents of the new cheap newspapers that began to be produced in the later nineteenth century

---

'Of Modern English Poetry', *Letters on Literature* (1889)

1 *'bright home in the setting sun'*: this phrase appears to be a quotation from William Dean Howells' novel *A Hazard of New Fortunes* which had appeared earlier in 1889. Given

Lang and Howell's antagonism, Lang is probably having a private joke at Howells' expense by imagining his naïve American correspondent as one of Howell's characters. However, *Letters on Literature* had originally appeared as separate columns in the New York magazine the *Independent*, also in 1889, so it is difficult to ascertain the precise timing. The joke may perhaps be the other way round.

2 *'I may write till they can spell'*: 'I may write till she can spell', Matthew Prior (1664–1721), 'To a Child of Quality, Five Years Old'. The poet is suggesting that he will continue to write to the child until she can comprehend the verses.

3 *to their address*: simply meaning 'directly'.

4 *soubrette*: stock character in drama or opera, a cheeky maidservant.

5 *Seniores priores*: Latin, 'elders first'.

6 *Rhamses*: now more usually spelt Rameses or Ramesses, Lang refers to Ramesses II, who ruled Egypt for more than 60 years between 1279 BCE and 1213 BCE.

7 *'None but minstrels list of sonneting'*: Shakespeare, *Love's Labours Lost*, act 4, scene 3.

8 *the faint embers on the altar of Apollo*: Frederick Furnivall (1825–1910) was one of the founders of the Oxford English Dictionary, as well as of a number of the societies that Lang mentions: the Early English Text Society (1864), the Chaucer Society (1868), the Ballad Society (1868), the New Shakspere Society (1873), the Browning Society (1881), the Wyclif Society (1882), and the Shelley Society (1885). Lang fancifully imagines Furnivall and his associates as priests of Apollo, the Greek god of music and poetry.

9 *during the war of Troy*: the remark made in line 352 of the first book of the *Odyssey*.

10 *'Homer is enough for all'*: Theocritus, *Idylls*, 12–18.

11 *the blind night that shall again receive it*: this is a reference to the description of human life as being like the flight of a small bird through the door of a nobleman's feast hall, briefly being in light and warmth and good company, and then flying out again into the cold, dark night. The story is recounted in Bede's *Ecclesiastical History of the English People*, completed in about 731. Lang would also probably have known the story from his folklore studies and comparative work on Northern European mythology.

12 *some unlucky gentleman*: quotation not identified, but Lang's vagueness about the gentleman suggests that he may have picked up the anecdote from Benjamin Jowett (see this volume, p. 360, n. 12) who had been his tutor at Oxford. See 'Benjamin Jowett' in *Personal Ethics*, ed. K. Kirk (London, 1934), pp. 37–8.

13 *Albert*: Prince Albert (1819–61), husband of Queen Victoria.

14 *'what the grain has been'*: the *Odyssey*, book 14.

15 *'Logic' of Hegel*: the philosopher Georg Hegel (1770–1831) published his *Science of Logic* in three parts (1811, 1812, 1816). It is a formidable work and Hegel is notoriously challenging to read.

16 *story of two clever girls*: source not identified.

17 *'a thousand hopes and fears'*: from Browning's poem, *Bishop Blougram's Apology* (1855).

18 *'a chain of highly valuable thoughts'*: this is not a quotation, but Lang's own words. It is also a version of the title of one of his own poems, 'A Highly Valuable Chain of Thoughts', *New Collected Rhymes* (London: Longmans, Green and Co., 1905).

19 *'wet, bird-haunted English lawns'*: Matthew Arnold, *Empedocles on Etna*, published anonymously in 1852.

20 *grassy harvest of the river yields'*: Matthew Arnold, 'Thyrsis'(1865), though the line actually reads 'harvest of the river fields.'

21 *while things subsist'*: Lang misquotes Arnold's poem 'Resignation' quite substantially here. The lines actually read: 'That life, whose dumb wish is not miss'd, / If birth proceeds, if things subsist'.

22 'lutin': an unthreatening imp-like figure in French folklore and fairy tale.

23 '*takes the pen from his hand and writes for him'*: quotation not identified, though it may be a description of Wordsworth by Arnold.

24 '*the surest-footed'*: in his review 'Mr. Arnold's New Poems', *Fortnightly Review*, 2:10 (October 1867), pp. 414–55

25 *Cadmus and Harmonia'*: Lang must be quoting from memory, as he misremembers the actual line from Arnold's 'Cadmus and Harmonia' which is 'two bright and aged snakes, who once were Cadmus and Harmonia'.

26 *'flutes of the Grecians'*: see this volume, p. 351, n. 47.

27 *Apollo and Marsyas*: in Greek mythology there are several versions of this story, but usually it is the satyr Marsyas who challenges the god Apollo to a musical contest. He loses and his punishment is to be flayed and his skin nailed to a tree.

28 *best foot, anapaest or trochee*: Lang puns (as does Browning in his poem 'Respectability' 1852) on two meanings of 'foot': the human foot of the proverbial phrase 'to put one's best foot forward' meaning to make a determined effort, and the foot of poetic metre, of which anapest and trochee are examples.

29 *Old Corporal Raddlebanes*: the reference is to Walter Scott's novel *Old Mortality* (1816), chapter 11.

30 fallentis semita vitae: the quotation is from Horace, *Epistles* I, 18, 102–3, but widely used by other later poets. It is usually translated from the Latin as 'the untrodden paths of life' though the Latin also carries a sense of secrecy rather than just unfamiliarity.

31 'Porphyria's Lover': dramatic monologue by Robert Browning, first published in 1836.

32 *Mr Burne-Jones*: Edward Burne-Jones (1833–98). English painter, illustrator and designer associated with the Pre-Raphaelite movement. A friend of William Morris at Oxford in the 1850s, he was a major figure in the revival of stained glass work in Britain.

33 *'art manufacture'*: Lang makes a contrast between 'art' by which he implies single works of genius, with 'art manufacture' meaning possibly good and beautiful things, but produced for sale. He is perhaps thinking of Morris's other career as a commercial producer of items of furniture and interior decoration.

34 *they are 'good, but copious'*: this seems to have been said of Gladstone's speeches, but the quotation has not been further identified.

35 *'The Mount is mute, the channel dry'*: Matthew Arnold, 'The Progress of Poesy' (1867).

36 'the meteoric poet': Robert Browning, *Balaustion's Adventure* (1871), line 203.

37 *'blue cold fields ... air'*: the line from Swinburne's 'Atalanta in Calydon' actually reads 'the blue sad fields and folds of air'.

38 *'mighty-mouthed inventer of harmonies'*: Tennyson's description of the poet John Milton, from his sonnet 'Milton'.

39 *Landor*: the poem is 'In Memory of Walter Savage Landor' and is not in Greek; Lang means to suggest that it is in the style of a Greek eulogy.

40 *rondels to small boys and girls*: Herod was King of Judea at the time of Jesus. In the biblical account he was responsible for the 'Massacre of the Innocents', the killing of male children in order to prevent Jesus becoming king. Victor Hugo went into political exile when Napoleon III assumed the throne and his works were banned under the regime.

41 Ne quid nimis: Latin, usually translated as 'nothing in excess' or more loosely as meaning 'moderation in all things'.

42 *Professor Freeman*: Edward Freeman (1823–92), Regius Professor of History at Oxford and the author of more than two hundred works. He also stood for Parliament and was known for the forthright expression of his views, both on politics and history.

'Victorian Literature', *Good Words* (January 1897)

1 *any* anointed *monarch*: Lang is referring to Queen Victoria; 1897 was her Diamond Jubilee year, marking sixty years on the throne. In his footnote, however, he is referring to James Stuart, 'The Old Pretender' (1688–1766) who was the son of the deposed James II of England (James VII of Scotland). He claimed the English, Scottish and Irish thrones after the death of his father in 1701, thus for those who believed in the legitimacy of his claim (the 'Jacobites') he would have been king for sixty-five years.

2 *Reynolds ... Cotman*: Lang names these eighteenth-century artists, all of whom were also members of the Royal Academy and much admired, in order to contrast what he thinks to be the inferior art and artists of his own period.

3 *Amuraths*: Lang may be recalling the line in *Henry IV Part 2*, act 5, scene 2: 'This is the English, not the Turkish court; Not Amurath an Amurath succeeds'. The reference is to sultans of the Ottoman Empire, beginning with Murad I (1326–89), who attempted to establish power by killing their own sons and brothers. Lang is suggesting that modern artists are similar in their bitter competitiveness.

4 *'standing ... where it should not.'* Matthew 24:151–6.

5 *Landor*: Walter Savage Landor (1775–1864). A writer and poet, his most celebrated work *Imaginary Conversations of Literary Men and Statesmen* (1824–9) is a collection of dialogues between historical characters on topics such as philosophy, politics and romance.

6 *Milman*: Henry Milman (1791–1868) wrote some fiction in the form of drama, but was principally known for translations of classical authors and religious history.

7 *'the abyssmal depths of personality'*: see this volume, p. 338, n. 20.

8 *George III ... Shakspeare*: presumably referring to this remark 'But was there ever such stuff as a great part of Shakespeare? Is there not sad stuff? But one must not say so.' Samuel Bent, *Familiar Short Sayings of Great Men* (Boston: Ticknor and Co., 1887).

9 *Lucretius*: Roman poet (*c.*99 BCE–55 BCE) whose work *De Rerum Natura* seeks to show that the world can be explained without recourse to notions of divine intervention.

10 flammantia moenia mundi: Latin, 'the flaming walls of the world'. Lucretius, *De Rerum Natura* (I, 73).

11 *flowering often in some lonely word'*: from Tennyson's poem 'To Virgil, Written at the Request of the Mantuans for the Nineteenth Centenary of Virgil's Death' (1882).

12 '*the Muse has gone away'*: the line is 'The Muse be gone away' and is the epigraph to Matthew Arnold's poem 'A Picture at Newstead' (1867).

13 *'booms'*: used in the nineteenth-century American slang sense, meaning promotions, advertising.

14 *Verlaine … the Decadents*: Lang uses these poets and playwrights to suggest writers and movements currently fashionable and discussed in the press. He does not admire them.

15 *'on admitted absurdity?':'* Alcibiades is speaking about democracy in Plato's *Alcibiades*, 1.

16 *the wind blowing as it listeth*: see this volume, p. 351, n. 46.

17 *'new Avatar,'*: in Hindu mythology, an avatar is an earthly form of a god.

18 *to do with literature?:* Augustine Birrell (1850–1933) was a politician and academic who expressed some very forthright views on literature. The remark is made in 'Dr Johnson', first published in 1887, *The Collected Essays and Addresses of Augustine Birrell* (New York: Scribner and Sons, 1925), p. 125.

19 *Mr. Gardiner*: Samuel Rawson Gardiner (1829–1902), academic and historian, whose huge history of the English Puritan revolution occupied nineteen volumes and was published over two decades (1883–1903).

20 *Jacobites*: see this volume, p. 383, n. 34.

21 *Mariolaters*: the usual sense of the word is a description of devotees of the Virgin Mary, but Lang may also be suggesting the cult of Mary, Queen of Scots.

22 *Ancient Pistol*: hard-drinking and belligerent character in Shakespeare's *Henry IV Part 2*.

23 *Mr. Freeman*: see this volume, p. 367, n. 42.

24 *Historical Manuscripts Commission*: a Royal Commission established in 1869 in order to locate, identify and catalogue manuscripts and papers of historical interest and importance. It is now part of the Public Records Office.

25 belles lettres: literally translated from the French, 'fine writing', but also often used to refer to prose writing that does not belong to a particular genre. It has also come to have a dismissive connotation, with a 'belles-lettrist' meaning a dilettante of literary culture.

26 spectacle *and* engouement: French, meaning 'performance' and 'devotion '. Lang means to suggest that the staging of the plays and the audience's infatuation with certain actors accounts for Shakespeare being played at all.

27 *Marlowe, … Webster*: Jacobean playwrights whose work was not much performed during the nineteenth century as it was seen as crude, violent and uninstructive.

28 '*Atalanta in Calydon,' or 'Chastelard'*: Swinburne's long dramatic poem and his poetic drama, both published in 1865.

29 '*Charley's Aunt' is still running*: a farce by Brandon Thomas (1848–1914), first performed in 1892 and achieving a record-breaking run of 1,466 performances.

30 *Mr. Henley*: William Ernest Henley (1849–1903), poet and critic. He was a friend and collaborator of Robert Louis Stevenson and a bold editor of the *New Review*, publishing Hardy, Kipling, Yeats, H. G.Wells and Henry James, among others.

31 *'Beau Austin?*: co-written by W. E. Henley and Stevenson, it was privately printed in 1884 and performed first in the winter of 1890. Although the noted actor Herbert Beerbohm Tree was enthusiastic about his part in it, the play was not a great success.

32 *'ettling at'*: Scots dialect, 'aiming for', 'attempting'.

33 *'A Remonstrance with Boz'*: the article's title is actually 'A Remonstrance with Dickens', *Blackwood's Edinburgh Magazine* 81:498 (April 1857), pp. 490–503.

34 *objections to Dickens*: the articles were anonymous and may well have been by different writers, but one example is 'Mr Dickens', *Saturday Review*, 5:132 (8 May 1858), pp. 474–5.

35 *their name, happily, is Legion*: the phrase comes from the Bible, 'My name is Legion, for we are many.' Mark 5:9.

36 bêtes noires: French, literally 'black beasts', meaning a person's particular dislikes or enemies.

37 *like Sir Richard Strachan, one is 'longing to be at them'*: Strachan (1760–1828) was an officer in the navy. After some confusion in an engagement under his command, a comic verse circulated: 'The Earl of Chatham, with his sword drawn, / Stood waiting for Sir Richard Strachan; / Sir Richard, longing to be at 'em, / Stood waiting for the Earl of Chatham'.

38 *Lovelace ... Graham of Gartmore*: poets, Lovelace and Suckling at the time of the English Civil War, William Hamilton in the early eighteenth century and Robert Graham in the late eighteenth century.

39 *Herbert Spencer... Mr. Green*: Spencer (1820–1903), philosopher and sociologist, much influenced by Darwin's ideas on evolution. Thomas Green (1836–82), philosopher and proponent of ethical socialism, disagreed profoundly with Spencer's position.

40 *The great Darwin*: Charles Darwin (1809–82). Naturalist who proposed that species evolved over time and originated from a common ancestor. His work in which this is elaborated, *On the Origin of Species* was published in 1859. Although he was not the first to suggest transmutation of species and his first paper on the topic (1858) drew little attention, his work became one of the profoundly transformational theories of modern science.

'Notes on Fiction', *Longman's Magazine* (February 1891)

1 *M. Jusserand*: Jusserand was the French ambassador to the US. His *English Novel during the Time of Shakespeare* (London: T. Fisher Unwin) was published in 1890.

2 *'live like other men, only more purely'*: quotation not identified.

3 *like King Candaules of Lydia, was 'in love with his wife,'*: Candaules was a king of the ancient Kingdom of Lydia from 735 BCE to 718 BCE. The earliest story, related by Herodotus in the fifth century BCE, tells how Candaules persuaded another man to spy on his naked wife. Shamed, his wife then arranged Candaules' death. Although Fielding

married his pregnant maid after the death of his first wife, it isn't quite clear what Lang is suggesting here.

4 *Dora*: in Charles Dickens, *David Copperfield* (1849–50) Dora is David's pretty but childish first wife.

5 *Mr. Black*: Charles Black (1841–98), Scottish writer of several novels, very popular in his time.

6 *Dahlia*: in George Meredith's novel *Rhoda Fleming* (1865) Dahlia is the sister of the title character, and is seduced by a worthless upper-class man.

7 *both the Kingsleys*: Charles (1819–75) author of *The Water Babies* (1863) amongst other books, and Henry (1830–1876) his less successful younger brother, also a writer of novels.

8 *Malory*: the line comes from Molière (*The School for Wives,* act 3, scene 4), rather than Malory. This is an odd mistake for Lang to make and may be a misprint.

9 '*Amaryllis … Neæra's hair*': from John Milton's *Lycidas* (1637) lines 69–70. Using figures from classical pastoral poetry, Milton is questioning whether it is better, in view of the shortness of life, to work hard or to enjoy oneself.

10 *Brynhild and Sigurd*: see this volume, p. 351, n. 49.

11 *Miss Broughton*: Rhoda Broughton (1840 –1920) was a romantic novelist, very popular in her time.

12 Miss Braddon: Mary Elizabeth Braddon (1835–1915) was a popular novelist. Her 1862 novel *Lady Audley's Secret* was among the first 'sensation' novels of the period, combining romance and mystery.

13 *£ s. d*: the symbols for pounds, shillings and pence, units of English currency.

14 *Hawley Smart*: Henry Hawley Smart (1833–93) was a prolific and best-selling writer.

15 *Manon Lescaut …. Maupassant*: *Manon Lescaut* (*L'Histoire du chevalier des Grieux et de Manon Lescaut*), novel by French author Abbé Prévost, published in 1731. Paul Bourget (1852–1935) was a French novelist and critic and Guy de Maupassant (1850–93) a French short story writer and novelist who was part of the group of young authors that formed around Zola.

16 *As if love were an affair … have any concern*: François, duc de La Rochefoucauld (1613–80), *Moral Maxims and Reflections,* maxim 418.

17 *Dotheboys Hall*: the dreadful school in Dickens' *Nicholas Nickleby* (1839), not in *David Copperfield* as Lang would seem to suggest.

18 *Mr Murdstone*: character in Dickens' *David Copperfield,* David's unpleasant and possibly murderous step-father.

19 *Berlin wools*: a style of embroidery.

'Behind the Novelist's Scenes', *Illustrated London News* (July 1892)

1 *The Wrecker,' Mr. Stevenson*: Stevenson's novel was written in collaboration with his stepson Lloyd Osbourne. It centres on an abandoned wrecked ship, and the mystery of the missing crew is solved by following clues in a stamp album. The same issue of

the *Illustrated London News* in which Lang's piece appears also contains an instalment of Stevenson's story 'Uma; or the Beach of Falesá'.

2 *'epilude'*: Robert Buchanan was the Scottish poet referred to by Swinburne as a 'writer of epiludes'. See also this volume, p. 347, n. 13.

3 *Lloyd Osborne*: see n. 1, above.

4 *Flying Scud ... Mr. Carthew*: the Flying Scud is the abandoned ship in the story, and Mr Carthew one of the characters.

5 *'Treasure Island'*: Stevenson's novel (1883) was originally serialised in the children's magazine *Young Folks* between 1881 and 1882 under a pseudonym, Captain George North.

6 *Numa Roumestan and Jack*: eponymous charatcters in Daudet's novels, published in 1880 and 1876 respectively.

7 *Ficelles*: French, 'strings'.

8 *'Robert Elsmere'*: novel by Mrs Humphrey Ward (1888). It is set in Oxford and concerns the crisis of faith experienced by the central character.

'The Mystery of Style', *Illustrated London News* (February 1893)

1 *'David Balfour'*: Stevenson's novel *Catriona* was first published under the title *David Balfour* in the American magazine *Atalanta* between December 1892 and September 1893. Thus Lang was in the middle of reading it at the time of writing this article and the book was yet to be re-named.

2 *Lyttelton ... Ayton*: Edward Lyttelton played cricket for Middlesex and football for England; Egerton Castle was an antiquarian and swordsman, Laurie Ayton a famous golfer.

3 *Dr Grace*: W. G. Grace (1848–1915) is considered by many to have been the greatest cricketer of all time and was important in the development of the game.

4 *Mrs Gamp*: Sairey Gamp is a drunken, dissolute nurse in Dickens' novel *Martin Chuzzlewit* (1844).

5 *Mr Mantalini*: disreputable character in Dickens's *Nicholas Nickleby* (1839)

6 *'army with banners'*: from the Bible, 'Thou *art* beautiful, O my love, as Tirzah, comely as Jerusalem, terrible as an army with banners', *Song of Solomon* 6:4.

7 *'roof and crown of things'*: from Tennyson's poem *The Lotus Eaters* (1832).

'The Supernatural in Fiction', *Adventures Among Books* (1905)

1 *'I leave it to yourself, sir'*: the taxi-driver would be subtly suggesting that a tip would be welcome, but leaving the amount to the passenger's discretion.

2 *'Christabel'*: The quotation is the description of Geraldine from stanza 29 of Coleridge's long, unfinished narrative poem *Christabel.* See this volume, p. 359, n. 1.

3 *Mr. Gilman*: Coleridge lived with Dr James Gillman (rather than Gilman) in the latter years of his life. Gillman, in his *Life of Samuel Taylor Coleridge* (London: Pickering, 1838)

suggested a synopsis of the missing part of the poem that he said Coleridge had planned.

4 *in the very first ... of a vision*: Coleridge makes this claim in the preface to the first published version of the poem in 1816.

5 speciosa miracula: Latin, 'impressive wonders', from Horace, *Ars Poetica*, 140–4.

6 *'but have passed ... the miracles they celebrate'*: *Letters of Charles Lamb* (London: J.M. Dent, 1909), vol. 1, p. 105.

7 *'It is as bad as ... of its truth?'*: Letter to Wordsworth, 30 January 1801, *Letters of Charles Lamb* (London: J. M. Dent, 1909), vol. 1, p. 177.

8 *'disliked all the miraculous part of it'*: ibid.

9 *'a character and a profession'*: ibid.

10 *'an excellent character'*: meaning 'a good reference'. This is not a quotation, but Lang continuing the idea that the Mariner should have had a job.

11 *Mr. Marshall ... was reading,'*: Letter to Thomas Manning, 24 September 1802, *Letters of Charles Lamb* (London: J. M. Dent, 1909), vol. 1, p. 202.

12 *'this monstrous apparition'*: William Shakespeare, *Julius Caesar*, act 4, scene 3.

13 *Les Dames Vertes*: For George Sand see this volume, p. 363, n. 19. Her novel *Les Dames Vertes* (1857) describes an encounter with the three 'green ladies' of the title, who are mysterious witch-like figures in an old mansion.

14 *'was that my master's voice?*: Robert Louis Stevenson, *The Strange Case of Dr Jekyll and Mr Hyde*, (London: Penguin, 1985), p. 64.

15 *ancestral Covenanter*: Covenanters were people in Scotland who signed the National Covenant in 1638, opposing the interference of the monarchy in the Church of Scotland. They were persecuted, often violently, by the English government and crown, and divisions between the Highland and Lowland Scots were widened over the issues involved. Their religious beliefs were strict and informed by the sense of the real presence of evil.

16 *Southey called that poem a Dutch piece of work*: 'We do not sufficiently understand the story to analyse it. It is a Dutch attempt at German sublimity. Genius has here been employed in producing a poem of little merit'. Robert Southey's review of *Lyrical Ballads, Critical Review* 24 (October 1798), p. 201.

17 et inania regna: Latin, 'in the kingdom of shadows', Virgil's term for the underworld, *Aeneid* 6.269.

18 '*But it needs Heaven-sent moments for this skill:*' Matthew Arnold, 'The Scholar Gipsy' (1852), stanza 5.

4 SCOTLAND, HISTORY AND BIOGRAPHY

'The Celtic Renascence', *Blackwood's Edinburgh Magazine* (February 1897)

1 *Celtic Movement ... agitation in Celtdom*: there were several movements during the nineteenth century that manifested an interest in the traditional literature, songs and culture of Ireland, Scotland and Wales, and to some extent Cornwall, the Isle of Man

and Brittany (the other 'Celtic nations'). In the latter years of the century, William Sharp was the best known of the Scottish writers and W. B. Yeats of the Irish. There were other significant figures; Douglas Hyde, for example, a scholar of the Irish language, who founded the Gaelic League in 1893, through which many of the Irish Nationalists became politicised. The question of Home Rule for Ireland was still a divisive topic in British politics.

2 *William Sharp, Miss Fiona Macleod*: these two writers are in fact the same person. The poet and biographer William Sharp (1855–1905) assumed an additional female literary identity from 1893, producing romantic and mystical Celtic stories. This fact remained almost unknown during Sharp's lifetime and it is obvious from his comment here that Lang was unaware of it.

3 *Professor Geddes*: Sir Patrick Geddes (1854–1932) had a very wide-ranging career. A biologist and sociologist, he was also important in re-thinking town planning and architecture for mass housing. A Scotsman, he was prominent in the promotion of Scottish culture and identity, founding the nationalist magazine *Evergreen* with William Sharp (see note 2, above). His manifesto, 'The Scots Renascence' was published in the first issue in the spring of 1895.

4 *Moses … Celtic Literature*: in the Biblical narrative Aaron is the elder brother of Moses and a persuasive orator on his behalf. Moses leads the people of Israel out of captivity in Egypt. Miriam is their sister. Here Lang is possibly only half-frivolously implying a comparison between the oppressed Jews and the Celts.

5 *Macpherson's 'Ossian'… critical opinion*: Macpherson began publishing what he claimed to be translations of Scots Gaelic epic poetry in 1760. Ossian was the narrator and supposedly the poet, but questions were raised about the authenticity of the works almost immediately. Despite that, many people continued to believe them genuine and they were influential on other writers and poets, including Goethe.

6 *'the claymore plied'*: a targe was a shield and a claymore a heavy sword, both used by Scottish fighters. The source of the quotation has not been identified.

7 *translated by Mr Hutchison*: William G. Hutchison was the translator of many of Renan's works into English, including the controversial *Life of Jesus* which was published in the same year as Lang's article.

8 *'Myvyrian Archaeology,'… Lady Charlotte Guest*: both are early Welsh literature. The three-volume 'Myvyrian' contains poetry and prose, a small amount of which was probably forged by one of its editors. Owen Jones funded the work, published 1801–7. Guest (1811–95) translated and published between 1838 and 1849 a large group of mediaeval Welsh stories, and gave them the title 'Mabinogi' by which they are now known.

9 *Gael and Cymry*: Scotsman and Welshman.

10 de la vient sa tristesse*:* French, 'from whence their sorrow comes.'

11 *The Celt … Harold Skimpole*: character in Charles Dickens' *Bleak House* (1852–3). Skimpole is not referring to the Celt, in fact he is discussing his butcher. Skimpole glosses over possible failings.

12 *hydromel*: water mixed with honey, when fermented it becomes an alcoholic drink, also known as mead.

13 *St Brandan and Peredur*: sixth century Irish saint and a hero from the *Mabinogion*.

14 *as the negro said*: this phrase seems to have been almost proverbial during the nineteenth century. No origin has been found, and it appears variously as spoken by 'a negro', 'Abdullah', a man from Madras, 'John Chinaman' and other non-white subjects.

15 enivrement de carnage: French, literally, 'intoxication of slaughter'.

16 *more Celtic than Christian*: Ernst Renan's description from *Poetry of the Celtic Races* (1896).

17 *Fairies of Domremy*: Domrémy was the birthplace of Joan of Arc. At her trial the judges emphasised the story of a 'fairy tree' near the village and magical practices associated with it.

18 *Henri Martin*: French historian (1813–83) whose nineteen-volume *Histoire de France* (1830–65) contained an account of Joan of Arc's life.

19 *La Pucelle*: Joan of Arc was also called La Pucelle d'Orléans – the Maid of Orleans.

20 *Taliesin*: an early Welsh poet, possibly sixth century. Though there are works by him that refer to apparently contemporary events there is no historical record of him. He becomes a somewhat mythologised figure, sometimes imagined as poet to King Arthur.

21 *Ugrians*: a people whose existence was hypothesised from the linguistic similarities of some languages in the regions of Finland, Hungary and Estonia.

22 *singular beauty and power*: Matthew Arnold, *On the Study of Celtic Literature* (London: Smith, Elder, 1867), p. 80.

23 *south of the Tweed*: the river Tweed is the historic boundary between Scotland and England.

24 *Nibelungen Lied*: epic poem in Middle High German, surviving in manuscripts from the thirteenth century, but possibly dating from much earlier in oral form. Episodes are also found in the Old Norse Eddas, see this volume, p. 339, n. 34.

25 *Lord Strangford denied the facts*: Percy Smyth, Lord Strangford (1826–69) was a philologist and friend of Arnold. He reviewed Arnold's 'On the Study of Celtic Literature' in the *Pall Mall Gazette* 346 (19 March 1866).

26 *Pindar*: Greek lyric poet (*c.*522 BCE–443 BCE).

27 Lywarch … *old age*: Llywarch Hen was a sixth-century poet. With Taliesin, Aneirin, and Myrddin he is thought of as one of the four great bards of Welsh poetry. His poem 'I was formerly fair of limb' is presumably the work to which Lang refers.

28 *Alcaeus … Ecclesiastes*: sixth-century BCE Greek lyric poet, seventh century BCE Greek elegiac poet and the anonymous author of the Old Testament Book of Ecclesiastes.

29 *Manfred … Prometheus*: all three are poems by Byron, written between 1810 and 1817.

30 *Alfieri or Leopardi*: Vittorio Alfieri (1749–1803), writer of poetry and drama and Giacomo Leopardi (1798–1837) poet and essayist.

31 *Verkovitch*: Stephen Verkovich (1827–93), Serbian Croat Franciscan monk and important collector of Bulgarian folk songs. His major collection, *Veda Slovena*, was published in two volumes in 1874 and 1881.

32 *Lönnrot*: Elias Lönnrot (1802–84), collector of Finnish oral poetry and the compiler of the *Kalevala*, see this volume, p. 338, n. 28.

33 *Nutt … Maclean*: Nutt (1856–1910), John Francis Campbell (1821–85) and Maclean (1818–93), were all contemporary Celtic scholars. The latter two worked closely together.

34 *Professor O'Curry*: Eugene O'Curry (1794–1862), scholar of Irish language and history, appointed chair of Irish history and archaeology on the establishment of the Catholic University of Ireland in 1854.

35 *Squire Western*: character in Henry Fielding's *Tom Jones*. The reference is not particularly relevant, Lang just means to suggest that the argument is not a logical one.

36 *Sassenach*: Gaelic word for Saxon, used now by Scots as a derogatory term for an English person.

37 *Slough of Despond*: In John Bunyan's allegory *Pilgrim's Progress* (1678) the Slough of Despond is a deep bog that Christian has to cross on his journey. It has come to mean an episode of depression or discouragement.

38 *omits the proof*: Robert Kirk (1644–92) was a minister, Gaelic scholar and collector of folklore. His book on folkore, ghosts and second sight was re-published by Scott in 1815 and Lang wrote the introduction to an edition published in 1893.

39 *poll-book … dog ate it*: Lang most likely found this incident in *Handy Andy* (1842) a novel by the Irish humourist Samuel Lover (1797–1868) rather than in Irish history.

40 *word-picture … Mr Whistler*: James McNeill Whistler (1834–1903), controversial painter of the 'art for art's sake' movement. He emphasised colour and tone rather than narrative or moral messages in his work.

41 &c.,*κ.τ.λ, u.s.w.*: English, Greek and German abbreviations, all meaning 'and so on'.

42 *Stuart Papers in the Scots College*: collection of documents of the Scottish court-in-exile held in the Scots College in Paris. Some were stolen and others lost in the French Revolution. Macpherson's pre-revolutionary 'transcripts' of these papers came under suspicion as forgeries.

43 *Ireland's … Chatterton's*: William Ireland (1775–1835) forged Shakespearean works and papers, Thomas Chatterton (1752–70) mediaeval poetry. Lang was interested in forgery and referred to it many times, see, for example 'Literary Forgeries', *Contemporary Review* 44 (December 1883), pp. 837–49.

44 *Amergin and Taliesin … Poet's Corner*: Lang is making a broad analogy here, in which he suggests that Sharp has taken the widest possible range of Celtic writers, from the great and almost mythical ancient bards to the recent and undistinguished. He compares that with a similar range in Greek.

45 *being a Stuart*: Oliver Cromwell's mother was Elizabeth Steward, though she appears not to be connected to the royal Stuarts beyond jokes about such a descent that Cromwell himself is supposed to have made.

46 *Maquet*: Auguste Maquet (1813–88) French writer, collaborator with Alexandre Dumas the Elder.

47 *Hereward the Wake*: eleventh-century rebel leader of resistance against the Norman Conquest.

48 *Picts*: ancient tribes of eastern and northern Scotland who were the ancestors of modern Scots.

49 *Quarterings … themselves*: quarterings appear on coats of arms and indicate families of ancestry. Scott's house at Abbotsford featured the quartering of his forebears, the families Lang names.

50 *Professor Brinton*: Daniel Garrison Brinton (1837–99) was an American ethnologist who published a number of works on American Indians.

51 *the poet says*: from the poem 'Sir Joseph Banks and the Boiled Fleas' by John Wolcot (1738–1819) who used the pen-name 'Peter Pindar'.

52 *Moidart*: remote area of western Scotland. Lang wrote about instances of second sight in Scotland in 'Opening the Gates of Distance', chapter 4 in *The Making of Religion* (1898).

53 *Tupper*: Martin Tupper (1810–9), author of the very popular *Proverbial Philosophy* (1837) which was not highly regarded as poetry.

54 *Grant Allen:* (1848–99) Canadian-born writer whose first books were on philosophy. His philosophy was influenced by the sociological evolutionary theories of Herbert Spencer. He published articles on scientific subjects in journals such the *Cornhill* and in the 1880s began writing fiction. His best-seller was *The Woman Who Did* (1895), a serious novel with an anti-marriage heroine that caused controversy on publication. Allen was a friend of Lang, though they often disagreed, sometimes publically as in the *Illustrated London News*. See Volume 1, p. 322.

55 voulu, *of* malice prepense: *voulu* means 'would-be' and *malice prepense* means 'deliberately intended'.

56 *Dr Hyde*: Douglas Hyde (186–949) founder of the Gaelic League, first President of Ireland (1938).

57 *Miss Fiona Macleod … Hopper*: poets of the Celtic Revival of the late nineteenth century. Mcleod (see this volume, p. 373, n. 2) was well-known. W. B. Yeats (1865–1939) became a very prominent literary figure, but at this time was quite early in his career. Hopper (1871–1906) wrote on Irish themes and Matheson (1863–1943) on Scottish, but were less well known.

58 Lyttonian: in the style of Edward Bulwer Lytton, that is, dramatic historical work.

59 *Mr Neil Munro*: Munro (1863–1930) was Scottish journalist and writer. He produced humourous short stories under his pen-name Hugh Foulis, but also historical stories and novels set in the Highlands. Only the first of these, *The Lost Pibroch* had been published at the time of Lang's article.

60 C'est de pur … Lytton: French, 'It is pure James Macpherson, doubled with Bulwer Lytton.' Lang is suggesting that the work is inauthentic and over-dramatic.

61 *sennachies*: traditional Irish story-tellers. The word is spelled with many variations, such as seanchaidhe in Gaelic, shanachie in English.

62 verae causae*:* Latin, 'true causes'.

Introduction to Sir Walter Scott, ***Waverley, Or 'Tis Sixty Years Since*** **(1893)**

1 *Wordsworth's sonnet*: 'On the Departure of Sir Walter Scott from Abbotsford, for Naples' (1835).

2 *Lady Louisa Stuart*: (1757–1851), aristocrat and writer of memoirs and biographies, grand-daughter of Lady Mary Wortley Montagu (see this volume, p. 357, n. 21).

3 *Mackenzie's 'Man of Feeling'*: sentimental novel by the Scottish author Henry Mackenzie (174–831) published in 1771. A series of short moral scenes, it was a best-seller at the time of publication.

4 *Rousseau's 'Nouvelle Heloise,'*: *Julie, ou la nouvelle Héloïse,* novel consisting of letters between two lovers by Jean-Jacques Rousseau, published in 1761 to sensational public reaction.

5 *Ellis, Erskine*: George Ellis (1753–1815) antiquary and critic and William Erskine (1768–1862) barrister, writer of songs and friend of Scott.

6 *'The Goodnatured Man'*: 1768 comedy by Irish writer Oliver Goldsmith (1730–74).

7 *'Modern Painters'*: the five volumes of Ruskin's work important work *Modern Painters* appeared between 1843 and 1860. Ruskin makes the statement about his writing in the essay 'Fiction Fair and Foul' (1881).

8 *stippler or niggler*: person working in tiny detail or preoccupied with trifling matters.

9 *out of his way*: source not identified.

10 dénouements: French, literally 'outcome', and now widely used to mean the resolution of a narrative plot.

11 *Joanna Baillie*: Joanna Baillie (1762–1851), Scottish poet and dramatist.

12 *in her hand:* the letter from Scott to Morritt, from which this quotation comes is reproduced in John Gibson Lockhart's *Memoirs of the Life of Sir Walter Scott*, 7 vols (Edinburgh: Robert Caddell, 1837–8), as are the remarks from Morritt that follow.

13 *blue-backed volumes*: referring to the colour of the book's cover. 'Yellow-backed' books were notoriously more sensational as French publishers tended to use the colour. Blue here indicates more 'serious' work.

14 *'Race to Derby'*: calamitous episode in the Jacobite campaign where Highland forces advanced to the town at great speed expecting a decisive engagement. It is described in Scott's novel *Waverley.*

15 *as the girl says in the nursery tale*: this is actually the evasive reply given by the eponymous villain of the English fairy tale 'Mr Fox' when he is told of a dream that exposes his crimes. The story was included by Joseph Jacobs in *English Fairy Tales* (1890), in which the rhyme reads: 'It is not so, nor it was not so. And God forbid it should be so.'

16 *Jemmy and Jessamy tribe*: *The History of Jemmy and Jenny Jessamy* by Eliza Haywood (1753) is the story of the romantic difficulties that beset a young couple.

17 *'Pelham'*: *Pelham, or Adventures of a Gentleman* (1823) is a novel by Bulwer Lytton, popular in its time and recounting the dramatic and not entirely plausible events of a young man's life as he clears his friend of an accusation of murder.

18 *'the big bow-wow strain'*: writing of Jane Austen in his journal in March 1826, Scott says 'The big bow-wow strain I can do myself like any now going; but the exquisite touch, which renders ordinary commonplace things and characters interesting, from the truth of the description and the sentiment, is denied to me'.

19 *Mr. Senior … 'Quarterly Review'*: this seems to have been Nassau Senior's review of *Peveril of the Peak* in the *London Review*. J. G. Lockhart quotes it in full in his biography and Lang perhaps took it from there, misrembering the publication's title.

20 *Vivaldi in the Inquisition*: an episode in Ann Radcliffe's novel *The Italian* (1797).

21 *Good Demon … Herrick*: Robert Herrick's poem 'The Departure of the Good Demon' laments his inability to write.

22 *bane-stuff*: something that is the cause of ruin or death to a particular person but not to others.

23 *'of Beatrice's mind'*: a reference to the character in Shakespeare's *Much Ado About Nothing* who is witty, but also capricious and contrary.

24 *Cromwell … Dunbar*: Oliver Cromwell, occupying Edinburgh in 1650 after the rout of Scottish armies at Dunbar.

25 *Men-ka-ra*: King from the fourth or fifth dynasty of rulers of Egypt.

26 *amusing as a fairy tale*: Johnson seems to have said this about Goldsmith's abridgement of a Roman history.

27 *Eyrbyggja Saga … romance*: the saga is Icelandic, surviving in written form from the thirteenth century. It contains accounts of ghosts, rituals and superstitious fear and Lang is here likening the reader distracted by new literary fashions to the credulous people of the saga.

28 *'Let it not …personal happiness'*: from Ruskin's essay 'Fiction Fair and Foul', from which Lang quotes earlier. See note 7 above.

29 *l'amor che move 'l sol e l'altre stelle*: Italian, 'the love that moves the sun and other stars'. It is from the last section of Dante's *Divine Comedy*, where it is referring to God.

30 *Julia de Roubigné*: 1777 novel by Henry Mackenzie.

31 *shepherd … rocks*: the shepherd in Theocritus's idylls is elusive, because he lives among the rocks. Lang is suggesting by analogy that Scott found love elusive in his own life.

32 *Virgilius Maro, 'Fuimus Troes'*: quotation from *Waverley*, from the speech of Brawardine to Waverley after the defeat at Culloden. The reference is to Virgil's *Aeneid* and the fall of Troy, where Maro says 'We are Trojans no longer.'

'At the Sign of the Ship', *Longman's Magazine* (November, 1887)

1 *Irish orator*: this orator has not been identified.

2 *Matthew Arnold … in literature*: From Arnold's poem *Memorial Verses April 1850*. He refers to Byron's 'fount of fiery life' as the source of strength for his 'Titanic strife' but the poem is also about Goethe and Wordsworth.

3 *Teuton*: person of the Germanic peoples of Northern Europe.

4 *Montrose's wars … the Argyles*: The Argyles were the clans of the Campbells, led by Archibald Campbell, 1st Marquis of Argyll, who also became the leader of the Scottish forces in the Civil Wars of the 1640s and 1650s and thus fiercely opposed to the Royalist Montrose.

5 *second sight*: Lang wrote about second sight using examples from Scotland. See, for example, 'Opening the Gates of Distance', chapter 4 in *the Making of Religion* (Longman's, Green and Co., 1898) and in 'At the Sign of the Ship', *Longman's Magazine* 18:108 (October 1891), pp. 662–6.

6 *gillie*: or ghillie is a Scots term for a servant attending a person engaged in hunting, shooting or fishing.

7 *delf dinner service*: 'Delft' china is blue and white patterned, in the style of the pottery first produced in the area of Delft in the Netherlands in the seventeenth century.

8 trop de zèle: French, 'excess of enthusiasm'.

9 *Messenger at Arms*: officer of the Scottish courts responsible for serving documents.

10 *Kingsley's poet of gamekeeping life*: Tregarva is the gamekeeper in Charles Kingsley's 1851 novel, *Yeast*, who shows the well-meaning hero the miserable conditions of contemporary rural life.

'At the Sign of the Ship', *Longman's Magazine* (July 1896)

1 *Dorians may talk Doric,' according to Praxinoë and Gorgo*: Lang explains further below that 'Praxinoë and Gorgo are Syracusan, Doric-speaking women in an idyll of Theocritus, a Greek poet'. Doric was a dialect of ancient Greek. There is a more complicated joke here as the rural Dorians were regarded as rough and unsophisticated by the urban Athenians and Doric came to be used in English to mean rustic and unpolished. It was also used to describe the dialects of Scots spoken in the northeast of Scotland. A number of the 'Kailyard' writers to whom Lang later refers used 'Doric' Scots.

2 *remarks of the critic:* Unsigned review of Stevenson's novel in the *Athenaeum* 3578 (23 May 1896), p. 673.

3 *Quarterly Review* ... Anglified Erse': the unsigned review, actually of Scott's *The Antiquary* rather than *Guy Mannering*, describes it as written in 'a dark dialect of Anglified Erse.' *Quarterly Review* 15 (1816), p. 139.

4 *as Ascham calls it*: Roger Ascham (1515/6–1668) scholar and courtier, approvingly described Thomas Malory's *Morte d'Arthur* as consisting principally of 'open manslaughter and bold bawdry' in *Books That Do Hurt*.

5 *Mr. Barrie's ... Mr. Crockett's novels*: J. M. (James Matthew) Barrie (1860–1937) is best remembered as the creator of Peter Pan, though he also wrote a number of novels set in his native Scotland. His success inspired Samuel Rutherford Crockett (1859–1914), who published under the name S. R. Crockett and whose Lowland Scots novels were popular in his time. Both were part of the 'Kailyard' school of fiction.

6 *'Kailyard novel'*: the 'Kailyard school' is the description of the sentimentalised novels of rural Scottish life fashionable in the late 1880s and early 1890s. The Scots word 'kailyard' means a cabbage patch or cottage vegetable garden. As well as Barrie and Crockett, some of the works of J. J. Bell, George MacDonald and Gabriel Setoun are often included under this title.

7 *Professor Goldwin Smith*: Goldwin Smith (1823–1910) was Regius Professor of History at Oxford but moved to the United States to support the anti-slavery cause in the Civil War. He published widely on history and politics. Smith did not write a full-length life of Scott and the location of his error has not been found.

'At the Sign of the Ship', *Longman's Magazine* (August 1896)

1 *Caledonia*: Latin name given to what is now Scotland by the Roman occupiers of the southern part of the British Isles.

2 *'rich Cyrene'*: a rather obscure reference. Battus, the founder of the city of Cyrene, was originally an inhabitant of Greece. He was advised by the Oracle at Delphi to go to Libya to found the city as a solution to the drought being experienced in his home city. Battus did not know where Libya was, so Lang is suggesting that Purcell knows Scotland only as a story, rather than a reality.

3 *'a poetic child' named Scott*: see this volume, p. 337, n. 2.

4 ben trovato, *if not* vero: the Italian expression '*Si non e vero, e ben trovato*' means 'If not true then well-invented' and the sense is that although something may not be true, it is an ingenious and thus attractive fiction.

5 *Walker London*: this was a play, first performed in 1892, by J.M.Barrie (1860 –1937), the Scottish writer best remembered today as the creator of Peter Pan.

6 *Kailyard School*: see note 6 below.

7 *Walton, an old English writer*: Izaak Walton (1539–1683), essayist whose prose style was much admired. His book *The Compleat Angler* (1653) is a mix of practical tips on fishing, folklore, quotations from a wide range of authors, ballads and accounts of idyllic rural life.

8 *gifted Gilfillian… sma' trading way*: character in Scott's *Waverley*, who has visited a number of countries, including Poland, France and Russia.

9 *excellent book*: see this volume, p. 376, n. 59.

10 proh pudor!: Latin, 'for shame!'

11 *Quintin Kennedy*: Kennedy (1520–64) was the abbot of Crossraguel and an anti-Reformation theologian who was involved in a public debate with John Knox at Maybole in 1562 that lasted three days.

12 *Professor Blackie*: John Stuart Blackie (1809–95) was a Scottish scholar and writer, professor of Greek at Edinburgh University and a strong advocate of the establishment of a chair of Celtic Studies there.

13 *friendship, regret, and national feeling:* Stevenson had died in December 1894 leaving *Weir* unfinished.

14 *Prince of Paper Lords …. Metre*: Francis Jeffrey's (see this volume, p. 337, n. 2) epitaph on Peter Robinson reads 'Here lies the preacher, judge, and poet, Peter / Who broke the laws of God, and man and metre.'

15 *how often …. time and trouble*: the writer and the quotation have not been identified.

16 *'nice derangement of epitaphs'*: see this volume, p. 350, n. 32.

17 *I do not know … epic poem*: quotation not identified.

18 *Herbert Spencer*: See this volume, p. 369, n. 39.

19 *ethnical ethics of our own idiosyncrasy*: quotation not identified.

Introduction to J. Vyrnwy Morgan, ***A Study in Nationality*** **(1911)**

1 *MacMillanites … and Sandemanians*: small religious groups formed by breaking away from the dominant Scottish Presbyterianism. Lang names some of them here though there were many more, a number of them named after their founders, such as John MacMillan.

2 *'boetry and bainting'*: George II (1683–1760) ruled Britain from 1727. He was born and brought up in Germany and this remark about poetry and painting mocks both his accent and his unsophisticated character. Lang, as a Jacobite, would have reason to dislike George as he was the king against whom the last Jacobite rebellions were directed.

3 *Council of Nicea*: conference of bishops, convened by the Emperor Constantine in 325 in order to try to achieve agreement on the tenets of Christianity.

4 *'the heathenish timepiece … Sabbath'*: quotation not further identified.

5 *Church of Geneva … Servetus*: Michael Servetus (*c.*1509–53), Spanish scholar whose theology asserted the singularity of God, in opposition to the orthodox idea of the Holy Trinity. He was burned as a heretic in Geneva, the centre of John Calvin's Protestant Reformation.

6 *Gardiner*: Stephen Gardiner (1497–1555) archbishop and Lord Chancellor under Mary Tudor. Her short reign briefly restored Catholicism as the faith of England and saw the persecution of Protestants.

7 *Mr Knox*: Lang's biography of John Knox, *John Knox and the Reformation* was published in 1905.

8 *put under sackcloth*: the wearing of sackcloth is referred to several times in the Bible, for example Genesis 37:34, and is part of a public display of penitence.

9 *'Love would still be lord of all'*: from Walter Scott's poem 'It was an English Ladye Bright' (1805).

10 *Laud*: William Laud (1573–1645), Archbishop of Canterbury during the reign of Charles I, opposed to Puritanism and executed during the English Civil War.

11 *'Not as their friend or child I speak'*: from Matthew Arnold's poem 'Stanzas from the Grande Chartreuse' (1855). The poem expresses Arnold's religious ambivalence and the line refers to the religious teachers of his youth.

12 *Solemn League and Covenant*: an agreement made in 1643, during the English Civil War, between the Scottish Covenanters and the leaders of the English Parliamentarians. The Protestant Parliamentarians, faced with the threat of Irish Catholic troops joining the Royalist army, requested the aid of the Scots. It was, in effect, a treaty between the English Parliament and Scotland for the preservation of the reformed religion in Scotland.

13 *'who's a deniging of it'*: the expression is used by Betsey Prig, a sharp-tongued character in Dickens' *Martin Chuzzlewit*. Lang is not quoting directly from the novel, but he is using Dickens's rendering of 'denying'.

14 *Ninian Winzet, or Quentin Kennedy*: Winzet (1518–92) and Kennedy (1520–64) were both Scottish Catholic priests and writers opposed to John Knox and his party.

15 *Father Pollen, S.J*: John Hungerford Pollen (1858–1925) was an English member of the Society of Jesus (Jesuits) and a historian of the Protestant Reformation.

16 *Observantine Friars*: a particularly austere branch of the Franciscan Order.

17 *idolaters must die the death'*: the phrase is attributed to John Knox.

18 '*kinless loons'*: meaning without friends, relations or clan. Walter Scott, in *Tales of a Grandfather*, records the remark of a Scottish judge referring to the impartial judges sent into Scotland by Oliver Cromwell as 'kinless loons'.

19 *Wishart ... Beaton*: the Scottish religious reformer George Wishart (*c.*1513–46) was burned at the stake in St Andrews after a show trial conducted by Cardinal David Beaton. Beaton was murdered three months later, also in St Andrews, partly in revenge for Wishart's death. A plaque in the path marks the site of the burning and Lang would have seen it often in St Andrews.

20 *Douglases*: old and powerful Scottish family. Archibald Douglas (Earl of Angus) was Lord Chancellor and became guardian of the infant James V by marrying his widowed mother, Margaret Tudor. Their daughter Margaret was the mother of Henry Stewart, Lord Darnley who later married to Mary, Queen of Scots. James Douglas (Earl of Morton) was Archibald's nephew and an enemy of Mary, being involved in both the murder of her secretary David Rizzio and Lord Darnley.

21 *Episcopacy in Scotland*: the history of Scottish churches is complex. The Scottish Episcopal Church is separate from the Presbyterian Church of Scotland, but was formed from the Church of Scotland after the Reformation, though it claims its origins in the first missions to Scotland. It is sometimes disparagingly called 'the English Kirk' because of its associations with the English monarchy and the conflicts of the Jacobite period. Episcopal means to have bishops as significant figures in its hierarchy.

22 *sacerdotalism*: attribution of excessive importance, even supernatural power, to priests and the priesthood.

23 *Hildebrandine claims*: the Hildebrandine or Gregorian Reforms were named after Archdeacon Hildrebrand (*c.*1015–85) who became Pope Gregory VII. He placed the Church as the highest power, with the Pope greater than any monarch and the priest in a consequently high position qualified even, as Lang quotes here, 'to judge angels.'

24 *Frank Bothwell*: Francis Stewart, Earl of Bothwell (1562–1612), Lang describes him in *James VI and the Gowrie Mystery* as a 'Protestant firebrand' and Walter Scott refers to him as 'mad Frank'. His stepfather was Archibald Douglas and his uncle was James Bothwell. He too was a violent conspirator and was accused of treason, but in 1593 forced his way into the King's bedchamber at Holyrood Palace and obliged the King to agree to his pardon.

25 *Charles Lamb*: In his essay, 'Imperfect Sympathies', published in the *London Magazine*, in August, 1821, Lamb declares 'I have been trying all my life to like Scotchmen, and am obliged to desist from the experiment in despair'.

26 *Higher Criticism*: see this volume, p. 345, n. 3.

27 *Apostles' Creed*: statement of the tenets of Christian faith, broadly accepted in Western Christian churches.

28 *paladins*: warriors of the Court of Charlemagne, explicitly Christian and opposed to the Muslim Saracens.

29 *prayers not extempore*: 'extempore' prayers would be those thought to spring directly from the religious experience of the person praying and resulting from their individual

relationship with God. The refusal of already-written prayers in favour of the extemporised was a central article of Reformation belief.

30 *Brodie of Brodie*: Alexander Brodie of Brodie (1617–79) a strong Presbyterian who took part in the destruction of the 'idolatrous' carvings and paintings in Elgin Cathedral.

31 *Erskine of Dun to Andrew Melville*: John Erskine of Dun (1509–91), friend of George Wishart and John Knox. Andrew Melville (1545–1622) taught at St Andrews for many years but in 1606 was imprisoned in the Tower of London by James I. He was forbidden to return to Scotland on his release four years later and spent the last decade of his life in France as Professor at the Hugenot Academy of Sedan.

32 *Henryson, Dunbar*: Robert Henryson was a poet writing in Scotland in the period *c.*1460–1500. William Dunbar (born 1459 or 1460) was a Scottish poet writing in the late fifteenth century and the early sixteenth century and associated with the court of King James IV of Scotland.

33 *Sir George Mackenzie*: Mackenzie (*c.*1636–91) also called Bluidy Mackenzie, was a Scottish lawyer, later Lord Advocate, and a writer on legal matters. He conducted witch trials, but gained his nickname from the persecution of Covenanters. After the Battle of Bothwell Bridge in 1679 over a thousand Covenanters were imprisoned in a field near Greyfriars Church in Edinburgh. Some were executed, but hundreds died of maltreatment.

34 *Jacobin and a Jacobite*: Jacobins were a political group important in the French Revolution and their name has come to mean radical and revolutionary. Jacobites were the supporters of the claim of the Stuarts to the throne of England and Scotland, their name derived from the Latin for James, the first of the Stuart claimants. The two words are not connected, but Lang jokes here on Burns' radical nature and Stuart sympathies.

35 *'Laddie, ye manna whustle on the Sabbath'*: you must not whistle on Sunday.

'History As She Ought To Be Wrote', *Blackwood's Edinburgh Magazine* (August 1899)

1 *Borrow's Quaker lady*: George Borrow writes of the 'Bruisers' (prize fighters) in *Lavengro* (1851).

2 *Mr J. R. Green*: John Richard Green (1837–83) was a clergyman who became a historian. *A Short History of the English People* appeared in 1874 and there were several other histories of England before his early death.

3 *author of 'Feudal England,'*: John Horace Round (1854–1928) whose *Feudal England* appeared in 1895.

4 *Professor Maitland*: Frederic William Maitland (1850–1906), important legal historian. The book Lang refers to was published in 1897.

5 notae variorum: Latin, meaning 'notes by various people', and referring to an edition of a work that contains notes and commentaries by different scholars.

6 *Mommsen*: Theodor Mommsen (1817–1903) was one of the most important German classical scholars of the nineteenth century, publishing major work on the history of Rome and on Roman law. He was also a politician and a member of the German parliament after unification. He won the Nobel Prize for literature in 1902.

7 *Harrison*: Frederic Harrison (1831–1923), barrister and historian. He makes these claims in *The Meaning of History* which had been re-published in an expanded edition in 1894.

8 *York Powell*: Frederic York Powell (1850–1904) had recently (1894) become Regius Professor of Modern History at Oxford.

9 contre-coeur: French, literally 'against the heart' meaning against his natural inclination.

10 *Mr Maitland's books*: Frederic William Maitland (1850–1906) was a lawyer and historian of English law, and the author of many books and essays on the topic.

11 *Clarendon … Mommsen*: Edward Hyde, Earl of Clarendon (1609–74), Thucydides (*c.*460 BCE–*c.*395 BCE), Edward Freeman (1823–92), Macaulay and Theodor Mommsen (1817–1903) were all respected historians.

12 *Caesar, his Gracchi, his Cicero*: Mommsen wrote on all these figures in his best-selling and much admired multi-volume *History of Rome* (1854–56). His ability to depict the characters of historical figures was often appreciatively noted, so Lang is being deliberately contentious here.

13 *Curtius*: Quintus Curtius Rufus, first century Roman historian, author of a long biography of Alexander the Great, but much criticised for his lack of attention to accurate facts.

14 *Claverhouse*: John Graham of Claverhouse (1648–89), Scottish nobleman and Jacobite whose actions and reputation were a matter of dispute among historians. Macaulay was critical of him.

15 *poffle or pendicle*: small properties that are part of larger estates. Scott uses the phrase in the opening pages of *Heart of Midlothian* (1818) which is perhaps where Lang recalls it from.

16 *Gibbon's great work*: Edward Gibbon's huge work, *The History of the Decline and Fall of the Roman Empire*, published in six volumes between 1776 and 1788.

17 *Where are the snows of yesteryear?:* this is Dante Gabriel Rossetti's translation of the French line, 'Mais où sont les neiges d'antan?', from the *Ballade des dames du temps jadis* by François Villon. The phrase has become almost proverbial.

18 *Knights' Fees …* Mulierum: Lang lists a number of topics discussed by historians of the mediaeval period. His description of them as exciting is sarcastic. He uses the example of Knights' Fees elsewhere to the same effect, see this volume, p. 360, n. 9.

19 *certain author's Theory of West African Religion*: Lang was at this time revising the two volumes of *Myth, Ritual and Religion*, first published in 1887, in the light of his discoveries of early monotheism as set out in *The Making of Religion* (1898). The second edition of *Myth, Ritual and Religion* was published in 1899. The work he refers to here may have been part of his revising.

20 oere perennius: Latin, 'lasting longer than bronze'.

21 *I have insisted … not invade Ireland*: Lang does not make any such statement in the first volume of his *History of Scotland*, published the following year (1900). Possibly he made a further correction before the volume reached the press.

22 *'Purple patches'*: over-elaborate writing.

23 *Solway Moss*: The Battle of Solway Moss, November 1542, where English forces defeated those of the Scottish king James, who had refused to follow Henry VIII in schism from the Roman Catholic Church.

24 *'men of the Merse … no more'*: quotation has not been further identified. The Merse is an area of eastern Scotland on the border with England.

25 *'Heuristik'*: this is not a slang word, but means an analytic approach based on limited information supplemented by assumptions.

26 *École des Chartes*: French institution (founded 1821) for the training of librarians and archivists.

27 *Matthew … Brompton*: during the nineteenth century the mediaeval chronicler Matthew of Westminster was discovered not to have existed. The reference below to 'Harris' is because the name Matthew Paris has been associated with the work previously thought to be his. Simeon was a twelfth century monk of Durham and also writer of chronicles. John of Brompton was abbot of Jervaulx in 1436 and supposed to have written another important chronicle.

28 *Dr Lingard*: John Lingard (1771–1851) English Catholic historian, author of *The History of England, From the First Invasion by the Romans to the Accession of Henry VIII* (1819).

29 *Winchester Chronicle*: Freeman, in his *History of the Norman Conquest of England* (1870) describes the Winchester Chronicle as being written in 'honest English.'

30 *honest Injun*: became a catchphrase from the works of Mark Twain, derived from term used by settlers of the American West who distrusted the native peoples.

31 *Barbour*: John Barbour (*c.*1320–95), was a Scottish poet who wrote in Scots. His major extant work is a long historical verse romance, *The Brus* (*The Bruce*),

32 *Bright's disease*: disease of the kidneys, first described by Richard Bright in 1827.

33 *late Mr Paget, in 'Maga'*: John Paget, unsigned review of Macaulay's *History of England*, *Blackwood's Edinburgh Magazine* 65:402 (April 1849), pp. 386–405. 'Maga' was the nickname of *Blackwood's*.

34 *Florence … Tytler*: Lang names a range of writers of history: Florence was a monk of Gloucester abbey (died 1118); Walter of Hemingburgh and John of Fordun were both fourteenth-century chroniclers; Thomas Carte (1686–1754) and Patrick Fraser Tytler (1791–1849) were more recent writers.

35 *Simancas*: Froude had used an archive in a village in Spain during the research for his twelve-volume *History of England* (published 1856–70).

36 *Scylla and Charybdis*: proverbial phrase meaning two equal dangers, derived from the rocks and a whirlpool negotiated by Odysseus on his voyage in Homer's *Odyssey*.

37 *Von Pflugk Harting*: Julius von Pflugk-Harttung (1848–1919) German writer on medieval history.

38 *tithes of mint and cumin*: from Matthew 23:23. The passage describes those who are scrupulous about small details but neglect the larger and more important issues.

'At the Sign of the Ship', *Longman's Magazine* (May 1896)

1 *Cardinal Manning*: probably E. S. Purcell's biography, *Henry Edward Manning* (London: Macmillan, 1896).

2 *Mr. Carlyle's essay*: the essay was a review of the Lockhart biography, published in the *London and Westminster Review* 12 (January 1837).

3 *Carlyle … hubbub*: Froude, who had been a friend of the Carlyles, was given correspondence and other material, including letters and writings by his wife, by Thomas Carlyle. Froude published the material in the early 1880s, culminating in the *Life of Carlyle* in 1884. The publications showed Carlyle in a poor light, especially in his unhappy marriage, and Froude was widely criticised.

4 *Dr. Johnson at Lichfield*: Samuel Johnson, moved by remorse by the memory of having failed on one occasion to help his father at his market stall, fifty years later visited the place in Uttoxeter market where the stall had been. He stood bare-headed in the rain in penance.

5 *every wart was photographed*: Lang is referring to the remark supposed to have been made by Oliver Cromwell on having his portrait painted: 'I desire you would use all your skill to paint your picture truly like me, and not flatter me at all; but remark all these roughness, pimples, warts, and everything as you see me.'

6 *Mr. W. B. Scott*: William Bell Scott (1811–90), Scottish painter and poet who also wrote introductory memoirs of Sir Walter Scott prefacing editions of the latter's work.

7 *troops in Flanders*: it is unclear to which troops Lang is referring. None were stationed in Flanders in 1896. Before World War I the best-known British engagement was the 1702–10 campaign of the Duke of Marlborough during the War of the Spanish Succession.

8 *Sir E. B. Jones*: Edward Burne-Jones (1833–98), artist and designer associated with the Pre-Raphaelite movement. At the time that Lang was writing this article Burne-Jones was the most venerable and respected of contemporary artists.

9 *Professor Wilson*: it is not clear whether Lang is referring to any particular work, but John Wilson (1785–1854) was a Scottish advocate, literary critic and a prolific author. He was the writer most frequently identified with the pseudonym Christopher North in *Blackwood's Edinburgh Magazine*.

10 *Lady Forbes*: Margaret Stuart Belches, whom for some years Scott hoped to marry. She married Sir William Forbes in 1796, but she and Scott remained friends.

11 *jesting Pilate … Truth?'*: chapter 18, verse 38 of the Gospel of John is often referred to as 'jesting Pilate' or 'Truth? What is truth?' from the questions that Pontius Pilate puts to Jesus.

12 *Poor, greedy … person*: this reference has not been further identified.

13 pulveris exigui jactu*:* Latin, 'throwing a little dust'. The quotation is from Virgil's *Georgics* IV.87.

14 *Mr. Pepys's autobiographic babble*: Samuel Pepys (1633–1703) was an English naval administrator and Member of Parliament. He kept a detailed diary in a shorthand code for almost a decade from 1660. The first published edition came out in 1825, but was only about a third of the text. More complete editions (though still with most of the accounts of Pepys's sexual adventures omitted) were published in the 1870s and from

1893–9. Lang is probably referring to the recent edition which was clearly still too candid for his taste.

15 *Tullus and Ancus*: third and fourth kings of Rome, in the seventh century BCE. They appear in the underworld in Virgil's *Aeneid* as figures from history whose wealth and power did not keep them from death.

16 per impossibile: Latin, 'the impossible'.

17 *Highland Mary*: Mary Campbell was a young women with whom Burns was in love, writing three poems about her. Lang writes about her again in his *Longman's* column in May and July 1897 where he decries speculation on the relationship and notes the 'idolatry' of a statue of her on the banks of the Clyde at Dunoon.

18 *If we can find out Junius... King over the water*: Junius was the pseudonym of the writer of a series of letters to the *Public Advertiser* from January 1769 to January 1772, criticising government figures and policy. His identity is not known, though there continues to be much speculation. Lang wrote on the question of who Junius may have been in 'Did Junius Commit Suicide?', *Blackwood's Edinburgh Magazine* 157:953 (March 1895), pp. 406–16. John Churchill's role in defeating the Monmouth Rebellion in 1685 helped secure James on the throne, but in 1688 he changed sides and supported William of Orange, who made him Duke of Marlborough. 'The King Over the Water' in the Jacobite toast, is the successor of James. Lang's point in putting these figures together is to suggest tantalising historical puzzles that could be solved (as he had with *Pickle the Spy*) by finding a relevant document.

'New Light on Mary Queen of Scots', *Blackwood's Magazine* (July 1907)

1 *1586*: Mary's trial for treason took place in 1586. She was sentenced to death in October and executed in February 1587.

2 *'searchers of records'*: this reference has not been identified.

3 *one-eyed calendars*: a kalandar, or qalandar, is a Sufi mystic. *The Arabian Nights*, which Lang knew well, contains the story of three qalandars, all blinded in one eye.

4 *Lemons ... Bains*: compilers of recently published calendars of documents. Bains'calendar of Scottish papers, for example, was published between 1881 and 1888.

5 *George Buchanan:* Buchanan (1506–82) was a Scottish historian, humanist and Latin scholar, known for his translations of Latin prose and poetry.

6 *Mary Fleming or Mary Beaton*: two of the 'Four Marys' who were the Queen's ladies-in-waiting. All were from aristocratic families; Mary Fleming married Sir William Maitland and Mary Beaton was the mistress of Thomas Randolph, who attempted to recruit her to spy on the Queen.

7 *William Kirkcaldy of Grange*: Sir William Kirkcaldy of Grange (1520–73), Scottish politician and soldier. A supporter of Mary, he was nevertheless opposed to both her second and third marriages.

8 *Tremaynes... Killegrew*: the Tremaynes were an old family from Cornwall in the south west of England, members of which had long held government positions and continued to so under Elizabeth. Sir Henry Killigrew (*c.*1528–1603), also from a Cornish family, was a diplomat employed by Elizabeth in Scottish affairs.

9 *Earl of Arran*: James Hamilton, 3rd Earl of Arran (*c.*1532–1609), Scottish nobleman who fought against French troops during the Scottish Reformation. Descended from James VI of Scotland through his mother's family, he was next in line to the Scottish throne. Marriages to both Mary and Elizabeth were suggested several times.

10 *Court of Holyrood*: Holyrood Palace in Edinburgh, built by Mary's grandfather James IV, was the residence of Scottish monarchs.

11 lettres inédits: French, 'unpublished letters'.

12 *Earl of Leicester*: Robert Dudley, 1st Earl of Leicester (1532–88), leading statesman and personal favourite of Elizabeth I. He hoped to marry her, but was also proposed as a husband for Mary.

13 *mysterious death … Amy Robsart*: she fell down some stairs and died in 1560. It was rumoured that Leicester had murdered her in order to clear the way to his marrying Elizabeth, but there is no evidence of this.

14 *dirked*: a dirk is the short dagger worn with Scottish traditional dress.

15 *ride at the ring*: a game played on horseback, the tilting ring was a suspended circle which the rider had to catch on the end of his lance as he rode towards it at speed.

16 *Labanoff's collection*: Alexandre Labanoff had published *Lettres, instructions et mémoires de Marie Stuart, Reine d'Écosse* in seven volumes in 1844.

17 *Cecil:* William Cecil, 1st Baron Burghley (1520–98) was a powerful statesman and the chief advisor of Queen Elizabeth I for most of her reign. He acted twice as Secretary of State (1550–3 and 1558–72) and Lord High Treasurer from 1572. His younger son, Sir Robert Cecil, took over the role as advisor on his father's death and oversaw the transfer of power to the House of Stuart on the accession of James I and VI.

18 *'a Holbein for oyl'*: 'a Dürer for proportion ... an Angelo for his happy fancy, and an Holbein for oyl works', David Lloyd, *State-worthies: or, the Statesmen and Favourites of England from the Reformation to the Revolution* (1766). No works of Killegrew's are now known.

19 *Norfolk*: Thomas Howard, 4th Duke of Norfolk (1536–72), courtier and official of Elizabeth, Norfolk was the Principal of the commission at York in 1568 to hear evidence of the Casket Letters, but was imprisoned by Elizabeth the following year for plotting to marry Mary. He continued to scheme for the overthrow of Elizabeth and was executed for treason in 1572.

20 les politiques*:* French, 'politicians'.

'M. Anatole France on Jeanne d'Arc', *Scottish Historical Review* (1908)

1 *M. Anatole France*: Anatole France (1844–1924) was a French writer and journalist. He was sceptical and anti-clerical. He strongly supported Émile Zola's defence of Alfred Dreyfus and became known as a Dreyfusard. In 1922 his works were put on the Index Librorum Prohibitorum (List of Prohibited Books) of the Catholic Church. He was awarded the Nobel Prize in 1921.The book Lang is responding to here is volume 1 of *Vie de Jeanne d'Arc*, vol. 1 (2 vols, Paris: Calmann Lévy, 1908).

2 *is in no hurry to canonise her*: Jeanne d'Arc was made venerable in 1894, beatified in 1909, and eventually canonised in 1920.

3 *Of M. France's inconsistencies*: the translations from France throughout must be Lang's own.

4 Hilarem vultum gerit: Latin, 'her face was glad'. See also this volume, p. 248.

5 *William…ogre*: Sir William Wallace (d.1305) was a leader during the Wars of Scottish Independence (1296–1328 and 1332–57). Napoleon Bonaparte (1769–1821) was a French military and political leader and Emperor of France from 1804 to 1814. He was born in Corsica.

6 *'The lusty bird takes every hour for dawn'*: From Alfred Lord Tennyson, 'Morte d'Arthur' (1842).

7 *Thoreau was not … wild birds*: Henry David Thoreau (1817–62) was an American writer. One of his best known works, *Walden, Or, Life in the Woods* (1854), is an account based on his two years living a simpler life, one more in tune with and responsive to the natural world.

8 *Morosini's reports*: Antonio Morosini (*c.*1365–*c.*1434) wrote *La chronique d'Antonio Morosini: Extraits relatifs à l'histoire de France.*

9 *In the pages of the* Procès: *Procès* is French for trial, and Lang here refers to the transcripts of the trial of Jeanne in 1431. These were translated into Latin from the minutes taken during the trial in French, and a number of copies were made. Three remain. In 1455–6 Jeanne's trial and its outcome were reconsidered in the Procès de Réhabilitation (trial of rehabilitation), during which this account of the original trial was used.

10 Le Roman de Brut: this is a history of Britain in verse by the poet Wace (*c.*1110–*c.*1174), written around 1155. It is written in Norman French, and is based on Geoffrey of Monmouth's (*c.*1100–*c.*1155) *Historia Regum Britanniae* (*c.*1136).

11 *Merlin … seer*: Merlin is a legendary wizard usually associated with Arthurian legend. The figure first appears in Geoffrey of Monmouth's *Historia Regum Britannia*. Michel de Nostradamus (1503–66) was a French apothecary and seer who published his prophecies as *Les Prophecies* (1555). For Thomas of Ercildoune (Thomas the Rhymer), see note 12 below. 'Nixon' comes from Charles Dickens's *The Pickwick Papers* (1836) where Sam Weller accuses his father of 'a prophesyin' away' like one. The Brahan seer (Coinneach Odhar in Gaelic) is reputed to have lived in Scotland in the seventeenth century and predicted, among other things, the building of the Caledonian Canal. There is no evidence for his existence.

12 *Thomas the Rhymer*: this is the name given to Thomas Learmonth (*c.*1220–*c.*1298), a thirteenth-century Scottish laird. He was believed to be a prophet, and was the protagonist of the ballad 'Thomas the Rhymer'. Sir Walter Scott wrote about him, and included 'Thomas the Rhymer' in his *Minstrelsy of the Scottish Border* (2 vols, 1802).

13 *Marie … says Quicherat*: Marie d'Avignon was Marie Robine (d.1399), whose prophecies were thought to have foretold the coming of Jeanne d'Arc. Jules Étienne Joseph Quicherat (1814–82) was a French historian and archaeologist. He published the text of the two trials of Jeanne d'Arc (the original of 1431 and the rehabilitation of 1455–6) as *Procès de condamnation et de réhabilitation de Jeanne d'Arc* in five volumes (1841–9), as well as his *Aperçus nouveaux sur l'histoire de Jeanne d'Arc* in 1850.

14 *'firent grand bruit'*: French, 'made a great noise'.

15 *Christ's silly vassal'*: for Andrew Melville see this volume, p. 383, n. 31.

16 Elle .... l'ouïr: Old French, 'She appears divine in her actions, when you see her and hear her.'

From *The Maid of France: Being the Story of the Life and Death of Jeanne d'Arc* (1908)

1 *If the Church canonises her:* during this period a debate was going on over the possible canonisation of Jeanne d'Arc by the Catholic Church. The Bishop of Orleans had led the campaign to have her canonised and first submitted a formal request to Rome in 1869. During the late nineteenth century the slow process begun, and during this period a number of very popular books were published which tracked it. Jeanne was given the title 'venerable' in 1894, beatified in 1909 and canonised in 1920.

2 *It has appeared to me ... not inquire*: on the main documentary evidence surrounding Jeanne's career, see this volume, p. 389, n. 9.

3 *It has pleased ... of History*: Lang here seems to have confused two French clerical writers on Jeanne d'Arc. Jean-Baptiste-Joseph Ayroles (1828–1921) was the author of *La Vraie Jeanne d'Arc* (5 vols, 1890–1901). Canon Philippe-Hector Dunand (1835–1912) wrote, among other works on Jeanne, *Histoire complète de Jeanne d'Arc* (3 vols, 1898–9). His *Études Critiques* appeared between 1903 and 1908.

4 *Fabyan, Holinshed, and Polydore Virgil*: Robert Fabyan (d. 1513) kept a diary of notable events which he then expanded into a chronicle, *The Concordance of Historyies*. It was printed in 1516 as *The New Chronicles of England and France*. Raphael Holinshed (1529–.*c.*80) was an English chronicler who was one of the main contributor's to *The Chronicles of England, Scotland, and Ireland* (1577). Polydore Virgil (or Vergil) (*c.*1470–1555) was an Italian historian who spent most of his life in England. His *Anglica Historia* was completed in 1513 and printed in 1534.

5 *but a page of Caxton*: William Caxton (*c.*1415/2–92) was a merchant and writer who introduced printing to England. He published *The Chronicles of England*, a version of the mediaeval *Brut* chronicle, in 1480. One continuation of the *Brut* contains an account of Jeanne, and this was copied by Caxton for his version of Ranulf Higden's *Polychronicon* (also from 1480).

6 *Such as Monstrelet ... du Haillan*: Enguerrand de Monstrelet (*c.*1400–53) was a French chronicler. He was present at the interrogation of Jeanne d'Arc, and was the author of *Chronique de Enguerrand de Monstrelet*. Bernard de Girard Haillan (*c.*1535–1610) was a French historian whose most well known work is *L'histoire general des rois de France jusqu'à Charles VII inclusivement* (1576).

7 *which is so conspicuous ... as 1642*: Jeanne d'Arc (as 'Joan La Pucelle') appears as a character in Shakespeare's *Henry VI, Part 1* which uses at its sources Raphael Holinshed's *Chronicles of England, Scotland, and Ireland* (1577), Edmund Hall's *The Union of Two Noble and Illustre Famelies of Lancastre and Yorke* (written in 1550) and Robert Fabyan's *New Chronicles of England and France* (1516), all of which mention Jeanne d'Arc. The play undermines her claims to divine authority for her mission. A number of events concerning Jeanne in the play, such as her foray into Rouen with her soldiers, all disguised as peasants, are not recorded in any historical source. Lang responded to the portrait of Jeanne in the play in the privately printed pamphlet, *The Voices of Jeanne d'Arc* (1895), which was reprinted in *The Valet's Tragedy* (1903). Thomas

Fuller (1608–61) was a cleric and prolific writer. He wrote a number of histories, including *The Holy State* (1642), which contains a chapter on Jeanne d'Arc.

8 *But, in the middle ... Jeanne d'Arc*: David Hume includes a section on Jeanne d'Arc in vol. II of his *The History of England* (6 vols, 1754–61), in which he writes that it is 'the business of history to distinguish between the miraculous and the marvellous' and acknowledges the story of Jeanne is the latter if not the former. John Lingard (1771–1851), who had been ordained as a Catholic priest, published his *The History of England, From the First Invasion by the Romans to the Accession of Henry VIII* (8 vols) in 1819.

9 *In 1790 ... two trials*: Clément Charles François de Laverdy (sometimes L'Averdy) (1724–93) discovered new documents surrounding the trials, and published his discoveries in volume 3 of *Notices et extraits des manuscripts du Roy* (1790).

10 *Henceforth the facts ... her honour*: Robert Southey's epic poem, *Joan of Arc*, appeared in 1796. Samuel Taylor Coleridge's 'Destiny of Nations: A Vision' originated as his contribution to Southey's poem, but was later extracted from it by Coleridge and expanded, parts published as 'The Visions of the Maid of Orleans: A Fragment' in 1797, abandoned, and finally published in full in 1817.

11 *and while America ... (1840–50)*: Francis C. Lowell, *Joan of Arc* (1896). Lang reviewed this book favourably in 'At the Sign of the Ship', *Longman's Magazine* 254, December 1903, pp. 187–8. In the review he regretted that it had taken so long for the book to come to his attention. Lowell in turn reviewed both Anatole France's book and Lang's *The Maid of France*, asserting that Lang's use of the evidence surpassed France's, even if Lowell does not agree fully with Lang's reading of it. See Francis C. Lowell, Review of Anatole France, *Vie de Jeanne d'Arc* and Andrew Lang, *The Maid of France*, *The American Historical Review*, July 1909, pp. 80–. Jules Étienne Joseph Quicherat, see this volume, p. 389, n. 13.

12 *We have, indeed ... and girls*: Janet Tuckey, *Joan of Arc, 'The Maid'* (1880). Lord Ronald Charles Sutherland Leveson-Gower (Lord Ronald Gower), *Joan of Arc* (1893). Lang wrote his own book on Jeanne d'Arc for children, *The Story of Joan of Arc* (1906).

13 *There is no ... with sword*: In his poem 'A Scot to Jeanne d'Arc', Lang aquits himself, because of his Scottishness, of any guilt for her death: 'Not upon us the shame / Whose sires were to the Auld Alliance true; / They, by the Maiden's side, / Victorious fought and died'. See Lang, *Ban and Arrière Ban: A Rally of Fugitive Rhymes* (London: Longmans, Green and Co., 1894), p. 1. Another poem, 'How the Maid Marched to Blois', is written in the voice of her Scottish banner painter. See Lang, *New Collected Rhymes*, London: Longmans, Green, & Co. (1904), pp. 7–8.

14 ... *Bothwell in Darnley's murder*: James Hepburn (*c.* 1534–78), the 4th Earl of Bothwell, was charged with and tried for the murder of Henry Stuart, Lord Darnley, the second husband of Mary, Queen of Scots, in early 1567. He was acquitted, and a few months later became Mary's third husband.

15 ... *St Catherine of Siena ... Dame Eleanor Raughton*: Catherine of Siena (1347–80) intervened in the question of bringing the papacy of Gregory XI back to Rome from Avignon, and was active in the politics of the Italian city states, travelling from city to city and writing letters to the powerful. Dame Emma (not Eleanor) Raughton was an anchoress in All Saints church in York in the fifteenth century. She had visions in 1421, given to her by the Virgin Mary, and her advice was sought by Richard Beauchamp, 13th Earl of Warwick (not the Duke of Bedford), the following year.

16 *Father Ayroles … Dunand*: see this volume, p. 390, n. 3.

17 *Lord Morley's Life … politician*: Lang wrote a short story, 'The Great Gladstone Myth', first published in *Macmillan's Magazine* in February 1886, which satirises historians' inability to separate myth from reality and the dangers of using evidence inappropriately. See 'The Great Gladstone Myth', *In the Wrong Paradise and Other Stories* (London: Kegan Paul, Trench & Co., 1886).

18 *Montrose… Mary of Guise*: James Graham, 1st Marquess of Montrose (1612–50) initially supported the Covenanters then switched to the side of Charles I. Claverhouse see this volume, p. 384, n. 14. Mary of Guise (1515–60) was the French second wife of James V of Scotland and the mother of Mary, Queen of Scots.

5 THE BUSINESS AND INSTITUTIONS OF LITERARY LIFE

'At the Sign of the Ship', *Longman's Magazine* (March 1886)

1 *Henri Murger's heroes*: Murger (1822–61) was a French novelist and poet, writer of *Scènes de la vie de Bohème* (1851). The hero referred to is Alexander Schaunard, a character in 'How the Bohemian Club was Formed', one of the 'Scenes'.

2 *Lord Salisbury*: (1830–1903) Conservative politician and three times Prime Minister. Lang's article was published in the brief period of Gladstone's government, as Salisbury had resigned in January 1886 but he and the Tories were re-elected six months later.

3 *Wolf and the Lamb*: one of Aesop's fables, a collection of tales ascribed to a Greek story-teller, Aesop, believed to have lived around 620 BCE–550 BCE. As these tales appear and are circulated in many forms it is very difficult to know with which versions Lang was familiar.

4 *Captain Kidd … John Silver*: pirates, one real – William Kidd, executed for piracy in 1701, though it has since been suggested he was not really guilty, and one fictional – Long John Silver from Stevenson's *Treasure Island* (1883).

5 *Great Pink Pearl*: a farce by R. C. Carton and Cecil Raleigh being performed in London at the time of Lang's writing. Despite his professed dislike of theatre it would appear that he may have seen it.

6 *American author*: this author has not been identified.

7 *Farrar's 'Life of Christ'*: see this volume, p. 344, n. 7.

8 *Lion and the Eagle*: national symbols of Britain and the United States.

9 *'The Dude'*: in the late nineteenth century this meant a fashionable city figure, rather shallow and stupid, ill-suited to country life. There is a good account of the origin and use of the term in Seth Lehrer, 'Hello, Dude', *American Literary History* 15:3 (2003) pp. 471–503.

'At the Sign of the Ship', *Longman's Magazine* (August 1886)

1 *ardour of politics*: William Gladstone's short-lived third government had just collapsed. See this volume, p. 392, n. 2.

2 *Mr. Shand*: Alexander Innes Shand (1832–97) writer and reviewer.

3 *Old Man, even Nicholas*: from advice given by a disreputable character in *Nicholas Notes*. William Jeffrey Prowse (1839–70) was a journalist and humourist; the majority of his poems were published after his death in a volume entitled *Nicholas Notes* (1870) edited by the poet Thomas Hood.

4 Called Back, … The Private Secretary: *Called Back* (1883), a best-seller by Hugh Conway, the pen name of Frederick John Fargus (1847–85); *John Inglesant* (1881), a popular historical novel by Joseph Shorthouse (1834–1903); George Eliot's *Romola* (1863); *The Private Secretary* (1881) by George Chesney (1830–95); and *Our Boys* (1875) by H. J. Byron (1835–84), the first play to achieve 500 consecutive stage performances. Lang uses them all as examples of best-selling literature.

5 *M. Ohnet*: Georges Ohnet (1848–1918) was a French novelist of great popularity, strongly opposed to the school of Zola.

6 feuilleton: see this volume, p. 353, n. 33.

7 *'Sappho' or 'Serge Panine'*: novel by Alphonse Daudet, *Sapho* (1884). Lang gives the title of the English version, published 1886. *Serge Panine* (1881) is by Georges Ohnet (1848–1918).

8 *Mr. Mudie*: see this volume, p. 352, n. 2.

9 *Folios … octavos*: sizes of book. A folio is a very large format of sheets of 12 by 15 inches, an octavo a smaller format of sheets 6 by 9 inches.

10 *grapes are often sour*: Br'er Fox is a character in the Uncle Remus stories. See this volume, p. 347, n. 7. Lang is referring to the tale 'How Brother Fox Failed to Get His Grapes'.

11 *Children of Gibeon of literature*: Walter Besant's novel *The Children of Gibeon* depicted the deprivation and injustice of the 'sweating' system, work carried out in 'sweat-shops' or in workers' own homes. It was paid by the piece and was notoriously hard and poorly paid work. The novel was published serially in *Longman's Magazine* between January and December 1886 and was placed immediately before Lang's 'At the Sign of the Ship' column.

12 *'Hints on Golf,' Mr. Horace Hutchinson*: published in 1886, in the same year as Lang's article here. Lang would have been keen to read a new book on golf.

13 tour de force*:* French, 'show of skill'.

14 ne faict ce tour qui veult: French, can be translated as 'cannot do this deed by wishing'.

'At the Sign of the Ship', *Longman's Magazine* (July 1893)

1 *Mr. Besant*: see this volume, p. 392, n. 11. See also Robert A. Colby, 'Harnessing Pegasus: Walter Besant, "The Author" and the Profession of Authorship', *Victorian Periodicals Review* 23:3 (Fall 1990), pp. 111–20.

2 sommité*s*: French, 'luminaries' or stars.

3 *Ecclesiastical revenues*: Pierre de Ronsard (1524–85) was a celebrated French poet from an aristocratic family. His income meant that he did not need the money from publishers. Lang repeats Ronsard's complaint in his essay on him in *Letters to Dead Authors* (London: Longmans, Green and co., 1886), pp. 22–33.

4 *Grub Street*: see this volume, p. 345, n. 10.

5 *Collins*: William Collins (1751–59), poet whose work was more widely recognised after his death. During his life he struggled on a low income and suffered episodes of depression and mental illness which obstructed his work.

6 '*...the booksellers of London'*: James Boswell, *Life of Samuel Johnson* (1791).

7 *'Life of Savage'*: Samuel Johnson, *Life of Mr Richard Savage* (1744).

8 *writes Horace Walpole*: this letter from Horace Walpole to George Montagu is quoted by George Birkbeck Hill in his edition of *Boswell's Life of Johnson*, 6 vols (New York: Harper and Brothers, 1889), vol. 1, p. 333. This is thus likely to be the edition of the biography that Lang is using.

9 *booksellers are generous, liberal-minded men*: see note 8 above, ibid., p. 352.

10 *Bohemia*: Waugh, and Lang, refer to the idea of the 'Bohemian' artist, socially unconventional and living on little money, dedicated to art.

11 *Higher Criticism*: see also this volume, p. 345, n. 3. Lang is here referring to the criticism of classical texts that is engaged in attempting to prove or disprove authorship and relies upon supposed differences of style or information in making the case. Lang was involved in these debates from his work on Homer.

12 *'The song ... that feast'*: from the third verse of the hymn, 'Jerusalem the Golden', originally written in Latin in 1146 by Bernard of Morlaix, translated from Latin to English (1858) by John M. Neale (1818–66). As it was in the first edition of *Hymns Ancient and Modern* (1861) it became very well known to the Victorians.

13 *Incorporated Authors' Society, at Chicago*: the Society of Authors was founded in Britain in 1884, Walter Besant was instrumental in its formation and active in it until his death. In 1893 he attended the Chicago World's Fair to represent the Society. Thomas Hardy was one of its early presidents.

14 bête noire: French, literally 'black beast', but meaning a particular enemy or disliked idea.

15 *'Omar Khayyam,' ... the original Keatses*: Edward FitzGerald (1809–83) translated the work of the Persian poet Omar Khayyám in the *Rubaiyat of Omar Khayyam* (1859); *The Strayed Reveller* (1849) was Matthew Arnold's first collection of poetry, he published 'Empedocles on Etna' anonymously in 1852. The Tennysons and Keatses to which Lang refers are the earliest works of both poets, before they had achieved any fame.

16 *Roxburghe, Bannatyne, Maitland, Abbotsford, Wodrow*: clubs formed for the purpose of re-printing rare books and historical manuscripts. The first was the Roxburghe, founded in in 1812 by Thomas Frognall Dibdin (1776–1847), author of *Bibliomania* (1809). It was named after the Duke of Roxburghe, the sale of whose library was the occasion of its first meeting.

17 abonnements: French, 'subscriptions'.

18 *the rectory of Mr. Samuel Wesley at Epworth*: Epworth Rectory was a famous haunted house where the family of the Reverend Samuel Wesley experienced mysterious noises over Christmas 1716 and into January 1717. The family, which included John Wesley, later the founder of Methodism, called the poltergeist 'Old Jeffrey'. Lang wrote about the phenomena several times. See, for example, *Cock Lane and Common Sense* (London: Longmans, Green and Co.,1894).

19 *'Betsy Prig, who's deniging of it?'*: see this volume, p. 381, n. 13.

20 *'Humpty Dumpty is Abracadabra'*: John Stuart Mill gives this as an example of a proposition which means nothing because both the terms mean nothing in themselves. J. S. Mill, *An Examination of Sir William Hamilton's Philosophy* (Boston: William Spencer, 1865), vol. I, p. 95.

21 *a month's mind*: this is an odd use of the phrase, which usually refers to the period of mourning after a death which was marked at its end by a special mass. Shakespeare mentions it in *Two Gentlemen of Verona* (act 1, scene 2): 'I see you have a month's mind for them', as does Pepys in his diary entry for 20 May 1660: 'there was a pretty Dutch woman in bed alone, but though I had a month's-mind I had not the boldness to go to her'. Both Shakespeare and Pepys use the term to mean 'a strong inclination'.

22 Wilkie Collins: William Wilkie Collins (1824–89) was a novelist and author of short stories. He was also a friend of Dickens, with whom he collaborated in writing drama. His best-known works *The Woman in White* (1859–60) and *The Moonstone* (1868) were among those that brought him popular and financial success. His addiction to opium, which he took as medication for gout, damaged both his health and his later writing.

23 *Savage*: Richard Savage (*c.*1697-1743). English poet and satirist whose biography was written by Samuel Johnson and published as *An Account of the Life of Mr Richard Savage, Son of the Earl Rivers* (1744). See note 7, above.

How to Fail in Literature (1890)

1 *College for Working Men and Women*: Morley College, which had been established in the previous year (1889), one of several institutions for the education of working-class people set up in the later nineteenth century; the first was the Working Men's College in 1854.

2 revu, corrigé, et considerablement augmenté: French, revised, corrected and considerably expanded.

3 *'in running to devour the way'*: from Shakespeare, *Henry IV Part 2*, act 1, scene 1.

4 *the shilling*: reference to the former practice of recruiting men for the army or navy in which the recruit would be given a shilling on enlisting.

5 *'many thyrsus bearers … chosen*: a *thyrsus* was a staff carried in ritual practices in ancient Greece. The proverb is also Greek (attributed to Plato), meaning that many may be involved but few have true gifts. The same idea is familiar from the Biblical quotation that follows, which is from Matthew 22:14.

6 *Pendennis*: novel by William Thackeray (1848–50) in which the eponymous character goes to London to make his fortune. He initially becomes a journalist.

7 *Marryat … away to sea*: Marryat's early novels, such as *Frank Mildmay* (1829), had naval settings.

8 *Famine and Fear … Hades*: in book six of Virgil's *Aeneid*, Aeneas is guided through the underworld.

9 *Maupassant … Flaubert*: Gustave Flaubert (1821–80), important French writer and author of *Madame Bovary* (1857). He was a friend of the family of Maupassant (see this volume, p. 358, n. 29) and was highly encouraging of the young writer's career.

10 *tea and good advice, as Keats said*: Keats wrote to his publisher in October 1818: 'In [writing] Endymion, I leaped headlong into the Sea, and thereby have become better acquainted with the Soundings, the quicksands, & the rocks, than if I had stayed upon the green shore, and piped a silly pipe, and took tea & comfortable advice.'

11 *Shakespeare … Gibbon*: Lang uses these writers as examples of excellent style. Francis Bacon (1561–1626) and Izaak Walton (1593–1683) were known for their essays, Richard Hooker (1553–1600) for his religious commentary and Edward Gibbon (1737–94) for his massive historical work, *The Decline and Fall of the Roman Empire*, which appeared in six volumes between 1776 and 1789.

12 *'break Priscian's head'*: Priscian was a sixth-century grammarian, so to break his head was to ignore the rules of grammar. Lang may have known the saying from Samuel Butler's use of it in his mock-heroic poem *Hudibras* (1684) lines 223–4.

13 *'… irridescence of the poetic afflatus'*: this review has not been identified.

14 *Wardour-street English*: the affected use of archaic words and phrases. The term was first applied by William Morris in 1888 to describe a translation of the *Odyssey*: he said the translation reminded him of the new but antique-style furniture sold in Wardour Street. There is an article by Archibald Ballantyne, 'Wardour Street English' in *Longman's Magazine* 12:72 (October 1888), pp. 585–94 that discusses the topic at length.

15 *Piers Plowman and Gabriel Harvey*: Piers Plowman is a Middle English poem written in the late fourteenth century, Gabriel Harvey a poet (*c.*1545–1631). Lang means to suggest that a mistaken idea of the language of 'merry England' is being aspired to.

16 *'made-up article'*: a piece of furniture constructed of bits of other items, rather than made as one piece.

17 Ornari … doceri: Lang translates the line himself below: 'The matter declines to be adorned, and is content with being clearly stated'. The poet is Marcus Manilius, a first century Roman writer.

18 *the two MM. Halévy*: there are in fact three writers by this name: Ludovic Halévy (1834–1908), a writer of operettas, farces and comedies, his father, Léon Halévy (1802–83), who wrote in a number of genres, and his uncle, Fromental Halévy, (1799–1862) who was a noted composer of opera. It is likely that Ludovic and Fromental are the two intended by Lang.

19 *Gibbon …* Histoire d' Israel*:* for Gibbon see this volume, p. 000, n. 000. Lang makes or repeats a pun where '*esprit*' can mean 'spirit' or 'joke', thus Montesquieu's (1689–1755) work, called 'The Spirit of the Law' can also be called 'A Joke Upon the Law'. The first two volumes of Joseph Ernst Renan's (1823–92) huge history had appeared by the time of Lang's writing.

20 *gravity … animal*: this a horse belonging to Parson Yorick in Laurence Sterne's novel *Tristram Shandy* (1759).

21 causeries: from French, meaning 'babble', the description of a type of newspaper column, light in style and of topical interest. See discussion in this volume, p. 20.

22 *Roundabout Papers*: Thackeray published a volume of 'occasional writings' by this title in 1862 and the term was used, as it is here by Lang, to refer to short, often humorous, magazine or newspaper columns.

23 *Montaigne*: Michel Eyquem de Montaigne (1533–92). Famous for popularising the essay as a literary genre, and a key figure in the development of modern sceptical

thought, Montaigne's *Essais*, published between 1580 and 1592, was among the most influential works of the Renaissance in France.

24 retombons à nos coches: French, meaning 'let us return to our coaches' and quoted from the last paragraph of Montaigne's essay 'On Coaches' (1580).

25 *'In this way ... save that'*: from Walter Pater's 1888 essay 'Style'.

26 *vagrom*: wandering.

27 *Miss Yonge ... Master of Balliol*: Lang names pairs of people whose writing styles are very different: the romantic novelist Charlotte Yonge and Charles Lever (1806–72) who produced rollicking tales; John Morley (1838–1923) wrote a series of biographies of statesmen and philosophers, whereas Uncle Remus is the fictional narrator of a series of African-American folk tales published in 1881. Haggard's stories of imperial adventure are contrasted with the work of Benjamin Jowett, the formidable Master of Balliol and Regius Professor of Greek.

28 Kalevala *and Lycophron, and the Scholiast on Apollonius Rhodius*: the *Kalevala* is the Finnish epic poem (see also this volume, p. 338, n. 28), Lycophron an ancient Greek writer and commentator in the third century BCE, Apollonius of Rhodes, also a third century BCE Greek writer about whom little is known, may have been the author of a poem, the *Argonautica*, and the Scholiast is the commentator on that poem.

29 *Grosvenor Gallery*: an art gallery in Bond Street, London that became synonymous with the Aesthetic movement and associated with figures like Oscar Wilde. It was satirised in Gilbert and Sullivan's comic opera *Patience* (1881).

30 *'Most can grow ... but a weed'*: quotation not identified.

31 *burned several plays of Shakespeare*: Lang is repeating this story from Walter Scott, *Reliquae Trotcosienses* in which the cook of the antiquarian John Warburton (1682–1759) supposedly burned some fifty early copies of plays by Shakespeare and his contemporaries.

32 *who is* not: Lang is speaking personally here as he was frequently taken to be the editor of *Longman's Magazine*, despite printing statements to the contrary in his column 'At The Sign of the Ship'.

33 *Paribanou treated Prince Ahmed*: Lang collected the tale 'Prince Ahmed and the Fairy Pari-Banou' in his *Blue Fairy Book* (London: Longmans, Green and Co.,1889).

34 *Mr. William Black's novels*: novelist (1841–98) born in Scotland. Prolific and popular in his time, many of his works were set in Scotland.

35 *your want of common sense*: this is said by the Athenians in the Melian Dialogue in Thucydides' *History of the Peloponnesian War.*

36 *clerks of St. Nicholas*: 'The Three Clerks of St Nicholas', a story by Honoré de Balzac in which three students cheat an innkeeper, published in *Contes Drolatiques* (1832–37)

37 *'have no use for them'*: Lang quotes here a generic statement from letters of rejection.

38 *Golden Helen*: Helen of Troy, whose abduction was the ostensible cause of the Trojan War, she was supposedly the most beautiful woman in the world. Lang wrote a long narrative poem about her (London: George Bell and Sons,1882).

39 *wrongs of the Arênians*: the harshly oppressive treatment of the minority Christian Armenians in the Ottoman Empire was a matter of international concern during the

later nineteenth century when there was much political pressure for a treaty designed to protect them.

40 like Saul … *discover a kingdom*: according to the Bible and the Qu'ran, Saul was commanded by his father, Kish, to locate the lost donkeys of the Israelites. God revealed to the prophet Samuel that Saul would become the first king of Israel.

41 *Memoir of* A Scotch Probationer: the book is actually called *The Life of a Scottish Probationer*, by James Brown (1889). It gives an account of the life of Thomas Davidson (1838–70), a minor poet, and Alison Hay Dunlop (1835–88), author of just the single text mentioned by Lang here.

'To A Young Journalist', *Essays in Little* (1891)

1 The Bull-dog: a single issue of a magazine entitled 'The Bulldog' is listed as published at Oxford University on 28 February 1896 (*Cambridge Bibliography of English Literature,* ed. Joanne Shattock, Cambridge: Cambridge University Press, 1999, p. 2963). This cannot be the magazine to which Lang refers, which is probably fictitious.

2 *put forth by members of the University*: it is difficult to tell whether Lang is referring to a real publication here. There were several short-lived magazines during the time Lang was at Oxford. See *Cambridge Bibliography of English Literature,* pp. 2962–4.

3 chronique scandaleuse*:* French, referring to a literary genre of narratives of sexual intrigue.

4 métier: French, 'business'.

5 chantage: French, 'blackmail'.

6 mouchards: French, 'informers'

7 éreintage: French, meaning a destructive personal attack.

8 *Memoirs of M. Blowitz*: Henri de Blowitz (1825–1903) was a journalist, known for obtaining and publishing secret state information, such as the text of the Treaty of Berlin in 1878, which he published at the moment it was being signed. He worked for a time for Marie Joseph Thiers, see note 9 below.

9 *M. Thiers*: Marie Joseph Thiers (1797–1877) was a French politician and historian, head of state between 1871–3.

10 *'St. Satan's Penitents'*: Lang uses the phrase repeatedly in the poem 'Ballade of the Penitents', *Scribner's Magazine,* 1:3 (March 1887), pp. 355–65. There he gives the source of the line as '"Le repentir de leur premier choix les rend des *Pénitens du Diable,* comme dit Tertullien." Pascal, 'Pensées' 1672, p. 178.'

11 Virtutem … relicta: Latin, 'let them see virtue, and rot away for having abandoned it'.

12 Vous irez loin?: French, literally 'will you go far', here meaning 'Do you wish to get on?'

13 *'with larger other eyes than ours'*: from Tennyson's *In Memoriam* (1850), stanza 51.

'The Science of Novels', *Illustrated London News* (November 1894)

1 *University Extension*: during the 1870s Cambridge, Oxford and London Universities all developed extension programmes, arranging lectures all over the country on topics of general interest and eventually offering formal courses.

2 *Mr. Walter Raleigh*: Walter Raleigh (1861–1922), Scottish critic who became an important figure in the development of English as a University subject. He was Professor of modern literature at Liverpool, then of English at Glasgow and was appointed Oxford's first professor of English literature in 1904. He was knighted in 1911.

3 *Balliol Essays*: Balliol College, Oxford, held a competition for the best essays on set topics.

4 *Mrs. Behn, Mrs. Haywood, Bluidy Mackenzie, Henry Mackenzie*: For Behn and Haywood see this volume, p. 356, n. 1 and p. 356, n. 32. George 'Bluidy' Mackenzie (*c.*1636–91) wrote on legal matters; Henry Mackenzie (1745–1831) was a Scottish novelist.

5 *Miss Jane Porter*: Scottish historical novelist and playwright (1779–1850).

6 *Schwegler ... to Hegel*: Albert Schwegler (1819–57), his *General Outline of the History of Philosophy* was published first in 1848, and very widely used.

7 *in whom Sidney Smith took no interest*: reference not identified.

8 *'Euphues' ... 'Sukey Shandy'*: Lang names several lesser-known novels, ranging from the sixteenth century to the present.

9 *Empedocles*: Empedocles (*c.*490 BCE–430 BCE), Greek philosopher and originator of the theory of the four elements.

10 *De Foe's Mrs. Veal*: Daniel Defoe (*c.*1660–1731) was a man of various careers, including that of spy. He is now considered one of the founders of the English novel. He published many short pamphlets, mostly on political topics, but one, entitled '*A True Relation of the Apparition of One Mrs. Veal the Next Day after her Death to One Mrs. Bargrave at Canterbury the 8th of September, 1705*' describes exactly what the title suggests: the encounter of with the ghost of a dead friend. This would have been of interest to Lang in his research on magical phenomena.

11 *Lord Orrery's masterpiece*: Roger Boyle, Lord Orrery was the author of *Parthenissa,* a six-volume novel published in 1654.

12 *Dunlop's 'History of Fiction'*: John Dunlop, *History of Fiction* (London: Longman, 1814).

13 *'Bootles' Baby' and Mr. Hawley Smart*: *Bootle's Baby: A Novel of the Scarlet Lancers* (1885) was by John Strange Winter (pen-name of Mrs Arthur Stannard.) It sold 2 million copies in ten years. Henry Hawley Smart (1833–93) was also a prolific and best-selling writer.

'The Teaching of English Literature', *Illustrated London News* (December 1891)

1 *Churton Collins's book*: John Churton Collins (1848–1908), literary critic who strongly supported the study of English literature at university. In 1904 he became Professor of English at Birmingham University. *The Study of English Literature* (London: Macmillan) was newly published in 1891 and Lang is effectively reviewing it here.

2 *Scott defined the virtuoso*: the anecdote is recorded in John Gibson Lockhart, *Memoirs of the Life of Sir Walter Scott* (Edinburgh: Robert Cadell, 1837), vol. 1, p. 51. Scott was apparently aged six at the time.

3 *literal forms of Christianity'*: A. Orr, 'The Religious Opinions of Robert Browning', *Contemporary Review* 60 (December 1891), p. 876. See also letters on Browning in Volume 1, pp. 317–27 and p. 333 where he again discusses Mrs Orr's article. Although Lang suggests here that the poet's beliefs would not be of interest, his letters demonstrate otherwise.

4 *Paulus Silentiarius*: Greek official (575–80), writer of series of epigrams and a poem in praise of the Church of St Sophia in Constantinople.

5 *skews*: distortions, errors.

6 *Taylorian scholarship*: examinations set in competition for scholarships in Modern Languages at the University of Oxford.

7 *'Greats'*: Oxford University slang term for the degree in Classics.

8 *Canon Farrar*: see this volume, p. 344, n. 7.

9 *'Atalanta in Calydon'*: poem by Swinburne. It was published in 1865, the year before the scandalising *Poems and Ballads*, and it is long and complex piece of work.

'The Teaching of Literature', *The Pilot* (April 1901)

1 genus: Latin, 'race', 'type'.

2 '*Ephemera Critica' of Mr. Churton Collins*: see this volume, p. 399, n. 1. *Ephemera Critica* (London: Constable, 1901) was newly published at the time of Lang's writing.

3 *mansuetude*: meekness, gentleness.

4 *'Tirocinium' ... 'Stalky and Co.,*: 'Tirocinium' (1785) is also a poem by William Cowper, urging a friend not to send his son to school because they are awful places. *Stalky and Co.* is Rudyard Kipling's 1899 book of short stories, the earliest of which are set in a boy's boarding school.

5 *Phillips ... Binyon*: the poetry of Phillips (1864–1915) was much praised in the 1890s; he published four collections in that decade and also began writing plays that were equally celebrated. His work fell from regard almost immediately after his death. Binyon (1869–1943) was Phillips's cousin, also a poet and later to write the poem 'For the Fallen', widely used in remembrance services and epitaphs for those killed in the First World War.

6 *Huchown*: or Huchoun, a fourteenth-century poet, about whom little is known.

7 *Pecock*: Reginald Pecock, a fifteenth-century writer. His writings led to accusations of heresy and he was removed from his bishopric and place on the Privy Council.

8 *Guy Boothby*: see this volume, p. 356, n. 5.

9 *Wolf ... Leaf*: Friedrich August Wolf (1759–1824) and August Fick (1833–1916) were both German philologists and classical scholars. Walter Leaf (1852–1927) was also a noted classical scholar with whom Lang collaborated on translations of the *Iliad* and the *Odyssey*.

10 *Nash … Sidney Lee*: figures associated with Shakespeare. Nash and Greene are playwrights, Quiney a friend and Lee a biographer.

11 *Chettle*: Henry Chettle (*c.*1564–*c.*1606) is a very minor figure in literature; a dramatist and writer of pamphlets.

12 *'in Greek was sadly to seek'*: Richard Porson (1759–1808) was a classicist at Cambridge, who wrote that 'the Germans in Greek are sadly to seek', suggesting the weakness of German classical scholarship. John Watson, *The Life of Richard Porson* (London: Longmans, 1861), p. 260.

13 scutum crystallinum *of Pallas Athene*: the crystalline shield of the Greek goddess Athene.

14 *'Hamlet is too thick'*: the barber is in fact referring to the play *Macbeth* as 'too thick', meaning that it is too full of gore to be enjoyable. Israel Zangwill, *Without Prejudice* (New York: Century, 1896), p. 147.

15 *Queen's Maries … 'Kittlerumpit'*: this can be found in the *Calendar of State Papers, Foreign Series for the Reign of Elizabeth 1564–5* (London: Longman, 1870), vol. 7, p. 340. As the book was published by Longman, Lang may well have obtained it from there, possibly he was using the volume for his research on Mary Queen of Scots.

16 *Mr. Darwin hated him*: Lang also makes this claim in 'Ghosts Up to Date', derived from Darwin's autobiography (published 1887) where Darwin says that in later life he tried to read Shakespeare 'and found it so intolerably dull that it nauseated me'.

17 *'…to do with literature?'*: Augustine Birrell (1850–1933) was a politician and academic who expressed some very forthright views on literature. The remark is made in 'Dr Johnson' [1887], *The Collected Essays and Addresses of Augustine Birrell* (New York: Scribner and Sons, 1925), p. 125.

INDEX

Numbers in the form 100n signal a footnote by Lang on the page indicated; numbers in the form 100 n.1 indicate an explanatory endnote.

A

B

D

E

H

I

J

M

N

O

P

Q

R

S

T

U

V

W

Y

Z